Geometry, Fields and Cosmology

Fundamental Theories of Physics

An International Book Series on The Fundamental Theories of Physics:
Their Clarification, Development and Application

Editor: ALWYN VAN DER MERWE
   University of Denver, U.S.A.

Volume 88

Geometry, Fields and Cosmology

Techniques and Applications

Edited by

B. R. Iyer

Raman Research Institute,
Bangalore, India

and

C. V. Vishveshwara

Indian Institute of Astrophysics,
Bangalore, India

KLUWER ACADEMIC PUBLISHERS

DORDRECHT / BOSTON / LONDON

A C.I.P. Catalogue record for this book is available from the Library of Congress

ISBN 978-90-481-4931-5

Published by Kluwer Academic Publishers,
P.O. Box 17, 3300 AA Dordrecht, The Netherlands.

Sold and distributed in the U.S.A. and Canada
by Kluwer Academic Publishers,
101 Philip Drive, Norwell, MA 02061, U.S.A.

In all other countries, sold and distributed
by Kluwer Academic Publishers,
P.O. Box 322, 3300 AH Dordrecht, The Netherlands.

Printed on acid-free paper

TABLE OF CONTENTS

viii

It may well wait a century for a reader, as God has waited six thousand years for an observer.

–JOHANNES KEPLER

Geometry enlightens the intellect and sets one's mind right. All its proofs are very clear and orderly. It is hardly possible for errors to enter into geometrical reasoning because it is well arranged and orderly. Thus, the mind that constantly applies itself to geometry is not likely to fall into error. In this convenient way, the person who knows geometry acquires intelligence. It has been assumed that the following statement was written upon Plato's door: 'No one who is not a geometrician may enter our house'.

–IBN KHALDUN

Mathematics is the door and the key to the sciences.

–ROGER BACON

Structures are the weapons of the mathematician.

–NICHOLAS BOURBAKI

God does not care about our mathematical difficulties. He integrates empirically.

–ALBERT EINSTEIN

Preface

This volume is based on the lectures given at the First Inter University Graduate School on Gravitation and Cosmology organized by IUCAA, Pune, in 1989. This series of Schools have been carefully planned to provide a sound background and preparation for students embarking on research in these and related topics. Consequently, the contents of these lectures have been meticulously selected and arranged. The topics in the present volume offer a firm mathematical foundation for a number of subjects to be developed later. These include Geometrical Methods for Physics, Quantum Field Theory Methods and Relativistic Cosmology. The style of the book is pedagogical and should appeal to students and research workers attempting to learn the modern techniques involved. A number of specially selected problems with hints and solutions have been included to assist the reader in achieving mastery of the topics. We decided to bring out this volume containing the lecture notes since we felt that they would be useful to a wider community of research workers, many of whom could not participate in the school. We thank all the lecturers for their meticulous lectures, the enthusiasm they brought to the discussions and for kindly writing up their lecture notes. It is a pleasure to thank G. Manjunatha for his meticulous assistence over a long period, in preparing this volume for publication. We appreciate the help given by Raju Verghese in preparing some of the line drawings and producing the photographic prints of all the diagrams appearing in the volume. We thank Sreejith Sukumaran and J. Raghunathan for producing the figures in Chapter I.

We gratefully acknowledge the financial support given by the U.G.C. and institutional support offered by IUCAA, RRI and IIA at various stages. And finally we acknowledge the cooperation of our publishers Kluwer Academic Publishers, The Netherlands and in particular Margaret Deignan in bringing out this volume.

B. R. Iyer

C. V. Vishveshwara

The simplicities of natural laws arise through the complexities of the languages we use for their expression.

–EUGENE WIGNER

The important thing in science is not so much to obtain new facts as to discover new ways of thinking about them.

–WILIAM LAWRENCE BRAGG

When it comes to atoms, language can be used only as in poetry. The poet too, is not nearly so concerned with describing facts as with creating images.

–J. BRONOWSKI

Where there is matter, there is geometry.

–JOHANNES KEPLER

There is nothing in the world except empty curved space. Matter, charge, electromagnetism and other fields are only manifestations of curvature of space.

–JOHN ARCHIBALD WHEELER

1.   GEOMETRICAL METHODS FOR PHYSICS

N.MUKUNDA
Centre for Theoretical Studies & Department of Physics
Indian Institute of Science
Bangalore 560 012 India

1. Introduction and scope

The purpose of these informal notes is to give an elementary introduction to a collection of mathematical methods which have a geometric flavour, and which have become very useful in relativity, quantum field theory, and elementary particle physics. They are characterised as being intrinsic, coordinate-free, component-free and global in nature. Once one becomes familiar with them, it is like acquiring a new language with which to express many physical ideas in a direct and concise manner.

Naturally it takes some initial effort to learn and become comfortable with these intrinsic methods; and in fact it has been only with passage of time that they have won wide appreciation and acceptance. It is amusing to recall that no less a mathematician than Hermann Weyl had written in 1921 in his book "Space-Time-Matter": "Various attempts have been made to set up a standard terminology in this branch of mathematics involving only the vectors themselves and not their components, analogous to that of vectors in vector analysis. This is highly expedient in the latter, but very cumbersome for the much more complicated framework of the tensor calculus. In trying to avoid continual reference to the components we are obliged to adopt an endless profusion of names and symbols in addition to an intricate set of rules for carrying out calculations, so that the balance of advantage is considerably on the negative side. An emphatic protest must be entered against these orgies of formalism which are threatening the peace of even the technical scientist". One concludes that these words are really a sign of those times!

In these notes the emphasis will be on clarity in motivating and understanding new concepts rather than on rigour for its own sake. Whenever an

1

argument or point is better grasped by falling back upon older coordinate
and component based methods, at least at first brush, we will not hesitate
to use them. We will be guided by Feynman's statement that there need
be no sense of defeat in working with local methods and components, if it
helps. Similarly we will freely use intuitive arguments whenever they are
appropriate.

Generally speaking, concepts and the strategy of calculations go better
and more efficiently with the newer methods. For practical problems, however, one must retain the ability to calculate in the older ways, but with
the advantage of a deeper understanding of things.

The initial Sections are rather brief. Their purpose is to recapitulate,
introduce terminology and matters of notation. Later Sections will be somewhat more substantial. Sometimes a new concept introduced at some point
may be taken up and developed further somewhat later on. This is unavoid-
able, but it serves the purpose of covering new ideas in small steps.

Here is an outline of the contents. Sections 2, 3 and 4 recall basic set-
theoretic notions and terminology, actions of groups on sets and some ideas
of linear algebra and vector space theory. Generally the properties of groups
and group operations are assumed known. Section 5 introduces the idea of a
topological space as the minimum framework needed to define continuous
maps. This is then gradually refined over sections 6, 7 and 8 to develop
the concept of a differentiable manifold; charts and atlases and transition
functions, smooth maps, functions, the pullback operation; the tangent,
cotangent and general tensor spaces over a given manifold.

Sections 9 and 10 cover the three kinds of differentiation processes on
manifolds: Lie, exterior and covariant differentiations. The motivating ideas
behind and the input necessary to define each one, along with their respective algebraic properties and a clear understanding of the objects on which
each can operate, are all brought out. In the case of an affine connection
the definition of torsion and curvature, Cartan's equations of structure and
the Bianchi identities are developed in detail. The case of the connection
on a (pseudo) Riemannian metric is treated as a particular case.

Section 11 deals with various kinds of submanifolds in a given differentiable manifold, congruences and foliations, and Frobenius' theorem on the
conditions for a set of vector fields to be surface-forming. The definitions
of closed and exact forms are given and the Poincaré Lemma on the local
exactness of a closed form is proved. Section 12 takes up the global concept
of orientability and choice of orientation on a manifold, and the integration of volume forms. Here the results on partitions of unity are stated and
freely used with no attempt at proving them.

Section 13 brings out those aspects of Lie groups that make them an
especially rich and attractive example of differentiable manifolds. This is

also useful preparation for the development of the fibre bundle (FB) and principal fibre bundle (PFB) concepts over sections 14 and 15. The latter deals in some detail with connection and curvature in a PFB; it is also shown in some detail that when one has in mind the Frame bundle (FM) on a manifold M, the results of section 10 are fully recovered. Sections 16 and 17 deal with a couple of global processes and properties – integration of differential forms of various degrees on a given manifold, leading upto Stokes' theorem; and the concepts of homotopy of a manifold, and holonomy in a PFB. In both cases the emphasis is on a step by step development of ideas with a fair amount of analytical detail. With homotopy we deal not only with general topological spaces but also in particular with Lie groups and their coset spaces pointing out the nice simplifications that occur.

This set of notes has grown out of a more limited amount of material originally presented as a course of lectures. It would have been desirable to include more examples than actually appear, but constraints of time and length intervened. We only hope that at least some readers will feel – though more could have been done, what has been done is done well.

2. Sets, Mappings, Equivalence Relations

The basic notions regarding sets and mappings are assumed to be familiar, and we shall only briefly recall some definitions. If two sets M, N are given, a mapping $\varphi : M \to N$ is a rule which assigns in an unambiguous way an element or point of N to each element or point of M :

$$\varphi : \quad M \to N :$$
$$m \in M \to \varphi(m) \in N \tag{2.1}$$

We may call m the initial, or *source*, point in M, while $\varphi(m)$ is its *image* in N under φ. The entire set M is the *domain* of φ - the place where it is defined - while the set of all images $\varphi(m)$ as m runs over all of M gives a portion or subset (in general) of N, called the *range* of φ :

$$\text{Domain of } \varphi = M;$$
$$\text{Range of } \varphi = \varphi(M) \subseteq N \tag{2.2}$$

The map φ from M to N is said to be *injective* if distinct source points in M have distinct images in N:

$$\text{Injective: } \varphi(m') = \varphi(m) \iff m' = m \tag{2.3}$$

It is said to be *surjective* if the range of φ is all of N :

$$\text{Surjective: } \varphi(M) = N \tag{2.4}$$

And if φ is both injective and surjective, in plain language one-to-one and onto, it is *bijective*:

> Bijective $\iff$ injective and surjective,
>
> for any $n \in N$, there is an unique $m \in M$ such that
>
> $\varphi(m) = n$ $\hspace{3cm}$ (2.5)

Clearly, for a bijective map $\varphi : M \to N$, there is a unique inverse map $\varphi^{-1} : N \to M$.

To understand this last remark properly, we need the concept of *composition of maps*. Let maps $\varphi : M \to N$ and $\psi : N \to K$ be given, where M, N and K are three sets. Then the composed map $\psi \circ \varphi$ from M to K is defined in the obvious way:

$$m \in M : (\psi \circ \varphi)(m) = \psi(\varphi(m)) \in K \hspace{2cm} (2.6)$$

This can clearly be extended to the composition of several maps, of course in a correct sequence, and the process is easily seen to be associative. Now one can go back to the inverse, φ^{-1}, of a bijective map $\varphi : M \to N$. On a given set M, we have the *identity map*

$$\mathcal{I}d_M : m \in M \to m \in M \hspace{2cm} (2.7)$$

This looks trivial, but it is a map. One can now say that the composition of φ and its inverse φ^{-1} gives the (appropriate) identity:

$$\begin{aligned} \varphi^{-1} \circ \varphi &= \mathcal{I}d_M, \\ \varphi \circ \varphi^{-1} &= \mathcal{I}d_N \end{aligned} \hspace{2cm} (2.8)$$

An *equivalence relation* on a set M is a rule, chosen in some particular way, which tells us when two elements m and m' are to be regarded as equivalent to one another. Such a rule must obey three conditions: it must be

(i) Reflexive: each $m \in M$ is equivalent to itself.

(ii) Symmetric: m is equivalent to $m' \implies m'$ is equivalent to m.

(iii) Transitive: m is equivalent to m', m' is equivalent to m''

$\hspace{4cm} \implies m$ is equivalent to m'' $\hspace{2cm}$ (2.9)

We may express the equivalence of m and m' by writing $m \sim m'$. One can easily see that when such a relation is given, it breaks M up into disjoint equivalence classes. Each element m belongs to a definite class consisting of all m' equivalent to it; and each class is determined by any one of its elements. Thus each equivalence relation on M breaks up M in a particular way into such nonoverlapping pieces or subsets of M .

Given two sets X and Y , the set of functions (with definite properties chosen according to the context) from X to Y , ie. maps from X to Y , may be denoted by $\mathcal{F}(X;Y)$. In case Y happens to be $\mathcal{R}$, the real line or the set of all real numbers, we are concerned with real-valued functions on X (possessing some specified properties). We would then write $\mathcal{F}(X;R)$ for this set of functions, or if there is no danger of confusion, we abbreviate it to $\mathcal{F}(X)$. In case X and Y are linear vector spaces, and in case we are dealing with linear maps from X to Y , we write $\mathcal{L}(X;Y)$ rather than $\mathcal{F}(X;Y)$. Necessary extensions of this notation will be introduced later.

We have interchangeably used the words 'element' and 'point' for the 'things' contained in a set M . In a more geometrical context, the word 'point' may be more appropriate.

3. Action of a Group on a Set

The basic notions concerning groups will be assumed known. This includes, apart from the laws of group structure, the notions of subgroups and coset spaces, etc.

Let a group G with elements g, g', ..., and identity e , be given. Let X be a set with points x, x', y, ... We say we have *an action of G on X* if for each $g \in G$, we have a map $\psi_g : X \to X$ obeying the following conditions:

$$(i) \; \psi_g : X \;\; \to \;\; X \;\; \text{is bijective;}$$
$$(ii) \; \psi_{g'} \, o \, \psi_g \;\; = \;\; \psi_{g'\,g} \, ,$$
$$i.e. \; \psi_{g'} \, (\psi_g \, (x) \,) \;\; = \;\; \psi_{g'\,g} \, (x) \, , \;\; \text{any } x \in X;$$
$$(iii) \; \psi_{g^{-1}} \;\; = \;\; (\,\psi_g\,)^{-1} \; ;$$
$$(iv) \; \psi_e \;\; = \;\; \mathcal{I} \, d_X \qquad\qquad (3.1)$$

(Here, $g'g$ is the element of G obtained by composing g' and g according to the law of G ; g^{-1} is the element inverse to g). Thus the group G is "realised" by a set of one-to-one onto mappings of X on to itself, with their composition rule following the law in G .

Given an action of G on X , several natural definitions follow. Some are concerned with the details of the action, others characterise the action as a whole and help classify actions into different kinds. We take up the former first.

For any point $x \in X$, the *stability group* is that subgroup $H(x) \subset G$ consisting of all group elements that do not move x :

$$H\,(x)\,=\,\{\,g\,\in\,G\,|\,\psi_g\,(x)\,=\,x\,\}\,\subset\,G \qquad (3.2)$$

We say that each $h \in H\,(x)$ leaves x *fixed* or *invariant* . On the other hand, each $g \notin H\,(x)$ definitely moves x to a distinct image point $\psi_g\,(x) \neq x$.

In the expression $\psi_g\,(x)$ let us keep x fixed, and let g run all over G . We then get a set of points in X which comprise the *orbit* of x under the given action by G , denoted $\vartheta\,(x)$:

$$\begin{aligned}\vartheta\,(x)\ &=\ \{\,x'\,\in\,X\,|\,x'\,=\,\psi_g\,(x)\,,\ \text{some}\ g\,\in\,G\,\}\\ &=\ \{\,\psi_g\,(x)\,|\,x\ \text{fixed}\,,\ g\,\in\,G\,\}\,\subset\,X \qquad (3.3)\end{aligned}$$

It is easy to convince oneself that an orbit is determined by any point on it; and any two orbits are either disjoint, or coincide in their entirety. There is no possibility of a partial overlap of orbits. All these facts suggest that we can bring in here the notion of an equivalence relation! This is indeed so. Given the action of G on X , let us say that two points $x,\ y \in X$ are equivalent if and only if one goes into the other under action by some group element:

$$x\,\sim\,y\,\Longleftrightarrow\,\psi_g\,(x)\,=\,y\ \text{for some g}\,\in\,G \qquad (3.4)$$

The set of conditions (3.1) on the ψ 's ensures that the properties (2.9) of an equivalence relation do obtain. Then the orbit $\vartheta\,(x)$ is just the equivalence class of x .

Let x and y lie on the same orbit, in other words $\vartheta\,(x)\,=\,\vartheta\,(y)$. Then their stability groups are conjugate sub-groups in G :

$$\begin{aligned}y\,\in\,\vartheta\,(x)\quad &\Rightarrow\,\psi_g\,(x)\,=\,y\,,\ \text{some}\ g\,\in\,G\\ &\Rightarrow\,H\,(y)\,=\,g\,H\,(x)\,g^{-1} \qquad (3.5)\end{aligned}$$

Of course the element g here is not necessarily unique. Examining the extent of its nonuniqueness, one can see that for any $x \in X$, there is a natural bijective map from $\vartheta\,(x)$ to the coset space $G\,/\,H\,(x)$. In other words, the orbit of x produced by the given action of G on X is "essentially the same" as the coset space:

$$\vartheta\,(x)\,\longleftrightarrow\,G\,/\,H\,(x)\ \text{bijectively} \qquad (3.6)$$

Now let us turn to the aspect of *various kinds* of group actions. In the expression $\psi_g\,(x)$, let us as before keep x fixed and vary g over G . Clearly we have a map from G to X , dependent on x :

$$\underline{x\,\in\,X}\ \ \psi.\,(x)\,:\quad G\,\to\,X\,,$$
$$g\,\in\,G\,\to\,\psi_g\,(x)\,\in\,X \qquad (3.7)$$

The domain of $\psi.\,(x)$ is G , the range is the orbit $\vartheta\,(x)$. We now characterise the G action in terms of the properties of $\psi.\,(x)$:

$$\psi.\,(x) \text{ surjective for each } x \iff G \text{ action is transitive,} \quad (a)$$
$$\psi.\,(x) \text{ injective for each } x \iff G \text{ action is free.} \quad (b)$$

$$(3.8)$$

We can draw out the meanings of these definitions thus. In the transitive case, we have:

$$\text{Transitive } G \text{ action} \iff \vartheta(x) = X \text{ for each } x$$
$$\iff \text{ any two points } x, y \in X$$
$$\text{are equivalent à la (3.4)}$$
$$\iff X \text{ is a single } G \text{ orbit} \quad (3.9)$$

In the free case, we have:

$$\text{Free } G \text{ action} \iff \{ \text{ for each } x, \; \psi_{g'}\,(x) = \psi_g\,(x) \Leftrightarrow g' = g \}$$
$$\iff H\,(x) = \{\, e \,\} \text{ for each } x \quad (3.10)$$

That is, all the stability groups are trivial, and each orbit $\vartheta\,(x)$ is essentially a replica of G itself.

Lastly we define what we mean by an *effective* action of G on X . This involves looking at the collection of maps $\{\psi_g\}$. We say:

$$G \text{ action is effective} \iff \{\, \psi_g = \mathcal{I} \, d_X \iff g = e \,\} \quad (3.11)$$

In other words, every nontrivial group element definitely moves some point in X :

$$\text{Effective G action} \iff \text{ for each } g \neq e, \text{ there is some } x \in X$$
$$\text{such that } \psi_g\,(x) \neq x$$
$$\iff \bigcap_x H\,(x) = \{\, e \,\} \quad (3.12)$$

We have thus defined three kinds of action of a group G on a set X : transitive, free and effective. A given action may of course not be of any one of these three kinds. A free action is certainly an effective one, as we see on comparing eqs. (3.10,12); but the converse does not hold, as the notion of being effective is weaker. A transitive action allows us to identify the entire space X with a suitable coset space G/H . In the case when G is a Lie group and H is a (closed Lie) subgroup of G , the coset space G/H is called a *homogeneous space* . It then carries a transitive G action.

4. Algebraic Operations on Vector spaces

We shall mainly deal with real linear vector spaces $\mathcal{V}$, $\mathcal{V}'$, $\mathcal{V}_1, \mathcal{V}_2$, ... of various finite dimensions. If occasionally we need to consider complex vector spaces, this will be clearly stated.

4.1. DIMENSION, LINEAR INDEPENDENCE, BASIS

In a real linear vector space $\mathcal{V}$, of dimension n say, the "elements" or "points" x, y, u, v, ... are *vectors* . We can multiply vectors by real numbers and form linear combinations, and the results are again vectors. A set of vectors x_1, $x_2, \ldots,$ $x_k \in \mathcal{V}$ is *linearly independent* if, the c's being real numbers,

$$c_1\, x_1 + c_2\, x_2 + \ldots + c_k\, x_k \;=\; 0 \iff c_1 \;=\; c_2 \;=\; \ldots \;=\; c_k \;=\; 0 \quad (4.1)$$

The meaning of the statement that $\mathcal{V}$ has dimension n is that the maximum number of linearly independent vectors is n , and that there are such sets of vectors. Any n linearly independent vectors $\{e_1, e_2, \ldots, e_n\} = \{e_a\}$ give us a basis for $\mathcal{V}$. Any $x \in \mathcal{V}$ can be uniquely expressed as a linear combination of the e_a , and then the coefficients are called the components of x in that basis:

$$
\begin{aligned}
x \in \mathcal{V}: x \;&=\; x^1\, e_1 + x^2\, e_2 \ldots + x^n\, e_n \\
&=\; x^a\, e_a
\end{aligned}
\quad (4.2)
$$

(Summation over repeated indices is understood). Multiplication of vectors by real numbers, and forming linear combinations of vectors, pass into corresponding operations on the components.

4.2. FRAMES, THE GROUP GL($n,\mathcal{R}$), ORIENTATION

A *frame* $\{e_a\}$ is an *ordered* set of basis vectors for $\mathcal{V}$. Thus, with the same n independent vectors, $\{e_1, e_2, e_3, \ldots, e_n\}$ and $\{e_2, e_1, e_3, \ldots, e_n\}$ define two different frames. The set of all frames for $\mathcal{V}$ is denoted by $F\,(\mathcal{V})$:

$$F\,(\mathcal{V}) \;=\; \{\ \{e_a\} \mid e_1, e_2, \ldots, e_n \;=\; \text{ordered basis for } \mathcal{V}\ \} \quad (4.3)$$

If we have two frames $\{e_a\}$, $\{e'_a\}$ for $\mathcal{V}$, there must be a unique linear relation from one to the other. This must correspond to some definite element of the general real linear group in n dimensions, denoted by $GL\,(n,\,\mathcal{R})$:

$$
\begin{aligned}
\{e_a\},\ \{e'_a\} \;&\in\; F\,(\mathcal{V}): \\
e'_a \;&=\; (A^{-1})^b{}_a\, e_b,
\end{aligned}
$$

$$A \quad = \quad (A^b{}_a) \in GL(n, \mathcal{R}),$$
$$A^a{}_b (A^{-1})^b{}_c \quad = \quad (A^{-1})^a{}_b A^b{}_c = \delta^a_c \tag{4.4}$$

Here we view superscripts (subscripts) as row (column) indices for matrix operations. The relations expressing e 's in terms of e' 's are:

$$e_a = A^b{}_a \, e'_b . \tag{4.5}$$

The reason for the form chosen for the relation between $\{e'_a\}$ and $\{e_a\}$ is this: if we have $A \in GL(n, \mathcal{R})$ taking $\{e_a\}$ to $\{e'_a\}$ and then $A' \in GL(n, \mathcal{R})$ taking $\{e'_a\}$ to $\{e''_a\}$, then the product $A'A$ (rather than AA') takes $\{e_a\}$ to $\{e''_a\}$. One can immediately see that the group $GL(n , \mathcal{R})$ acts both *freely* and *transitively* on $F(\mathcal{V})$, the set of all frames for $\mathcal{V}$!

The fact that the group $GL(n, \mathcal{R})$ has many significant subgroups leads to new and natural notions. Let $GL^+(n, \mathcal{R})$ be the subgroup of transformations with positive determinant:

$$GL^+(n, \mathcal{R}) = \{ A \in GL(n, \mathcal{R}) \mid \det A > 0 \} \subset GL(n, \mathcal{R}) \tag{4.6}$$

This is clearly an invariant or normal subgroup, and the quotient $GL(n, \mathcal{R}) / GL^+(n, \mathcal{R})$ is a two-element group. We shall say that two frames $\{e_a\}$, $\{e'_a\}$ for $\mathcal{V}$ *have the same orientation* if the unique $A \in GL(n, \mathcal{R})$ carrying $\{e_a\}$ to $\{e'_a\}$ belongs to $GL^+(n, \mathcal{R})$; they have *opposite* orientations if this $A \notin GL^+(n, \mathcal{R})$, which means $\det A < 0$. Thus, while $F(\mathcal{V})$ is a single orbit under the transitive $GL(n, \mathcal{R})$ action, the action by $GL^+(n, \mathcal{R})$ is *not* transitive; instead we have two disjoint orbits. Any two frames on the same orbit have the same orientation. On each of these two orbits, of course, the action by $GL^+(n, \mathcal{R})$ is transitive and free. We consider other subgroups of $GL(n, \mathcal{R})$ later.

Given the vector space $\mathcal{V}$, its *dual* $\mathcal{V}^*$ is another vector space, of the same dimension as $\mathcal{V}$. It consists of all real linear functionals on $\mathcal{V}$, so $\mathcal{V}^* = \mathcal{L}(\mathcal{V}; \mathcal{R})$. Thus any vector $\alpha \in \mathcal{V}^*$ is a function or map from $\mathcal{V}$ to $\mathcal{R}$ with the properties

$$\alpha \in \mathcal{V}^*, x \in \mathcal{V} \quad : \quad \alpha(x) \in \mathcal{R} ,$$
$$\alpha(c_1 x_1 + c_2 x_2) \quad = \quad c_1 \alpha(x_1) + c_2 \alpha(x_2) \tag{4.7}$$

Such α 's themselves form a real linear space, with scalar multiplication and linear combinations defined as expected:

$$(c_1 \alpha_1 + c_2 \alpha_2)(x) = c_1 \alpha_1(x) + c_2 \alpha_2(x). \tag{4.8}$$

We may write $< \alpha , x >$ or $< x , \alpha >$ or $\alpha(x)$ for the *value* of $\alpha \in \mathcal{V}^*$ *on* or *at* $x \in \mathcal{V}$. It is easy to convince oneself that

$(\mathcal{V}^*)^* = \mathcal{V}$: in a canonical and intrinsic way the dual to $\mathcal{V}^*$ is $\mathcal{V}$ itself; just "read" $\alpha\,(x)$ in the opposite direction!

Given a frame $\{e_a\} \in F\,(\mathcal{V})$, a unique dual frame $\{e^a\} \in F\,(\mathcal{V}^*)$ is determined by setting

$$e^a\,(e_b) \quad = \quad \delta_b^a \,,$$
$$\text{i.e.,} < e^a\,, e_b > \quad = \quad \delta_b^a \tag{4.9}$$

The change of frame (4.4) under an element of $GL\,(n,\,\mathcal{R})$ induces a corresponding change of dual frame for $\mathcal{V}^*$:

$$e_a \rightarrow e'_a \quad = \quad (A^{-1})^b{}_a\, e_b \Longrightarrow$$
$$e^a \rightarrow e'^a \quad = \quad A^a{}_b\, e^b \tag{4.10}$$

Therefore, if $\{e_a\}$ and $\{e'_a\}$ have the same orientation as frames for $\mathcal{V}$, then $\{e^a\}$ and $\{e'^a\}$ have the same orientation as frames for $\mathcal{V}^*$.

4.3.   DIRECT SUMS AND PRODUCTS OF VECTOR SPACES

The *direct sum* of two real linear vector spaces $\mathcal{V}_1$ and $\mathcal{V}_2$ is defined to be the space $\mathcal{V} = \mathcal{V}_1 \oplus \mathcal{V}_2$ of *ordered pairs* subject to the following familiar rules:

$$x \in \mathcal{V}_1, y \in \mathcal{V}_2 \quad \Longleftrightarrow \quad (x,y) \in \mathcal{V}\,;$$
$$c\,(x,y) \quad = \quad (cx,cy)\,;$$
$$c_1\,(x_1,y_1) + c_2\,(x_2,y_2) \quad = \quad (c_1\,x_1 + c_2\,x_2, c_1\,y_1 + c_2\,y_2) \tag{4.11}$$

We must take care to note here that (x,y) is an ordered pair, not an inner product! So it may be simpler to write $x+y$ rather than (x,y) , and understand the meaning of the addition sign properly. The fact that $\mathcal{V}$ is a real vector space is evident; its dimension is the sum of the dimensions of $\mathcal{V}_1$ and of $\mathcal{V}_2$. A frame for $\mathcal{V}_1$ along with one for $\mathcal{V}_2$, put together, certainly provide us with a frame for $\mathcal{V}$. However the most general frame for $\mathcal{V}$ is not of this special kind!

To deal next with the *direct product* or *tensor product* of two vector spaces $\mathcal{V}_1$ and $\mathcal{V}_2$, a little more effort is needed. At first sight the construction we shall now describe may seem somewhat cumbersome, but after some reflection it should become evident that this is the most economical and convenient procedure. First we pass from $\mathcal{V}_1$ and $\mathcal{V}_2$ to their duals $\mathcal{V}_1^*, \mathcal{V}_2^*$. Then we form the *Cartesian product* $\mathcal{V}_1^* \times \mathcal{V}_2^*$ of $\mathcal{V}_1^*$ and $\mathcal{V}_2^*$, namely the set of ordered pairs:

$$\mathcal{V}_1^* \times \mathcal{V}_2^* = \{\,(\alpha\,,\beta) \mid \alpha \in \mathcal{V}_1^*,\, \beta \in \mathcal{V}_2^*\,\} \tag{4.12}$$

(This kind of set of ordered pairs was just what we used earlier to form the direct sum $V_1 \oplus V_2$, in eq.(4.11), but here we use it for a different purpose). Now consider all bilinear functionals from $V_1^* \times V_2^*$ to $\mathcal{R}$, namely maps $f : V_1^* \times V_2^* \to \mathcal{R}$ obeying:

$$\alpha \in V_1^*, \beta \in V_2^* \quad : \quad f(\alpha, \beta) \in \mathcal{R};$$
$$f(c_1 \alpha_1 + c_2 \alpha_2 , \beta) = c_1 f(\alpha_1, \beta) + c_2 f(\alpha_2, \beta),$$
$$f(\alpha, c_1 \beta_1 + c_2 \beta_2) = c_1 f(\alpha, \beta_1) + c_2 f(\alpha, \beta_2) \quad (4.13)$$

The set of all such functionals can be denoted as $\mathcal{L}(V_1^* \times V_2^*; \mathcal{R})$ or, as the meaning is clear, by $\mathcal{L}(V_1^*, V_2^*; \mathcal{R})$. These then are the elements of the *tensor product* or *direct product* $V_1 \otimes V_2$:

$$V_1 \otimes V_2 = \mathcal{L}(V_1^*, V_2^*; \mathcal{R}) \quad (4.14)$$

Forming the tensor product of vector spaces is best done in this way via linear functionals on the cartesian product of their duals. The dimension of $V_1 \otimes V_2$ is the product of the dimensions of V_1 and V_2 .

The properties demanded of f in eqs.(4.13) can be summed up by saying that f is a real-valued multi-linear functional.

Particular vectors of $V_1 \otimes V_2$ arise as the tensor products of vectors in V_1 and V_2 thus:

$$x \in V_1, y \in V_2 \Rightarrow x \otimes y \in V_1 \otimes V_2 :$$
$$(x \otimes y)(\alpha, \beta) = \alpha(x) \beta(y), \alpha \in V_1^*, \beta \in V_2^* \quad (4.15)$$

Of course the most general vector in $V_1 \otimes V_2$ is not of this special kind, but is a sum of such single products. From a basis for V_1 and one for V_2 , we can form a special basis for $V_1 \otimes V_2$:

$$\{e_a\} \in F(V_1), \{e_j'\} \in F(V_2) \Rightarrow \{e_a \otimes e_j'\} \in F(V_1 \otimes V_2) \quad (4.16)$$

But again the most general frame for $V_1 \otimes V_2$ is not of this kind.

4.4.   TENSORS OVER V

Let us now revert to a single vector space V and its dual V^* . We can use the idea of multilinear functionals to set up various kinds of tensors over V . The space $\mathcal{J}^{(r,s)}(V)$ of tensors over V , of contravariant rank r and covariant rank s , is a linear space of real valued multilinear functionals having r arguments from V^* and s from V . This may be indicated as follows:

$$\mathcal{J}^{(r,s)}(\mathcal{V}) \qquad = \mathcal{L}(\mathcal{V}^*,\ \mathcal{V}^*,\dots,\ \mathcal{V}^*,\ \mathcal{V},\mathcal{V},\dots,\ \ \mathcal{V};\ \mathcal{R})$$
$$\leftarrow\ r\ \text{slots}\ \rightarrow\ \ \leftarrow\ \ s\ \text{slots}\ \ \ \rightarrow$$

$$= \mathcal{V}\otimes\mathcal{V}\otimes\dots\otimes\mathcal{V}\otimes\mathcal{V}^*\otimes\mathcal{V}^*\otimes\dots\otimes\mathcal{V}^*;$$
$$\leftarrow\ r\ \text{factors}\ \rightarrow\ \ \leftarrow\ \ s\ \text{factors}\ \ \rightarrow$$

$$A\in\mathcal{J}^{(r,s)}(\mathcal{V})\quad:\quad A(\alpha_1,\ \alpha_2,\ \dots,\ \alpha_r;\ x_1,\ x_2,\dots,\ x_s)\in\mathcal{R},$$
$$\alpha's\in\mathcal{V}^*,\ x's\in\mathcal{V},$$

A separately linear in each argument (4.17)

As a matter of convention, we regard $\mathcal{J}^{(0,0)}(\mathcal{V})$ as being just $\mathcal{R}$. Then $\mathcal{J}^{(1,0)}(\mathcal{V})$ and $\mathcal{J}^{(0,1)}(\mathcal{V})$ are respectively $\mathcal{V}$ and $\mathcal{V}^*$. With a basis or frame $\{e_a\}$ for $\mathcal{V}$, and the dual frame $\{e^a\}$ for $\mathcal{V}^*$, we can construct a particular frame for $\mathcal{J}^{(r,s)}(\mathcal{V})$ of the tensor product kind; its members are

$$e_{a_1}\otimes\dots\otimes e_{a_r}\ \ \otimes e^{b_1}\otimes\dots\otimes e^{b_s}\in\mathcal{J}^{(r,s)}(\mathcal{V}):$$
$$(e_{a_1}\otimes\dots\otimes e_{a_r}\ \ \otimes e^{b_1}\otimes\dots\otimes e^{b_s})(\alpha_1,\dots,\alpha_r;\ x_1,\dots,\ x_s)$$
$$= \alpha_1(e_{a_1})\ ..\ \alpha_r(e_{a_r})\,e^{b_1}(x_1)..\ e^{b_s}(x_s)\qquad(4.18)$$

In the last line here each factor has been written as the value of an element of $\mathcal{V}^*$ on an element of $\mathcal{V}$. A general tensor A in $\mathcal{J}^{(r,s)}(\mathcal{V})$ can then be expanded in the above basis, bringing in its components:

$$A\ \ = A^{a_1\,\cdots\,a_r}{}_{b_1\,\dots\,b_s}\ \ e_{a_1}\otimes\dots\otimes e_{a_r}\otimes e^{b_1}\otimes\dots\otimes e^{b_s},$$
$$A^{a_1\,\cdots\,a_r}{}_{b_1\,\dots\,b_s}\ \ = A(\dots e^a\,\dots;\ \dots e_b\,\dots)\qquad(4.19)$$

Clearly, the dimension of $\mathcal{J}^{(r,s)}(\mathcal{V})$ is given by

$$\dim.\ \mathcal{J}^{(r,s)}(\mathcal{V})\ =\ (\dim.\ \mathcal{V})^{(r+s)}\qquad(4.20)$$

Now we turn to two important, and familiar, algebraic operations with tensors: tensor multiplication, and "contraction of indices". Both of these yield new tensors from old. Given two tensors, A and B, of some ranks, we set up their tensor product using the method of multilinear functionals:

$$A\in\mathcal{J}^{(r,s)}(\mathcal{V}),B\in\mathcal{J}^{(r',s')}(\mathcal{V})\ \Rightarrow$$
$$A\otimes B\in\mathcal{J}^{(r+r',\ s+s')}(\mathcal{V}):$$
$$(A\otimes B)(\alpha_1,\ \dots,\ \alpha_{r+r'};\ x_1,\ \dots,\ x_{s+s'})\ =$$
$$A(\alpha_1,\dots,\alpha_r;\ x_1,\dots\ x_s)\,B(\alpha_{r+1},\dots,\alpha_{r+r'};\ x_{s+1},\dots,\ x_{s+s'})\qquad(4.21)$$

It is evident that $A \otimes B$ is indeed a tensor of the kind indicated. Tensor multiplication is associative: for any three (or more) tensors over $\mathcal{V}$,

$$\begin{aligned} A \otimes (B \otimes C) &= (A \otimes B) \otimes C \\ &= A \otimes B \otimes C \end{aligned} \qquad (4.22)$$

Turning to contraction: let $A \in \mathcal{J}^{(r,s)}(\mathcal{V})$, and choose some pth contravariant and qth covariant "index" on A . This means we focus on the pth $\mathcal{V}^*$ - argument and the qth - $\mathcal{V}$ - argument in A as a multilinear functional. Let $\{e_a\}$, $\{e^a\}$ be dual bases for $\mathcal{V}$ and $\mathcal{V}^*$. Then we get a tensor $B \in \mathcal{J}^{(r-1,\ s-1)}(\mathcal{V})$ out of A by the rule:

$$B(\ldots; \ldots) = A(\ldots \quad \underset{\downarrow}{e^a} \ _{\ldots;\ \ldots} \quad \underset{\downarrow}{e_a} \ \ldots)$$

$$pth \text{ slot} \quad qth \text{ slot}$$

i.e., $B(\alpha_1, \ldots, \alpha_{r-1}; x_1, \ldots, x_{s-1}) =$
$A(\alpha_1, \ldots, e^a, \ldots, \alpha_{r-1};\ x_1 \ \ldots, e_a,\ \ldots\ x_{s-1})$ \qquad (4.23)

Here the sum on a is understood. The significant point is that because of the mutually related transformation laws (4.10) of dual bases in $\mathcal{V}$ and $\mathcal{V}^*$, we see that B arises solely from A and the choices of positions p and q , but is independent of the frames $\{e_a\}$, $\{e^a\}$ used in the contraction process. In component form we have the well-known rule:

$$B^{a_1 \ \cdots \ a_{,}-1}{}_{b_1 \ \ldots \ b_{s-1}} = A^{a_1 \ \cdots \ a_{p-1} \ a \ a_p \ \cdots \ a_{r-1}}{}_{b_1 \ \ldots \ b_{q-1} \ a \ b_q \ \ldots \ b_{s-1}} \quad (4.24)$$

The several ways in which to pass from $\mathcal{J}^{(r,s)}(\mathcal{V})$ to $\mathcal{J}^{(r-1,\ s-1)}(\mathcal{V})$ via contraction are distinguished by the choices of p and q .

4.5.   FORMS OVER $\mathcal{V}$

A particularly important role is played in general theory by the *covariant* tensors $\mathcal{J}^{(0,s)}(\mathcal{V})$ of various ranks, and more particularly the *completely antisymmetric* ones. These latter are called *forms* over the vector space $\mathcal{V}$. They constitute an interesting mathematical system on their own, an associative algebra, with a characteristic new rule of composition or "multiplication". This is denoted by the wedge symbol, $\wedge$, distinct from the direct or tensor product $\otimes$ but related to it. The space of k-forms over $\mathcal{V}$, denoted by $C^k(\mathcal{V})$, is a subspace of the space of k-th rank covariant tensors $\mathcal{J}^{(0,k)}(\mathcal{V})$:

$$C^k(\mathcal{V}) \subset \mathcal{J}^{(0,k)}(\mathcal{V}) \qquad (4.25)$$

A tensor $A \in \mathcal{J}^{(0,k)}(\mathcal{V})$ is a k-form if for any permutation $p \in S_k$ on k objects we have

$$A(x_{p(1)}, \; x_{p(2)}, \; \cdots \; , x_{p(k)}) \;\; = \;\; \delta_p \, A(x_1, x_2, \; \cdots \; , \; x_k)$$
$$x's \in \mathcal{V}, \; \delta_p \;\; = \;\; \text{signature of } p \qquad (4.26)$$

Given this total antisymmetry property, we can carry the expansion (4.19) one step further to exploit it:

$$A \;\; \in \;\; C^k(\mathcal{V}):$$
$$A_{a_{p(1)} \, a_{p(2)} \, \cdots \, a_{p(k)}} \;\; = \;\; \delta_p \, A_{a_1 \, a_2 \, \cdots \, a_k};$$
$$A \;\; = \;\; A_{a_1 \, a_2 \, \cdots \, a_k} \, e^{a_1} \otimes e^{a_2} \otimes \cdots \otimes e^{a_k}$$
$$= \;\; \frac{1}{k!} A_{a_1 \, a_2 \, \cdots \, a_k} \, e^{a_1} \wedge e^{a_2} \wedge \cdots \wedge e^{a_k},$$
$$e^{a_1} \wedge e^{a_2} \wedge \cdots \wedge e^{a_k} \;\; \equiv \;\; \sum_{p \in S_k} \delta_p \, e^{\,a_{p(1)}} \otimes e^{\,a_{p(2)}} \otimes \cdots \otimes e^{\,a_{p(k)}}$$

$$(4.27)$$

What we have done is to set up a new "wedge product" of k basis vectors for $\mathcal{V}^*$, such that this product is explicitly anti- symmetric in the indices $a_1, a_2, \ldots, a_k$, matching the antisymmetry of the components of A: the last line defines $\wedge$ in terms of $\otimes$.

It is clear from this discussion that the spaces of forms $C^k(\mathcal{V})$ can be defined only for $k = 0, 1, \ldots, n$; for $k > n$, a totally antisymmetric covariant tensor vanishes identically.(For $k = 0$, we take $C^o(\mathcal{V}) = \mathcal{R}$). Moreover the dimensions are:

$$\dim C^k(\mathcal{V}) \;=\; n! \, / \, k! \, (n-k)! \qquad (4.28)$$

And the wedge products of the elements of a basis for $\mathcal{V}^*$ give bases for forms.

Given a k-form $A \in C^k(\mathcal{V})$ and an l-form $B \in C^l(\mathcal{V})$, we can produce a $(k+l)$-form $A \wedge B$ out of them (nonvanishing only if $k + l \leq n$) by taking the direct product and totally antisymmetrising it:

$$A \in C^k(\mathcal{V}), \; B \in C^l(\mathcal{V}) \; \rightarrow \; A \wedge B \in C^{k+l}(\mathcal{V}):$$
$$(A \wedge B)\,(x_1, \, x_2, \, \ldots, \, x_{k+l}) \;=\;$$
$$\frac{1}{k! \, l!} \sum_{p \in S_{k+l}} \delta_p \, A(x_{p(1)}, \, \ldots, \, x_{p(k)}) \, B(x_{p(k+1)}, \, \ldots, \, x_{p(k+l)})$$

$$(4.29)$$

This definition and the numerical factors have been chosen so that in $A \wedge B$ we may recognise a *leading term* with coefficient unity, and then a *retinue* uniquely determined by antisymmetry:

$$(A \wedge B)(x_1, x_2, \ldots, x_{k+l}) = A(x_1, x_2, \ldots, x_k) \, B(x_{k+1}, \ldots, x_{k+l})$$
$$+ \text{ unique remainder} \qquad (4.30)$$

Recognition of this structure helps us to easily verify several important properties of the wedge product:

(i) $A \in C^k(\mathcal{V}),\ B \in C^l(\mathcal{V}):$
      $A \wedge B = (-1)^{kl} \, B \wedge A.$

(ii) $A \in C^k(\mathcal{V}),\ B \in C^l(\mathcal{V}),\ C \in C^m(\mathcal{V}):$
      $A \wedge (B \wedge C) = (A \wedge B) \wedge C = A \wedge B \wedge C.$

(iii) $\alpha_1, \alpha_2, \ldots, \alpha_k \in \mathcal{V}^* \Rightarrow \alpha_1 \wedge \alpha_2 \wedge \ldots \wedge \alpha_k \in C^k(\mathcal{V}):$
      $(\alpha_1 \wedge \alpha_2 \wedge \ldots \wedge \alpha_k)(x_1, x_2, \ldots, x_k) = \det(\alpha_j(x_l)),\ x's \in \mathcal{V}$
$$(4.31)$$

In each case the proof consists in isolating the unique leading term and identifying its coefficient carefully: the rest then follows automatically.

Sometimes the space $C^k(\mathcal{V})$ is written as $\wedge^k \mathcal{V}^*$. The direct sum of all these spaces, from $k = 0$ to $k = n$, is called the space of forms over $\mathcal{V}$, or the *Grassmann algebra over* $\mathcal{V}$:

$$\mathcal{G}(\mathcal{V}) = \text{Grassmann algebra over } \mathcal{V}$$
$$= \sum_{k=0}^{n} \oplus\, C^k(\mathcal{V})$$
$$= \mathcal{R} \oplus \mathcal{V}^* \oplus C^2(\mathcal{V}) \oplus \ldots \oplus C^n(\mathcal{V}),$$
$$C^o(\mathcal{V}) = \mathcal{R},\ C^1(\mathcal{V}) = \mathcal{V}^* \qquad (4.32)$$

The wedge product makes $\mathcal{G}(\mathcal{V})$ an *associative* but *noncommutative* algebra.

4.6.   INNER CONTRACTION, SIMPLE FORMS

An important algebraic operation on forms is that of *inner contraction with a vector*, ie., with an element of $\mathcal{V}$. This lowers the rank of the form by one. Given a k-form $A \in C^k(\mathcal{V})$ (for $k \geq 1$) and a vector $x \in \mathcal{V}$, we define

$$i_x A \in C^{(k-1)}(\mathcal{V}) \quad :$$
$$(i_x A)(x_1, x_2 \ldots, x_{k-1}) = A(x, x_1, x_2, \ldots, x_{k-1}) \quad (4.33)$$

The algebraic properties of inner contraction are:

$$(i) \quad i_x \, i_y = - \, i_y \, i_x \, ;$$

$$(ii) \quad i_x \, (A \wedge B) = (i_x \, A) \wedge B + (-1)^k \, A \wedge i_x \, B,$$
$$A \in C^k(\mathcal{V}), \; B \in C^l(\mathcal{V}) \qquad (4.34)$$

The first is evident from the antisymmetry of forms; the second is easily seen by keeping track of the relevant leading terms in the sense of eq.(4.30). For the wedge product of three (or more) forms A, B, C, .. of degrees $k, l, m, \ldots$ we obtain:

$$
\begin{aligned}
i_x \, (A \wedge B \wedge C) \;=\;& i_x \, A \wedge B \wedge C + (-1)^k \, A \wedge i_x \, B \wedge C \\
&+ (-1)^{k+l} \, A \wedge B \wedge i_x \, C, \qquad (4.35)
\end{aligned}
$$

and so on.

A single term or monomial type k-form $A = \alpha_1 \wedge \alpha_2 \wedge \ldots \wedge \alpha_k$ has a nice geometrical interpretation. Of course, to be non-zero, the α 's must be linearly independent elements in $\mathcal{V}^*$. Then A is called a *simple* or *decomposable* k-form. It determines uniquely an $(n - k)$ dimensional linear subspace $\mathcal{V}_1 \subset \mathcal{V}$, and conversely $\mathcal{V}_1$ determines A up to a multiplicative factor:

$$
\begin{aligned}
&A \in C^k(\mathcal{V}), \; A = \alpha_1 \wedge \alpha_2 \wedge \ldots \wedge \alpha_k \neq 0 : \\
&\mathcal{V}_1 = \{ x \in \mathcal{V} \mid i_x \, A = 0 \} \\
&= \{ x \in \mathcal{V} \mid \alpha_1 \, (x) = \alpha_2 \, (x) = \ldots = \alpha_k \, (x) = 0 \} \subset \mathcal{V}, \\
&\dim . \; \mathcal{V}_1 = (n - k) \qquad (4.36)
\end{aligned}
$$

4.7. n-FORMS AND VOLUME ELEMENTS FOR $\mathcal{V}$

We saw that $C^k(\mathcal{V})$ is of dimension $n! \, / k! \, (n - k)!$. Thus this dimension increases as k goes from zero to about $n/2$, then it decreases and becomes unity for $C^n(\mathcal{V})$. If $\{e_a\}$ is any frame for $\mathcal{V}$ and $\{e^a\}$ is its dual for $\mathcal{V}^*$, then

$$e^1 \wedge e^2 \wedge \ldots \wedge e^n \in C^n(\mathcal{V}), \qquad (4.37)$$

and any n-form ω is some real multiple of this one:

$$
\begin{aligned}
\omega \in C^n(\mathcal{V}) \quad : \quad \omega =\;& \omega_{12 \ldots n} \, e^1 \wedge e^2 \wedge \ldots \wedge e^n, \\
&\omega_{12 \ldots n} \in \mathcal{R} \qquad (4.38)
\end{aligned}
$$

If via an element $A \in GL(n, \mathcal{R})$ we switch to a new frame $\{e'_a\}$ for $\mathcal{V}$ and its dual $\{e'^a\}$ for $\mathcal{V}^*$, according to eqs.(4.10), we find:

$$
\begin{aligned}
e'^a =\;& A^a{}_b \, e^b \Rightarrow \\
e'^{\,1} \wedge e'^{\,2} \wedge \ldots \wedge e'^{\,n} =\;& (\det A) \, e^1 \wedge e^2 \wedge \ldots \wedge e^n \quad (4.39)
\end{aligned}
$$

So for a general n-form ω we have:

$$
\begin{aligned}
\omega &= \omega_{12\,\ldots\,n}\; e^1 \wedge e^2 \wedge \ldots \wedge e^n \\
&= \omega'_{12\,\ldots\,n}\; e'^{\,1} \wedge e'^{\,2} \wedge \ldots \wedge e'^{\,n}, \\
\omega'_{12\,\ldots\,n} &= (\det\,A)^{-1}.\,\omega_{12\,\ldots\,n}
\end{aligned}
\tag{4.40}
$$

On the basis of these results we say: any nonzero n-form η on $\mathcal{V}$ defines an *oriented volume element* for $\mathcal{V}$. A frame $\{e_a\}$ for $\mathcal{V}$ is "well-oriented" or "positively oriented" (with respect to η, of course) if $\eta_{12\,\ldots\,n}$ is positive. Such frames are connected to one another by elements of $GL^+(n,\,\mathcal{R})$. (The "other half" of $F(\mathcal{V})$ consists of negatively oriented frames, with respect to η; they too are related to one another by elements of $GL^+(n,\,\mathcal{R})$). With respect to a given volume form η, the parallelopiped formed by n vectors $x_1,\ x_2,\ \ldots,\ x_n \in \mathcal{V}$ has a volume which has a magnitude and a sign:

$$
\text{Vol.}\,\{x_1,\ x_2,\ \ldots,\ x_n\} \;=\; \eta\,(x_1,\ x_2,\ \ldots,\ x_n)
\tag{4.41}
$$

Of course, if the x's are linearly dependent, the volume becomes zero; and interchanging any two of them switches the sign.

Among all well-oriented frames are the unimodular frames: these are those in which $\eta_{12\,\ldots\,n} = 1$. Such frames are related to one another by elements of the subgroup $SL(n,\,\mathcal{R})$. Thus one can make the series of statements:

$$
\begin{aligned}
F(\mathcal{V}) \quad &= \text{all frames for V:} &\quad &\text{admits free transitive } GL(n,\mathcal{R}) \text{ action;} \\
&\text{Orientation on } \mathcal{V} \equiv &\quad &\text{a } GL^+(n,\,\mathcal{R}) \text{ orbit in } F(\mathcal{V}); \\
&\text{Volume form } \eta \text{ on } \mathcal{V} \Rightarrow &\quad &\text{choice of orientation,} \\
& & &\text{class of unimodular frames,} \\
& & &\text{i.e., an } SL(n,\mathcal{R}) \text{ orbit within } F(\mathcal{V})
\end{aligned}
\tag{4.42}
$$

We see illustrated here some of the notions introduced in Section 3 concerning the action of a group on a set.

4.8.   INTRODUCTION OF A METRIC ON $\mathcal{V}$

As a last item in this Section let us suppose that a nondegenerate (pseudo) Euclidean metric g on $\mathcal{V}$ is given. This is a rank two symmetric tensor of covariant type. Apart from being a bilinear functional, the other specific properties are:

(i) $x,\,y \in \mathcal{V}:\ g(x,\,y) = g(y,\,x) \in \mathcal{R}:$ symmetry;

(ii) $g(x,\,y) = 0$ for all $y \in \mathcal{V} \Rightarrow x = 0:$ nondegeneracy

$$
\tag{4.43}
$$

With respect to frames $\{e_a\}$, $\{e^a\}$ for $\mathcal{V}$, $\mathcal{V}^*$ we can write:

$$
\begin{aligned}
g &= g_{ab}\, e^a \otimes e^b, \\
g(x,\, y) &= g_{ab}\, e^a(x)\, e^b(y) \\
&= g_{ab}\, x^a\, y^b
\end{aligned}
\tag{4.44}
$$

Under the change of frame (4.10) the components g_{ab} transform thus:

$$
\begin{aligned}
g &= g'_{ab}\, e'^{\,a} \otimes e'^{\,b}, \\
g'_{ab} &= (A^{-1})^c{}_a\, (A^{-1})^d{}_b\, g_{cd}
\end{aligned}
\tag{4.45}
$$

By a standard theorem in matrix theory, by a suitable choice of frame we can bring the matrix (g_{ab}) to diagonal form, and arrange that the diagonal elements are ± 1. The *signature* $(p,\, n-p)$, where p is the number of $+1$'s and $n-p$ is the number of -1's in this diagonal form, is an intrinsic property of the metric g. Based on this, a special class of frames in $F(\mathcal{V})$ is singled out, namely the *orthonormal frames* :

$$
\{e_a\} \text{ an orthonormal frame} \Leftrightarrow
$$
$$
(g_{ab}) = \mathrm{diag.}(+1,+1,\ldots,+1,\ -1,-1,-1\ldots,-1)
$$
$$
\longleftarrow \quad p \quad \longrightarrow \longleftarrow \quad (n-p) \quad \longrightarrow
\tag{4.46}
$$

Such frames are related to one another by the group $O(p,\, n-p)$ of (pseudo) orthogonal rotations. This is of course a subgroup of $GL(n,\, \mathcal{R})$.

If we go one step further and pick an orientation, then half the orthonormal frames are declared to be well or positively oriented, the other half negatively oriented. Each class in this case is an orbit under the group $SO(p,\, n-p)$ of unimodular (pseudo) orthogonal transformations. Thus a nondegenerate metric plus a choice of orientation determine a *natural volume element* or *natural volume form* η :

$$
\begin{aligned}
\{e_a\} &= \text{well-oriented orthonormal frame,} \\
\{e'_a\} &= \text{general well-oriented frame:} \\
\eta &\equiv e^1 \wedge e^2 \wedge \ldots \wedge e^n \\
&= |\det(g'_{ab})|^{1/2}\, e'^{\,1} \wedge e'^{\,2} \wedge \ldots \wedge e'^{\,n}
\end{aligned}
\tag{4.47}
$$

We can recapitulate the roles played by various groups in this manner:

$$
GL^+(n, \mathcal{R}) \longleftrightarrow \text{ choice of an orientation;}
$$

$$
SL(n, \mathcal{R}) \longleftrightarrow \text{ unimodular frames with respect to a volume form } \eta;
$$

$$
O(p,\, n-p) \longleftrightarrow \text{ orthonormal frames for a pseudo Euclidean metric;}
$$

$SO(p,\ n-p)\ \longleftrightarrow$ oriented orthonormal frames with a metric,
i.e., natural volume element

4.9. THE DUALITY OPERATION

If a metric g and an orientation are both in hand, then a new relation among, or operation on, forms becomes available. This is the passage to the dual of a form, or the Hodge duality operation. It maps k-forms to $(n-k)$ - forms in an invertible manner, and in a way determined by both metric and orientation.

To begin, we reinterpret the given metric $g \in \mathcal{J}^{(0,2)}(\mathcal{V})$ in the following way: If we choose and keep fixed some $x \in \mathcal{V}$, then $g(x, y)$ is a linear function of y with real values:

$$x \in \mathcal{V} \text{ fixed } : \quad g\,(x,\, \cdot) \in \mathcal{L}(\mathcal{V};\, \mathcal{R}),$$
$$\text{ie.,} \quad g(x,\, \cdot) \in \mathcal{V}^* \tag{4.48}$$

Thus one can view the metric $g \in \mathcal{J}^{(0,2)}(\mathcal{V})$ as a linear map, $\tilde{g}$ say, from $\mathcal{V}$ to $\mathcal{V}^*$: the linearity of $g(x,\, \cdot)$ in x is obvious. In explicit detail we say:

$$\tilde{g}: \mathcal{V} \to \mathcal{V}^* \quad : \quad x \in \mathcal{V} \to \tilde{g}\,(x) \in \mathcal{V}^*,$$
$$< \tilde{g}\,(x),\, y > = g(x,\, y),\, y \in \mathcal{V} \tag{4.49}$$

The nondegeneracy of g reads:

$$x \neq 0 \Leftrightarrow \tilde{g}(x) \neq 0 \tag{4.50}$$

Now let us work in any well-oriented frame, and let η be the natural volume element determined by g and the chosen orientation. The Hodge map is then defined as follows:

$$A \in C^k(\mathcal{V}) \quad \to \quad \tilde{A} \in C^{(n-k)}(\mathcal{V}):$$
$$\tilde{A}\,(x_1,\, x_2,\, \ldots,\, x_{n-k})\, \eta \quad = \quad A \wedge \tilde{g}(x_1) \wedge \tilde{g}(x_2) \wedge \ldots \wedge \tilde{g}(x_{n-k})$$
$$\tag{4.51}$$

We can easily get an explicit relation between the components of $\tilde{A}$ and of A in any well-oriented frames $\{e_a\}$, $\{e^a\}$ in which we have the expressions

$$\eta \quad = \quad |\det g\,|^{1/2}\, e^1 \wedge e^2 \wedge \ldots \wedge e^n\,;$$
$$\tilde{g}(x) \quad = \quad g_{ab}\, x^a\, e^b \in \mathcal{V}^* \text{ for } x = x^a\, e_a \in \mathcal{V}\,;$$
$$A \quad = \quad \frac{1}{k!}\, A_{a_1\, a_2\, \ldots\, a_k}\, e^{a_1} \wedge e^{a_2} \wedge \ldots \wedge e^{a_k}\,,$$
$$\tilde{A} \quad = \quad \frac{1}{(n-k)!}\, \tilde{A}_{b_1\, b_2\, \ldots\, b_{n-k}} e^{b_1} \wedge e^{b_2} \wedge \ldots \wedge e^{b_{n-k}} \tag{4.52}$$

Here the numerical factors are as agreed upon in eq.(4.27). In the ensuing calculations we shall, merely as a shorthand notation, freely use the completely antisymmetric Levi-Civita symbols normalised to

$$\epsilon^{12\ \cdots\ n} = \epsilon_{12\ \cdots\ n} = +1 \ .$$

Relabelling the x 's in eq.(4.51) for convenience as $x_{k+1}, x_{k+2}, \ldots, x_n$, we have:

$$A \wedge \tilde{g}\,(x_{k+1}) \wedge \tilde{g}\,(x_{k+2}) \wedge \ldots \wedge \tilde{g}\,(x_n) =$$

$$\frac{1}{k!}\, A_{a_1\,a_2\,\cdots\,a_k}\ e^{a_1} \wedge e^{a_2} \wedge \ldots \wedge e^{a_k} \wedge$$

$$g_{b_{k+1}\,a_{k+1}}\, x_{k+1}^{b_{k+1}}\ e^{a_{k+1}} \wedge \ldots\ g_{b_n\,a_n}\ x_n^{b_n}\ e^{a_n}$$

$$= \frac{1}{k!}\, A_{a_1\,a_2\,\cdots\,a_k}\ g_{a_{k+1}\,b_{k+1}}\ \cdots\ g_{a_n\,b_n}\, x_{k+1}^{b_{k+1}}\ \cdots\ x_n^{b_n} \times$$

$$\epsilon^{a_1\,a_2\,\cdots\,a_n} \cdot e^1 \wedge e^2 \wedge \ldots \wedge e^n,$$

$$\text{ie.,}\quad \tilde{A}\,(x_{k+1}, \ldots, x_n) = \frac{|\det g|^{-1/2}}{k!}\ \epsilon^{a_1\,\cdots\,a_n} \times$$

$$A_{a_1\,\cdots\,a_k}\ g_{a_{k+1}\,b_{k+1}}\ \cdots\ g_{a_n\,b_n} x_{k+1}^{b_{k+1}}\ \cdots\ x_n^{b_n} \tag{4.53}$$

On the other hand, from the way the components of $\tilde{A}$ are defined in eq.(4.52), we would have,

$$\tilde{A}\,(x_{k+1}, \ldots, x_n) = \frac{1}{(n-k)!}\, \tilde{A}_{b_{k+1}\,\cdots\,b_n} \times$$

$$(e^{b_{k+1}} \wedge \ldots \wedge e^{b_n})\,(x_{k+1}, \ldots, x_n)$$

$$= \tilde{A}_{b_{k+1}\,\cdots\,b_n}\ x_{k+1}^{b_{k+1}}\ \cdots\ x_n^{b_n} \tag{4.54}$$

Comparing the above two equations we read off the relation:

$$A \in C^k(\mathcal{V}) \quad \to \quad \tilde{A} \in C^{(n-k)}(\mathcal{V}) :$$

$$\tilde{A}_{b_{k+1}\,\cdots\,b_n} = \frac{|\det g|^{-1/2}}{k!}\ \epsilon^{a_1\,\cdots\,a_n}\ A_{a_1\,\cdots\,a_k} \times$$

$$g_{a_{k+1}\,b_{k+1}}\ \cdots\ g_{a_n\,b_n} \tag{4.55}$$

The earlier eq.(4.51) is the intrinsic definition of the duality operation, involving both the metric g and the oriented natural volume form η . The component form is in eq.(4.55). The latter makes it quite easy to calculate the effect of the double dual:

$$A \in C^k(\mathcal{V}) \quad \to \quad \tilde{A} \in C^{(n-k)}(\mathcal{V}) \quad \to \quad \tilde{\tilde{A}} \in C^k(\mathcal{V}) :$$

$$\tilde{A}_{c_1 \ldots c_k} = \frac{|\det g|^{-1/2}}{(n-k)!} \epsilon^{b_{k+1} \ldots b_n \; b_1 \ldots b_k} \times$$

$$\tilde{A}_{b_{k+1} \ldots b_n} g_{b_1 c_1} \cdots g_{b_k c_k}$$

$$= \frac{|\det g|^{-1}}{k!(n-k)!} (-1)^{k(n-k)} \epsilon^{b_1 \ldots b_n} \epsilon^{a_1 \ldots a_n} A_{a_1 \ldots a_k} \times$$

$$g_{c_1 b_1} \cdots g_{c_k b_k} \cdot g_{a_{k+1} b_{k+1}} \cdots g_{a_n b_n}$$

$$= \frac{|\det g|^{-1}}{k! \, (n-k)!} (-1)^{k \, (n-k)} \epsilon^{a_1 \ldots a_n} \times$$

$$\epsilon_{c_1 \ldots c_k \, a_{k+1} \ldots a_n} \det g \cdot A_{a_1 \ldots a_k}$$

$$= (-1)^{k(n-k)} \text{Sign} \det g \cdot A_{c_1 \ldots c_k},$$

$$\text{i.e., } \tilde{\tilde{A}} = (-1)^{k(n-k)} \text{Sign} \det g \cdot A. \qquad (4.56)$$

5. Topological Spaces

The concept of a topology on a given set M is the minimum framework needed to discuss the notions of convergence of sequences, and of continuity of functions and mappings. In the brief review given in this Section, we look only at the basic ideas and terms, without going into any detail. We will define topology on a set via the notion and properties of open sets.

5.1. OPEN SETS

A set M becomes a *topological space* by defining the concept of open sets in it. For this, we must choose some collection τ of subsets of M with the following three properties:

(i) $M \in \tau$, $\phi = $ empty set $\in \tau$;

(ii) $A_\alpha \in \tau$, any index set $\alpha \Rightarrow$

$$\bigcup_\alpha A_\alpha \in \tau;$$

(iii) A_1, $A_2 \in \tau \Rightarrow A_1 \cap A_2 \in \tau$ (5.1)

Then, open sets are the members of the collection τ. One can convey in words the content of the three properties above: the whole set and the empty set must belong to τ; arbitrary unions and finite intersections of open sets must also be open. The pair (M, τ) is then a topological space, and τ is a topology on M.

Of course this idea is an abstraction and refinement of what one knows and does with $\mathcal{R}$, $\mathcal{R}^2$, $\mathcal{R}^3$, ... in an intuitive way. As we shall see, a given set M may admit several topologies, ie., there may be many ways of choosing the collection τ .

A subset $A \subset M$ is open if and only if $A \in \tau$. It is closed if its complement A' is open. So M and ϕ are both open and closed. The closure of A is the smallest closed set containing A: it is denoted by $\overline{A}$. (All these definitions are relative to the given topology τ). A given subset $A \subset M$ need not be either open or closed.

5.2. CONTINUITY OF MAPS

Now topology is designed to allow a definition of continuity of functions or mappings. Let then (M, τ) and (N, τ') be two topological spaces, and $f : M \to N$ a map from M to N. We say f is continuous (relative to τ and τ') if and only if inverse images of open sets in N are open in M:

$$f : M \to N \text{ is continuous} \iff f^{-1}(B) \in \tau \text{ for every } B \in \tau' \quad (5.2)$$

Here we do not require f to be injective or surjective or both. The symbol f^{-1} denotes the *total inverse* : $f^{-1}(B)$ is the subset of M containing all points m such that $f(m) \in B$. Even if f were bijective, so that f^{-1} does define a map $N \to M$, *continuity of f does not imply that of* f^{-1} .

5.3. EQUIVALENT TOPOLOGIES

Now let us return to a single set M and a topology τ on it. For any point $m \in M$, a *neighbourhood* of m is any open set $\mathcal{U}$ containing m :

$$m \in M : \quad m \in \mathcal{U} \in \tau \iff \mathcal{U} \text{ is a neighbourhood of } m \quad (5.3)$$

(If we want to be specific we may say that $\mathcal{U}$ is a τ -neighbourhood of m). We can now define a notion of equivalence among topologies on M . Two topologies τ_1 and τ_2 on M are equivalent if the two concepts of continuity coincide. That is, if a function f from M to some topological space (possibly M itself with a specific topology) is continuous with respect to τ_1 , it is so with respect to τ_2 as well, and conversely. The criterion turns out to be this: for each $m \in M$, every τ_1 -neighbourhood $\mathcal{U}_1$ of m must contain a τ_2 -neighbourhood $\mathcal{U}_2$, and conversely:

τ_1 **equivalent to** τ_2

$$m \in \mathcal{U}_1 \in \tau_1 \Rightarrow \text{there is } \mathcal{U}_2 \text{ such that}$$
$$m \in \mathcal{U}_2 \in \tau_2 , \quad \mathcal{U}_2 \subset \mathcal{U}_1 ,$$
$$\text{and vice versa} \quad (5.4)$$

Thus one need not distinguish between equivalent topologies.

5.4. COMPARING TOPOLOGIES

Suppose two topologies τ_1 and τ_2 on M are not equivalent. Can they be compared in some way? In principle they can, and this involves the notions of stronger (finer) and weaker (coarser) topologies. The topology τ_1 is stronger (finer) than τ_2 if every τ_2-open set is also τ_1-open. That is, the τ_1-open sets are all the τ_2-open sets, and some more:

$$\tau_1 \text{ stronger than } \tau_2 \quad \Longleftrightarrow \quad \{ A \in \tau_2 \Rightarrow A \in \tau_1\}$$
$$\Longleftrightarrow \quad \tau_2 \text{ weaker than } \tau_1 \qquad (5.5)$$

Let us indicate the reason for these names. Continuity of some map f with respect to τ_1 or τ_2 means different things. Let $f : X \rightarrow M$ be a given map, (X, τ_o) being a *fixed* topological space. We want to compare (M, τ_1) and (M, τ_2). Clearly, if τ_1 is stronger than τ_2, continuity of f under τ_1 imposes *more* conditions on f than under τ_2, just because there are more τ_1-open sets in M! So if f is τ_1-continuous, it is certainly also τ_2-continuous, but not the other way around. There are thus fewer τ_1-continuous functions from X to M than τ_2-continuous ones:

$$\tau_1 \text{stronger than } \tau_2 \Rightarrow \{\tau_1 - \text{ continuity of } f : (X, \tau_o) \rightarrow (M, \tau_1) \Rightarrow$$
$$\tau_2 - \text{ continuity of } f : (X, \tau_o) \rightarrow (M, \tau_2) \}$$
$$(5.6)$$

(Remember that τ_o on X is kept fixed!). Of course, given two topologies τ_1 and τ_2 on M, it need not happen that one is stronger than the other.

On a given M, clearly the *strongest* topology is the one with the *most* open sets. This is called the *discrete* topology on M: in it, τ includes *all* subsets of M. So each subset in M, even each single point $m \in M$, is declared to be open. Of course, all the conditions (5.1) are obeyed, so we do have a topology. Obviously, any other topology on M is weaker than the discrete topology. At the other extreme, the *weakest* topology on M is obtained by saying that τ consists only of M and ϕ: this is the absolute minimum needed to fulfill (5.1). And this is called the *indiscrete* (*not* indiscreet!) or *trivial* topology on M. So any other topology on M is stronger than the indiscrete, and weaker than the discrete, topology on M.

5.5. TOPOLOGY ON A SUBSET

Given the topology τ on M , let $A \subset M$ be any subset, not necessarily either open or closed. Then through τ , A also becomes a topological space. We say A inherits a topology τ_A from τ on M . The definition of τ_A is very simple:

$$\mathcal{U} \in \tau_A \iff \mathcal{U} = A \cap \mathcal{U}', \ \mathcal{U}' \in \tau \tag{5.7}$$

That is, $\mathcal{U}$ is a τ_A -open subset of A if it is the intersection of A with a τ -open subset of M . It is easy to check that all the conditions (5.1) are obeyed, so $(A, \ \tau_A)$ is indeed a topological space.

5.6. BASIS FOR A TOPOLOGY

So far we viewed a topology τ on M as being given when *all* the open sets, *all* members of the collection τ , are displayed or enumerated. But this can be unwieldy and tiresome. Can we in principle exhibit τ by actually giving something less? Indeed we can, via the concept of a *basis* or *base* for τ . Let us now describe this notion.

First, at a point $m \in M$: an *open base* $\mathcal{B}_m$ is a *selected* set of neighbourhoods of M (τ -open sets containing m) such that if $\mathcal{U}$ is *any* neighbourhood of m , $\mathcal{U}$ contains a neighbourhood drawn from $\mathcal{B}_m$:
$\underline{\mathcal{B}_m = \text{open base at } m}$:

$$m \in \mathcal{U} \in \tau \Rightarrow \exists \ \mathcal{U}' \in \mathcal{B}_m \text{ such that } m \in \mathcal{U}' \subset \mathcal{U}$$
$$\tag{5.8}$$

In other words: inside *any* neighbourhood of m , we can find a *selected* one belonging to $\mathcal{B}_m$.

Next, moving to all of M : an open base $\mathcal{B}$ for the topology τ of M is a collection of open bases $\mathcal{B}_m$ for each $m \in M$. Thus, in brief, an open base $\mathcal{B}$ for (M, τ) is a collection of open sets (may be "far fewer" than τ itself) such that

$$m \in \mathcal{U} \in \tau \Rightarrow m \in B \subset \mathcal{U}, \ \text{ some } B \in \mathcal{B} \tag{5.9}$$

If the topology τ on M is given by specifying *all* open sets, we may then choose more economical bases $\mathcal{B}$ in many ways. Conversely, we may attempt to define τ itself by first choosing the base $\mathcal{B}$ for it, and then showing how to build up τ . In that case, we have to proceed as follows: Choose a family $\mathcal{B}$ of subsets of M such that:

(*i*) $M = $ union of members of $\mathcal{B}$;

(ii) $\quad B_1$, $B_2 \in \mathcal{B}$, $m \in B_1 \cap B_2 \Rightarrow$

$\exists \; B_3 \in \mathcal{B}$ such that

$$m \in B_3 \subset B_1 \cap B_2 \qquad (5.10)$$

These are the conditions we put on the *basic open sets* . We now say that a subset $A \subset M$ is open, and so belongs to τ, if and only if

$$m \in A \Rightarrow \exists \; B \in \mathcal{B} \text{ such that}$$
$$m \in B \subset A \qquad (5.11)$$

This definition of members of τ, plus the properties (5.10) for the basic open sets, ensures that all the conditions (5.1) are obeyed.

5.7. HAUSDORFF, COUNTABILITY PROPERTIES

In the theory of differentiable manifolds, which will be our main concern later, particular kinds of topological spaces are involved, namely those having the *Hausdorff* property, and those obeying the *Second Axiom of Countability*. Let us define these, and just hint at their significance.

A topological space (M, τ) is said to be *Hausdorff* if for any two distinct points $m, m' \in M$, we can find nonoverlapping neighbourhoods:

$$m \neq m' : \quad m \in \mathcal{U} \in \tau, \; m' \in \mathcal{U}' \in \tau,$$
$$\mathcal{U} \cap \mathcal{U}' = \phi \qquad (5.12)$$

The motivation here is that with this property a convergent sequence of points in M will have a unique limit. This is called a *separation* property.

Next, (M, τ) obeys the *Second Axiom of Countability* if we can find an open base $\mathcal{B}$ for τ, which is countable or denumerable. (First countability means that at each $m \in M$, a countable open base $\mathcal{B}_m$ can be chosen). These countability axioms are designed to make the concepts of continuity of functions and of convergence of sequences agree.

5.8. CONNECTEDNESS, COMPACTNESS

Among characterisations of topological spaces, the last two of interest to us are those of *connectedness* and *compactness*. A topological space (M, τ) is *connected* if and only if we *cannot* express M as the union of two disjoint open sets. On the other hand, if we can, then M is disconnected. The topological space (M, τ) is *compact* if *every* covering of M by open sets (an open covering) contains a finite subcover. Two notions related to this definition are these: (a) (M, τ) is *locally compact* if for every $m \in M$, we can find a neighbourhood $\mathcal{U}$ of m, $m \in \mathcal{U} \in \tau$, such that the closure $\overline{\mathcal{U}}$ of $\mathcal{U}$ is compact. But to make sense of this definition we need (b): A subset $A \subset M$ is compact if the topological space $(A, \ \tau_A)$ with the inherited topology τ_A is compact. If $(M, \ \tau)$ is compact, then it is also locally compact, but not conversely.

5.9. HOMEOMORPHISMS

Now let us go back to the definition of a continuous mapping $f : M \to N$, carrying topologies τ, τ' respectively. We mentioned that even if f were bijective, so that the inverse map $f^{-1} : N \to M$ makes sense, f^{-1} need not be continuous. Bijective maps which are continuous in both directions are special and are specially named: they are called bicontinuous functions or *homeomorphisms* . Thus, τ and τ' being given, $f : M \to N$ is a homeomorphism if it is bijective and

$$
\begin{aligned}
\mathcal{U} \in \tau \quad &\Rightarrow \quad f(\mathcal{U}) \in \tau', \\
\mathcal{U}' \in \tau' \quad &\Rightarrow \quad f^{-1}(\mathcal{U}') \in \tau
\end{aligned}
\tag{5.13}
$$

Just as in group theory we say that isomorphic groups are "one and the same", in the case of topology homeomorphic spaces are, in all topological respects, identical and not intrinsically distinguishable from one another.

5.10. THE CASE OF A METRIC

One can construct examples of topological spaces quite easily from experience with $\mathcal{R}$, the plane $\mathcal{R}^2$, space $\mathcal{R}^3$ etc. In these cases, the idea of topology arises from that of distance, or a metric. A *metric space* is *always* an example of a topological space. A space X is called a metric space if we have a real distance function $d(x, y)$ for $x, \ y \in X$ obeying:

(i) $d(x, \ y) = d(y, x) \geq 0$;

(ii) $d(x, y) = 0 \Longleftrightarrow x = y$;

(iii) $d(x, y) + d(y, z) \geq d(x, z)$ for any $x, \ y, \ z \in X$ (5.14)

Then one can define an open base $\mathcal{B}_x$ at any $x \in X$ to be all "open spheres" centred on x , ie.,

$$
\begin{aligned}
\mathcal{B}_x &= \{\, S_x(\rho) \mid \rho > 0 \,\}, \\
S_x(\rho) &= \{ y \in X \mid d(x, \ y) < \rho \,\}
\end{aligned}
\tag{5.15}
$$

From here one can build up the entire topology τ . By applying this idea of passing from a metric to a topology, all the concepts mentioned earlier can be viewed in a concrete fashion.

5.11.   COMPOSITION OF CONTINUOUS MAPS, HOMEOMORPHISMS

The composition of continuous maps is easily seen to preserve continuity. Thus if we have three (or more) topological spaces (M_1, τ_1), (M_2, τ_2), (M_3, τ_3),... and two (or more) continuous maps $\varphi_1 : M_1 \to M_2$, $\varphi_2 : M_2 \to M_3$,..., then the composed maps $\varphi_2 \circ \varphi_1 : M_1 \to M_3$, ... are also continuous. Similarly when homeomorphisms are composed, the result is again a homeomorphism.

6.   Differentiable Manifolds, Smooth Maps, Diffeomorphisms, Smooth Functions and Curves, Pullback of Functions

We will now work our way up step by step to the concept of a differentiable manifold.

6.1.   CHARTS

Let (M, τ) be a given topological space. A *chart* on M is a triple $(\mathcal{U}, \psi, n)$ where $\mathcal{U} \in \tau$ is an open set, n is a positive integer, and ψ is a homeomorphism from $\mathcal{U}$ to some open set in real Euclidean space $\mathcal{R}^n$. (Here and in the following we often use $\mathcal{R}^n$ as a topological space : the topology is always the *usual* one given by the Euclidean definition of distance or metric on $\mathcal{R}^n$). A chart thus assigns coordinates *in a continuous way* to points $m \in \mathcal{U} \subset M$; it gives us a local patch or coordinate system over $\mathcal{U}$. The continuity of this assignment, contained in the statement that ψ is a homeomorphism, means no more and no less than that both ψ and ψ^{-1} are continuous with respect to the topology τ on M and the usual one on $\mathcal{R}^n$. Of course, since a homeomorphism is injective, distinct points in $\mathcal{U}$ are assigned distinct coordinates. We may depict the situation as in Figure 1. The domain of the chart is the open set $\mathcal{U}$; its dimension is n ; and its range is the open set $\psi(\mathcal{U}) \subset \mathcal{R}^n$. We may denote the coordinates assigned by ψ to $m \in \mathcal{U} \subset M$ by $x^\mu(m)$, $\mu = 1, 2, ..., n$:

 Chart $(\mathcal{U}, \psi, n)$

$$m \in \mathcal{U} \subset M \overset{\psi}{\to} x^\mu(m) \in \psi(\mathcal{U}) \subset \mathcal{R}^n \qquad (6.1)$$

For definiteness we include in this definition of a chart the condition that $\mathcal{U}$ and $\psi(\mathcal{U})$ both be connected.

6.2.   ATLAS

An *atlas* $\mathcal{A}$ for M is a collection of charts $\{(\mathcal{U}_\alpha, \psi_\alpha, n_\alpha)\}$, such that the open sets $\mathcal{U}_\alpha$ provide an open cover for M. In an atlas, the dimen-

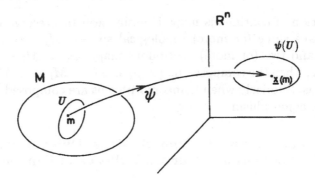

Figure 1. A chart on a topological space M

sion n_α could vary from chart to chart. But if the domains $\mathcal{U}_\alpha$, $\mathcal{U}_\beta$ of two charts intersect, from topological properties of Euclidean spaces and homeomorphisms we can conclude that their dimensions must be the same, $n_\alpha = n_\beta$. In particular, if M is a connected topological space and it admits an atlas, all the n_α must be equal. In any case, if we have an atlas on M , for every $m \in M$ we can find some $\mathcal{U}_\alpha$ such that $m \in \mathcal{U}_\alpha$, and over this neighbourhood of m we can "put up a local coordinate system" via the homeomorphism ψ_α to $\mathcal{R}^{n_\alpha}$. If M admits an atlas such that all $n_\alpha = n$, we say n is the dimension of M as well as of the atlas.

6.3. MANIFOLD OF DIMENSION n

An $n - dimensional\ manifold$ is a topological space (M, τ) which: admits an atlas $\mathcal{A} = \{(\mathcal{U}_\alpha, \psi_\alpha, n)\}$ with a definite common dimension n for all the charts; has the Hausdorff property; and obeys the Second Axiom of Countability. Thus each "portion" $\mathcal{U}_\alpha$ of M can be bicontinuously mapped, via ψ_α , to some open set in $\mathcal{R}^n$; we can say that all of M is covered by a patchwork of local coordinate systems or descriptions.

Let us note that in order to define a chart, its dimension, and then an atlas, we only require that (M, τ) be a topological space admitting these things on it. In case an atlas has a definite dimension common to all its charts, we assign that dimension to M as well. At the next stage, to define an n -dimensional manifold, we require more of (M, τ) : it must be a Hausdorff second countable topological space, and must admit an n -dimensional atlas. Then it is an n -dimensional manifold. Note also that while connectedness would have led to a unique dimension n , the converse is not true!

6.4. DIFFERENTIABLE MANIFOLD OF DIMENSION n

Now we impose more conditions on an n-dimensional manifold which we just defined, and move towards the definition of a *differentiable manifold of dimension n*. Two charts $(\mathcal{U},\ \psi)$ and $(\mathcal{U}',\ \psi')$ on an n-dimensional manifold are said to be C^∞-compatible if either (i) $\mathcal{U} \cap \mathcal{U}' = \phi$, the empty set, or (ii) $\mathcal{U} \cap \mathcal{U}' \neq \phi$ and in the overlap the two systems of coordinates assigned by ψ and ψ' are related by C^∞ functions, that is, infinitely differentiable functions. (In the entire discussion C^∞ can be replaced by C^k − k times differentiable - or C^ω -real analytic, and the manifold gets a corresponding name). In greater detail: suppose $\mathcal{U} \cap \mathcal{U}' = \phi$; then for convenience we agree to declare that the two charts are compatible. If $\mathcal{U} \cap \mathcal{U}' \neq \phi$, then each point m in the open set $\mathcal{U} \cap \mathcal{U}'$ receives two sets of coordinates : $x^\mu(m)$ via ψ, $x'^{\,\mu}(m)$ via ψ'. This may be pictured as in Figure 2. Then we have by composition

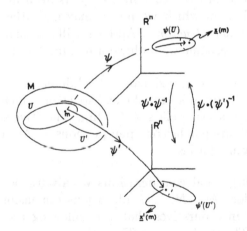

Figure 2. Conditions on the overlap of two charts

the homeomorphisms

$$\psi' \circ \psi^{-1} \ :\ \psi(\mathcal{U} \cap \mathcal{U}') \subset \mathcal{R}^n \ \to\ \psi'(\mathcal{U} \cap \mathcal{U}') \subset \mathcal{R}^n,$$
$$\psi \circ (\psi')^{-1} \ :\ \psi'(\mathcal{U} \cap \mathcal{U}') \subset \mathcal{R}^n \ \to\ \psi(\mathcal{U} \cap \mathcal{U}') \subset \mathcal{R}^n,$$

between the two open sets of $\mathcal{R}^n$ as indicated. And of course these two homeomorphisms are inverses of one another. In plain language, for points $m \in \mathcal{U} \cap \mathcal{U}'$, the overlap region, one set of coordinates $x^\mu(m)$ can be expressed as functions of the other set $x'^\mu(m)$, and vice versa. We now say that $(\mathcal{U}, \psi)$ and $(\mathcal{U}', \psi')$ are C^∞-compatible if in this overlap, the x^μ are infinitely differentiable functions of x'^μ and conversely. An atlas $\mathcal{A} = \{(\mathcal{U}_\alpha, \psi_\alpha)\}$ on an n-dimensional manifold is said to be of class C^∞ if every two of its charts are C^∞-compatible. Finally a C^∞ *differentiable manifold of dimension* n is an n-dimensional manifold M admitting an atlas $\mathcal{A}$ of class C^∞.

One often carries the definition of an atlas one step further to a *maximal atlas* in this way. Given a C^∞ atlas $\mathcal{A} = \{(\mathcal{U}_\alpha, \psi_\alpha)\}$, if we have some chart $(\mathcal{U}, \psi)$ which is C^∞-compatible with each $(\mathcal{U}_\alpha, \psi_\alpha) \in \mathcal{A}$, we may as well add $(\mathcal{U}, \psi)$ to $\mathcal{A}$ and get an augmented C^∞-atlas! More generally, two C^∞-atlases $\mathcal{A}$ and $\mathcal{A}'$ are said to be *equivalent* if each chart in $\mathcal{A}$ is C^∞-compatible with each chart in $\mathcal{A}'$. Now on a given C^∞-differentiable manifold of dimension n (defined as above via a single atlas $\mathcal{A}$), we can take *all the atlases* equivalent to the given $\mathcal{A}$, put all their charts together, and form one grand atlas - this is called a *maximal atlas* $\mathcal{A}_{max}$. The advantage now is that any chart $(\mathcal{U}, \psi)$ which is C^∞-compatible with the charts in $\mathcal{A}_{max}$ is itself in $\mathcal{A}_{max}$. An n-dimensional manifold on which we put a maximal atlas is then said to possess a *differentiable structure*. And we will see that it is sometimes technically helpful to assume we do have a maximal atlas at hand.

To summarise, an n-dimensional C^∞-differentiable manifold M is a (Hausdorff second countable) topological space on which we have an n-dimensional maximal atlas of class C^∞. In an intuitive sense, *all possible* local smooth coordinate patches on open portions of M are admitted and included in the maximal atlas.

Hereafter in all general considerations we always deal with such differentiable manifolds M, N, ... of various dimensions. As examples, we can easily convince ourselves that the following are such manifolds: $\mathcal{R}$, $\mathcal{R}^2$, ..., $\mathcal{R}^n$; $\mathcal{C}$, ..., $\mathcal{C}^n$; the circle S^1 , the two-sphere S^2, ..., S^n ; the cylinder $S^1 \times \mathcal{R}$; the torus $S^1 \times S^1$; the projective spaces $\mathcal{R}P^n$, $\mathcal{C}P^n$.

A differentiable manifold M which can be covered by a single chart atlas is called a **simple** manifold.

We can also see in an easy and obvious way that the *Cartesian product* of two C^∞-differentiable manifolds M, M' , denoted by $M \times M'$, is again such a manifold. The dimensionalities simply add. At the first step, the atlas one would arrive at for $M \times M'$ reflects its being a Cartesian product, but one can then easily pass to general atlases.

6.5.   SMOOTH MAPS BETWEEN MANIFOLDS

A continuous map or function from one topological space M to another N has been defined in Section 5. Now if both M and N are differentiable manifolds, of any dimensions, we can refine this notion and define a *smooth map* or $C^\infty - function$ from M to N .

Let φ be a given map from M to N :

$$\varphi \; : \; M \; \to \; N \; : \; m \; \in \; M \; \to \; \varphi(m) \; = \; n \; \in \; N \qquad (6.2)$$

We introduce a chart $(\mathcal{U}, \; \psi)$ around m , and a chart $(\mathcal{V}, \chi)$ around the image $n \; \in \; N$. So the composite map $\chi \circ \varphi \circ \psi^{-1}$ expresses the coordinates y of $\varphi(m) \; = \; n$ in terms of the coordinates x of m :

$$\psi : m \in \mathcal{U} \; \longrightarrow x^\mu \in \psi(\mathcal{U}) \subset \mathcal{R}^{n_1}, \mu = 1, 2, \ldots, n_1 = \dim .M;$$
$$\chi : n \in \mathcal{V} \; \longrightarrow y^\alpha \in \chi(\mathcal{V}) \subset \mathcal{R}^{n_2}, \alpha = 1, 2, \ldots, n_2 = \dim .N;$$
$$\chi \circ \varphi \circ \psi^{-1} \; : x^\mu \longrightarrow y^\alpha = \varphi^\alpha(x^1, x^2, \ldots, x^{n_1}), \alpha = 1, 2, \ldots, n_2 \; (6.3)$$

We now say that the map $\varphi \; : \; M \; \to \; N$ is a C^∞ or smooth map if the y^α are C^∞ functions of the x^μ around each $m \; \in \; M$; that is, the functions $\varphi^\alpha(x)$ must be infinitely often differentiable. While the definition of a smooth map φ uses in an inescapable way local coordinates or charts around each $m \; \in \; M$ and $\varphi(m) \; \in \; N$, it makes no difference which charts are used since in a maximal atlas any two charts are C^∞ - compatible. In this sense, smoothness of $\varphi \; : \; M \; \to \; N$ is an intrinsic notion exploiting only the differentiable structures on M and N . The set of all smooth maps $\varphi \; : \; M \; \to \; N$ could be denoted by $\mathcal{F}(M \; ; \; N)$: function on M , value in N.

6.6.   DIFFEOMORPHISMS

We will later classify, in a useful way, some interesting kinds of smooth maps between manifolds. Of course composition of smooth maps results again in smooth maps. A particular case of a smooth map is a *diffeomorphism* . This is when $\varphi \; : \; M \; \to \; N$ is bijective, and *both* φ and φ^{-1} are smooth. This is the analogue, for differentiable manifolds, of homeomorphisms among topological spaces or of isomorphisms among groups. Again to define a diffeomorphism we need to use charts, but the notion is intrinsic. Two differentiable manifolds M and N which are diffeomorphically related are in all respects "essentially the same", as far as their differential structures go. Of course with such a mapping the dimensions must be the same:

$$\varphi : M \rightarrow N \qquad \text{a diffeomorphism} \Rightarrow$$
$$\dim . M = \dim . N ,$$
$$\varphi \quad \text{bijective} ,$$
$$\varphi \text{ and } \varphi^{-1} \text{ smooth} \qquad (6.4)$$

One can have in particular $M = N$: then φ maps M diffeomorphically *onto itself* . This is a very important instance, which will be used later on.

In a general way one can see that once we have a differentiable manifold with a maximal atlas, various objects and operations can always be looked at using local coordinates, but as long as one is sure that the relevant properties are chart-independent, one is confident that those properties are intrinsic. Thus there is no defeat involved in using local coordinates if at the same time one is conscious of the intrinsic nature of the argument. Whenever we are able to express ourselves without using charts at all - so much the better, we have mastered the language, like using the Dirac bra and ket notation instead of Schrodinger wave functions in quantum mechanics.

6.7.   SMOOTH REAL - VALUED FUNCTIONS ON A MANIFOLD – AN EXAMPLE

To get at home with C^∞ maps let us look at two important cases, when one of the two spaces M and N is the real line $\mathcal{R}$. We take up first the case $N = \mathcal{R}$, later the case $M = \mathcal{R}$. We are dealing then with smooth real-valued functions on M . The set of all such functions is often denoted by $\mathcal{F}(M ; \mathcal{R})$ or more simply by $\mathcal{F}(M)$ when it is implicit that we are dealing with real-valued functions. Formally,

$$f \in \mathcal{F}(M) \quad : \quad f = M \rightarrow \mathcal{R} \quad :$$
$$m \in M \rightarrow f(m) \in \mathcal{R} \qquad (6.5)$$

The smoothness of f is expressed using charts on M . For each $m \in M$, pick a chart $(\mathcal{U}, \psi)$ containing m . Over $\mathcal{U}$, we can "express f in terms of the coordinates of m ". This means we look at the composite map from an open subset in $\mathcal{R}^n$, where $n = \dim . M$, to $\mathcal{R}$:

$$\psi \quad : \quad m \in \mathcal{U} \longrightarrow x^\mu(m) \in \psi(\mathcal{U}) \subset \mathcal{R}^n \quad ;$$
$$f \circ \psi^{-1} \quad : \quad \psi(\mathcal{U}) \rightarrow \mathcal{R} \quad :$$
$$(f \circ \psi^{-1}) \, (x(m)) = f(m) \, . \qquad (6.6)$$

(This is a simple instance of eq.(6.3). Notice in passing that in the casual physicist's manner we might have just written $f(x)$ for the value of f at a general point m in $\mathcal{U}$ expressed in a local coordinate system; but this notation would conceal the fact that a choice of chart is needed before we can so express f ! With familiarity with the processes involved, we may later allow ourselves the luxury of many such abuses of notation). We now say f is a smooth function on M if in each such chart-based description the function $f \circ \psi^{-1}$ is infinitely differentiable with respect to each of the Euclidean coordinates x^μ (over the range $\psi(\mathcal{U}) \subset \mathcal{R}^n$). Having defined smoothness of f via charts, we then realise that the notion is chart independent.

Constant numerical multiples, ordinary pointwise products and linear combinations of smooth functions on M again belong to $\mathcal{F}(M)$.

6.8.   THE PULL-BACK OF FUNCTIONS

Now we describe an *extremely important relationship* between smooth functions on two differentiable manifolds M and N, which arises when a smooth map $\varphi : M \to N$ is given. Namely, the map φ gives rise to a unique map φ^*, called the *pull* − *back*, from $\mathcal{F}(N)$ to $\mathcal{F}(M)$:

$$\varphi \;:\; M \to N \Rightarrow \varphi^* \;:\; \mathcal{F}(N) \to \mathcal{F}(M) \;;$$
$$g \in \mathcal{F}(N) \to \varphi^* g \in \mathcal{F}(M) \;;$$
$$m \in M \;:\; (\varphi^* g)(m) \;=\; g(\varphi(m)) \tag{6.7}$$

Notice that φ and φ^* work in opposite directions. In words: given any smooth function on N, its pull-back is a smooth function on M, whose value at any point of M equals the value of the original function at the image point. Smoothness of φ and of g (in their respective senses) leads to that of $\varphi^* g$. What is involved here is the composition of smooth maps, since the operation (6.7) can be expressed thus:

$$\varphi \;:\; M \to N, \; g : N \to \mathcal{R} \longrightarrow$$
$$\varphi^* g \equiv g \circ \varphi : M \to \mathcal{R} \tag{6.8}$$

Notice, by the way, that no charts have been used in eqs.(6.7, 6.8)!

The pull-back operation seen here is in its simplest version; it has extensions to objects other than functions, which we take up in detail later. Even in the present version, we easily establish the following result concerning the pull-back of composite maps:

$$\varphi \;:\; M \to N, \; \varphi' : N \to P \Rightarrow \varphi' \circ \varphi : M \to P \;;$$
$$(\varphi' \circ \varphi)^* \;=\; \varphi^* \circ \varphi'^* \;:\; \mathcal{F}(P) \to \mathcal{F}(M) \tag{6.9}$$

The point to note is that the sequence gets switched!

6.9. SMOOTH PARAMETRISED CURVES ON A MANIFOLD

Now let us go back to maps between spaces, one of which is $\mathcal{R}$, and consider the case where the first space rather than the second is $\mathcal{R}$. To conserve notation, let us consider smooth maps $\mathcal{R} \to M$, the latter being an n -dimensional differentiable manifold. The set of all such maps may be denoted by $\mathcal{F}(\mathcal{R};\ M)$. These are actually just *smooth curves* in M . To be modest, let us describe them in this way. Take an open interval in $\mathcal{R}$:

$$I \ = \ (a,b) \ = \ \{s \ \in \ \mathcal{R} \mid a < s < b\}, \qquad (6.10)$$

and denote by γ a smooth map from I to M :

$$\gamma \ : \ I \to M :$$
$$s \ \in \ I \ \to \ m\,(s) \ \in M \qquad (6.11)$$

The image of I under this map, the set of points $\gamma\,(I) \equiv \{\,m\,(s)\,\}$ in M , is a *parametrised smooth curve* in M . Of course here we use the usual topology of $\mathcal{R}$ and I . And smoothness of γ , as already set up, means that if in a chart on M (which may not cover all of $\gamma\,(I)$!) we have coordinates $x^{\mu}\,(m\,(s))$ for the point $m\,(s)$, then these coordinates are infinitely often differentiable with respect to s .

We may retain the set of points $\gamma\,(I)$ in M but change the parametrisation by s in some smooth way : in that case the "trace" is the same but as a parametrised curve we have a change!

Smooth curves in a differentiable manifold have many important uses, so we shall meet them often in the sequel.

We have had a first look at smooth maps in the examples of real-valued functions $\mathcal{F}\,(M;\ \mathcal{R}) \ \equiv \ \mathcal{F}\,(M)$, and smooth curves $\mathcal{F}\,(\mathcal{R};\ M)$. Now we can combine the two in a useful way. Let γ be a smooth curve in M parametrised by $s \in I \subset \mathcal{R}$, and f a real valued function on M . Since $\gamma : I \to M$ has M as the image space, we can apply the pull back γ^{*} to f on M ! The result would be a smooth function on $I \subset \mathcal{R}$, that is, an infinitely differentiable function of the parameter s . All we have done is to take the function f defined all over M , restricted attention to its values along the curve $\gamma\,(I)$, and thus turned it into a function of s :

$$\gamma \ : \ I \subset \mathcal{R} \ \to \ M, \quad \text{a smooth curve ;}$$
$$f \ : \ M \to \mathcal{R}, \quad \text{a smooth function ;}$$
$$\gamma^{*} f \ = \ f \circ \gamma : \ I \subset \mathcal{R} \to \mathcal{R},$$
$$(f \circ \gamma)\,(s) \ = \ f\,(m\,(s)) \qquad (6.12)$$

Here no charts have been used. If now around $m\,(0)\;=\;m_0$, say, we choose a chart $(\mathcal{U},\;\psi)$, then we get an expression of $f\;(m\;(s))$ as a function of the "time-dependent" coordinates $x^\mu(m\;(s))$ of a "moving point" on the curve. Combining eqs.(6.6, 6.12), and to save on symbols writing $x^\mu(s)$ instead of the more proper $x^\mu(m\;(s))$, we have :

$$f(m\;(s))\;=\;(f\circ\gamma)\;(s)\;=\;(f\circ\psi^{-1})\;(x\;(s)) \qquad (6.13)$$

Having seen how the notation works, it will be hereafter an excusable and understandable abuse of notation if we slip back to physicists' methods and just write $f(x\;(s))$ for the above!

7. Tangent, Cotangent and Tensor Spaces at a Point; Smooth Tensor Fields on a Manifold; Orientability

In the previous Section we have developed the concept of a differentiable manifold. Now we proceed to build up various structures on it.

7.1. TANGENT SPACE AT A POINT

The first and most basic geometric construction is that of the *tangent space*, or the *space of tangent vectors*, to a differentiable manifold M at a point $m\;\in\;M$. This is denoted by $T_m\,M$. Towards its construction, we look first at all smooth parametrised curves on M that pass through m at, say, parameter value $s\;=\;0$ (see eq.(6.11)):

$$\begin{aligned} \gamma\;&:\quad I\subset\mathcal{R}\to M\;:\\ &\quad s\in I\to m(s)\in M\;,\\ &\quad m(0)\;=\;m \end{aligned} \qquad (7.1)$$

Let $(\mathcal{U},\;\psi)$ be a chart containing m , "large enough" so that $m(s)$ lies in it and has coordinates $x^\mu(s)$:

$$\begin{aligned} \psi\;(m(s))\;&=\;\{x^\mu(s)\}\;,\\ \psi(m)\;&=\;\{x^\mu(0)\}\;=\;\text{coordinates of } m \end{aligned} \qquad (7.2)$$

We shall say two such smooth parametrised curves $\gamma,\;\overline{\gamma}$ are equivalent if their "time derivatives" are equal at $s=0$, ie., as they pass through m :

$$\begin{aligned} \gamma\;&:\;s\quad\to\;x^\mu(s)\;;\;\overline{\gamma}\;:\;s\;\to\;\overline{x}^\mu(s)\;;\;x^\mu(0)\;=\;\overline{x}^\mu(0)\;;\\ \gamma\;&\sim\;\overline{\gamma}\;\Leftrightarrow\;\frac{dx^\mu(s)}{ds}\Big|_{s=o}\;=\;\frac{d\overline{x}^\mu(s)}{ds}\Big|_{s=o} \end{aligned} \qquad (7.3)$$

It is immediately verified that this is an acceptable equivalence relation. Morever, though it has been defined using a chart, the notion is chart-independent. If γ and $\bar{\gamma}$ are equivalent in one chart $(\mathcal{U}, \psi)$, so are they in any other chart $(\mathcal{U}', \psi')$ compatible with $(\mathcal{U}, \psi)$.

Next let us suppose we have a smooth function f defined over some neighbourhood $\mathcal{U}$ of m , $f \in \mathcal{F}(\mathcal{U})$, which in the chart $(\mathcal{U}, \psi)$ "appears as" $f(x)$. Given a smooth curve γ as in (7.1), we can use eqs.(6.12,13) to evaluate f along γ , thus getting a smooth function of s . Then we can calculate its rate of change with respect to s at $s = 0$, ie., at m :

$$\frac{d}{ds} f(x(s)) \Big|_{s=o} = (\frac{\partial f(x)}{\partial x^\mu})_{x(o)} (\frac{dx^\mu(s)}{ds})_{s=o} \tag{7.4}$$

For a given γ we have here a map F_γ from $\mathcal{F}(\mathcal{U})$ to $\mathcal{R}$, acting as a *derivation at m* :

$$F_\gamma : \quad \mathcal{F}(\mathcal{U}) \rightarrow \mathcal{R} :$$
$$F_\gamma(f) = \frac{d}{ds} f(x(s)) \Big|_{s=o} ;$$
$$F_\gamma(fg) = F_\gamma (f) g(m) + f(m) F_\gamma(g) \tag{7.5}$$

It is easily verified that: (i) the derivation F_γ is determined by γ alone, and is independent of the chart $(\mathcal{U}, \psi)$; (ii) if γ and $\bar{\gamma}$ are equivalent in the sense of eq.(7.3), then F_γ and $F_{\bar{\gamma}}$ are the same.

Now we are ready to define what we mean by a *tangent vector* u to M at m , $u \in T_m M$. There are in fact three ways to do this: a tangent vector u to M at m is

(i) an equivalence class of smooth parametrised curves passing through m at $s = 0$;

(ii) a derivation (i.e., a map obeying the Liebnitz rule) on functions over U , at m , written as $u(f)$ and obeying the Liebnitz rule (7.5);

(iii) in each chart $(\mathcal{U}, \psi)$ containing m , an assignment of n numbers u^μ such that under a change of chart to $(\mathcal{U}', \psi')$ these numbers change to u'^μ according to the rule

$$u'^\mu = (\frac{\partial x'^\mu}{\partial x^\nu})_m u^\nu \tag{7.6}$$

The set of all tangent vectors to M at m , defined in any one of these ways, is a real n -dimensional vector space. Definition (i) works with equivalence classes of curves, and one must show that the vector space operations and properties preserve the equivalence relation; in a sense, at first sight, forming linear combinations of equivalence classes of curves is "unnatural". Definition (ii) is intrinsic and in fact the best : the linear space property is *immediate* , and it is chart independent, though initially a bit unfamiliar. The Liebnitz rule is what makes the connection with first (partial) derivatives of functions. Definition (iii) is familiar and easy but chart based; a little effort is needed to use it and abstract the notion of a vector in itself independent of charts! After having seen all three, one realises the true merits of Definition (ii).

Having set up the tangent space $T_m M$ at a point $m \in M$, much of the remaining constructions are smooth sailing. In a formal sense, each $u \in T_m M$ is a possible directional derivative of functions defined at and around m . In a chart $(\mathcal{U}, \psi)$ around m , we see that by taking in turn each one of the coordinates x^μ to vary while the rest stay constant we get a corresponding parametrised curve or directional derivative. In this way, we get a *coordinate based frame* for $T_m M$:

$$\{(\frac{\partial}{\partial x^\mu})_m\} \quad = \quad \text{basis for } T_m M \text{ ,}$$

$$u \in T_m M \quad \Rightarrow \quad u = u^\mu \, (\frac{\partial}{\partial x^\mu})_m \qquad (7.7)$$

Under a change of chart $(\mathcal{U}, \psi) \to (\mathcal{U}', \psi')$, this frame for $T_m M$ changes as:

$$(\frac{\partial}{\partial x^\mu})_m \to (\frac{\partial}{\partial x'^\mu})_m \quad = \quad (\frac{\partial x^\nu}{\partial x'^\mu})_m \, (\frac{\partial}{\partial x^\nu})_m \qquad (7.8)$$

Here the Jacobian of the inverse coordinate transformation $x' \to x \, (x')$, has naturally appeared.

We are not obliged to use always a coordinate-based frame for $T_m M$. Any other frame made up of n linearly independent tangent vectors $e_a, a = 1, 2, \ldots, n$, at m can be used. We will generally write:

General frame $\qquad \{e_a(m)\} \in F(T_m M);$

Coordinate frame $\qquad \{(\frac{\partial}{\partial x^\mu})_m\} \in F(T_m M);$

$$e_a(m) \quad = \quad e^\mu{}_a(m) \, (\frac{\partial}{\partial x^\mu})_m \text{ ,}$$

$$e^\mu{}_a(m) \in \mathcal{R}, \qquad a = 1, 2, \ldots, n, \quad \mu = 1, 2, \ldots, n \qquad (7.9)$$

(Recall the notation of eq.(4.3) for the set of all frames on a vector space)

7.2. COTANGENT SPACE AT A POINT

Once the space $T_m M$ is in hand, one can pass to its dual, written as $T_m^* M$. Vectors in $T_m^* M$ are called $co - vectors$ or $cotangent\ vectors\ to$ M at m. By definition, each $\alpha \in T_m^* M$ is a linear functional $T_m M \to R$. We can construct a coordinate-based frame for $T_m^* M$ as follows. Recall from the previous work that each $u \in T_m M$ defines, in fact *is* , a derivation at m on functions f around m . Choose a function f , evaluate $u(f)$, and "read this backwards": evidently, for fixed f and variable u we have here a linear functional of u with values in $\mathcal{R}$! Hence $u(f)$ "becomes", or leads to, an element of $T_m^* M$ evaluated on u . We write it as $< (df)(m), u >$, thus formally denoting by $(df)(m)$ the element of $T_m^* M$ determined in this way by $f \in \mathcal{F}(\mathcal{U})$. Using a chart $(\mathcal{U}, \psi)$ to convey this construction, we have:

$$
u \in T_m M, f \in \mathcal{F}(\mathcal{U}) \quad \Rightarrow \quad u(f) = u^\mu \left(\frac{\partial f(x)}{\partial x^\mu} \right)_m
$$
$$
= \; < (df)(m), u >,
$$
$$
(df)(m) \in T_m^* M \qquad (7.10)
$$

The cotangent vector $(df)(m)$ determined by $f \in \mathcal{F}(\mathcal{U})$ is called the *differential of f at m*. One has thus a definite way to pass from functions to cotangent vectors - really the familiar notion of the gradient! Now in a chart $(\mathcal{U}, \psi)$, each coordinate x^μ can also be viewed as a smooth function over $\mathcal{U}$! These are the coordinate functions for that chart. So using each of the x^μ in turn as the f of the above discussion, we get a set of cotangent vectors $(dx^\mu)(m)$ in $T_m^* M$. The various equations above easily show that this is the dual frame to $\left(\frac{\partial}{\partial x^\mu} \right)_m$ for $T_m M$:

$$
< (dx^\mu)(m), \left(\frac{\partial}{\partial x^\nu} \right)_m > \quad = \quad \left(\frac{\partial}{\partial x^\nu} \right)_m \text{ acting as a derivation}
$$
$$
\text{on the "function" } x^\mu, \text{ evaluated at } m ,
$$
$$
= \delta_\nu^\mu \qquad (7.11)
$$

To repeat: in a chart, we get coordinate-based dual frames $\left\{ \left(\frac{\partial}{\partial x^\mu} \right)_m \right\}$ and $\{ (dx^\mu)(m) \}$ for $T_m M$ and $T_m^* M$ respectively.

The frame $\{ e^a(m) \}$ for $T_m^* M$ dual to the general frame $\{ e_a(m) \}$ for $T_m M$ is fixed by the conditions

$$
< e^a(m), e_b(m) > \quad = \quad \delta_b^a ,
$$
$$
\{ e^a(m) \} \quad \in \quad F(T_m^* M) ,
$$
$$
\{ e_a(m) \} \quad \in \quad F(T_m M) \qquad (7.12)
$$

To accompany the relations (7.9) we have

$$
(dx^\mu)(m) \quad = \quad e^\mu{}_a(m) \, e^a(m) ,
$$
$$
e^a(m) \quad = \quad e_\mu{}^a(m) \, (dx^\mu)(m) ;
$$
$$
e_\mu{}^a(m) \, e^\mu{}_b(m) \quad = \quad \delta_b^a ,
$$
$$
e_\mu{}^a(m) \, e^\nu{}_a(m) \quad = \quad \delta_\mu^\nu . \qquad (7.13)
$$

Thus we have "created" tangent and cotangent spaces $T_m M$, $T_m^* M$ at any $m \in M$; described chart based and general frames for each; and found a way to pass from *functions* to their *differentials* at each $m \in M$. All this machinery belongs intrinsically and automatically to M: once a differentiable manifold M is "given", all these structures (and more!) are "already there"!

7.3.   TENSOR SPACES AT A POINT

The space of tensors $\mathcal{J}_m^{(r,s)}(M)$ "to M at m" is, as in Section 4, set up via multilinear functionals over $T_m M$ and $T_m^* M$. We can express a general $A \in \mathcal{J}_m^{(r,s)}(M)$ in various by now familiar ways:

$$A \in \mathcal{J}_m^{(r,s)}(M) :$$
$$A(\alpha_1, \ldots, \alpha_r; \, u_1, \, \ldots, \, u_s) \in \mathcal{R}, \; \alpha \in T_m^* M, \; u \in T_m M,$$
linear separately in each argument ;
$$A = A^{\mu_1 \cdots \mu_r}{}_{\nu_1 \ldots \nu_s} (\partial_{\mu_1})_m \otimes \ldots \otimes (\partial_{\mu_r})_m \otimes (dx^{\nu_1})(m) \otimes \ldots \otimes (dx^{\nu_s})(m)$$
$$= A^{a_1 \cdots a_r}{}_{b_1 \ldots b_s} \, e_{a_1}(m) \otimes \ldots \otimes e_{a_r}(m) \otimes e^{b_1}(m) \otimes \ldots \otimes e^{b_s}(m);$$
$$A^{\cdots \mu \cdots}{}_{\cdots \nu \cdots} = A(\ldots (dx^\mu)(m) \ldots; \ldots (\partial_\nu)_m \ldots);$$
$$A^{\cdots a \cdots}{}_{\cdots b \cdots} = A(\ldots e^a(m) \ldots; \ldots e_b(m) \ldots) \qquad (7.14)$$

(Here for simplicity we have written ∂_μ in place of $\partial / \partial x^\mu$). On any tensor $A \in \mathcal{J}_m^{(r,s)}(M)$ we can apply the contraction process on the pth covector and q^{th} contravector arguments and get a tensor $B \in \mathcal{J}_m^{(r-1,s-1)}(M)$:

$$B(\alpha_1, \ldots, \alpha_{r-1}; u_1, \ldots, u_{s-1}) =$$
$$A(\alpha_1, \ldots, \alpha_{p-1}, e^a(m), \ldots \alpha_{r-1}; u_1, \ldots, u_{q-1}, e_a(m), \ldots, u_{s-1}),$$
$$\alpha \in T_m^* M, \; u \in T_m M \qquad (7.15)$$

Of course as a particular case we could have used coordinate based frames to carry out this contraction. Tensor products of tensors at m are also defined as before, pointwise.

The space of k -forms at $m \in M$,ie., totally antisymmetric elements of $\mathcal{J}_m^{(0,k)}(M)$, is usually denoted by $C_m^k(M)$. For $k = 0$, we simply have $\mathcal{R}$; and for $k > n$, this space vanishes! The wedge product of forms, defined in Section 4, works at each $m \in M$.

7.4.   TENSOR FIELDS

Having thus set up vectors, covectors and general tensors at each point $m \in M$, we are now able to define *smooth fields* of such objects all over

M . In general, a smooth tensor field of type (r,s) over M is a choice for each $m \in M$ of an element $A(m) \in \mathcal{J}_m^{(r,s)}(M)$, such that this choice varies smoothly with m . This smoothness is, as always, specified and checked by using, around each m , a chart $(\mathcal{U}, \psi)$ and ensuring that the components of A so determined are smooth, ie., C^∞ -functions of the coordinates x^μ . The set of smooth tensor fields of type (r,s) over M is naturally denoted by $\mathcal{J}^{(r,s)}(M)$. If now $\{(\mathcal{U}_\alpha, \psi_\alpha)\}$ is an atlas for M , a field $A \in \mathcal{J}^{(r,s)}(M)$ is specified by giving its components over the domain of each chart, and by ensuring that in each overlap $\mathcal{U}_\alpha \cap \mathcal{U}_\beta$ the components are correctly related. The easily understood scheme of equations is:

$$A \in \mathcal{J}^{(r,s)}(M) \ :$$
Over $\mathcal{U}_\alpha$,
$$A \ = \ A^{(\alpha)\cdots\mu\cdots}{}_{\cdots\nu\cdots}(x)\cdots \otimes \partial_\mu \cdots \otimes dx^\nu \cdots \ ;$$
Over $\mathcal{U}_\beta$,
$$A \ = \ A^{(\beta)\cdots\mu\cdots}{}_{\cdots\nu\cdots}(x')\cdots \otimes \partial'_\mu \cdots \otimes dx'^\nu \cdots \ ;$$
Over $\mathcal{U}_\alpha \cap \mathcal{U}_\beta$,
$$A^{(\beta)\cdots\mu\cdots}{}_{\cdots\nu\cdots}(x') \ = \ \cdots \frac{\partial x'^\mu}{\partial x^\rho}\cdots \frac{\partial x^\sigma}{\partial x'^\nu}\cdots A^{(\alpha)\cdots\rho\cdots}{}_{\cdots\sigma\cdots}(x)$$

$$(7.16)$$

Here the variable point m previously indicated in $\left(\frac{\partial}{\partial x^\mu}\right)_m$ and $(dx^\mu)(m)$ has been omitted.

It is instructive to compare the above with the usual definitions in tensor analysis. There the *transformation law* in the last line of eqs.(7.16) is taken as the *definition* of a tensor field, and usually no attention is paid to the question whether the entire manifold M can be covered by a single chart or not. Here, this transformation law is built into, or is part of, the specification of even a single tensor field A all over M . We admit that in general an atlas for M may consist of many charts, so to define an $A \in \mathcal{J}^{(r,s)}(M)$ we need to pick $A(m) \in \mathcal{J}_m^{(r,s)}(M)$ over each $\mathcal{U}_\alpha$, and then ensure the transformation law in each overlap $\mathcal{U}_\alpha \cap \mathcal{U}_\beta$. In particular, in the present intrinsic approach, if M could be covered by a single chart, (a simple manifold) there would be no need to use this transformation law at all in defining or specifying a tensor field A !

Partly repeating what has been introduced before, some common notations are as follows:

$$\mathcal{J}^{(0,0)}(M) \ \equiv \ \mathcal{F}(M) \ = \text{ smooth functions on } M \ ;$$
$$\mathcal{J}^{(1,0)}(M) \ \equiv \ \mathcal{X}(M) \ = \text{ smooth vector fields on } M \ ;$$

$$\mathcal{J}^{(0,1)}(M) \equiv \mathcal{X}^*(M) = \text{smooth covector fields on } M$$
$$= \text{smooth one forms on } M \; ;$$
$$(\mathcal{J}^{(0,k)}(M))_{\text{antisymmetric}} \equiv C^k(M) = \text{smooth } k - \text{forms on } M$$

$$(7.17)$$

To gain familiarity with these and see how our constructions have been extended from single points to fields of quantities on all of M , we list a series of easily understood results:

$$f, g \in \mathcal{F}(M) \quad , \quad X \in \mathcal{X}(M), \alpha \in \mathcal{X}^*(M) \Rightarrow$$
$$df \in \mathcal{X}^*(M) \quad , \quad fX \in \mathcal{X}(M), f\alpha \in \mathcal{X}^*(M);$$
$$< \alpha, X > \; = \; i_X \alpha \in \mathcal{F}(M);$$
$$X(f) \; = \; < df, X > = i_X df \in \mathcal{F}(M);$$
$$X(fg) \; = \; X(f)g + fX(g);$$
$$d(fg) \; = \; gdf + fdg \tag{7.18}$$

The process of contraction of a tensor field $A \in \mathcal{J}^{(r,s)}(M)$ to get a tensor field $B \in \mathcal{J}^{(r-1,s-1)}(M)$ is done pointwise following eq.(7.15), once the locations p and q are specified. Similarly tensor products of tensor fields give tensor fields. Over the domain $\mathcal{U}$ of a chart $(\mathcal{U}, \psi)$ we can use either the coordinate-based objects $\partial/\partial x^\mu$ and dx^μ , or mutually dual *fields of frames* $\{e_a\}, \{e^a\}$, to expand tensors. Each e_a is a smooth vector field over $\mathcal{U}$, and each e^a a smooth one form or covector field over $\mathcal{U}$. Whether a smooth field of frames can be found for all of M is a global question, and in general this is not possible!

7.5.   ORIENTABILITY

The Jacobian involved in a change of chart $(\mathcal{U}, \psi) \to (\mathcal{U}', \psi')$, of course defined only over the intersection $\mathcal{U} \cap \mathcal{U}'$, has arisen several times, in eqs.(7.6,8,16). We now use it to define the concept of *orientability* of a differentiable manifold. Such a manifold M is said to be *orientable* if we can find an atlas $\mathcal{A} = \{(\mathcal{U}_\alpha, \psi_\alpha)\}$ such that on *each nontrivial overlap* $\mathcal{U}_\alpha \cap \mathcal{U}_\beta$ this Jacobian is *positive definite* :

<u>*M orientable*</u> $m \in \mathcal{U}_\alpha \cap \mathcal{U}_\beta :$

$$\psi_\alpha(m) \; = \; (x^1, x^2, \ldots, x^n) \in \psi_\alpha(\mathcal{U}_\alpha) \subset \mathcal{R}^n,$$
$$\psi_\beta(m) \; = \; (x'^1, x'^2, \ldots, x'^n) \in \psi_\beta(\mathcal{U}_\beta) \subset \mathcal{R}^n,$$

$$\det\left(\frac{\partial x'}{\partial x}\right) \; \equiv \; \det \begin{vmatrix} \frac{\partial x'^1}{\partial x^1} & \cdots & \frac{\partial x'^1}{\partial x^n} \\ \cdots\cdots\cdots \\ \frac{\partial x'^n}{\partial x^1} & \cdots & \frac{\partial x'^n}{\partial x^n} \end{vmatrix} > 0 \tag{7.19}$$

A simple manifold, *i.e*, one possessing a single chart atlas, is trivially orientable – there is no overlap in which to impose the condition (7.19)! And it possesses two distinct orientations. You can convince yourself that each $\mathcal{R}^n$, each S^n , the cylinder, the torus are all orientable, while the Mobius band is not!

7.6. COMMUTATOR OF VECTOR FIELDS

Functions, vector fields and forms on a differentiable manifold play key roles in geometrical methods. Once one learns how to handle them in various contexts, the extension to handling general tensor fields is more or less straightforward. Among vector fields $X \in \mathcal{X}(M)$ there is a special operation: the *commutator* of two vector fields is also a vector field. We set up the operation of forming the commutator thus:

$$
\begin{aligned}
X, Y \in \mathcal{X}(M) \quad &\Rightarrow \quad [X, Y] \in \mathcal{X}(M), \\
[X, Y](f) \quad &= \quad X(Y(f)) - Y(X(f)), \\
&\quad \text{any } f \in \mathcal{F}(M)
\end{aligned}
\tag{7.20}
$$

One must verify that $[X, Y]$ so defined is indeed a vector field, ie., that it obeys the Liebnitz rule. But this is quite easy:

$$
\begin{aligned}
[X, Y](fg) \quad &= \quad X(Y(fg)) - Y(X(fg)) \\
&= \quad X(Y(f)g + fY(g)) - Y(X(f)g + fX(g)) \\
&= \quad X(Y(f))g + Y(f)X(g) + X(f)Y(g) + fX(Y(g)) - \\
&\qquad Y(X(f))g - X(f)Y(g) - Y(f)X(g) - fY(X(g)) \\
&= \quad (X(Y(f)) - Y(X(f)))g + f(X(Y(g)) - Y(X(g))) \\
&= \quad [X, Y](f) \cdot g + f[X, Y](g)
\end{aligned}
\tag{7.21}
$$

Thus, $[X, Y]$ is indeed a vector field, so the set $\mathcal{X}(M)$ of all smooth vector fields on M forms a Lie algebra.

In a chart $(\mathcal{U}, \psi)$, the commutator takes the following explicit form:

$$
\begin{aligned}
X \quad &= \quad X^\mu(x)\partial_\mu, \; Y = Y^\mu(x)\partial_\mu \Rightarrow \\
[X, Y] \quad &= \quad [X, Y]^\mu(x)\partial_\mu , \\
[X, Y]^\mu(x) \quad &= \quad X^\nu(x)\partial_\nu Y^\mu(x) - Y^\nu(x)\partial_\nu X^\mu(x)
\end{aligned}
\tag{7.22}
$$

Independent of charts we have the following intrinsic algebraic laws for commutators among vector fields:

$$
\begin{aligned}
[X, Y] \quad &= \quad - [Y, X]; \\
[c_1 X_1 + c_2 X_2, Y] \quad &= \quad c_1[X_1, Y] + c_2[X_2, Y], \; c \in R; \\
[[X, Y], Z] + [[Y, Z], X] &+ [[Z, X], Y] = 0; \\
[fX, Y] \quad &= \quad f[X, Y] - Y(f)X
\end{aligned}
\tag{7.23}
$$

All these follow easily from the definition (7.20); and the third result, namely the Jacobi identity, is what makes for the Lie algebra property.

7.7. WEDGE PRODUCT OF FIELDS OF FORMS

Just as for general tensor fields tensor multiplication is to be done point-wise, so also the wedge product for forms works pointwise. Thus all the properties in eqs.(4.26,27,29,30,31) hold at each $m \in M$, and then by smooth extension for a field of forms. As samples, and to gain familiarity, here are some results:

$$\alpha \in C^k(M), X_1, X_2, \ldots, X_k \in \mathcal{X}(M) \Rightarrow$$
$$\alpha(X_1, X_2, \ldots, X_k) \in \mathcal{F}(M), \text{antisymmetric in } X's ;$$
$$\alpha \in C^k(M), \beta \in C^l(M) \;\Rightarrow\; \alpha \wedge \beta = (-1)^k \beta \wedge \alpha \in C^{k+l}(M);$$
$$X \in \mathcal{X}(M), \alpha \in C^k(M) \;\Rightarrow\; i_X \alpha \in C^{k-1}(M);$$
$$i_X(\alpha \wedge \beta) = (i_X \alpha) \wedge \beta + (-1)^k \alpha \wedge i_X \beta \qquad (7.24)$$

Expansions of a form in a coordinate-based or other field of frames take these appearances:

$$\alpha \in C^k(M) :$$
$$\alpha(x) = \frac{1}{k!} \alpha_{\mu_1 \ldots \mu_k}(x) dx^{\mu_1} \wedge dx^{\mu_2} \wedge \ldots \wedge dx^{\mu_k},$$
$$\alpha(m) = \frac{1}{k!} \alpha_{a_1 \ldots a_k}(m) e^{a_1}(m) \wedge e^{a_2}(m) \wedge \ldots \wedge e^{a_k}(m) \qquad (7.25)$$

Such expansions naturally are valid only over the domain of the chart or of the field of frames as the case may be.

8. The Tangent Map; Classifying Smooth Maps; Pull-back Extended; Case of Diffeomorphisms

On any differentiable manifold M , all the geometric objects, structures and operations described in the previous Section (and others to follow!) are automatically available. Suppose now we have two such manifolds, M and N , possibly of different dimensions n_1 and n_2 , and a smooth map $\varphi : M \to N$. On M and on N we have functions, vectors, tensors, forms. Does the map φ lead to natural relations between them? For functions we have already seen the operation of the pull-back φ^* . Are there useful ways to analyse φ itself? We now explore these questions.

8.1. THE TANGENT MAP

Given the smooth map $\varphi : M \to N$, the *tangent map* φ_* (also called the *derived map* , and also sometimes denoted by $T \varphi$) is a collection of linear mappings which, for each $m \in M$, takes $T_m M$ into $T_{\varphi(m)} N$:

Tangent Map φ_*

$$m \in M \xrightarrow{\varphi} \varphi(m) \in N \Rightarrow$$
$$(\varphi_*)_m : T_m M \longrightarrow T_{\varphi(m)} N :$$
$$u \in T_m M \longrightarrow v = (\varphi_*)_m(u) \in T_{\varphi(m)} N \qquad (8.1)$$

How do we define the image v, under $(\varphi_*)_m$, of $u \in T_m M$? We know
that this image is a derivation, at $\varphi(m)$, on smooth functions defined at
and around $\varphi(m)$. Let $\mathcal{V}$ be a neighbourhood of $\varphi(m)$, and g a smooth
function over $\mathcal{V}$. Then as we already know how to apply the pull back
to g, we are in possession of the smooth function $\varphi^* g$ defined over the
neighbourhood $\varphi^{-1}(\mathcal{V})$ of m. We then define v in eq.(8.1) thus:

$$v(g) \equiv (\varphi_*)_m (u) (g) = u(\varphi^* g) \qquad (8.2)$$

The Liebnitz law for v is an immediate consequence of that law for u,
and of $\varphi^*(fg) = \varphi^* f . \varphi^* g$ for functions. Pictorially we have the situation
shown in Figure 3.

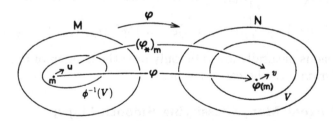

Figure 3. Illustrating the action of the tangent map

All this is coordinate or chart-free. If however we assign local coordinates
x^μ around m in M and y^α around $\varphi(m)$ in N, and we use the
notations of eq.(6.3), we have:

$$y^\alpha = \varphi^\alpha(x^1, \ldots, x^{n_1}), \; (\varphi^* g)(x) = g(y) \equiv g(\varphi(x)) \;;$$
$$u = u^\mu \left(\frac{\partial}{\partial x^\mu}\right)_m, \; v = (\varphi_*)_m(u) = v^\alpha \left(\frac{\partial}{\partial y^\alpha}\right)_{\varphi(m)} \;;$$
$$v^\alpha \frac{\partial}{\partial y^\alpha} g(y) \bigg|_{\varphi(m)} = u^\mu \frac{\partial}{\partial x^\mu} g(\varphi(x)) \bigg|_m \,,$$
$$\text{i.e., } v^\alpha = \left(\frac{\partial \varphi^\alpha(x)}{\partial x^\mu}\right)_m u^\mu, \; \alpha = 1, \ldots, n_2 \qquad (8.3)$$

Thus the Jacobian matrix of the map φ appears as the linear transformation that carries vectors in $T_m\,M$ into vectors in $T_{\varphi(m)}\,N$. In eq.(8.2) we have the intrinsic, and in eq.(8.3) the chart-based, version of the point-to-point linear map of tangent spaces arising from the smooth map φ. In local coordinates this Jacobian matrix has smooth, finite, matrix elements.

It is *extremely important* to realize that the tangent map φ_* is in general only defined in this point-to-point manner, taking $T_m\,M$ for each $m\,\in\,M$ into $T_{\varphi(m)}\,N$. One cannot suppose in general that φ_* acts in a well-defined way on vector fields over M to yield vector fields over N. There are two quite elementary reasons for this. Firstly, φ may not be injective; so if a vector field $X\,\in\,\mathcal{X}\,(M)$ is given, at each point $\varphi(m)\,\in\,N$ we may end up with more than one tangent vector as a result of the maps φ_*, and we would not know which one to take. Secondly, φ may not be surjective, so at points in N outside $\varphi(M)$ we do not get any tangent vector at all. For these reasons, in the general case we have to be content with having only the well-defined point-to-point maps $(\varphi_*)_m$ for each $m\,\in\,M$. Subject to this, we can see that composition of smooth maps leads to similar composition of their tangent maps in the same sequence:

$$\varphi_1\,:\,M\,\to\,N\,,\quad \varphi_2\,:\,N\,\to\,P\,\Rightarrow$$
$$(\varphi_2\,\circ\,\varphi_1)_*\,=\,(\varphi_2)_*\,\circ\,(\varphi_1)_*\,;$$
$$((\varphi_1)_*)_m\,:\,T_m\,M\,\to\,T_{\varphi_1(m)}\,N\,,$$
$$((\varphi_2)_*)_{\varphi_1(m)}\,:\,T_{\varphi_1(m)}\,N\,\to\,T_{(\varphi_2\circ\varphi_1)(m)}\,P\,\Rightarrow$$
$$((\varphi_2\,\circ\,\varphi_1)_*)_m=((\varphi_2)_*)_{\varphi_1(m)}\circ((\varphi_1)_*)_m\,:T_mM\to T_{(\varphi_2\circ\varphi_1)(m)}P$$
$$(8.4)$$

This is just the chain rule of matrix multiplication for the Jacobians of successive maps. And this composition rule for φ_* must be contrasted with the rule (6.9) for composing pull-backs φ^* !

8.2. EXAMPLES OF TANGENT MAPS

To see simple examples of the tangent map in action, let us go back to the two cases of maps $\mathcal{F}(M;\mathcal{R})\,\equiv\,\mathcal{F}(M)$, ie., smooth functions on M; and $\mathcal{F}(\mathcal{R};M)$, ie., smooth curves in M. In the former case, let us use the natural single coordinate s for $\mathcal{R}$. We view a function f as a map:

$$f\,:\,M\quad\to\quad\mathcal{R}\,:$$
$$m\,\in\,M\quad\to\quad f(m)\,\in\,\mathcal{R}\qquad(8.5)$$

Then $(f_*)_m$ maps, in a linear fashion, the n-dimensional tangent space $T_m\,M$ into the one-dimensional tangent space $T_{f(m)}\,\mathcal{R}$. (Here dim.$M\,=$

n). But in an obvious sense we know that:

$$s \in \mathcal{R} : T_s \mathcal{R} \simeq \mathcal{R} \qquad (8.6)$$

So we can say that $(f_*)_m$ is just a linear real-valued functional on $T_m M$, ie., an element of $T_m^* M$! Use of a chart around $m \in M$, if necessary, combined with eqs.(7.10,8.2), shows very easily that we have here just the differential of f at m :

$$u \in T_m M : (f_*)_m(u) \;=\; < (df)(m), u > \in \mathcal{R},$$

$$\text{more precisely,} (f_*)_m(u) \;=\; < (df)(m), u > (\frac{d}{ds})_{f(m)} \in T_{f(m)} \mathcal{R}$$

$$(8.7)$$

Thus we recover the differential of a function as a special case of the notion of the tangent map!

Turning to the case of smooth parametrised curves in M, these were defined in Section 6, and then used in Section 7 as an ingredient in the definition of tangent vectors. Now such a curve γ is a smooth map from $\mathcal{R}$ (or from some $I \subset \mathcal{R}$) to M, and we are using the natural coordinate s for $\mathcal{R}$. At each $s \in \mathcal{R}$, we have $(\frac{d}{ds})_s$ as a basis vector for $T_s \mathcal{R}$. Then applying $(\gamma_*)_s$ to it must result in a vector in $T_{m(s)}M$, where we are denoting $\gamma(s)$ by $m(s)$. This vector is just the tangent to the curve γ at the point $m(s)$! This is the content of eqs.(6.12, 7.4, 7.5) combined:

$$\gamma : s \in \mathcal{R} \;\longrightarrow\; m(s) \in M :$$

$$(\gamma_*)_s \, (\frac{d}{ds})_s \;=\; X_s \in T_{m(s)}M \;;$$

$$X_s(f) \;=\; (\frac{d}{ds})_s \, (\gamma^* f)(s)$$

$$=\; \frac{d}{ds} \, (f \circ \gamma) \, (s)$$

$$=\; \frac{d}{ds} \, f(m(s)) \;,\; \text{any } f \in \mathcal{F}(M) \qquad (8.8)$$

These examples of the tangent map in the two cases of functions on M and curves in M should familiarise one with its properties, and ways to handle it in practice. Now let us use the general notion of the tangent map φ_* for any smooth map $\varphi : M \to N$ to classify the possible pointwise behaviours and natures of φ.

8.3. RANK OF A SMOOTH MAP

Given two differentiable manifolds M and N of (possibly different) dimensions n_1 and n_2, and a smooth map $\varphi : M \to N$, the *rank* of

φ_* at $m \in M$ is the dimension of the subspace of $T_{\varphi(m)}N$ obtained by applying $(\varphi_*)_m$ to all of $T_m M$:

$$\text{Rank of } \varphi_* \text{ at } m \in M \; = \; \text{Dimension of } (\varphi_*)_m (T_m M) \subset T_{\varphi(m)} N \tag{8.9}$$

In local coordinates x^μ around m and y^α around $\varphi(m)$, we have the $n_1 \times n_2$ Jacobian matrix appearing in eq.(8.3), and it is the rank of this matrix that is involved here. Clearly,

$$\text{Rank of } \varphi_* \text{ at } m \in M \leq (n_1, n_2)_< \tag{8.10}$$

Here now are some local and global definitions and names for maps φ :

(a) φ is regular at $m \in M \iff (\varphi_*)_m$ has maximal rank, ie. $(n_1, n_2)_<$.

(b) φ is a regular map $\iff \varphi$ is regular at each $m \in M$

(c) $n \in N$ is a regular value of $\varphi \iff$ either $n \notin \varphi(M)$, or φ is regular at each $m \in \varphi^{-1}(n)$

(d) $n \in N$ is a critical value of $\varphi \iff n$ is not a regular value of φ $\iff n \in \varphi(M)$ but φ is not regular at some $m \in \varphi^{-1}(n)$

Each point $n \in N$ is definitely either a regular or a critical value of φ. If φ is regular, all $n \in N$ are regular values of φ. If φ is not regular, then some $n \in N$ are critical values of φ.

8.4.   CLASSIFYING SMOOTH REGULAR MAPS

The nicest maps are the smooth and regular ones. (Note carefully that "not regular" does not at all mean "not smooth"!). In this case, depending on the relative dimensions of M and N, distinctive names are used. We describe them now.

Dim. $M = n_1 <$ Dim. $N = n_2$
     Locally, M is a "smaller" space than N, and φ is called an *immersion*. For each $m \in M$ we have:

$$
\begin{aligned}
(\varphi_*)_m (T_m M) &= \text{ proper } n_1 - \text{dimensional subspace of } T_{\varphi(m)} N, \\
\text{rank } (\varphi_*)_m &= n_1 , \\
(\varphi_*)_m &\text{ is injective} \tag{8.11}
\end{aligned}
$$

Dim. $M = n_1 =$ Dim. $N = n_2$

Locally, M and N are of the "same size", and for each $m \in M$, $(\varphi_*)_m$ maps $T_m M$ bijectively on to $T_{\varphi(m)} N$. The rank of $(\varphi_*)_m$ is of course $n_1 = n_2$.

Dim. $M = n_1 >$ Dim. $N = n_2$

Locally, M is "bigger" than N, and φ is called a *submersion*. For each $m \in M$ we have:

$$(\varphi_*)_m (T_m M) = T_{\varphi(m)} N ,$$
$$\text{rank } (\varphi_*)_m = n_2 ,$$
$$(\varphi_*)_m \qquad \text{is surjective} \qquad (8.12)$$

In this case, there is an $(n_1 - n_2)$ dimensional subspace of $T_m M$ which is annihilated by $(\varphi_*)_m$.

The purpose of presenting these definitions is certainly not to submerge or immerse or overwhelm you with them, but only to show ways in which, using the tangent map φ_*, we can explore both the small scale and the large scale nature of a smooth regular map φ.

8.5.   EXTENDING THE PULLBACK

Now we look at the pull-back φ^* of a smooth map $\varphi : M \to N$. In Section 6 we saw how φ^* allows us to pass from smooth functions on N to smooth functions on M, $\mathcal{F}(N)$ to $\mathcal{F}(M)$. This is *opposite* to the direction in which φ operates. Now the action of φ^* can be extended to all *covariant* tensor fields on N, ie., all elements of $\mathcal{J}^{(0,s)}(N)$. The results are similar fields on M. For this we simply exploit the tangent map φ_* which is well-defined pointwise!

For any $A \in \mathcal{J}^{(0,s)}(N)$, the pull-back $\varphi^* A$ is an element of $\mathcal{J}^{(0,s)}(M)$ defined point by point on M thus:

$$A \in \mathcal{J}^{(0,s)}(N) \to \varphi^* A \in \mathcal{J}^{(0,s)}(M) :$$
$$m \in M, X_1, X_2, \ldots, X_s \in T_m M :$$
$$(\varphi^* A)(m)(X_1, \ldots, X_s) = A(\varphi(m))((\varphi_*)_m (X_1), \ldots, (\varphi_*)_m(X_s))$$
$$(8.13)$$

Notice that *none* of the problems that arose in trying to make φ_* act on a vector field on M to get a vector field on N arise here. Since the map $\varphi : M \to N$ is *given*, for each $m \in M$ there is an unambiguous image $\varphi(m) \in N$; and that is really all we have used in setting up $\varphi^* A$ on M. It is easy to convince oneself, using charts for instance, that as A and

φ are both smooth, so is $\varphi^* A$. The continued validity of the pull-back composition law (6.9) is also easy to see.

The interplay and alternating uses of pull-back φ^* and tangent map φ_* are well brought out if we record the sequence in which we set up successive processes or maps. For ease in writing we sometimes omit the generic point $m \in M$ and its image $\varphi(m) \in N$ at which various operations are understood to be carried out; corresponding to eqs.(6.2, 6.7, 8.2, 8.13) we have in sequence:

$$m \in M \quad \overset{\varphi}{\longrightarrow} \quad \varphi(m) \in N$$

$$f = \varphi^* g \in \mathcal{F}(M) \quad \overset{\varphi^*}{\longleftarrow} \quad g \in \mathcal{F}(N)$$
$$f(m) = g(\varphi(m))$$

$$u \in T_m M \quad \overset{\varphi_*}{\longrightarrow} \quad v = (\varphi_*)_m(u) \in T_{\varphi(m)} N$$
$$v(g) = u(\varphi^* g)$$

$$\varphi^* A \in \mathcal{J}^{(0,s)}(M) \quad \overset{\varphi^*}{\longleftarrow} \quad A \in \mathcal{J}^{(0,s)}(N)$$
$$(\varphi^* A)(X_1, \dots, X_s) = A(\varphi_* X_1, \dots, \varphi_* X_s)$$

This display should make clear the organization of ideas involved.

8.6.   PULL-BACK VERSUS DIFFERENTIAL AND WEDGE PRODUCT

We can use the above display to get a crucial result. For any $g \in \mathcal{F}(N)$, we know that its differential is a one-form on N, while its pull-back is a function on M:

$$g \in \mathcal{F}(N) \implies dg \in \mathcal{X}^*(N), \ \varphi^* g \in \mathcal{F}(M) \qquad (8.14)$$

Then, omitting the arguments m, $\varphi(m)$ in various expressions, we have:
$u \in T_m M$:

$$
\begin{aligned}
< \varphi^* dg, u > \ &= \ < dg, \varphi_* u > \quad \text{by eq. (8.13)} \\
&= \ (\varphi_* u)(g) \quad \text{by eq. (7.10)} \\
&= \ u(\varphi^* g) \quad \text{by eq. (8.2)} \\
&= \ < d \varphi^* g, u > \quad \text{by eq. (7.10) },
\end{aligned}
$$

$$\text{ie., } \varphi^* dg \ = \ d \varphi^* g \qquad\qquad (8.15)$$

Thus, recalling that the differential of a function is a $\mathcal{J}^{(0,1)}$ tensor and so the pull-back is defined on it, we have the theorem: *the pull-back of the differential of a function equals the differential of the pull-back of the function:* φ^* and d commute on functions. We will exploit and extend this result later.

Since forms are particular cases of covariant tensors, the pull-back works on them too. The results are forms again, since antisymmetry is preserved. So:

$$\omega \in C^k(N) \implies \varphi^* \omega \in C^k(M) \tag{8.16}$$

The interesting question is whether wedge products behave nicely under pull-back. Of course they do, as we see by judiciously combining eqs.(8.13, 4.29):

$$A \in C^k(N),\ B \in C^\ell(N) \Rightarrow A \wedge B \in C^{(k+\ell)}(N)\ ;$$
$$X_1, \ldots, X_{k+\ell} \in T_m\ M\ :$$
$$(\varphi^* (A \wedge B))\,(X_1, \ldots, X_{k+\ell}) = (A \wedge B)\,(\varphi_*\,X_1, \ldots, \varphi_*\,X_{k+\ell})$$
$$= \frac{1}{k!\ \ell!} \sum_{P \in S_{k+\ell}} \delta_P\,A(\varphi_*\,X_{P(1)}, \ldots, \varphi_*\,X_{P(k)})$$
$$B(\varphi_*\,X_{P(k+1)}, \ldots, \varphi_*\,X_{P(k+\ell)})$$
$$= \frac{1}{k!\ \ell!} \sum_{P \in S_{k+\ell}} \delta_P\,(\varphi^*\,A)\,(X_{P(1)}, \ldots, X_{P(k)})$$
$$(\varphi^* B)\,(X_{P(k+1)}, \ldots, X_{P(k+\ell)})$$
$$= ((\varphi^* A) \wedge (\varphi^* B))\,(X_1, \ldots, X_{k+\ell})\ ,$$
$$\varphi^*(A \wedge B) = (\varphi^*\,A) \wedge (\varphi^*\,B) \tag{8.17}$$

So φ^* and $\wedge$ also "commute".

8.7.   THE CASE OF DIFFEOMORPHISMS

With respect to *general* smooth maps $\varphi\ :\ M\ \to\ N$, then, the privileged status or role of covariant tensor fields (and in particular fields of forms) is clear: the pull-back is available for them, carrying such fields on N to similar fields on M. (Functions of course are "scalar fields" or "zero forms"). Vector fields, and generally fields with any contravariant character, do not have any similar well-defined behaviours under φ_*.

The *exception* is when we have a *diffeomorphism* $\varphi : M \to N$. In that case, both φ^* and φ_* work beautifully and naturally! *All* tensor fields $\mathcal{J}^{(r,s)}$ can be handled. The two maps φ and φ^{-1}, from M to N and N to M respectively, are both smooth and bijective. It is then easy to visualize that : (i) φ_* carries vector fields on M to vector fields on N ; (ii) the pull-back φ^* can be extended so that tensor fields in $\mathcal{J}^{(r,s)}(N)$ are taken to tensor fields in $\mathcal{J}^{(r,s)}(M)$. The following family of results, catalogued here, are easy to establish:

$$g \in \mathcal{F}(N), \ f = \varphi^* g \in \mathcal{F}(M) \ \Rightarrow \ g = (\varphi^{-1})^* f \ ; \qquad (a)$$

$$u \in T_m M, \ v = (\varphi_*)_m(u) \in T_{\varphi(m)} N \ \Rightarrow \ u = ((\varphi^{-1})_*)_{\varphi(m)} (v) \ ; \quad (b)$$

$$X \in \mathcal{X}(M) \ \Rightarrow \ Y = \varphi_* (X) \in \mathcal{X}(N) \ ; \qquad (c)$$

$$X \in \mathcal{X}(M), \ \beta \in \mathcal{X}^*(N) \ \Rightarrow$$

$$< \varphi^* \beta, \ X > = \varphi^* (< \beta, \ \varphi_* (X) >) \in \mathcal{F}(M) \ ; \qquad (d)$$

$$A \in \mathcal{J}^{(r,s)}(N) \ \Rightarrow \ \varphi^* A \in \mathcal{J}^{(r,s)}(M) \ :$$

$$(\varphi^* A) (\ldots \alpha \ldots ; \ldots X \ldots) = \varphi^*(A (\ldots (\varphi^{-1})^* \alpha \ldots ; \ldots \varphi_* (X) \ldots)) \ ,$$

$$\alpha \in \mathcal{X}^*(M), \ X \in \mathcal{X}(M) \ ; \qquad (e)$$

$$Y \in \mathcal{X}(N) \ \Rightarrow \ \varphi^* Y = (\varphi^{-1})_* Y \in \mathcal{X}(M) \ ; \qquad (f)$$

$$\alpha \in \mathcal{X}^*(M), \ X \in \mathcal{X}(M) \ :$$

$$< \alpha, \ X > = \varphi^* (< (\varphi^{-1})^* \alpha, \ \varphi_* (X) >) \ ; \qquad (g)$$

$$A \in \mathcal{J}^{(r,s)}(N), \ B \in \mathcal{J}^{(r',s')} (N) \ :$$

$$\varphi^* (A \otimes B) = \varphi^* A \otimes \varphi^* B \ . \qquad (h)$$

$$(8.18)$$

In addition to all these, we also have the result that φ^* carries dual frames for $T_{\varphi(m)} N$ and $T^*_{\varphi(m)} N$ (and also fields of dual frames over an open set $\mathcal{V} \subset N$), to dual frames for $T_m M$ and $T^*_m M$ (and fields of dual frames over $\varphi^{-1}(\mathcal{V}) \subset M$). Therefore the process of contraction of indices commutes with the pull-back via φ^* of general tensor fields from N to M . For practice with the set of results (8.18), one can try to establish the following additional ones:

$$Y \in \mathcal{X}(N), \ g \in \mathcal{F}(N) \ \Rightarrow$$

$$\varphi^* (Y (g)) = (\varphi^* Y) (\varphi^* g) \in \mathcal{F}(M) \ ; \qquad (a)$$

$$Y, Z \in \mathcal{X}(N) \ \Rightarrow$$

$$\varphi^* [Y, Z] = [\varphi^* Y, \varphi^* Z] \ ; \qquad (b)$$

$$X \in \mathcal{X}(M), \ \alpha \in C^k(N) \ \Rightarrow$$

$$i_X \ \varphi^* \ \alpha \ = \ \varphi^*(i_{\varphi_*(X)} \ \alpha) \ \in \ C^{(k-1)}(M) \qquad (c)$$

$$(8.19)$$

In brief, then, all natural and intrinsic geometric objects and operations on M and N are faithfully mapped onto one another when φ is a diffeomorphism.

9. Intrinsic Differentiation Processes on a Differentiable Manifold

We have already met two "processes of differentiation", processes obeying a Liebnitz law, in the development so far. Let us recall them. On a differentiable manifold M of dimension n , given a vector field X , we are able to map smooth functions f to other smooth functions in such a way that

$$X(fg) \ = \ X(f)g + f \ X(g) \qquad (9.1)$$

Next, we have the process of passing from a function f to its differential df , which is a one-form or covector field on M . This process obeys

$$d(fg) \ = \ g \ df + f \ dg \qquad (9.2)$$

These two Liebnitz laws are mutually consistent, or in harmony with one another, namely they respect the identity

$$X(f) \ = \ < \ df, X \ > \ = \ i_X \ df \qquad (9.3)$$

The process of acting on a function with a vector field is a process "labelled by" or "parametrised by" that vector field. In contrast the process of forming the differential of a function stands on its own - it is "autonomous". Each of these generalises in a very useful way. The former leads to the process of *Lie differentiation*: this is labelled by a vector field and is applicable to *all* tensor fields on M . The latter leads to the process of *exterior differentiation*, which is autonomous but is *applicable only to forms on M.*

We will study these two generalisations in this order, and then turn to their mutual relationship. At first we work on a single manifold M , and then later we consider the behaviours with respect to maps between two manifolds.

9.1.   THE LIE DERIVATIVE

Let us begin by supposing that we have a diffeomorphism φ of a differentiable manifold M onto itself, and let us recall the way the pull-back φ^* acts on various objects. On smooth functions we know that

$$f \in \mathcal{F}(M) \quad \rightarrow \quad \varphi^* f \in \mathcal{F}(M) :$$
$$(\varphi^* f)(m) \quad = \quad f(\varphi(m)) \tag{9.4}$$

Let us think of f as the "old" and $\varphi^* f$ as the "new" function; similarly of m as the "old" and its image $\varphi(m)$ as the "new" point. We can then express eq.(9.4) in this way: the value of the new function at the old point equals the value of the old function at the new point. With the pull-back of tensor fields on M we have a similar situation. Let $A, \varphi^* A \in \mathcal{J}^{(r,s)}(M)$. Then the "value" of the new tensor $\varphi^* A$ *as a multilinear map* at an old point m is *determined by* the "value" of the old tensor A at the new point $\varphi(m)$:

$$A \in \mathcal{J}^{(r,s)}(M) :$$
$$(\varphi^* A)(m)(\ldots \alpha \ldots; \ldots u \ldots) = A(\varphi(m))(\ldots (\varphi^{-1})^* \alpha \ldots; \ldots \varphi_*(u) \ldots),$$
$$\alpha \in T_m^* M, \ u \in T_m M ,$$
$$(\varphi^{-1})^* \alpha \in T_{\varphi(m)}^* M , \ \varphi_*(u) \in T_{\varphi(m)} M \tag{9.5}$$

We have also the following general properties:

$$A \in \mathcal{J}^{(r,s)}(M), \ B \in \mathcal{J}^{(r',s')}(M) :$$
$$\varphi^*(A \otimes B) = \varphi^* A \otimes \varphi^* B \in \mathcal{J}^{(r+r',s+s')}(M) ;$$
$$\varphi^* \text{ (contracted tensor from } A) = \text{similarly contracted tensor from } \varphi^* A \tag{9.6}$$

We will now use these results in the following context. Let us have a *one parameter group* of diffeomorphisms $\{\varphi_s\}$ of M onto M. That is, for each $s \in \mathcal{R}, \varphi_s : M \rightarrow M$ is a diffeomorphism; and we have the composition rules:

$$s_1, s_2 \in \mathcal{R} \quad : \quad \varphi_{s_1} \circ \varphi_{s_2} = \varphi_{s_2} \circ \varphi_{s_1} = \varphi_{s_1+s_2},$$
$$\varphi_0 = \mathcal{I}d_M = \text{identity map on } M \cdot \tag{9.7}$$

We will see that such a family $\{\varphi_s\}$ has associated with it a unique vector field $X \in \mathcal{X}(M)$.

A general point $m \in M$ is taken by φ_s to an image $\varphi_s(m) \in M$. When in a certain argument the point m is kept fixed and there is no danger of confusion, we may simply write $m(s)$ for this image:

$$s \in \mathcal{R}, m \in M : \varphi_s(m) = m(s) \in M \tag{9.8}$$

Now to define $X \in \mathcal{X}(M)$ means to give its effect on any $f \in \mathcal{F}(M)$. We set it up this way:

$$f \in \mathcal{F}(M):$$
$$X(f) = \frac{d}{ds} \varphi_s^* f \big|_{s=o} \in \mathcal{F}(M) \qquad (9.9)$$

We must check that X is indeed a vector field, namely a derivation on functions. But this is easy, on account of the product of the pull-back of functions being the pull back of the product:

$$
\begin{aligned}
X(fg) &= \frac{d}{ds} \varphi_s^*(fg) \big|_{s=o} = \frac{d}{ds} \varphi_s^* f \cdot \varphi_s^* g \big|_{s=o} \\
&= X(f) \, g + f \, X(g) \qquad (9.10)
\end{aligned}
$$

Thus, given a one-parameter group of diffeomorphisms $\{\varphi_s\}$ on M, the X defined in eq.(9.9) is indeed a vector field on M.

We now want to extend the action of X on functions and make it act in a proper way on all tensor fields on M. As a matter of notation, we hereafter write L_X for the "operator" to be defined presently as this extension of X. In the case of functions, then, we agree that

$$f \in \mathcal{F}(M) : L_X f \equiv X(f) \qquad (9.11)$$

The idea now is that from any $A \in \mathcal{J}^{(r,s)}(M)$, we want to produce an $L_X A \in \mathcal{J}^{(r,s)}(M)$. It is probably simplest to define how L_X acts on any general tensor field, then subsequently gain familiarity by looking at vector fields, one-forms etc. We define the action by L_X in this way:

$$A \in \mathcal{J}^{(r,s)}(M) \;\rightarrow\; L_X A = \frac{d}{ds} \varphi_s^* A \big|_{s=o} \in \mathcal{J}^{(r,s)}(M) \qquad (9.12)$$

Formally the rule is exactly as for action on functions given in eq.(9.9). The only point is to carefully extract the $meaning$ of L_X ! One can use eqs.(9.5,6) to give $L_X A$ in more explicit detail, and also to express the most important properties of L_X :

$$(L_X A)(m) (\ldots \alpha \ldots; \ldots u \ldots) = \frac{d}{ds} (\varphi_s^* A)(m)(\ldots \alpha \ldots; \ldots u \ldots) \big|_{s=0}$$

$$= \frac{d}{ds} A(m(s))(\ldots \varphi_{-s}^* \, \alpha \ldots; \ldots (\varphi_s)_* \, u \ldots) \big|_{s=o} : \qquad (a)$$

$$A \in \mathcal{J}^{(r,s)}(M), \; B \in \mathcal{J}^{(r',s')}(M) :$$

$$L_X(A \otimes B) = L_X A \otimes B + A \otimes L_X B \in \mathcal{J}^{(r+r',s+s')}(M) ; \qquad (b)$$

$$L_X(\text{Contracted tensor obtained from } A) =$$

$$\text{Similarly contracted tensor obtained from } L_X \ A \qquad (c)$$

$$(9.13)$$

The object or operator L_X is called the *Lie derivative* determined by $X \in \mathcal{X}(M)$, which in turn comes from the one-parameter group $\{\varphi_s\}$. Application of L_X to any tensor field A is called "Lie differentiation of A along X". We see from eqs.(9.13b,c) that L_X is a derivation on tensors, respecting contraction. For this reason, given these properties, the action of L_X on functions and on vector fields, $\mathcal{F}(M)$ and $\mathcal{X}(M)$, completely determines its action on *all* tensor fields on M. We already have in eq.(9.11) the action on functions. Thus in principle all we need now is the action on vector fields.

From eq.(9.13a) we can see that L_X depends on X in two qualitatively different ways: (i) there is an *algebraic* dependence coming from the fact that on the right hand side we have A at the moving point $m(s) \in M$; (ii) there is a *differential* dependence because of the appearances of the pull-back φ^*_{-s} and the tangent map $(\varphi_s)_*$ acting on the arguments of A, and these bring in the Jacobian of the diffeomorphism φ_s. This latter kind of dependence on X is absent in eq.(9.11), since no arguments drawn from $T_m M$ or $T^*_m M$ occur in that case. Both kinds of dependences will now be seen when we calculate the effect of L_X on a vector field Y.

Actually, instead of directly using eq.(9.13a) to get $L_X Y$, we will use an even simpler method by evaluating $L_X Y$ on a general *function* ! Thus we develop:

$$Y \in \mathcal{X}(M) \ , \quad f \in \mathcal{F}(M) :$$

$$(L_X \ Y)(f) = \frac{d}{ds} (\varphi^*_s Y)(f) \ |_{s=0}$$

$$= \frac{d}{ds} (\varphi^*_s (Y(\varphi^*_{-s} f))) \ |_{s=0}$$

$$= \frac{d}{ds} \varphi^*_s (Y(f)) \ |_{s=0} + Y \left(\frac{d}{ds} \varphi^*_{-s} f \right) |_{s=0}$$

$$(9.14)$$

Here in the second step we used the identity (8.19a). Now both terms here are at the level of eq.(9.9), involving action of L_X on functions alone, and the net result is:

$$(L_X \ Y)(f) = X(Y(f)) - Y(X(f))$$

$$= [X, Y](f),$$

$$\text{ie., } L_X \ Y = [X, Y] . \qquad (9.15)$$

Thus, on functions L_X is simply action by X , and on vector fields it is the commutator with X ! The first term in the commutator indicates the algebraic, the second term the differential, dependence on X as we had anticipated.

At this stage we can eliminate the dependence on the one-parameter group of diffeomorphisms $\{\varphi_s\}$, and for *any* $X \in \mathcal{X}(M)$ we can directly define L_X action on any tensor field by the following set of self-consistent rules: eq.(9.11) for action on functions; eq.(9.15) on vector fields; and the algebraic laws (9.13b,c). This suffices to fix L_X action on *all* tensors, and therefore also on all forms too. For a general $X \in \mathcal{X}(M)$, there may not be a corresponding group of diffeomorphisms $\{\varphi_s\}$; but the view now taken frees us from this requirement anyway. As an example, let us work out the effect of L_X on a one-form α. We find:

$$\alpha \in \mathcal{X}^*(M), \ Y \in \mathcal{X}(M) \ ;$$
$$L_X < \alpha, Y > \ = \ < L_X \, \alpha, Y > \ + \ < \alpha, L_X \, Y > \ ,$$
$$\text{ie., } (L_X \, \alpha)(Y) \ = \ X(\alpha(Y)) \ - \ \alpha \, ([X,Y]) \tag{9.16}$$

This completely determines the one-form $L_X \, \alpha$, and we see again both algebraic and differential dependences on X present. In principle, by repeated use of eqs.(9.15,16), explicit expressions for $L_X \, A$ for all kinds of tensor fields A on M can be developed. With eq.(9.16) one can also convince oneself that the right hand side depends on Y only algebraically and not in a differential manner.

In a chart $(\mathcal{U}, \psi)$ around a point $m \in M$, these various results of Lie differentiation can be expressed in terms of coordinate-based components:

$$f \in \mathcal{F}(M) \quad \to \quad f(x), \ X \text{ or } Y \in \mathcal{X}(M) \ \to \ (X^\mu(x) \text{ or } Y^\mu(x)) \ \partial_\mu \ ,$$
$$\alpha \in \mathcal{X}^*(M) \quad \to \quad \alpha_\mu \, (x) \ dx^\mu \ :$$
$$(L_X \, f)(x) \quad = \quad X^\mu(x) \ \partial_\mu \, f(x) \ ;$$
$$(L_X \, Y)^\mu(x) \quad = \quad X^\nu(x) \ \partial_\nu \, Y^\mu(x) \ - \ Y^\nu(x) \ \partial_\nu \, X^\mu(x) \ ;$$
$$(L_X \, \alpha)_\mu(x) \quad = \quad X^\nu(x) \ \partial_\nu \, \alpha_\mu(x) \ + \ \alpha_\nu(x) \ \partial_\mu \, X^\nu(x) \ ;$$
$$L_X \, (\partial_\mu) \quad = \quad - \ \partial_\mu \, X^\nu(x) \, . \, \partial_\nu \ ;$$
$$L_X \, (dx^\mu) \quad = \quad \partial_\nu \, X^\mu(x) \ dx^\nu$$
$$\quad = \quad d \, X^\mu(x)$$
$$\quad = \quad d \, L_X \, (x^\mu) \tag{9.17}$$

This last result here suggests that if in the intrinsic, chart-independent statement (9.16) the one-form α is the differential df of a function f , there would be an important simplification. This is indeed so, as a short calculation shows. From eq.(9.16) we get:

$$
\begin{aligned}
f \in \mathcal{F}(M),\ \alpha &= df \in \mathcal{X}^*(M) : \\
(L_X\, df)(Y) &= X((df)(Y)) - (df)([X,Y]) \\
&= X(Y(f)) - [X,Y](f) \\
&= Y(X(f)) \\
&= (d(X(f)))(Y) \\
&= (d\, L_X\, f)(Y)\,, \\
\text{ie.,}\quad L_X\, df &= dL_X\, f
\end{aligned}
\tag{9.18}
$$

Thus, on functions, *Lie differentiation and taking the differential commute!*

9.2. RELATION TO A DIFFEOMORPHISM

We have derived the basic properties of Lie differentiation on a given differentiable manifold M starting from the concept of action of a one-parameter group of diffeomorphisms of M onto itself. Now let $\varphi : M \to N$ be a *fixed* diffeomorphism between *two* differentiable manifolds M and N, and let $\{\varphi_s\}$ as before be the one-parameter group acting on M. Then a similar group $\{\varphi_s'\}$ acting on N arises by composition or conjugation with φ :

$$
s \in \mathcal{R} : \qquad \varphi_s' = \varphi \circ \varphi_s \circ \varphi^{-1}
\tag{9.19}
$$

The vector field X' on N associated with this group is immediately given by the vector field X on M determined by φ_s :

$$
\begin{aligned}
X' &= \varphi_*\,(X)\,, \\
X &= \varphi^*\, X'
\end{aligned}
\tag{9.20}
$$

More generally, the action of $L_{X'}$ on tensors on N is related to the action of L_X on tensors on M by:

$$
L_{\varphi_*(X)} = (\varphi^{-1})^* \circ L_X \circ \varphi^*
\tag{9.21}
$$

These are all easily established results. As a matter of notation, we have used the same symbol L to denote Lie operators both on M and on N, rather than, say, L and L' or $L^{(M)}$ and $L^{(N)}$. This should cause no confusion.

9.3. EXTERIOR DIFFERENTIATION

While Lie differentiation is a concept and a process intrinsically available on any differentiable manifold and applicable to *all* tensor fields, we develop next the process of exterior differentiation which works *only on forms* , more precisely on fields of forms. As a first step, let us gather the important properties of Lie differentiation and inner contraction on forms:

$$X \in \mathcal{X}(M) , \; \alpha \in C^k(M) , \; \beta \in C^\ell(M) :$$

$$L_X \, \alpha \in C^k(M) ,$$

$$L_X \, (\alpha \wedge \beta) = (L_X \, \alpha) \wedge \beta + \alpha \wedge L_X \, \beta ; \qquad (a)$$

$$i_X \, \alpha \in C^{(k-1)}(M) ,$$

$$i_X \, (\alpha \wedge \beta) = (i_X \, \alpha) \wedge \beta + (-1)^k \, \alpha \wedge i_X \, \beta \qquad (b)$$

$$(9.22)$$

We see that L_X preserves the degree of a form and obeys a Liebnitz rule; the latter is of course a consequence of the general tensor product rule (9.13(b)). On the other hand, i_X lowers the degree of a form by one, and obeys what we may call an anti Liebnitz rule with respect to wedge multiplication of forms. These facts motivate the setting up of the concepts of derivations and antiderivations on the space of forms on a differentiable manifold M .

A *derivation* $\mathcal{D}$ *of degree* r is a rule which carries each form α of degree k to a form of degree $k + r$, and obeys a Liebnitz rule:

$$\mathcal{D} \; : \; \alpha \in C^k(M) \to \mathcal{D} \, \alpha \in C^{(k+r)}(M) ,$$
$$\mathcal{D}(\alpha \wedge \beta) = (\mathcal{D} \, \alpha) \wedge \beta + \alpha \wedge \mathcal{D} \, \beta \qquad (9.23)$$

An *antiderivation* $\mathcal{A}$ *of degree* r differs only in the form of the Liebnitz rule:

$$\mathcal{A} \; : \; \alpha \in C^k(M) \to \mathcal{A} \, \alpha \in C^{(k+r)}(M) ,$$
$$\mathcal{A}(\alpha \wedge \beta) = (\mathcal{A} \, \alpha) \wedge \beta + (-1)^k \, \alpha \wedge \mathcal{A} \, \beta \qquad (9.24)$$

In this language: for each $X \in \mathcal{X}(M)$, L_X *is a derivation of degree zero*, while i_X *is an antiderivation of degree* -1. Two elementary facts now emerge: (i) on account of the Liebnitz and anti Liebnitz laws, any derivation $\mathcal{D}$ or antiderivation $\mathcal{A}$ is completely determined if we know its action on functions and on one-forms; (ii) since $\alpha \wedge \beta$ and $\beta \wedge \alpha$ differ only by the factor $(-1)^{k\ell}$, where k and ℓ are the degrees of α and β , the degree r of a derivation $\mathcal{D}$ must be even and that of an antiderivation $\mathcal{A}$ must be odd. Property (i) implies that we cannot have a nontrivial $\mathcal{D}$ or $\mathcal{A}$ on forms, of degree $r \leq -2$: it would necessarily have to vanish on functions and one-forms, and so would vanish identically. Property (ii) is consistent with what we know about L_X and i_X .

Now the process of forming the differential of a function $f \in \mathcal{F}(M)$, thus getting a one-form $df \in \mathcal{X}^*(M) = C^1(M)$, suggests that this might be the tip of an iceberg: an antiderivation of degree one! This is indeed so. The axiomatic definition of the process of exterior differentiation is as follows: knowing how to pass from $f \in \mathcal{F}(M)$ to $df \in C^1(M)$, we declare:

$$(i) \quad \alpha \in C^k(M) \rightarrow d\alpha \in C^{(k+1)}(M);$$

$$(ii) \quad \alpha \in C^k(M), \beta \in C^\ell(M):$$
$$d(\alpha \wedge \beta) = (d\alpha) \wedge \beta + (-1)^k \alpha \wedge d\beta;$$

$$(iii) \quad d\, d = 0 \qquad (9.25)$$

The last addition may come as somewhat of a surprise! We shall convince ourselves, by means of a local coordinate calculation, that it is necessary. Indeed we shall see the consistency of the entire notion of exterior differentiation.

Over a chart $(\mathcal{U}, \psi)$ on M, let us expand the k-form α in the manner of eq.(7.25):

$$\alpha = \frac{1}{k!} \alpha_{\nu_1 \ldots \nu_k}(x)\, dx^{\nu_1} \wedge \ldots \wedge dx^{\nu_k} \qquad (9.26)$$

In the overlap with another chart $(\mathcal{U}', \psi')$ using coordinates x', we have components $\alpha'_{\mu_1 \ldots \mu_k}(x')$ related to the above by eq.(7.16):

$$\alpha'_{\mu_1 \ldots \mu_k}(x') = \frac{\partial x^{\nu_1}}{\partial x'^{\mu_1}} \ldots \frac{\partial x^{\nu_k}}{\partial x'^{\mu_k}} \alpha_{\nu_1 \ldots \nu_k}(x) \qquad (9.27)$$

If we now calculate $\beta = d\alpha$ based on the axioms (9.25), the third axiom shows that there are no terms ddx^ν, and in the chart $(\mathcal{U}, \psi)$ the form β is:

$$\begin{aligned} \beta &= d\alpha = \frac{1}{k!} (d\, \alpha_{\nu_1 \ldots \nu_k}(x)) \wedge dx^{\nu_1} \wedge \ldots \wedge dx^{\nu_k} \\ &= \frac{1}{k!} \alpha_{\nu_1 \ldots \nu_k, \, \nu_{k+1}}(x)\, d\, x^{\nu_{k+1}} \wedge d\, x^{\nu_1} \wedge \ldots \wedge dx^{\nu_k} \\ &= \frac{(-1)^k}{k!} \alpha_{\nu_1 \ldots \nu_k, \nu_{k+1}}(x)\, d\, x^{\nu_1} \wedge \ldots \wedge d\, x^{\nu_{k+1}} \qquad (9.28) \end{aligned}$$

Here a comma followed by an index means the partial derivative with respect to that coordinate. To extract the components of β we have to antisymmetrize explicitly in *all* indices $\nu_1, \nu_2, \ldots, \nu_{k+1}$. This is seen to give:

$$\begin{aligned} \beta_{\nu_1 \ldots \nu_{k+1}}(x) = \quad & (-1)^k (\alpha_{\nu_1 \ldots \nu_k, \, \nu_{k+1}}(x) \\ & - \sum_{r=1}^{k} \alpha_{\nu_1 \ldots \nu_{r-1} \nu_{k+1} \nu_{r+1} \ldots \nu_k, \, \nu_r}(x)) \qquad (9.29) \end{aligned}$$

The basic question now is: when in the overlap $\mathcal{U} \cap \mathcal{U}'$ the components of α transform in the linear homogeneous fashion (9.27) appropriate for a (completely antisymmetric) covariant tensor field of rank k , will the completely antisymmetric components $\beta_{\nu_1...\nu_{k+1}}$ transform likewise, with the rank being $k+1$ instead of k ? Indeed they do! From the transformation rule (9.27) for α , we get on differentiation:

$$\alpha'_{\mu_1...\mu_k,\mu_{k+1}}(x') = \frac{\partial x^{\nu_1}}{\partial x'^{\mu_1}} \cdots \frac{\partial x^{\nu_k}}{\partial x'^{\mu_k}} \frac{\partial x^{\nu_{k+1}}}{\partial x'^{\mu_{k+1}}} \alpha_{\nu_1...\nu_k,\nu_{k+1}}(x) +$$

$$\sum_{r=1}^{k} \frac{\partial x^{\nu_1}}{\partial x'^{\mu_1}} \cdots \frac{\partial^2 x^{\nu_r}}{\partial x'^{\mu_r} \partial x'^{\mu_{k+1}}} \cdots \frac{\partial x^{\nu_k}}{\partial x'^{\mu_k}} \alpha_{\nu_1...\nu_k}(x)$$

$$(9.30)$$

When we next form $\beta'_{\mu_1...\mu_{k+1}}(x')$ by explicit antisymmetrisation of $\alpha'_{\mu_1...\mu_k,\mu_{k+1}}(x')$ with respect to *all* the indices $\mu_1 \ldots \mu_{k+1}$, we see that the second collection of terms in (9.30) *cannot survive* since the rth term there is *symmetric* under $\mu_r \longleftrightarrow \mu_{k+1}$! Thus from (9.30) we find that

$$\beta'_{\mu_1...\mu_{k+1}}(x') = \frac{\partial x^{\nu_1}}{\partial x'^{\mu_1}} \cdots \frac{\partial x^{\nu_{k+1}}}{\partial x'^{\mu_{k+1}}} \beta_{\nu_1...\nu_{k+1}}(x) , \qquad (9.31)$$

demonstrating that our axioms (9.25) do indeed turn a k -form into a $(k+1)$ -form as intended.

Having thus satisfied ourselves that the exterior differentiation d is a well defined antiderivation on forms, of degree $+1$, we realise that it is completely fixed once we know how it acts on functions and on one- forms. But even for the latter, the action on functions and the antiderivation law suffice! As is evident in a chart, the action of d on a one-form of the type $f \, dg$, where f and g are both functions on M , fixes its action on all one-forms, and then on all forms. Thus the minimal complete set of properties of d is this:

(i) $\quad f \in \mathcal{F}(M) \rightarrow df \in \mathcal{X}^*(M) = C^1(M)$
$\quad\quad$ according to eqs.(7.10,18) ;

(ii) $\quad f, g \in \mathcal{F}(M) : d(f \, dg) = df \wedge dg \in C^2(M) ;$

(iii) $\quad \alpha \in C^k(M), \beta \in C^\ell(M) :$
$\quad\quad d(\alpha \wedge \beta) = d\alpha \wedge \beta + (-1)^k \alpha \wedge d\beta ;$

(iv) $\quad d^2 = 0 .$ $\qquad\qquad\qquad\qquad\qquad\qquad\qquad\quad (9.32)$

9.4. RELATION BETWEEN PULL-BACK AND EXTERIOR DIFFERENTIATION

This reduction of the d -operation to its bare essentials leads to an important result. Let $\varphi : M \to N$ be a smooth map, M and N being differentiable manifolds of any dimensions; in particular, φ *need not be a diffeomorphism*. Now on each of M and N , an exterior differentiation is available, $d^{(M)}$ and $d^{(N)}$ say. Each is *fully fixed* by the way it operates on *functions* , plus the other common laws given in eq.(9.32). On the other hand, on *functions* we know from eq.(8.15) that pull-back commutes with exterior differentiation; and also from eq.(8.17) we know that wedge multiplication commutes with the pull-back. Putting all this together we conclude: if $\varphi : M \to N$ is a smooth map, then

$$
\begin{aligned}
\alpha \in C^k(N) \quad &\Rightarrow \quad \varphi^* \alpha \in C^k(M) \,, \\
d^{(M)} \varphi^* \alpha \quad &= \quad \varphi^* d^{(N)} \alpha \in C^{(k+1)}(M) \,, \\
\text{ie., } d^{(M)} \varphi^* \quad &= \quad \varphi^* d^{(N)}
\end{aligned}
\tag{9.33}
$$

Thus, exterior differentiation on *all* forms commutes with pull-back! We are thus justified in using a common symbol for this process both on M and on N , and simply writing:

$$
d \, \varphi^* = \varphi^* d
\tag{9.34}
$$

This is expressed by saying that *exterior differentiation is natural with respect to pull-back.*

9.5. THE CARTAN FAMILY IDENTITY AND OTHER RELATIONS AMONG L_X, i_X AND d

We have seen that Lie differentiation is a derivation on all tensors (and so on forms too) with degree zero. It is an easy algebraic fact that commutators of derivations are again derivations, with the ranks adding up. (In eq.(7.21) we saw this for vector fields in their action on functions). So for two vector fields $X, Y \in \mathcal{X}(M)$, the commutator $[L_X, L_Y]$ is again a derivation, of degree zero, *on all tensors*. Suspiciously like another Lie derivative! Indeed it is. We have seen that the Lie derivative operator is completely determined by action on functions and on vector fields; so let us evaluate the above commutator on them. We find:

$$
X, Y, Z \in \mathcal{X}(M), f \in \mathcal{F}(M) :
$$

$$
\begin{aligned}
[L_X, L_Y] f &= L_X(L_Y \, f) - L_Y(L_X \, f) \\
&= L_X(Y(f)) - L_Y(X(f))
\end{aligned}
$$

$$= X(Y(f)) - Y(X(f))$$
$$= [X, Y] f$$
$$= L_{[X,Y]} f ;$$ $\qquad (a)$
$$[L_X, L_Y] Z = L_X(L_Y Z) - L_Y(L_X Z)$$
$$= L_X([Y, Z]) - L_Y([X, Z])$$
$$= [X, [Y, Z]] - [Y, [X, Z]]$$
$$= [[X,Y], Z]$$
$$= L_{[X,Y]} Z$$ $\qquad (b)$
$$(9.35)$$

In $(9.35(a))$ we used eq.(9.11), while in $(9.35(b))$ we used eq.(9.15) and the Jacobi identity (7.23). We conclude that *on all tensors* we have

$$[L_X, L_Y] = L_{[X,Y]} \qquad (9.36)$$

Next let us turn to i_X and d. We must now confine ourselves to the set of all forms $C^k(M)$ of all degrees $k = 0, 1, \ldots, n = \dim.M$. On them we know that i_X and d are antiderivations, of degrees -1 and +1 respectively. Again it is a general algebraic result that the commutator of a derivation and an antiderivation is another anti- derivation; while the anticommutator of two antiderivations is a derivation. In both cases the degrees add up. Thus we are led to examine the combinations

$$L_X i_Y - i_Y L_X , \ L_X d - d L_X , \ i_X d + d i_X \qquad (9.37)$$

We may expect the first, an antiderivation of degree -1, to be an i_Z ; the second, judging from eq.(9.18), to vanish; and the third, being a derivation of degree zero, to be a Lie derivative! In all three cases, we need only calculate the effects on functions and one-forms of the simple type $f \, dg$. We then find:

$$(L_X i_Y - i_Y L_X) f = - i_Y X(f) = 0 ,$$

$$(L_X i_Y - i_Y L_X) f \, dg = L_X(f Y(g)) - i_Y(X(f)dg + f \, d X(g))$$
$$= X(f)Y(g) + f X(Y(g)) - X(f)Y(g) - f Y(X(g))$$
$$= i_{[X,Y]} f \, dg ; \qquad (a)$$
$$(L_X d - dL_X) f = 0 ,$$
$$(L_X d - dL_X)f \, dg = L_X(df \wedge dg) - d(X(f)dg + f \, d X(g))$$

$$= d\,X(f)\wedge dg \,+\, df\wedge dX(g) \,-\, d\,X(f)\wedge dg \,-\, df\wedge dX(g)$$

$$= 0\;;\qquad\qquad (b)$$

$$(i_X d + d\,i_X)\,f \,=\, i_X\,df \,=\, X(f) \,=\, L_X\,f\;,$$

$$(i_X d + d\,i_X)f\,dg \,=\, i_X(df\wedge dg) \,+\, d(f\,X(g))$$

$$= X(f)dg \,-\, X(g)df \,+\, X(g)df \,+\, f\,dX(g)$$

$$= (L_X f)\cdot dg \,+\, f\,dL_X\,g$$

$$= L_X(f\,d\,g)\;.\qquad\qquad (c)$$

$$(9.38)$$

Here we used the vanishing of i_X applied to any function, and also the result (9.18). We have thus obtained the following three results valid *on all forms* :

$$[L_X,\,i_Y] \,=\, i_{[X,Y]}\;;\qquad\qquad (a)$$

$$L_X\,d \,=\, d\,L_X\;;\qquad\qquad (b)$$

$$i_X\,d \,+\, d\,i_X \,=\, L_X\;.\qquad\qquad (c)$$

$$(9.39)$$

The last of these, which is really pretty, is called the *Cartan family identity.*

We conclude this Section by deriving a useful consequence of these results. It is an expression, in explicit form, for $d\,\theta$ where θ is any one-form:

$$\begin{aligned}
(d\theta)(X,Y) \,&=\, i_Y\,i_X\,d\theta\\
&=\, i_Y\,(L_X\,\theta \,-\, d\,i_X\,\theta)\\
&=\, <\,L_X\,\theta,\,Y\,> \,-\, Y(\theta(X))\\
&=\, L_X\,<\,\theta,\,Y\,> \,-\, <\,\theta,\,L_X\,Y\,> \,-\, Y(\theta(X))\\
&=\, X(\theta(Y)) \,-\, Y(\theta(X)) \,-\, \theta([X,\,Y])\qquad (9.40)
\end{aligned}$$

This relation will be of help in analysing torsion and curvature in a manifold with an affine connection.

10. Covariant Differentiation, Parallel Transport and Affine Connection; Torsion, Curvature; Cartan Equations, Bianchi Identities; Metric Geometry

We have just studied two intrinsic differentiation processes - Lie derivatives and exterior differentiation - that come naturally and automatically with any differentiable manifold, "at no extra cost". Let us follow it up with a study of a third differentiation process which is not intrinsic to a manifold, but is something we can impose upon it by giving it additional structure. This is the idea of *a covariant differentiation* or *an affine connection*. This idea brings along with it a host of other concepts, some listed in the title of this Section. So this will be a longer Section than earlier ones but shorter than some later ones.

10.1. COVARIANT DIFFERENTIATION - AN AFFINE CONNECTION

We saw in the case of Lie derivatives that for each $X \in \mathcal{X}(M)$ the operator L_X is a derivation on all tensor fields, with rather subtle dependences on X: there are both algebraic and differential dependences. A *process of covariant differentiation* on a differentiable manifold M again associates with each $X \in \mathcal{X}(M)$ a derivation ∇_X on all tensor fields, but now the dependence on X is purely algebraic and linear. Thus it is quite different from the case of L_X. Note for emphasis that we keep saying "*a* process of ..." – there is no unique, intrinsic, canonical one that comes naturally with a differentiable manifold. We put down many desirable properties, and any definition that obeys them all is acceptable!

We give the laws for a covariant differentiation, symbolised by ∇_X, by saying how it must depend on X; and then for fixed X, how it must act on tensor fields. The full list of laws is this:

i) $X \in \mathcal{X}(M) : \nabla_X = $ a derivation on tensors.

ii)   Dependence on X : for any $f, g \in \mathcal{F}(M)$, and $X, Y \in \mathcal{X}(M)$,
$$\nabla_{f\,X\,+\,g\,Y} = f\,\nabla_X + g\,\nabla_Y .$$

iii)   Action on tensor fields :

(a) $f \in \mathcal{F}(M) \rightarrow \nabla_X f = X(f)$;

(b) $f \in \mathcal{F}(M), Y \in \mathcal{X}(M) \rightarrow \nabla_X(fY) = X(f)Y + f\nabla_X Y$;

(c) $Y, \mathcal{Z} \in \mathcal{X}(M) \rightarrow \nabla_X(Y + \mathcal{Z}) = \nabla_X Y + \nabla_X \mathcal{Z}$;

(d) $A \in \mathcal{J}^{(r,s)}(M) \rightarrow \nabla_X A \in \mathcal{J}^{(r,s)}(M), \; c - $ linear in A

iv)   Derivation property : for any tensor fields A, B,
$$\nabla_X(A \otimes B) = \nabla_X A \otimes B + A \otimes \nabla_X B$$

v)   Preservation of contraction :

∇_X (contracted form of tensor field A) =

similarly contracted form of tensor field$\nabla_X A$.   (10.1)

Any rule or assignment of a ∇_X operation to each $X \in \mathcal{X}(M)$, obeying all these conditions, is called a covariant differentiation on M or an affine connection on M.

We repeat that the differences between L_X and (any) ∇_X lie in the natures of dependence on X, and the fact that the former is intrinsic and unique to M while the latter is not. Of course both are applicable to all tensor fields (unlike d), respect tensor products and contractions.

10.2.   LOCAL COORDINATE DESCRIPTION OF AN AFFINE CONNECTION

We can understand "what it takes" to set up an affine connection – which can abstractly be denoted by ∇ – by expressing the above requirements in the several charts making up an atlas. As past experience shows, on account of requirements (iii a, iv, v) of (10.1), the operation ∇_X is *completely determined* once one knows its action on *vector fields*. To make immediate contact with the approach familiar in traditional tensor calculus, let us denote by $(\mathcal{U}, \psi)$ and $(\mathcal{U}', \psi')$ a pair of (overlapping) charts in an atlas for M. Over $\mathcal{U}$, let the homeomorphism ψ assign coordinates x^μ to a generic point $m \in \mathcal{U}$. Then the local specification of ∇ over $\mathcal{U}$ is fully contained in a set of n^3 functions $\Gamma^\lambda{}_{\nu\mu}(x)$ defined over $\psi(\mathcal{U})$ in this way:

$$(\mathcal{U}, \psi): \qquad X \quad = \quad X^\mu(x)\partial_\mu \in \mathcal{X}(\mathcal{U}):$$
$$\nabla_X \quad = \quad X^\mu(x)\,\nabla_{\partial_\mu},$$
$$\nabla_{\partial_\mu}\partial_\nu \quad = \quad \Gamma^\lambda{}_{\nu\mu}(x)\,\partial_\lambda \qquad (10.2)$$

We are using here the coordinate based frame for vectors at each $m \in \mathcal{U}$; and expanding both the vector field X, and the result of applying ∇_X to ∂_ν, in terms of ∂_λ. So, to *give*, or to *know*, the covariant differentiation law over $\mathcal{U}$ is to give, or to know, these functions $\Gamma^\lambda{}_{\nu\mu}(x)$ all over $\psi(\mathcal{U})$, loosely all over $\mathcal{U}$. Now in the overlap $\mathcal{U} \cap \mathcal{U}'$ of the domains of two charts we have the system of equations

$$\partial'_\mu \quad = \quad \frac{\partial x^\lambda}{\partial x'^\mu}\,\partial_\lambda,$$
$$\partial_\lambda \quad = \quad \frac{\partial x'^\nu}{\partial x^\lambda}\,\partial'_\nu;$$
$$\nabla_{\partial_\mu}\partial_\nu \quad = \quad \Gamma^\lambda{}_{\nu\mu}(x)\,\partial_\lambda,$$
$$\nabla_{\partial'_\mu}\partial'_\nu \quad = \quad \Gamma'^\lambda{}_{\nu\mu}(x')\,\partial'_\lambda. \qquad (10.3)$$

Compatibility of these connecting relations with the requirements (10.1) on ∇ means:

$$\Gamma'^\lambda{}_{\nu\mu}(x')\partial'_\lambda \quad = \quad \frac{\partial x^\lambda}{\partial x'^\mu}\,\nabla_{\partial_\lambda}\left(\frac{\partial x^\rho}{\partial x'^\nu}\,\partial_\rho\right)$$

$$= \frac{\partial x^\lambda}{\partial x'^\mu} \left(\frac{\partial x^\rho}{\partial x'^\nu} \Gamma^\sigma{}_{\rho\lambda}(x)\partial_\sigma + \frac{\partial}{\partial x^\lambda} \left(\frac{\partial x^\rho}{\partial x'^\nu}\right) \cdot \partial_\rho \right)$$

$$= \frac{\partial x^\rho}{\partial x'^\nu} \frac{\partial x^\lambda}{\partial x'^\mu} \Gamma^\sigma{}_{\rho\lambda}(x)\partial_\sigma + \frac{\partial^2 x^\rho}{\partial x'^\mu \partial x'^\nu} \partial_\rho ,$$

$$\text{ie.,} \Gamma'^\lambda{}_{\nu\mu}(x') = \frac{\partial x'^\lambda}{\partial x^\sigma} \left(\frac{\partial x^\rho}{\partial x'^\nu} \frac{\partial x^\tau}{\partial x'^\mu} \Gamma^\sigma{}_{\rho\tau}(x) + \frac{\partial^2 x^\sigma}{\partial x'^\nu \partial x'^\mu} \right) \cdot \quad (10.4)$$

This is the familiar linear inhomogeneous nontensorial transition rule, usually called the transformation law for the connection coefficients.

Now we can say: in a local approach, what it takes to define or set up an affine connection on a given differentiable manifold M is to give, on *each* chart of an atlas, a set of n^3 functions $\Gamma^\lambda{}_{\nu\mu}$, such that in the overlap of *any two* charts the transition relations (10.4) are obeyed. In the traditional approach we tend to work with just one chart, and to say that Γ is an affine connection if on changing the coordinate system it behaves in such and such a way, ie., according to eq.(10.4). Here, that equation is part of the process of setting up Γ in its totality all over M. If we had a one-chart atlas, (a simple manifold), in the present approach there would be no need to use or "check" eq.(10.4) at all!

Continuing with the coordinate based description over a chart $(\mathcal{U}, \psi)$, we can see that the effect of ∇ on the basis of one forms dx^μ is fixed by the derivation law and preservation of contractions:

$$\nabla_{\partial_\mu} dx^\nu = -\Gamma^\nu{}_{\lambda\mu}(x)dx^\lambda \qquad (10.5)$$

Notice by the way that we have nowhere demanded the symmetry of Γ in its two lower indices!

10.3. PARALLEL TRANSPORT

The reinterpretation of affine connection as a process of parallel transport is made in this way. Take two vector fields $X, Y \in \mathcal{X}(M)$, and apply ∇_X to Y: the result is another vector field. In a local coordinate system, we write:

$$
\begin{aligned}
X = \ & X^\nu(x)\partial_\nu, \ Y = Y^\mu(x)\partial_\mu \Rightarrow \\
(\nabla_X Y)^\mu(x)\partial_\mu = \ & X^\nu(x)\nabla_{\partial_\nu}(Y^\mu(x)\partial_\mu) \\
= \ & X^\nu(x)(Y^\mu{}_{,\nu}(x)\partial_\mu + Y^\rho(x)\nabla_{\partial_\nu}\partial_\rho) \\
= \ & X^\nu(x)(Y^\mu{}_{,\nu}(x) + Y^\rho(x)\Gamma^\mu_{\rho\nu}(x))\partial_\mu , \\
(\nabla_X Y)^\mu(x) = \ & X^\nu(x)Y^\mu{}_{,\nu}(x) + \Gamma^\mu_{\rho\nu}(x)Y^\rho(x)X^\nu(x) .
\end{aligned}
$$

$$(10.6)$$

Now, both $Y^\mu(x)$ and $(\nabla_X Y)^\mu(x)$ are the components of tangent vectors located at the point in $\mathcal{U}$ assigned the coordinates x in this chart. Therefore for an infinitesimal parameter ε, the expressions

$$Y^\mu(x) \; - \; \varepsilon \, X^\nu(x) \, Y^\mu_{,\nu}(x) \; - \; \varepsilon \, \Gamma^\mu_{\rho\nu}(x) \, Y^\rho(x) \, X^\nu(x) \qquad (10.7)$$

are the components of a vector again "located at x". But writing $\varepsilon \, X^\nu(x) = \delta x^\nu$ and thinking of this as a small displacement from x in the direction of $X(x)$, to first order in ε we can say:

$$Y^\mu(x - \delta x) - \Gamma^\mu_{\rho\nu}(x) \, Y^\rho(x)\delta x^\nu \; = \text{components of a vector at } x \; ;$$

or shifting $x \to x + \delta x$ and again to lowest order :

$$Y^\mu(x) - \Gamma^\mu_{\rho\nu}(x)Y^\rho(x)\delta x^\nu = \text{components of a vector at } x + \delta x.$$

$$(10.8)$$

This is the way an affine connection is introduced in traditional tensor analysis, based on the idea of "carrying $Y^\mu(x)$ from x to $x + \delta x$" by parallel transport.

Let us now apply this notion of affine connection or parallel transport to study smooth curves on M, then come back to the further analysis of ∇ itself.

10.4.   INTEGRAL CURVES OF A VECTOR FIELD, PARALLEL TRANSPORT ALONG A CURVE, GEODESICS

As in Section 6, let

$$\gamma : I = (a,b) \subset \mathcal{R} \to M : s \in I \to m(s) \in M \qquad (10.9)$$

be a smooth parametrised curve in a differentiable manifold M. We know that at each point on $\gamma(I)$, there is a unique tangent vector X_s to the curve:

$$X_s = \gamma_*(\frac{d}{ds}) \in T_{m(s)} M \qquad (10.10)$$

In local coordinates we have:

$$m(s) \to x^\mu(s) : \quad X_s \to \frac{dx^\mu(s)}{ds} \qquad (10.11)$$

Now we introduce a notion (which could have been brought in earlier) which will be useful later. If a smooth vector field $X \in \mathcal{X}(M)$ were given, then a smooth parametrised curve $\gamma(I)$ is *an integral curve of the vector field* X if and only if

$$s \in I : \quad X_s = X(m(s)) \in T_{m(s)} M \qquad (10.12)$$

That is, at each point on the curve, the tangent to the curve is the same as the "value" of the vector field X at that point. In local coordinates, such an integral curve obeys a system of ordinary first order differential equations (which incidentally show that there is no freedom of nontrivial reparametrisation here):

$$X = X^\mu(x)\partial_\mu :$$
$$\frac{dx^\mu(s)}{ds} = X^\mu(x(s)), \quad \mu = 1, 2, \ldots, n \qquad (10.13)$$

We follow up this idea later. Notice that ∇ has played no role here!

Now let us revert to a general smooth parametrised curve γ, and assume an affine connection ∇ is given on M. At each "time" $s \in I$, we have the point $m(s)$ on the curve and the tangent X_s there. Let $Y \in \mathcal{X}(M)$ be some vector field over M, and consider how the "values" $Y(m(s))$ of Y along the curve vary as we travel along it. We say Y is parallel transported along γ, or Y is covariantly constant along γ, if for each s, $\nabla_{X_s} Y$ vanishes at $m(s)$. (Realise here that the tangent vectors X_s are available only along γ, they do not come from any vector field $X \in \mathcal{X}(M)$!). So:

$$Y \in \mathcal{X}(M) \quad : \quad (\nabla_{X_s} Y)(m(s)) = 0 \text{ for all } s \iff$$
$$Y(m(s)) \text{ is parallel transported along } \gamma \iff$$
$$Y \text{ is covariantly constant along } \gamma \qquad (10.14)$$

In local coordinates this clearly means that, on adapting eq.(10.6) to this situation:

$$\frac{d}{ds} Y^\mu(x(s)) + \Gamma^\mu{}_{\rho\nu}(x(s)) Y^\rho(x(s)) \frac{dx^\nu(s)}{ds} = 0 \qquad (10.15)$$

The expression on the left hand side here is the component-wise description of the covariant rate of change of Y along γ.

Now in this discussion, we imagined Y to be a vector field, defined both on and off γ, while of course the tangent vector X_s was defined only along γ. Let us now specialise further and ask how we might compute the covariant rate of change of X_s itself: in that case all we have is the smooth curve γ and the connection ∇. Taking X_s for Y in eq.(10.15) we shall say in local coordinates:

Covariant rate of change of the tangent to γ along γ
$$= \nabla_{X_s} X_s$$
$$= \frac{d^2 x^\mu(s)}{ds^2} + \Gamma^\mu{}_{\rho\nu}(x(s)) \frac{dx^\rho(s)}{ds} \frac{dx^\nu(s)}{ds} \qquad (10.16)$$

We now say that γ is a *geodesic with respect to the given affine connection* if $\nabla_{X_s} X_s$ is proportional to X_s by some function of the parameter s. In other words, the tangent vector must stay covariantly parallel to itself. So:

$$\gamma \text{ is a geodesic with respect to} \nabla \iff$$

$$\nabla_{X_s} X_s = a(s)X_s, \ a(s) \text{ real} \iff$$

$$\frac{d^2 x^\mu(s)}{ds^2} + \Gamma^\mu_{\ \rho\nu}(x(s)) \frac{dx^\rho(s)}{ds} \frac{dx^\nu(s)}{ds} = a(s) \frac{dx^\mu(s)}{ds}$$

$$(10.17)$$

Given a geodesic defined in this way, it is easy to see that by a suitable change in the parameter s we can reduce the function $a(s)$ to zero! One only has to pass from s to s' via the monotonic reparametrisation

$$s \rightarrow s' = \int ds \ e^{\int a(s)ds} \qquad (10.18)$$

We may as well assume then that such a parametrisation of γ has been employed from the start. In that case a geodesic curve with respect to a given affine connection is defined very simply as one obeying

$$\nabla_{X_s} X_s = 0 \ ,$$

i.e., $$\frac{d^2 x^\mu(s)}{ds^2} + \Gamma^\mu_{\ \rho\nu}(x(s)) \frac{dx^\rho(s)}{ds} \frac{dx^\nu(s)}{ds} = 0 \qquad (10.19)$$

In both eqs.(10.17,19) we have given an intrinsic as well as a local coordinate description of the situation.

We note that (i) geodesic here means "as straight as possible" in the sense that the tangent vector X_s stays parallel to itself as we go along γ, so the notion of *distance* is *not* involved here; (ii) with proper choice of parameter X_s even becomes covariantly constant, and with such an "affine parametrisation" (see eq.(10.19)) the only freedoms left are constant scale changes and shifts of the origin; (iii) a geodesic is only "sensitive to" the symmetric part of the connection coefficients $\Gamma^\mu_{\ \rho\nu}$.

After we introduce a metric, the idea of a geodesic as set up here can under suitable conditions acquire another meaning as well. Now we revert to the study of a general affine connection ∇ on M.

10.5.   THE ANHOLONOMIC CONNECTION COEFFICIENTS

In eqs.(10.2,5) we gave a local coordinate based description of the elementary processes of action of covariant derivatives on vectors and one-forms, using $\partial / \partial x^\mu$ and dx^μ as bases for these objects. Now we set up the formalism using general fields of frames for $T_m M$ and $T_m^* M$ as m varies over some open set $\mathcal{U} \subset M$. While what we will do is coordinate-free, it is in general still local, since M may not admit a global field of frames!

Leaving implicit their domain of definition, let $\{e_a\}$ and $\{e^a\}$ be smooth dual fields of frames for the tangent and cotangent spaces at various points $m \in M$. Any vector fields $X, Y \in \mathcal{X}(M)$ possess the expansions

$$
\begin{aligned}
X &= X^a \, e_a, \;\; Y = Y^a \, e_a, \\
X^a &= < e^a, X >, \;\; Y^a = < e^a, Y >
\end{aligned} \tag{10.20}
$$

We can see that the action of ∇_X on Y is completely determined if we know the effect of each ∇_{e_a} on each e_b. We therefore define:

$$
\nabla_{e_a} e_b = \omega^c{}_{ba} \, e_c \tag{10.21}
$$

The n^3 functions $\omega^c{}_{ba}$ (over the domain of the frames) are called the *anholonomic connection coefficients*. The counterpart equation for forms is

$$
\nabla_{e_a} e^b = - \omega^b{}_{ca} \, e^c \tag{10.22}
$$

This is fixed by the derivation and contraction laws for ∇. Then on a general vector field $Y \in \mathcal{X}(M)$ and a general one-form $\alpha \in \mathcal{X}^*(M)$ the effect of ∇_X is as follows:

$$
\begin{aligned}
Y &= Y^a \, e_a, \;\; \alpha = \alpha_a \, e^a \Rightarrow \\
\nabla_X Y &= (\nabla_X Y)^a \, e_a \, , \\
(\nabla_X Y)^a &= X(Y^a) + \omega^a{}_b \, (X) \, Y^b \, , \\
\omega^a{}_b \, (X) &\equiv \omega^a{}_{bc} \, X^c \, ; \\
\nabla_X \alpha &= (\nabla_X \alpha)_a \, e^a \, , \\
(\nabla_X \alpha)_a &= X(\alpha_a) - \omega^b{}_a \, (X) \, \alpha_b
\end{aligned} \tag{10.23}
$$

In eq.(10.21) we had introduced n^3 *functions* $\omega^a{}_{bc}$ as giving a complete account of the affine connection ∇ (over a certain domain). Now we have gone one step further and in eqs.(10.23) we have organised them into n^2 *one-forms* $\omega^a{}_b$ (over the same domain) as giving an equally good and complete account of ∇! Using the elements e^a of the dual frame $\{e^a\}$ of forms, we can in fact write:

$$
\begin{aligned}
\nabla_X e_a &= \omega^b{}_a \, (X) \, e_b \, , \\
\omega^b{}_a &= \omega^b{}_{ac} \, e^c \, , \\
\omega^b{}_a \, (X) &= \omega^b{}_{ac} < e^c, X > \\
&= \omega^b{}_{ac} \, X^c
\end{aligned} \tag{10.24}
$$

If as a particular choice of dual frames we use those provided by the coordinates in a chart, then we recover the earlier Γ's in this way:

$$a \;\rightarrow\; \mu, \;\; b \rightarrow \nu, \;\; c \rightarrow \lambda :$$
$$e_a \;\rightarrow\; \partial_\mu, \;\; e^a \rightarrow dx^\mu ,$$
$$\omega^a{}_{bc} \;\rightarrow\; \Gamma^\mu{}_{\nu\lambda} \tag{10.25}$$

In the local coordinate description of ∇, we encountered the linear inhomogeneous transition formula (10.4) for the connection coefficients Γ in the overlap of the domains of two charts. This is why the Γ's are nontensorial quantities. In the description of ∇ relative to general dual fields of frames $\{e_a\}$, $\{e^a\}$ we have a chart-independent way of handling ∇, but now the freedom to change these frames (even if they are not coordinate based!) causes the ω's to change in linear inhomogeneous fashion! This however in no way conflicts with $\omega^a{}_b$ being a set of one-forms (defined over the domain of the fields of frames), hence (local) tensorial objects. If we make a general smooth $GL(n,R)$ transformation $(A^a{}_b)$ over the domain concerned, we get new frames (cf.eq.(4.10)).

$$e'{}_a \;=\; (A^{-1})^{a'}{}_a \; e_{a'} ,$$
$$e'^a \;=\; A^a{}_{a'} \; e^{a'} , \tag{10.26}$$

so the new ω's are:

$$\begin{aligned}
\omega'^a{}_{bc} \;&=\; <\, e'^a, \nabla_{e'_c} e'{}_b \,> \\
&=\; A^a{}_{a'} < e^{a'}, (A^{-1})^{c'}{}_c \nabla_{e_{c'}} ((A^{-1})^{b'}{}_b \, e_{b'}) > \\
&=\; A^a{}_{a'} (A^{-1})^{c'}{}_c < e^{a'}, e_{c'}((A^{-1})^{b'}{}_b) \cdot e_{b'} + \\
&\quad (A^{-1})^{b'}{}_b \, \omega^d{}_{b'c'} \, e_d > \\
&=\; A^a{}_{a'} (A^{-1})^{c'}{}_c \, (e_{c'}((A^{-1})^{a'}{}_b) + (A^{-1})^{b'}{}_b \, \omega^{a'}{}_{b'c'}) .
\end{aligned} \tag{10.27}$$

This is a linear inhomogeneous law of change $\omega \;\rightarrow\; \omega'$. In terms of the one-forms $\omega^a{}_b$, we have a neater result:

$$\begin{aligned}
\omega'^a{}_b \;&=\; \omega'^a{}_{bc} \, e'^c = A^a{}_{a'} \, e^{c'} (e_{c'} ((A^{-1})^{a'}{}_b) + (A^{-1})^{b'}{}_b \, \omega^{a'}{}_{b'c'}) \\
&=\; A^a{}_{a'} (A^{-1})^{b'}{}_b \, \omega^{a'}{}_{b'} + A^a{}_{a'} \, d \, (A^{-1})^{a'}{}_b \tag{10.28}
\end{aligned}$$

This may be interpreted as follows: the inhomogeneous law of change has been shifted from being the coordinate dependence of nontensorial objects to a frame dependence of a collection of tensorial objects!

10.6. TORSION AND CURVATURE

Now we turn to the concepts of *torsion* and *curvature*, which are geometrical notions intimately associated with any affine connection ∇ on a differentiable manifold M. They are determined once ∇ is given. In fact Cartan's two *equations of structure* determine them in terms of the n^2 one-forms $\omega^a_{\ b}$ which, as we have seen, contain all information about ∇. We first define torsion and curvature, then study them in that sequence.

Given ∇, the torsion T is a tensor of type $\mathcal{J}^{(1,2)}(M)$. Thus for any two vector fields $X, Y \in \mathcal{X}(M)$, $T(X,Y)$ is also a vector field on M defined in this way:

$$T(X,Y) \ = \ \nabla_X Y \ - \ \nabla_Y X \ - \ [X,Y] \ \in \ \mathcal{X}(M) \qquad (10.29)$$

Using the postulated properties of ∇ and the known properties of the commutator of vector fields, we easily see that

$(i) \quad T(X,Y) = - \, T(Y,X) \, ,$

$(ii) \quad T(fX + gY, Z) = fT(X,Z) + gT(Y,Z), \ f, g \in \mathcal{F}(M)$

$$(10.30)$$

So the dependence of $T(X,Y)$ on each argument is linear algebraic, not differential, and the tensor character of T is evident. Taking account of the antisymmetry as well, we can say: *the torsion is a vector-valued two-form on M*.

Next, the curvature. This too is a "function" of two vector fields X, Y as arguments, but the "result" or the "value" is not a tensor of some definite type; rather, it is a derivation on tensors! We define it thus:

$$X, \quad Y \in \mathcal{X}(M) :$$

$$R(X,Y) \ = \ [\nabla_X, \nabla_Y] \ - \ \nabla_{[X,Y]} \qquad (10.31)$$

And we realise that its action on tensor fields is governed by these properties:

$(i) \qquad A \in \mathcal{J}^{(r,s)}(M) \ \Rightarrow \ R(X,Y)\, A \in \mathcal{J}^{(r,s)}(M) \, ;$

$(ii) \qquad$ for any two tensor fields A and B,

$\qquad\qquad R(X,Y)\, (A \otimes B) \ = \ R(X,Y)\, A \otimes B \ + \ A \otimes R(X,Y)\, B \, ;$

$(iii) \qquad R(X,Y)\, \text{(Contracted form of } A) \ =$

$\qquad\qquad$ similarly contracted form of $R(X,Y)\, A$ $\qquad\qquad\qquad (10.32)$

Thus, as past experience tells us, the action of $R(X,Y)$ on *all* tensor fields is completely determined by its actions on *functions* $f \in \mathcal{F}(M)$ and on *vector fields* $Z \in \mathcal{X}(M)$; all else is obtainable from here. Now the action on functions, on which ∇_X reduces to action by X, simplifies dramatically:

$$
\begin{aligned}
R(X,Y)f &= \nabla_X (\nabla_Y f) - \nabla_Y (\nabla_X f) - \nabla_{[X,Y]} f \\
&= X(Y(f)) - Y(X(f)) - [X,Y]f \\
&= 0
\end{aligned} \tag{10.33}
$$

So to the properties (10.32) we can now add this one:

$$
f, g \in \mathcal{F}(M), \; A, B \in \mathcal{J}^{(r,s)}(M) \; :
$$
$$
R(X,Y)(fA + gB) = fR(X,Y)A + gR(X,Y)B \in \mathcal{J}^{(r,s)}(M) \tag{10.34}
$$

We are therefore entitled to say : $R(X,Y)A$ depends on A in a linear algebraic, *not differential,* manner; and *all information* concerning $R(X,Y)$ is contained in its action on *vector fields.* As for the dependences on the arguments X and Y, we find as with torsion that:

$$
(i) \quad R(X,Y) = - R(Y,X) ,
$$
$$
(ii) \quad R(fX + gY, \; Z) = f \, R(X,Z) + gR(Y, \; Z), \; f, g \in \mathcal{F}(M) \tag{10.35}
$$

We are then justified in calling the curvature a *derivation-valued two-form on M,* vanishing in its action on functions and respecting contraction.

Comparing torsion and curvature: both are two-forms; the former is vector-valued, the latter is derivation-valued. With respect to general dual fields of frames $\{e_a\}$, $\{e^a\}$ (over some domain in M) we can expand both T and R:

$$
\begin{aligned}
(i) \quad & T(X,Y) = T^a(X,Y)e_a , \\
& T^a(X,Y) \in \mathcal{F}(M) ; \\
(ii) \quad & R(X,Y)Z = \Omega^a{}_b (X,Y) \, Z^b \, e_a , \\
& \Omega^a{}_b (X,Y) \in \mathcal{F}(M) .
\end{aligned} \tag{10.36}
$$

Thus while ∇ is "coded" in the n^2 one-forms $\omega^a{}_b$, torsion T is expressed through the n two-forms T^a, and curvature R through the n^2 two-forms $\Omega^a{}_b$. We know that ∇ determines both T and R. Cartan's equations of structure give us T^a and $\Omega^a{}_b$ in terms of $\omega^a{}_b$ and the fields of frames. Going one step backwards, we can reduce T and R to systems of functions (rather than forms) in this way:

$$
T^a(X,Y) \quad = T^a{}_{bc} \, X^b \, Y^c ,
$$

$$T^a{}_{bc} = T^a(e_b, e_c) \,,$$
$$T^a = \tfrac{1}{2} T^a{}_{bc} \, e^b \wedge e^c \,; \qquad (a)$$
$$\Omega^a{}_b(X,Y) = R^a{}_{bcd} \, X^c \, Y^d \,,$$
$$R^a{}_{bcd} = \Omega^a{}_b(e_c, e_d) \,,$$
$$\Omega^a{}_b = \tfrac{1}{2} R^a{}_{bcd} \, e^c \wedge e^d \,. \qquad (b)$$

$$(10.37)$$

Thus the "content of torsion" is in the $\frac{1}{2} n^2(n-1)$ functions $T^a{}_{bc}$, and of curvature in the $\frac{1}{2} n^3(n-1)$ functions $R^a{}_{bcd}$: in each set there is antisymmetry in the (last) pair of subscripts.

To sum up we can say:

Torsion $T \sim n$ two-forms $T^a \sim \dfrac{1}{2} n^2(n-1)$ functions $T^a{}_{bc}$;

Curvature $R \sim n^2$ two-forms $\Omega^a{}_b \sim \dfrac{1}{2} n^3(n-1)$ functions $R^a{}_{bcd}$.

$$(10.38)$$

10.7. THE CARTAN EQUATIONS OF STRUCTURE

Now we obtain Cartan's equations. First, for torsion, using the result (9.40) on the way:

$$
\begin{aligned}
T^a(X,Y) &= \; < e^a, \nabla_X Y - \nabla_Y X - [X,Y] > \\
&= \; < e^a, X^b \nabla_{e_b}(Y^c \, e_c) - Y^b \nabla_{e_b}(X^c \, e_c) - [X,Y] > \\
&= \; < e^a, X^b Y^c \omega^d{}_{cb} \, e_d + X^b \, e_b(Y^c) \, e_c - \\
&\quad\; Y^b X^c \omega^d{}_{cb} \, e_d - Y^b \, e_b(X^c) e_c - [X,Y] > \\
&= \; \omega^a{}_{cb} \, Y^c X^b + X(Y^a) - \omega^a{}_{cb} \, X^c Y^b - Y(X^a) - \\
&\quad\; e^a([X,Y]) \\
&= \; X(e^a(Y)) - Y(e^a(X)) - e^a([X,Y]) + \\
&\quad\; \omega^a{}_c(X) \, e^c(Y) - \omega^a{}_c(Y) \, e^c(X) \\
&= \; (de^a + \omega^a{}_b \wedge e^b)(X,Y) \,,
\end{aligned}
$$

ie., $\quad T^a = de^a + \omega^a{}_b \wedge e^b \,.$ $\qquad (10.39)$

This is *Cartan's First Equation of Structure* - the torsion two-forms are expressed in terms of the dual frame and affine connection one-forms.

Next, for curvature, we exploit eq.(9.40) as well as eq.(10.24):

$$
\begin{aligned}
\Omega^a{}_b\,(X,Y) &= \;\; < e^a,\; R(X,Y)\, e_b > \\
&= \;\; < e^a,\; \nabla_X(\nabla_Y\, e_b) - (X \leftrightarrow Y)\; > - \\
&\qquad < e^a,\; \nabla_{[X,Y]}\, e_b\; > \\
&= \;\; < e^a,\; \nabla_X(\omega^c{}_b\,(Y)\, e_c) - (X \leftrightarrow Y) > - \omega^a{}_b\,([X,Y]) \\
&= \;\; < e^a,\; X(\omega^c{}_b\,(Y))\, e_c + \omega^c{}_b\,(Y)\,\omega^d{}_c\,(X)\, e_d - \\
&\qquad (X \leftrightarrow Y) > -\omega^a{}_b\,([X,Y]) \\
&= \;\; X(\omega^a{}_b\,(Y)) - Y(\omega^a{}_b\,(X)) - \omega^a{}_b\,([X,Y]) + \\
&\qquad \omega^a{}_c\,(X)\,\omega^c{}_b\,(Y) - \omega^a{}_c\,(Y)\,\omega^c{}_b\,(X) \\
&= \;\; (d\,\omega^a{}_b + \omega^a{}_c \wedge \omega^c{}_b)\,(X,Y)\;, \\
\text{i.e., } \Omega^a{}_b &= \;\; d\,\omega^a{}_b + \omega^a{}_c \wedge \omega^c{}_b\,.
\end{aligned}
\tag{10.40}
$$

This is *Cartan's Second Equation of Structure* - the curvature two- forms are given in terms of the affine connection one-forms.

10.8. CONNECTION TO FAMILIAR NOTATIONS

Let us see how these equations of structure reduce to the familiar ones in a local coordinate system with its coordinate-based dual frames. The transcription must be done with some care. We follow the rules of eqs.(10.25) and set:

$$ a \to \mu,\; b \to \nu,\; c \to \lambda : $$

$$ e^a \to dx^\mu\;; \tag{a} $$

$$ \omega^a{}_b \to \Gamma^\mu{}_\nu = \Gamma^\mu{}_{\nu\lambda}\, dx^\lambda\;; \tag{b} $$

$$ T^a \to T^\mu = \frac{1}{2}\, T^\mu{}_{\nu\lambda}\, dx^\nu \wedge dx^\lambda\;, $$

$$ T(\partial_\nu,\, \partial_\lambda) = \frac{1}{2}\, T^\mu{}_{\nu\lambda}\, \partial_\mu\;; \tag{c} $$

$$ \Omega^a{}_b \to R^\mu{}_\nu = \frac{1}{2}\, R^\mu{}_{\nu\rho\sigma}\, dx^\rho \wedge dx^\sigma\;, $$

$$ R(\partial_\rho,\, \partial_\sigma)\, \partial_\nu = R^\mu{}_{\nu\rho\sigma}\, \partial_\mu\,. \tag{d} $$

$$ \tag{10.41} $$

Then the First Equation of Structure, (10.39), says:

$$
\begin{aligned}
T^\mu &= \Gamma^\mu{}_\nu \wedge dx^\nu\;, \\
\text{ie. } T^\mu{}_{\nu\lambda} &= \Gamma^\mu{}_{\lambda\nu} - \Gamma^\mu{}_{\nu\lambda}\,.
\end{aligned}
\tag{10.42}
$$

Thus, in coordinate language, torsion is the *antisymmetric part of the connection*, so it is *algebraic* in the latter.

Next, the Second Equation of Structure, (10.40), says:

$$R^\mu{}_\nu = d\,\Gamma^\mu{}_\nu + \Gamma^\mu{}_\lambda \wedge \Gamma^\lambda{}_\nu ,$$

$$\text{ie., } R^\mu{}_{\nu\rho\sigma} = \Gamma^\mu{}_{\nu\sigma,\rho} - \Gamma^\mu{}_{\nu\rho,\sigma} + \Gamma^\mu{}_{\lambda\rho}\,\Gamma^\lambda{}_{\nu\sigma} - \Gamma^\mu{}_{\lambda\sigma}\,\Gamma^\lambda{}_{\nu\rho}$$

$$(10.43)$$

This has both algebraic and differential dependences on Γ. Such an expression, in the case of a symmetric Γ, is of course quite familiar.

In conventional tensor analysis, a covariant differentiation process on tensor fields is indicated by a *semicolon* followed by a covariant index, and in this the Γ's are used. The curvature comes in when we calculate second covariant derivatives in opposite orders and look at the difference. From the present intrinsic point of view, working in a chart, let us see how we can systematically recover the results of the "semicolon notation". Let us begin by symbolically defining an action by ∇, not by ∇_X, on a general tensor field. It is natural to say:

$$A \in \mathcal{J}^{(r,s)}(M) \rightarrow \nabla A \in \mathcal{J}^{(r,s+1)}(M) :$$
$$(\nabla A)(\ldots\alpha\ldots;\ldots Y\ldots,X) \equiv (\nabla_X A)(\ldots\alpha\ldots;\ldots Y\ldots) ,$$
$$\alpha \in \mathcal{X}^*(M) ,$$
$$X, Y \in \mathcal{X}(M) .$$

$$(10.44)$$

Recalling the definitions (10.2,5), we can introduce the semicolon notation in a chart by expressing the idea of ∇ acting on A thus:

$$A \in \mathcal{J}^{(r,s)}(M) :$$

$$A = A^{\cdots\mu\cdots}{}_{\cdots\nu\cdots}(x) \ldots \otimes \partial_\mu \ldots \otimes dx^\nu \ldots \Rightarrow$$

$$\nabla A = (\nabla_{\partial_\rho} A) \otimes dx^\rho , \tag{a}$$

$$\nabla_{\partial_\rho} A = A^{\cdots\mu\cdots}{}_{\cdots\nu\cdots;\rho} \ldots \otimes \partial_\mu \ldots \otimes dx^\nu \ldots , \tag{b}$$

$$A^{\cdots\mu\cdots}{}_{\cdots\nu\cdots;\rho} = A^{\cdots\mu\cdots}{}_{\cdots\nu\cdots,\rho} + \ldots \Gamma^\mu{}_{\lambda\rho}\,A^{\cdots\lambda\cdots}{}_{\cdots\nu\cdots} -$$
$$\ldots \Gamma^\lambda{}_{\nu\rho}\,A^{\cdots\mu\cdots}{}_{\cdots\lambda\cdots} \tag{c}$$

$$(10.45)$$

It is consistent here to place dx^ρ at the last extreme right position in ∇A, since in eq.(10.44) we agreed to place X in such a position among the arguments of ∇A. Appreciate also two other points: in $\nabla_{\partial_\rho} A$ there is (naturally) *no factor dx^ρ*; in the semicolon notation there is, after the plain derivative, one term induced by each contravariant μ index and one by each covariant ν index, arising from $\nabla_{\partial_\rho} \partial_\mu$ and $\nabla_{\partial_\rho} dx^\nu$ respectively.

Now let us apply ∇_{∂_σ} to $\nabla_{\partial_\rho} A$:

$$\nabla_{\partial_\sigma} \nabla_{\partial_\rho} A = (A^{\cdots\mu\cdots}{}_{\cdots\nu\cdots;\rho;\sigma} + \Gamma^\lambda{}_{\rho\sigma} A^{\cdots\mu\cdots}{}_{\cdots\nu\cdots;\lambda}) \cdots \otimes \partial_\mu \cdots \otimes dx^\nu \cdots$$
$$(10.46)$$

The reason for the appearance of the second term here is interesting: it is *to compensate for* or *cancel* a term which the "semicolon derivative with respect to σ" would have automatically produced on account of the index ρ on the right hand side in eq.(10.45b), if we follow the *rule* given in eq.(10.45c); but this term is *not wanted* because in $\nabla_{\partial_\rho} A$ there is no dx^ρ factor! Antisymmetrising the left hand side of eq.(10.46) in ρ and σ we get (remember $[\partial_\rho, \partial_\sigma] = 0$):

$$R(\partial_\sigma, \partial_\rho) A = (A^{\cdots\mu\cdots}{}_{\cdots\nu\cdots;\rho;\sigma} - A^{\cdots\mu\cdots}{}_{\cdots\nu\cdots;\sigma;\rho} - T^\lambda{}_{\rho\sigma} A^{\cdots\mu\cdots}{}_{\cdots\nu\cdots;\lambda}) \cdots \otimes \partial_\mu \cdots \otimes dx^\nu \cdots$$
$$(10.47)$$

This "master result" holds for all tensor fields $A \in \mathcal{J}^{(r,s)}(M)$, for any ranks r and s. Let us look at a few simple cases.

Scalar fields, $r = s = 0$. Here the left hand side of eq.(10.47) vanishes by eq.(10.33), so we get the result:

$$f \in \mathcal{F}(M) : f_{,\rho;\sigma} - f_{,\sigma;\rho} = T^\lambda{}_{\rho\sigma} f_{,\lambda} . \qquad (10.48)$$

This is then yet another way of isolating the torsion for a given affine connection.

Vector fields, $r = 1$, $s = 0$. Here we have $A \in \mathcal{J}^{(1,0)}(M) = \mathcal{X}(M)$ and can write $A = A^\mu(x)\partial_\mu$. Then using eq.(10.41d) we get from eq.(10.47):

$$A^\mu{}_{;\rho;\sigma} - A^\mu{}_{;\sigma;\rho} = R^\mu{}_{\lambda\sigma\rho} A^\lambda + T^\lambda{}_{\rho\sigma} A^\mu{}_{;\lambda} \qquad (10.49)$$

In the case of vanishing torsion (symmetric Γ's), this is the way the curvature is usually introduced. For the most general situation, however, we see that both curvature and torsion figure in the difference of two "semicolon derivatives" in opposite orders.

One $-$ forms, $r = 0$, $s = 1$. Now we have $A \in \mathcal{J}^{(0,1)}(M) = \mathcal{X}^*(M)$ and can write $A = A_\mu(x)dx^\mu$. It is a consequence of eq.(10.41d) and the properties of the curvature that

$$R(\partial_\sigma, \partial_\rho) dx^\nu = - R^\nu{}_{\lambda\sigma\rho} dx^\lambda . \qquad (10.50)$$

Using this, eq.(10.47) becomes:

$$A_{\nu;\rho;\sigma} - A_{\nu;\sigma;\rho} = - R^\lambda{}_{\nu\sigma\rho} A_\lambda + T^\lambda{}_{\rho\sigma} A_{\nu;\lambda} \qquad (10.51)$$

This is a companion to eq.(10.49).

After seeing these examples, it is apparent that in component form the "master formula" (10.47) for any tensor field $A \in \mathcal{T}^{(r,s)}(M)$ becomes:

$$A^{\cdots\mu\cdots}{}_{\ldots\nu\ldots;\rho;\sigma} - A^{\cdots\mu\cdots}{}_{\ldots\nu\ldots;\sigma;\rho} =$$
$$T^\lambda{}_{\rho\sigma}\, A^{\cdots\mu\cdots}{}_{\ldots\nu\ldots;\lambda} +$$
$$\cdots\, R^\mu{}_{\lambda\sigma\rho}\, A^{\cdots\lambda\cdots}{}_{\ldots\nu\ldots} -$$
$$\cdots\, R^\lambda{}_{\nu\sigma\rho}\, A^{\cdots\mu\cdots}{}_{\ldots\lambda\ldots} \qquad (10.52)$$

10.9. THE BIANCHI IDENTITIES

These consist of both an *algebraic* and a *differential* statement: both are obeyed by the curvature, and are consequences of the Jacobi identities for commutators of vector fields, and of ∇_X viewed as derivations on tensors. First we derive them in intrinsic form, then we give their local coordinate versions. Take $X, Y, Z \in \mathcal{X}(M)$ and consider the effect of $R(X,Y)$ on Z :

$$R(X,Y)Z = (\nabla_X \nabla_Y - \nabla_Y \nabla_X)Z - \nabla_{[X,Y]}Z$$

If we indicate by $\sum_c$ a cyclic sum on X, Y and Z, we find:

$$\begin{aligned}
\sum_c R(X,Y)Z &= \nabla_X \nabla_Y Z - \nabla_Y \nabla_X Z - \nabla_{[X,Y]}Z + \\
&\quad \nabla_Y \nabla_Z X - \nabla_Z \nabla_Y X - \nabla_{[Y,Z]}X + \\
&\quad \nabla_Z \nabla_X Y - \nabla_X \nabla_Z Y - \nabla_{[Z,X]}Y \\
&= \sum_c \{\nabla_X (T(Y,Z) + [Y,Z]) - \nabla_{[Y,Z]}X\} \\
&= \sum_c \{\nabla_X T(Y,Z) + T(X,[Y,Z]) + \\
&\quad [X,[Y,Z]]\} \ ,
\end{aligned}$$

$$\text{ie.,} \ \sum_c R(X,Y)Z = \sum_c \{\nabla_X T(Y,Z) + T(X,[Y,Z])\} \ . \quad (10.53)$$

This is the *algebraic* Bianchi identity, and in its derivation we have used the Jacobi identity for commutators of vector fields (apart from the definitions of R and T)

In a chart, we take

$$X \to \partial_\lambda, \quad Y \to \partial_\mu, \quad Z \to \partial_\nu \ ,$$

so that $\sum_c$ will mean a cyclic sum over $(\lambda\mu\nu)$. Then eq.(10.53) boils down to

$$\sum_{(\lambda\mu\nu)} R(\partial_\lambda,\, \partial_\mu)\, \partial_\nu = \sum_{(\lambda\mu\nu)} \nabla_{\partial_\lambda} T(\partial_\mu,\, \partial_\nu\,) \ ,$$

$$\text{ie., } \sum_{(\lambda\mu\nu)} R^\sigma{}_{\nu\lambda\mu} \, \partial_\sigma = \sum_{(\lambda\mu\nu)} \nabla_{\partial_\lambda} T^\sigma{}_{\mu\nu} \, \partial_\sigma$$

$$= \sum_{(\lambda\mu\nu)} (T^\sigma{}_{\mu\nu;\lambda} + \Gamma^\rho{}_{\mu\lambda} T^\sigma{}_{\rho\nu} + \Gamma^\rho{}_{\nu\lambda} T^\sigma{}_{\mu\rho}) \, \partial_\sigma \, .$$

Here, both "extra" terms on the right are to compensate with respect to μ and ν in the use of the semicolon notation. After using the antisymmetry of $T^{\cdot}{}_{..}$ we end up with the local coordinate form of the first Bianchi identity for the curvature:

$$\sum_{(\lambda\mu\nu)} R^\sigma{}_{\lambda\mu\nu} = \sum_{(\lambda\mu\nu)} (T^\sigma{}_{\lambda\mu;\nu} + T^\rho{}_{\lambda\mu} T^\sigma{}_{\rho\nu}) \, . \tag{10.54}$$

Turning to the differential Bianchi identity, here we directly use the Jacobi identity for three ∇ symbols:

$$\sum_c [\nabla_X, [\nabla_Y, \nabla_Z]] = 0 \, ,$$

$$\text{ie., } \sum_c [\nabla_X, R(Y,Z) + \nabla_{[Y,Z]}] = 0 \, ,$$

$$\text{ie., } \sum_c \{[\nabla_X, R(Y,Z)] + R(X,[Y,Z]) + \nabla_{[X,[Y,Z]]}\} = 0,$$

$$\text{ie., } \sum_c [R(X,Y), \nabla_Z] = \sum_c R(X,[Y,Z]) \, . \tag{10.55}$$

This is the intrinsic statement of the second Bianchi identity. We see that the left hand side is not purely algebraic in R.

In a chart, if we set

$$X \to \partial_\sigma, \quad Y \to \partial_\rho, \quad Z \to \partial_\tau,$$

the terms on the righthand side vanish, and the identity reads:

$$\sum_{(\rho\tau\sigma)} R(\partial_\sigma, \partial_\rho) \nabla_{\partial_\tau} = \sum_{(\rho\tau\sigma)} \nabla_{\partial_\tau} R(\partial_\sigma, \partial_\rho) \tag{10.56}$$

Now both sides are applicable to any tensor field $A \in \mathcal{J}^{(r,s)}(M)$. Exposing one typical contravariant and one typical covariant index on A, it suffices to take

$$A = A^\mu{}_\nu \, \partial_\mu \otimes dx^\nu \, . \tag{10.57}$$

We use the general formulas

$$\nabla_{\partial_\tau} A = A^\mu{}_{\nu;\tau} \, \partial_\mu \otimes dx^\nu \, ,$$

$$R(\partial_\sigma, \partial_\rho) A = (A^\lambda{}_\nu R^\mu{}_{\lambda\sigma\rho} - A^\mu{}_\lambda R^\lambda{}_{\nu\sigma\rho}) \, \partial_\mu \otimes dx^\nu \tag{10.58}$$

to develop the two sides of (10.56) applied to A:

$$R(\partial_\sigma,\partial_\rho)\,\nabla_{\partial_\tau}\,A \;=\; R(\partial_\sigma,\partial_\rho)\,A^\mu{}_{\nu;\tau}\,\partial_\mu \otimes dx^\nu$$
$$=\; (A^\lambda{}_{\nu;\tau}\,R^\mu{}_{\lambda\sigma\rho} - A^\mu{}_{\lambda;\tau}\,R^\lambda{}_{\nu\sigma\rho})\partial_\mu \otimes dx^\nu \;;$$
$$\nabla_{\partial_\tau}\,R(\partial_\sigma,\partial_\rho)\,A \;=\; \nabla_{\partial_\tau}\,(A^\lambda{}_\nu\,R^\mu{}_{\lambda\sigma\rho} - A^\mu{}_\lambda\,R^\lambda{}_{\nu\sigma\rho})\,\partial_\mu \otimes dx^\nu$$
$$=\; \{A^\lambda{}_{\nu;\tau}\,R^\mu{}_{\lambda\sigma\rho} + A^\lambda{}_\nu\,R^\mu{}_{\lambda\sigma\rho;\tau} -$$
$$A^\mu{}_{\lambda;\tau}\,R^\lambda{}_{\nu\sigma\rho} - A^\mu{}_\lambda\,R^\lambda{}_{\nu\sigma\rho;\tau} +$$
$$A^\lambda{}_\nu\,(\Gamma^\xi{}_{\sigma\tau}\,R^\mu{}_{\lambda\xi\rho} + \Gamma^\xi{}_{\rho\tau}\,R^\mu{}_{\lambda\sigma\xi}) -$$
$$A^\mu{}_\lambda\,(\Gamma^\xi{}_{\sigma\tau}\,R^\lambda{}_{\nu\xi\rho} + \Gamma^\xi{}_{\rho\tau}\,R^\lambda{}_{\nu\sigma\xi})\}\,\partial_\mu \otimes dx^\nu \;.$$
$$(10.59)$$

In the first statement, the index τ on $A^\mu{}_{\nu;\tau}$ just goes along for the ride since in any case R vanishes on functions. In the second statement we have compensating terms with respect to ρ and σ alone, and not with respect to the dummy index λ. Equating the two cyclic sums over $(\rho\tau\sigma)$ we get:

$$\sum_{(\rho\tau\sigma)} (R^\mu{}_{\lambda\sigma\rho;\tau} + \Gamma^\xi{}_{\sigma\tau}\,R^\mu{}_{\lambda\xi\rho} + \Gamma^\xi{}_{\rho\tau}\,R^\mu{}_{\lambda\sigma\xi})\,A^\lambda{}_\nu \;=\;$$
$$\sum_{(\rho\tau\sigma)} (R^\lambda{}_{\nu\sigma\rho;\tau} + \Gamma^\xi{}_{\sigma\tau}\,R^\lambda{}_{\nu\xi\rho} + \Gamma^\xi{}_{\rho\tau}\,R^\lambda{}_{\nu\sigma\xi})\,A^\mu{}_\lambda \;,$$

ie., $$\sum_{(\rho\tau\sigma)} (R^\mu{}_{\lambda\sigma\rho;\tau} + T^\xi{}_{\tau\sigma}\,R^\mu{}_{\lambda\xi\rho}) = 0 \qquad (10.60)$$

Here we have taken advantage of the antisymmetry of $R^\mu{}_{\lambda\xi\rho}$ in ξ and ρ, and the presence of a cyclic sum.

For the most general affine connection, then, we can collect together in one place the basic identities obeyed by the curvature, as described in local coordinates:

$$R^\sigma{}_{\lambda\mu\nu} \;=\; -\,R^\sigma{}_{\lambda\nu\mu} \;; \qquad (a)$$

$$\sum_{(\lambda\mu\nu)} R^\sigma{}_{\lambda\mu\nu} \;=\; \sum_{(\lambda\mu\nu)} (T^\sigma{}_{\lambda\mu;\nu} + T^\sigma{}_{\rho\mu}\,T^\rho{}_{\nu\lambda}) \;; \qquad (b)$$

$$\sum_{(\lambda\mu\nu)} R^\sigma{}_{\tau\lambda\mu;\nu} \;=\; \sum_{(\lambda\mu\nu)} T^\rho{}_{\lambda\mu}\,R^\sigma{}_{\tau\nu\rho} \;. \qquad (c)$$

$$(10.61)$$

In case ∇ is free of torsion, the right hand sides in (b) and (c) vanish.

10.10.   INTRODUCTION OF METRIC - RIEMANNIAN STRUCTURE

Let M be as always an n-dimensional differentiable manifold. A *metric g* on M is a tensor field belonging to $\mathcal{J}^{(0,2)}(M)$, smooth as always, which is symmetric and nondegenerate. Thus at each point $m \in M$ we demand of $g(m)$:

$$(i) \quad u, v \in T_m\, M \;:\; g(m)\,(u, v) \;=\; g(m)(v, u) \;\in \mathcal{R}\;;$$
$$(ii) \quad g(m)(u, v) = 0 \text{ for all } v \in T_m\, M \;\Rightarrow\; u = 0\;. \qquad (10.62)$$

Over the domain of a chart $(\mathcal{U}, \psi)$ we can express g as

$$g(m) \;=\; g_{\mu\nu}(x)\, dx^{\mu} \otimes dx^{\nu}\;; \qquad (10.63)$$

and then the conditions (10.62) are

$$g_{\mu\nu}\,(x) \;=\; g_{\nu\mu}\,(x)\,,$$
$$\det |\,g_{\mu\nu}\,(x)\,| \;\neq\; 0\,. \qquad (10.64)$$

A manifold M carrying such a metric is a *(pseudo) Riemannian manifold.*

At each point $m \in M$, $g(m)$ is a nondegenerate symmetric bilinear form on $T_m\, M$. Many natural operations carried out algebraically at each point then lead to corresponding operations on fields of tensors. As in Section 4, the nondegeneracy allows us to reinterpret g as a linear invertible map $\tilde{g}(m)$ from $T_m\, M$ to $T_m^*\, M$ at each $m \in M$:

$$\tilde{g}(m) \quad : \quad T_m\, M \;\rightarrow\; T_m^*\, M \;:$$
$$u \in T_m\, M \;\rightarrow\; \tilde{g}(m)(u) \;\in T_m^*\, M \;:$$
$$<\tilde{g}(m)(u),\; v > \;=\; g(m)(u,\; v),\; v \in T_m\, M\;. \;(10.65)$$

We denote the inverse to $\tilde{g}$ by $\tilde{g}^{-1}$; it obeys:

$$\tilde{g}^{-1}(m) \quad : \quad T_m^*\, M \;\rightarrow\; T_m\, M \;:$$
$$\alpha \in T_m^*\, M \;\rightarrow\; \tilde{g}^{-1}(m)(\alpha) \;\in T_m\, M \;:$$
$$<\tilde{g}(m)(u),\; \tilde{g}^{-1}(m)(\alpha) > \;=\; <\alpha,\; u >,\; u \in T_m\, M\;.$$
$$(10.66)$$

Finally, g^{-1} as a tensor field of type $\mathcal{J}^{(2,0)}(M)$, again symmetric and non-degenerate, is set up pointwise as follows:

$$\alpha,\; \beta \in \quad T_m^*\, M \;:$$
$$g^{-1}(m)(\alpha,\; \beta) \;=\; <\alpha,\; \tilde{g}^{-1}(m)(\beta) > \;\in \mathcal{R} \quad (10.67)$$

In a chart, to accompany eq.(10.63), we have

$$g^{-1}(m) \;=\; g^{\mu\nu}(x)\, \partial_{\mu} \otimes \partial_{\nu}\,,$$
$$(g^{\mu\nu}(x)) \;=\; (g_{\mu\nu}(x))^{-1}\,. \qquad (10.68)$$

Moving from operations at single points to fields, we have the pattern of smooth maps:

$$
\begin{aligned}
g \in \mathcal{J}^{(0,2)}(M) &\quad : \quad & \mathcal{X}(M) \times \mathcal{X}(M) &\to \mathcal{F}(M) \,; \\
\tilde{g} \in \mathcal{J}^{(0,2)}(M) &\quad : \quad & \mathcal{X}(M) &\to \mathcal{X}^*(M) \,; \\
\tilde{g}^{-1} \in \mathcal{J}^{(2,0)}(M) &\quad : \quad & \mathcal{X}^*(M) &\to \mathcal{X}(M) \,; \\
g^{-1} \in \mathcal{J}^{(2,0)}(M) &\quad : \quad & \mathcal{X}^*(M) \times \mathcal{X}^*(M) &\to \mathcal{F}(M) \,. \quad (10.69)
\end{aligned}
$$

It is understood here that g and $\tilde{g}$ are "two names for the same thing", and likewise for $\tilde{g}^{-1}$ and g^{-1}.

Usually all the above "formalities" are indicated as rules for raising and lowering of indices, and contracting them. We leave it as an exercise for the reader to express these rules in the language of multilinear forms. One can picture the usual raisings and lowerings - "the only exercises for a theoretical physicist now a days" - as just the formation of the tensor products $g^{-1} \otimes A$ and $g \otimes A$, where A is a general tensor, followed by suitable contractions.

Going back to $g(m)$ at a point, we can always choose a frame $\{e_a\} \in F(T_m M)$ such that $g(m)(e_a, e_b)$ becomes diagonal, and each diagonal element is normalised to ± 1. This "spectrum" or "signature" of $g(m)$, ie., the number of $+1$'s and the remaining number of -1's, is an intrinsic property of $g(m)$. Given the smoothness and nondegeneracy of g, if M is connected the signature of g must be constant over M. Depending on whether g is (positive or negative) definite or indefinite, we say g is a Riemannian or pseudo Riemannian metric, and correspondingly M is a Riemannian or pseudo Riemannian manifold.

10.11.   METRIC COMPATIBLE AFFINE CONNECTION

Now consider imposing an affine connection ∇ on an M already carrying a metric g. If we can ensure that

$$
X \in \mathcal{X}(M) \,:\, \nabla_X \, g = 0 \,, \qquad (10.70)
$$

then we say that the metric and the connection are compatible. The main advantage of such compatibility is that covariant differentiation or parallel transport will then commute with "raising and lowering of indices", i.e., passing from $\mathcal{J}^{(r.s)}(M)$ to $\mathcal{J}^{(r+1,s-1)}(M)$ via $\tilde{g}^{-1}$ or to $\mathcal{J}^{(r-1,s+1)}(M)$ via $\tilde{g}$.

For a given metric, let us see by using a chart what compatibility means for the connection. We have:

$$\nabla g = 0 \iff g_{\mu\nu;\lambda} = 0 \iff$$

$$g_{\mu\nu,\lambda} = \Gamma^\rho{}_{\mu\lambda} g_{\rho\nu} + \Gamma^\rho{}_{\nu\lambda} g_{\mu\rho},$$

$$g_{\nu\lambda,\mu} = \Gamma^\rho{}_{\nu\mu} g_{\rho\lambda} + \Gamma^\rho{}_{\lambda\mu} g_{\nu\rho},$$

$$g_{\lambda\mu,\nu} = \Gamma^\rho{}_{\lambda\nu} g_{\rho\mu} + \Gamma^\rho{}_{\mu\nu} g_{\lambda\rho}. \qquad (10.71)$$

The last three relations are identical in content, being obtained by cyclic permutation of $\lambda\mu\nu$. Adding the first two and then subtracting the third gives:

$$\begin{aligned}
g_{\mu\nu,\lambda} + g_{\nu\lambda,\mu} - g_{\lambda\mu,\nu} &= g_{\lambda\rho} T^\rho{}_{\mu\nu} + g_{\mu\rho} T^\rho{}_{\lambda\nu} + \\
&\quad g_{\nu\rho} (\Gamma^\rho{}_{\mu\lambda} + \Gamma^\rho{}_{\lambda\mu}) \\
&= 2g_{\nu\rho} \Gamma^\rho{}_{\lambda\mu} + g_{\lambda\rho} T^\rho{}_{\mu\nu} + \\
&\quad g_{\mu\rho} T^\rho{}_{\lambda\nu} + g_{\nu\rho} T^\rho{}_{\lambda\mu} \qquad (10.72)
\end{aligned}$$

This can be solved algebraically for the connection coefficients $\Gamma^\rho{}_{\lambda\mu}$ in terms of torsion T and the well-known symmetric Christoffel connection coefficients $\Gamma^{(0)\rho}{}_{\lambda\mu}$ which are completely determined by the metric:

$$\Gamma^{(0)\rho}{}_{\lambda\mu} = \frac{1}{2} g^{\rho\nu} (g_{\mu\nu,\lambda} + g_{\lambda\nu,\mu} - g_{\lambda\mu,\nu}). \qquad (10.73)$$

Namely, Γ is given in terms of $\Gamma^{(0)}$ and T by

$$\begin{aligned}
\Gamma^\rho{}_{\lambda\mu} &= \Gamma^{(0)\rho}{}_{\lambda\mu} - \frac{1}{2} g^{\rho\nu} (g_{\lambda\sigma} T^\sigma{}_{\mu\nu} + g_{\mu\sigma} T^\sigma{}_{\lambda\nu} + g_{\nu\sigma} T^\sigma{}_{\lambda\mu}) \\
&= \Gamma^{(0)\rho}{}_{\lambda\mu} - \frac{1}{2} (T_{\lambda\mu}{}^\rho + T_{\mu\lambda}{}^\rho + T^\rho{}_{\lambda\mu}) \qquad (10.74)
\end{aligned}$$

One must keep careful track of the relative positions of indices on the torsion tensor components! As expected we get for the antisymmetric part of Γ, which is a tensor,

$$\Gamma^\rho{}_{\lambda\mu} - \Gamma^\rho{}_{\mu\lambda} = T^\rho{}_{\mu\lambda}. \qquad (10.75)$$

For the symmetric part, which is *not* a tensor, we find:

$$\Gamma^\rho{}_{\lambda\mu} + \Gamma^\rho{}_{\mu\lambda} = 2\Gamma^{(0)\rho}{}_{\lambda\mu} - T_{\lambda\mu}{}^\rho - T_{\mu\lambda}{}^\rho. \qquad (10.76)$$

In general, then, if an affine connection leaves a metric covariantly constant (is compatible with it), the antisymmetric part of Γ is just the torsion; while the symmetric part is the Christoffel connection plus a tensorial piece from the torsion. If the torsion vanishes we can say: a given metric determines a unique compatible torsion-free affine connection, namely the Christoffel connection.

10.12. NEW INTERPRETATION FOR GEODESICS

The use of a metric-compatible connection on a manifold allows us to give a new meaning to geodesics. Previously we said: if a smooth curve $\gamma : I \subset \mathcal{R} \to M$ is given, a vector $Y(s)$ defined along γ is *covariantly constant* if $\nabla_{X_s} Y$ vanishes along γ. Here X_s is the tangent to γ at the point with parameter s. In local coordinates, covariant constancy of Y along γ is expressed by eq.(10.15). We can see clearly that here *torsion can play a role*. Next when we defined a *geodesic*, we required that $\nabla_{X_s} X_s$ be parallel to X_s, and this led to eq.(10.17). By suitable change of parametrisation, we then saw that this could be reduced to the vanishing of $\nabla_{X_s} X_s$ along γ, as in eq.(10.19). However even though in this geodesic equation only the symmetric part of Γ is involved, this *does not mean* that torsion plays no role in determining geodesics! This is clear from eq.(10.76), which holds if a compatible metric is also specified. Therefore, given a metric and a connection compatible with one another, the previous definition of geodesics *cannot* be related to or obtained from the metric alone *unless we set the torsion equal to zero.*

Let us then do so, in which case the affine connection reduces to the familiar Christoffel connection. *Then* the previous geodesic equations (10.17, 19) become the equations of the Euler-Lagrange variational principle for a suitable functional of the curve γ. Namely, for a given smooth curve γ, we define its length to be

$$
\begin{aligned}
L\left[\gamma\right] &= \int_I ds \, (g(m(s)) \, (X_s, \, X_s))^{\frac{1}{2}} \\
&= \int_I ds \, (\phi(s))^{\frac{1}{2}} , \\
\phi(s) &= g_{\mu\nu} \, (x(s)) \, \dot{x}^{\mu}(s) \, \dot{x}^{\nu}(s) .
\end{aligned}
\tag{10.77}
$$

We assume for simplicity that $\phi(s)$ does not vanish along γ. Then the requirement that $L\left[\gamma\right]$ be stationary against small changes in γ leads to the Euler-Lagrange equations

$$
\begin{aligned}
\frac{d^2 x^{\mu}(s)}{ds^2} &+ \Gamma^{(0)\mu}{}_{\rho\sigma} \, (x(s)) \, \frac{dx^{\rho}(s)}{ds} \, \frac{dx^{\sigma}(s)}{ds} \\
&= -\frac{dx^{\mu}(s)}{ds} \, \phi(s)^{\frac{1}{2}} \, \frac{d}{ds} \, \phi(s)^{-\frac{1}{2}}
\end{aligned}
\tag{10.78}
$$

This is of just the same form as the previous general geodesic equation (10.17), where no conditions are imposed on the choice of the parameter s. Choosing it so that $\phi(s)$ becomes a constant along γ thus corresponds to the previous passage to eq.(10.19). With a metric and its preferred Christoffel connection, "as straight as possible" is the same thing as "as short, or as long, as possible"!

We summarise by repeating: even if a metric and an affine connection are mutually compatible, in general they lead to distinct concepts of geodesics: the former gives curves of stationary length, the latter gives curves as straight as possible, and the two are not the same. Only when torsion vanishes do the two coincide.

11. Congruences, submanifolds, foliations, Frobenius' Theorem; closed and exact forms; Poincare's lemma

In the two preceding Sections we have studied three distinct kinds of differentiation processes on a differentiable manifold. Whereas Lie differentiation and exterior differentiation require no additional input, covariant differentiation does - an affine connection. Now for a while we revert to things that can be done intrinsically on a differentiable manifold, not assuming any additional structure. We will look at some aspects of (systems of) vector fields, and then of forms. Our account will be heuristic and qualitative. By and large what we say will have a local flavour, ie., be restricted to suitable open sets in the manifold.

11.1. INTEGRAL CURVES, CONGRUENCES OF A VECTOR FIELD

Let us begin with a single vector field $X \in \mathcal{X}(M)$. We work in some open set $\mathcal{U} \subset M$, the domain of a chart $(\mathcal{U}, \psi)$. An integral curve γ for X has been defined in eqs. (10.12,13), and we recapitulate:

$$\gamma : I = (a, b) \subset \mathcal{R} \to M :$$
$$s \in I \to m(s) \in \mathcal{U} \subset M;$$
$$\gamma_* \left(\frac{d}{ds} \right) \equiv X_s = X(m(s)) \in T_{m(s)}M;$$
$$\text{ie.,} \frac{dx^\mu(s)}{ds} = X^\mu(x(s)) \tag{11.1}$$

Given the smooth vector field X, and an initial point $m(0)$, from the theory of solutions to ordinary differential equations we know that a definite and unique integral curve γ (for some range of parameter s around zero) is determined. (So here we are assuming $0 \in (a, b)$, ie., $a < 0$ and $b > 0$ in eq.(11.1)). Of course if $X(m_0)$ vanishes at some point $m_0 \in M$, and we take $m(0) = m_0$ as the "starting point", we have a degenerate situation - no curve at all, just a single point. Leaving this aside, we see that two distinct integral curves can never cross or even be tangent to one another at a common point - the former conflicts with $X(m)$ having a definite "value" at each m, the latter with the curve being unique for given $m(0)$!

A *congruence* is a family of integral curves of a given $X \in \mathcal{X}(M)$, filling a given open region $\mathcal{U} \subset M$. In such a family there is a unique integral curve γ passing, at parameter value $s = 0$, through each point $m \in \mathcal{U} \subset M$. We introduce now the useful and expressive *exponential notation*. Let γ be the integral curve passing through m at $s = 0$, and let it reach $m(s)$ at "time" s. Then we formally write:

$$m(s) = e^{sX} m. \tag{11.2}$$

This is well-defined for s in some open interval (a, b) around zero.

We have seen in Section 9, eq.(9.9), that if we have in hand a one-parameter group of diffeomorphisms $\{\varphi_s\}$ on M, it defines a unique $X \in \mathcal{X}(M)$. Conversely at least locally we can say that if an $X \in \mathcal{X}(M)$ is given, by solving eqs.(11.1) and building up a congruence over an open region $\mathcal{U}$, we have a family of "local" diffeomorphisms $\{\varphi_s\}$ identified by eq.(11.2):

$$\varphi_s(m) = e^{sX} m \tag{11.3}$$

11.2. LIE DRAGGING OF TENSOR FIELDS

Let us now use the above notions to see how a tensor field A behaves along the integral curves of a given vector field $X \in \mathcal{X}(M)$. We say that $A \in \mathcal{J}^{(r,s)}(M)$ is "constant along these integral curves" if, in terms of φ_s defined by eq.(11.3), we have:

$$\begin{aligned} \varphi_s^* A &= A, \\ \text{ie., } L_X A &= 0. \end{aligned} \tag{11.4}$$

This means that the "value" of A at a point $m(s)$ on an integral curve of X is related to its "value" at the starting point m in a definite way. Rewriting the previous eq.(9.5) is the present context, we have:

$$A \text{ is constant with respect to} X \iff$$

$$\begin{aligned} L_X A &= 0 \iff \\ \varphi_s^* A &= A \iff \\ (\varphi_s^* A)(m) &= A(m) \iff \\ A(m)(\ldots \alpha \ldots ; \ldots u \ldots) &= A(m(s))(\ldots \varphi_{-s}^* \alpha \ldots ; \ldots (\varphi_s)_*(u) \ldots), \\ \alpha \in T_m^* M \quad &, \quad u \in T_m M, \\ \varphi_{-s}^* \alpha \in T_{m(s)}^* M, \quad &(\varphi_s)_*(u) \in T_{m(s)} M. \end{aligned} \tag{11.5}$$

We must appreciate that if A is constant with respect to X, then on each integral curve of X, *as a multilinear functional $A(m)$ determines $A(m(s))$ algebraically.* It is only to be able to compute the pullbacks $\varphi^*_{-s}\alpha$ and the tangent maps $(\varphi_s)_*(u)$ acting on the arguments of $A(m)$ that we need to know, or have available, a "few nearby integral curves", ie., we need to know how φ_s acts near and around a given integral curve.

We can convey all this in more graphic and explicit form thus: Since $X^\mu(x(s))$ in eq.(11.1) has no "explicit" time dependence, on a given integral curve γ we have

$$m(s_2) = \varphi_{s_2-s_1}(m(s_1)) = e^{(s_2-s_1)X}m(s_1). \qquad (11.6)$$

Let us concentrate on two general points on γ, and for simplicity write

$$\varphi_{s_2-s_1} \equiv \varphi;$$
$$m(s_2) = m_2, m(s_1) = m_1;$$
$$m_2 = \varphi(m_1), m_1 = \varphi^{-1}(m_2). \qquad (11.7)$$

Then, if a tensor field A is constant along γ, *i.e.*, constant with respect to X, $A(m_1)$ and $A(m_2)$ determine one another. We need to use the associated maps $\varphi^*, \varphi_*, (\varphi^{-1})^*, (\varphi^{-1})_*$, for which purpose we need to draw a few neighbouring integral curves taken from a congruence. Then we have this picture indicated in Figure 4. The accompanying equations are these:

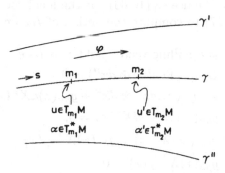

Figure 4. Illustrating Lie-dragging of a tensor field

$$\varphi_*(T_{m_1}M) = T_{m_2}M,$$
$$(\varphi^{-1})_*(T_{m_2}M) = T_{m_1}M;$$
$$\varphi^*(T^*_{m_2}M) = T^*_{m_1}M,$$
$$(\varphi^{-1})^*(T^*_{m_1}M) = T^*_{m_2}M;$$

$$A(m_2)(\ldots\alpha'\ldots;\ldots u'\ldots) = A(m_1)(\ldots\varphi^*\alpha'\ldots;\ldots(\varphi^{-1})_*(u')\ldots),$$
$$A(m_1)(\ldots\alpha\ldots;\ldots u\ldots) = A(m_2)(\ldots(\varphi^{-1})^*\alpha\ldots;\ldots\varphi_*(u)\ldots).$$

$$(11.8)$$

By this construction, then, if $A(m_1)$ were known only at one point $m_1 \in \gamma$, we can determine $A(m_2)$ at all other $m_2 \in \gamma$ using the requirement that A *be constant with respect to* X. Moreover we could do this all over a congruence! If we know A at *one* point on *each* γ in the congruence, ie., over all points of a "transverse cross section" of the congruence, we can determine A all over the region $\mathcal{U}$ filled by the congruence. This process is called *Lie dragging* of a tensor field.

From now on, as we will often have to deal with several vector fields $X, Y, \ldots$ simultaneously, we shall introduce this terminology: an integral curve γ with respect to $X \in \mathcal{X}(M)$ will be called *an X - line*; similarly Y-lines and so on.

11.3. KILLING VECTOR FIELDS WITH RESPECT TO A METRIC

A particular and important instance of the above situation, namely constancy of a tensor field with respect to a vector field, arises when we have a (pseudo) Riemannian manifold. Let a symmetric nondegenerate tensor field $g \in \mathcal{J}^{(0,2)}(M)$ be given on a manifold M. If g is constant with respect to some $X \in \mathcal{X}(M)$, then X is called a *Killing vector field* (of course for g). The Killing condition on X can be obtained in local coordinates in differential form quite easily. We use eq.(10.63) for the local coordinate expression of g, and then eq.(9.17) to compute the action of L_X on g:

$$
\begin{aligned}
X \quad &\text{is a Killing vector field} \Longleftrightarrow L_X g = 0 \\
&\Longleftrightarrow L_X(g_{\mu\nu}(x)dx^\mu \otimes dx^\nu) = 0 \\
&\Longleftrightarrow X(g_{\mu\nu}(x))dx^\mu \otimes dx^\nu + g_{\mu\nu}(x)dX^\mu(x) \otimes dx^\nu \\
&+ \quad g_{\mu\nu}(x)dx^\mu \otimes dX^\nu(x) = 0, \\
\text{ie.,} \quad &g_{\mu\nu,\lambda}(x)X^\lambda(x) + g_{\lambda\nu}(x)X^\lambda{}_{,\mu}(x) \\
&+ \quad g_{\mu\lambda}(x)X^\lambda{}_{,\nu}(x) = 0
\end{aligned}
$$

$$(11.9)$$

Now the metric g determines its associated unique symmetric Christoffel connection $\Gamma^{(0)\lambda}{}_{\mu\nu}(x)$ by eq.(10.73). Using this for covariant differentiation, and adopting the "semicolon notation" of eq.(10.45c), we can write the partial derivatives of $X^\lambda(x)$ as

$$
\begin{aligned}
X^\lambda{}_{,\mu}(x) &= X^\lambda{}_{;\mu}(x) - \Gamma^{(0)\lambda}{}_{\nu\mu}(x)X^\nu(x), \\
X^\lambda{}_{,\nu}(x) &= X^\lambda{}_{;\nu}(x) - \Gamma^{(0)\lambda}{}_{\mu\nu}(x)X^\mu(x).
\end{aligned}
$$

$$(11.10)$$

If we substitute these expressions in eq.(11.9), we see that on account of eq.(10.73) the terms algebraic in X cancel. Since g is compatible with its $\Gamma^{(0)}$, the Killing condition becomes:

$$X \text{ is a Killing vector field for metric } g \iff$$
$$L_X \, g = 0 \iff$$
$$X_{\mu;\nu}(x) + X_{\nu;\mu}(x) \quad = \quad 0 \qquad (11.11)$$

This differential statement upon integration leads to "constancy of g along each X-line" in the sense of eq.(11.8).

11.4. SUBMANIFOLDS

At this point, let us digress a little to define the notion of a *submanifold* in a given differentiable manifold. There are two subtly different notions here: the wider one of a submanifold in general, and the narrower one of a *regular submanifold* which is in a way nicer to handle.

Let $N \subset M$ be an open subset of M. Then it is called a submanifold of M with dimension equal to the dimension of M. This is a rather trivial case.

The wider definition of a submanifold is this. Let K be a differentiable manifold of some dimension $n_1 \le n =$ dimension of M. Let $\varphi : K \to M$ be a smooth map such that

$$(i) \quad \varphi \text{ is a regular map, ie., } \mathrm{rank}(\varphi_*)_k = n_1 \text{ at each } k \in K;$$
$$(ii) \quad \varphi \text{ is injective, ie., } \varphi(k_1) = \varphi(k_2) \Rightarrow k_1 = k_2. \qquad (11.12)$$

In that case, both the topology of K (notion of open sets in K) and the differentiable structure on K (a maximal atlas) can be "bodily transferred" to the image $\varphi(K) \subset M$; in fact then φ is a diffeomorphism $K \to \varphi(K)$. We then say that $\varphi(K)$ is a n_1-*dimensional submanifold of M*. Conversely if N is a subset of M, it is a submanifold of dimension $n_1 (\le n)$ if and only if it is the image of a smooth regular injective map φ of some n_1-dimensional differentiable manifold K into M. In a sense, given $N \subset M$, the burden is on us to find K and φ before we can decide whether N is a submanifold! The regularity of φ makes N "sit nicely" within M, and the injective nature of φ allows us to transfer the topology, charts and atlases on K on to N.

We can see in this sense that for a given vector field $X \in \mathcal{X}(M)$, as long as we stay away from points where X vanishes, each X-line is a one-dimensional submanifold in M.

11.5. REGULAR SUBMANIFOLDS

Now in the sense of the definition just given, let N be a n_1 -dimensional submanifold in M. Being a subset of M, it *inherits* a topology from the topology of M. At the same time, from the manifold K appearing in the definition of a submanifold, it gets what we may call an *induced* topology by mere transfer from K via φ. These two topologies on N may or may not be equivalent!

We say N is a *regular submanifold* in M if these two topologies, the one inherited from M and the other induced from K via φ, are equivalent. It turns out that in that case, N can be described in an "easier" way, so let us spell it out. This is the method of *local locking of coordinates*, or equally well of *local constraints*.

A subset $N \subset M$ is a n_1-dimensional regular submanifold in M if for each point $q \in N$ we can find an open set $\mathcal{U} \subset M$, containing q, and a chart $(\mathcal{U}, \psi)$ from the *maximal* atlas $\mathcal{A}_{max}$ of M, such that the *portion* of N contained in $\mathcal{U}$ just corresponds to locking each of the last $(n - n_1)$ coordinates to the value zero:

$$
\begin{aligned}
q \in N \quad &\to \quad q \in \mathcal{U} \subset M, (\mathcal{U}, \psi) \in \mathcal{A}_{max} : \\
N \cap \mathcal{U} \quad &= \quad \psi^{-1}\{(x^1, x^2, \ldots, x^{n_1}, 0, \ldots, 0) \in \psi(\mathcal{U}) \subset \mathcal{R}^n\} \quad (11.13)
\end{aligned}
$$

If we wish to avoid using charts in this way, we do it via a *smooth independent local family of constraints*. Then, $N \subset M$ is a regular submanifold of dimension $n_1 \leq n$ if, for each $q \in N$, we can find an open set $\mathcal{U}$ containing q, and $(n - n_1)$ smooth and algebraically independent functions $f_1, f_2, \ldots, f_{n-n_1}$ over $\mathcal{U}$, such that $N \cap \mathcal{U}$ is just that part of $\mathcal{U}$ where all the f's vanish:

$$
\begin{aligned}
q \in N \quad &\to \quad q \in \mathcal{U} \subset M; f_1, f_2, \ldots, f_{n-n_1} \in \mathcal{F}(\mathcal{U}); \\
&\quad df_1 \wedge df_2 \wedge \ldots \wedge df_{n-n_1} \neq 0 \text{ over } \mathcal{U}; \\
N \cap \mathcal{U} \quad &= \quad \{m \in \mathcal{U} | f_1(m) = f_2(m) = \ldots = f_{n-n_1}(m) = 0\}
\end{aligned}
$$

$$(11.14)$$

Notice that the algebraic independence of a system of functions, usually stated in terms of the rank of a jacobian matrix, has a neat and intrinsic geometric expression! Notice also that the earlier "locking" definition is actually a particular case of the second "constraint" version: just take the functions $f_1, f_2, \ldots, f_{n-n_1}$ to be the coordinates $x^{n_1+1}, x^{n_1+2}, \ldots, x^n$ respectively.

We have not actually proved above that the first definition of a regular submanifold is the same as the second and third, more convenient, ones. But it is good to know that they are the same. By way of further motivation for refining the notion of a submanifold to that of a regular submanifold, we can refer to the case of one-dimensional submanifolds: then what the regularity does is that we avoid self-crossings!

11.6. EXAMPLES OF REGULAR SUBMANIFOLDS

The method of defining a regular submanifold via local independent constraints can be used to show the following. Let $\varphi : M \to N'$ be a *submersion* (see Section 8):φ is a smooth map; dim$.M = n >$ dim$.N' = n_2$ say; and at each $m \in M, (\varphi_*)_m$ has maximal rank n_2. We expect that for any fixed image point $n' \in \varphi(M) \subset N'$, we have many source points in M. In fact, for each fixed $n' \in \varphi(M) \subset N'$, it turns out that $\varphi^{-1}(n')$ is a $(n - n_2)$-dimensional regular submanifold of M!

We can see this using charts in N' and in M. Keep $n' \in \varphi(M)$ fixed, and let m_0 be some point in the inverse image $\varphi^{-1}(n') \subset M$. Continuity of φ assures us that if $\mathcal{V}'$ is any open set in N' containing n', then $\varphi^{-1}(\mathcal{V}') = \mathcal{U}_0$ is open in M. Choose $\mathcal{V}'$ to be the domain of a chart $(\mathcal{V}', \psi')$ around n', and write y^α for the local coordinates. With no loss of generality we can take a $\mathcal{U}$ to be the domain of a chart $(\mathcal{U}, \psi)$ around m_0, such that $\varphi(\mathcal{U}) \subset \mathcal{V}'$: this may involve restricting ourselves to intersections of open sets around m_0, with $\mathcal{U}_0$. Over $\mathcal{U}$ we use local coordinates x^μ. So all in all we have:

$$n' \in \varphi(M), \text{ kept fixed}; (\mathcal{V}', \psi') = \text{chart around } n';$$
$$m_0 \in \varphi^{-1}(n'), \text{ kept fixed}; (\mathcal{U}, \psi) = \text{chart around } m_0 \text{ with } \varphi(\mathcal{U}) \subset \mathcal{V}';$$
$$m \in \mathcal{U}, \text{coordinates } x^\mu \xrightarrow{\varphi} \varphi(m) \in \mathcal{V}', \text{coordinates } y^\alpha = \varphi^\alpha(x^\mu)$$
$$(11.15)$$

All this is depicted in Figure 5.

Now these functions $\varphi^\alpha(x^\mu)$ defined over $\mathcal{U}$ are smooth, and the regularity of φ means that they are algebraically independent:

$$d\varphi^1 \wedge d\varphi^2 \wedge \ldots \wedge d\varphi^{n_2} \neq 0 \text{ over } \mathcal{U} \qquad (11.16)$$

On the other hand, $\mathcal{U} \cap \varphi^{-1}(n')$ consists of just those points in $\mathcal{U}$ for which each φ^α has a fixed value, namely the αth coordinate of n' in the chart $(\mathcal{V}', \psi')$:

$$\psi'(n') = \{y_0^\alpha\} :$$
$$\varphi^{-1}(n') \cap \mathcal{U} = \{m \in \mathcal{U} | \varphi^\alpha(x) - y_0^\alpha = 0, \alpha = 1, 2, \ldots, n_2\} \quad (11.17)$$

Comparing the above two equations with eqs.(11.14), and realising that all this can be done around each $m_0 \in \varphi^{-1}(n')$, we see that $\varphi^{-1}(n')$ for

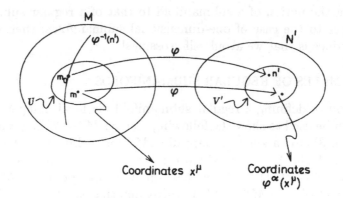

Figure 5.   Submersion leading to regular submanifolds

each fixed $n' \in \varphi(M) \subset N'$ is a regular submanifold in M, with dimension $n - n_2$.

11.7. INTEGRAL CURVES AND COMMUTATORS OF VECTOR FIELDS

Now that we have understood the meaning of a submanifold in a differentiable manifold, let us begin our study of some interesting properties of systems of vector fields.

We take two independent vector fields $X, Y \in \mathcal{X}(M)$ and first develop a simple geometrical meaning for their commutator. We freely use local coordinates. Start at a point $m = \{x^\mu\}$ and travel for a "short time ε" along the X-line through m, arriving at $m' = \{x'^\mu\}$. Then travel for a short time ε' along the Y-line through m', to reach $m'' = \{x''^\mu\}$. Now you can do this also in the opposite sequence:

$$m \xrightarrow{Y} m''' \xrightarrow{X} m'''' \tag{11.18}$$

from m to m''' along the Y-line for a spell ε', then m''' to m'''' along the X-line for a spell ε. Retaining terms only up to first order in ε and ε', the coordinates of the various points are:

$$
\begin{aligned}
m' &= e^{\varepsilon X} m : x'^\mu = x^\mu + \varepsilon X^\mu(x); \\
m'' &= e^{\varepsilon' Y} m' = e^{\varepsilon' Y} e^{\varepsilon X} m : \\
&\qquad x''^\mu = x'^\mu + \varepsilon' Y^\mu(x + \varepsilon X(x)); \\
m''' &= e^{\varepsilon' Y} m : x'''^\mu = x^\mu + \varepsilon' Y^\mu(x); \\
m'''' &= e^{\varepsilon X} m''' = e^{\varepsilon X} e^{\varepsilon' Y} m : \\
&\qquad x''''^\mu = x'''^\mu + \varepsilon X^\mu(x + \varepsilon' Y(x)) \cdot
\end{aligned}
\tag{11.19}
$$

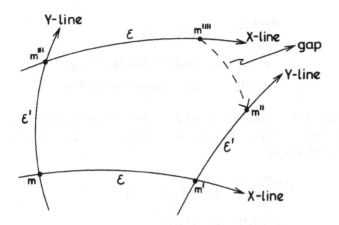

Figure 6. The commutator of two vector fields

In general, we do not find $m'''' = m''$: the "quadrilateral" need not close! If we calculate the differences in the coordinates of the two alternative end points we find:

$$
\begin{aligned}
x''''^{\mu} - x''^{\mu} &= \varepsilon\varepsilon'(Y^{\nu}(x)X_{,\nu}^{\mu}(x) - X^{\nu}(x)Y_{,\nu}^{\mu}(x)) \\
&= -\varepsilon\varepsilon'[X,Y]^{\mu}(x), \\
(e^{\varepsilon'Y}e^{\varepsilon X}m)^{\mu} - (e^{\varepsilon X}e^{\varepsilon'Y}m)^{\mu} &\simeq \varepsilon'\varepsilon[X,Y]^{\mu}(x).
\end{aligned}
\tag{11.20}
$$

This then is the geometrical meaning of the commutator - it tells us the extent to which two alternative sequences of short travel along X and Y lines starting from a given point lead to different end points. Of course, these X and Y lines are separately members of congruences. We see that *in general these congruences are not surface - forming.*

If however the two vector fields X and Y *commute*, we *do* have a closing of the figure in Figure 6, and the two points m'' and m'''' obtained in alternative pathways *do* coincide! In that case, by a process of integration we can pass from an *infinitesimal* to a *finite*, though still *local*, construction. It is worthwhile to see the argument. Let us start with some $m_0 \in \mathcal{U} \subset M$, and write:

$$
m(\alpha,\beta) = e^{\beta Y}e^{\alpha X}m_0
\tag{11.21}
$$

The meaning is: first build up the X-line through m_0, ie., solve the differential equations

$$\frac{dx^{\mu}(\alpha)}{d\alpha} \;=\; X^{\mu}(x(\alpha)),$$

$$x^{\mu}(\alpha) \;=\; \text{coordinates of } e^{\alpha X} m_0;$$

$$x^{\mu}(0) \;=\; x_0^{\mu} = \text{coordinates of } m_0. \tag{11.22}$$

Having done this, choose some α and keep it fixed. Then construct the Y-line through $e^{\alpha X} m_0$. This involves solving, at fixed α, the system of differential equations

$$\frac{\partial x^{\mu}(\alpha,\beta)}{\partial \beta} \;=\; Y^{\mu}(x(\alpha,\beta)),$$

$$x^{\mu}(\alpha,0) \;=\; x^{\mu}(\alpha),$$

$$x^{\mu}(\alpha,\beta) \;=\; \text{coordinates of } e^{\beta Y} e^{\alpha X} m_0 \tag{11.23}$$

We now show: if $[X,Y] = 0$, then we get the *same point* $m(\alpha,\beta)$ if we travel first along a Y-line from m_0 upto a "time" β, then switch to an X-line for a "time" α! In other words, we will show that, having constructed $m(\alpha,\beta)$ with coordinates $x^{\mu}(\alpha,\beta)$ in the specific sequence given in eqs.(11.22,23), if we now keep β fixed in $m(\alpha,\beta)$ and vary α, we get an X-line! We show this relying on the (local) uniqueness of solutions to systems of ordinary differential equations with given initial conditions.

Take $x^{\mu}(\alpha,\beta)$ obtained above, and consider its derivative with respect to α. From eq.(11.23) and the assumption $[X,Y] = 0$ we find:

$$\frac{\partial}{\partial \beta}\frac{\partial x^{\mu}(\alpha,\beta)}{\partial \alpha} = \frac{\partial}{\partial \alpha} Y^{\mu}(x(\alpha,\beta))$$

$$= Y^{\mu}{}_{,\nu}(x(\alpha,\beta))\frac{\partial x^{\nu}(\alpha,\beta)}{\partial \alpha} \quad ,$$

$$\frac{\partial x^{\mu}(\alpha,\beta)}{\partial \alpha}\Big|_{\beta=0} = \frac{\partial x^{\mu}(\alpha)}{\partial \alpha}$$

$$= X^{\mu}(x(\alpha,0)); \tag{11.24a}$$

$$\frac{\partial}{\partial \beta} X^{\mu}(x(\alpha,\beta)) = X^{\mu}{}_{,\nu}(x(\alpha,\beta))\frac{\partial x^{\nu}(\alpha,\beta)}{\partial \beta}$$

$$= Y^{\nu}(x(\alpha,\beta))X^{\mu}{}_{,\nu}(x(\alpha,\beta))$$

$$= Y^{\mu}{}_{,\nu}(x(\alpha,\beta))X^{\nu}(x(\alpha,\beta)),$$

$$X^{\mu}(x(\alpha,\beta))\big|_{\beta=0} = X^{\mu}(x(\alpha,0)). \tag{11.24b}$$

On comparing (a) and (b) above we see that *with respect to β* both $\frac{\partial x^\mu(\alpha,\beta)}{\partial \alpha}$ and $X^\mu(x(\alpha,\beta))$ obey the same first order ordinary differential equations and boundary conditions (the variable α remaining a "silent spectator"), so *they must be equal*:

$$\frac{\partial x^\mu(\alpha,\beta)}{\partial \alpha} = X^\mu(x(\alpha,\beta)),$$

ie.,for fixed β,

$$m(\alpha,\beta) \equiv \{x^\mu(\alpha,\beta)\} \text{ is an } X - \text{line},$$

$$\text{ie.,} m(\alpha,\beta) \equiv e^{\beta Y} e^{\alpha X} m_0$$

$$= e^{\alpha X} m(0,\beta)$$

$$= e^{\alpha X} e^{\beta Y} m_0. \tag{11.25}$$

The above construction can be easily extended to more than two vector fields. Thus suppose we have $k(\leq n)$ independent commuting vector fields $X_1, X_2, \ldots, X_k \in \mathcal{X}(M)$. Starting at some point $m_0 \in M$, we can travel in any sequence along the integral curves of the k separate congruences. We can thus "reach out" to a (small) region of dimension k around m_0 in M:

$$m(\xi^1, \xi^2, \ldots, \xi^k) = e^{\xi^k X_k} e^{\xi^{k-1} X_{k-1}} \ldots e^{\xi^1 X_1} m_0,$$

$$= \left\{ x^\mu(\xi^1, \xi^2, \ldots, \xi^k) \right\},$$

$$\frac{\partial x^\mu(\xi)}{\partial \xi^r} = X^\mu_r(x(\xi)), r = 1, 2, \ldots, k \tag{11.26}$$

If at any point in this region we keep all the ξ's *except* ξ^r fixed, and vary only ξ^r, we get an X_r-line! And it is an easy matter to verify that, with the precise meaning we have given to the exponential of a vector field, we have

$$m(\xi^1, \xi^2, \ldots, \xi^k) = exp.(\xi^1 X_1 + \xi^2 X_2 + .. + \xi^k X_k).m_0. \tag{11.27}$$

11.8. FOLIATIONS

Now this leads to a beautiful generalisation of the idea of a congruence - a family of X-lines determined by a single vector field X and filling a region $\mathcal{U} \subset M$, one through each point in $\mathcal{U}$- to a *foliation*. In the construction just described using several commuting vector fields, for $\boldsymbol{\xi}$ varying in a suitably chosen small neighbourhood of the origin in $\mathcal{R}^k$, we get a k-dimensional submanifold in M built up from the initial point m_0. (This submanifold is the generalisation of the unique X-line through m_0, in the case of a single vector field). Call it $S^{(k)}(m_0; \{X_r\})$:

$$S^{(k)}(m_0; \{X_r\}) = \left\{ \exp(\xi^1 X_1 + \ldots + \xi^k X_k) m_0 \mid (\xi^1, \ldots \xi^k) \in \vartheta \subset \mathcal{R}^k \right\} \tag{11.28}$$

where ϑ is a suitable neighbourhood of the origin in $\mathcal{R}^k$. We can repeat this construction for other points in $\mathcal{U}$ not contained in $S^{(k)}(m_0; \{X_r\})$. And so we build up a family of k-dimensional submanifolds, a unique one $S^{(k)}(m; \{X_r\})$ passing through each $m \in \mathcal{U}$, and which together fill out $\mathcal{U}$. This family is itself evidently an $(n-k)$ parameter family. This is called a *foliation* of $\mathcal{U}$, and each $S^{(k)}(m; \{X_r\})$ is a *leaf* of the foliation. Note that, within the limits of applicability of the results on solutions to systems of ordinary differential equations, each $m \in \mathcal{U}$ determines a unique leaf $S^{(k)}(m; \{X_r\})$ on which it lies; so two such distinct leaves cannot have any points in common - no crossing or touching!

11.9. FROBENIUS' THEOREM

We arrived at the idea of a foliation by assuming we had *mutually commuting* vector fields $X_1, X_2, \ldots, X_k$. But this is unnecessarily strong! Suppose we have some k independent vector fields $X_1, \ldots, X_k$, not necessarily commuting with one another. Over some open region $\mathcal{U} \subset M$, we build up k congruences. Starting from any point $m_0 \in \mathcal{U}$, we have the freedom to travel along various integral curves in various sequences. The question is - when do these different congruences "mesh together" to form a foliation, so that starting out from m_0 we always stay on one definite k -dimensional submanifold determined by m_0?

The answer is contained in the celebrated *Theorem of Frobenius*. We describe heuristically the content of the theorem, and then sketch a simple-minded proof of it. The congruences of a set of k independent vector fields $X_r, r = 1, 2, \ldots, k$, are *surface- forming* and lead to a family of non-intersecting, non-touching k- dimensional submanifolds giving a foliation of $\mathcal{U}$, if and only if the vector fields are *closed under commutation* in the sense:

$$X_r \in \mathcal{X}(M) : \quad [X_r, X_s] = f_{rst} X_t,$$
$$f_{rst} \in \mathcal{F}(M) \tag{11.29}$$

Note that we allow *functions*, not merely *constants*, to appear as coefficients on the righthand side.

Qualitatively speaking we can say: linear independence of the vector fields means that at each $m \in \mathcal{U}$, the X_1-line, the X_2-line,..., the X_k-line start off in k different directions. So at each m, they determine a k-dimensional linear subspace of the complete n-dimensional tangent space $T_m M$ there. Now if and only if condition (11.29) is satisfied, these "small spaces" or "pieces of surfaces" at each m will combine together nicely to form one smooth surface of dimension k through each m. This is the meaning of "meshing together".

One can appreciate what is happening by going back to the geometrical picture (Figure 6) of the commutator : if condition (11.29) is obeyed, then the "gap" between the points m'' and m'''' in that figure *can be closed* by another integral curve belonging to one of the X's in the collection $\{X_r\}$, or a linear combination thereof! It is this that helps weld together small pieces of a submanifold into a true submanifold.

Now we sketch the proof of the theorem, which is based on induction. The idea is to show that if we are given a certain number of independent vector fields closed under commutation, we can always replace them by independent linear combinations which commute pairwise. Once this is achieved, the previous construction of the submanifolds $S^{(k)}(m; \{X_r\})$ as in eq.(11.28) shows that we do have a foliation. We will assume that the transition - closed under commutation $\rightarrow$ commuting - can be made for $k-1$ independent vector fields; then we shall prove it for k independent vector fields.

Given the k independent vector fields $X_1, \ldots, X_k$ satisfying eq.(11.29), let us first build the congruence of X_k-lines over the open region $\mathcal{U} \subset M$. On each X_k-line we have a parameter τ chosen in the manner of eq.(11.2) and measured from some point on that line as origin. Thus, as the congruence fills $\mathcal{U}$, we can regard τ as a function over $\mathcal{U}$. Therefore $d\tau$ is a well-defined one-form over $\mathcal{U}$, and with respect to X_k we have

$$i_{X_k} d\tau = X_k(\tau) = 1 \qquad (11.30)$$

(Notice by the way that while $d\tau$ is well-defined, there is no meaning to $\partial/\partial\tau$. This would involve making τ one of the coordinates in a chart over $\mathcal{U}$, ie., supplementing τ with $(n-1)$ other independent functions over $\mathcal{U}$ all of which together give a chart. This we do not do, so we certainly cannot write $X_k = \partial/\partial\tau$).

Now we use the freedom to replace the X_r by independent linear combinations of themselves to do the following: from each of $X_1 \ldots, X_{k-1}$ we subtract a multiple of X_k and define

$$
\begin{aligned}
X_r' &= X_r - i_{X_r} d\tau \cdot X_k \\
&= X_r - X_r(\tau) \cdot X_k \quad , r = 1, \ldots, k-1 \cdot
\end{aligned}
\qquad (11.31)
$$

Each of these has the property of annihilating τ: by eq.(11.30),

$$i_{X_r'} d\tau = X_r'(\tau) = 0, \quad r = 1, \ldots, k-1 \cdot \qquad (11.32)$$

This then means that in each of the commutators $[X_r', X_s'], 1 \le r, s \le k-1$, which in any case is a linear combination of $X_1', \ldots, X_{k-1}', X_k$, there is no piece involving X_k because from eq.(11.32) follows

$$[X_r', X_s'](\tau) = 0, \quad r, s = 1, \ldots, k-1 \qquad (11.33)$$

So we have the closure relations

$$[X'_r, X'_s] = f'_{rst} X'_t \quad , r, s = 1, \ldots, k-1, \tag{11.34}$$

the sum on t being over the range $1, \ldots, k-1$. Now by the inductive hypothesis, these $(k-1)$ independent vector fields can be replaced by independent commuting combinations of themselves. After doing so, and to save on symbols, let us write the resulting vector fields as $X_1, \ldots, X_{k-1}$:

$$[X_r, X_s] = 0, \quad r, s = 1 \ldots, k-1 \tag{11.35}$$

. The question now is: what can be said about the commutators $[X_r, X_k]$ for $r = 1, \ldots, k-1$? Since $X_r(\tau) = 0$ while $X_k(\tau) = 1$, it is easy to see that each of these commutators has no X_k piece in it, so let us write

$$[X_r, X_k] = f_{rs} X_s, \quad r = 1, \ldots, k-1, \tag{11.36}$$

the sum on s being over the range $1, \ldots, k-1$. We now exploit eq.(11.35) and the Jacobi identity to find:

$$\begin{aligned}
[X_t, [X_r, X_k]] &= [X_r, [X_t, X_k]], \\
\text{ie.,} \ X_t(f_{rs}) &= X_r(f_{ts}), \quad r, s, t = 1, \ldots, k-1 \cdot
\end{aligned} \tag{11.37}$$

These relations can be examined on each leaf $S^{(k-1)}(m; X_1, \ldots, X_{k-1})$ of the foliation of $\mathcal{U}$ generated by the independent commuting vector fields $X_1, \ldots, X_{k-1}$. It is easy to see that, in an obvious notation, they imply, for each fixed s, that

$$\frac{\partial}{\partial \xi^t} f_{rs}(\xi \ldots) = \frac{\partial}{\partial \xi^r} f_{ts}(\xi \ldots) \tag{11.38}$$

Here the ξ's are independent parameters over a leaf introduced as in eq.(11.28). We thus see that the various functions f_{rs} arise from a smaller set f_s by action with X_r:

$$f_{rs} = X_r(f_s), \tag{11.39}$$

and the commutators $[X_r, X_k]$ become

$$[X_r, X_k] = X_r(f_s) X_s \tag{11.40}$$

At this point we shift X_k to X'_k suitably:

$$X'_k = X_k - f_s X_s \cdot \tag{11.41}$$

This commutes with each X_r:

$$[X_r, X_k'] = [X_r, X_k] - X_r(f_s)X_s$$
$$= 0 \qquad (11.42)$$

We have thus proved that k independent vector fields closed under commutation can be linearly transformed to k commuting independent ones, given by assumption that this could be done for $(k-1)$ fields. Now for $k = 2$ the original hypothesis definitely works: a single vector field commutes with itself. So we are done.

We can also relate the present discussion to the possibility of describing a (regular) submanifold by a system of local constraints. Evidently we are concerned here with finding a maximal independent set of functions $\{f_\alpha\}$ over $\mathcal{U}$ obeying

$$X_r\, f_\alpha = 0, r = 1, 2, \ldots, k,$$
$$\alpha = k+1, \ldots, n \qquad (11.43)$$

If such can be found, then setting each f_α equal to a suitable constant value will define a corresponding submanifold. The conditions (11.29) can now be seen as being the *integrability conditions* for the system of first order partial differential equations (11.43) for each function f_α.

Once we have grasped the content of Frobenius' Theorem, given here in its vector-field formulation (there is a dual formulation using one-forms, but that is another story), we see that a foliation of $\mathcal{U}$ need not arise only from a system of mutually commuting vector fields : any more general system obeying (11.29) will do.

11.10. CONDITIONS FOR COORDINATE-BASED FRAMES

Let us go back for a moment to the case of mutually commuting vector fields, and consider the case $k = n$. With respect to a chart $(\mathcal{U}, \psi)$, the field of coordinate-based frames $\{\partial/\partial x^\mu\}$ gives us a family of n independent vector fields, commuting pairwise. Is the converse true? In other words: suppose $\{e_a(m)\}$ is a field of frames over a region $\mathcal{U} \subset M$. What are the necessary and sufficient conditions for $\{e_a\}$ to be the coordinate-based frame associated with some chart $(\mathcal{U}, \psi)$ using coordinates x^μ? It is clearly *necessary* that they commute pairwise:

$$\{e_a\} \equiv \{\partial/\partial x^\mu\} \Rightarrow [e_a, e_b] = 0 \text{ over } \mathcal{U} \qquad (11.44)$$

But these conditions are also *sufficient*! For, via the exponential maps, we can put a new chart over $\mathcal{U}$, in the manner of eq.(11.26). Starting from some $m_0 \in \mathcal{U}$, we set

$$m(\xi) = e^{\xi^a e_a} m_0 \qquad (11.45)$$

Given the smoothness of the solutions to the relevant differential equations, the passage from (any originally given) chart or coordinates $\{x^\mu\}$ to $\{\xi^a\}$ is (at least locally!) an allowed one. And in the latter chart, eqs. (11.26,27) ensure that each e_a is just $\partial/\partial\xi^a$!

In terms of the dual frames $\{e^a(m)\}$ defined over $\mathcal{U}$, the commutator conditions (11.44) become very simple and attractive. Recall from eq.(9.40) that the differential of each e^a is determined thus:

$$(de^a)(X,Y) = X(e^a(Y)) - Y(e^a(X)) - e^a([X,Y]) \qquad (11.46)$$

All knowledge about de^a is contained in the values of these expressions when X and Y are chosen to be members of the frame $\{e_b\}$. But since $e^a(e_b)$ is a pure number, we immediately see:

$$de^a = 0, \text{all } a \Leftrightarrow [e_a, e_b] = 0, \text{all } a, b \qquad (11.47)$$

In other words, a given set of dual fields of frames over a region $\mathcal{U}$ is a coordinate-based one if either the vector fields e_a commute with one another, or the one-forms e^a have vanishing exterior derivatives. These conditions are equivalent. A nice way of understanding this result will emerge after we digest the Poincaré Lemma.

11.11. CLOSED AND EXACT FORMS, SIMPLE FORMS

On the n-dimensional differentiable manifold M, we can consider forms of various degrees k, from 0 upto n. The space of k- forms was denoted by $C^{(k)}(M)$. Exterior differentiation takes us from $C^{(k)}(M)$ to $C^{(k+1)}(M)$:

$$\alpha \in C^{(k)}(M) \Rightarrow d\alpha \in C^{(k+1)}(M) \qquad (11.48)$$

But a second application of d gives a vanishing result:

$$d\,d\,\alpha = 0 \qquad (11.49)$$

Based on this we define the following: a k-form α is *closed* if $d\alpha = 0$, it is *exact* if in addition it is $d\beta$ for some $\beta \in C^{(k-1)}(M)$:

$$\alpha \in C^{(k)}(M) : \alpha \text{ is closed} \quad \Leftrightarrow \quad d\alpha = 0;$$
$$\alpha \text{ is exact} \quad \Leftrightarrow \quad \alpha = d\beta,$$
$$\beta \in C^{(k-1)}(M);$$
$$\alpha \text{ is exact} \quad \Rightarrow \quad \alpha \text{ is closed} \cdot \qquad (11.50)$$

We denote the spaces of closed and of exact k-forms thus:

Closed $\quad Z^{(k)}(M) \;=\; \{\alpha \in C^{(k)}(M) | d\,\alpha = 0\};$

Exact $\quad B^{(k)}(M) \;=\; \{\alpha \in C^{(k)}(M) | \alpha = d\,\beta, \beta \in C^{(k-1)}(M)\};$

$$B^{(k)}(M) \;\subset\; Z^{(k)}(M) \subset C^{(k)}(M). \qquad (11.51)$$

Remember that while a k-form can be multiplied by a function and it remains a k-form, its closed or exact nature will generally be lost in the process. One can now refine the obvious statement

$$d : C^{(k)}(M) \to C^{(k+1)}(M) \tag{11.52}$$

to say:

$$d : C^{(k)}(M) \to B^{(k+1)}(M) \subset C^{(k+1)}(M). \tag{11.53}$$

We shall come back to a study of these matters a little later after we study the integration of differential forms in Section 16.

Another useful notion is that of a *simple* form. A k-form α on M is said to be simple if it consists of a monomial like

$$\begin{aligned} \alpha &= df^1 \wedge df^2 \wedge \ldots \wedge df^k, \\ & f's \in \mathcal{F}(M). \end{aligned} \tag{11.54}$$

In that case α is seen to be exact, hence also closed:

$$\begin{aligned} \alpha &= d(f^1 df^2 \wedge df^3 \wedge \ldots \wedge df^k), \\ d\alpha &= 0. \end{aligned} \tag{11.55}$$

So,

$$\alpha \text{ simple} \Rightarrow \alpha \text{ exact} \Rightarrow \alpha \text{ closed} \tag{11.56}$$

11.12. POINCARE'S LEMMA

This is the assertion that while globally a closed form need not be exact, locally it is! That is, given a closed $\alpha \in C^{(k)}(M)$, and a point $m \in M$, we can find a neighbourhood $\mathcal{U}$ around m, and a $(k-1)$-form β defined over $\mathcal{U}$, such that $\alpha = d\beta$ over $\mathcal{U}$. The problem is that *in general* β cannot be smoothly defined all over M.

We shall give a proof of this result because it is quite instructive. It is by explicit construction over a suitable chart taken from a maximal atlas for M. Around a point $m_0 \in M$, choose a neighbourhood $\mathcal{U}$ and a chart $(\mathcal{U}, \psi)$ such that ψ maps $\mathcal{U}$ homeomorphically onto the interior of the unit sphere in $\mathcal{R}^n$. Such a range for the chart, $\psi(\mathcal{U})$, is chosen because it is *topologically trivial*. More specifically, it is *star-shaped* : starting from m_0, we are able to travel "radially outwards" in every direction to some extent, and remain

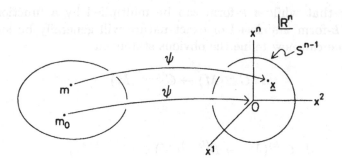

Figure 7.   Chart used in proving Poincaré's Lemma

within $\mathcal{U}$. For simplicity, we let ψ map m_0 to the origin in $\mathcal{R}^n$. A general $m \in \mathcal{U}$ goes into $x \in \mathcal{R}^n$:

$$m \in \mathcal{U} : \psi(m) = x,$$
$$|x|^2 = \sum_1^n (x^\mu)^2 < 1. \tag{11.57}$$

The situation in schematically pictured in Figure 7. All our constructions and calculations will be done using this chart. We expand $\alpha \in C^{(k)}(M)$ as in eq. (9.26):

$$\alpha = \frac{1}{k!}\alpha_{\mu_1\mu_2\ldots\mu_k}(x)dx^{\mu_1}\wedge dx^{\mu_2}\wedge\ldots\wedge dx^{\mu_k}. \tag{11.58}$$

As seen from eqs. (9.28,29), the exterior derivative of α is given in components as

$$d\alpha = \frac{1}{(k+1)!}(d\alpha)_{\mu_1\mu_2\ldots\mu_{k+1}}(x)dx^{\mu_1}\wedge dx^{\mu_2}\wedge\ldots\wedge dx^{\mu_{k+1}},$$

$$(d\alpha)_{\mu_1\ldots\mu_{k+1}}(x) = (-1)^k\Big\{\alpha_{\mu_1\ldots\mu_k,\mu_{k+1}}(x)-$$

$$\sum_{r=1}^{k}\alpha_{\mu_1\ldots\mu_{r-1}\mu_{k+1}\mu_{r+1}\ldots\mu_k,\mu_r}(x)\Big\}$$

$$= (-1)^k\sum_{r=1}^{k+1}(-1)^{kr}\alpha_{\mu_{r+1}\mu_{r+2}\ldots\mu_k\mu_{k+1}\mu_1\ldots\mu_{r-1},\mu_r}(x). \tag{11.59}$$

In this last form we have expressed the sum as a *cyclic series of terms* and we see that for even k all terms come with a positive sign, while for odd

k they alternate with r. Now if α is closed, $d\alpha = 0$, the right hand side vanishes; it is convenient to express this as:

$$\alpha_{\mu_1...\mu_k,\lambda}(\boldsymbol{x}) = \sum_{r=1}^{k} \alpha_{\mu_1...\mu_{r-1}\lambda\mu_{r+1}...\mu_k,\mu_r}(\boldsymbol{x}). \tag{11.60}$$

We will now show by a process of *radial outward integration* within the interior of the unit sphere S^{n-1} in $\mathcal{R}^n$, that we can set up a $(k-1)$ form β over $\mathcal{U}$, such that $\alpha = d\beta$ over $\mathcal{U}$. We define β by

$$\beta = \frac{1}{(k-1)!}\beta_{\mu_1\mu_2...\mu_{k-1}}(\boldsymbol{x})dx^{\mu_1} \wedge dx^{\mu_2} \wedge ... \wedge dx^{\mu_{k-1}},$$

$$\beta_{\mu_1...\mu_{k-1}}(\boldsymbol{x}) = \int_0^1 dt \cdot f(t)x^\lambda \alpha_{\mu_1...\mu_{k-1}\lambda}(t\boldsymbol{x}), \tag{11.61}$$

and find a suitable function $f(t)$ that will do the trick. To calculate $d\beta$ we use (11.59) with the changes $\alpha \to \beta, k \to k-1$:

$$(d\beta)_{\mu_1...\mu_k}(\boldsymbol{x}) = (-1)^{k-1} \{\beta_{\mu_1...\mu_{k-1},\mu_k}(\boldsymbol{x}) -$$

$$\sum_{r=1}^{k-1} \beta_{\mu_1...\mu_{r-1}\mu_k\mu_{r+1}...\mu_{k-1},\mu_r}(\boldsymbol{x}) \}. \tag{11.62}$$

Now a general partial derivative of any component of β can be computed from eq.(11.61):

$$\beta_{\mu_1...\mu_{k-1},\rho}(\boldsymbol{x}) = \int_0^1 dt \cdot f(t) \cdot \{\alpha_{\mu_1...\mu_{k-1}\rho}(t\boldsymbol{x}) +$$

$$tx^\lambda \alpha_{\mu_1...\mu_{k-1}\lambda,\rho}(t\boldsymbol{x}) \}. \tag{11.63}$$

For the first term on the righthand side of eq.(11.62) we have to set $\rho = \mu_k$. For the general term in the sum on r, we have to take $\mu_1 \to \mu_1, \ldots, \mu_{r-1} \to \mu_{r-1}, \mu_r \to \mu_k, \mu_{r+1} \to \mu_{r+1}, \ldots, \mu_{k-1} \to \mu_{k-1}, \rho \to \mu_r$ in eq.(11.63). In this way we get:

$$(d\beta)_{\mu_1...\mu_k}(\boldsymbol{x}) = (-1)^{k-1} \int_0^1 dt \cdot f(t) \cdot \{\alpha_{\mu_1...\mu_k}(t\boldsymbol{x}) + tx^\lambda \alpha_{\mu_1...\mu_{k-1}\lambda,\mu_k}(t\boldsymbol{x}) -$$

$$\sum_{r=1}^{k-1} (\alpha_{\mu_1...\mu_k...\mu_{k-1}\mu_r} \ (t\boldsymbol{x}) + tx^\lambda \alpha_{\mu_1...\mu_k...\mu_{k-1}\lambda,\mu_r} \ (t\boldsymbol{x}))\}$$

$$\downarrow \qquad\qquad\qquad \downarrow$$
$$\text{rth place} \qquad\qquad \text{rth place}$$

$$= (-1)^{k-1} \int_0^1 dt \cdot f(t) \{k\alpha_{\mu_1\ldots\mu_k}(t\boldsymbol{x}) + tx^\lambda \alpha_{\mu_1\ldots\mu_k,\lambda}(t\boldsymbol{x})\}$$

$$= (-1)^{k-1} \int_0^1 dt \cdot f(t) \cdot \left(k + t\frac{d}{dt}\right) \alpha_{\mu_1\ldots\mu_k}(t\boldsymbol{x}). \tag{11.64}$$

Here the undifferentiated terms in α were simplified using the total anti-symmetry of the components $\alpha_{\mu_1\ldots\mu_k}(\boldsymbol{x})$; while for the derivative terms we used eq.(11.60) with λ and μ_k interchanged. Now we see that by choosing $f(t) = (-t)^{k-1}$ we can achieve our goal:

$$\beta_{\mu_1\ldots\mu_{k-1}}(\boldsymbol{x}) = (-1)^{k-1} \int_0^1 dt \cdot t^{k-1} \cdot x^\lambda \alpha_{\mu_1\ldots\mu_{k-1}\lambda}(t\boldsymbol{x}),$$

$$\alpha = d\beta \tag{11.65}$$

This is the Poincaré Lemma: locally, in a suitable star-shaped neighbour-hood of any point $m \in M$, a closed form is exact.

With this result in hand, let us go back to the earlier eqs.(11.47), the necessary and sufficient conditions for a field of dual frames $\{e_a\}, \{e^a\}$ to be coordinate-based. Locally, if de^a vanishes, each e^a is expressible as the differential of some function $\xi^a \in \mathcal{F}(\mathcal{U})$. As the e^a form a frame, these functions must be algebraically independent:

$$de^a = 0 \quad \Rightarrow \quad e^a = d\xi^a, \xi^a \in \mathcal{F}(\mathcal{U});$$
$$\{e^a\} \text{ a frame} \quad \Longleftrightarrow \quad e^1 \wedge e^2 \wedge \ldots \wedge e^n \neq 0$$
$$\Longleftrightarrow \quad d\xi^1 \wedge d\xi^2 \wedge \ldots \wedge d\xi^n \neq 0$$
$$\Longleftrightarrow \quad \{\xi^a\} \text{are independent functions} \tag{11.66}$$

From here it immediately follows that we can use these ξ's as local coordinates over $\mathcal{U}$, and indeed then

$$e_a = \partial/\partial\xi^a \tag{11.67}$$

12. Orientation, Volume forms, Pseudo Riemannian metric, Hodge duality

Let us continue our study of "things that can be done" on an n-dimensional differentiable manifold M, sometimes with the help of additional structures. As defined in Section 7, the manifold M is said to be *simple* if and only if we can find a single chart atlas for it:

$$M \text{ simple} \quad \Longleftrightarrow \quad \text{there exists a homeomorphism } \psi :$$
$$M \quad \longrightarrow \quad \psi(M) = \text{connected open set in } \mathcal{R}^n. \tag{12.1}$$

Thus there are no overlaps, no transition rules or transition functions. On the other hand, as we defined in Section 7, M is *orientable* if we can find a *positively oriented* (so certainly *not* a maximal) atlas $\mathcal{A}$ for M satisfying eq.(7.19): on each overlap of charts the Jacobian is positive. (One can speak of a *maximal oriented atlas*, roughly one half of a maximal atlas!). We now easily see that

$$M \text{ simple} \implies M \text{ orientable},$$
$$M \text{ not orientable} \implies M \text{ not simple} \qquad (12.2)$$

12.1. DEFINING AN n-FORM

Let us see "what it takes" to define an n-form on a general n-dimensional differentiable manifold M. Let $\omega \in C^{(n)}(M)$ and let $\mathcal{A} = \{(\mathcal{U}_\alpha, \psi_\alpha)\}$ be an atlas for M. Over each open set $\mathcal{U}_\alpha$, with points m assigned coordinates $\{x^\mu\}$ in $\mathcal{R}^n$ via the homeomorphism ψ_α, we can describe ω in this way:

$$(\mathcal{U}_\alpha, \psi_\alpha): \quad \omega = \frac{1}{n!}\omega^{(\alpha)}_{\mu_1\mu_2\ldots\mu_n}(x)dx^{\mu_1} \wedge dx^{\mu_2} \wedge \ldots \wedge dx^{\mu_n}$$
$$= \omega^{(\alpha)}_{12\ldots n}(x)\, dx^1 \wedge dx^2 \wedge \ldots \wedge dx^n$$
$$= S^{(\alpha)}(x)\, dx^1 \wedge dx^2 \wedge \ldots \wedge dx^n,$$
$$S^{(\alpha)}(x) = \omega^{(\alpha)}_{12\ldots n}(x) \qquad (12.3)$$

Thus over each $\mathcal{U}_\alpha$, with the help of the local coordinates there, ω reduces to or is describable by a *single real-valued function* $S^{(\alpha)}(x)$. In the overlap of two open sets $\mathcal{U}_\alpha$ and $\mathcal{U}_\beta$, $S^{(\alpha)}(x)$ and $S^{(\beta)}(x')$ must be related by a *transition rule*:

$$x \in \psi_\alpha(U_\alpha \cap U_\beta) \subset \mathcal{R}^n$$

$$\psi_\alpha$$

$$\mathcal{U}_\alpha \cap \mathcal{U}_\beta \neq \phi: \quad m \in \mathcal{U}_\alpha \cap \mathcal{U}_\beta$$

$$\psi_\beta$$

$$x' \in \psi_\beta(U_\alpha \cap U_\beta) \subset \mathcal{R}^n,$$

$$S^{(\beta)}(x') = \left(\det\left(\frac{\partial x'^\mu}{\partial x^\nu}\right)\right)^{-1} S^{(\alpha)}(x). \qquad (12.4)$$

Throughout an overlap region, the determinant here never vanishes, so it has a definite sign, which may be positive or negative. So, to define an n-form ω on a general manifold M means to give a function $S^{(\alpha)}(x)$ on each

$\mathcal{U}_\alpha$, obeying (12.4) in overlap regions.

12.2. INTEGRAL OF AN n-FORM

Now let us assume M is orientable, let the atlas $\mathcal{A}$ above be a positively oriented one, and let ω be any n-form on M. We can then in an intrinsic way speak of *the integral of ω over M*. First we define the integral of ω over each open set $\mathcal{U}_\alpha$ involved in the atlas. We express ω via eq.(12.3) in terms of a function $S^{(\alpha)}(x)$ over $\psi_\alpha(\mathcal{U}_\alpha) \subset \mathcal{R}^n$ and set:

$$\int_{\mathcal{U}_\alpha} \omega \equiv \int_{\psi_\alpha(\mathcal{U}_\alpha)} S^{(\alpha)}(x)dx^1 dx^2 \ldots dx^n = \text{ordinary numerical}$$

$$\text{Riemann integral over } \psi_\alpha(\mathcal{U}_\alpha) \subset \mathcal{R}^n \qquad (12.5)$$

Keeping $\mathcal{U}_\alpha$ fixed, any change in the choice of local coordinates, ie., any change in the homeomorphism ψ_α into $\mathcal{R}^n$ *which remains positively oriented* will not alter the right hand side of (12.5). This is because while $S^{(\alpha)}$ changes according to eq.(12.4) involving the Jacobian determinant, the "ordinary volume element" $dx^1 \ldots dx^n$ changes by the modulus of this Jacobian determinant; but these changes *exactly cancel* one another because the determinant is positive:

$$x \in \psi_\alpha(\mathcal{U}_\alpha) \subset \mathcal{R}^n$$

$$\psi_\alpha \nearrow$$

$$m \in \mathcal{U}_\alpha$$

$$\psi'_\alpha \searrow$$

$$x' \in \psi'_\alpha(\mathcal{U}_\alpha) \subset \mathcal{R}^n :$$

$$S^{(\alpha)\prime}(x') = \left(\det \left(\frac{\partial x'^\mu}{\partial x^\nu} \right) \right)^{-1} S^{(\alpha)}(x),$$

$$dx'^1 \ldots dx'^n = \left| \det \left(\frac{\partial x'^\mu}{\partial x^\nu} \right) \right| dx^1 \ldots dx^n$$

$$= \det \left(\frac{\partial x'^\mu}{\partial x^\nu} \right) dx^1 \ldots dx^n,$$

$$\int_{\mathcal{U}_\alpha} \omega = \int_{\psi_\alpha(\mathcal{U}_\alpha)} S^{(\alpha)}(x)dx^1 \ldots dx^n = \int_{\psi'_\alpha(\mathcal{U}_\alpha)} S^{(\alpha)\prime}(x')dx'^1 \ldots dx'^n .$$

$$(12.6)$$

So indeed the expression $\int_{\mathcal{U}_\alpha} \omega$ is correctly written in a coordinate-free manner.

Now to complete the story we must carefully put together the individual integrals of ω over each $\mathcal{U}_\alpha$ to get the integral of ω over M. Here there may be problems of convergence which must be taken care of and which we assume can be handled properly. More important for us is the fact that a simple-minded sum over α of the individual integrals of ω over each $\mathcal{U}_\alpha$ would be incorrect, because there would be double or multiple counting of contributions in each overlap! This is however very cleverly handled by the trick of "partitions of unity". Under suitable conditions on M (which we do not go into in detail as our aim is only to get the main idea across) we can find a partition of unity, that is, a set of smooth functions $\{e_\alpha(m)\}$, one on each open set $\mathcal{U}_\alpha$ in the oriented atlas $\mathcal{A}$, which obey:

$$i) \qquad e_\alpha(m) = 0 \text{ if } m \notin \mathcal{U}_\alpha;$$
$$ii) \qquad 0 \leq e_\alpha(m) \leq 1;$$
$$iii) \qquad \sum_\alpha e_\alpha(m) = 1 \text{ for any } m \in M \qquad (12.7)$$

Here in the third condition the extra requirements on M (alluded to but not spelt out above) ensure that for any given m there is only a finite number of nonzero terms. (The point is that if a certain $m \in M$ is in the overlap of several $\mathcal{U}_\alpha$, all those e_α's contribute to the sum, and the number of such $\mathcal{U}_\alpha$'s is finite for each given m). Then the integral of ω over M is defined as

$$\int_M \omega = \sum_\alpha \int_{\mathcal{U}_\alpha} e_\alpha \omega. \qquad (12.8)$$

It requires a little "fancy footwork" to convince oneself that the right hand side here is independent of the choice of the partition of unity and even of the choice of oriented atlas $\mathcal{A}$, but we leave the details as exercises. In any case the quite beautiful and intrinsic way in which one integrates an n-form over an n-manifold with orientation must be clear.

Later on, in Section 16, we shall return to this theme and take up the question of integrating general k-forms on M over suitable domains of integration.

12.3.   VOLUME FORMS

Now revert to a general n-dimensional differentiable manifold M. A *volume form* Ω on M is *any* nowhere vanishing n-form on M. It is easy to show that a volume form can exist only if M *is orientable*:

$$\text{Volume form } \Omega \text{ exists} \implies M \text{ is orientable,}$$
$$M \text{ is nonorientable} \implies \text{no volume form exists} \qquad (12.9)$$

The proof being quite elementary, we give it! Being an n-form, over each $\mathcal{U}_\alpha$ of an atlas $\mathcal{A}$ for M, Ω is represented by a function $S^{(\alpha)}(x)$. Being always non-zero, each $S^{(\alpha)}(x)$ is strictly positive or strictly negative over its domain of definition. Divide the $\mathcal{U}_\alpha$'s into those $\mathcal{U}_\alpha^{(+)}$'s over each of which $S^{(\alpha)}$ is positive, and the remaining $\mathcal{U}_\alpha^{(-)}$'s over each of which $S^{(\alpha)}$ is negative. Then eq.(12.4) shows that in the various kinds of overlaps the Jacobian determinant has the following signs:

$$\mathcal{U}_\alpha^{(+)} \cap \mathcal{U}_\beta^{(+)} \text{ or } \mathcal{U}_\alpha^{(-)} \cap \mathcal{U}_\beta^{(-)} \quad : \quad \det\left(\frac{\partial x'}{\partial x}\right) > 0;$$

$$\mathcal{U}_\alpha^{(+)} \cap \mathcal{U}_\beta^{(-)} \quad : \quad \det\left(\frac{\partial x'}{\partial x}\right) < 0 \qquad (12.10)$$

Now all we do is to switch, say, the first two coordinates x^1 and x^2 in each $\mathcal{U}_\alpha^{(-)}$, and also change from $S^{(\alpha)}(x)$ to - $S^{(\alpha)}(x)$ in them: we then get a new atlas for M which is positively oriented, so M is orientable. And with respect to this atlas Ω is represented by a *positive* function on each open set $\mathcal{U}_\alpha$, consistent with eq.(12.4). Thus the claims (12.9) are established.

12.4. BRINGING IN A METRIC

Let the n-dimensional manifold M carry a pseudo Riemannian metric g, as defined in Section 10. Over each chart $(\mathcal{U}_\alpha, \psi_\alpha)$ of an atlas $\mathcal{A}$ for M, g is described by a "symmetric covariant second rank tensor field":

$$\mathcal{U}_\alpha : g = g_{\mu\nu}^{(\alpha)}(x)dx^\mu \otimes dx^\nu;$$

$$\mathcal{U}_\alpha \cap \mathcal{U}_\beta : g_{\mu\nu}^{(\beta)}(x') = \frac{\partial x^\rho}{\partial x'^\mu}\frac{\partial x^\sigma}{\partial x'^\nu} g_{\rho\sigma}^{(\alpha)}(x),$$

$$\det\left(g_{\mu\nu}^{(\beta)}(x')\right) = \left(\det\left(\frac{\partial x'}{\partial x}\right)\right)^{-2} \det\left(g_{\rho\sigma}^{(\alpha)}(x)\right).$$

$$(12.11)$$

Now at each point $m \in M, g(m)$ has an intrinsically defined *signature*, namely the numbers of positive and negative diagonal entries when g is brought to diagonal form. We hereafter assume M to be *connected*, so this signature of g, and hence also the sign of $\det\left(g_{\mu\nu}^{(\alpha)}(x)\right)$, *is constant all over*

M. If in addition M is *also orientable*, let us assume the atlas $\mathcal{A}$ is oriented. Then we can take square roots on both sides of eq.(12.11) to get:

$$| \det \left(g_{\mu\nu}^{(\alpha)}(x) \right) |^{1/2} = \left(\det \left(\frac{\partial x'}{\partial x} \right) \right) \cdot | \det \left(g_{\mu\nu}^{(\beta)}(x') \right) |^{1/2}.$$

$$(12.12)$$

Realise that here the Jacobian is *given* to be positive. So we have a "solution" to eq.(12.4) provided by the metric itself, namely a nowhere vanishing n-form on M. Thus a pseudo Riemannian metric on M plus the orientability and connectedness of M lead to a preferred volume form Ω which appears in local (oriented) coordinates as:

$$
\begin{aligned}
\Omega &= \frac{1}{n!}\Omega_{\mu_1\mu_2\ldots\mu_n}(x)dx^{\mu_1} \wedge dx^{\mu_2} \wedge \ldots \wedge dx^{\mu_n} \\
&= \Omega_{12\ldots n}(x)dx^1 \wedge dx^2 \wedge \ldots \wedge dx^n, \\
\Omega_{\mu_1\mu_2\ldots\mu_n}(x) &= \epsilon_{\mu_1\mu_2\ldots\mu_n} | \det \left(g_{\mu\nu}(x) \right) |^{1/2}, \\
\epsilon_{12\ldots n} &= +1, \text{ totally antisymmetric}
\end{aligned}
$$

$$(12.13)$$

It must be realised that the existence of a metric on M *does not mean* that M is orientable; *that* is an independent property which M may or may not possess. We can say:

Metric plus orientation $\longrightarrow$ preferred (Levi-Civita) volume form Ω;

Metric but nonorientable $\longrightarrow$ no volume form at all   (12.14)

Often for brevity in the sequel we shall write in the domain of each chart:

$$g(x) = \det \left(g_{\mu\nu}(x) \right) : \text{ constant sign all over } \mathcal{U}_\alpha \qquad (12.15)$$

12.5.   THE HODGE DUALITY OPERATION

In Section 4, one of the algebraic operations on a vector space which we studied was the *Hodge duality operation*. This is defined when both a metric and an orientation are available. For orientable manifolds carrying a metric we can take over the procedures of Section 4 at each point; and "doing things smoothly" as always, we can set up the duality operation on fields of forms on M. Conventionally this is denoted by a star $*$ on the upper left of the relevant form, so we adopt this notation in place of the tilde used in Section 4.

For convenience we quickly recapitulate notations and factors needed in dealing with forms and wedge products, using local coordinates when convenient.

$$\underline{A \in \mathcal{J}^{(0,k)}(M)}:$$
$$A = A_{\mu_1 \mu_2 \ldots \mu_k}(x) dx^{\mu_1} \otimes dx^{\mu_2} \otimes \ldots \otimes dx^{\mu_k},$$
$$A(X_1, X_2, \ldots, X_k) = A_{\mu_1 \mu_2 \ldots \mu_k} X_1^{\mu_1} X_2^{\mu_2} \ldots X_k^{\mu_k},$$
$$X_1, \ldots, X_k \in T_m M; \tag{12.16a}$$
$$\underline{A \in C^{(k)}(M) \subset \mathcal{J}^{(0,k)}(M)}:$$
$$A = \frac{1}{k!} A_{\mu_1 \ldots \mu_k}(x) \sum_{P \in S_k} \delta_P \, dx^{\mu_{P(1)}} \otimes \ldots \otimes dx^{\mu_{P(k)}}$$
$$= \frac{1}{k!} A_{\mu_1 \ldots \mu_k}(x) dx^{\mu_1} \wedge \ldots \wedge dx^{\mu_k},$$
$$(dx^{\mu_1} \wedge \ldots \wedge dx^{\mu_k})(X_1, \ldots, X_k) = \sum_{P \in S_k} \delta_P \, X_1^{\mu_{P(1)}} \ldots X_k^{\mu_{P(k)}};$$

$$\tag{12.16b}$$

$$\underline{A \in C^{(k)}(M), \; B \in C^{(\ell)}(M)}:$$
$$(A \wedge B)(X_1, \ldots, X_{k+\ell}) = (A \wedge B)_{\mu_1 \ldots \mu_{k+\ell}} X_1^{\mu_1} \ldots X_{k+\ell}^{\mu_{k+\ell}}$$
$$= \frac{1}{k! \ell!} \sum_{P \in S_{k+\ell}} A\left(X_{P(1)}, \ldots, X_{P(k)}\right) B\left(X_{P(k+1)}, \ldots, X_{P(k+\ell)}\right)$$
$$= \frac{1}{k! \ell!} \sum_{P \in S_{k+\ell}} \delta_P A_{\nu_1 \ldots \nu_k} B_{\nu_{k+1} \ldots \nu_{k+\ell}} X_1^{\nu_{P(1)}} \ldots X_{k+\ell}^{\nu_{P(k+\ell)}},$$
$$(A \wedge B)_{\mu_1 \ldots \mu_{k+\ell}} = \frac{1}{k! \ell!} \sum_{P \in S_{k+\ell}} \delta_P A_{\mu_{P(1)} \ldots \mu_{P(k)}} B_{\mu_{P(k+1)} \ldots \mu_{P(k+\ell)}}$$
$$= A_{\mu_1 \ldots \mu_k} B_{\mu_{k+1} \ldots \mu_{k+\ell}} + \text{unique retinue.} \tag{12.16c}$$

Here, P is a permutation, an element of S_k or $S_{k+\ell}$ as the case may be, and δ_P is its signature.

Now we define duality as in Section 4, point by point on M. Given the metric g, at each $m \in M$ we view it as a nondegenerate symmetric bilinear form on $T_m M$. Then we produce the map $\tilde{g}$ from $T_m M$ to $T_m^* M$; next $\tilde{g}^{-1}$ from $T_m^* M$ to $T_m M$; and finally the bilinear form g^{-1} on $T_m^* M$. All this being understood: for each $\alpha \in C^{(k)}(M)$, duality gives us an $(n - k)$-form denoted by $^*\alpha$. This is an *algebraic* operation carried out at each point $m \in M$, using both $\tilde{g}(m)$ and the volume form $\Omega(m)$ defined in eq.(12.13):

$$\alpha \in C^{(k)}(M) \quad \rightarrow \quad {}^*\alpha \in C^{(n-k)}(M):$$
$${}^*\alpha(m)(X_1,\ldots,X_{n-k})\Omega(m) \;=\; \alpha(m) \wedge \tilde{g}(m)(X_1)\wedge\ldots\wedge\tilde{g}(m)(X_{n-k}),$$
$$X_1,\ldots,X_{n-k} \in T_m M,$$
$$\tilde{g}(m)(X_1),\ldots,\tilde{g}(m)(X_{n-k}) \in T_m^* M \cdot$$

$$\text{(12.17)}$$

Clearly, for sums of forms and on multiplication by functions we have:

$$\alpha, \beta \in C^{(k)}(M) :{}^* (\alpha + \beta) \;=\; {}^*\alpha + {}^*\beta \in C^{(n-k)}(M);$$
$$\alpha \in C^{(k)}(M), \; f \in \mathcal{F}(M) :{}^* (f\alpha) \;=\; f\,{}^*\alpha \in C^{(n-k)}(M) \cdot \quad \text{(12.18)}$$

Always using charts from an oriented atlas, we read off from Section 4 the local component description of this Hodge duality operation, and the effect of the double dual:

$$({}^*\alpha)_{\mu_{k+1}\ldots\mu_n}(x) \;=\; \frac{|g(x)|^{-1/2}}{k!}\epsilon^{\lambda_1\ldots\lambda_n}\alpha_{\lambda_1\ldots\lambda_k}(x)g_{\lambda_{k+1}\mu_{k+1}}(x)\cdots g_{\lambda_n\mu_n}(x);$$
$${}^*({}^*\alpha) \;=\; \sigma \cdot (-1)^{k(n-k)}\alpha,$$
$$\sigma \;=\; \operatorname{sign} g(x) \qquad \text{(12.19)}$$

Since we have a metric on hand, if we wish we can use it to raise and lower indices, and can even speak of "the contravariant components of a k-form"! In that sense, the passage to the dual $\alpha \rightarrow {}^*\alpha$ can be expressed slightly more neatly. We also need some identities obeyed by the metric matrix $(g_{\mu\nu})$:

$$\epsilon^{\lambda_1\lambda_2\ldots\lambda_n}g_{\lambda_1\mu_1}\,g_{\lambda_2\mu_2}\cdots g_{\lambda_n\mu_n} \;=\; \epsilon_{\mu_1\mu_2\ldots\mu_n}\det g \implies$$
$$\epsilon^{\lambda_1\lambda_2\ldots\lambda_n}g_{\lambda_{k+1}\mu_{k+1}}\cdots g_{\lambda_n\mu_n} \;=\; g \cdot \epsilon_{\mu_1\mu_2\ldots\mu_n}g^{\mu_1\lambda_1}\ldots g^{\mu_k\lambda_k}$$

$$\text{(12.20)}$$

Then eq.(12.19) appears as

$$({}^*\alpha)_{\mu_{k+1}\ldots\mu_n}(x) \;=\; \frac{\sigma}{k!}|g(x)|^{1/2}\epsilon_{\mu_1\ldots\mu_n}\alpha^{\mu_1\ldots\mu_k}(x)$$
$$=\; \frac{\sigma}{k!}\Omega_{\mu_1\ldots\mu_n}(x)\alpha^{\mu_1\ldots\mu_k}(x) \cdot \qquad \text{(12.21)}$$

Here are some simple examples of taking the dual, for functions, one-forms, two-forms, $(n-1)$ forms, and n forms:

$\underline{f \in \mathcal{F}(M)}$:

$^*f = \sigma \cdot f \cdot \Omega \in C^{(n)}(M)$,

$^*1 = \sigma \, \Omega$;   (12.22a)

$\underline{\alpha = \alpha_\mu(x)dx^\mu \in C^{(1)}(M)}$:

$^*\alpha = \alpha_\mu(x)^*dx^\mu \in C^{(n-1)}(M)$,

$$^*dx^\mu = \frac{\sigma|g|^{1/2}}{(n-1)!} \cdot g^{\mu\mu_1}(x)\epsilon_{\mu_1\mu_2\ldots\mu_n}dx^{\mu_2} \wedge \ldots \wedge dx^{\mu_n};$$ (12.22b)

$\underline{\alpha = \dfrac{1}{2}\alpha_{\lambda\rho}(x)dx^\lambda \wedge dx^\rho \in C^{(2)}(M)}$:

$^*\alpha = \dfrac{1}{2}\alpha_{\lambda\rho}(x) \, ^*(dx^\lambda \wedge dx^\rho)$,

$$^*(dx^\lambda \wedge dx^\rho) = \frac{\sigma|g|^{1/2}}{(n-2)!}g^{\lambda\mu_1}(x)g^{\rho\mu_2}(x)\epsilon_{\mu_1\mu_2\ldots\mu_n}dx^{\mu_3} \wedge \ldots \wedge dx^{\mu_n};$$

(12.22c)

$$^*(dx^{\mu_2} \wedge dx^{\mu_3} \wedge \ldots \wedge dx^{\mu_n}) = (-1)^{n-1}|g|^{-1/2} \cdot \epsilon^{\mu_1\mu_2\ldots\mu_n} \cdot g_{\mu_1\mu}(x)dx^\mu;$$

(12.22d)

$\underline{\omega \in C^{(n)}(M)}$:

$^*\omega = \omega_{12\ldots n}(x)/|g(x)|^{1/2} \in \mathcal{F}(M)$,

$^*\Omega = 1 \cdot$ (12.22e)

12.6.   INNER PRODUCT FOR FORMS, DUALITY AND THE WEDGE

Now the metric g has given us the object g^{-1} which, at each $m \in M$, is a bilinear form on T_m^*M. It is natural and possible to extend this to a pointwise symmetric nondegenerate inner product on k-forms at each $m \in M$. This is done as follows:

$$\alpha, \beta \in C^{(k)}(M) : (\alpha, \beta)_m = \frac{\sigma}{k!}\alpha_{\mu_1\ldots\mu_k}(x)\beta^{\mu_1\cdots\mu_k}(x) \in \mathcal{R} \qquad (12.23)$$

You can easily convince yourself that this is chart and coordinate independent, and is an operation involving only the metric. Quite generally we can say:

$$\alpha, \beta \in C^{(k)}(M) \rightarrow (\alpha, \beta) \in \mathcal{F}(M),$$
$$(\alpha, \beta)(x) = \frac{\sigma}{k!}g^{\mu_1\lambda_1}(x)\ldots g^{\mu_k\lambda_k}(x)\alpha_{\mu_1\ldots\mu_k}(x)\beta_{\lambda_1\ldots\lambda_k}(x) \cdot$$

(12.24)

A general query can now be raised: is there a natural (metric and orientation dependent) relation between the dual of the wedge product and the wedge product of the duals? For a k-form α and an ℓ-form β, can we expect a connection between $^*(\alpha \wedge \beta)$ and $^*\alpha \wedge {}^*\beta$? Possibly surprisingly, and for rather elementary reasons, the answer is : No! It is just a matter of counting up dimensions:

$$\alpha \in C^{(k)}(M), \beta \in C^{(\ell)}(M) \quad \Rightarrow \quad {}^*\alpha \in C^{(n-k)}(M), {}^*\beta \in C^{(n-\ell)}(M);$$
$$\alpha \wedge \beta, \, {}^*(\alpha \wedge \beta) \neq 0 \quad \Rightarrow \quad k + \ell \leq n;$$
$$^*\alpha \wedge {}^*\beta \neq 0 \quad \Rightarrow \quad k + \ell \geq n. \tag{12.25}$$

So we can expect a relation only if $k + \ell = n$. In that case, each of $\alpha \wedge \beta$ and $^*\alpha \wedge {}^*\beta$ is an n-form, so each is proportional to the volume form Ω. How do they compare? If we write $\beta = {}^*\gamma$ with γ a k-form, we are seeking a relation between $\alpha \wedge {}^*\gamma$ and $^*\alpha \wedge \gamma$ or $\gamma \wedge {}^*\alpha$. Let us expand $\alpha \wedge {}^*\gamma$ and see what multiple of Ω we get; omitting the argument x:

$$\alpha, \gamma \in C^{(k)}(M) \quad \Rightarrow \quad \alpha \wedge {}^*\gamma = f\Omega, f \in \mathcal{F}(M);$$

$$(\alpha \wedge {}^*\gamma)_{\mu_1\ldots\mu_n} = f\Omega_{\mu_1\ldots\mu_n} = f\epsilon_{\mu_1\ldots\mu_n}|g|^{1/2} \Rightarrow$$

$$f = \frac{|g|^{-1/2}}{n!}\epsilon^{\mu_1\ldots\mu_n}(\alpha \wedge {}^*\gamma)_{\mu_1\ldots\mu_n}$$

$$= \frac{|g|^{-1/2}}{n!}\frac{\epsilon^{\mu_1\ldots\mu_n}}{k!(n-k)!}\sum_{P\in S_n}\delta_P\,\alpha_{\mu_{P(1)}\ldots\mu_{P(k)}}\times$$

$$(*\gamma)_{\mu_{P(k+1)}\ldots\mu_{P(n)}}$$

$$= \frac{|g|^{-1/2}}{k!(n-k)!}\epsilon^{\mu_1\ldots\mu_n}\alpha_{\mu_1\ldots\mu_k}(^*\gamma)_{\mu_{k+1}\ldots\mu_n}$$

$$= \frac{|g|^{-1/2}}{k!(n-k)!}\epsilon^{\mu_1\ldots\mu_n}\alpha_{\mu_1\ldots\mu_k}\frac{\sigma}{k!}\Omega_{\lambda_1\ldots\lambda_k\mu_{k+1}\ldots\mu_n}\gamma^{\lambda_1\ldots\lambda_k}$$

$$= \frac{\sigma}{k!k!(n-k)!}\epsilon^{\mu_1\ldots\mu_k\mu_{k+1}\ldots\mu_n}\epsilon_{\lambda_1\ldots\lambda_k\mu_{k+1}\ldots\mu_n}\alpha_{\mu_1\ldots\mu_k}\times$$

$$\gamma^{\lambda_1\ldots\lambda_k}$$

$$= \frac{\sigma}{k!}\alpha_{\lambda_1\ldots\lambda_k}\gamma^{\lambda_1\ldots\lambda_k},$$

$$\alpha \wedge {}^*\gamma = (\alpha, \gamma)\Omega \tag{12.26}$$

Here the local inner product of forms, defined in eq.(12.24), has been used. Now since (α, γ) is symmetric in α and γ, we have obtained:

$$\alpha, \gamma \in C^{(k)}(M) : \alpha \wedge {}^*\gamma = \gamma \wedge {}^*\alpha = (\alpha, \gamma)\Omega \tag{12.27}$$

Rewriting this in terms of $\beta = {}^*\gamma \in C^{(n-k)}(M)$ we can say:

$$
\begin{aligned}
\alpha \wedge \beta &= \alpha \wedge {}^*\gamma = (\alpha, \gamma)\Omega; \\
{}^*\alpha \wedge {}^*\beta &= \sigma \cdot (-1)^{k(n-k)} {}^*\alpha \wedge \gamma \\
&= \sigma \cdot \gamma \wedge {}^*\alpha \\
&= \sigma \cdot \alpha \wedge {}^*\gamma \\
&= \sigma(\alpha, \gamma)\Omega; \\
{}^*\alpha \wedge {}^*\beta &= \sigma\alpha \wedge \beta = \sigma^*(\alpha \wedge \beta)\Omega \qquad (12.28)
\end{aligned}
$$

Returning to the general query raised earlier we can say in summary:

$$
\begin{aligned}
&\alpha \in C^{(k)}(M), \qquad \beta \in C^{(\ell)}(M): \\
&k + \ell < n \quad : \quad {}^*\alpha \wedge {}^*\beta \doteq 0; \\
&k + \ell > n \quad : \quad \alpha \wedge \beta = 0; \\
&k + \ell = n \quad : \quad {}^*\alpha \wedge {}^*\beta = \sigma \ {}^*(\alpha \wedge \beta)\Omega. \qquad (12.29)
\end{aligned}
$$

An interesting relation exists only when $k + \ell = n$.

From all this you can get a good feeling for the *algebraic* properties of the Hodge duality operation. Remember always that it is a smooth local operation on M: both a metric and orientability, together giving a special volume form, are needed to set it up.

12.7.   THE CO-DIFFERENTIAL OPERATOR

Now we go on to the idea of the *co-differential*: another kind of differentiation process on forms, depending on both metric and orientation. What we do is combine these assumed extra structures or properties of M with the plain exterior differentiation of forms, the d-operation which M carries on its own. So the co-differential is the non-algebraic but analytic side of Hodge duality. There are some variations in the way different books define the co-differential, though all write δ for it. We adopt the following definition:

$$
\begin{aligned}
\alpha \in C^{(k)}(M) \quad &\Rightarrow \quad {}^*\alpha \in C^{(n-k)}(M) \Rightarrow d^*\alpha \in C^{(n-k+1)}(M) \\
&\Rightarrow \quad {}^*d^*\alpha \in C^{(k-1)}(M); \\
\delta\alpha \quad &\equiv \quad \sigma(-1)^{k(n-k+1)} {}^*d^*\alpha \\
&= \quad \sigma(-1)^{nk} {}^*(d({}^*\alpha)) \in C^{(k-1)}(M). \qquad (12.30)
\end{aligned}
$$

While δ is thus a differentiation process which lowers the order of a form by unity, it unfortunately does *not* possess a derivation or Liebnitz-type property with respect to the wedge product, such as d possesses; this is a consequence of our *algebraic* result found earlier that there is no available way to simplify $^*(\alpha\wedge\beta)$ for general α and β. So one *cannot* work out the effect of δ on a general k-form in a step-by-step manner starting with its effect on something elementary, say on one-forms. For each order k, one has to laboriously apply the definition (12.30) of δ. Here are some useful results following from the fact that the double dual of a form is essentially the same form:

$$
\begin{aligned}
\alpha \in C^{(k)}(M) \quad & : \\
^*\delta\alpha \;&=\; (-1)^{n-k+1} d^*\alpha, \\
\delta^*\alpha \;&=\; (-1)^{n-k}\, {}^*d\alpha, \\
\delta\delta\alpha \;&=\; 0 \qquad\qquad\qquad\qquad\text{(12.31)}
\end{aligned}
$$

We can obtain the effects of δ on functions, one-forms, two-forms in turn by using the duality relations given in eq.(12.22). Omitting all details, we have:

$$
f \in \mathcal{F}(M) \quad : \quad \delta f = 0; \tag{12.32a}
$$

$$
\alpha \;=\; \alpha_\mu(x)dx^\mu \in C^{(1)}(M) : \delta\alpha \in \mathcal{F}(M),
$$

$$
\delta\alpha \;=\; \frac{(-1)^n}{|g|^{1/2}}(|g|^{1/2}\alpha^\mu)_{,\mu}; \tag{12.32b}
$$

$$
\alpha \;=\; \frac{1}{2}\alpha_{\lambda\rho}(x)dx^\lambda \wedge dx^\rho \in C^{(2)}(M) : \delta\alpha \in C^{(1)}(M),
$$

$$
\delta\alpha \;=\; \frac{(-1)^{n-1}}{|g|^{1/2}}(|g|^{1/2}\alpha^{\lambda\rho})_{,\rho}\, g_{\lambda\mu}dx^\mu. \tag{12.32c}
$$

These give you some idea how the co-differential works: result of combining exterior differentiation, (pseudo) Riemannian metric, and orientation. Not hard to conceive of and define, but a bit cumbersome to work out in detail due to absence of a derivation-like property.

12.8.   THE LAPLACIAN ON FORMS

One thing the δ operation gives in a natural way is the notion of the *Laplacian* on forms: basically, in local coordinates, a distinguished second order differential operator. The Laplacian, written Δ, acts thus:

$$
\alpha \in C^{(k)}(M) : \Delta\alpha \equiv (\delta d + d\delta)\alpha \in C^{(k)}(M). \tag{12.33}
$$

One might wonder why both terms are needed here, but an example will show the reason. On functions we have in fact only one of the two terms operative:

$$f \in \mathcal{F}(M) : \Delta f = \delta df$$
$$= \frac{(-1)^n}{|g|^{1/2}} (|g|^{1/2} g^{\mu\nu} f_{,\mu})_{,\nu}. \qquad (12.34)$$

This should be familiar from the way the Klein-Gordon equation gets generalized in Riemannian space-time. Next when we look at one-forms we find using the results in eq.(12.32):

$$\alpha = \alpha_\mu(x) dx^\mu \in C^{(1)}(M) :$$
$$(d\alpha)_{\mu\nu} = \alpha_{\nu,\mu} - \alpha_{\mu,\nu};$$
$$\delta d\alpha = \frac{(-1)^{n-1}}{|g|^{1/2}} \left(|g|^{1/2} g^{\lambda\mu_1} g^{\rho\mu_2} (\alpha_{\mu_2,\mu_1} - \alpha_{\mu_1,\mu_2}) \right)_{,\rho} g_{\lambda\mu} dx^\mu,$$
$$d\delta\alpha = (-1)^n d \left(\frac{1}{|g|^{1/2}} \left(|g|^{1/2} g^{\lambda\mu} \alpha_\lambda \right)_{,\mu} \right). \qquad (12.35)$$

Now in the limit of flat Euclidean space with constant positive definite diagonal metric, these two terms become:

$$\delta d\alpha \rightarrow (-1)^{n-1} (\alpha_{\rho,\lambda\rho} - \alpha_{\lambda,\rho\rho}) dx^\lambda,$$
$$d\delta\alpha \rightarrow (-1)^n d(\alpha_{\rho,\rho}) = (-1)^n \alpha_{\rho,\lambda\rho} dx^\lambda,$$
$$\Delta\alpha \rightarrow (-1)^n \left(\frac{\partial}{\partial x^\rho} \frac{\partial}{\partial x^\rho} \alpha_\lambda \right) dx^\lambda. \qquad (12.36)$$

This indicates why both terms are needed in defining Δ on general k-forms unlike on functions alone.

12.9.   THE HODGE DECOMPOSITION THEOREM

One can relate the properties of δ to a suitable inner product for forms involving an integration over M, produce the positivity (or negativity depending on convention!) of Δ, and so on. We do not pursue these further developments but rest content with having explained the essential starting ideas. We only mention a beautiful theorem. First, some terminology:

$$\alpha \in C^{(k)}(M) \quad : \quad \alpha \text{ co closed} \iff \delta\alpha = 0;$$
$$\alpha \text{ co exact} \iff \alpha = \delta\beta;$$
$$\alpha \text{ harmonic} \iff \Delta\alpha = 0 \qquad (12.37)$$

Then the *Hodge decomposition theorem* says: On a *compact manifold M with no boundary* (this we have yet to explain but we do in Section 16!), *any k-form* α is the *unique* sum of an exact, a co-exact and a harmonic form.

$$\alpha \in C^{(k)}(M) \quad : \quad \alpha = d\beta + \delta\gamma + \alpha_0,$$
$$\beta \in C^{(k-1)}(M), \qquad \gamma \in C^{(k+1)}(M), \Delta\alpha_0 = 0,$$
$$\beta, \gamma, \alpha_0 \quad \text{unique·} \tag{12.38}$$

13. Lie Groups as Differentiable Manifolds

Lie groups are a very pretty example of differentiable manifolds possessing special additional features. They are also an important ingredient in the theory of fibre bundles which we will take up in the next Section. We devote this Section to a brief description of the geometrical aspects of Lie groups.

A Lie group G is simultaneously a differentiable manifold, of some dimension n, and a group, such that the basic group operations are smooth in the manifold sense. We restrict ourselves to the connected component of G containing the identity. The dimension n of the manifold is also called the order of the group. The smoothness of group operations is conveyed in this way: the map

$$G \times G \to G : (g, g') \to g^{-1} g', \ g \text{ and } g' \in G \tag{13.1}$$

from the product manifold $G \times G$ back to G must be smooth. (Actually it is regular). This requirement ensures at once the smoothness of the operation of taking the inverse of a group element:

$$\text{Inversion} : G \to G \ : \ g \to g^{-1}; \tag{13.2}$$

and the product or composition law:

$$\text{Product} : G \times G \to G : (g, g') \to g \, g'· \tag{13.3}$$

13.1. LEFT AND RIGHT TRANSLATIONS, CONJUGATION

The group structure together with the smoothness of these algebraic processes combine to give us *two* sets of diffeomorphisms of G onto itself, *each* giving a faithful realisation of G. The *left translation* diffeomorphisms L_g are set up this way:

$$g \in G \ : \ L_g \text{ is a diffeomorphism } G \to G :$$
$$g' \to L_g(g') = g \, g' \tag{13.4}$$

Clearly all the laws for group realisation are obeyed. Similarly the *right translation* diffeomorphisms are defined as:

$$g \in G \quad : \quad R_g \text{ is a diffeomorphism } G \to G :$$
$$g' \to R_g(g') = g' \, g^{-1}. \tag{13.5}$$

The composition laws read the same in both cases, and the two actions commute:

$$
\begin{aligned}
L_{g'} \circ L_g &= L_{g'g}, \\
R_{g'} \circ R_g &= R_{g'g}, \\
L_{g'} \circ R_g &= R_g \circ L_{g'}.
\end{aligned} \tag{13.6}
$$

Out of these two we easily produce a third action via diffeomorphisms, namely the *action by conjugation* which may not be faithful:

$$
\begin{aligned}
I_g &= L_g \circ R_g : g' \to I_g(g') = g \, g' \, g^{-1}, \\
I_{g'} \circ I_g &= I_{g'g}.
\end{aligned} \tag{13.7}
$$

13.2. RIGHT AND LEFT INVARIANT VECTOR FIELDS, COMMUTATORS, THE LIE ALGEBRA

Now let us look at the space of all vector fields $X \in \mathcal{X}(G)$. If $\varphi : G \to G$ is any diffeomorphism, its pull-back on any tensor on G is determined by eqns.(8.18e, 9.5). In particular the effect on any $X \in \mathcal{X}(G)$ is given by

$$(\varphi^* X)(g)(\alpha) = X(\varphi(g)) \left(\left(\varphi^{-1} \right)^* \alpha \right),$$
$$\alpha \in T_g^* G, \qquad \left(\varphi^{-1} \right)^* \alpha \in T_{\varphi(g)}^* G. \tag{13.8}$$

Suppose we take φ to be one of the right translations R. A vector field X is said to be *right invariant* if under pull-back by every R_g it is unaltered:

$$X \in \mathcal{X}(G) \qquad \text{is right invariant} \iff$$
$$R_g^* X = X, \text{ all } g \in G. \tag{13.9}$$

One then sees on using eqn.(13.8) that for a vector field of this kind, $X(g) \in T_g G$ is algebraically determined at each $g \in G$ by its "value" at the identity $e \in G$:

$$R_g^* X = X \text{ for all } g \iff$$
$$X(g) = \left(R_{g^{-1}*} \right)_e X(e) \in T_g G,$$
$$X(e) \in T_e G. \tag{13.10}$$

One can go one step further and relate such an X at any two points in G as well:

$$(R_{g'*})_g \, X(g) = X\left(g \, g'^{-1}\right). \qquad (13.11)$$

In an entirely similar way, we can define *left invariant* vector fields on G, and show that any such is determined all over G once it is known at the identity:

$$
\begin{aligned}
X \in \mathcal{X}(G) \qquad &\text{is left invariant} \Longleftrightarrow \\
L_g^* X \;=\; & X \text{ for all } g \Longleftrightarrow \\
X(g) \;=\; & (L_{g*})_e \, X(e) \in T_g \, G, \\
X(e) \;\in\; & T_e \, G; \\
(L_{g'*})_g \, X(g) \;=\; & X(g' \, g). \qquad (13.12)
\end{aligned}
$$

Notice, by the way, that both $\left(R_{g^{-1}*}\right)_e$ and $(L_{g*})_e$ carry $T_e \, G$ to $T_g \, G$.

Now let us look at commutators. In general, for any diffeomorphism φ on a manifold M, we know from eqn.(8.19) that

$$
\begin{aligned}
\varphi^*[X,Y] \;=\; & [\varphi^* X, \varphi^* Y], \\
X,Y \;\in\; & \mathcal{X}(M). \qquad (13.13)
\end{aligned}
$$

This immediately means: the commutator of two right-invariant (left-invariant) vector fields on G is again right-invariant (left-invariant).

We can now tie up matters. Notice from eqn.(13.6) that the left and the right translations commute. We also know from our previous work that if we have a one-parameter group of diffeomorphisms $\{\varphi_s\}$ on a manifold M, with generator $X \in \mathcal{X}(M)$; and with a *fixed* diffeomorphism φ we define another one-parameter group $\{\varphi_s'\} = \{\varphi \circ \varphi_s \circ \varphi^{-1}\}$; then the generator of the latter is $X' = (\varphi^{-1})^* \, X = \varphi_* \, X$:

$$
\begin{aligned}
\varphi_{s'} \circ \varphi_s \;=\; & \varphi_{s'+s}, \\
X(f) \;=\; & \frac{d}{ds}\varphi_s^* f \Big|_{s=0}, \quad f \in \mathcal{F}(M); \\
\varphi_s' = \varphi \circ \varphi_s \circ \varphi^{-1} \;:\; & X'(f) = \frac{d}{ds}\varphi_s'^* f \Big|_{s=0} \\
\;=\; & \frac{d}{ds}\left(\varphi \circ \varphi_s \circ \varphi^{-1}\right)^* f \Big|_{s=0} \\
\;=\; & \frac{d}{ds}\varphi^{-1*}\left(\varphi_s^*(\varphi^* f)\right)\Big|_{s=0} \\
\;=\; & \varphi^{-1*}\left(X(\varphi^* f)\right)
\end{aligned}
$$

$$= \left(\varphi^{-1*}X\right)(f),$$

$$X' = \text{generator of } \varphi'_s = \left(\varphi^{-1}\right)^* X. \tag{13.14}$$

So all in all the vector fields generating the one-parameter subgroups of left translations must be right invariant, and vice versa the generators of right translations must be left-invariant! In either case there is only a finite number, n, of such independent vector fields, because in either case the "value" at the identity determines everything. Choose a frame $\{e_a\}$ for $T_e G$. Then a basis for right invariant vector fields is given by

$$X_a^{(\ell)}, \qquad a = 1, \dots, n :$$

$$X_a^{(\ell)}(g) = \left(R_{g^{-1}*}\right)_e (e_a),$$

$$X_a^{(\ell)}(e) = e_a,$$

$$R_g^* X_a^{(\ell)} = X_a^{(\ell)}. \tag{13.15}$$

These are the generators of L_g! Any other right-invariant vector field $X \in \mathcal{X}(G)$ is a *constant* linear combination of these:

$$R_g^* X = X \Longleftrightarrow X = x^a X_a^{(\ell)},$$

$$x^a = \text{constants} \cdot \tag{13.16}$$

And now the commutator of any two of these $X_a^{(\ell)}$ must be a constant linear combination of them again:

$$\left[X_a^{(\ell)}, X_b^{(\ell)}\right] = f_{ab}{}^c X_c^{(\ell)}. \tag{13.17}$$

These coefficients are the *structure constants* of G, subject to the laws

$$f_{ab}{}^c = -f_{ba}{}^c,$$

$$f_{ab}{}^d f_{dc}{}^e + f_{bc}{}^d f_{da}{}^e + f_{ca}{}^d f_{db}{}^e = 0, \tag{13.18}$$

which follow from the antisymmetry and Jacobi property for commutators.

Let us recapitulate. Starting with a basis $\{e_a\}$ for $T_e G$, with the help of the right translations R_g and their tangent maps R_{g*} we get a set of n-independent nowhere vanishing right-invariant vector fields $X_a^{(\ell)}$. In fact since $\{e_a\}$ is a basis, a frame, for $T_e G$, we see that at each g, $\left\{X_a^{(\ell)}(g)\right\}$ gives a basis for $T_g G$! Thus by transporting the frame $\{e_a\}$ at the identity to all points via right translations, we have built up a globally smooth set of frames for all $T_g G$.

We mentioned in Section 7 that for a general differentiable manifold M we cannot be sure that a globally smooth set of frames for all the tangent spaces $T_m M$ exists. This depends on the global properties of M. We see here that in case M is a Lie group, it *is* possible to build up such a smooth set of frames at all points. This is a special property of Lie groups as manifolds; they are said to be *parallelizable*. We shall return to this notion in the next Section.

A general vector field $X \in \mathcal{X}(G)$ is a function-dependent, or better position-dependent, linear combination of the $X_a^{(\ell)}$:

$$X \in \mathcal{X}(G) \quad \Rightarrow \quad X = x^a X_a^{(\ell)},$$
$$x^a \in \mathcal{F}(G);$$
$$T_g G = Sp\left\{X_a^{(\ell)}(g)\right\}, \text{ each } g \in G. \tag{13.19}$$

As stated in eqn.(13.16), the x^a are constants if and only if X is right invariant.

Exactly similar statements can be made, *mutatis mutandis*, for the left-invariant vector fields $X_a^{(r)}$ which generate the right translations R_g:

$$X_a^{(r)}(g) = (L_{g*})_e(-e_a),$$
$$X_a^{(r)}(e) = -e_a;$$
$$L_g^* X_a^{(r)} = X_a^{(r)};$$
$$\left[X_a^{(r)}, X_b^{(r)}\right] = f_{ab}{}^c X_c^{(r)};$$
$$T_g G = Sp\left\{X_a^{(r)}(g)\right\}. \tag{13.20}$$

Since the two families of diffeomorphisms commute, so do their generators:

$$\left[X_a^{(\ell)}, X_b^{(r)}\right] = 0. \tag{13.21}$$

It is in order that the $X_a^{(r)}$ may obey the *same* commutation relations (13.17) as the X_a^ℓ that we have had to use $-e_a$ in eqn.(13.20) at the identity, in contrast to e_a in eqn.(13.15). A brief argument reinforcing this point will be presented shortly.

One now defines the *Lie algebra* $\underline{G}$ of G to be the set of all right-invariant vector fields, or equally well the set of all left-invariant vector fields, or finally and most simply the tangent space $T_e G$ at the identity, a real linear n-dimensional vector space equipped with the Lie bracket operation

$$[e_a, e_b] = f_{ab}{}^c e_c. \tag{13.22}$$

13.3. AN ALTERNATIVE VIEW OF THE GENERATORS

Consider the actions of the left and right translations on a general element in G:

$$
\begin{aligned}
L_g(g') &= g\,g', \\
R_g(g') &= g'\,g^{-1}.
\end{aligned}
\tag{13.23}
$$

In each of $L_g(g')$ and $R_g(g')$ if we keep *one* group element fixed and allow the *other* to vary, the result may be viewed as a definite map of G onto itself. Thus, denoting the variable element by a dot, we have four maps $L.(g)$, $L_g(\cdot)$, $R.(g)$, $R_g(\cdot)$, each "indexed" by g. Let us also bring in the "inversion" map $\mathcal{I}$:

$$
\mathcal{I} : g \in G \to g^{-1} \in G.
\tag{13.24}
$$

Then we easily check the equalities and composition relations

$$
\begin{aligned}
L.(g) &= R_{g^{-1}}(\cdot), \\
R.(g) &= L_g(\cdot) \circ \mathcal{I}
\end{aligned}
\tag{13.25}
$$

The generators $\left(X_a^{(\ell)}\right)$ of the left translations are built up all over G starting from $T_e\,G$ and applying $L.(g)_*$:

$$
\begin{aligned}
X_a^{(\ell)}(g) &= (L.(g)_*)_e\,(e_a) \\
&= \left(R_{g^{-1}*}\right)_e(e_a),
\end{aligned}
\tag{13.26}
$$

where we used the first of eqns.(13.25). We have recovered eqn.(13.15)!

Next let us use a strictly similar procedure to get the generators $X_a^{(r)}$ of the right translations. We now recover eqns.(13.20):

$$
\begin{aligned}
X_a^{(r)}(g) &= (R.(g)_*)_e(e_a) \\
&= ((L_g(\cdot) \circ \mathcal{I})_*)_e\,(e_a) \\
&= (L_{g*})_e \circ (\mathcal{I}_*)_e(e_a) \\
&= (L_{g*})_e\,(-e_a),
\end{aligned}
\tag{13.27}
$$

since, as one can convince oneself, the map $(\mathcal{I}_*)_e$ is just the negative of the identity map. Thus it is the difference in the structures of the two relations in eqns.(13.25) that accounts for the different ways in which the two sets of generators are built up all over G starting from $T_e\,G$

13.4. CONJUGATION, THE ADJOINT REPRESENTATION AND FURTHER RELATIONS

Action by conjugation was defined in eqn.(13.7). Since it is the product of commuting factors, its generators are the sums of the commuting sets $X_a^{(\ell)}$, $X_a^{(r)}$:

$$\text{Generators of } I_g : X_a = X_a^{(\ell)} + X_a^{(r)} \in \mathcal{X}(G). \qquad (13.28)$$

By taking the tangent map that follows from the definition of I_g, several useful results follow. To begin with, eqn.(13.7) gives:

$$\begin{aligned}(I_{g*})_{g'} &= (L_{g*})_{g'g^{-1}} \circ (R_{g*})_{g'} \\ &= (R_{g*})_{gg'} \circ (L_{g*})_{g'} : T_{g'}G \to T_{gg'g^{-1}} G. \end{aligned} \qquad (13.29)$$

Setting $g' = e$ here we see that $(I_{g*})_e$ is a g-dependent map of $T_e G$ onto itself. Thus its action on each member of the basis $\{e_a\}$ is expressible as a g-dependent linear combination of e_b:

$$(I_{g*})_e \, e_a = \mathcal{D}^b{}_a \, (g) \, e_b. \qquad (13.30)$$

From the composition law

$$(I_{g'*})_e \circ (I_{g*})_e = (I_{g'g*})_e \qquad (13.31)$$

follows the representation property of the matrices $\mathcal{D}(g)$:

$$\mathcal{D}(g') \, \mathcal{D}(g) = \mathcal{D}(g'g). \qquad (13.32)$$

This is called the *adjoint representation* of the Lie group G. Here superscripts (subscripts) on $\mathcal{D}(g)$ function as row (column) indices.

We can exploit the relations (13.29,30) in other ways to derive useful transformation laws for the vector fields $X_a^{(\ell)}$ and $X_a^{(r)}$. Start from

$$(L_{g*})_{g^{-1}} \circ (R_{g*})_e \, e_a = \mathcal{D}^b{}_a \, (g) \, e_b \qquad (13.33)$$

and use (13.26) to write it as

$$(L_{g*})_{g^{-1}} X_a^{(\ell)} \left(g^{-1} \right) = \mathcal{D}^b{}_a \, (g) \, e_b \qquad (13.34)$$

Now apply $(R_{g'*})_e$ to both sides, use (13.26) again, and the commutativity of the L's and the R's as well as the right invariance of the $X_a^{(\ell)}$:

$$\mathcal{D}^b{}_a(g)X_b^{(\ell)}\left(g'^{-1}\right) = (R_{g'*})_e \circ (L_{g*})_{g^{-1}}X_a^{(\ell)}\left(g^{-1}\right)$$

$$= \left((R_{g'} \circ L_g)_*\right)_{g^{-1}}X_a^{(\ell)}\left(g^{-1}\right)$$

$$= \left((L_g \circ R_{g'})_*\right)_{g^{-1}}X_a^{(\ell)}\left(g^{-1}\right)$$

$$= (L_{g*})_{g^{-1}g'^{-1}} \circ (R_{g'*})_{g^{-1}}X_a^{(\ell)}\left(g^{-1}\right)$$

$$= (L_{g*})_{g^{-1}g'^{-1}}X_a^{(\ell)}\left(g^{-1}g'^{-1}\right),$$

$$\text{ie., } L_{g^{-1}}^* X_a^{(\ell)} = \mathcal{D}^b{}_a(g)X_b^{(\ell)}. \tag{13.35}$$

Thus while the left translation generators are right invariant, under "their own" translations they change according to the matrices of the adjoint representation!

In an exactly similar manner, by manipulating the second form of eqn.(13.29) we can derive

$$R_{g^{-1}}^* X_a^{(r)} = \mathcal{D}^b{}_a(g)X_b^{(r)}, \tag{13.36}$$

as a companion to (13.35).

Combining invariance under one translation with adjoint behaviour under the other gives behaviour under conjugation. We can collectively display all these properties thus:

$$L_g^*\left(X_a^{(\ell)},X_a^{(r)}\right) = \left(\mathcal{D}^b{}_a\left(g^{-1}\right)X_b^{(\ell)},X_a^{(r)}\right),$$

$$R_g^*\left(X_a^{(\ell)},X_a^{(r)}\right) = \left(X_a^{(\ell)},\mathcal{D}^b{}_a\left(g^{-1}\right)X_b^{(r)}\right),$$

$$I_g^*\left(X_a^{(\ell)},X_a^{(r)}\right) = \left(\mathcal{D}^b{}_a\left(g^{-1}\right)X_b^{(\ell)},\mathcal{D}^b{}_a\left(g^{-1}\right)X_b^{(r)}\right) \tag{13.37}$$

Lastly we can relate the two bases $\left\{X_a^{(\ell)}(g)\right\},\left\{X_a^{(r)}(g)\right\}$ for $T_g\,G$ at each g; here too the adjoint representation comes in:

$$X_a^{(\ell)}(g) = \left(R_{g^{-1}*}\right)_e e_a$$

$$= \left(\left(L_g \circ I_{g^{-1}}\right)_*\right)_e e_a$$

$$= (L_{g*})_e \circ \left(I_{g^{-1}*}\right)_e e_a$$

$$= (L_{g*})_e \mathcal{D}^b{}_a\left(g^{-1}\right)e_b$$

$$= -\mathcal{D}^b{}_a\left(g^{-1}\right)X_b^{(r)}(g) \tag{13.38}$$

13.5. THE MAURER-CARTAN FORMS AND RELATIONS

We arrived at the Lie algebra $\underline{G}$ of G by considering right (and left) invariant vector fields on G and their commutators. An entirely equivalent description exists using forms instead. Let us restrict ourselves to right-invariant forms. Since the $X_a^{(\ell)}$ give a global set of frames all over G, we can define a dual global set of one-forms $\theta^{(\ell)a}$ by setting at each g:

$$< \theta^{(\ell)a}(g), X_b^{(\ell)}(g) > = \delta_b^a. \tag{13.39}$$

Clearly these forms share the right-invariance of $X_a^{(\ell)}$, and each $\theta^{(\ell)a}$ is built up all over G by starting with the dual frame $\{e^a\}$ for $T_e^* G$:

$$\theta^{(\ell)a}(g) = R_g^* e^a \in T_g^* G.$$
$$< \theta^{(\ell)a}(g), X > = < e^a, (R_{g*})_g X > \text{ for } X \in T_g G,$$
$$R_g^* \theta^{(\ell)a} = \theta^{(\ell)a}. \tag{13.40}$$

Thus the right-invariant one-forms $\theta^{(\ell)a}$ give a global basis for all one-forms on G, a general right-invariant one being a constant linear combination of them.

And now, with the help of the general formula (9.40), we can express the content of the commutation relations (13.17) in this way:

$$\left(d\theta^{(\ell)a}\right)\left(X_b^{(\ell)}, X_c^{(\ell)}\right) = X_b^{(\ell)}(\delta_c^a) - X_c^{(\ell)}(\delta_b^a) - \theta^{(\ell)a}\left(\left[X_b^{(\ell)}, X_c^{(\ell)}\right]\right)$$

$$= -f_{bc}{}^d \delta^a{}_d$$

$$= -\frac{1}{2}f_{b'c'}{}^a \left(\delta_b^{b'}\delta_c^{c'} - \delta_c^{b'}\delta_b^{c'}\right)$$

$$= -\frac{1}{2}f_{b'c'}{}^a \left(\theta^{(\ell)b'} \wedge \theta^{(\ell)c'}\right)\left(X_b^{(\ell)}, X_c^{(\ell)}\right),$$

$$d\theta^{(\ell)a} + \frac{1}{2}f_{bc}{}^a \theta^{(\ell)b} \wedge \theta^{(\ell)c} = 0 \tag{13.41}$$

These are called the *Maurer-Cartan equations* for the Lie group G. They convey the local structure of G as well as do the vector field commutation relations (13.17): the two are precisely equivalent.

One can convey the content of these Maurer-Cartan equations even more compactly by the following device. We have so far dealt with the one-forms $\theta^{(\ell)a}$: they are real number valued one-forms, in that the result of evaluating any one of them on any vector is a number. We can define Lie-algebra valued one-forms as well. For this, go back to a general differentiable manifold M, and let $\underline{G}$ be the Lie algebra of some Lie group G, taken for definiteness to be "realised" as the tangent space T_e G.$\underline{G}$-valued forms on M are expressions of the form

$$\alpha = \alpha^a e_a, \quad \alpha^a \in C^{(k)}(M), \tag{13.42}$$

namely formal linear combinations of the basis elements e_a of $\underline{G}$, with the coefficients α^a being "ordinary" number-valued forms (of some common degree k) on M. Now among the coefficients we have the wedge product, and among the e_a the Lie bracket. Putting the two together we define a bracket for $\underline{G}$-valued forms in this way:

$$\begin{aligned} \alpha = \alpha^a e_a, \qquad \beta &= \beta^a e_a \longrightarrow \\ [\alpha, \beta] &= \alpha^a \wedge \beta^b [e_a, e_b] \\ &= f_{ab}{}^c \, \alpha^a \wedge \beta^b e_c \end{aligned} \tag{13.43}$$

If α and β are $\underline{G}$-valued k- and ℓ- forms respectively, then $[\alpha, \beta]$ is a $\underline{G}$-valued $(k + \ell)$-form.

Now go back to the case of a Lie group and take $M = G$. We combine all the right-invariant "number-valued" one-forms $\theta^{(\ell)a}$ to define the Maurer-Cartan Lie-algebra valued one-form ω_0 on G as

$$\omega_0 = \theta^{(\ell)a} e_a. \tag{13.44}$$

And in terms of it the n Maurer-Cartan equations (13.41) appear as the single Lie-algebra valued equation

$$d\omega_0 + \frac{1}{2}[\omega_0, \omega_0] = 0 \tag{13.45}$$

Very compact and elegant, but all the content is hidden in the definitions!

13.6. THE EXPONENTIAL MAP $\underline{G} \to G$

In passing we describe briefly some aspects of the exponential mapping by which one goes from $\underline{G}$ to (a suitable neighbourhood of the identity e in) G. The task of proving the statements to be made is left to the interested reader.

For any tangent vector $t \in T_e G = \underline{G}$ with components t^a, we have both a right-invariant vector field $X_t^{(\ell)}$ defined all over G:

$$\begin{aligned} X_t^{(\ell)} &= t^a X_a^{(\ell)}, \\ X_t^{(\ell)}(e) &= t, \end{aligned} \tag{13.46}$$

and a left-invariant vector field $X_t^{(r)}$ likewise defined all over G:

$$X_t^{(r)} = -t^a X_a^{(r)} .$$
$$X_t^{(r)}(e) = t.$$

(13.47)

These two vector fields are defined to share the same "value" at e, but generally differ elsewhere. Using each of them in turn, by exponentiation in the manner described in Section 11, we build up one-parameter groups of diffeomorphisms of G onto itself. It is not hard to guess that by exponentiating $X_t^{(\ell)}$ we in fact get one of the L_g, ie., a left translation on G; and by exponentiating $X_t^{(r)}$ we build up a right translation $R_{g'}$. (To be more precise, we get one-parameter subgroups of these respective translations). The content of the exponential mapping from $\underline{G}$ to G is then contained in these statements:

$$\exp\left(sX_t^{(\ell)}\right) = L_{\exp(st)},$$
$$\exp\left(sX_t^{(r)}\right) = R_{\exp(-st)},$$
$$\exp(st) = (\exp(-st))^{-1}$$
$$= \left(\exp\left(sX_t^{(\ell)}\right)\right)(e)$$
$$= \left(\exp\left(sX_t^{(r)}\right)\right)(e) \in G.$$

(13.48)

In words: for any $t \in T_e G = \underline{G}$, $\exp(t)$ is the element of G we reach at parameter value unity, by starting at the identity $e \in G$ and following the integral curve of the right-invariant vector field $X_t^{(\ell)}$. It is also the element at parameter value unity, of the integral curve of the left-invariant vector field $X_t^{(r)}$ starting out at e. In fact, if the starting point is the identity element, both $X_t^{(\ell)}$ and $X_t^{(r)}$ lead to the *same* integral curve, and elements on that curve form the one-parameter subgroup $\{\exp(st)\}$ in G!

13.7.   ACTION OF A LIE GROUP ON A DIFFERENTIABLE MANIFOLD

So much for the basic differential geometric machinery associated with a Lie group. In case the group G is semisimple, we could go further and define a metric on it and pursue further developments, but we do not do so here. Instead we recall briefly some terminology associated with a smooth action of a Lie group G on a manifold M.

In Section 3 we described in a preliminary way the action of a group on a set and introduced some definitions. Now we specialise to the case of a Lie group G acting through diffeomorphisms on a differentiable manifold

M. This means that for each $g \in G$, we have a diffeomorphism ψ_g of M onto itself, satisfying the standard composition laws:

$$\psi_{g'} \circ \psi_g = \psi_{g'g},$$
$$\psi_e = \mathcal{I}d_M. \qquad (13.49)$$

Then one says that M is a G-space. In this context, the stability group at any point $m \in M$ is a *closed* subgroup $H(m)$ in G, and the orbit $\vartheta(m)$ of m is a *closed* submanifold in M. There are some technical niceties here which we do not go into.

If the action of G on M is transitive, then M is called a *homogeneous space*: in that case it is essentially the coset space G/H where H is a *closed* subgroup in G, the stability group of some point in M. If the action is free, ie., the stability groups $H(m)$ are all trivial, then M is called a *principal space*. Gathering these various terms, we have:

G acts on M by diffeomorphisms $-$ M is a $G-$ space;

  Action is transitive $-$ M is a homogeneous G $-$ space,

  a coset space G/H;

  Action is free $-$ M is a principal G $-$ space $\cdot$

$$(13.50)$$

In any such smooth G action on M, $\underline{G}$ gets realized by a set of smooth vector fields on M. The idea is quite simple. Within G, via the exponential map we have a one-parameter group of elements corresponding to each vector $t \in \underline{G}$:

$$t \in T_e\, G = \underline{G} \;\; : \;\; \exp(st)\,\exp(s't) = \exp((s+s')t) \in G,$$
$$s,\, s' \in \mathcal{R}\cdot \qquad (13.51)$$

Then the diffeomorphisms ψ_g on M representing these elements form a one-parameter group of diffeomorphisms, so they define a vector field on M:

$$\psi_{\exp(st)} = \exp(sX_t), \quad X_t \in \mathcal{X}(M);$$
$$X_t(f) = \frac{d}{ds}\psi_{\exp(st)}{}^* f\Big|_{s=0}, \quad f \in \mathcal{F}(M)\cdot \qquad (13.52)$$

(Here we have no left and right actions of G on M, just the *given* action by ψ_g. Even if M were G itself, we would have to take ψ_g to be a *specific* action!). Thus, corresponding to a basis $\{e_a\}$ for $\underline{G}$, we have n vector fields

$X_a \in \mathcal{X}(M)$ which generate ψ_g upon exponentiation, and which obey the commutation relations for $\underline{G}$:

$$e_a \in \underline{G} \longrightarrow X_a \in \mathcal{X}(M):$$
$$[X_a, X_b] = f_{ab}{}^c X_c. \qquad (13.53)$$

In an intuitively clear sense one can say that at any $m \in M$, the vectors $X_a(m)$ span a subspace of $T_m M$ tangent to the orbit $\vartheta(m)$.

There is another way to "read" the diffeomorphisms ψ_g which is sometimes useful. In the relation

$$\psi_g(m) = m', \qquad (13.54)$$

we can keep m fixed and allow g to vary all over G. Then m' also varies, and we have a map $\psi.(m) : G \to M$, indexed by m. The domain of $\psi.(m)$ is G, the range is the orbit $\vartheta(m) \subset M$. Then we obtain $X_a(m) \in T_m M$ by applying the tangent map:

$$(\psi.(m)_*)_e : T_e G \to T_m M;$$
$$(\psi.(m)_*)_e (e_a) = X_a(m). \qquad (13.55)$$

This procedure can be applied, when $M = G$, to L_g and R_g as well. This is exactly what we did in eqns.(13.23-27)!

14. The Bundle Concept - Fibre, Principal, Associated and Vector Bundles

We now take up a study of the general idea of a bundle, and the kinds of bundles indicated in the title. When we initially defined the notion of a differentiable manifold, we noted briefly that in an obvious and natural way the Cartesian product of two such manifolds is again such a manifold. The fibre bundle idea allows us to construct new "product" manifolds from given ones in a nontrivial and richer way, differing from the plain Cartesian product. We may say we have a way of forming a "twisted product". In the new process, it is as though locally we are dealing with an ordinary product of manifolds, but globally it need not be so; we leave room for a twist or two to be thrown in! Here different authors work their way up to the main concept of a principal fibre bundle in different ways. We shall follow a particular route which may differ in detail from some of the references.

We need to limit ourselves in the choice of concepts to cover, and yet this Section will be rather long. We shall try to give qualitative descriptions of the main constructions, to convey the motivating ideas. We may also mention in a general way that several notions relating to fibre bundles and principal fibre bundles are generalisations of corresponding notions familiar from group theory on the one hand, and manifold theory on the other.

14.1.   THE BUNDLE CONCEPT

Let us begin by defining a plain *bundle*. By this we mean a collection of three objects, a triple (E, π, M): E and M are topological spaces, and $\pi : E \to M$ a continuous onto map. We call E the *total space*, M the *base space*, and π the *projection*. For each $m \in M$ we say that $\pi^{-1}(m)$, the part of E that projects onto m, is the "fibre" sitting on top of the point m in the base. There is however no implication here that each fibre is a one-dimensional object!

We emphasize that it would not be correct to picture the base M as situated somewhere inside, or embedded within, the total space E. Rather, they must be viewed as separate objects, with π going from E to M.

In a general bundle, the fibres $\pi^{-1}(m)$ on top of different base points m need not be similar to one another in any way. If however they all are, we arrive at the concept of a Fibre Bundle. Here at the same time we sharpen our conditions on E and M and require that they be differentiable manifolds.

14.2.   FIBRE BUNDLES

A *fibre bundle* - hereafter FB - is a collection of the following four objects with indicated properties: a differentiable manifold E, the total space; another differentiable manifold M, the base space; a smooth onto projection map $\pi : E \to M$ (which will be seen to be regular); and a differentiable manifold F called the *typical fibre*. The triple (E, π, M) is already a bundle. The additional properties involve F. For each point $m \in M$, there must be an open set $\mathcal{U} \subset M$ containing m, and a diffeomorphism $h : \mathcal{U} \times F \to \pi^{-1}(\mathcal{U})$ such that the composite map $\pi \circ h$ is trivial on the first factor:

$$m \in M \to m \in \mathcal{U} \subset M, \; h : \mathcal{U} \times F \to \pi^{-1}(\mathcal{U}) \text{ a diffeomorphism,}$$
$$\pi(h(m,q)) = m \in \mathcal{U},$$
$$\text{ie., } h(m,q) \in \pi^{-1}(m), \text{ any } q \in F. \tag{14.1}$$

Note that no charts are involved in this set-up.

Let us say in words what is being demanded. Given any point $m \in M$, we are demanding that over a suitable neighbourhood $\mathcal{U}$ of it, if we look at the portion $\pi^{-1}(\mathcal{U})$ of the total space sitting on top of $\mathcal{U}$ (all the fibres on top of all points in $\mathcal{U}$), it must "look like" the ordinary Cartesian product of $\mathcal{U}$ with the typical fibre F. Since π is smooth, $\pi^{-1}(\mathcal{U})$ is an open set in

E. This property of $\pi^{-1}(\mathcal{U})$ "looking like" $\mathcal{U} \times F$ is to be accomplished by a *diffeomorphism* h from $\mathcal{U} \times F$ to $\pi^{-1}(\mathcal{U})$. So by using h^{-1}, any point $e \in \pi^{-1}(\mathcal{U})$ can be uniquely described by, or pictured as, a *pair* $(m, q) : m = \pi(e)$ is the base point "below" e, and $q \in F$ is a suitable point in the typical fibre F. Continuing the notation of eqn.(14.1) we say:

$$e \in \pi^{-1}(\mathcal{U}), \qquad \pi(e) = m \in \mathcal{U} \subset M \Rightarrow$$
$$e = h(m, q), \quad q \in F \text{ unique.} \qquad (14.2)$$

Thus each sufficiently small portion of the total space E (some collection of entire fibres) looks like the Cartesian product of the corresponding portion of the base, with F. But as a whole this need not be so! The requirements expressed in eqns.(14.1,2) are that it should be possible to *locally trivialize* the total space E into a product structure, but not necessarily globally.

Given base M and fibre F, one trivial way to combine them to get an FB is to take E to be their Cartesian product $M \times F$, and π the projection onto the first factor. But the set-up above allows other possibilities!

We see that we have gone beyond the plain bundle idea: each fibre $\pi^{-1}(m)$ looks like the typical fibre F, so they also all look like one another.

With all these ingredients we say that "E is an F-bundle over M". As manifolds, the dimension of E is the sum of those of M and F. With the help of the local trivializations we see immediately that π is regular: at each $e \in E$, $(\pi_*)_e$ has maximal rank, namely the dimension of M.

We have assumed that like E and M, the typical fibre F is also a differentiable manifold. In some simple cases it is necessary to relax this and allow F to be a finite or a discrete set. Then the previous discussion must be suitably modified. For the most part, though, we do assume that F is a differentiable manifold.

14.3.   SECTIONS IN A FIBRE BUNDLE

A *section* in a $F B$ (E, π, M, F) is a smooth map $\sigma : M \to E$ such that $\pi \circ \sigma$ reduces to the identity on M. For each $m \in M$, we need to choose a point $\sigma(m) \in \pi^{-1}(m)$, "sitting somewhere" in the fibre on top of m, and varying smoothly as m varies:

$$\sigma : M \to E : m \to \sigma(m) \in \pi^{-1}(m). \qquad (14.3)$$

If σ is defined all over M, we have a *global section*. On the other hand, if σ is defined only over some open set $\mathcal{U} \subset M$, then we have a *local section*.

14.4.   MORPHISMS AND ISOMORPHISMS AMONG FB'S

It is natural to say, as we did, that a FB is trivial if the total space E is simply the Cartesian product of the base M and the typical fibre F. More generally it would be appropriate to say that we have a trivial FB if it is "essentially the same" as the product bundle. What precise meaning should we give to this notion?

Let us for a moment go back to the situations with groups and manifolds. As we know, two groups G and G' are "essentially the same" if there is an isomorphism $f : G \rightarrow G'$. This is an injective and surjective - one to one and onto - map which respects the two group composition laws. An isomorphism is a particular case of a homomorphism : a map from G to G', not necessarily one to one and onto, such that "the image of the product is the product of the images". Similarly with differentiable manifolds we have the two notions of smooth maps (like homomorphisms between groups) and diffeomorphisms (like isomorphisms between groups). Two manifolds are "essentially the same" if there is a diffeomorphism connecting them. What we need is to set up corresponding relationships among FB's, and give them nice names.

Given two FB's (E, π, M, F) and (E', π', M', F'), a *bundle morphism* from the former to the latter is a pair of smooth maps $u : E \rightarrow E'$ and $f : M \rightarrow M'$ such that u carries all points on one fibre in E to points on one fibre in E':

$$(E, \pi, M, F) \xrightarrow{(u,f)} (E', \pi', M', F') :$$
$$\pi' \circ u = f \circ \pi. \tag{14.4}$$

We say that the map $u : E \rightarrow E'$ is *fibre-preserving*, and this is what the above condition ensures:

$$e_1, e_2 \in E, \qquad \pi(e_1) = \pi(e_2) \Rightarrow$$
$$\pi'(u(e_1)) = f(\pi(e_1)) = f(\pi(e_2)) = \pi'(u(e_2)). \tag{14.5}$$

This is indicated in the following "commutative diagram": We must bear

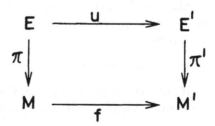

Figure 8. The commutative diagram for a morphism between two fibre bundles

in mind, however, that $u(E)$ may not include all fibres in E', and may not also include entire fibres in E' : $u(E)$ need only consist of parts of some fibres in E'. To stress again just what we are demanding:

$$u \text{ (each entire fibre in } E) \subset \text{ some corresponding single fibre in } E'. \quad (14.6)$$

We do not require identity of the typical fibres F, F' or a fixed map from F to F'.

Such a bundle morphism is the FB analogue of group homomorphisms and smooth maps between manifolds. We must appreciate that the map f in the pair (u, f) is determined by u and cannot be chosen independently! For, given a fibre-preserving u : for each $m \in M$ choose *any* $e \in \pi^{-1}(m)$; then $f(m)$ is determined by the effect of u on e:

$$f(m) = f(\pi(e)) = \pi'(u(e)) \in M'. \quad (14.7)$$

This means that in order to set up a bundle morphism (u, f) between two FB's it is enough to specify the fibre preserving map u, and then f follows. We need only ensure that f is smooth.

Successive bundle morphisms can be composed in sequence to give new bundle morphisms. This is like composition of group homomorphisms, or maps between manifolds.

A *bundle isomorphism* between two FB's is but one step away. We need bundle morphisms both ways, inverse to each other:

$$(E, \pi, M, F) \xrightarrow{(u,f)} (E', \pi', M', F') \xrightarrow{(u',f')} (E, \pi, M, F) :$$
$$u' \circ u = \mathcal{I}d_E, \qquad u \circ u' = \mathcal{I}d_{E'},$$
$$f' \circ f = \mathcal{I}d_M, \qquad f \circ f' = \mathcal{I}d_{M'}. \quad (14.8)$$

Then the two FB's are "essentially the same". So here both u and f are one to one onto maps. And we can say in a more sophisticated way than before: a fibre bundle is trivial if it is bundle isomorphic to the product of the base by the typical fibre.

14.5. PULLBACK OF A FB - INDUCED FB

The important pull-back operation associated with maps between manifolds - working on functions and forms in the reverse direction - generalises very nicely to the FB context. Let (E, π, M, F) be a given FB, and let $\varphi : M' \to M$ be a smooth map from some differentiable manifold M' into the base space M. Then one can "pull back" the bundle in hand to create a new one with M' as base:

$$\varphi^*(E, \pi, M, F) = (E', \pi', M', F') = \text{new } FB. \quad (14.9)$$

We need to spell out how E', π', F' are constructed. The new total space E' is defined to be a carefully chosen subset of the Cartesian product of the new base M' with the old total space E:

$$E' = \left\{(m',e)|m' \in M', \, e \in \pi^{-1}(\varphi(m')) \subset E\right\} \subset M' \times E. \quad (14.10)$$

The new projection π' works in the obvious way:

$$(m',e) \in E' : \pi'((m',e)) = m' \in M'. \quad (14.11)$$

The new fibre $\pi'^{-1}(m')$ on top of any $m' \in M'$ consists of all pairs (m',e) with m' fixed and e running all over the old fibre $\pi^{-1}(\varphi(m'))$:

$$m' \in M' : \pi'^{-1}(m') = \left\{(m',e)|m' \text{ fixed}, \, e \in \pi^{-1}(\varphi(m'))\right\}. \quad (14.12)$$

This means really that we take the fibre in E on top of the base point $\varphi(m')$ and "pull it back and attach it" to $m' \in M'$! Thus the new typical fibre F' is the same as the old one, F.

In general, $\varphi(M') \subset M$. For each $m' \in M'$, we get a well-defined unique fibre on top of it. We may say loosely that $\pi'^{-1}(m') \simeq \pi^{-1}(\varphi(m'))$: they are not *really* the same but are *morally* so! In this sense, if two points $m'_1, m'_2 \in M'$ have a common image $\varphi(m'_1) = \varphi(m'_2) = m \in M$, they end up having the "same" fibre $\pi^{-1}(m)$ stuck on top of each of them. The tasks of establishing the manifold structure of E', local trivializations etc. are left to the reader.

This FB (E', π', M', F') obtained from (E, π, M, F) by pull back φ^* is also called the *induced bundle*, induced by φ. Successive pull backs work as with maps between manifolds:

$$\begin{aligned}
\varphi : M' \to M &\Rightarrow (E',\pi',M',F') &=& \quad \varphi^*(E,\pi,M,F); \\
\varphi' : M'' \to M' &\Rightarrow (E'',\pi'',M'',F'') &=& \quad \varphi'^*(E',\pi',M',F'); \\
\varphi \circ \varphi' : M'' \to M &\Rightarrow (E'',\pi'',M'',F'') &=& \quad \varphi'^*(\varphi^*(E,\pi,M,F)), \\
&(\varphi \circ \varphi')^* &=& \quad \varphi'^* \circ \varphi^*. \quad (14.13)
\end{aligned}$$

A section σ in the FB (E, π, M, F), local or global, can be subjected to the pull-back operation, and leads to a section σ' in $\varphi^*(E, \pi, M, F)$:

$$\sigma' = \varphi^*\sigma : m' \in M' \to \sigma'(m') = (m',\sigma(\varphi(m'))) \subset \pi'^{-1}(m'). \quad (14.14)$$

14.6. SUBBUNDLE IN, RESTRICTION OF, A FB

With groups and manifolds we have the subgroup and submanifold notions - in each case a part of the whole having the essential properties of the whole. For FB's the corresponding concept is that of a *sub bundle*, or a *restriction* of the given bundle. The FB (E', π', M', F') is a subbundle of (E, π, M, F) if E' is a submanifold of E containing complete fibres in E. More precisely:

$$
\begin{aligned}
(E',\pi',M',F') &= \text{subbundle of } (E,\pi,M,F) \Rightarrow \\
M' &= \text{submanifold in } M, \\
E' &= \text{submanifold in } E = \pi^{-1}(M'), \\
\pi' &= \pi \text{ restricted to } E' = \pi|_{E'}, \\
F' &= F.
\end{aligned}
\tag{14.15}
$$

To *restrict* a given FB (E, π, M, F) is to take a submanifold $M' \subset M$, and "by hand" define $E' = \pi^{-1}(M')$, $\pi' = \pi|_{E'}$:

$$
\begin{aligned}
M' &= \text{submanifold in } M: \\
\left(\pi^{-1}(M'), \pi|_{\pi^{-1}(M')}, M', F \right) &= \text{restriction of } (E, \pi, M, F) \\
&= \text{subbundle of } (E, \pi, M, F).
\end{aligned}
\tag{14.16}
$$

So a subbundle and a restriction of a FB are one and the same: we limit ourselves to a submanifold in the base, and take all and only the corresponding fibres to make up the new FB.

Formally the subbundle concept is a particular case of the pull back operation. Given a submanifold $M' \subset M$, we denote by $i_{M'}$ the "identification map" written as a hooked arrow:

$$
i_{M'} : M' \hookrightarrow M.
\tag{14.17}
$$

In a sense we pull M' out of M, look at it on its own, and then put it back where it was to begin with! Then the subbundle built up on M', and the pull back via $i_{M'}^*$, coincide:

$$
\left(\pi^{-1}(M'), \pi|_{\pi^{-1}(M')}, M', F \right) = i_{M'}^*(E, \pi, M, F).
\tag{14.18}
$$

Summarising the various operations with FB's: in a bundle morphism no map or connection between the typical fibres is demanded. With both pull back and sub bundle constructions the typical fibre remains the same, and we end up with a new FB, the base having been altered.

14.7. PRINCIPAL FIBRE BUNDLES

In our build-up of concepts we move on next to that of a *Principal Fibre Bundle* - hereafter PFB. For this more inputs and structures are required. At the FB level, no group was involved in any essential

way. Now we bring in a Lie group in two crucial roles: it functions as the
typical fibre, and also acts on the total space in a specific manner.

We shall now write P rather than E for the total space; and p, p',...
rather than e, e',... for points in P. We require for a start that the typical
fibre F be a Lie group G. Then we ask for the following properties *in
addition to* those that are needed to make P a FB over M:

(i) The group G must act *freely* on the total space P via
          diffeomorphisms $\psi_g : g \in G$, $p \in P \Rightarrow p' = \psi_g(p) \in P$,
          $$\psi_e = \mathcal{I}d_P,$$
          $$\psi_{g'} \circ \psi_g = \psi_{g'g},$$
          $$g \neq e \Leftrightarrow p' \neq p. \tag{14.19a}$$

Here e is the identity element in $G \cdot$ So for each $p \in P$, the stability
subgroup $H(p)$ (see eqn.(3.2)) is trivial $\cdot$

(ii) This G action must preserve each fibre, it should just
          produce *motions* or *translations* along fibres :
          $$\pi \circ \psi_g = \pi,$$
          ie., $\pi(\psi_g(p)) = \pi(p)$, $g \in G$, $p \in P \cdot$ $\tag{14.19b}$

(iii) The action of G on each fibre must be *transitive* $\cdot$
          p, $p' \in P$, $\pi(p) = \pi(p') \Rightarrow p' = \psi_g(p)$, some $g \in G \cdot$ $\tag{14.19c}$
          Then because the action is free, by eqn.(14.19a), this g is also
          unique $\cdot$

(iv) With respect to the local trivializations $h : \mathcal{U} \times G \to \pi^{-1}(\mathcal{U}) \subset P$
          that come with the FB (P, π, M, G), the free G action (14.19a)
          must appear as a right translation on the G factor :
          $$\psi_{g'}(h(m,g)) = h\left(m, g\,g'^{-1}\right),$$
          $$m \in \mathcal{U} \subset M, \qquad g, g' \in G \cdot \tag{14.19d}$$

If the FB (P, π, M, G) has all these additional properties, we say P
is a PFB over the base M with structure group and typical fibre G.

Sometimes in the interest of compactness the symbol ψ_g for G action
on P is omitted; one just says that $g \in G$ maps $p \in P$ to $p\,g^{-1} \in P$.
This is consistent with eqn.(14.19d). With familiarity one can switch to this
simpler notation.

We must note that the action of G on P is global. It is even stated
without any reference to local trivializations. With respect to the latter, we
only demand that on each fibre this global action appear in a simple manner

as a *right translation* of the kind we studied in Section 13. Clearly this is a convention. We mention this here only because we will soon encounter a different manner of action by G, a *local* action *on the left*, which must be carefully distinguished from the one so far discussed.

For a PFB the definitions of triviality and of local and global sections are the same as for any FB. As we will see, however, in the case of a PFB the existence of a global section implies triviality of the bundle!

14.8.   TRANSITION FUNCTIONS IN A PFB

Now let us be given a PFB and let us examine its local structure a little more closely. Let $\mathcal{U},\mathcal{U}'$ be two overlapping open sets in the base M, and let $\pi^{-1}(\mathcal{U})$ and $\pi^{-1}(\mathcal{U}')$ be trivialized by diffeomorphisms h and h' respectively to look like the products $\mathcal{U} \times G$ and $\mathcal{U}' \times G$:

$$p \in \pi^{-1}(\mathcal{U}) \cap \pi^{-1}(\mathcal{U}') \;\Rightarrow\; \pi(p) = m \in \mathcal{U} \cap \mathcal{U}',$$
$$p = h(m,g) \;=\; h'(m,g') \tag{14.20}$$

Here it must happen that as g varies all over G, and so p moves all over the fibre $\pi^{-1}(m)$, g' also varies all over G. But $(m, h$ and h' being given) g' must always be determined by m and g. We can now pin down the form of such dependence. For any $g'' \in G$, we consider $\psi_{g''}$ acting on p in accordance with eqn.(14.19d) and get:

$$\psi_{g''}(p) = h\left(m,\; g\, g''^{-1}\right) = h'\left(m,\; g'\, g''^{-1}\right). \tag{14.21}$$

This relation must hold for all g''. For a start set $g'' = g$ to get:

$$h(m,\; e) = h'\left(m,\; g'\, g^{-1}\right), \tag{14.22}$$

where we know that g' depends on m and g. Since m alone appears on the left, for each $m \in \mathcal{U} \cap \mathcal{U}'$ there *must be* an element $t(m) \in G$ such that

$$h(m,\; e) = h'(m,\; t(m)). \tag{14.23}$$

We can now apply ψ_g, for any $g \in G$, to both sides and invoke (14.19d) to get

$$h(m,\; g) = h'(m,\; t(m)g). \tag{14.24}$$

In words: the two local trivializations over $\mathcal{U}$ and $\mathcal{U}'$ are *matched in the overlap* $\mathcal{U} \cap \mathcal{U}'$ by a *transition rule* involving a *transition function* $t(m) \in G$ depending only on the base point m. If a given $p \in P$ is "described by h" as "being the pair (m, g)", then at the same time h' "describes p" as "being the pair $(m,\ t(m)g)$". Note carefully that this transition group element stands *on the left*, and so in no way interferes with the global (right) action by G on P given by the ψ_g. Had we used the convention that ψ_g appear as a left translation on each fibre, then the transition rule would have involved a right action.

14.9. CONSTRUCTING A *PFB* FROM TRANSITION FUNCTIONS

We have *derived* the existence and meaning of transition functions in overlaps by starting from our original definition of a *PFB* in which they did not explicitly appear. It is however possible and common to base the *construction* of a *PFB* on a set of transition functions with suitable properties. It is good to learn to use both approaches in a flexible way.

We set up laws for transition functions as follows. We demand that the base manifold M be covered by a family of open sets $\mathcal{U}_\alpha$, such that each $\pi^{-1}(\mathcal{U}_\alpha)$ is trivialized by a corresponding diffeomorphism h_α:

$$M = \bigcup_\alpha \mathcal{U}_\alpha, \qquad P = \bigcup_\alpha \pi^{-1}(\mathcal{U}_\alpha);$$

$$h_\alpha : \mathcal{U}_\alpha \times G \ \rightarrow \ \pi^{-1}(\mathcal{U}_\alpha) \text{ a diffeomorphism;}$$

$$p \in \pi^{-1}(\mathcal{U}_\alpha) \ \Rightarrow \ p = h_\alpha(\pi(p),\ g);$$

$$\psi_{g'}(h_\alpha(m,g)) \ = \ h_\alpha\left(m, g\, g'^{-1}\right),\ m \in \mathcal{U}_\alpha. \tag{14.25}$$

Then over each nonempty overlap $\mathcal{U}_\alpha \cap \mathcal{U}_\beta$ these must be defined a transition function $t_{\alpha\beta}(m)$ with these properties:

$$m \in \mathcal{U}_\alpha \cap \mathcal{U}_\beta \ : \ t_{\alpha\beta}(m) = t_{\beta\alpha}(m)^{-1} \in G,$$

$$h_\alpha(m,g) = h_\beta(m, t_{\beta\alpha}(m)g); \tag{14.26a}$$

$$m \in \mathcal{U}_\alpha \cap \mathcal{U}_\beta \cap \mathcal{U}_\gamma \ : \ t_{\alpha\beta}(m)t_{\beta\gamma}(m)t_{\gamma\alpha}(m) = e,$$

$$\text{ie.,} \qquad t_{\alpha\gamma}(m) = t_{\alpha\beta}(m)t_{\beta\gamma}(m). \tag{14.26b}$$

One can now take the point of view that to *give* or to *define* a *PFB P* over M with structure group G is to *choose* an open covering $\{\mathcal{U}_\alpha\}$ for M, and then to *specify* a set of smooth transition functions $t_{\alpha\beta}(\cdot) \in G$ in overlaps $\mathcal{U}_\alpha \cap \mathcal{U}_\beta$, obeying the laws (14.26). That P can be built up "from scratch" is not hard to see, though we do not enter into the details. But it is good to realise that this is a possible approach, and we shall freely use it in the sequel.

As a matter of notation, once one is familiar with the set up, one can simply write $(m,g)_\alpha$ for a general element $p \in \pi^{-1}(\mathcal{U}_\alpha)$ rather than the more elaborate $h_\alpha(m,\ g)$. Then the transition rule (14.26a) has the simple form

$$(m,\ g)_\alpha = (m,\ t_{\beta\alpha}(m)\ g)_\beta. \tag{14.27}$$

14.10. EQUIVALENT TRANSITION FUNCTIONS, TRIVIAL PFB AND GLOBAL SECTIONS

We have derived the existence and properties of transition functions by examining the relation between two local trivializations and matching them in the overlap; then we made this the starting point for constructing a PFB. Now in the original definition we could very well make changes in the way the individual diffeomorphisms work, causing no essential change in the PFB but only some changes in the transition functions. This idea is now reflected in the notion of equivalence of two sets of transition functions $\{t_{\alpha\beta}(m)\}$, $\{t'_{\alpha\beta}(m)\}$, both being defined relative to the same open cover $\{\mathcal{U}_\alpha\}$ for M. Namely we can show that the two sets of transition functions are *equivalent* if over each $\mathcal{U}_\alpha$ we can define a smooth function $t_\alpha(m) \in G$ such that

$$m \in \mathcal{U}_\alpha \cap \mathcal{U}_\beta : t'_{\alpha\beta}(m) = t_\alpha(m)\, t_{\alpha\beta}(m)\, t_\beta(m)^{-1}. \qquad (14.28)$$

Now the PFB is surely trivial if all $t'_{\alpha\beta}(m) = e$, the identity in G. So we can see that a given PFB with transition functions $\{t_{\alpha\beta}(m)\}$ is equivalent to the trivial PFB $M \times G$, or is essentially trivial in itself, if we are able to find $t_\alpha(m) \in G$ over each $\mathcal{U}_\alpha$ such that in each overlap we have:

$$t_{\alpha\beta}(m) = t_\alpha(m)^{-1}\, t_\beta(m). \qquad (14.29)$$

In other words, a *separable system* of transition functions is essentially trivial.

With this last result in hand, we can easily show that in a PFB, existence of a smooth global section and triviality mean the same thing. For, if such a section $\sigma : M \to P$ exists, for each $m \in M$ we have in a smooth manner a point in the fibre on top of m:

$$\sigma : M \to P : m \to \sigma(m) \in \pi^{-1}(m). \qquad (14.30)$$

Over $\mathcal{U}_\alpha$ we write this as

$$m \in \mathcal{U}_\alpha : \sigma(m) = h_\alpha\left(m,\, t_\alpha(m)^{-1}\right),\, t_\alpha(m) \in G, \qquad (14.31)$$

thus identifying $t_\alpha(m)$. In an overlap $\mathcal{U}_\alpha \cap \mathcal{U}_\beta$, use of eqn.(14.26a) immediately gives:

$$
\begin{aligned}
\sigma(m) &= h_\alpha(m,\, t_\alpha(m)^{-1}) = h_\beta(m,\, t_\beta(m)^{-1}) \Rightarrow \\
t_\beta(m)^{-1} &= t_{\beta\alpha}(m)\, t_\alpha(m)^{-1} \Rightarrow \\
t_{\alpha\beta}(m) &= t_\alpha(m)^{-1}\, t_\beta(m),
\end{aligned}
\qquad (14.32)
$$

which is just the triviality condition (14.29)!

14.11. EXAMPLES OF PFB'S - FRAME BUNDLES, LIE GROUP COSET SPACES

Let us now describe two naturally occurring types of PFB's - frame bundles on manifolds, and Lie group coset spaces. Here we introduce them, later we come back to study them further.

Take an n-dimensional (connected) differentiable manifold M, and let $\mathcal{A} = \{(\mathcal{U}_\alpha, \psi_\alpha)\}$ be an atlas for it. At each $m \in M$ we have the tangent and cotangent spaces $T_m M$, $T_m^* M$, and the corresponding spaces of frames $F(T_m M)$, $F(T_m^* M)$. The *frame bundle FM over M* is defined as

$$FM = \bigcup_{m \in M} F(T_m M) \cdot \tag{14.33}$$

Thus it just consists of all possible frames for the tangent spaces at all possible points of M. We will soon see that FM is a differentiable manifold of dimension $n(n + 1)$, and that it is a PFB over M with structure group and typical fibre $G = GL(n, R)$. Moreover it is a PFB whose structure, ie., whose $\{t_{\alpha\beta}(m)\}$, is *totally determined by M itself!* We have no freedom to choose or assign the transition functions. Thus the triviality or otherwise of FM is an intrinsic property of M itself.

Excusing the over use of the letter e, a "point" $e \in FM$ is a frame $\{e_a(m)\}$ for $T_m M$ at some $m \in M$, so the projection π is defined:

$$
\begin{aligned}
e \in FM &\Longleftrightarrow e = \{e_a(m)\} \in F(T_m M), \text{ some } m \in M \Longrightarrow \\
\pi(e) &= m \cdot
\end{aligned}
\tag{14.34}
$$

Thus the fibre on top of m is

$$\pi^{-1}(m) = F(T_m M) \cdot \tag{14.35}$$

The free transitive action of $GL(n, R)$ on each fibre is known to us from eqn.(4.4):

$$
\begin{aligned}
(A^a{}_b) \in GL(n, R) \,, \; e &= \{e_a(m)\} \in \pi^{-1}(m) \longrightarrow \\
e' &= \{e'_a(m)\} \in \pi^{-1}(m), \\
e'_a(m) &= e_b(m) \, (A^{-1})^b{}_a \cdot
\end{aligned}
\tag{14.36}
$$

Here we have intentionally placed A^{-1} on the right.

Now consider the domain $\mathcal{U}_\alpha$ of one of the charts in $\mathcal{A}$. At each $m \in \mathcal{U}_\alpha$, we have a particular coordinate-based frame for $T_m M$, namely $\left\{\left(\frac{\partial}{\partial x^\mu}\right)_m\right\}$. So a general frame $\{e_a(m)\}$ is expressible as

$$
\begin{aligned}
e_a(m) &= e^\mu{}_a(m) \, (\partial/\partial x^\mu)_m \,, \\
e^\mu{}_a(m) &= \; < (dx^\mu)_m \,, e_a(m) > \cdot
\end{aligned}
\tag{14.37}
$$

Thus from the chart $(\mathcal{U}_\alpha, \psi_\alpha)$ on M, we have produced a chart for the portion $\pi^{-1}(\mathcal{U}_\alpha) \subset FM$; we have a "coordinate description" for all possible frames for $T_m M$ at all possible $m \in \mathcal{U}_\alpha$:

$$\pi^{-1}(\mathcal{U}_\alpha) \equiv \widehat{\mathcal{U}}_\alpha \subset FM :$$
$$\widehat{\psi}_\alpha : \widehat{\mathcal{U}}_\alpha \rightarrow \psi_\alpha(\mathcal{U}_\alpha) \times GL(n, R) \subset \mathcal{R}^{n(n+1)};$$
$$e \in \widehat{\mathcal{U}}_\alpha, \ \pi(e) = m \in \mathcal{U}_\alpha \Longrightarrow$$
$$\widehat{\psi}_\alpha(e) = (\psi_\alpha(m), e^\mu{}_a(m))$$
$$\equiv (x^\mu, e^\mu{}_a) . \tag{14.38}$$

So from each chart $(\mathcal{U}_\alpha, \psi_\alpha)$ on M we have produced a chart $\left(\widehat{\mathcal{U}}_\alpha, \widehat{\psi}_\alpha\right)$ on FM. In the overlap of two charts $\widehat{\mathcal{U}}_\alpha \cap \widehat{\mathcal{U}}_\beta$, ie., for $m \in \mathcal{U}_\alpha \cap \mathcal{U}_\beta$, on FM we have this transition rule:

$$e \in \widehat{\mathcal{U}}_\alpha \cap \widehat{\mathcal{U}}_\beta, \ \pi(e) = m \in \mathcal{U}_\alpha \cap \mathcal{U}_\beta :$$
$$x'^\mu = c^\infty - \text{functions of } x^\mu;$$
$$e'^\mu{}_a = \frac{\partial x'^\mu}{\partial x^\nu} e^\nu{}_a . \tag{14.39}$$

This is the *transition function* acting, as it should, on the left as in eqn.(14.26). We see that the Jacobian matrices of the coordinate transformations on overlaps $\mathcal{U}_\alpha \cap \mathcal{U}_\beta$ in M are directly used as the transition functions for the PFB FM. It is in this sense that the structure of FM is totally determined by M. Whether or not FM is trivial depends completely on the nature of these Jacobians in an atlas for M, ie., whether or not they are of the factorisable kind in the sense of eqn.(14.32).

The next important family of examples of PFB's arises as follows. Let G be a (connected) Lie group of dimension n, and H a (closed and connected) Lie subgroup of G of dimension k. We can split G up into, say, right cosets with respect to H: the coset determined by and containing $g \in G$ is the subset gH defined by

$$g H = \{g h \mid g \text{ fixed}, h \in H\} \subset G. \tag{14.40}$$

Each coset is determined by any element in it, and two cosets are either disjoint or coincide completely. Then the *coset space* G/H is the space, or collection, of these cosets. It is a manifold of dimension $(n - k)$. One can easily see that G acts on G/H on the left, mapping cosets on to each other; while H acts on the elements of each coset on the right, preserving the coset as a whole. These two actions are:

$$g \in G : g' H \in G/H \rightarrow g g' H \in G/H; \tag{14.41a}$$
$$h \in H : g' \in g H \rightarrow g' h^{-1} \in g H. \tag{14.41b}$$

These actions of course obey the respective composition laws. We can see that this H action on each coset is free and transitive. Each coset is "as large as", or looks just like, H itself, except that it may not be a subgroup of G. Of all the cosets, the one determined by $e \in G$ is special: it is H itself viewed as a subset of G, and it alone is a subgroup.

Given all these features, we see that the original group G can be viewed as a PFB over G/H as base, with H as structure group and typical fibre. In the standard (P, π, M, G) notation we have:

$$P \longrightarrow \text{group } G ;$$
$$M \longrightarrow \text{coset space } G/H ;$$
$$\pi : g \in G \longrightarrow \pi(g) = g\,H \in G/H ;$$
$$G \longrightarrow \text{subgroup } H \cdot \qquad (14.42)$$

Here we see that as far as the PFB structure goes, no use is made of the action (14.41a) of G on G/H.

As examples : (i) for $G = SO(n)$ and $H = SO(n-1)$ in the natural way (subgroup leaving nth coordinate invariant), we find $G/H = S^{n-1}$, the unit sphere in n-dimensional Euclidean space, so $SO(n)$ is an $SO(n-1)$ PFB over S^{n-1}; (ii) for $G = SU(n)$ and $H = SU(n-1)$ in the natural way, G/H is the unit sphere in complex n-dimensional space with the usual hermitian scalar product, which can also be regarded as the real unit sphere S^{2n-1}, so $SU(n)$ is an $SU(n-1)$ PFB over S^{2n-1}. In the $SU(n)$ case we can also consider the coset space $SU(n)/U(n-1)$ which is quite different from $SU(n)/SU(n-1)$, and set up the PFB structure accordingly. The coset spaces $SO(3)/SO(2)$ and $SU(2)/U(1)$ both happen to be the "Poincare sphere" S^2, so $SO(3)$ is an $SO(2)$ PFB, and $SU(2)$ a $U(1)$ PFB, over S^2 as base. Two more examples familiar from special relativity may be mentioned. Starting from the homogeneous (proper orthochronous) Lorentz group $SO(3,1)$, we can construct the two coset spaces $SO(3,1)/SO(3)$ and $SO(3,1)/SO(2,1)$. These may be identified respectively with the unit positive timelike hyperboloid, and the unit spacelike hyperboloid, in Minkowski space. Therefore $SO(3,1)$ is an $SO(3)$ PFB over the timelike hyperboloid as base, as well as an $SO(2,1)$ PFB over the spacelike one as base - new ways of picturing familiar things! It happens that the former is trivial while the latter is not.

14.12. MORPHISMS AND ISOMORPHISMS AMONG PFB'S

After these two important examples, let us revert to our study of general properties of PFB's. For FB's we have described the notions of bundle morphisms and isomorphisms. The key idea was that of a fibre-preserving mapping. To extend these notions to PFB's we must naturally take into account, and respect, the additional structures involved - a Lie group as typical fibre and structure group.

Given two PFB's (P, π, M, G) and (P', π', M', G'), we have a *principal morphism* from the former to the latter if we have a triple (u, f, ϕ) of smooth maps $u : P \to P'$, $f : M \to M'$, $\phi : G \to G'$ with these properties:

(i) The pair (u, f) must give a bundle morphism as defined earlier in eqn.(14.9), namely u must be fibre preserving:

$$\pi' \circ u = f \circ \pi \cdot \tag{14.43}$$

(ii) ϕ must be a homomorphism from G to G'.

(iii) The (right) actions of G, G' on fibres in P, P' respectively must be respected by u:

$$\text{for any } p \in P, g \in G \quad :$$
$$u(\psi_g(p)) \;=\; \psi'_{\phi(g)}\, (u(p)),$$
$$\text{ie., } u \circ \psi_g \;=\; \psi'_{\phi(g)} \circ u \cdot \tag{14.44}$$

Items (ii) and (iii) here are new compared to the FB situation. The need for the homomorphism ϕ means that we require a fixed map from G to G' in their roles as structure groups rather than as typical fibres.

As a particular case we may have $G' = G$ and ϕ the identity. Then we have two PFB's built on possibly different base spaces M and M' but with a common structure group. Then eqn.(14.44) simplifies to

$$u \circ \psi_g = \psi'_g \circ u \cdot \tag{14.45}$$

Now with this principal morphism, the image of each old fibre is exactly one new fibre, not a (variable) part of it.

To graduate to the idea of a *principal isomorphism* between two PFB's is easy, as in the FB case. Namely we need two principal morphisms, one in each direction, and one the inverse of the other. Clearly then the two structure groups have to be isomorphic. The triviality of a PFB, earlier defined via factorisability of the transition functions, can be restated in this way: there has to be a principal isomorphism between the given PFB and the trivial product PFB.

We mention next a nice result: Suppose two PFB's have both $G' = G$ and $M' = M$. In general, then, the two PFB's would be two different or distinct ways of forming "twisted products" of M and G. But now it turns out that if there is any principal morphism at all connecting these two PFB's, with $f = \mathcal{I}d_M$ and $\phi = \mathcal{I}d_G$, it has to be an isomorphism! The map $u : P \to P'$ is onto and a diffeomorphism.

14.13. PULLBACKS AND RESTRICTIONS OF PFB'S

Let (P, π, M, G) be a given PFB, and $\varphi : M' \to M$ a smooth map from a differentiable manifold M' into M. Then as with FB's we can pull back (P, π, M, G) via φ^* to get a new PFB (P', π', M', G). The procedure is the same as before, except that we have to give the action of G on P':

$$P' = \left\{ (m',p) \,|m' \in M', p \in \pi^{-1}(\varphi(m')) \subset P \right\} \subset M' \times P;$$

$$\tag{14.46a}$$

$$\pi'(m',p) = m'; \tag{14.46b}$$

$$g \in G, \; p' = (m',p) \in P' : \psi'_g(p') = (m', \, \psi_g(p)) \cdot \tag{14.46c}$$

That G acts freely and transitively on each fibre in P' is obvious. The point to appreciate is that the pullback of a PFB is another PFB, with altered base but unaltered structure group.

Turning to the subbundle or restriction concept for PFB's, we use the same definition as in the FB case. More easily, since we know that a subbundle is a particular case of pullback via the identification map, as in eqn.(14.18), we can see that here too a subbundle of a PFB is another PFB, with restricted base but the same structure group as before.

14.14. ASSOCIATED BUNDLES, VECTOR BUNDLES

Given a PFB (P, π, M, G) with transition functions $\{t_{\alpha\beta}(m)\}$, one can pass to other nonprincipal FB's which are called *associated bundles* (AB). In these, both the group G and the functions $\{t_{\alpha\beta}(m)\}$ play essential roles; so these are FB's with more structure than is assumed in the general FB definition given earlier. In this sense we may say that AB's lie midway between FB's and PFB's. The construction can be carried out in two ways, one elegant and aristocratic, the other down-to-earth and practical. We begin with the former.

Let F be a differentiable manifold on which the group G of the given PFB acts via diffeomorphisms, as described in the previous Section:

$$g \in G : q \in F \to q' = \varphi_g(q) \in F \cdot \tag{14.47}$$

First form the Cartesian product $P \times F$ consisting of all pairs (p,q). On these there is the natural G action:

$$g \in G : (p,q) \in P \times F \to (\psi_g(p), \, \varphi_g(q)) \in P \times F \cdot \tag{14.48}$$

In a local trivialization of P this appears thus:

$$g \in G : \; (h_\alpha(m,g'),q) \in \pi^{-1}(\mathcal{U}_\alpha) \times F \longrightarrow$$
$$\left(h_\alpha \left(m, g' \, g^{-1} \right), \varphi_g(q) \right) \in \pi^{-1}(\mathcal{U}_\alpha) \times F \cdot \tag{14.49}$$

Now introduce on $P \times F$ the equivalence relation

$$(p, q) \sim (\psi_g(p), \varphi_g(q)), \tag{14.50}$$

and denote the quotient by E:

$$E = P \times F / \sim \tag{14.51}$$

Points in E are equivalence classes $(p, q)^\sim$ in $P \times F$ - these are just the orbits in $P \times F$ under the G action (14.48). Clearly, since the G action on P is a motion along fibres, the projection $\pi : P \to M$ passes over to a projection $\pi_E : E \to M$:

$$\pi_E \left((p, q)^\sim\right) = \pi(p) \in M. \tag{14.52}$$

Using the description of pairs appearing in eqn.(14.49), over $\pi_E^{-1}(\mathcal{U}_\alpha) \subset E$ we can choose a representative element in each equivalence class in this way:

$$m \in \mathcal{U}_\alpha : (h_\alpha(m, g), q)^\sim = (h_\alpha(m, e), \varphi_g(q))^\sim. \tag{14.53}$$

In other words, we can regard the pairs $(h_\alpha(m, e), q)$ for $m \in \mathcal{U}_\alpha$ and $q \in F$ as representing, in a one-to-one and smooth manner, the equivalence classes in $P \times F / \sim$ contained within $\pi_E^{-1}(\mathcal{U}_\alpha)$. So we have

$$E = \bigcup_\alpha \left(\pi^{-1}(\mathcal{U}_\alpha) \times F / \sim\right)$$

$$= \bigcup_\alpha \{(h_\alpha(m, e), q)^\sim \mid m \in \mathcal{U}_\alpha, q \in F\}. \tag{14.54}$$

And since from P we know that in an overlap $\mathcal{U}_\alpha \cap \mathcal{U}_\beta$

$$h_\alpha(m, e) = h_\beta\left(m, t_{\beta\alpha}(m)\right), \tag{14.55}$$

in the overlap of corresponding portions of E we have the identification

$$m \in \mathcal{U}_\alpha \cap \mathcal{U}_\beta : (h_\alpha(m, e), q)^\sim = \left(h_\beta(m, e), \varphi_{t_{\beta\alpha}(m)}(q)\right)^\sim. \tag{14.56}$$

Looking at eqns.(14.54,56) we see that it is simpler to say: each portion $\pi_E^{-1}(\mathcal{U}_\alpha) \subset E$ is diffeomorphic to $\mathcal{U}_\alpha \times F$ via a map h'_α:

$$(m, q) \in \mathcal{U}_\alpha \times F : h'_\alpha(m, q) \equiv (h_\alpha(m, e), q)^\sim. \tag{14.57}$$

And in the overlap $\mathcal{U}_\alpha \cap \mathcal{U}_\beta$ these local trivializations of E are related by the rule

$$m \in \mathcal{U}_\alpha \cap \mathcal{U}_\beta : h'_\alpha(m, q) = h'_\beta\left(m, \varphi_{t_{\beta\alpha}(m)}(q)\right). \tag{14.58}$$

The secret of the construction is now clear! In a sense we have first put the fibres of P, namely G, into the product $P \times F$. Then by quotienting with respect to the G action (14.48) we have removed these fibres and replaced them by F as the typical fibre on top of each point of M. But in this process the transition functions $\{t_{\alpha\beta}(m)\}$ of P have been retained; they go into the structure of E as seen in eqn.(14.58). In other words, dropping P right at the beginning and retaining only $\{t_{\alpha\beta}(m)\}$, we can say: E is a FB with base M and typical fibre F, trivializable over each $\mathcal{U}_\alpha \subset M$; and in each overlap the "identification" of points of E is by the transition rule (14.58).

The space E is then called an *Associated Bundle*, built up using the space F carrying a G action. It is associated to P, as they share the same base and transition functions. To display all the ingredients we may write it as the quintet (E, π_E, M, F, G) - three for a bundle, four for a FB and PFB, and now five! Sometimes for simplicity we may just refer to the total space E as the associated bundle, the rest being clear from the context.

We must appreciate that in an AB there is (in general) no room for any global right action of the structure group G on E, a moving up and down each fibre. The given action of G on F is *totally used up* in stating the matching rule (14.58) in each overlap.

Just as with PFB's in eqn.(14.27), here too we could simplify the notation somewhat and denote the point $h'_\alpha(m, q)$ of eqn.(14.57) by $(m, q)_\alpha$. Then the matching rule (14.58) reads

$$(m, q)_\alpha = \left(m, \; \varphi_{t_{\beta\alpha}(m)}(q)\right)_\beta .\tag{14.59}$$

Given an AB, it is said to be trivial if and only if the transition functions are separable and can be eliminated as in eqn.(14.29), ie., if and only if the parent PFB is itself trivial. Existence of a smooth global section in the AB is no indication of its triviality. Conversely, a trivial PFB gives rise only to trivial AB's. If an AB is trivial in the sense just described, it is certainly also trivial as a FB as it reduces to a Cartesian product of base M by fibre F. But the converse need not be true: an AB might be trivial in the FB sense of being trivial, yet its parent PFB could have nontrivial transition functions. One need only consider the case when the action of G on F is trivial, ie., all the maps $\varphi_g : F \to F$ reduce to the identity!

The case of a *vector bundle* arises if F is a *linear vector space*, and the diffeomorphisms φ_g giving the action of G are *linear transformations*. So vector bundles are particular cases of AB's and are descendants from the same parent PFB. If F is a space of tensors of some kind with respect to G, we could call E a *tensor bundle*, or in a general sense we could still call it a vector bundle. Always the secret of the structure lies in the set $\{t_{\alpha\beta}(m)\}$ belonging to the parent PFB!

14.15.   MORPHISMS AND PULL BACKS FOR AB'S

At the FB level we saw that a morphism involves a pair of maps $u : E \to E'$ and $f : M \to M'$ tied together by the fibre-preserving condition (14.4). When we move up to the PFB level, a principal morphism involves one more map, a homomorphism $\phi : G \to G'$ involving the two structure groups. What is the situation with AB's? Here the most useful definition of a morphism goes beyond the plain bundle morphism given by a pair (u, f): we need not only the homomorphism ϕ, but also a suitable map $\chi : F \to F'$ involving the two typical fibres. Thus a morphism between two AB's (E, π_E, M, F, G) and $(E', \pi_{E'}', M', F', G')$, descended from respective PFB's (P, π, M, G) and (P', π', M', G'), consists of a quartet of maps (u_F, f, ϕ, χ). It begins with a principal morphism (u, f, ϕ) between the two PFB's; requires that there be a smooth map $\chi : F \to F'$ intertwining the two group actions:

$$g \in G : \chi \circ \varphi_g = \varphi'_{\phi(g)} \circ \chi, \tag{14.60}$$

and defines the map $u_F : E \to E'$ by

$$p \in P, q \in F, \qquad (p, q)^\sim \in E:$$
$$u_F((p, q)^\sim) = (u(p), \chi(q))^\sim \in E' \tag{14.61}$$

The property (14.60) of χ ensures that this is a well-defined map from E to E'. We have to keep track of the fact that points of E are G-orbits in $P \times F$, points of F' are G'-orbits in $P' \times F'$, and $u : P \to P'$ obeys not only the fibre preservation condition (14.4) but also the intertwining relation (14.44). An AB morphism is then the set of maps (u_F, f, ϕ, χ) with all the above properties. This goes well beyond the pair (u_F, f) needed to just define a bundle morphism at the FB level, since the maps ϕ, χ and the intertwining properties of u and χ are all needed to fit together coherently. There are obvious simplifications if $G' = G$, $F' = F$, $\phi = Id_G$ and $\chi = Id_F$.

Since by now you must have entered into the spirit of things, let us mention (but not prove) a nice result: start with a PFB (P, π, M, G) and do two things: (i) apply the pull-back operation to produce a new PFB (P', π', M', G) as in eqn.(14.46) with a new base M'; (ii) pass to an AB (E, π_E, M, F, G). What is the effect of carrying out these operations one after the other, and does the result depend on the sequence? The answer is that the result is an AB, the pull-back of (E, π_E, M, F, G), with base M', fibre F and group G; it is associated to (P', π', M', G); and the order of operations does not matter!

14.16. BUNDLES ASSOCIATED TO THE FRAME BUNDLE

For a differentiable manifold M of dimension n, the frame bundle FM is a PFB with base M, group $GL(n, R)$, and structure determined by M. We now get some important and natural associated bundles also with base M and determined totally by M. One is the *tangent bundle* TM, and another is the *cotangent bundle* T^*M. Let us look first at the former.

We defined FM by taking the union, for all $m \in M$, of the space of all frames $F(T_m M)$ at each point. Now we just take the union of all the tangent spaces:

$$T M = \bigcup_{m \in M} T_m M. \tag{14.62}$$

A point $u \in TM$ means a tangent vector $u \in T_m M$ for some $m \in M$, so the projection π is defined:

$$u \in T M \iff u \in T_m M, \text{ some } m \in M \Longrightarrow$$
$$\pi(u) = m. \tag{14.63}$$

Taking an atlas $\mathcal{A} = \{(\mathcal{U}_\alpha, \psi_\alpha)\}$ for M we get, as in the case of FM, a particular atlas $\hat{\mathcal{A}}$ for TM. Over $\pi^{-1}(\mathcal{U}_\alpha)$, each $u \in TM$ is expandible in the coordinate-based frame $\{(\partial_\mu)_m\}$:

$$u \in \pi^{-1}(\mathcal{U}_\alpha), \ \pi(u) = m \in \mathcal{U}_\alpha \Longrightarrow u = u^\mu \left(\frac{\partial}{\partial x^\mu}\right)_m. \tag{14.64}$$

So we have a coordinate description for all of $\pi^{-1}(\mathcal{U}_\alpha)$ by a homeomorphism ψ'_α:

$$\psi'_\alpha : \pi^{-1}(\mathcal{U}_\alpha) \ \rightarrow \ \psi_\alpha(\mathcal{U}_\alpha) \times \mathcal{R}^n \subset \mathcal{R}^{2n};$$
$$u \in \pi^{-1}(\mathcal{U}_\alpha), \qquad \pi(u) = m \in \mathcal{U}_\alpha \Rightarrow$$
$$\psi'_\alpha(u) \ = \ (\psi_\alpha(m), u^\mu) \equiv (x^\mu, u^\mu). \tag{14.65}$$

In the overlap of two charts on M, $m \in \mathcal{U}_\alpha \cap \mathcal{U}_\beta$, on TM we have the transition rules

$$u \in \pi^{-1}(\mathcal{U}_\alpha \cap \mathcal{U}_\beta), \qquad \pi(u) = m \in \mathcal{U}_\alpha \cap \mathcal{U}_\beta :$$
$$\psi_\alpha(u) \ = \ (x^\mu, u^\mu), \ \psi_\beta(u) = (x'^\mu, u'^\mu),$$
$$x'^\mu \ = \ C^\infty \text{ functions of } x^\mu,$$
$$u'^\mu \ = \ \frac{\partial x'^\mu}{\partial x^\nu} u^\nu. \tag{14.66}$$

Notice that the *same* transition functions that appeared in eqn.(14.39) in the case of FM are used here as well, so TM *is an* AB *of* FM. The action of $G = GL(n, R)$ by diffeomorphisms φ_g as needed in eqn.(14.47) becomes here the defining linear representation of $GL(n, R)$, so TM is also a vector bundle. As a differentiable manifold, TM is of dimension $2n$, twice that of M.

For the case of T^*M, we just take the union of all the pointwise cotangent spaces:

$$
\begin{aligned}
T^*M &= \bigcup_{m \in M} T_m^* M \; ; \\
\alpha \in T^*M &\iff \alpha \in T_m^* M, \text{ some } m \in M \implies \\
\pi(\alpha) &= m; \\
\alpha \in \pi^{-1}(\mathcal{U}_\alpha) &: \quad \alpha \sim (x^\mu, \alpha_\mu), \\
\alpha &= \alpha_\mu \, dx^\mu; \\
\alpha \in \pi^{-1}(\mathcal{U}_\alpha \cap \mathcal{U}_\beta), &\qquad m \in \mathcal{U}_\alpha \cap \mathcal{U}_\beta : \\
x'^\mu &= C^\infty - \text{functions of } x^\mu, \\
\alpha'_\mu &= \frac{\partial x^\nu}{\partial x'^\mu} \, \alpha_\nu .
\end{aligned}
\tag{14.67}
$$

Here for simplicity we again used π for the projection $T^* M \to M$. We see again that the transition functions of FM determine the transition rules in overlaps in $T^* M$; as an AB, we use here the action of $GL(n, R)$ on $\mathcal{R}^n$ contragredient to the one used for TM. The dimension of T^*M is $2n$, and it too is a vector bundle intrinsically determined by M.

The general tensor bundle $T^{(r,s)}M$ is built up along the same lines; it involves using, via the representation of $GL(n, R)$ appropriate to tensors of type (r, s), the transition rules determined by Jacobians in an atlas for M. The dimension of $T^{(r,s)}M$ is $n + n^{r+s} = n(n^{r+s-1} + 1)$. And of course it is a vector bundle associated to FM.

In the context of Hamiltonian mechanics the cotangent bundle T^*M has a special significance. There we usually write Q, rather than M, for the n-dimensional configuration space manifold of a physical system; a general configuration is a point $q \in Q$. A general co-vector at q, an element of $T_q^* Q$, is written as $p \in T_q^* Q$. So p is also a point in T^*M, carrying with it the information that its base point is $\pi(p) = q$. The distinguishing feature of T^*Q is the existence of a canonical one-form θ_0 on it. For clarity, denote a general point of T^*Q by the pair (q,p):

$$
\begin{aligned}
(q,p) \in T^*Q &: \quad q \in Q, \, p \in T_q^* Q; \\
\pi((q,p)) &= q.
\end{aligned}
\tag{14.68}
$$

Then, if $X \in T_{(q,p)} T^*Q$, the tangent map π_* produces a vector in $T_q Q$:

$$
X \in T_{(q,p)} T^*Q \longrightarrow \pi_*(X) \in T_q Q.
\tag{14.69}
$$

The canonical one-form $\theta_0 \in \mathcal{X}^*(T^*Q)$ is then defined as

$$< \theta_0(q,p),\, X > = < p, (\pi_*)_{(q,p)}\,(X) > \cdot \qquad (14.70)$$

In a local coordinate system q^j for Q, we can write these in more familiar forms:

$$p = p_j\, dq^j,\ X = \alpha^j\, \frac{\partial}{\partial q^j} + \beta_j\, \frac{\partial}{\partial p_j},$$

$$\pi_*(X) = \alpha^j\, \frac{\partial}{\partial q^j}$$

$$< \theta_0,\, X > = < p,\, \pi_*(X) > = p_j\, \alpha^j,$$

$$\text{ie.,}\ \theta_0 = p_j\, dq^j \qquad (14.71)$$

Here q^j are the (local) generalised coordinates and p_j the components of canonical momentum conjugate to q^j.

A similar construction exists in the case of the frame bundle FQ as well, leading to n distinguished one-forms on FQ.

14.17. PARALLELIZABLE MANIFOLDS

A differentiable manifold M is said to be *parallelizable* if the frame bundle FM is trivial. This means that there exist global smooth sections in FM, ie., global smooth choices of frames for each $m \in M$. If M is parallelizable, then both TM and T^*M, indeed all $T^{(r,s)}M$, are trivial AB's. But in these cases, as we have emphasized earlier, their triviality is not the same as existence of smooth global sections! For instance, in *any* TM (or $T^{(r,s)}M$) we have the zero section which is certainly smooth; and this exists whether or not M is parallelizable. So this just reiterates the point that triviality of an AB means triviality of the PFB from which it came, *not* existence of a global section in it.

If M possesses a single chart atlas, ie., M is simple, then certainly it is parallelizable as there are no overlaps and transition functions at all! But the converse need not be true! The circle S^1 is parallelizable, but cannot be covered by any single-chart atlas. An interesting fact is that the only compact parallelizable manifolds are the compact semisimple Lie groups, and the sphere S^7. In particular, both $S^1 \sim U(1)$ and $S^3 \sim SU(2)$ are parallelizable, while S^2 is not! That every Lie group G is parallelizable, and not just the compact semi-simple ones, was pointed out in the previous Section: the set of left (or right) invariant vector fields $X_a^{(r)}$ (or $X_a^{(\ell)}$) gives us a smooth choice of n independent nonvanishing vectors at each $g \in G$, hence a globally smooth choice of frames.

In this connection, the spheres S^n exhibit the following interesting behaviours. For each even n, S^n is not parallelizable and there does not exist
a smooth everywhere nonvanishing vector field. For each odd $n \geq 5$ (apart
from $n = 7$), S^n is not parallelizable (as we have seen above), but there
does exist an everywhere nonvanishing smooth vector field.

14.18.   ANOTHER LOOK AT LIE GROUP COSET SPACES AS PFB'S

We have earlier seen briefly that coset spaces of Lie groups G with respect
to Lie subgroups H are a nice source of PFB's. Let us now look at them
a little more closely, bringing out the role of transition functions as an
instructive example of the general situation.

We have an n-dimensional connected Lie group G, and a k-dimensional
closed connected Lie subgroup H in G. In eqn.(14.42) we have indicated the
way in which G can be viewed as a PFB with base $M = G/H$, structure
group and typical fibre H. In line with our general notations, a point in M
will be denoted by m; the special point corresponding to the identity coset
$e\,H$ in G will be denoted by m_0. We may think of it as a distinguished
"origin" in M.

The global (right) action of the structure group H on the total space G
is just the action by right translations defined in Section 13, now limited
to H. Thus the diffeomorphisms ψ_h for $h \in H$, needed for the PFB
structure, act on G as follows:

$$\psi_h \equiv R_h : g \in G \longrightarrow \psi_h(g) = gh^{-1} \in G. \qquad (14.72)$$

This preserves each right H-coset in G as it should, ie., it is a translation
along fibres in G viewed as a PFB.

Let us now ask whether we can choose in a globally smooth way a coset
representative $\ell(m) \in G$ for each point $m \in M$, such that $\pi(\ell(m)) = m$.
If we could, this would be a global section in the PFB, which would then
have to be a trivial bundle. In general we do not expect this to be so. Let us
then regard M as the union of a set of open subsets $\mathcal{U}_\alpha$, chosen so that over
each of them we are able to choose a smoothly varying coset representative:

$$M = \bigcup_\alpha \mathcal{U}_\alpha\,;$$
$$m \in \mathcal{U}_\alpha \;\to\; \ell_\alpha(m) \in \pi^{-1}(m) \subset \pi^{-1}(\mathcal{U}_\alpha) \subset G. \qquad (14.73)$$

Then each map $\ell_\alpha : \mathcal{U}_\alpha \to \pi^{-1}(\mathcal{U}_\alpha) \subset G$ gives us a local section in the
PFB. Naturally for any $h \in H$ we have

$$\pi(\ell_\alpha(m)h) = m \qquad (14.74)$$

And once $\ell_\alpha(m)$ is chosen over $\mathcal{U}_\alpha$, any $g \in G$ such that $\pi(g) = m \in \mathcal{U}_\alpha$ can be uniquely written as the product

$$g = \ell_\alpha(m)\, h \qquad\qquad (14.75)$$

for a definite $h \in H$, since g and $\ell_\alpha(m)$ are in the same coset.

Next consider a nonempty overlap $\mathcal{U}_\alpha \cap \mathcal{U}_\beta$. Clearly for $m \in \mathcal{U}_\alpha \cap \mathcal{U}_\beta$, $\ell_\alpha(m)$ and $\ell_\beta(m)$ lie in the same coset; so by eqn.(14.75) they are related by a suitable element of H on the right:

$$m \in \mathcal{U}_\alpha \cap \mathcal{U}_\beta \;\; : \;\; \ell_\beta(m) = \ell_\alpha(m)\, h_{\alpha\beta}(m),$$
$$h_{\alpha\beta}(m) \in H. \qquad\qquad (14.76)$$

These $h_{\alpha\beta}(m)$ are precisely the transition functions of the general theory in the present case! One easily establishes the necessary properties

$$m \in \mathcal{U}_\alpha \cap \mathcal{U}_\beta : h_{\alpha\beta}(m) \;\; = \;\; h_{\beta\alpha}(m)^{-1};$$
$$m \in \mathcal{U}_\alpha \cap \mathcal{U}_\beta \cap \mathcal{U}_\gamma : h_{\alpha\gamma}(m) \;\; = \;\; h_{\alpha\beta}(m)\, h_{\beta\gamma}(m). \qquad (14.77)$$

And one can see that an element $g \in \pi^{-1}(m)$ for $m \in \mathcal{U}_\alpha \cap \mathcal{U}_\beta$ can be regarded as a pair $(m, h)_\alpha$ or as a pair $(m, h')_\beta$ in the notation of eqn.(14.27), with h and h' related by the transition function:

$$g \in G, \; \pi(g) \;\; = \;\; m \in \mathcal{U}_\alpha \cap \mathcal{U}_\beta :$$
$$g \;\; = \;\; (m, h)_\alpha = (m, h')_\beta,$$
$$h' \;\; = \;\; h_{\beta\alpha}(m)\, h. \qquad\qquad (14.78)$$

This is the connection between two local trivializations, and it is consistent with eqns.(14.75,76).

Suppose we alter the local choices of coset representatives from $\ell_\alpha(m)$ to $\ell'_\alpha(m)$ in the following manner:

$$m \in \mathcal{U}_\alpha \;\; : \;\; \ell'_\alpha(m) = \ell_\alpha(m)\, h_\alpha(m)^{-1},$$
$$h_\alpha(m) \in H. \qquad\qquad (14.79)$$

Then the transition functions change as follows:

$$h'_{\alpha\beta}(m) = h_\alpha(m)\, h_{\alpha\beta}(m)\, h_\beta(m)^{-1}. \qquad\qquad (14.80)$$

This is an instance of eqn.(14.28), and we see why we should regard $\{h_{\alpha\beta}(m)\}$ and $\{h'_{\alpha\beta}(m)\}$ as equivalent systems of transition functions.

In this way all the main ingredients and properties of a general PFB are well illustrated by the coset space example. There is however a further aspect here which is missing in the case of a general PFB. Namely here the total space itself is a Lie group G, and this certainly acts in a well defined way on the base space $M = G/H$! Such action is neither needed nor contemplated for a general PFB. It is worth describing briefly this action of G on M, and its generating vector fields.

Recall that G brings with it both right translations R_g and left translations L_g acting on itself. For the PFB structure we used the former with g limited to elements $h \in H$. Now as mentioned earlier in this Section the left translations L_g clearly act in a well-defined way on the right cosets $g H \in G/H$, mapping them on to one another. We can now say that the mappings $L_g : G \to G$ *descend* to a family of mappings $\tilde{L}_g : G/H \to G/H$ in the obvious way. This is the action given in eqn.(14.41a):

$$g \in G, \ \{g'H\} \in M : \tilde{L}_g\{g'H\} = \{g\,g'\,H\} \in M. \tag{14.81}$$

With the use of the projection $\pi : G \to M$ we see the relationship

$$\pi \circ L_g = \tilde{L}_g \circ \pi \tag{14.82}$$

linking left translations on G to G action on G/H.

The question that now naturally arises is whether the vector fields $X_a \in \mathcal{X}(M)$ generating $\tilde{L}_g$ are related to or obtainable from the (right invariant) vector fields $X_a^{(\ell)} \in \mathcal{X}(G)$ generating L_g. This is indeed so as the following brief calculation shows. Let us replace g by g_0 in eqn.(14.82), apply both sides to some $g \in G$, and write the result as

$$\pi\left(L_{g_0}\left(g\right)\right) = \tilde{L}_{g_0}\left(m\right),$$
$$\pi(g) = m \in M. \tag{14.83}$$

Now if we keep g (and so m) fixed and regard g_0 as variable, we can write this in the language of composition of maps as

$$\pi \circ L.\ (g) = \tilde{L}.\ (m), \ \pi(g) = m \tag{14.84}$$

Both sides are to be read as maps $G \to M$ indexed by g and $m = \pi\ (g)$, the dot symbolizing the argument drawn from G. We are using here the notation introduced in eqn.(13.25). For the associated tangent maps applied at $e \in G$ we have:

$$\pi_* \circ (L.\ (g)_*)_e = \left(\tilde{L}.\ (m)_*\right)_e,$$
$$\pi(g) = m. \tag{14.85}$$

On the left the first map takes us from $T_e\,G$ to $T_g\,G$, then π_* takes us finally to $T_m\,M$; on the right we go directly from $T_e\,G$ to $T_m\,M$. Now apply both sides to a vector e_a in a basis $\{e_a\}$ for $T_e\, G$: from eqns.(13.26,55) we get

$$\pi_* \left(X_a^{(\ell)}\,(g) \right) = X_a(m) = X_a(\pi(g)). \tag{14.86}$$

(There is a minor change of notation involved here : we must replace ψ in eqn.(13.55) by $\tilde{L}$). This is the result we are after, and we also learn something about the (right invariant) vector fields $X_a^{(\ell)}$ on G. In the result above, for given $m \in M$ on the right, we are free to choose any $g \in \pi^{-1}(m)$ on the left, and the result is the same. We saw in Section 8, however, that in general the tangent map φ_* induced by a map $\varphi : M \to N$ between two manifolds is only defined pointwise. We do not generally expect a vector field on M to be mapped by φ_* to a well-defined vector field on N. If however a particular vector field X on M is such that via φ_* we obtain a definite well defined vector field on N, then we say X is *projectable*. We see in the present context: just as the left translations L_g on G descend to an action $\tilde{L}_g$ of G on $M = G/H$, so too the generators $X_a^{(\ell)}$ of the former are projectable; and upon projection they give us the generators X_a of $\tilde{L}_g$!

Here are some further interesting and useful properties of the action $\tilde{L}.$ of G on G/H. The distinguished point $m_0 \in M$ corresponds to the identity coset $e\,H = H \subset G$. The corresponding stability group is H itself:

$$H(m_0) = \left\{ g \in G | \tilde{L}_g(m_0) = m_0 \right\} = H. \tag{14.87}$$

Since G acts transitively on M, any other point $m \in M$ is $\tilde{L}_g(m_0)$ for (many) suitable choices of g. Then the stability group of m is obtained by conjugating H with g:

$$m = \vec{\tilde{L}}_g(m_0):$$
$$H(m) = \left\{ g \in G | \tilde{L}_g(m) = m \right\} = g\,H\,g^{-1}. \tag{14.88}$$

Returning to $\tilde{L}_g$, its tangent map $\tilde{L}_{g*}$ maps each $T_m\, M$ linearly onto $T_{g(m)}\, M$, where for simplicity we have denoted $\tilde{L}_g(m)$ by $g(m)$:

$$\left(\tilde{L}_{g*} \right)_m : T_m\, M \to T_{g(m)}\, M. \tag{14.89}$$

From eqn.(14.87), if we now set $m = m_0$ here and restrict g to elements $h \in H$, then $g(m) \to h(m_0) = m_0$ again. Thus the maps $\left(\tilde{L}_{h*} \right)_{m_0}$ are linear transformations of $T_{m_0}\, M$ on to itself. Moreover they form a linear representation of H since

$$\tilde{L}_{h_1} \circ \tilde{L}_{h_2} = \tilde{L}_{h_1 h_2} \Longrightarrow$$
$$\left(\tilde{L}_{h_1 *} \right)_{m_0} \circ \left(\tilde{L}_{h_2 *} \right)_{m_0} = \left(\tilde{L}_{h_1 h_2 *} \right)_{m_0}. \tag{14.90}$$

Thus a certain linear representation of H, of dimension $(n-k)$, comes naturally from the action of G on G/H: it is called the *isotopy representation
of H*. We leave it to the reader to check that this arises also in the following way: start with the adjoint representation of G on its Lie algebra $\underline{G}$
(described in the previous Section); restrict it to elements in H; then pass
to the quotient vector space $\underline{G}/\underline{H}$!

14.19.   LIFTING LIE GROUP ACTION TO TANGENT AND COTANGENT SPACES

In Section 13 we have described some aspects of the action of a Lie group
G on a differentiable manifold M via a group of diffeomorphisms $\psi_.$. In
the present Section we have learnt that any M automatically brings with
it the PFB FM, and then the tangent and cotangent bundles TM, T^*M
associated with FM. Let us now see briefly how a given G action on M
can be canonically or naturally "lifted" to actions on TM and T^*M. First
we look at the case of TM.

For each $g \in G$, ψ_g is a map from M on to M. So ψ_{g*} maps the
tangent spaces at various points of M linearly on to one another:

$$(\psi_{g*})_m \quad : \quad T_m\,M \to T_{m'}\,M,$$
$$m' = \psi_g(m). \tag{14.91}$$

Now denote a point in TM (for clarity and some redundancy!) by a pair
(m, u):

$$(m, u) \in T\,M \iff m \in M,\, u \in T_m\,M. \tag{14.92}$$

Then we define the lift of $\psi_g : M \to M$ to an action $\psi'_g : TM \to TM$ as
follows:

$$\psi'_g(m, u) = (m', u'),$$
$$m' = \psi_g(m),$$
$$u' = (\psi_{g*})_m(u). \tag{14.93}$$

It is easy to check that, given the composition property of the ψ's, the ψ''s
also obey the right laws:

$$\psi_{g'} \circ \psi_g = \psi_{g'g} \implies$$
$$\psi_{g'*} \circ \psi_{g*} = \psi_{g'g*} \implies$$
$$\psi'_{g'} \circ \psi'_g = \psi'_{g'g}. \tag{14.94}$$

This is the lifted action of G on TM.

For the case of T^*M, we have to follow a path "contragredient" to the above. In place of eqn.(14.91) we start with the fact that the pull-backs $\psi^*_{g^{-1}}$ work as follows:

$$\psi^*_{g^{-1}} \quad : \quad T^*_m\, M \to T^*_{m'}\, M,$$
$$m' \;=\; \psi_g(m). \tag{14.95}$$

Then a point in T^*M being a pair,

$$(m,\, \alpha) \in T^*M \Longleftrightarrow m \in M,\, \alpha \in T^*_m\, M, \tag{14.96}$$

the lift of ψ_g to ψ''_g acting on T^*M is given by

$$\psi''_g(m,\, \alpha) \;=\; (m',\, \alpha'),$$
$$m' \;=\; \psi_g(m),$$
$$\alpha' \;=\; \psi^*_{g^{-1}}(\alpha). \tag{14.97}$$

This is again checked to be acceptable and to have the right composition property as pullbacks and composition of maps behave properly:

$$\psi_{g^{-1}} \circ \psi_{g'^{-1}} \;=\; \psi_{(g'g)^{-1}} \Longrightarrow$$
$$\psi^*_{g'^{-1}} \circ \psi^*_{g^{-1}} \;=\; \psi^*_{(g'g)^{-1}} \Longrightarrow$$
$$\psi''_{g'} \circ \psi''_g \;=\; \psi''_{g'g}. \tag{14.98}$$

The vector fields X'_a, X''_a on TM, T^*M respectively, generating ψ'_g and ψ''_g, are clearly determined by the generators $X_a \in \mathcal{X}(M)$ of ψ_g. Naturally X'_a and X''_a are called the appropriate lifts of X_a. The case of $X''_a \in \mathcal{X}(T^*M)$ is particularly interesting, because as a "classical phase space" T^*M carries the distinguished one-form θ_0 defined by eqns.(14.70,71). We develop the significant properties in some detail. With $\pi : T^*M \to M$ being the canonical projection, the manner in which ψ_g has been lifted in eqn.(14.97) to ψ''_g ensures that

$$\pi \circ \psi''_g = \psi_g \circ \pi. \tag{14.99}$$

(A similar result holds for ψ'_g in the case of TM, of course). Now we will show that θ_0 is preserved under pull-back by any ψ''^*_g. With the replacements $q \to m$, $p \to \alpha$ in eqns.(14.70), and letting ψ''_g map $(m,\, \alpha)$ to $(m',\, \alpha')$ according to eqn.(14.97), we have:

$$X(m, \alpha) \in T_{(m, \alpha)} \, T^* M :$$

$$< \left(\psi_g''^* \theta_0 \right) (m, \alpha), X(m, \alpha) > =$$

$$= \, < \theta_0(m', \alpha'), \left(\psi_{g*}'' \right)_{(m, \alpha)} (X(m, \alpha)) >$$

$$= \, < \alpha', (\pi_*)_{(m', \alpha')} \circ \left(\psi_{g*}'' \right)_{(m, \alpha)} (X(m, \alpha)) >$$

$$= \, < \alpha', \left(\left(\pi \circ \psi_g'' \right)_* \right)_{(m, \alpha)} (X(m, \alpha)) >$$

$$= \, < \alpha', ((\psi_g \circ \pi)_*)_{(m, \alpha)} (X(m, \alpha)) >$$

$$= \, < \alpha', (\psi_{g*})_m \circ (\pi_*)_{(m, \alpha)} (X(m, \alpha)) >$$

$$= \, < \psi_g^* \, \alpha', (\pi_*)_{(m, \alpha)} (X(m, \alpha)) >$$

$$= \, < \alpha, (\pi_*)_{(m, \alpha)} (X(m, \alpha)) >$$

$$= \, < \theta_0(m, \alpha), X(m, \alpha) >,$$

$$\psi_g''^* \, \theta_0 \, = \, \theta_0 \tag{14.100}$$

Here we used the definition (14.70) of θ_0 at the beginning and at the end, and in between we used both (14.99) and the $\alpha - \alpha'$ connection given in eqn.(14.97). Thus the lifted action of G on $T^* M$ has a special property with respect to θ_0 : the ψ_g'' are canonical transformations. Now considering various one-parameter subgroups in G and appealing to the definition of the Lie derivative in eqn.(9.12) we see that

$$L_{X_a''} \, \theta_0 = 0 \cdot \tag{14.101}$$

We are now almost home in our characterisation of $X_a'' \in \mathcal{X}(T^* M)$. Since obviously

$$(\pi_*)_{(m, \alpha)} \, (X_a'' \, (m, \alpha)) = X_a(m) \in T_m \, M, \tag{14.102}$$

the functions $i_{X_a''} \, \theta_0 \in \mathcal{F}(T^* M)$ are easy to calculate:

$$(i_{X_a''} \, \theta_0) \, (m, \, \alpha) \, = \, < \theta_0(m, \alpha), X_a''(m, \, \alpha) >$$

$$= \, < \alpha, X_a(m) > \tag{14.103}$$

Essentially the calculation is done point by point on M and the result then viewed as a function on $T^* M$! We now finally use the Cartan family identity (9.39c) in eqn.(14.101) to get:

$$(i_{X_a''} \, d \, + \, d \, i_{X_a''}) \, \theta_0 = 0,$$

$$\text{ie.,} \, i_{X_a''} \, \omega_0 \, = \, d \, (-i_{X_a''} \, \theta_0) \,,$$

$$\omega_0 \, = \, d \, \theta_0 \cdot \tag{14.104}$$

Here ω_0 is a (closed, nondegenerate) two-form on T^*M; and point by point on T^*M we see that the generators X_a'' of ψ_g'' are related to the differentials of a set of corresponding functions on T^*M! The nondegeneracy of ω_0 means that X_a'' are *algebraically determined* by the above result. This is what is referred to in classical Hamiltonian dynamics by saying that the X_a'' are "Hamiltonian vector fields" on T^*M.

It should be easy to trace the generalisation of the above two lifts to get actions of G on FM and on the general tensor bundle $T^{(r,s)}M$: all these are various lifts of the G action on M as starting point.

The particular case where the manifold M is G itself is of special interest! Here for ψ_g we have several choices: left translations L_g, right translations R_g, or conjugation I_g. Purely for purposes of illustration let us see how to lift the left translations L_g from G to L_g'' acting on the "phase space" T^*G.

We have noted that every Lie group is a parallelizable manifold. Thus the cotangent bundle T^*G has globally the structure of the trivial Cartesian product $G \times \underline{G}^*$ where the real linear vector space $\underline{G}^*$ is dual to the Lie algebra $\underline{G}$ of G. There is a natural way in which we can display this fact. We begin with eqn.(14.67) in the case $M = G$:

$$T^*G = \bigcup_{g \in G} T_g^* G$$
$$= \left\{ (g, \alpha) | g \in G, \alpha \in T_g^* G \right\}. \tag{14.105}$$

The globally defined (right invariant) one-forms $\theta^{(\ell)a} \in \mathcal{X}^*(G)$ give us a basis $\left\{ \theta^{(\ell)a}(g) \right\}$ for $T_g^* G$ at each $g \in G$; at $g = e$ this reduces to the basis $\{e^a\}$ for $T_e^*G = \underline{G}^*$ dual to the basis $\{e_a\}$ for T_eG. In the pair $(g, \alpha) \in T^*G$ we can expand α in the $\theta^{(\ell)a}(g)$, then use the coefficients to define an $\tilde{\alpha} \in \underline{G}^*$:

$$(g, \alpha) \in T^*G : \alpha = \alpha_a \, \theta^{(\ell)a}(g) \longrightarrow$$
$$\tilde{\alpha} = \alpha_a \, e^a \in \underline{G}^*. \tag{14.106}$$

That is, for each fixed g, we have an isomorphism $T_g^* G \longleftrightarrow \underline{G}^*$:

$$T_g^* G \to \underline{G}^* : \alpha \to \tilde{\alpha} = <\alpha, \, X_a^{(\ell)}(g) > e^a \; ;$$
$$\underline{G}^* \to T_g^* G : \tilde{\alpha} \to \alpha = <\tilde{\alpha}, \, e_a > \theta^{(\ell)a}(g). \tag{14.107}$$

We can even regard α_a for each $a = 1, 2, \ldots, n$ as a function on T^*G, $\alpha_a \in \mathcal{F}(T^*G)$; its value at (g, α) is just the ath component of α in an expansion in $\theta^{(\ell)a}(g)$:

$$\alpha_a(g, \alpha) = <\alpha, \, X_a^{(\ell)}(g) > \tag{14.108}$$

With these preliminaries we can see how $T^*G \simeq G \times \underline{G}^*$. We have

$$(g, \alpha) \in T^*G \longleftrightarrow (g, \tilde{\alpha}) \in G \times \underline{G}^*, \qquad (14.109)$$

the two-way passage between α and $\tilde{\alpha}$ being given by eqn.(14.107). In the second way of describing T^*G, we do not have to view $\tilde{\alpha}$ as being "tied to" the point $g \in G$, as we have to in the case of α. And to set up the lifted action L''_g on T^*G we can use either description of T^*G. Specialising eqn.(14.97) we have in the first instance:

$$
\begin{aligned}
L''_{g_0}(g, \alpha) &= (g', \alpha'), \\
g' &= L_{g_0} g = g_0 g, \\
\alpha' &= L^*_{g_0^{-1}} \alpha \in T^*_{g'} G.
\end{aligned}
\qquad (14.110)
$$

To switch to the second description of T^*G we expand α in the $\theta^{(\ell)a}(g)$ and see how the coefficients α_a change in going to α'. Here we need an easily established converse to eqn.(13.35) giving the behaviour of $\theta^{(\ell)a}$ under pull back by left translations:

$$L^*_{g_0^{-1}} \theta^{(\ell)b} = \mathcal{D}^b{}_a\left(g_0^{-1}\right) \theta^{(\ell)a}. \qquad (14.111)$$

Therefore the change $\alpha \to \alpha'$ is given by:

$$
\begin{aligned}
\alpha = \alpha_a\, \theta^{(\ell)a}(g) \to \alpha' &= \alpha'_a\, \theta^{(\ell)a}(g') \\
&= \alpha_b\left(L^*_{g_0^{-1}} \theta^{(\ell)b}\right)(g') \\
&= \alpha_b\, \mathcal{D}^b{}_a\left(g_0^{-1}\right) \theta^{(\ell)a}(g'), \\
\alpha'_a &= \mathcal{D}^b{}_a\left(g_0^{-1}\right) \alpha_b.
\end{aligned}
\qquad (14.112)
$$

So in a compact and "decoupled" form we have the action L''_g in the description $G \times \underline{G}^*$ of T^*G:

$$L''_{g_0}(g, \alpha_a) = \left(g_0\, g, \quad \mathcal{D}^b{}_a\left(g_0^{-1}\right) \alpha_b\right) \qquad (14.113)$$

What happens to the characterisation of the generators of L''_g as Hamiltonian vector fields? Here the functions $\alpha_a \in \mathcal{F}(T^*G)$ set up in eqn.(14.108) come into play. Namely one can nicely exhibit the one-form θ_0 on T^*G, and characterise the vector fields X''_a generating L''_g, in these ways:

$$
\begin{aligned}
\theta_0 &= \alpha_a\, \pi^*\, \theta^{(\ell)a}, \\
i_{X''_a}\, \omega_0 &= -d\,\alpha_a.
\end{aligned}
\qquad (14.114)
$$

Establishing these is an easy exercise based on the formulae assembled above.

15. Connections and Curvature on a Principal Fibre Bundle

Our aim in this Section is to describe what is meant by a *connection*, or a *law of parallel transport*, on a general PFB. As we shall see, the concept of an affine connection on a differentiable manifold M, studied in Section 10, is a particular case of what we shall develop now, when the PFB is the frame bundle FM on M.

A connection on a PFB is not part of the PFB structure which we learnt about in the previous Section. It does not automatically or uniquely come with the PFB itself. Rather, it is an additional structure which we can impose on a PFB. Just as with an affine connection on a differentiable manifold, here too a connection on a PFB involves additional geometrical objects which must obey certain general conditions. Beyond this it is up to us to choose or specify one or another connection.

By way of preparation we begin by collecting some useful properties of tangent spaces to a PFB - these are actually implicit in the PFB structure, we merely draw them out and make them explicit.

15.1. TANGENT SPACES TO A PFB - SOME PROPERTIES

Let (P, π, M, G) be a PFB with all its associated machinery: diffeomorphisms ψ_g implementing the global G action; local trivializations h_α; transition functions $t_{\alpha\beta}(m)$. When necessary we write dim$\cdot M = n$, dim$\cdot G = n'$, dim$\cdot P =$ dim$\cdot M +$ dim$\cdot G = n + n'$. We have seen in Section 13 that if a Lie group acts on a differentiable manifold via diffeomorphisms, we can "read" these diffeomorphisms in two ways, depending on which of the two "arguments" is held fixed and which is varied. Thus we have exploited this freedom in dealing with the left and right translations $L_g(g')$, $R_g(g')$ on G (see eqs.(13.25-27)); and also with the maps $m \to \psi_g(m)$ giving G action on some M (see eqs.(13.54,55)). Now we obtain some results along these lines in the PFB context.

The (right) global action of G on P is through the diffeomorphisms ψ_g. A point $p \in P$ is carried by $g \in G$ to $p' = \psi_g(p) \equiv p\, g^{-1}$ on the same fibre as p. If we keep g fixed and vary p, we have the fibre-preserving map $\psi_g : P \to P$. Alternatively we can keep p fixed and vary g. Then we have a map indexed by p, $\psi_\cdot(p) : G \to P$, with domain G and range the entire fibre containing p, namely $\pi^{-1}(\pi(p))$. Now we can easily establish three composition relations involving these two ways of viewing ψ, each relation connecting maps between two of the three manifolds P, M and G:

$$P \to M : \pi \circ \psi_g \;\; = \;\; \pi \; ; \tag{15.1a}$$

$$G \to M : \pi \circ \psi.(p) \;\; = \;\; \pi(p) = \text{constant} \; ; \tag{15.1b}$$

$$G \to P : \psi_g \circ \psi.(p) \;\; = \;\; \psi.(p\,g^{-1}) \circ I_g \; . \tag{15.1c}$$

The first relation, indexed by g, merely confirms that ψ_g preserves fibres. The second relation, indexed by p, is really the same statement: as g varies in $\pi(\psi_g(p))$, the base point $\pi(p)$ stays constant. The third relation, indexed by both g and p, is a useful link between the two ways of "reading" ψ; here the action I_g of G on itself by conjugation comes in.

The next step is to take the tangent map relations that follow from each of eqs.(15.1) and interpret them carefully. The projection $\pi : P \to M$ leads to π_* which maps each tangent space T_pP linearly onto T_mM at $m = \pi(p) \in M$. As we saw in Section 14 already with a FB, this is an onto map because the projection π is always regular. So we have:

$$p \in P, \; \pi(p) \;\; = \;\; m \in M \; :$$

$$(\pi_*)_p(T_pP) \;\; = \;\; T_mM \; ,$$

$$\dim \cdot T_pP \;\; = \;\; \dim \cdot T_mM + \dim \cdot \underline{G} \cdot \tag{15.2}$$

Here we have (surreptitiously!) brought in the Lie algebra $\underline{G}$ of G. We see that the null space of $(\pi_*)_p$, a linear subspace of T_pP, has dimension equal to $\dim \cdot \underline{G}$. This is also intuitively clear for the following reason: $(\pi_*)_p$ maps to zero all those directions at p which correspond to "motions within the fibre", since then no change in base point is involved; and there are as many independent "directions within the fibre" as the dimension of $\underline{G}$, since the typical fibre is G itself. The subspace involved, called the "vertical subspace at p", is denoted by V_p:

$$V_p \;\; = \;\; \{X \in T_pP | (\pi_*)_p(X) = 0\} \subset T_pP \; ,$$

$$\dim \cdot V_p \;\; = \;\; \dim \cdot \underline{G} \cdot \tag{15.3}$$

Now let us begin exploiting the relations (15.1) one by one. Since ψ_g mapping p to pg^{-1} is invertible, to begin with we have:

$$(\psi_{g*})_p(T_pP) = T_{pg^{-1}}P \; ; \tag{15.4}$$

that is, $(\psi_{g*})_p$ carries the full tangent space at p linearly *onto* that at pg^{-1}. The relation

$$(\pi_*)_{pg^{-1}} \circ (\psi_{g*})_p = (\pi_*)_p \tag{15.5}$$

following from eq.(15.1a), combined again with invertibility of ψ_{g*}, then tells us that

$$(\psi_{g*})_p(V_p) = V_{pg^{-1}} \cdot \tag{15.6}$$

That is, $(\psi_{g*})_p$ takes the vertical subspace at p linearly *onto* that at pg^{-1}.

Next let us see how to exploit eq.(15.1b). For a start we have that $(\psi.(p)_*)_e$ takes T_eG into T_pP. Identifying T_eG with $\underline{G}$ we write:

$$(\psi.(p)_*)_e : \underline{G} \to T_pP \cdot \tag{15.7}$$

But from the constancy of the right hand side of eq.(15.1b) we have

$$(\pi_*)_p \circ (\psi.(p)_*)_e = 0 \cdot \tag{15.8}$$

Therefore eq.(15.7) can be sharpened to

$$(\psi.(p)_*)_e : \underline{G} \to V_p \subset T_pP \cdot \tag{15.9}$$

At this point we appeal to the invertibility of $\psi.(p)$ (as a map $G \to \pi^{-1}(\pi(p))$) which follows from G being the typical fibre, and to $\dim \cdot V_p = \dim \cdot \underline{G}$, to conclude that

$$(\psi.(p)_*)_e(\underline{G}) = V_p \subset T_pP. \tag{15.10}$$

The vertical subspace V_p at p, earlier defined "passively" as that subspace of T_pP on which $(\pi_*)_p$ vanishes, is now "actively" seen to be the range of the map $(\psi.(p)_*)_e$:

$$V_p = \text{null space of } (\pi_*)_p = \text{range of } (\psi.(p)_*)_e \cdot \tag{15.11}$$

Thus in an intrinsic and canonical manner, for each p we have an *isomorphism* between $\underline{G}$ and V_p. It is useful to denote this by a special symbol ρ_p:

$$\begin{aligned} t \in \underline{G} &\to \rho_p(t) = (\psi.(p)_*)_e(t) \in V_p \,, \\ v \in V_p &\to \rho_p^{-1}(v) \in \underline{G} \cdot \end{aligned} \tag{15.12}$$

Thus ρ_p is just the invertible map $(\psi.(p)_*)_e$ from $\underline{G}$ to V_p.

The two statements (15.6,10) are consequences, for vertical subspaces, of eqs.(15.1a,b) respectively. When we turn next to the consequences of eq.(15.1c) we get a relation between the natural isomorphisms $\rho_p : \underline{G} \to V_p$, $\rho_{pg^{-1}} : \underline{G} \to V_{pg^{-1}}$ at any two points on the same fibre. From eq.(13.30) we know that $(I_{g*})_e$ subjects each vector $t \in \underline{G}$ to action by the adjoint representation $\mathcal{D}(g)$ of G:

$$t = t^a e_a \in \underline{G} \quad , \quad g \in G :$$
$$(I_{g*})_e \, t \;=\; t' = \mathcal{D}(g)t \, ,$$
$$t'^a \;=\; \mathcal{D}^a{}_b(g) \, t^b \cdot \qquad (15.13)$$

Taking the tangent map on both sides of eq.(15.1c),

$$(\psi_{g*})_p \circ (\psi.(p)_*)_e = (\psi.(pg^{-1})_*)_e \circ (I_{g*})_e \, , \qquad (15.14)$$

applying both sides to some $t \in \underline{G}$ and using eqs.(15.12,13) we see that

$$(\psi_{g*})_p(\rho_p(t)) = \rho_{pg^{-1}}(\mathcal{D}(g)t) \cdot \qquad (15.15)$$

In words: the result of first passing from $\underline{G}$ to V_p via the canonical isomorphism ρ_p and then from V_p to $V_{pg^{-1}}$ via $(\psi_{g*})_p$, is the same as first applying the adjoint representation to $\underline{G}$ and then going straight to $V_{pg^{-1}}$ via *its* canonical isomorphism $\rho_{pg^{-1}}$:

$$(\psi_{g*})_p \circ \rho_p = \rho_{pg^{-1}} \circ \mathcal{D}(g) \cdot \qquad (15.16)$$

This can also be expressed by a commutative diagram:

$$
\begin{array}{ccc}
 & \mathcal{D}(g) & \\
\underline{G} & \longrightarrow & \underline{G} \\
\rho_p \downarrow & & \downarrow \rho_{pg^{-1}} \\
V_p & \longrightarrow & V_{pg^{-1}} \\
 & (\psi_{g*})_p &
\end{array}
$$

We emphasize that the concept and properties of vertical subspaces at points in a PFB, assembled above, all follow from the basic PFB structure; nothing additional is required. With this preparation, we go on to discuss connections.

15.2. DEFINING A CONNECTION ON A PFB

There are three ways to do this. We call them definitions A, B and C; look at them in sequence; and prove their equivalence.

   <u>Definition A</u> A connection consists in giving, for each $p \in P$ with $\pi(p) = m \in M$, a linear map σ_p from $T_m M$ to $T_p P$, varying smoothly with p and obeying two conditions:

$$\sigma_p \; : \; T_m M \to T_p P \; :$$
$$(i) \qquad (\pi_*)_p \circ \sigma_p = \mathcal{I}d_{T_m M} \, ,$$
$$(ii) \qquad (\psi_{g*})_p \circ \sigma_p = \sigma_{pg^{-1}} \cdot \qquad (15.17)$$

Let us spell out the consequences. The range of σ_p is a subspace of T_pP. We call it the *horizontal subspace at p* (corresponding of course to the given connection) and denote it by H_p:

$$\sigma_p(T_mM) = H_p \subset T_pP \, . \tag{15.18}$$

We can show immediately using condition (15.17(i)) that:

$$\begin{aligned}
\dim \cdot H_p &= \dim \cdot T_mM \, , \\
V_p \cap H_p &= \phi \, , \\
T_pP &= V_p \oplus H_p \, .
\end{aligned} \tag{15.19}$$

For, the first condition on σ_p means that the image under σ_p of any nonzero vector in T_mM is nonzero in T_pP; therefore the range of σ_p is of maximum dimension, namely $\dim \cdot T_mM$. In other words, $\sigma_p : T_mM \to H_p$ is non-singular. For these same reasons V_p and H_p have only the null vector in common. Combining all these facts leads to the last of eqs.(15.19).

The second condition (15.17(ii)) controls the behaviour of σ_p as p varies over a fibre in P. Equivalently, the horizontal subspaces at different points on a fibre get related:

$$(\psi_{g*})_p(H_p) = H_{pg^{-1}} \, , \tag{15.20}$$

to be compared with the known behaviour (15.6) of the vertical subspaces. So we are free only to assign H_p at one point on each fibre, and then elsewhere on that fibre it is determined by the PFB itself.

We can summarise Definition A thus: a connection is a way of smoothly supplementing the vertical subspaces V_p at points $p \in P$ by horizontal subspaces H_p, such that the full tangent space T_pP is the direct sum of vertical and horizontal parts, and the "equivariance" condition (15.20) holds along each fibre.

<u>Definition B</u> Now we deal directly with the horizontal subspaces H_p rather than view them as ranges of maps σ_p. A connection then consists of an assignment of a linear subspace $H_p \subset T_pP$ at each p, varying smoothly with p, such that:

$$\begin{aligned}
(i) \quad & T_pP = V_p \oplus H_p \, , \\
(ii) \quad & (\psi_{g*})_p(H_p) = H_{pg^{-1}} \, .
\end{aligned} \tag{15.21}$$

From the first condition it is clear that V_p and H_p have only the null vector in common, and $\dim \cdot H_p = \dim \cdot T_mM$. The second condition is the same "equivariance" statement, or law of variation along a fibre, as before. We can now see that, since V_p is the null space of $(\pi_*)_p$, the image under $(\pi_*)_p$ of any nonzero vector in H_p must be nonzero in $T_m M$. Thus, $(\pi_*)_p : H_p \to T_m M$ is an isomorphism; the map σ_p of definition A is just the inverse of this! The equivalence of definitions A and B is evident.

Definition C The vertical subspaces V_p are the null spaces of the maps $(\pi_*)_p$. Now the third way of defining a connection arises by characterizing each horizontal subspace H_p as the null space of a suitable linear map from $T_p P$ to something! Here is how we achieve this. We need to choose the "target space" of the map, the space into which the map leads us, appropriately; and we must ensure that exactly on nonvanishing vectors in V_p it has nonzero values. But we *know* that there is a canonical isomorphism ρ_p^{-1} from V_p to $\underline{G}$, given by the PFB itself. We exploit this fact and achieve our goal.

To give a connection on a PFB is to assign a linear map $\omega_p : T_p P \to \underline{G}$ for each $p \in P$, varying smoothly with p and obeying two conditions:

$$(i) \qquad \omega_p \circ \rho_p = \mathcal{I}d_{\underline{G}} \,,$$

$$(ii) \qquad \omega_{pg^{-1}} \circ (\psi_{g*})_p = \mathcal{D}(g) \circ \omega_p \cdot \qquad (15.22)$$

The first condition ensures that if $v \in V_p$ is nonzero, then $\omega_p(v)$ is also nonzero, and is in fact the vector $\rho_p^{-1}(v) \in \underline{G}$ assigned to v by the canonical $V_p \longleftrightarrow \underline{G}$ isomorphism. The second condition controls the behaviour of ω_p as p varies over a fibre; its specific form is fixed by requiring consistency with eq.(15.16) and the first condition on ω_p: we see this easily by composing each side of (15.22(ii)) with ρ_p on the right.

Given such an ω_p (at each p), we define H_p as its null space:

$$H_p = \{X \in T_p P \mid \omega_p(X) = 0\} \cdot \qquad (15.23)$$

Then from the nonvanishing of ω_p on V_p, the fact that it carries V_p exactly to $\underline{G}$, and eq.(15.2) relating dimensions, we see that $\dim \cdot H_p = \dim \cdot T_m M$ *exactly*, and also that V_p and H_p have no nonzero overlap. So we obtain

$$T_p P = V_p \oplus H_p. \qquad (15.24)$$

Finally (15.22(ii)) shows, since $(\psi_{g*})_p$ is nonsingular, that

$$H_{pg^{-1}} = (\psi_{g*})_p(H_p) \cdot \qquad (15.25)$$

Thus definition C is equivalent to definition B, and so in turn to definition A.

The reverse passage from definition B to definition C is also easy. Given the horizontal subspaces H_p obeying eqs.(15.21), any $X \in T_p P$ can be uniquely decomposed into vertical and horizontal components:

$$X \in T_p P : \quad X = X_{\text{hor}} + v \,,$$
$$X_{\text{hor}} \in H_p \,, \, v \in V_p \cdot \qquad (15.26)$$

The isomorphism $\rho_p^{-1} : V_p \to \underline{G}$ takes v to its image in $\underline{G}$. So we simply define ω_p by

$$\omega_p(X) = \rho_p^{-1}(v) \cdot \tag{15.27}$$

The conditions (15.22) on ω_p are easily seen to be satisfied.

Now ω_p is a linear map from T_pP to $\underline{G}$. Thus definition C for a connection amounts to giving a $\underline{G}$-valued one-form ω on P, reducing on each V_p to the canonical ρ_p^{-1}, and "transforming properly" under G. The condition (15.22(ii)) can be expressed neatly as

$$\psi_g^* \omega = \mathcal{D}(g) \circ \omega \cdot \tag{15.28}$$

15.3. LOCAL DESCRIPTIONS OF A CONNECTION

In the spirit of our study of affine connections in Section 10, let us see "what it takes" to set up a connection on a PFB, by working out the foregoing conditions and the matching formulae in overlaps, in their local forms. We use the notations of eqs.(14.25,26) for a set of overlapping trivializations of P. The diffeomorphism h_α^{-1} takes the portion $\pi^{-1}(\mathcal{U}_\alpha) \subset P$ to the Cartesian product $\mathcal{U}_\alpha \times G$:

$$
\begin{aligned}
h_\alpha^{-1} : \pi^{-1}(\mathcal{U}_\alpha) \;&\to\; \mathcal{U}_\alpha \times G \,, \\
p \in \pi^{-1}(\mathcal{U}_\alpha) \;&\Leftrightarrow\; p = h_\alpha(m, g_0) \equiv (m, g_0)_\alpha \,,
\end{aligned}
$$

$$
\begin{aligned}
h_\alpha^{-1}(p) \;&=\; (m, g_0) \,, \\
m \in \mathcal{U}_\alpha \;,\quad g_0 &\in G \cdot
\end{aligned}
\tag{15.29}
$$

(Here as in eq.(14.27) for brevity we denote p by an ordered pair with subscript α). Therefore the tangent map $(h_{\alpha *}^{-1})_p$ allows us to describe vectors in T_pP as "sums" of vectors in T_mM and $T_{g_0}G$. We introduce a notation for tangent vectors to accompany eq.(14.27) for points:

$$
\begin{aligned}
m \in \mathcal{U}_\alpha \;,\quad & p = (m, g_0)_\alpha \;: \\
\left(h_{\alpha *}^{-1} \right)_p \;&:\; T_pP \to T_mM \oplus T_{g_0}G \;; \\
X \in T_pP \;&:\; (h_{\alpha *}^{-1})_p(X) = u + t_{g_0} \,, \\
& \quad u \in T_mM \,,\; t_{g_0} \in T_{g_0}G \;; \\
X \;&=\; (u + t_{g_0})_\alpha \,, \\
(\pi_*)_p(X) \;&=\; u \cdot
\end{aligned}
\tag{15.30}
$$

We have here the locally trivialized form of eqs.(15.2) and in this sense we can exhibit elements of V_p explicitly:

$$p = (m, g_o)_\alpha \in \pi^{-1}(\mathcal{U}_\alpha) : V_p = \{(t_{g_o})_\alpha \in T_p P | t_{g_o} \in T_{g_o} G\} \cdot \quad (15.31)$$

It is also useful to work out the local forms of eqs. (15.4,6,12). For this, the following consequence of the machinery of Section 13 is needed:

$$(R_{g*})_{g_o} X_a^{(r)}(g_o) = \mathcal{D}^b{}_a (g) X_b^{(r)}(g_o g^{-1}) \cdot \quad (15.32)$$

Then, when necessary writing $t_{g_o} \in T_{g_o} G$ as the linear combination

$$t_{g_o} = t^a X_a^{(r)}(g_o) , \quad (15.33)$$

we get the local forms of eqs. (15.4,6,12) in that sequence (with $p = (m, g_o)_\alpha$ and $g \in G$ throughout):

$$\begin{aligned}
(\psi_{g*})_p : X &= (u + t_{g_o})_\alpha \in T_p P \to (u + (R_{g*})_{g_o} t_{g_o})_\alpha \\
&= \left(u + t^a \mathcal{D}^b{}_a (g) X_b^{(r)} \left(g_o g^{-1}\right)\right)_\alpha \in T_{pg^{-1}} P ;
\end{aligned}$$

$$(15.34a)$$

$$(\psi_{g*})_p : v = (t_{g_o})_\alpha \in V_p \to ((R_{g*})_{g_o} t_{g_o})_\alpha \in V_{pg^{-1}} ; \quad (15.34b)$$

$$t^a e_a \in \underline{G} : \rho_p (t^a e_a) = \left(t^a X_a^{(r)}(g_o)\right)_\alpha = (t_{g_o})_\alpha \in V_p ,$$

$$\rho_p^{-1} ((t_{g_o})_\alpha) = t^a e_a = e_a i_{t_{g_o}} \theta^{(r)a}(g_o) \in \underline{G} \cdot \quad (15.34c)$$

The local form of eq.(15.15) is clearly subsumed in the above. As is to be expected, under the map $(\psi_{g*})_p$ the "u part" of a tangent vector is unchanged, while the components of the "t_{g_o} part" get transformed by the adjoint representation of G.

Now we can see "what it takes" to define a connection locally over $\pi^{-1}(\mathcal{U}_\alpha)$. We write:

$$p = (m, g_o)_\alpha , \ X = \left(u + t^a X_a^{(r)}(g_o)\right)_\alpha \in T_p P :$$

$$\begin{aligned}
\omega_p(X) &= \omega_p((u)_\alpha) + \omega_p \left(\left(t^a X_a^{(r)}(g_o)\right)_\alpha\right) \\
&= \left(t^a - A^{(\alpha)a}(m, g_o)(u)\right) e_a \in \underline{G} ,
\end{aligned}$$

$$\omega_p \left(\left(X_a^{(r)}(g_o)\right)_\alpha\right) = e_a ,$$

$$A^{(\alpha)a}(m, g_o) \in T_m^* M \cdot \quad (15.35)$$

The effect of ω_p on the vertical part is fixed by the condition (15.22(i)); the only freedom is in the choice of the co-vectors $A^{(\alpha)a}(m, g_o)$. Now we bring in the "equivariance" condition (15.22(ii)): it essentially determines the dependence of $A^{(\alpha)a}(m, g_o)$ on g_o! Apply both sides of condition (15.22(ii)) to some $X \in T_p P$ expressed in the form above, use eq.(15.34(a)) and simplify to get:

$$A^{(\alpha)a}\left(m, g_o g^{-1}\right) = \mathcal{D}^a{}_b (g) A^{(\alpha)b}(m, g_o) \cdot \qquad (15.36)$$

We can now set $g_o \to e$, $g \to g^{-1}$ and conclude:

$$\begin{aligned} A^{(\alpha)a}(m, g) &= \mathcal{D}^a{}_b (g^{-1}) A^{(\alpha)b}(m) , \\ A^{(\alpha)a}(m) &\equiv A^{(\alpha)a}(m, e) \in T_m^* M \cdot \end{aligned} \qquad (15.37)$$

Then from eq.(15.35) $\omega_p(X)$ and ω_p become:

$$\begin{aligned} \omega_p(X) &= \left(t^a - \mathcal{D}^a{}_b \left(g_o^{-1}\right) A^{(\alpha)b}(m)(u)\right) e_a , \\ \omega_p &= \left(\theta^{(r)a}(g_o) - \mathcal{D}^a{}_b \left(g_o^{-1}\right) A^{(\alpha)b}(m)\right) e_a \cdot \end{aligned} \qquad (15.38)$$

Thus the specification of ω over each $\pi^{-1}(\mathcal{U}_\alpha)$ involves the choice of the set of (local) one-forms $A^{(\alpha)a} \in \mathcal{X}^*(\mathcal{U}_\alpha)$: these are completely free except for the compatibility conditions in overlaps $\mathcal{U}_\alpha \cap \mathcal{U}_\beta$ to which we now turn.

Let $\pi(p) = m \in \mathcal{U}_\alpha \cap \mathcal{U}_\beta$. Then both p and any $X \in T_p P$ can be given two local descriptions. For the former, the relation between them is known from eq.(14.27):

$$\begin{aligned} p &= (m, g)_\alpha = (m, g')_\beta , \\ g' &= t_{\beta\alpha}(m) g \cdot \end{aligned} \qquad (15.39)$$

From here we should deduce the relation between the two local descriptions of X. In the manner of eq.(15.30) write:

$$\begin{aligned} X &= (u + t_g)_\alpha = (u' + t'_{g'})_\beta , \\ u, u' &\in T_m M , \\ t_g &\in T_g G , \ t'_{g'} \in T_{g'} G \cdot \end{aligned} \qquad (15.40)$$

If $u = 0$, then $X \in V_p$ and the canonical isomorphism to $\underline{G}$ determines u', $t'_{g'}$:

$$u = 0, \ t_g = t^a X_a^{(r)}(g) \Leftrightarrow u' = 0, t'_{g'} = t^a X_a^{(r)}(g') \cdot \qquad (15.41)$$

So we only need to find the "β description" of $(u)_\alpha$. For this we recognize from eq.(15.39) that if we imagine a smooth curve passing through p, along which (in the α description) m varies while g does not, so that its tangent at p is some $(u)_\alpha$, then (in the β description) the element g' does vary. It is this that has to be suitably expressed; that is, a nonzero u with a vanishing t_g induces nonzero u' as well as $t'_{g'}$. We now view the transition group element $t_{\beta\alpha}(m)$ as a map $\mathcal{U}_\alpha \cap \mathcal{U}_\beta \to G$:

$$t_{\beta\alpha} : \mathcal{U}_\alpha \cap \mathcal{U}_\beta \to G : m \in \mathcal{U}_\alpha \cap \mathcal{U}_\beta \to t_{\beta\alpha}(m) \in G \cdot \qquad (15.42)$$

Then we can see that, by imagining a smooth curve through p with tangent $(u)_\alpha$ there:

$$t_g = 0 \Rightarrow u' = u \,,$$
$$t'_{g'} = \left((R_{g^{-1}} \circ t_{\beta\alpha})_*\right)_m (u) \in T_{g'}G \cdot \qquad (15.43)$$

Putting together these results, we get the tangent vector counter part of eq.(15.39):

$$\left(u + t^a X_a^{(r)}(g)\right)_\alpha = \left(u + \left((R_{g^{-1}} \circ t_{\beta\alpha})_*\right)_m (u) + t^a X_a^{(r)}(g')\right)_\beta \,,$$
$$g' = \left(R_{g^{-1}} \circ t_{\beta\alpha}\right)(m) = t_{\beta\alpha}(m)\, g \cdot \qquad (15.44)$$

Now we compute $\omega_p(X)$ separately over $\pi^{-1}(\mathcal{U}_\alpha)$ and $\pi^{-1}(\mathcal{U}_\beta)$ using eqs. (15.38), and equate the results in the overlap. This gives:

$$m \in \mathcal{U}_\alpha \cap \mathcal{U}_\beta \,,\ u \in T_m M \,,\ g \in G \,,\ g' = t_{\beta\alpha}(m)g \,:$$

$$\mathcal{D}^a{}_b (g^{-1}) A^{(\alpha)b}(m)(u) = \mathcal{D}^a{}_b (g'^{-1}) A^{(\beta)b}(m)(u)$$
$$- \left\langle \theta^{(r)a}(g'), \left((R_{g^{-1}} \circ t_{\beta\alpha})_*\right)_m (u)\right\rangle \cdot$$
$$(15.45)$$

Here we have allowed p to be any point $(m, g)_\alpha$ on the fibre $\pi^{-1}(m)$. Let us set $g = e$ here; then we get the transition rule we are after:

$$A^{(\alpha)a}(m) = \mathcal{D}^a{}_b \left(t_{\beta\alpha}^{-1}(m)\right) A^{(\beta)b}(m) - \left(t_{\beta\alpha}^* \theta^{(r)a}\right)(m) \cdot \qquad (15.46)$$

We summarise: to assign a connection ω on a PFB is to choose a set of one-forms $A^{(\alpha)a} \in \mathcal{X}^*(\mathcal{U}_\alpha)$ over each $\mathcal{U}_\alpha$, such that the choices in any two overlapping regions are connected by the linear inhomogeneous law (15.46).

Returning to a single $\mathcal{U}_\alpha$, we can "isolate" $A^{(\alpha)a}$ from ω over it by setting up a local section σ_α in the PFB, and applying the pull-back to ω:

$$\sigma_\alpha : \mathcal{U}_\alpha \to \pi^{-1}(\mathcal{U}_\alpha) : m \in \mathcal{U}_\alpha \to (m,\, e)_\alpha \; ;$$

$$(\sigma_\alpha^* \omega)\,(m) = -e_a \, A^{(\alpha)a}(m) \cdot \tag{15.47}$$

In effect, σ_α "freezes" the group element involved in the local trivialization, so after pull back only $A^{(\alpha)}$ remains.

Once a connection ω is given, we can locally exhibit the horizontal subspaces H_p explicitly, as V_p was in eq. (15.31). Working over $\pi^{-1}(\mathcal{U}_\alpha)$, we have from eq. (15.38) (after replacing g_o by g):

$$X = \left(u + t^a X_a^{(r)}(g)\right)_\alpha \in T_p P \; :$$

$$X \in H_p \;\Leftrightarrow\; \omega_p(X) = 0$$
$$\Leftrightarrow\; t^a = \mathcal{D}^a{}_b\,(g^{-1}) A^{(\alpha)b}(m)(u) \; ;$$

$$\begin{aligned} H_p &= \left\{ \left(u + X_a^{(r)}(g)\mathcal{D}^a{}_b\,(g^{-1}) A^{(\alpha)b}(m)(u)\right)_\alpha \Big| \; u \in T_m M \right\} \\ &= \left\{ \left(u - X_a^{(\ell)}(g) A^{(\alpha)a}(m)(u)\right)_\alpha \Big| \; u \in T_m M \right\} \cdot \end{aligned} \tag{15.48}$$

Here eq.(13.38) has been used. Thus the isomorphism $H_p \leftrightarrow T_m M$ is made explicit. In the sense of definition A of a connection, the map $\sigma_p : T_m M \to T_p P$ is locally given as follows:

$$u \in T_m M : \sigma_p(u) = \left(u - X_a^{(\ell)}(g) A^{(\alpha)a}(m)(u)\right)_\alpha \in H_p \subset T_p P \cdot$$
$$\tag{15.49}$$

15.4. SOME USEFUL RESULTS FROM LIE GROUP REPRESENTATION THEORY

At this point we assemble some formulae from the theory of linear (matrix) representations of Lie groups and Lie algebras, which make it possible to express the basic relationships such as the transition rule (15.46), and other results needed later, in a compact manner. Thus our more or less purely geometrical treatment upto this point gets supplemented by a collection of algebraic techniques as well. These are a counterpart to the description in Section 13 of Lie group action on a differentiable manifold, generating vector fields etc.

Given a Lie group G with Lie algebra $\underline{G}$ spanned by basis vectors e_a, a linear representation of G associates to each $g \in G$ a nonsingular linear operator $D(g)$ (a matrix) acting on a (real or complex finite dimensional) linear vector space $\mathcal{V}$, obeying the appropriate composition laws:

$$g \in G \ \rightarrow \ D(g) \text{ acting on } \mathcal{V} \ ,$$
$$D(g') \, D(g) \ = \ D(g'g) \ ,$$
$$D(e) \ = \ 1 \text{ on } \mathcal{V} \cdot \qquad (15.50)$$

At the Lie algebra level we have a correspondence $e_a \rightarrow T_a$, the (matrix) generators of the representation $D(\cdot)$. These generators are linear operators on $\mathcal{V}$ obeying the commutation relations

$$[T_a, \ T_b] \equiv T_a \, T_b - T_b \, T_a = -f_{ab}{}^c \, T_c \ \cdot \qquad (15.51)$$

Thus the abstract Lie bracket relations (13.22) are realised in a linear representation by operator commutation relations.

To go from the T_a to the $D(g)$ involves a process of integration or exponentiation. Here global aspects can intervene. While a representation $D(\cdot)$ of G always leads to a representation $\{T_a\}$ of $\underline{G}$, the converse need not be the case. In general, a set $\{T_a\}$ obeying eqs.(15.51) leads upon exponentiation to a representation of the so-called simply connected universal covering group $\overline{G}$ of G, not necessarily of G itself. (The general properties of $\overline{G}$, and of the relation between G and $\overline{G}$, are studied in Section 17). This may be regarded as a "multivalued representation" of G. We shall hereafter assume that we actually obtain a true representation of G itself. Then the commutation relations (15.51) are an expression of, and ensure, the group composition law in (15.50).

With this specific assumption we can say: elements in G on a one-parameter subgroup $\{\exp(st)\}$, $t = t^a e_a \in \underline{G}$, are represented by the corresponding "ordinary" exponential of a linear combination of the generators T_a:

$$t = t^a e_a \in \underline{G} : D(\exp(s \, t)) = \exp(s \, t^a T_a) \ \cdot \qquad (15.52)$$

If we take s to be an infinitesimal δs, $|\delta s| \ll 1$, then $\exp(\delta s.t)$ is an element in G close to e, and to leading order it is represented as

$$D\left(\exp\left(\delta s. \ t^a e_a\right)\right) \simeq 1 + \delta s. t^a T_a \cdot \qquad (15.53)$$

One can now check that the presence of the negative sign on the right hand side of Eq.(15.51) follows from consistency between the group representation property (15.50) and the manner in which the generators T_a have been related to the $D(g)$ in Eqs.(15.52, 53).

Now we can develop in a nice way the rule to handle tangent vectors at general points $g \in G$, in the representation $D(\cdot)$. Let $g_o(s)$ be a smooth curve in G, passing through e at $s = 0$, and with tangent $t = t^a e_a \in T_e G$ there. Applying L_g for some $g \in G$ to the elements $g_o(s)$ we get another smooth curve $g_\ell(s)$ passing through g at $s = 0$:

$$
\begin{aligned}
g_\ell(s) &= L_g g_o(s) = g\, g_o(s)\,, \\
g_\ell(o) &= g\,\cdot
\end{aligned}
\tag{15.54}
$$

The tangent to $g_\ell(s)$ at $s = 0$ is then given by

$$
\begin{aligned}
(L_{g*})_e(t) &= t^a (L_{g*})_e(e_a) \\
&= -t^a X_a^{(r)}(g) \in T_g G\,,
\end{aligned}
\tag{15.55}
$$

where we used eq.(13.20). Now we argue as follows. If $g_o(\delta s)$ is an element on $g_o(\cdot)$ close to $g_o(0) = e$, the vector in $T_e G$ leading from e to $g_o(\delta s)$ is $\delta s.t^a e_a$. Therefore the tangent vector in $T_g G$ leading from $g_\ell(o) = g$ to the nearby element $g_\ell(\delta s)$ is $-\delta s.t^a X_a^{(r)}(g)$. By the group composition law, however,

$$
\begin{aligned}
D(g_\ell(\delta s)) &= D(g\, g_o(\delta s)) \\
&= D(g) D(g_o(\delta s)) \\
&\simeq D(g)\,(1 + \delta s.t^a T_a)\,\cdot
\end{aligned}
\tag{15.56}
$$

This can now be "read backwards": if g' is any element close to g, and the vector leading from g to g' is $\delta\ s.t_g \in T_g G$, then

$$
D(g') \simeq D(g)\left(1 - \delta s.i_{t_g}\theta^{(r)a}(g)T_a\right)
\tag{15.57}
$$

Thus the change in $D(g)$, a matrix function on G, in going from g to g' is

$$
\begin{aligned}
\delta\ D(g) &= D(g') - D(g) \\
&\simeq \delta s.i_{t_g} d\ D(g) \\
&= -\delta s.D(g) i_{t_g}\theta^{(r)a}(g)T_a\,, \\
d\ D(g) &= -D(g)T_a \theta^{(r)a}(g)\,\cdot
\end{aligned}
\tag{15.58}
$$

Here $d\ D(g)$ is a matrix of one-forms on G, obtained by applying d to each matrix element which is a (complex valued) function on G.

In a similar way, if we apply $R_{g^{-1}}$ to the curve $g_o(s)$, we produce the curve

$$
g_r(s) = R_{g^{-1}}g_o(s) = g_o(s)\,g\,,
\tag{15.59}
$$

again passing through g at $s = o$. Its tangent at g is

$$
\begin{aligned}
(R_{g^{-1}*})e(t) &= t^a (R_{g^{-1}*})e(e_a) \\
&= t^a X_a^{(\ell)}(g) \in T_g G \cdot
\end{aligned}
\tag{15.60}
$$

Now in place of eq.(15.56) we have from the group composition law:

$$
\begin{aligned}
D(g_r(\delta s)) &= D(g_o(\delta s)\, g) \\
&= D(g_o(\delta s))\, D(g) \\
&\simeq (1 + \delta s.t^a T_a)\, D(g)
\end{aligned}
\tag{15.61}
$$

Correspondingly if the vector $\delta s.t_g \in T_g G$ leads from g to a nearby g' we can say:

$$
D(g') \simeq \left(1 + \delta s.i_{t_g}\theta^{(\ell)a}(g)T_a\right) D(g) \cdot
\tag{15.62}
$$

This gives a companion to eq. (15.58):

$$
d\, D(g) = T_a \theta^{(\ell)a}(g)D(g) \cdot
\tag{15.63}
$$

Collecting our results we have the key formulae

$$
\begin{aligned}
D(g)^{-1}d\, D(g) &= -T_a \theta^{(r)a}(g) , \\
d\, D(g)\, D(g)^{-1} &= T_a \theta^{(\ell)a}(g) \cdot
\end{aligned}
\tag{15.64}
$$

By comparing these two forms for $dD(g)$ and bringing in the dual to eq.(13.38), namely

$$
\theta^{(\ell)a}(g) = -\mathcal{D}^a{}_b(g)\theta^{(r)b}(g) ,
\tag{15.65}
$$

we see that in any linear representation of G the generators transform upon conjugation according to the adjoint representation:

$$
D(g)\, T_a D(g)^{-1} = \mathcal{D}^b{}_a(g)\, T_b \cdot
\tag{15.66}
$$

One last item in this collection of useful results. Let

$$
\gamma : s \in (a, b) \to g(s) \in G
\tag{15.67}
$$

be a smooth parametrised curve in G. The tangent vector to it at $g(s)$ is

$$
X(s) = (\gamma_*)_s \left(\frac{d}{ds}\right) \in T_{g(s)}G \cdot
\tag{15.68}
$$

Thus the infinitesimal vector leading from $g(s)$ to the nearby element $g(s + \delta s)$ is $\delta s.X(s)$. By the "converse relations" (15.57,62) we can say:

$$D(g(s + \delta s)) \;\simeq\; D(g(s)) \left(1 - \delta s.T_a i_{X(s)} \theta^{(r)a}(g(s))\right)$$

$$\simeq\; \left(1 + \delta s.T_a i_{X(s)} \theta^{(\ell)a}(g(s))\right) D(g(s)) \cdot \quad (15.69)$$

So the matrix representative $D(g(s))$ of a smooth curve of elements $g(s)$ in G obeys two ordinary differential equations:

$$\frac{d}{ds} D(g(s)) \;=\; i_{X(s)} \theta^{(\ell)a}(g(s)) T_a\, D(g(s))$$

$$=\; -i_{X(s)} \theta^{(r)a}(g(s))\, D(g(s))\, T_a \cdot \quad (15.70)$$

In any application we can use either one of these depending on convenience.

As immediate illustrations of uses of these formulae, let us express the local description (15.38) of a connection, and the transition rule (15.46), in compact matrix forms. Using the generators $\{T_a\}$ of an (unspecified) matrix representation $D(\cdot)$ of G, over each $\mathcal{U}_\alpha$ we define the ($\underline{G}$-valued) matrix one-form $A^{(\alpha)}$ as

$$m \in \mathcal{U}_\alpha : A^{(\alpha)}(m) = A^{(\alpha)a}(m) T_a \cdot \quad (15.71)$$

Similarly we picture $\omega_p(X)$, ω_p of eq.(15.38) as matrices in the representation of $\underline{G}$ rather than as abstract vectors in $\underline{G}$:

$$p = (m, g)_\alpha\,,\; X \;=\; \left(u + t^a X_a^{(r)}(g)\right)_\alpha \in T_p P :$$

$$\omega_p(X) \;=\; \left(t^a - \mathcal{D}^a{}_b\, (g^{-1}) A^{(\alpha)b}(m)(u)\right) T_a$$

$$=\; t^a T_a - D(g)^{-1} A^{(\alpha)}(m)(u) D(g) ;$$

$$\omega_p \;=\; \left(\theta^{(r)a}(g) - \mathcal{D}^a{}_b\, (g^{-1}) A^{(\alpha)b}(m)\right) T_a$$

$$=\; -D(g)^{-1} \left(A^{(\alpha)}(m) + d\right) D(g) \cdot \quad (15.72)$$

Here we made use of eqs.(15.64,66) and the definition (15.71). To put the transition rule (15.46) into similar form, we can either multiply both sides of (15.46) by T_a and exploit (15.64,66), or more simply combine (15.72) with the transition rule (15.39) for local trivializations. The net result is:

$$m \in \mathcal{U}_\alpha \cap \mathcal{U}_\beta : A^{(\beta)}(m) = D(t_{\beta\alpha}(m))(A^{(\alpha)}(m) + d) D(t_{\alpha\beta}(m)) \cdot \quad (15.73)$$

We may make here a remark which could well have been made at eq.(15.46). Namely, that transition rule for the local descriptions of a connection can be used not only in a "genuine" overlap $\mathcal{U}_\alpha \cap \mathcal{U}_\beta$ where $\mathcal{U}_\beta \neq \mathcal{U}_\alpha$,

but also in case over a given $\mathcal{U}_\alpha$ we change the diffeomorphism h_α trivial-
ising the portion $\pi^{-1}(\mathcal{U}_\alpha)$ in P. For this purpose, in the previous formulae
we just take $\mathcal{U}_\beta = \mathcal{U}_\alpha$ but let h_β be different from h_α and write h'_α for it!
Then the transition group element $t_{\beta\alpha}(m)$ boils down to $t_\alpha(m)$ defined over
$\mathcal{U}_\alpha$, and we have:

$$p \in P , \ \pi(p) = m \in \mathcal{U}_\alpha \ :$$
$$p = h_\alpha(m,g) \ = \ h'_\alpha(m, t_\alpha(m)g) ,$$
$$t_\alpha(m) \in G \cdot \tag{15.74}$$

Thus the change $h_\alpha \to h'_\alpha$ is determined by a map $t_\alpha : \mathcal{U}_\alpha \to G$. The two
local sections σ_α, σ'_α over $\mathcal{U}_\alpha$, both defined in the manner of eq.(15.47), are
related pointwise by

$$m \in \mathcal{U}_\alpha : \sigma'_\alpha(m) \ = \ h'_\alpha(m, e)$$
$$= \ h_\alpha\left(m, t_\alpha(m)^{-1}\right)$$
$$= \ \psi_{t_\alpha(m)}(\sigma_\alpha(m)) \cdot \tag{15.75}$$

And the two $\underline{G}$-valued one-forms $A^{(\alpha)}$ and $A'^{(\alpha)}$, both defined over $\mathcal{U}_\alpha$, are
related by the same kind of formula as (15.73):

$$m \in \mathcal{U}_\alpha : A'^{(\alpha)}(m) = D(t_\alpha(m))(A^{(\alpha)}(m) + d)D(t_\alpha(m))^{-1} \cdot \tag{15.76}$$

15.5.   THE CASE OF FM - RECOVERING AFFINE CONNECTIONS

As an important illustration of the above developments we consider now the
case of the frame bundle FM over an n-dimensional differentiable manifold
M. In Section 10 we have seen how to define an affine connection on M,
namely as a differentiation process - a derivation - on tensor fields. Then
in Section 14 we have recognised that FM is a PFB of dimension $n(n+1)$,
with base M and n^2-dimensional structure group (and typical fibre) $G =
GL(n, R)$. Now we will show that the general definition of a connection on a
PFB reduces in the FM case to the definition of an affine connection on M
- there will be complete agreement with the formalism of Section 10. Once
this is done, we can consider whether and to what extent and in what form
the other ideas of Section 10 - parallel transport, covariant differentiation,
curvature, ...- generalise to any PFB carrying a connection.

Let us briefly recall the PFB structure of FM, exhibited in Section 14.
Using a redundant notation, a point $e \in FM$ is a pair consisting of a base
point in M and a frame for the tangent space there:

$$e \in FM \ , \quad \pi(e) = m \in M \ :$$
$$e = (m, \{e_a(m)\}) ,$$
$$\{e_a(m)\} \in F(T_m M) \cdot \tag{15.77}$$

Denote elements of $GL(n,R)$ by matrices $A = (A^a{}_b)$, A', $A_0,...$ in the defining representation. Then as in eq.(14.36) the right global group action is by fibre-preserving maps ψ_A:

$$A \in GL(n,R), \; e \in FM :$$
$$
\begin{aligned}
e' &= \psi_A(e) \equiv e\, A^{-1} \\
&= (m, \{e'_a(m)\}) , \\
e'_a(m) &= e_b(m)(A^{-1})^b{}_a ; \\
\psi_{A'} \circ \psi_A &= \psi_{A'A} .
\end{aligned}
\tag{15.78}
$$

We come to local descriptions, transition rules, in a moment.

At this point let us collect expressions and objects relating to $GL(n,R)$ and its Lie algebra, working in the defining (rather than in an unspecified) representation. (We also switch to Greek indices rather than $a, b, \ldots$, to be prepared for the later use of local coordinates $x^\mu, x'^\mu, \ldots$ on M). The generators $\{T_a\}$ of $GL(n,R)$ are written as $\{T^\mu{}_\nu\}$. Their definitions via matrix elements, and commutation relations, are:

$$
\begin{aligned}
(T^\mu{}_\nu)^\rho{}_\sigma &= \delta^\mu{}_\sigma \delta^\rho{}_\nu ; \\
[T^\mu{}_\nu, T^\rho{}_\sigma] &= \delta^\mu{}_\sigma T^\rho{}_\nu - \delta^\rho{}_\nu T^\mu{}_\sigma .
\end{aligned}
\tag{15.79}
$$

The two sets of vector fields over $GL(n,R)$ must correspondingly be written as $X^{(r)\mu}{}_\nu (A), X^{(\ell)\mu}{}_\nu (A)$. Their dual one-forms can then also be consistently written as $\theta^{(r)\mu}{}_\nu (A)$, $\theta^{(\ell)\mu}{}_\nu(A)$. Since the only condition on the real matrix A is that it be nonsingular, its n^2 elements can be used as independent coordinates over $GL(n,R)$. Then starting from eqs.(15.64) we easily find the following expressions at a general element $A \in GL(n,R)$:

$$
\begin{aligned}
\theta^{(\ell)\mu}{}_\nu (A) &= (A^{-1})^\lambda{}_\nu \, dA^\mu{}_\lambda , \\
\theta^{(r)\mu}{}_\nu (A) &= -(A^{-1})^\mu{}_\lambda \, dA^\lambda{}_\nu ; \\
X^{(\ell)\mu}{}_\nu (A) &= A^\mu{}_\lambda \, \partial/\partial A^\nu{}_\lambda , \\
X^{(r)\mu}{}_\nu (A) &= -A^\lambda{}_\nu \, \partial/\partial A^\lambda{}_\mu ; \\
\langle \theta^{(\ell)\rho}{}_\sigma (A), X^{(\ell)\mu}{}_\nu (A) \rangle &= \langle \theta^{(r)\rho}{}_\sigma (A), X^{(r)\mu}{}_\nu (A) \rangle \\
&= \delta^\rho{}_\nu \, \delta^\mu{}_\sigma .
\end{aligned}
\tag{15.80}
$$

From eq.(15.66) we get the elements of the n^2-dimensional adjoint representation matrices $\mathcal{D}(A)$:

$$
\begin{aligned}
A\, T^\mu{}_\nu \, A^{-1} &= \mathcal{D}(A)^\rho{}_\sigma{}^\mu{}_\nu \, T^\sigma{}_\rho , \\
\mathcal{D}(A)^\rho{}_\sigma{}^\mu{}_\nu &= A^\rho{}_\nu \, (A^{-1})^\mu{}_\sigma .
\end{aligned}
\tag{15.81}
$$

Now we can work out the local descriptions (trivializations) and transition formulae for FM, adapted to an atlas $\mathcal{A} = \{(\mathcal{U}_\alpha, \varphi_\alpha)\}$ for M, as already outlined in Section 14. (We use φ_α in place of ψ_α since the group acts via maps ψ_A). The map φ_α assigns coordinates to points $m \in \mathcal{U}_\alpha$ and also provides a coordinate-basis for $T_m M$:

$$m \in \mathcal{U}_\alpha \longrightarrow \varphi_\alpha(m) = x \equiv \{x^\mu\} = \text{local coordinates of } m \, ;$$
$$\{(\partial/\partial x^\mu)_m\} = \text{basis for } T_m M \cdot \qquad (15.82)$$

Then the local description of FM over $\pi^{-1}(\mathcal{U}_\alpha)$ looks thus:

$$m \in \mathcal{U}_\alpha \, , \, e = (m, \{e_\mu(m)\}) \in \pi^{-1}(m) \subset \pi^{-1}(\mathcal{U}_\alpha) \, :$$
$$e = h_\alpha(x, A) \equiv (x, A)_\alpha \, ,$$
$$x \in \varphi_\alpha(\mathcal{U}_\alpha) \subset \mathcal{R}^n \, ,$$
$$e_\mu(m) = A^\nu_{\ \mu} (\partial/\partial x^\nu)_m \, , \, A \in G \cdot \qquad (15.83)$$

(So we have here a further extension of the notation introduced at eq. (14.27): the base point m has been represented by its local coordinates). In the overlap $\mathcal{U}_\alpha \cap \mathcal{U}_\beta$ of two open sets in M carrying coordinates x, x' we easily find the transition rule (14.39) as an instance of (14.26,27):

$$\pi(e) = m \in \mathcal{U}_\alpha \cap \mathcal{U}_\beta \, :$$
$$e = (x, A)_\alpha = (x', A')_\beta \, ,$$
$$A' = J_{\beta\alpha}(x'|x) \, A \, ,$$
$$J_{\beta\alpha}(x'|x) = (\partial x'^\mu/\partial x^\nu) \in GL(n, R) \cdot \qquad (15.84)$$

That is, the transition group element $t_{\beta\alpha}(m)$ is the Jacobian matrix of the local coordinate transformation. The right global action is locally seen as

$$\psi_B(x, A)_\alpha = (x, AB^{-1})_\alpha \cdot \qquad (15.85)$$

The tangent spaces to FM, the tangent maps $(\psi_{B*})_e$, the vertical subspaces and canonical isomorphisms can all be similarly expressed. Thus eqs.(15.30,34(a)) take the forms (using the notation of eq.(15.33)):

$$e = (x, A)_\alpha, \, X \in T_e(FM) \, :$$
$$X = (u + t_A)_\alpha \, ,$$
$$u = u^\mu \frac{\partial}{\partial x^\mu} \in T_m M \, ,$$
$$t_A = t^\mu_{\ \nu} \, X^{(r)\nu}_{\ \mu} (A) \in T_A G \, ;$$
$$(\psi_{B*})_e(X) = X' \in T_{eB^{-1}}(FM) \, ,$$
$$X' = (u + t'_{AB^{-1}})_\alpha \, ,$$

(15.86a)

$$t'_{AB^{-1}} = t'^{\mu}{}_{\nu} X^{(r)\nu}{}_{\mu} (AB^{-1}) \in T_{AB^{-1}}G ,$$
$$t'^{\mu}{}_{\nu} = \mathcal{D}(B)^{\mu}{}_{\nu}{}^{\rho}{}_{\sigma} t^{\sigma}{}_{\rho} ,$$
$$\text{i.e., } t' = B t B^{-1} . \tag{15.86b}$$

The vertical subspace V_e and the canonical isomorphism $\rho_e : \underline{G} \to V_e$ follow from eqs. (15.31,34c) in the present case:

$$V_e = \{(t_A)_\alpha | t_A \in T_A G\}$$
$$= \left\{ \left(t^{\mu}{}_{\nu} X^{(r)\nu}{}_{\mu} (A) \right)_\alpha \middle| t \in \underline{G} \right\} ;$$
$$\rho_e (T^{\mu}{}_{\nu}) = \left(X^{(r)\mu}{}_{\nu} (A) \right)_\alpha \in V_e . \tag{15.87}$$

Viewing FM as a PFB over M, we can now see what it takes to define a connection on it. To avoid clashing with the use of A, A',... for elements of $GL(n, R)$, we write Γ in place of the (one-form) A locally describing a connection. Further, in the spirit of Section 10 and to facilitate comparison, we avoid superscripts α, β, ... on Γ: thus over $\mathcal{U}_\alpha$, respectively $\mathcal{U}_\beta$, we simply write Γ, respectively Γ'. The correspondence with the general notation is:

$$A^{(\alpha)a}(m) \to \Gamma^{\mu}{}_{\nu} (x) = \Gamma^{\mu}{}_{\nu\lambda} (x) \, dx^{\lambda} ,$$
$$A^{(\alpha)}(m) = A^{(\alpha)a}(m)T_a \to \Gamma(x) = \Gamma^{\mu}{}_{\nu} (x)T^{\nu}{}_{\mu}$$
$$= (\Gamma^{\mu}{}_{\nu} (x)) . \tag{15.88}$$

So $\Gamma(x)$ is a matrix with each element $\Gamma^{\mu}{}_{\nu} (x)$ a one-form over $\mathcal{U}_\alpha$. Then eq.(15.72) giving the local description of a connection ω at e, and its action on any $X \in T_e(FM)$, are in the FM case:

$$e = (x, A)_\alpha, \ X = \left(u + t^{\mu}{}_{\nu} X^{(r)\nu}{}_{\mu} (A) \right)_\alpha :$$
$$\omega(e) = \omega^{\mu}{}_{\nu} (e) \, T^{\nu}{}_{\mu}$$
$$= -A^{-1}(\Gamma(x) + d) \, A ,$$
$$\omega^{\mu}{}_{\nu}(e) = \theta^{(r)\mu}{}_{\nu} (A) - (A^{-1})^{\mu}{}_{\rho} A^{\sigma}{}_{\nu} \Gamma^{\rho}{}_{\sigma\lambda} (x) \, dx^{\lambda} ;$$
$$\omega^{\mu}{}_{\nu} (e)(X) = t^{\mu}{}_{\nu} - (A^{-1})^{\mu}{}_{\rho} A^{\sigma}{}_{\nu} \Gamma^{\rho}{}_{\sigma\lambda} (x) \, u^{\lambda} . \tag{15.89}$$

So the horizontal subspace H_e is a collection of vectors in $T_e(FM)$, in one-to-one correspondence with $u \in T_m M$:

$$H_e = \{X \in T_e(FM) | \omega(e)(X) = 0\}$$
$$= \left\{ \left(u + (A^{-1})^{\mu}{}_{\rho} A^{\sigma}{}_{\nu} \Gamma^{\rho}{}_{\sigma\lambda} (x) u^{\lambda} X^{(r)\nu}{}_{\mu} (A) \right)_\alpha \middle| u \in T_m M \right\} .$$
$$\tag{15.90}$$

The final and crucial step is to work out the transition formula (15.73) and see if we recover eq.(10.4) for an affine connection on M. The translation of eq.(15.73) is:

$$A^{(\beta)}(m) = D(t_{\beta\alpha}(m))(A^{(\alpha)}(m) + d)D(t_{\alpha\beta}(m)) \longrightarrow$$
$$\Gamma'(x') = J(x'|x)(\Gamma(x) + d)J(x|x') \cdot \qquad (15.91)$$

We can calculate the general matrix element of the left hand side:

$$
\begin{aligned}
\Gamma'^{\mu}{}_{\nu\lambda}(x')dx'^{\lambda} &= \frac{\partial x'^{\mu}}{\partial x^{\rho}} \left(\Gamma(x) + d\right)^{\rho}{}_{\sigma} \frac{\partial x^{\sigma}}{\partial x'^{\nu}} \\
&= \frac{\partial x'^{\mu}}{\partial x^{\rho}} \left(\Gamma^{\rho}{}_{\sigma\tau}(x) \, dx^{\tau} \frac{\partial x^{\sigma}}{\partial x'^{\nu}} + d \frac{\partial x^{\rho}}{\partial x'^{\nu}}\right), \\
\text{i.e., } \Gamma'^{\mu}{}_{\nu\lambda}(x') &= \frac{\partial x'^{\mu}}{\partial x^{\rho}} \left(\frac{\partial x^{\sigma}}{\partial x'^{\nu}} \frac{\partial x^{\tau}}{\partial x'^{\lambda}} \Gamma^{\rho}{}_{\sigma\tau}(x) + \frac{\partial^2 x^{\rho}}{\partial x'^{\nu} \partial x'^{\lambda}}\right) \cdot
\end{aligned}
$$

$$(15.92)$$

This agrees exactly with eq.(10.4)! Thus indeed we have recovered in full detail the earlier "calculus-based" definition of an affine connection on M, starting from the more geometrical definition of a connection on any PFB. The two approaches have been reconciled.

15.6. PARALLEL TRANSPORT - HORIZONTAL LIFTS - IN A PFB

Now we examine which of the main developments of Section 10, based on an affine connection on a differentiable manifold M, can be carried over to a general PFB. Recall briefly the situation in Section 10: subject to the list of requirements (10.1) that any affine connection must satisfy, a specific one is completely determined by the action of ∇_X, for any $X \in \mathcal{X}(M)$, on any $Y \in \mathcal{X}(M)$; the action on vector fields fixes all other actions. This then led to the following natural concepts and constructions: (i) given a smooth parametrised curve $\gamma = \{m(s), \, s \in [a, b]\} \subset M$, the idea of a vector field $Y \in \mathcal{X}(M)$ being "covariantly constant" along γ, or being "parallel transported" along γ, is defined (and described locally by the ordinary differential equations (10.15)); (ii) taking Y to be the tangent to γ itself, the idea of γ being a geodesic or "as straight as possible" arises; (iii) the torsion tensor T is defined via eq.(10.30); (iv) the curvature R (a derivation valued two-form) is given by eq.(10.31); (v) Cartan's equations of structure (10.39,40) determine, in general dual fields of frames, the "components" of T and R in terms of the anholonomic connection components; (vi) the two Bianchi identities (10.53,55) hold. We can now appreciate that the geodesic concept, the definition of torsion, and the first Bianchi identity are all dependent on the fact that basically both derivations ∇_X and $R(X, Y)$ *act on vector fields over* M. Indeed in each of these three items, such actions on chosen vector fields are used explicitly in the arguments of Section 10. It is these therefore that will not be expected to generalise to an arbitrary PFB.

We now motivate the notion of parallel transport (or horizontal lift) in a general PFB, by starting with the treatment in Section 10, working our way upto FM, and then examining the resulting structure. Let the affine connection ∇ on M have local components $\Gamma^\rho{}_{\sigma\lambda}$ and let

$$\gamma \; : \; I = [a, b] \subset \mathcal{R} \to M \; :$$
$$s \in I \to m(s) \in M , \tag{15.93}$$

be a smooth curve in M. Described locally as in eqs.(10.10-13), the point $m(s)$ has coordinates $\{x^\mu(s)\}$; and the tangent to γ at $m(s)$ is $\gamma_* \left(\frac{d}{ds} \right) = u(s)$ with components $u^\mu(s) = dx^\mu(s)/ds$. (The notation of Section 10 has been changed, with u rather than X being the tangent vector to γ). A vector $Y(s) \in T_{m(s)} M$, with components $Y^\mu(s)$, is covariantly constant along γ, or experiences parallel transport along γ, if these components obey the ordinary differential equations (10.15):

$$\frac{d}{ds} Y^\rho(s) + \Gamma^\rho{}_{\sigma\lambda} \left(x(s) \right) Y^\sigma(s) u^\lambda(s) = 0 \cdot \tag{15.94}$$

Such $\{Y^\rho(s)\}$ is uniquely determined by choice of $\{Y^\rho(a)\}$, and is nonvanishing everywhere on γ if it is nonvanishing at one point. Now consider a frame $\{e_\nu(a)\}$ for $T_{m(a)} M$, expanded as in eq.(15.83) in the coordinate basis:

$$e_\nu(a) \;\; = \;\; A^\rho{}_\nu(a) \left(\frac{\partial}{\partial x^\rho} \right)_{m(a)} ,$$
$$A(a) \;\; \in \;\; GL(n, R) \cdot \tag{15.95}$$

We can parallel transport each e_ν along γ using eq.(15.94), obtaining a unique $e_\nu(s) \in T_{m(s)} M$; and since linear independence is maintained, we produce a frame $\{e_\nu(s)\}$ for $T_{m(s)} M$ at points along γ. Clearly we have produced a curve Γ in FM, determined by $\gamma \subset M$, the affine connection, and the initial point (or frame) $\{e_\nu(a)\}$ or $A(a)$. The ordinary differential equations determining this curve are based on (15.94) above:

$$e_\nu(s) \;\; = \;\; A^\rho{}_\nu(s) \, (\partial/\partial x^\rho)_{m(s)} ,$$
$$\frac{d}{ds} A^\rho{}_\nu(s) \;\; + \;\; \Gamma^\rho{}_{\sigma\lambda} \left(x(s) \right) A^\sigma{}_\nu(s) u^\lambda(s) = 0 \cdot \tag{15.96}$$

The case of covariant constancy of a single vector Y being transported along γ is now recovered by saying that its expansion coefficients in the above *parallel transported frame* stay constant along γ.

What is the tangent to Γ "at the point s"? In the local description this is determined by the "velocities" of $x(s)$ and $A(s)$ and is the following expression:

$$
\begin{aligned}
\Gamma_* \left(\frac{d}{ds} \right) &= u^\mu(s) \frac{\partial}{\partial x^\mu} + \frac{d}{ds} A^\rho {}_\nu(s) \frac{\partial}{\partial A^\rho {}_\nu} \\
&= u^\mu(s) \frac{\partial}{\partial x^\mu} - \Gamma^\rho {}_{\sigma\lambda} (x(s)) A^\sigma {}_\nu (s) u^\lambda(s) \frac{\partial}{\partial A^\rho {}_\nu} \\
&= u^\mu(s) \frac{\partial}{\partial x^\mu} + (A^{-1}(s))^\mu {}_\rho A^\sigma {}_\nu (s) \times \\
&\quad \Gamma^\rho {}_{\sigma\lambda} (x(s)) u^\lambda(s) X^{(r)\nu} {}_\mu (A(s)) \cdot
\end{aligned}
\tag{15.97}
$$

Here we used eq.(15.80,96). Comparison with eq. (15.90) tells us: this is a horizontal vector at the point $(x(s),\; A(s))$ in FM! Therefore, parallel transporting each member of a frame along γ, in the sense of Section 10, leads to a curve in the PFB FM with a horizontal tangent vector at each point. Trivially of course each point on this "lifted curve" $\Gamma \subset FM$ sits on top of a corresponding point on the base space curve $\gamma \subset M$. This gives us the key to the definition of parallel transport or *horizontal lift* in a general PFB. We now describe this carefully.

Let ω be a connection on a PFB $(P,\; \pi,\; M,\; G)$. Given a smooth base space curve γ as in eq.(15.93), with tangent $u(s)$ at $m(s)$, we say that a curve $\Gamma \subset P$ given by

$$
\begin{aligned}
\Gamma : I &= [a,b] \subset R \to P : \\
s &\in I \to p(s) \in P,
\end{aligned}
\tag{15.98}
$$

is " a horizontal lift" of γ if it obeys:

$$
\begin{aligned}
(i) \; \pi(p(s)) &= m(s)\,,\; s \in I\,; \\
(ii) \; (\Gamma_*)_s \left(\frac{d}{ds} \right) &\equiv X(s) \equiv \text{tangent to } \Gamma \text{ at } p(s) \\
&\in H_{p(s)}\,, \\
\text{i.e., } X(s) &= \sigma_{p(s)}(u(s)) \cdot
\end{aligned}
\tag{15.99}
$$

Here σ_p is the map $T_m M \to T_p P$ occurring in definition (A), eq.(15.17), of the connection on P. It is clear that such a lift Γ of γ is uniquely determined by the choice of an initial point $p(a) \in \pi^{-1}(m(a))$. Once this is chosen, we build up Γ smoothly by always "sitting on top of γ" and "travelling horizontally".

We can see that there are infinitely many horizontal lifts of a given γ, one for each $p(a)$. There is no such thing as *the* horizontal lift of γ. Moreover we can easily see that the global G action on P preserves the horizontal property, so it maps one horizontal lift onto another:

$$g \in G, \Gamma \ = \ \text{a horizontal lift of } \gamma \Rightarrow$$
$$\Gamma' \ = \ \psi_g[\Gamma] = \text{another horizontal lift of } \gamma \cdot \quad (15.100)$$

The proof is very simple, it only uses the fact that the tangent map ψ_{g*} takes the horizontal subspace H_p onto $H_{pg^{-1}}$ as in eq.(15.20). Viewing Γ, Γ' as maps $I = [a, b] \to P$, we have:

$$\Gamma' \ = \ \psi_g \circ \Gamma,$$
$$X'(s) \ = \ (\Gamma'_*)_s\left(\frac{d}{ds}\right)$$
$$= \ (\psi_{g*})_{p(s)} \circ (\Gamma_*)_s\left(\frac{d}{ds}\right)$$
$$= \ (\psi_{g*})_{p(s)}(X(s)) \ \in \ H_{p(s)g^{-1}},$$
$$\text{or } X'(s) \ = \ (\psi_{g*})_{p(s)}(\sigma_{p(s)}(u(s)))$$
$$= \ ((\psi_{g*})_{p(s)} \circ \sigma_{p(s)})(u(s))$$
$$= \ \sigma_{p(s)g^{-1}}(u(s)) \ \in \ H_{p(s)g^{-1}}, \quad (15.101)$$

where eq.(15.20) has been used.

Just as in Section 10, here too in a general PFB the process of constructing a horizontal lift can be expressed locally by a system of ordinary differential equations. Over $\mathcal{U}_\alpha \subset M$, where the connection ω is described by the set of one-forms $A^{(\alpha)a}(m) \in \mathcal{X}^*(\mathcal{U}_\alpha)$, we know that the map σ_p takes any $u \in T_m M$ into $\sigma_p(u)$ given in eq. (15.49). Now let the portion of a horizontal lift Γ lying in $\pi^{-1}(\mathcal{U}_\alpha)$ be described locally as follows:

$$\Gamma \cap \pi^{-1}(\mathcal{U}_\alpha) : p(s) = (m(s), g(s))_\alpha \cdot \quad (15.102)$$

In a general unspecified representation of G, the matrix $D(g(s))$ obeys in any case the ordinary differential equation (15.70) which we write again:

$$\frac{d}{ds} D(g(s)) \ = \ i_{X(s)}\theta^{(\ell)a}(g(s)) T_a D(g(s)),$$
$$X(s) \ = \ \text{tangent to curve } \{g(s)\} \subset G \cdot \quad (15.103)$$

The horizontal property of Γ means that this $X(s)$ is determined by $u(s)$ by eq.(15.49):

$$X(s) = -A^{(\alpha)a}(m(s))(u(s))X_a^{(\ell)}(g(s)) \cdot \quad (15.104)$$

Using this in eq.(15.103) we see that in its passage through $\pi^{-1}(\mathcal{U}_\alpha)$, Γ obeys the ordinary differential equation

$$\left(\frac{d}{ds} + A^{(\alpha)}(m(s))(u(s))\right) D(g(s)) = 0 \cdot \tag{15.105}$$

Naturally we expect that, since the definition (15.99) of a horizontal lift is global, two such overlapping local descriptions will match properly in the transition region. This is indeed easily verified on the basis of eq.(15.73):

$$\Gamma \cap \pi^{-1}(\mathcal{U}_\alpha \cap \mathcal{U}_\beta) : p(s) \;=\; (m(s),\, g(s))_\alpha = (m(s),\, g'(s))_\beta \,,$$
$$g'(s) \;=\; t_{\beta\alpha}(m(s))g(s) \,;$$

$$\left(\frac{d}{ds} + A^{(\beta)}(m(s))(u(s))\right) D(g'(s))$$
$$= D(t_{\beta\alpha}(m(s))) \left(\frac{d}{ds} + A^{(\alpha)}(m(s))(u(s))\right) D(g(s)) \,;$$

$$\left(\frac{d}{ds} + A^{(\alpha)}(m(s))(u(s))\right) D(g(s)) = 0 \Leftrightarrow$$
$$\left(\frac{d}{ds} + A^{(\beta)}(m(s))(u(s))\right) D(g'(s)) = 0 \cdot \tag{15.106}$$

We can wrap up this discussion with these additional remarks. Given the base space curve $\gamma : I = \lfloor a, b \rfloor \to M$, for each initial point $p(a) \in \pi^{-1}(m(a))$ we can construct a unique horizontal lift of γ starting out at $p(a)$; if necessary this can be done piece-meal by solving eq.(15.105) locally and exploiting eq.(15.106) to "switch tracks" when needed. All these horizontal lifts of γ are related to one another by the maps ψ_g via eq.(15.100), so they are not all "independent". For each $p(a) \in \pi^{-1}(m(a))$ there is a unique $p(b) \in \pi^{-1}(m(b))$ reached along the horizontal lift starting out at $p(a)$. Thus we produce a map, a *parallel translation of the fibre* $\pi^{-1}(m(a))$ *to the fibre* $\pi^{-1}(m(b))$, determined by γ running from $m(a)$ to $m(b)$ in the base. And this map is equivariant under ψ_g:

$$p(a) \in \pi^{-1}(m(a)) \;\longrightarrow\; p(b) \in \pi^{-1}(m(b)) \text{ by parallel translation}$$
$$\text{along } \gamma,$$
$$\psi_g(p(a)) = p(a)g^{-1} \;\longrightarrow\; \psi_g(p(b)) = p(b)\,g^{-1} \cdot \tag{15.107}$$

We shall return to this construction later in Section 17.

15.7. COVARIANT DIFFERENTIATION IN THE PFB CONTEXT

In Section 10 the covariant derivative appeared from the start as a derivation - a differentiation process -applicable to all tensor fields on a differentiable manifold M. Thus for any $X \in \mathcal{X}(M)$, ∇_X when applied to
any tensor field belonging to $\mathcal{J}^{(r,s)}(M)$ gave another such field. Moreover,
tensor fields form a linear space, and they can also be multiplied pointwise
by functions on M (scalar fields) to give new tensor fields of the same type.

Now we have seen in detail that an affine connection on M - which
is what a covariant differentiation involves - is an instance of a PFB connection in the case of FM. In any PFB, as in FM, the typical fibre is the
structure group G which in general has no natural linear space structure.
A little reflection then shows that if from a connection on a general PFB
we wish to construct something like a covariant differentiation process, we
must deal, not with the PFB itself, but with an associated bundle which
is also a vector bundle: thus the typical fibre F should be a linear space,
with G represented and acting linearly on it. Indeed this is consistent, as
we now see, with the situation in Section 10: ∇_X acts on tensor fields and
not on FM itself; and the tensor bundles $\mathcal{J}^{(r,s)}(M)$ are associated vector
bundles obtained by the procedure described in Section 14, with $GL(n, R)$
acting linearly on them.

In short, given a connection ω on a PFB (P, π, M, G), we can set
up a covariant differentiation process on (sections in) any associated vector
bundle E, whose typical fibre is a linear vector space $\mathcal{V}$ carrying a linear
representation $D(\cdot)$, real or complex, of the structure group G. We now
sketch the details. The introduction of the machinery of linear representations of Lie groups and algebras, recapitulated earlier in this Section, gives
us the necessary tools.

In Section 14 the associated bundle (E, π_E, M, F, G) was constructed
by replacing the fibres in the PFB (P, π, M, G) by copies of the space
F on which G acts via diffeomorphisms φ_g. In the process the system of
transition functions $\{t_{\alpha\beta}(m)\}$ was retained. Now we take for F and φ_g
the linear space $\mathcal{V}$ and linear transformations (matrices) $D(g)$. We denote
vectors in $\mathcal{V}$ by $\Psi, \Psi', \Phi, \dots$. Corresponding to the covering of M by open
sets $\mathcal{U}_\alpha$, we have in eqs.(14.57,58) a set of overlapping local trivializations
of E along with transition rules:

$$
\begin{aligned}
h'_\alpha : \mathcal{U}_\alpha \times \mathcal{V} &\rightarrow \pi_E^{-1}(\mathcal{U}_\alpha) , \\
h'_\alpha(m, \Psi) &\equiv (m, \Psi)_\alpha \in \pi_E^{-1}(m) \subset \pi_E^{-1}(\mathcal{U}_\alpha) \\
&\quad \text{for all } m \in \mathcal{U}_\alpha, \Psi \in \mathcal{V} ; \quad \text{(15.108a)}
\end{aligned}
$$

$m \in \mathcal{U}_\alpha \cap \mathcal{U}_\beta$, $\Psi \in \mathcal{V}$:

$$(m, \Psi)_\alpha \ = \ (m, \Psi')_\beta \ ,$$
$$\Psi' \ = \ D(t_{\beta\alpha}(m)) \, \Psi \ . \qquad (15.108b)$$

This transition rule is just eq.(14.59) in the present case. A (global) section of the bundle E is a smooth assignment, for each $m \in M$, of a point in $\pi_E^{-1}(m)$. This amounts to giving, over each $\mathcal{U}_\alpha$, a smooth function $\Psi^{(\alpha)}(m) \in \mathcal{V}$, such that in overlaps eq. (15.108b) is obeyed:

$$\text{Section in } E \ : \ m \in \mathcal{U}_\alpha \to \Psi^{(\alpha)}(m) \in \mathcal{V} \ ,$$
$$(m, \Psi^{(\alpha)}(m))_\alpha \in \pi_E^{-1}(m) \ ;$$
$$m \in \mathcal{U}_\alpha \cap \mathcal{U}_\beta \ : \ \Psi^{(\beta)}(m) = D(t_{\beta\alpha}(m))\Psi^{(\alpha)}(m) \ ,$$
$$\text{i.e.,} \quad (m, \Psi^{(\alpha)}(m))_\alpha = (m, \Psi^{(\beta)}(m))_\beta \ . \qquad (15.109)$$

Dealing with a section in E is exactly analogous to dealing with a particular tensor field over M.

Now we set up the covariant derivative operation on E. For any $u \in \mathcal{X}(M)$ we define the derivation $D_u(\cdot)$ which acts on any section to produce another section:

$$\Psi^{(\alpha)}(m) \to \Psi'^{(\alpha)}(m) \ = \ D_u(A^{(\alpha)})\Psi^{(\alpha)}(m)$$
$$= \ i_{u(m)}(d + A^{(\alpha)}(m)) \ \Psi^{(\alpha)}(m) \ . \quad (15.110)$$

Thus over each $\mathcal{U}_\alpha, D_u(A^{(\alpha)})$ carries $(m, \ \Psi^{(\alpha)}(m))_\alpha$ to $(m, \ \Psi'^{(\alpha)}(m))_\alpha$. And in the overlap $\mathcal{U}_\alpha \cap \mathcal{U}_\beta$ eq. (15.73) assures us that

$$\Psi'^{(\beta)}(m) \ = \ i_{u(m)}(d + A^{(\beta)}(m))\Psi^{(\beta)}(m)$$
$$= \ i_{u(m)}D(t_{\beta\alpha}(m))(d + A^{(\alpha)}(m))D(t_{\alpha\beta}(m))\Psi^{(\beta)}(m)$$
$$= \ D(t_{\beta\alpha}(m))\Psi'^{(\alpha)}(m) \ ,$$
$$\text{i.e.,} \quad (m, \Psi'^{(\alpha)}(m))_\alpha = (m, \Psi'^{(\beta)}(m))_\beta \ . \qquad (15.111)$$

So $D_u(\cdot)$ is a well-defined differentiation rule which acts on sections in E to produce new sections. As with ∇_X in Section 10, here too the dependence of $D_u(\cdot)$ on u is purely algebraic and linear.

We remark that the action of d on $\Psi^{(\alpha)}(m)$ in eq.(15.110) is to be understood as follows: choose some fixed basis for $\mathcal{V}$, expand $\Psi^{(\alpha)}(m)$ in it using m-dependent coefficients, and apply d to these coefficients alone. Added to this, we remark that the transition rule $A^{(\alpha)} \to A^{(\beta)}$ for the local $\underline{G}$-valued one forms, as given in eq.(15.73), uses the d operation which acts just on the factor $D(t_{\alpha\beta}(m))$ there, whereas in eq.(15.111) above we need to allow d to act on "anything else standing to its right", namely here $\Psi^{(\beta)}(m)$ as well. In other words, we have rewritten eq.(15.73) as a one-form operator relation:

$$A^{(\beta)}(m) + d = D(t_{\beta\alpha}(m))(A^{(\alpha)}(m) + d)D(t_{\alpha\beta}(m)) \cdot \qquad (15.112)$$

We clarify very briefly the sense in which $D_u(\cdot)$ is a *derivation*. The representation $D(g)$ of G on $\mathcal{V}$ was not required to be irreducible. Its generators $\{T_a\}$ appear in the construction of $A^{\alpha)}(m)$ - this is just the combination $A^{(\alpha)a}(m)\, T_a$. Now the generators of the *direct product* of two representations of G are the *sums* of the two sets of individual generators. All these statements put together clearly show that $D_u(\cdot)$ acts as a derivation.

Suppose we have charts over the open sets $\mathcal{U}_\alpha \subset M$, ie., local coordinate systems with $m \in \mathcal{U}_\alpha$ being assigned coordinates $\varphi_\alpha(m) = \{x^\mu\}$. Then the various objects and operations acquire the following local forms:

$$
\begin{aligned}
A^{(\alpha)}(m) &\rightarrow A_\mu^{(\alpha)a}(x)dx^\mu T_a \; ; \\
\Psi^{(\alpha)}(m) &\rightarrow \Psi^{(\alpha)}(x) \; ; \\
u(m) &\rightarrow u^\mu(x)\,\frac{\partial}{\partial x^\mu} \; ; \\
D_u(A^{(\alpha)})\Psi^{(\alpha)}(m) &\rightarrow u^\rho(x)D_\rho(A^{(\alpha)}(x))\Psi^{(\alpha)}(x) \; , \\
D_\rho(A^{(\alpha)}(x)) &= \frac{\partial}{\partial x^\rho} + T_a\, A_\rho^{(\alpha)a}(x) \cdot
\end{aligned}
\qquad (15.113)
$$

Thus we recover the more familiar covariant derivative operator of gauge theory.

We can also easily check that from this setup we recover ∇_X in the FM case. We consider just the associated vector bundle TM, sections in which are vector fields $Y \in \mathcal{X}(M)$. Here we deal with the defining representation of $GL(n,R)$. According to eqs.(15.79,88) the rules of translation are:

$$
\begin{aligned}
T_a &\rightarrow T^\lambda{}_\sigma \, , \; \left(T^\lambda{}_\sigma\right)^\mu{}_\nu = \delta^\mu_\sigma \delta^\lambda_\nu \; ; \\
A^{(\alpha)}(m) &\rightarrow T^\lambda{}_\sigma \, \Gamma^\sigma{}_{\lambda\rho}(x)\, dx^\rho \; ;
\end{aligned}
$$

$$
\begin{aligned}
\left(\partial_\rho + T_a A^{(\alpha)a}{}_\rho(x)\right)\Psi^{(\alpha)}(x) &\rightarrow \left(\partial_\rho + T^\lambda{}_\sigma \, \Gamma^\sigma{}_{\lambda\rho}(x)\right)^\mu{}_\nu Y^\nu(x) \\
&= \partial_\rho Y^\mu(x) + \Gamma^\mu{}_{\lambda\rho}(x) Y^\lambda(x) \cdot
\end{aligned}
\qquad (15.114)
$$

This agrees exactly with eq.(10.45) (for each contravariant index).

Going back to the general situation, we exhibit the sense in which the derivative $D_u(\cdot)$ behaves covariantly under local G-actions. This is in the spirit of eq.(15.76), and leads to the 'gauge transformation" concept. What is involved is a choice of smooth functions

$$t_\alpha \;\; : \;\; \mathcal{U}_\alpha \to G \,,$$
$$m \in \mathcal{U}_\alpha \to t_\alpha(m) \in G \,, \qquad (15.115)$$

over each of the open sets $\mathcal{U}_\alpha \subset M$. This induces a chain of consistent changes in the transition functions $\{t_{\beta\alpha}(m)\}$ (cf.eq.(14.28)), the local one-forms $A^{(\alpha)}(m)$ for a connection, the local descriptions of a section in E, the transition rules, and the covariant derivative:

$$t_{\beta\alpha}(m) \to t'_{\beta\alpha}(m) \;=\; t_\beta(m) t_{\beta\alpha}(m) t_\alpha(m)^{-1} \,;$$
$$A^{(\alpha)}(m) \to A'^{(\alpha)}(m) \;=\; D(t_\alpha(m))(A^{(\alpha)}(m) + d) \times$$
$$D\left(t_\alpha(m)^{-1}\right) ,$$
$$A'^{(\beta)}(m) \;=\; D\left(t'_{\beta\alpha}(m)\right) (A'^{(\alpha)}(m) + d) \times$$
$$D\left(t'_{\alpha\beta}(m)\right) ;$$
$$\Psi^{(\alpha)}(m) \to \Psi'^{(\alpha)}(m) \;=\; D(t_\alpha(m))\Psi^{(\alpha)}(m) \,,$$
$$\Psi'^{(\beta)}(m) \;=\; D\left(t'_{\beta\alpha}(m)\right) \Psi'^{(\alpha)}(m) ;$$
$$u \in \mathcal{X}(M) : D_u(A'^{(\alpha)}(m))\Psi'^{(\alpha)}(m) \;=\; D(t_\alpha(m))D_u(A^{(\alpha)}(m))\Psi^{(\alpha)}(m) \;\cdot$$
$$(15.116)$$

Thus $D_u(A^{(\alpha)}(m)) \, \Psi^{(\alpha)}(m)$ "transforms in the same way" as $\Psi^{(\alpha)}(m)$ itself.

One final item before going on to curvature and the Bianchi identities. How does parallel transport, set up by eqs.(15.99,105) at the PFB level, appear in an associated vector bundle? Given a parametrised base space curve $\gamma \subset M$, we need to "lift" this to E, ie.,

$$m(s) \in \gamma \cap \mathcal{U}_\alpha \;\to\; (m(s), \Psi^{(\alpha)}(s))_\alpha \,;$$
$$m(s) \in \gamma \cap \mathcal{U}_\alpha \cap \mathcal{U}_\beta \;\; : \;\; \Psi^{(\beta)}(s) = D(t_{\beta\alpha}(m(s)))\Psi^{(\alpha)}(s) \;\cdot$$
$$(15.117)$$

And then over each portion the covariant derivative of $\Psi(s)$ along γ must vanish:

$$m(s) \in \gamma \cap \mathcal{U}_\alpha \;\; :$$
$$D_{u(s)}(A^{(\alpha)}(m(s)))\Psi^{(\alpha)}(s) \;=\; \left(\frac{d}{ds} + A^{(\alpha)}(m(s))(u(s))\right) \Psi^{(\alpha)}(s) = 0 \;\cdot$$
$$(15.118)$$

Here $u(s)$ is the tangent to γ at $m(s)$. Then we say that $\Psi(s)$ *experiences parallel transport*, or is *covariantly constant*, along γ.

15.8. THE CURVATURE TWO-FORM AND THE CARTAN THEOREM

We can arrive at the concept of curvature in a PFB carrying a connection in two ways: (i) in the spirit of Section 10, exploit the properties of covariant differentiation, or equivalently of the parallel transport law, on a general associated vector bundle; (ii) work directly on the PFB itself. We outline the former first, as it is close to the treatment of Section 10.

Let us carry out the calculations locally over $\mathcal{U}_\alpha \subset M$ and $\pi_E^{-1}(\mathcal{U}_\alpha) \subset E$, the associated vector bundle, also omitting α for the moment; we reinstate it later when we come to the transition formula. Given a section $m \to (m, \Psi(m)) \in E$, $\Psi(m) \in \mathcal{V}$, and a vector field $u \in \mathcal{X}(\mathcal{U}_\alpha)$, the covariant derivative (15.110) of Ψ gives another section which may be compactly written (at $m \in \mathcal{U}_\alpha$, which is also omitted):

$$D_u(A)\ \Psi = u(\Psi) + A(u)\ \Psi \cdot \qquad (15.119)$$

(Here in the first term on the right we imagine Ψ expanded in a fixed basis for $\mathcal{V}$, and u acting on each coefficient). So for any smooth function $f \in \mathcal{F}(\mathcal{U}_\alpha)$ we have:

$$D_u(A)\ f\ \Psi = u(f)\ \Psi + f\ D_u(A)\ \Psi \cdot \qquad (15.120)$$

If $u' \in \mathcal{X}(\mathcal{U}_\alpha)$ is another vector field we can next apply $D_{u'}(A)$ to get:

$$\begin{aligned} D_{u'}(A)D_u(A)\ f\ \Psi \ = \ & u'(u(f))\Psi + u(f)D_{u'}(A)\Psi + \\ & u'(f)D_u(A)\Psi + f\ D_{u'}(A)D_u(A)\Psi \cdot \end{aligned}$$
$$(15.121)$$

For the commutator we get a simpler result:

$$[D_{u'}(A),\ D_u(A)]\ f\ \Psi = [u',u](f)\Psi + f[D_{u'}(A),\ D_u(A)]\Psi \cdot \quad (15.122)$$

Compare this with

$$D_{[u',u]}(A)\ f\ \Psi = [u',u](f) \cdot \Psi + f\ D_{[u',u]}(A)\ \Psi\ , \qquad (15.123)$$

and subtract to find:

$$\begin{aligned} \Big\{[D_{u'}(A),\ D_u(A)] - D_{[u',u]}(A)\Big\}\ f\ \Psi\ = \ & f\ \{[D_{u'}(A),\ D_u(A)]- \\ & D_{[u',u]}(A)\Big\}\ \Psi \cdot \end{aligned}$$
$$(15.124)$$

This shows that the "operator" within curly brackets does not involve any differentiation at all and is purely multiplicative (and matrix valued). We then define a $\underline{G}$-valued two-form $\mathcal{G}$ (over $\mathcal{U}_\alpha$) by

$$\mathcal{G}(u', u) = [D_{u'}(A), \ D_u(A)] - D_{[u',u]}(A) \cdot \qquad (15.125)$$

Calculating it is quite easy as the steps are similar to those above:

$$
\begin{aligned}
D_{u'}(A)D_u(A)\Psi &= D_{u'}(A)\{u(\Psi) + A(u)\Psi\} \\
&= u'(u(\Psi)) + u'(A(u))\Psi + A(u)u'(\Psi) + \\
&\quad A(u')u(\Psi) + A(u')A(u)\Psi \ ; \\
[D_{u'}(A), D_u(A)]\Psi &= [u', u](\Psi) + \{u'(A(u)) - u(A(u')) + \\
&\quad [A(u'), A(u)]\}\Psi \ ; \\
D_{[u',u]}(A)\Psi &= [u', u](\Psi) + A([u', u]) \ \Psi \ ; \\
\text{i.e., } \mathcal{G}(u', u) &= u'(A(u)) - u(A(u')) - A([u', u]) + \\
&\quad [A(u'), A(u)] \\
&= (dA)(u', u) + [A(u'), \ A(u)] \\
&= (dA)(u', u) + A^a(u') \ A^b(u) \ [T_a, T_b] \quad (15.126)
\end{aligned}
$$

where eq.(9.40) has been used. We can now bring in the compact notation of eq.(13.43) and express $\mathcal{G}$ itself as

$$
\begin{aligned}
\mathcal{G} &= d \, A + \frac{1}{2} \, A^a \wedge A^b \, [T_a, \ T_b] \\
&= d \, A + \frac{1}{2} \, [A, \ A] \ , \qquad (15.127)
\end{aligned}
$$

the bracket here implying both the matrix commutator and the wedge product of one-forms.

The similarity of the above constructions to the way we defined curvature in Section 10 based on eq.(10.31) is quite evident.

Now we bring back the superscript α on $\mathcal{G}$ to indicate that we are working on some $\mathcal{U}_\alpha$; and since $D_u(A^{(\alpha)}) \ \Psi^{(\alpha)}$ obeys the transition rule (15.109) if $\Psi^{(\alpha)}$ does, we easily obtain:

$$
m \in \mathcal{U}_\alpha : \mathcal{G}^{(\alpha)}(m) = (d \, A^{(\alpha)})(m) + \frac{1}{2} \left[A^{(\alpha)}(m), \ A^{(\alpha)}(m) \right] \ ;
$$

$$
m \in \mathcal{U}_\alpha \cap \mathcal{U}_\beta, \ u', \ u \in T_m M \quad :
$$

$$
\begin{aligned}
\mathcal{G}^{(\beta)}(m)(u', u) &= D(t_{\beta\alpha}(m))\mathcal{G}^{(\alpha)}(m)(u', u)D(t_{\alpha\beta}(m)) \ , \\
\mathcal{G}^\beta(m) &= D(t_{\beta\alpha}(m))\mathcal{G}^{(\alpha)}(m)D(t_{\alpha\beta}(m)) \cdot
\end{aligned}
$$

$$(15.128)$$

The collection of $\underline{G}$-valued two-forms $\{\mathcal{G}^{(\alpha)}\}$ defined over the open sets $\mathcal{U}_\alpha \subset M$, obeying the above transition rules, all together defines the curvature associated with the connection $\{A^{(\alpha)}\}$ on the PFB.

If we use a chart over $\mathcal{U}_\alpha$, assigning coordinates x^μ to $m \in \mathcal{U}_\alpha$, we get expressions familiar from gauge theory:

$$u \to u^\mu \partial_\mu,\ u' \to u'^\mu \partial_\mu\ ,$$
$$A^{(\alpha)} \to A^{(\alpha)a}_\mu(x)dx^\mu T_a\ ,$$
$$\mathcal{G}^{(\alpha)}(m)(u',u) \to u'^\mu u^\nu \mathcal{G}^{(\alpha)}_{\mu\nu}(x)\ :$$
$$\mathcal{G}^{(\alpha)}_{\mu\nu}(x) = \mathcal{G}^{(\alpha)a}_{\mu\nu}(x)T_a$$
$$= \partial_\mu A^{(\alpha)}_\nu(x) - \partial_\nu A^{(\alpha)}_\mu(x) + \left[A^{(\alpha)}_\mu(x), A^{(\alpha)}_\nu(x)\right]\ ,$$
$$\mathcal{G}^{(\alpha)a}_{\mu\nu}(x) = \partial_\mu A^{(\alpha)a}_\nu(x) - \partial_\nu A^{(\alpha)a}_\mu(x) - f_{bc}{}^a\, A^{(\alpha)b}_\mu(x)A^{(\alpha)c}_\nu(x)\ .$$
$$(15.129)$$

Of course in a local coordinate description the expression in terms of covariant derivatives simplifies:

$$D_u\left(A^{(\alpha)}\right) = u^\mu D_\mu\left(A^{(\alpha)}\right)\ ,$$
$$D_\mu\left(A^{(\alpha)}\right) = \partial_\mu + A^{(\alpha)}_\mu(x)\ ;$$
$$\left[D_\mu\left(A^{(\alpha)}\right), D_\nu\left(A^{(\alpha)}\right)\right] = \mathcal{G}^{(\alpha)}_{\mu\nu}(x)\ .\qquad(15.130)$$

Next let us see how this same two-form $\mathcal{G}$ emerges via the parallel transport argument. Take $m \in \mathcal{U}_\alpha \subset M$, and $u',\ u \in \mathcal{X}(M)$. For two infinitesimal quantities $\varepsilon,\ \varepsilon'$ (and retaining only terms proportional to $\varepsilon,\ \varepsilon'$, and $\varepsilon\,\varepsilon'$), we imagine travelling from m to m' to m'' by "amounts" $\varepsilon\, u(m),\ \varepsilon'u'(m')$ respectively. In the opposite sequence we travel from m to m''' to m'''' by "amounts" $\varepsilon'u'(m),\ \varepsilon\, u(m''')$ respectively. The two end points m'' and m'''' do not coincide in general; according to eq.(11.20), this "gap" involves the commutator of u and u':

$$\text{Route I}\ :\ m \xrightarrow{\varepsilon\,u} m' \xrightarrow{\varepsilon'u'} m''\ ;$$
$$\text{Route II}\ :\ m \xrightarrow{\varepsilon'u'} m''' \xrightarrow{\varepsilon\,u} m''''\ ;$$
$$m'''' \longrightarrow m''\ :\ \varepsilon'\varepsilon[u,\,u'](m)\ .\qquad(15.131)$$

Now start with $\Psi \in V$ at m; use the parallel transport law (15.118) to obtain Ψ' at m' followed by Ψ'' at m'' along route I; and Ψ''' at m''' followed by Ψ'''' at m'''' along route 2. All these are shown in this composite Figure 9.

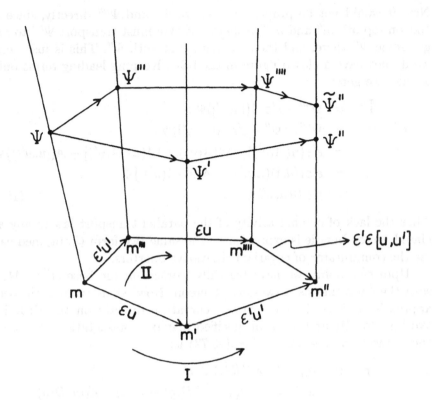

Figure 9. The parallel transport construction

The expressions for Ψ', Ψ'', ... are:

Route I :

$$\Psi \text{ at } m \rightarrow \Psi' \text{ at } m' = \Psi - \varepsilon\, A(m)(u(m))\, \Psi$$
$$\rightarrow \Psi'' \text{ at } m'' = \Psi' - \varepsilon'\, A(m')(u'(m'))\Psi'$$
$$= \Psi - \varepsilon\, A(u)\Psi - \varepsilon'(A(u') + \varepsilon\, u(A(u'))) \times$$
$$(\Psi - \varepsilon\, A(u)\Psi)\,,\text{ all at } m\,;$$

Route II :

$$\Psi \text{ at } m \rightarrow \Psi''' \text{ at } m''' = \Psi - \varepsilon'\, A(m)(u'(m))\Psi$$
$$\rightarrow \Psi'''' \text{ at } m'''' = \Psi''' - \varepsilon\, A(m''')(u(m'''))\Psi'''$$
$$= \Psi - \varepsilon'\, A(u')\Psi - \varepsilon(A(u) + \varepsilon'\, u'(A(u))) \times$$
$$(\Psi - \varepsilon'\, A(u')\Psi)\,,\text{ all at } m\,;$$

$$\Psi'' = \Psi - \{\varepsilon\, A(u) + \varepsilon'\, A(u')\}\Psi - \varepsilon'\varepsilon\{u(A(u')) - A(u')A(u)\}\Psi\,,$$
$$\Psi'''' = \Psi - \{\varepsilon\, A(u) + \varepsilon'\, A(u')\}\Psi - \varepsilon'\varepsilon\{u'(A(u)) - A(u)A(u')\}\Psi \cdot$$

$$(15.132)$$

Now it would not be proper to compare Ψ'' and Ψ'''' directly, since they "sit on top of" m'' and m'''' respectively. We must transport Ψ'''' to m'' to get some $\tilde{\Psi}''$ there, and then compare that with Ψ''. This is just because we do not have a closed figure in the base. Keeping leading terms only as always, we get:

$$
\begin{aligned}
\tilde{\Psi}'' &= \Psi'''' - \varepsilon'\varepsilon \, A([u, u'])\Psi \; ; \\
\tilde{\Psi}'' - \Psi'' &= \Psi'''' - \Psi'' - \varepsilon'\varepsilon \, A([u, u'])\Psi \\
&= \varepsilon'\varepsilon\{u(A(u')) - u'(A(u)) + [A(u), A(u')] - A([u, u'])\}\Psi \\
&= \varepsilon'\varepsilon\{(dA)(u, u') + [A(u), A(u')]\}\Psi \\
&= \varepsilon'\varepsilon \, \mathcal{G}(u, u')\Psi \cdot
\end{aligned}
\tag{15.133}
$$

Thus the lack of commutativity of the parallel transport law in any associated vector bundle is expressed by the same two-form $\mathcal{G}$ obtained earlier for the commutator of covariant derivative opertors.

Upto this point, we have basically worked on the base space M, and seen the curvature as a two-form thereon. Now let us turn to the second approach, and see how to express curvature directly on the PFB itself. Working locally and in an unspecified matrix representation of G and $\underline{G}$, the connection one-form ω of eq.(15.72) is:

$$
\begin{aligned}
p = (m, g)_\alpha &\in \pi^{-1}(\mathcal{U}_\alpha) \subset P : \\
\omega_p &= -D(g)^{-1} d\, D(g) - D(g)^{-1}A(m)D(g) \\
&= \theta^{(r)a}(g) \, T_a - D(g)^{-1}A(m)D(g) \cdot
\end{aligned}
\tag{15.134}
$$

Now ω_p is constructed so as to reduce to the canonical isomorphism ρ_p^{-1} on vertical vectors, while its kernel defines horizontal vectors:

$$
\begin{aligned}
X \in V_p &: \quad i_X\omega_p = \rho_p^{-1}(\underline{X}) \in \underline{G} \; ; \\
X \in H_p &\Leftrightarrow \quad i_X\omega_p = 0 \cdot
\end{aligned}
\tag{15.135}
$$

How do these statements translate into properties of the $\underline{G}$-valued two-form $d\omega$ over P? Calculation of $d\omega$ is easy enough: sometimes omitting arguments m and g for simplicity,

$$
\begin{aligned}
(d\omega)_p &= D(g)^{-1}d\, D(g)\wedge D(g)^{-1}d\, D(g) + \\
&\quad D(g)^{-1}d\, D(g)\wedge D(g)^{-1}A(m)D(g) - \\
&\quad D(g)^{-1}d\, A(m)D(g) + D(g)^{-1}A(m)\wedge d\, D(g) \\
&= \theta^{(r)a} \wedge \theta^{(r)b}T_aT_b - T_a\theta^{(r)a} \wedge D^{-1}A\, D - \\
&\quad D^{-1}d\, A\, D - D^{-1}A\, D\wedge\theta^{(r)a}T_a \\
&= \theta^{(r)a} \wedge \theta^{(r)b}T_aT_b + \theta^{(r)a} \wedge A^b\left[D^{-1}T_bD \, , \, T_a\right] - D^{-1}d\, A\, D \cdot
\end{aligned}
\tag{15.136}
$$

Now a basis for V_p is given by $\left\{X_a^{(r)}\right\}$. Contracting ω, $d\omega$ with each of these gives:

$$i_{X_a^{(r)}}\omega_p = T_a\ ;$$

$$i_{X_a^{(r)}}(d\,\omega)_p = \theta^{(r)b}[T_a, T_b] + A^b\left[D^{-1}T_bD\ ,\ T_a\right]$$

$$= [T_a\ ,\ \omega] = \left[i_{X_a^{(r)}}\,\omega\ ,\ \omega\right]\ ,$$

i.e., $X \in V_p\ \Rightarrow\ i_X\, d\omega = [i_X\, \omega,\, \omega]$ \hfill (15.137)

Next consider contraction with $X = \sigma_p(u) \in H_p$:

$$X = u + t^a X_a^{(r)} \in H_p \Leftrightarrow X = \sigma_p(u) \Leftrightarrow$$

$$i_X\omega = 0 \Leftrightarrow t^a T_a = D(g)^{-1}A(u)D(g)\ ;$$

$$i_X(d\omega)_p = i_u(d\omega)_p + t^a i_{X_a^{(r)}}(d\omega)_p$$

$$= A^b(u)\theta^{(r)a}[T_a, D^{-1}T_bD] - D^{-1}i_u d\,A\,D + t^a[T_a, \omega]$$

$$= \left[D^{-1}A(u)D\ ,\ \omega - \theta^{(r)a}T_a\right] - D^{-1}i_u d\,A\,D$$

$$= -D^{-1}\{i_u d\,A + [A(u), A]\}\,D\cdot \hfill (15.138)$$

Contracting this with another horizontal $Y = \sigma_p(u')$ gives:

$$i_Y\, i_X(d\omega)_p = -D(g)^{-1}\{(dA)(u, u') + [A(u), A(u')]\}\,D(g)$$

$$= -D(g)^{-1}\mathcal{G}(u, u')D(g)\cdot \hfill (15.139)$$

Collecting the results in eq.(15.137-139) we have:

$$(d\omega)(X, Y) = \begin{cases} [\omega(X), \omega(Y)] & \text{if } X, Y \in V_p\ ; \\ 0 & \text{if } X \in V_p,\ Y \in H_p\ ; \\ -D(g)^{-1}\mathcal{G}(u, u')D(g) & \text{if } X = \sigma_p(u),\ Y = \sigma_p(u')\cdot \end{cases} \hfill (15.140)$$

Quite generally, for any $X, Y \in T_p P$, we can say:

$$(d\omega)(X, Y) = [\omega(X), \omega(Y)] - D(g)^{-1}\mathcal{G}(\pi_*(X),\ \pi_*(Y))D(g)\cdot \hfill (15.141)$$

With this preparation we define the $\underline{G}$-valued curvature two-form Ω on the PFB P itself in this way:

$$X, Y \in T_p P : \Omega_p(X, Y) = (d\omega)_p(X_{\text{hor}}, Y_{\text{hor}})\ , \hfill (15.142)$$

where X_{hor}, Y_{hor} are the horizontal components of X and Y. But the right hand side here can be computed and expressed in terms of X and Y

themselves:

$$
\begin{aligned}
\Omega_p(X,Y) &= (d\omega)_p(\sigma_p(\pi_*(X)),\ \sigma_p(\pi_*(Y))) \\
&= -D(g)^{-1}\mathcal{G}(\pi_*(X),\ \pi_*(Y))D(g) \text{ by (15.140)} \\
&= (d\omega)_p(X,Y) - [\omega(X),\omega(Y)] \text{ by (15.141)} \\
\text{i.e., } \Omega(X,Y) &= (d\omega)(X,Y) - [\omega(X),\omega(Y)] \cdot \qquad (15.143)
\end{aligned}
$$

This is the Cartan structural theorem for a PFB carrying a connection: the curvature two-form Ω on P is obtained by this formula from the connection one-form on P.

Both ω and Ω are $\underline{G}$-valued. If we work with their components ω^a, Ω^a in an expansion in the generators T_a, we free ourselves from any representations and the Cartan formula (15.143) becomes:

$$
\begin{aligned}
\omega &= \omega^a T_a,\ \Omega = \Omega^a T_a : \\
\Omega^a &= d\,\omega^a + \frac{1}{2} f_{bc}{}^a\,\omega^b \wedge \omega^c \cdot \qquad (15.144)
\end{aligned}
$$

We can see from eq.(15.143) that even though Ω is defined over P, the "core" of this two-form is really the two-form $\mathcal{G}$ defined on the base M, "decorated" with $D(g)^{-1}$ and $D(g)$ to appear as living on P. This is in fact to be expected because, like the equivariance law (15.28) for ω, Ω too obeys an equivariance law. We see this by a series of simple calculations:

$$
\begin{aligned}
g_o \in G, \text{ fixed} : \psi_{g_o}^*\omega &= \mathcal{D}(g_o) \circ \omega \Rightarrow \\
\psi_{g_o}^* d\,\omega &= \mathcal{D}(g_o) \circ d\,\omega \cdot \qquad (15.145)
\end{aligned}
$$

So, at $p = (m,\ g)_\alpha$ (and α suppressed):

$$
\begin{aligned}
X,Y \in T_pP : \left(\psi_{g_o}^* d\,\omega\right)_p(X,Y) &= \mathcal{D}(g_o)(d\,\omega)_p(X,Y) \\
\text{i.e., } (d\,\omega)_{pg_0^{-1}}(\psi_{g_o\,*}(X),\psi_{g_o\,*}(Y)) &= \mathcal{D}(g_o)(d\,\omega)_p(X,Y) ;
\end{aligned}
$$

$$
\begin{aligned}
\mathcal{D}(g_o)\Omega_p(X,Y) &= \mathcal{D}(g_o)(d\omega)_p\left(X_{\text{hor}},Y_{\text{hor}}\right) \\
&= (d\omega)_{pg_0^{-1}}\left(\psi_{g_o\,*}(X_{\text{hor}}),\ \psi_{g_o\,*}(Y_{\text{hor}})\right) \\
&= (d\omega)_{pg_0^{-1}}\left((\psi_{g_o\,*}X)_{\text{hor}},(\psi_{g_o\,*}Y)_{\text{hor}}\right) \\
&= \Omega_{pg_0^{-1}}(\psi_{g_o\,*}X,\ \psi_{g_o\,*}Y) \\
&= (\psi_{g_o}^*\Omega)_p(X,\ Y) , \\
\text{i.e., } \psi_{g_o}^*\Omega &= \mathcal{D}(g_o) \circ \Omega \qquad (15.146)
\end{aligned}
$$

Here we used the property (15.20,25) of the horizontal subspaces at points on a fibre. In an (unspecified) matrix representation, we have:

$$\psi_{g_o}^*(\omega \text{ or } d\,\omega \text{ or } \Omega) = D(g_o)(\omega \text{ or } d\,\omega \text{ or } \Omega)D(g_o)^{-1} \cdot \tag{15.147}$$

Thus in the domain of a local trivialization of P, Ω_p for all $p = (m,g)_\alpha$ is really determined by its "values" over $(m,\ e)_\alpha$. In this way the two approaches to the curvature on a PFB get reconciled!

15.9. THE BIANCHI IDENTITIES

As with curvature, the Bianchi identities too can be handled at two levels - the PFB itself, or using covariant differentiation on sections on any associated vector bundle E. We present the latter in detail, and only indicate the structure of the former.

Over the base space M, locally, the curvature two-form $\mathcal{G}$ is given by eq.(15.125) in terms of commutators of covariant derivative operators. The Bianchi identities for $\mathcal{G}$ are simply consequences of the Jacobi identity for double commutators. Using eq.(15.125) twice we find:

$$\begin{aligned} &[[D_u(A), D_{u'}(A)],\ D_{u''}(A)] \\ = &\left[D_{[u,u']}(A) + \mathcal{G}(u,u'), D_{u''}(A)\right] \\ = &D_{[[u,u'],u'']}(A) + \mathcal{G}([u,u'],\ u'') + [\mathcal{G}(u,u'),\ D_{u''}(A)] \cdot \end{aligned} \tag{15.148}$$

If we now sum cyclically over the three vector fields u, u', u'', the initial left hand side and the first term on the final right hand side both yield zero (Jacobi identity!) and we are left with the statement:

$$\sum_{\substack{\text{cyclic} \\ (u,u',u'')}} [D_u(A), \mathcal{G}(u',u'')] = \sum_{\substack{\text{cyclic} \\ (u,u',u'')}} \mathcal{G}([u,u'],u'') \cdot \tag{15.149}$$

This is the Bianchi identity for the curvature two-form $\mathcal{G}$ on a PFB: it is a differential statement.

In a local coordinate sysem $m \to \{x^\mu\}$, if we represent $\mathcal{G}$ by eq.(15.129) as $\mathcal{G}_{\mu\nu}(x)$ and choose for u, u' and u'' the commuting vectors $\partial_\lambda, \partial_\mu, \partial_\nu$, the right hand side of eq.(15.149) vanishes and the Bianchi relations become:

$$\sum_{\substack{\text{cyclic} \\ (\lambda\mu\nu)}} \{\partial_\lambda \mathcal{G}_{\mu\nu}(x) + [A_\lambda(x), \mathcal{G}_{\mu\nu}(x)]\} = 0 \cdot \tag{15.150}$$

We leave it to the devoted reader to check that an equivalent treatment at the PFB level is as follows: starting from the Cartan relations (15.144) we obtain the three-form relation

$$d\,\Omega^a = -f_{bc}{}^a\,\omega^b \wedge d\,\omega^c \cdot \tag{15.151}$$

We see that in each term on the right one factor ω^b stands alone. Therefore contracting $d\,\Omega^a$ on three horizontal vectors automatically gives zero:

$$X,\,Y,\,Z \in H_p \Rightarrow (d\,\Omega^a)_p(X,Y,Z) = 0 \cdot \tag{15.152}$$

This property can be shown to be identical in content to the relations (15.149,150) for $\mathcal{G}$!

Let us at this point emphasize once more the major differences between the developments of Section 10 with an affine connection on M, and the general setting of a PFB P on base M in this Section. The torsion tensor T basically arose from an examination of the expression $\nabla_X Y - \nabla_Y X$, eq.(10.29); and the curvature R arose out of the very different expression $[\nabla_X, \nabla_Y]$, eq.(10.31). In a general PFB, the role of ∇_X is played by $D_u(A)$ acting on sections in an associated vector bundle. However the objects $\Psi \in \mathcal{V}$ on which $D_u(A)$ can act are not in any way similar to u at all: in the expression $D_u(A)\,\Psi$, it makes no sense to interchange u and Ψ! It is for this reason that only curvature, not torsion, can be set up with a connection in a general PFB: then indeed the constructions of eqs.(10.31,15.125) are very similar. And $R(X,Y)$ is a special instance of the more general $\mathcal{G}(u,u')$. Turning to the Bianchi identities, in Section 10 we found both an algebraic one, (10.53), by developing $R(X,Y)Z$; and a differential one, (10.55), by developing the double commutator $[[\nabla_X,\nabla_Y], \nabla_Z]$. One can see again that for a connection and curvature on a general PFB, the former identities are unavailable; and the latter generalise to the differential identities (15.149,150) on $\mathcal{G}$.

A parting shot: why is the object obtained above (in various ways) from a connection on a PFB called the "curvature"? The answer goes back to the Frobenius Theorem of Section 11! There we proved that the congruences of a set of independent vector fields on a manifold are surface-forming if and only if these vector fields are closed under commutation, in the sense of eq.(11.29). As mentioned there, a dual version of the theorem exists, stated in terms of one-forms. Now in the present context of defining a connection on a PFB P, we have the geometrical route (as distinct from the covariant differentiation approach) based on choosing smoothly the horizontal subspaces H_p at points $p \in P$. These are alternately viewed as the kernels, or null spaces, of the one-forms ω^a on P. The dual formulation of Frobenius' Theorem then says that these "individual subspaces" H_p mesh together to form smooth surfaces if and only if the two-forms $d\,\omega^a$ are expressible in terms of the ω's themselves (and something else). But this is just what happens if the curvature components Ω^a vanish, for then by eq.(15.144) each $d\,\omega^a$ is the linear combination $\frac{1}{2}f_{bc}{}^a\,\omega^b \wedge \omega^c$ and we have an "integrable connection". Thus the curvature two-form Ω is a quantitative expression of the extent to which the horizontal subspaces H_p do *not* mesh together to form smooth submanifolds in P leading to a foliation of P!

16. Integration of differential forms, Stokes' theorem

16.1. INTRODUCTION

We have studied several properties of differential forms in earlier Sections, largely from a local point of view. We have also looked at several differentiation processes - exterior, Lie, covariant - applicable to them. Now we consider the "converse" process of integration of differential forms. Our treatment - as earlier - will be intuitive and sometimes heuristic, without any pretence to rigour. Consistent with this, we shall develop and examine various expressions in some detail, and also permit some redundancy in expression if it serves to clarify ideas.

 We shall be concerned with the following natural questions: what are the domains over which differential forms of various degrees can be integrated; what are all the ingredients necessary before one has a well-defined and unambiguous integral expression; and what happens to the fundamental theorem of integral calculus in this context, i.e., how can one simplify the integral of an exact form? Throughout this Section our ambient space will be a connected differentiable manifold M of dimension n. For definiteness we will always assume that M is orientable, that a definite orientation has been chosen, and that $\mathcal{A}_{\max}$ is a maximal atlas for M compatible with this orientation. All the forms to be integrated will be forms on M, and their domains of integration will be suitably characterized subsets of M. No attention will be paid to problems of convergence of integrals, since that is not the focus of attention here.

16.2. INTEGRATING AN n-FORM OVER M

We have seen in Section 12 that if $\omega \in C^{(n)}(M)$, then having chosen an orientation on M the integral $\int_M \omega$ is unambiguously defined. The key expressions, using a covering of M by a family of oriented charts $\{(\mathcal{U}_\alpha, \psi_\alpha)\}$ drawn from $\mathcal{A}_{\max}$, are given in eqns.(12.3, 6, 8):

$$\text{over } \mathcal{U}_\alpha : \omega = S^{(\alpha)}(\boldsymbol{x}) dx^1 \wedge dx^2 \wedge \ldots \wedge dx^n \; ;$$

$$\int_{\mathcal{U}_\alpha} \omega \equiv \int_{\psi_\alpha(\mathcal{U}_\alpha) \subset \mathcal{R}^n} S^\alpha(\boldsymbol{x}) dx^1 dx^2 \ldots dx^n \; ;$$

$$\int_M \omega = \int_M \sum_\alpha e_\alpha \omega = \sum_\alpha \int_M e_\alpha \omega = \sum_\alpha \int_{\mathcal{U}_\alpha} e_\alpha \omega \cdot \qquad (16.1)$$

Here the smooth functions $\{e_\alpha\}$ give a partition of unity "subordinate to" the covering $\{\mathcal{U}_\alpha\}$ of M. In the second line here we have the basic step of connecting $\int_{\mathcal{U}_\alpha} \omega$ to an ordinary Riemann integral over the open set $\psi_\alpha(\mathcal{U}_\alpha)$ in $\mathcal{R}^n$, so there are no wedges in the volume element $dx^1 dx^2 \ldots dx^n$ occurring in the integral: the order of the dx's here is immaterial. In the final set of equations defining $\int_M \omega$, each $e_\alpha \omega$ is an n-form on M vanishing outside of $\mathcal{U}_\alpha$. The overall sign of $\int_M \omega$ is determined by the orientation chosen on M.

16.3. INTEGRATING AN n-FORM OVER A PORTION OF M

Given $\omega \in C^{(n)}(M)$, we are not obliged to integrate it over all of M, but can do so over only a part of M! Such a portion, D say, must be an n-dimensional submanifold in M. We recall from Section 11 that a subset $D \subseteq M$ is an n-dimensional submanifold if and only if D is open. Using charts from $\mathcal{A}_{\max}$ to cover D we see that D is also orientable, and the orientation on M passes over to a definite orientation on D as well. As examples we have: $D = M$; $M = \mathcal{R}$, $D = (0,1)$; $M = \mathcal{R}^2$, $\mathcal{R}^3, \ldots, D =$ interior of S^1, $S^2, \ldots$, of a square, cube, ..., annulus, torus,...; $M = S^2$, D=region strictly above the equator;....

If D is a proper subset of M, $D \subset M$, then its closure $\overline{D}$ will determine its boundary which we denote by ∂D. It consists of those points of $\overline{D}$ which are not in D. $\overline{D}$ is a closed subset of M, while D being open is the interior of $\overline{D}$. We see that ∂D is closed because we can express it as the intersection of the two closed sets $\overline{D}$ and D', $\partial D = \overline{D} \cap D'$, where D' is the complement of D in M. We record these facts here since they will be needed later:

$$
\begin{aligned}
D &= n - \dim.\ \text{submanifold in } M \Longleftrightarrow D = \text{open subset of } M \; ; \\
\overline{D} &= \text{closure of } D = \text{closed subset of } M \; ; \\
D &= \text{interior of } \overline{D} = \text{largest open subset of } \overline{D} \; ; \\
\partial D &= \overline{D} \text{ "minus" } D = \overline{D} \cap D' = \text{boundary in } \overline{D} = \text{boundary of } D \\
&= \text{closed subset of } M \cdot \qquad\qquad\qquad\qquad\qquad\qquad (16.2)
\end{aligned}
$$

As is intuitively plausible we will see later with suitable additional machinery that ∂D is an $(n-1)$-dimensional orientable submanifold in M. In the limiting case $D = M$, $\overline{D} = D$, $\partial M = 0$ as M is both open and closed.

Now returning to the problem of integrating ω over D, we use the identification map $i_D : D \hookrightarrow M$ (this concept has been defined in Section 14 at eqn.(14.17)). Thus we obtain an n-form $i_D^*\omega$ over D, and we can then define the integral of ω over D as

$$\int\limits_{D \subset M} \omega \equiv \int\limits_D i_D^* \, \omega \, , \tag{16.3}$$

this being evaluated (in principle) exactly as in eqn.(16.1). Everything is well-defined since D is both orientable and oriented.

16.4.   INTEGRATING A 0-FORM OVER M?

At the other end of the scale we might ask: given a 0-form, a smooth function $f \in \mathcal{F}(M)$, can we define in an intrinsic sense its integral over M? The answer is evidently "no", since there is no natural or intrinsic volume element on M, given only its manifold structure. The situation would of course be different if we were given a metric on M.

16.5.   INTEGRATING A ONE-FORM $\alpha \in \mathcal{X}^*(M)$

Beginning our climb back towards forms of higher degree, we can next ask whether and over what kinds of domains a one-form $\alpha \in \mathcal{X}^*(M) \equiv C^{(1)}(M)$ can be integrated. It is not hard to see that the domain must be a *directed connected smooth curve in* M. Denote such a curve by γ and let it be parametrised by a real monotonic variable s. So we write:

$$\gamma : I \;=\; (a,b) \subset \mathcal{R} \longrightarrow M \;:$$
$$s \in (a,b) \xrightarrow{\;\gamma\;} m(s) \in M \, . \tag{16.4}$$

So here we use the symbol γ for both the map $I \to M$ and for the *image* of this map, a smooth open parametrised directed connected curve in M. Then (in the same spirit as eqn.(16.3) but in a lower dimension) we define the integral of α over γ by

$$\int\limits_\gamma \alpha = \int\limits_I \gamma^* \alpha = \int\limits_a^b ds (\gamma^* \alpha)(s) \left(\frac{d}{ds} \right) \, . \tag{16.5}$$

If γ lies in the domain of a single chart, and $\alpha = \alpha_\mu(x)dx^\mu$ in this chart, then we have the completely explicit local expression

$$\int_\gamma \alpha = \int_a^b ds \; \alpha_\mu(x(s)) \frac{dx^\mu(s)}{ds} \; , \tag{16.6}$$

where the point $m(s) \in \gamma$ has coordinates $x^\mu(s)$. Several features are evident: (i) the choice of a direction along γ (orientation in one dimension) is needed to define this integral, a change in direction switching its sign; (ii) only the pull-back of α from M to $I \subset \mathcal{R}$, namely the "value" of α along γ evaluated on the tangent vector to γ, is needed; (iii) as long as the direction is respected, the integral is independent of the choice of parameter s, ie, it is reparametrisation invariant. Thus, just as with eqns.(16.1,3), we have the coordinate free expression $\int_\gamma \alpha$ - this *is* the natural way to denote this integral!

The open curve γ is a one-dimensional submanifold in M (but, for $n \geq 2$, it is *not* an open subset of M!). Its closure adds the two end points $m(a)$, $m(b)$ which are not contained in γ but constitute its boundary: $m(b)$ is the "upper" end and $m(a)$ the "lower" one. These will be directly relevant now.

16.6. CASE OF AN EXACT ONE-FORM

In the integral (16.5), what happens if $\alpha = df$ for some $f \in \mathcal{F}(m)$? Clearly we have a simplification, a reduction to boundary terms alone:

$$\begin{aligned}
\int_\gamma \alpha &= \int_\gamma df = \int_a^b ds(\gamma^* df)(s) \left(\frac{d}{ds}\right) = \int_a^b ds(d\gamma^* f)(s) \left(\frac{d}{ds}\right) \\
&= \int_a^b ds \frac{d}{ds}(\gamma^* f)(s) = (\gamma^* f)(b) - (\gamma^* f)(a) \\
&= f(m(b)) - f(m(a)) \; . \tag{16.7}
\end{aligned}$$

This is just the fundamental theorem of integral calculus, the lowest dimensional version of Stokes' Theorem which we will prove in generality later on. As expected, the boundary of the domain of integration γ is needed here, and the orientation chosen on γ fixes the sign of the difference of boundary terms.

16.7.   INTEGRATING FORMS OF GENERAL DEGREE - BASIC QUESTIONS

Next let $\alpha \in C^{(k)}(M)$. We want to handle its integrals, in the cases $k = 2, 3, \ldots, n-1$ since the two extreme cases $k = 1$ and $k = n$ have been dealt with. Two natural questions arise: (i) over what kinds of domains $D \subset M$ can α be integrated; (ii) in case $\alpha = d\beta$ for some $\beta \in C^{(k-1)}(M)$, is there a simplification in $\int_D \alpha$? We appreciate that domains of integration, their boundaries, and orientability and orientations of both, need to be carefully dealt with. We do this in easy stages.

16.8.   DOMAINS OF INTEGRATION AND THE INTEGRAL OF A FORM OF GENERAL DEGREE

We have defined a k-dimensional submanifold $D \subset M$ as the image of a smooth regular injective map $\varphi : K \to M$, $\varphi(K) = D$, where K is a differentiable manifold of dimension k. If furthermore D is a regular submanifold, which we assume from now on, it can be described locally by the process of "locking of coordinates". Then for each $p \in D$ we can find a chart $(\mathcal{U}, \psi) \in \mathcal{A}_{\max}$ such that $p \in \mathcal{U}$ and the portion of D contained in $\mathcal{U}$, $D \cap \mathcal{U}$, consists exactly of those points which have their last $(n-k)$ coordinates "locked to zero":

$$\psi(D \cap \mathcal{U}) = \{(x^1, x^2, \ldots, x^k, 0, \ldots, 0) \in \psi(\mathcal{U}) \subset \mathcal{R}^n\} \ . \tag{16.8}$$

The homeomorphism $\psi : \mathcal{U} \to \psi(\mathcal{U}) \subset \mathcal{R}^n$ establishes a one-to-one correspondence between points in $D \cap \mathcal{U}$ and points of the above form in $\psi(\mathcal{U})$. We introduce here the following suggestive notation: $x_{\|} = (x^1, x^2, \ldots, x^k)$, $x_\perp = (x^{k+1}, \ldots, x^n)$; thus to a general point in $\mathcal{U}$ the map ψ assigns coordinates $x = (x_{\|}, x_\perp)$, while those in $D \cap \mathcal{U}$ have $x_\perp$ locked to zero and for them $x = (x_{\|}, 0)$ and vice versa. Such charts $(\mathcal{U}, \psi) \in \mathcal{A}_{\max}$ are "adapted to D".

Now in the case $k = n$, D being an open subset of M is part of the submanifold definition. However for $k \leq n-1$, such a property does not hold. Nevertheless we still have the property of D being open and not containing any boundary points, though not in the sense of the topology on M. If we view D as the image $\varphi(K)$ of a map $\varphi : K \to M$, the fact that K is open must be reflected in D. We can convey this in a simple-minded way as follows.

We wish to extract for $D \cap \mathcal{U}$ (and so for D) the consequence of the fact that $\psi(\mathcal{U})$ is open in $\mathcal{R}^n$. If $q \in \mathcal{U}$ and $\psi(q) = (x_{\|}, x_\perp) \in \psi(\mathcal{U})$, then for small enough $\varepsilon > 0$, if $(y_{\|} - x_{\|})^2 + (y_\perp - x_\perp)^2 < \varepsilon^2$, $y = (y_{\|}, u_\perp) \in \psi(\mathcal{U})$ too. Such y are coordinates of points within an "open sphere of dimension n, radius ε, centre q", totally contained in $\mathcal{U}$. Now take for q a point $p \in D \cap \mathcal{U}$, then $x_\perp = 0$. Then for sufficiently small $\varepsilon > 0$, if $\boldsymbol{y} = (y_{||}, 0)$ is such that $(y_{||} - x_{||})^2 < \varepsilon^2$, this $\boldsymbol{y}$ too denotes a point in $D \cap \mathcal{U}$. Thus around every $p \in D$ we can always find, for small enough $\varepsilon > 0$, an "open sphere of dimension k, radius ε, centre p" totally contained in D. In this way every point in D is surrounded by an open neighbourhood also in D, so D *has no boundary points in itself.* We are evidently dealing here with the topology induced on D as a subset of M.

Next for purposes of integration we assume D is orientable. (For $k = n$ this separate assumption was unnecessary). Using charts $(\mathcal{U}, \psi) \in \mathcal{A}_{\max}$ adapted to D, we see that $x_{||} = (x^1, x^2, \ldots, x^k)$ become local coordinates for D. Consider two such overlapping adapted charts $(\mathcal{U}, \psi)$ and $(\mathcal{U}', \psi')$ yielding overlapping local coordinates $x_{||}$ and $x'_{||}$ for $D \cap \mathcal{U} \cap \mathcal{U}'$. Since $\mathcal{A}_{\max}$ consists of oriented charts for M, in the overlap we have:

$$\mathcal{U} \cap \mathcal{U}' : \begin{vmatrix} \partial x'_{||}/\partial x_{||} & \partial x'_{||}/\partial x_\perp \\ \partial x'_\perp/\partial x_{||} & \partial x'_\perp/\partial x_\perp \end{vmatrix} > 0 . \qquad (16.9)$$

Now here we set $x_\perp = 0$ and remember that $x'_\perp(x_{||}, x_\perp = 0) = 0$. Then we get:

$$(D \cap \mathcal{U}) \cap (D \cap \mathcal{U}') \ : \ |\partial x'_{||}/\partial x_{||}|_{x_\perp = 0} \cdot |\partial x'_\perp/\partial x_\perp|_{x_\perp = 0} > 0 . \quad (16.10)$$

So in the overlap of two adapted charts, the k-dimensional Jacobian $|\partial x'_{||}/\partial x_{||}|_{x_\perp=0}$ never changes sign, and is throughout either positive or negative. At this stage we bring in the assumption that D is orientable. It must then be possible to further restrict the choices of D-adapted charts $(\mathcal{U}, \psi)$, $(\mathcal{U}', \psi')$, ... such that in every overlap each factor in (16.10) is positive, ie., $|\partial x'_{||}/\partial x_{||}|_{x_\perp=0} > 0$. This still leaves the freedom to choose such restricted adapted charts in two possible ways, corresponding to the two possible orientations on D- for $k \leq n - 1$, the orientation on M does not automatically determine an orientation on an orientable D! For example, if $k = 1$ we have a curve $\gamma \subset M$ and (assuming $n \geq 2$) we can run along γ in one direction or its opposite. Similarly, over a two-dimensional plane in $\mathcal{R}^3$ we easily see the possibility of choosing one of two opposite orientations. So, out of all the charts $(\mathcal{U}, \psi) \in \mathcal{A}_{\max}$ adapted to D, we pick "one half" such that $|\partial x'_{||}/\partial x_{||}|_{x_\perp=0} > 0$ in every overlap, and thereby fix an orientation on D.

After these preliminaries, we are prepared to define the integral of any $\alpha \in C^{(k)}(M)$ over D. Using the identification map $i_D : D \hookrightarrow M$, we produce the k-form $i_D^* \alpha$ on D, ie., a form of maximal degree. Then we can set up the integral of α over D by the same method as of an n-form over

M:

$$\int_{D\subset M} \alpha \equiv \int_D i_D^* \, \alpha \; . \tag{16.11}$$

So, k-forms on M have as natural domains of integration regular k-dimensional orientable oriented submanifolds D in M. Switching the orientation on D (for $k \leq n-1$) changes the sign of the integral.

Locally the contribution to (16.11) has the following appearance. Over the chart $(\mathcal{U}, \psi)$ let α be expanded in the manner of eqn.(7.25):

$$\mathcal{U} : \alpha = \frac{1}{k!} \alpha_{\mu_1\mu_2\ldots\mu_k}(x_\parallel, x_\perp) dx^{\mu_1} \wedge dx^{\mu_2} \wedge \ldots \wedge dx^{\mu_k} \; . \tag{16.12}$$

The pull-back i_D^* amounts to setting $x_\perp = (x^{k+1}, \ldots, x^n) = 0$ "by hand". So we have over $D \cap \mathcal{U}$:

$$\begin{aligned}
i_D^* \, \alpha &= \frac{1}{k!} \alpha_{\mu_1\mu_2\ldots\mu_k}(x_\parallel, 0) dx^{\mu_1} \wedge dx^{\mu_2} \wedge \ldots \wedge dx^{\mu_k}\Big|_{dx_\perp = 0} \\
&= \alpha_{12\ldots k}(x_\parallel, 0) dx^1 \wedge dx^2 \wedge \ldots \wedge dx^k \; .
\end{aligned} \tag{16.13}$$

Then the elementary contribution to $\int_D \alpha$ from the region $D \cap \mathcal{U}$ has the ordinary Riemann form

$$\int_{D\cap\mathcal{U}} \alpha = \int_{\psi(D\cap\mathcal{U})\subset\mathcal{R}^k} \alpha_{12\ldots k}(x_\parallel, 0) dx^1 dx^2 \ldots dx^k \; . \tag{16.14}$$

16.9.   INTEGRATING AN EXACT FORM-TOWARDS STOKES' THEOREM

To generalise eqn.(16.7) for exact forms of higher degree, we need to develop machinery to deal carefully with boundaries of integration domains. We would like to limit ourselves to domains whose boundaries are 'nice' in a suitable sense, allowing integration over them in a neat fashion. Then we will be able to formulate and prove Stokes' Theorem. We have to do this in several stages. For reasons which will become clear as we proceed, we begin with the case of exact forms of maximal degree n, then work our way down.

So we begin with an n-dimensional submanifold $D \subset M$, which is automatically open in M, oriented, and a regular submanifold as well since no coordinates have to be locked to zero. We have already listed, in eqn. (16.2), the main properties of the closure $\overline{D}$, and of the boundary ∂D, of D. Now we will define when $\overline{D}$ is a *regular domain*, of dimension n, in M.

This includes a careful characterisation of ∂D. While open subsets in $\overline{D}$ can be handled via open subsets in $\mathcal{R}^n$, for ∂D we have to work with a "half Euclidean space" H^n, which incorporates the notion of a boundary. So we define

$$
\begin{aligned}
H^n &= \{x \in \mathcal{R}^n | x^1 \leq 0\} \\
&= \{x = (x^1, \tilde{x}) \in \mathcal{R}^n | x^1 \leq 0, \tilde{x} = (x^2, \ldots, x^n) \in \mathcal{R}^{n-1}\} \subset \mathcal{R}^n \cdot
\end{aligned}
$$

(16.15)

Points in the interior of H^n have $x^1 < 0$, those on the boundary have $x^1 = 0$. We need a basis of open sets in H^n - these are just the intersections of H^n with a basis of open sets in $\mathcal{R}^n$, namely open spheres. Depending on whether the centre of the sphere is an interior or a boundary point of H^n, we get two kinds of basic open sets for H^n:

First kind Around $x = (x^1 < 0, \tilde{x})$ in the interior of H^n: open spheres of radii ε in the range $0 < \varepsilon < |x^1|$, centred at x, so consisting of all points $y = (y^1, \tilde{y}) \in H^n$ such that

$$
(y^1 - x^1)^2 + (\tilde{y} - \tilde{x})^2 < \varepsilon^2 \text{ , some } \varepsilon \text{ in } (0, |x^1|) \cdot
$$

(16.16)

So automatically $y^1 < 0$, and these are also open sets in $\mathcal{R}^n$. It suffices for our purposes to limit the radius ε in this way, so that the resulting basic open sets for H^n are also open in $\mathcal{R}^n$.

Second kind Around $x = (0, \tilde{x})$ on the boundary of H^n: open hemispheres, lying within H^n, of any radii $\varepsilon > 0$, centred at x, including the "circular face" but not *its* boundary; so consisting of all $y \in H^n$ such that

$$
(y^1)^2 + (\tilde{y} - \tilde{x})^2 < \varepsilon^2, \ y^1 \leq 0 \text{ , any } \varepsilon > 0 \cdot
$$

(16.17)

The points with $y^1 < 0$ give us the interior of the hemisphere, lying within the interior of H^n; while the points with $y^1 = 0$ give us the "circular face" excluding *its* boundary, lying in the boundary of H^n. Such a basic open set in H^n is *not* an open set in $\mathcal{R}^n$. We can depict it pictorially as in Figure 10.

We can now define when $\overline{D}$ is a *regular domain*. This requires that each $p \in \overline{D}$ must be of Type (1) or Type (2) as defined below, *but not both*:

Type (1) points There exists a chart $(\mathcal{U}, \psi) \in \mathcal{A}_{\max}$ such that

$$
p \in \mathcal{U}, \ \psi(\overline{D} \cap \mathcal{U}) \text{ is an open set in } \mathcal{R}^n \cdot
$$

(16.18a)

Type (2) points No chart of the above type exists, but there exists a chart $(\mathcal{U}, \psi) \in \mathcal{A}_{\max}$ such that

$$
p \in \mathcal{U}, \ \psi(\overline{D} \cap \mathcal{U}) \text{ is an open set in } H^n \cdot
$$

(16.18b)

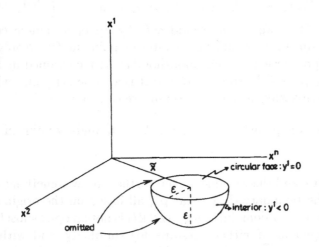

Figure 10.   Second kind open set in H^n

We will examine these alternatives and exploit the stipulation that *only one* of them must hold for each $p \in \overline{D}$. Then we will find, as we might expect: Type (1) points belong to D=interior of $\overline{D}$, Type (2) points belong to ∂D=boundary in $\overline{D}$.

Here is a subtle point: suppose for some $p \in \overline{D}$ we succeed in finding a chart $(\mathcal{U}, \psi)$ fulfilling eqn.(16.18b). Can we conclude that p is a Type (2) point? Not until we have also shown that no chart obeying (16.18a) exists!

Let $p \in \overline{D}$ be a Type (1) point, and $(\mathcal{U}, \psi)$ a chart realising eqn.(16.18a). Write $\psi(p) = x^{(p)} = (x^{(p)1}, \tilde{x}^{(p)}) \in \psi(\overline{D} \cap \mathcal{U})$. We have now the chain of arguments: $\psi(\overline{D} \cap \mathcal{U})$ open in $\mathcal{R}^n \Rightarrow$ we can surround $x^{(p)}$ by an open sphere contained within $\psi(\overline{D} \cap \mathcal{U}) \Rightarrow$ applying ψ^{-1} to this open sphere we get a neighbourhood of p contained within $\overline{D} \cap \mathcal{U} \Rightarrow p \notin \partial D \Rightarrow p \in D$, the interior of $\overline{D}$. Conversely, if $p \in D$ to begin with, we can see easily that it is of Type (1). Therefore we have established the two-way implications

$$p \text{ is a Type (1) point} \iff p \in D \cdot \qquad (16.19)$$

Incidentally, since H^n has not entered the picture at all, we can say nothing about the sign of $x^{(p)1}$, indeed it is irrelevant for Type (1) points.

Next let $p \in \overline{D}$ be a Type (2) point, so it is definitely not of Type (1). Then if the chart realising eqn.(16.18b) is $(\mathcal{U}, \psi)$, $\psi(\overline{D} \cup \mathcal{U})$ cannot be an open subset of $\mathcal{R}^n$, so we must be dealing here essentially with a basic open set for H^n of the second kind. From eqn.(16.19) we see that $p \in \partial D$ and vice versa:

$$p \text{ is a Type (2) point} \iff p \in \partial D \cdot \qquad (16.20)$$

We can go further in this case. In $\psi(p) = \boldsymbol{x}^{(p)} = \left(x^{(p)1}, \tilde{x}^{(p)}\right)$ suppose $x^{(p)1} < 0$. Then we can surround $\boldsymbol{x}^{(p)}$ by an open sphere contained in $\psi(\overline{D} \cap \mathcal{U})$, since $\boldsymbol{x}^{(p)}$ would be an interior point in H^n. Applying ψ^{-1} to this open sphere we get a neighbourhood $\mathcal{U}'$ of p contained in $\overline{D} \cap \mathcal{U}$. This would mean $p \notin \partial D$, so $p \in D$ and it is a Type (1) point, which cannot happen. Necessarily then $x^{(p)1} = 0$ and we can say:

$$p \text{ is a Type (2) point} \implies \psi(p) = \boldsymbol{x}^{(p)} = \text{ boundary point in } H^n \; .$$

$$(16.21)$$

We can extend this argument even further to say something about other points of the boundary ∂D "near p", all based on the original definition (16.18) of a regular domain! Since $\psi(\overline{D} \cap \mathcal{U})$ is not an open subset of $\mathcal{R}^n$, $\overline{D} \cap \mathcal{U}$ is not open in M either. Assume for simplicity, and with no loss of generality, that $\psi(\overline{D} \cap \mathcal{U})$ is a second kind basic open set in H^n, as depicted in Figure 10, and denote it by h:

$$
\begin{aligned}
\psi(\overline{D} \cap \mathcal{U}) \;=\; & h \\
=\; & \text{open hemisphere plus 'circular face' in } H^n \\
& \text{centred at } \boldsymbol{x}^{(p)} = \left(0, \tilde{x}^{(p)}\right) \\
=\; & \Big\{ \boldsymbol{x} = (x^1, \tilde{x}) \in \mathcal{R}^n \big| x^1 \le 0, \tilde{x} \in \mathcal{R}^{n-1}, \\
& \quad (x^1)^2 + \left(\tilde{x} - \tilde{x}^{(p)}\right)^2 < \varepsilon^2, \text{ some } \varepsilon > 0 \Big\} \; .
\end{aligned}
$$

$$(16.22)$$

Each $q \in \overline{D} \cap \mathcal{U}$ is mapped by ψ uniquely to some $\psi(q) = \boldsymbol{x}^{(q)} = \left(x^{(q)1}, \tilde{x}^{(q)}\right) \in h$. Consider all those $q \in \overline{D} \cap \mathcal{U}$ for which $x^{(q)1} = 0$. Then $\boldsymbol{x}^{(q)} = \left(0, \tilde{x}^{(q)}\right)$ obeys

$$\left(\tilde{x}^{(q)} - \tilde{x}^{(p)}\right)^2 < \varepsilon^2 \qquad\qquad (16.23)$$

and lies in the 'circular face' of h, away from *its* boundary. We argue that q is then a Type (2) point, belonging to ∂D as does p. Certainly we can exhibit a chart realising (16.18b) for q: just take the same $(\mathcal{U}, \psi)$ as we had for p to begin with! To clinch the argument, we must show the nonexistence of any other chart $(\mathcal{U}', \psi')$ realising (16.18a) for q. Suppose such a chart $(\mathcal{U}', \psi')$ was available. Without loss of generality we can suppose $\mathcal{U}' \subset \mathcal{U}$. Next since we have the maximal atlas $\mathcal{A}_{\max}$ at our disposal, we may assume with no loss of generality that ψ' is simply ψ restricted to $\mathcal{U}'$. We have then the statements:

(i) $x^{(q)} \in \psi(\overline{D} \cap \mathcal{U}') =$ open subset of $\mathcal{R}^n$;

(ii) $\psi(\overline{D} \cap \mathcal{U}') \subset \psi(\overline{D} \cap \mathcal{U}) = h$;

(iii) $x^{(q)} \in$ circular face of h ·   (16.24)

Statement (i) would imply that we can surround $x^{(q)}$ by an (n-dimensional!) open sphere contained within $\psi(\overline{D} \cap \mathcal{U}')$ and so by (ii) within h; but this conflicts with (iii)! Therefore no chart realising (16.18a) can be found for q, which is then a Type (2) point.

We can collect these results concerning type (2) points in these statements: for every point $p \in \overline{D}$ of Type (2), ie., for every $p \in \partial D$, there is a chart $(\mathcal{U}, \psi)$ realising (16.18b), in which *all* points with vanishing first coordinate are points in ∂D:

$$\psi(p) = x^{(p)} = \left(0, \tilde{x}^{(p)}\right) ,$$

$$\psi(\partial D \cap \mathcal{U}) = \left\{ x = (0, \tilde{x}) \in \mathcal{R}^n \middle| \tilde{x} \in \mathcal{R}^{n-1} , \left(\tilde{x} - \tilde{x}^{(p)}\right)^2 < \varepsilon^2 \right\} .$$

(16.25)

Many results concerning the boundary ∂D follow immediately from here! We see that $\tilde{x} = (x^2, \dots, x^n)$ are local coordinates over ∂D. We have a local description of ∂D by locking the first coordinate to zero (no harm in the variation from our earlier convention!). So ∂D is a regular submanifold of dimension $(n-1)$ in M. Next if we have an overlap of two such local coordinate systems arising from two charts $(\mathcal{U}, \psi)$, $(\mathcal{U}', \psi')$ both realising eqn.(16.18b) around different Type (2) points, we get at first as in eqn.(16.10), in the overlap:

$$\left(\frac{\partial x^{1'}}{\partial x^1}\right)_{x^1=0} \left.\left|\frac{\partial \tilde{x}'}{\partial \tilde{x}}\right|\right|_{x^1=0} > 0 \qquad (16.26)$$

But in each chart arising via eqn.(16.18b) we have arranged that x^1 is negative inside $\overline{D}$, ie. in D, vanishes on ∂D, and is positive just outside $\overline{D}$. So the first factor in the inequality (16.26) is positive by itself. This proves that ∂D is also orientable, though that still leaves two possible orientations we could choose over ∂D. Certainly all those charts $(\mathcal{U}, \psi)$ that arise via eqn.(16.18b) lead to the same orientation on ∂D, since in all of them x^1 increases monotonically through zero as we move from inside $\overline{D}$ to the outside.

The upshot is that if $\overline{D}$ is a regular domain of dimension n in M, its boundary ∂D is a regular orientable $(n-1)$ dimensional submanifold in M, over which it is possible to integrate forms of degree $(n-1)$. Is ∂D also a regular domain? Our earlier definition based on eqns.(16.18) concerns only n-dimensional regular domains, so some more preparation would be needed to answer this question. However at this stage we are ready to prove Stokes' Theorem for exact forms of degree n.

16.10.   STOKES' THEOREM FOR EXACT n-FORMS

Let $\omega \in C^{(n-1)}(M)$, and $\overline{D}$ be a regular domain of dimension n in M, with all the properties of ∂D we have assembled. Then Stokes' Theorem is the assertion that we can choose an orientation on ∂D, independent of ω, such that

$$\int_D d\omega = \int_{\partial D} \omega \cdot \qquad (16.27)$$

We prove this using the detailed pictures we have developed for local descriptions of D and ∂D, and exploiting the properties of a partition of unity $\{e_\alpha\}$ subordinate to a "large enough" covering of M by charts $\{(\mathcal{U}_\alpha, \psi_\alpha)\}$ each taken from $\mathcal{A}_{\max}$, to handle points in $\overline{D}$ of both Types (1) and (2). Then to begin with we have

$$\int_D d\omega = \int_D d\left(\sum_\alpha e_\alpha \omega\right) = \sum_\alpha \int_D d(e_\alpha \omega) = \sum_\alpha \int_{D \cap \mathcal{U}_\alpha} d(e_\alpha \omega) ,$$

$$\int_{\partial D} \omega = \int_{\partial D} \sum_\alpha e_\alpha \omega = \sum_\alpha \int_{\partial D} e_\alpha \omega = \sum_\alpha \int_{\partial D \cap \mathcal{U}_\alpha} e_\alpha \omega , \qquad (16.28)$$

with the orientation on ∂D still free. We will prove the equality of individual terms,

$$\int_{D \cap \mathcal{U}_\alpha} d(e_\alpha \omega) = \int_{\partial D \cap \mathcal{U}_\alpha} e_\alpha \omega , \qquad (16.29)$$

with the orientation on ∂D independent of α.

Three and only three mutually exclusive cases Ia, Ib, II - as indicated in Figure 11 - can arise. In two of them, both sides of eqn.(16.29) will be seen to vanish, so there is something nontrivial only in one case.

Case Ia Here $\partial D \cap \mathcal{U}_\alpha = \phi$ and $\mathcal{U}_\alpha \subset \overline{D}'$. So both sides of (16.29) vanish identically, and we are done without yet choosing an orientation on ∂D.

Case Ib Now $\partial D \cap \mathcal{U}_\alpha = \phi$ and $\mathcal{U}_\alpha \subset D$. The right hand side of eqn.(16.29) again vanishes, independent of orientation on ∂D, and we

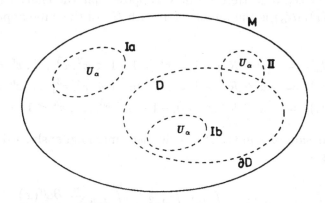

Figure 11.   Situations occurring in proving Stokes' Theorem

need only to evaluate the left hand side. We may assume without loss of generality that $\psi_\alpha(\mathcal{U}_\alpha)$ is the interior of a cube of side two units in $\mathcal{R}^n$:

$$\psi_\alpha(\mathcal{U}_\alpha) = \{x \in \mathcal{R}^n | -1 < x^\mu < 1, \mu = 1, 2, \ldots, n\} \qquad (16.30)$$

Expand $e_\alpha\omega$ over $\mathcal{U}_\alpha$ as

$$e_\alpha\omega = \sum_{\mu=1}^n (-1)^{\mu-1} a^\mu(x) dx^1 \wedge dx^2 \wedge \ldots \wedge \widehat{dx}^\mu \wedge \ldots \wedge dx^n ,$$

$$a^\mu(x)\big|_{\text{any } x^\nu = \pm 1} = 0 \cdot \qquad (16.31)$$

Here the caret $\hat{}$ atop any differential $\widehat{dx}^\mu$ is a signal to omit that factor. Then

$$d(e_\alpha\omega) = \left(\sum_{\mu=1}^n \frac{\partial a^\mu(x)}{\partial x^\mu}\right) dx^1 \wedge dx^2 \wedge \ldots \wedge dx^n \cdot \qquad (16.32)$$

The left hand side of eqn.(16.29) reduces to an ordinary Riemann integral over a cube:

$$\int_{D\cap\mathcal{U}_\alpha} d(e_\alpha\omega) = \int_{\mathcal{U}_\alpha} d(e_\alpha\omega) = \int_{-1}^{+1} dx^1 \ldots \int_{-1}^{+1} dx^n \sum_{\mu=1}^n \frac{\partial a^\mu(x)}{\partial x^\mu} = 0$$

$$(16.33)$$

on account of the boundary conditions appearing in eqn.(16.31). Only one case remains.

<u>Case II</u> $\partial D \cap \mathcal{U}_\alpha \neq \phi$. Here we may suppose that the chart $(\mathcal{U}_\alpha, \psi_\alpha)$ is such that $\psi_\alpha(\overline{D} \cap \mathcal{U}_\alpha)$ is the intersection with H^n of the cube appearing in eqn.(16.30):

$$\begin{aligned}
\psi_\alpha(\overline{D} \cap \mathcal{U}_\alpha) &= \{x \in \mathcal{R}^n | -1 < x^1 \leq 0, -1 < x^2, x^3, \ldots, x^n < 1\}, \\
\psi_\alpha(D \cap \mathcal{U}_\alpha) &= \{x \in \mathcal{R}^n | -1 < x^1 < 0, -1 < x^2, x^3, \ldots, x^n < 1\}, \\
\psi_\alpha(\partial D \cap \mathcal{U}_\alpha) &= \{x \in \mathcal{R}^n | x^1 = 0, -1 < x^2, x^3, \ldots, x^n < 1\} \cdot \quad (16.34)
\end{aligned}$$

The left hand side of eqn.(16.29) is defined unambiguously: using again eqns. (16.31,32).

$$\begin{aligned}
\int_{D \cap \mathcal{U}_\alpha} d(e_\alpha \omega) &= \int_{-1}^{0} dx^1 \int_{-1}^{+1} dx^2 \ldots \int_{-1}^{+1} dx^n \sum_{\mu=1}^{n} \frac{\partial a^\mu(x)}{\partial x^\mu} \\
&= \int_{-1}^{+1} dx^2 \ldots \int_{-1}^{+1} dx^n \, a^1(0, \tilde{x}) \cdot \quad (16.35)
\end{aligned}$$

To compute the right hand side of eqn.(16.29), we must fix the orientation on ∂D, and get the pullback of $e_\alpha \, \omega$ from M to ∂D. The latter involves setting $x^1 = 0$ "by hand":

pull-back of $e_\alpha \omega$ from M to $\partial D = a^1(0, \tilde{x}) dx^2 \wedge dx^3 \wedge \ldots \wedge dx^n$,

$$(16.36)$$

so

$$\int_{\partial D \cap \mathcal{U}_\alpha} e_\alpha \omega = \int_{\partial D \cap \mathcal{U}_\alpha} a^1(0, \tilde{x}) dx^2 \wedge dx^3 \wedge \ldots \wedge dx^n \cdot \quad (16.37)$$

The message is clear: choose the orientation over ∂D as that given by the charts $(\mathcal{U}, \psi)$ appearing in eqns. (16.18b, 25), and which have been used in eqns.(16.31, 32) as well! In this statement there is no reference to ω or α, so we have achieved our goal. The local coordinates $\tilde{x}$ for ∂D obtained as in eqn.(16.25) by locking x^1 to zero, define the orientation for ∂D, and the right hand side of eqn.(16.37) reduces to an ordinary Riemann integral:

$$\int_{\partial D \cap \mathcal{U}_\alpha} e_\alpha \omega = \int_{-1}^{+1} dx^2 \int_{-1}^{+1} dx^3 \ldots \int_{-1}^{+1} dx^n \, a^1(0, \tilde{x}) \cdot \quad (16.38)$$

The equality (16.29) follows in this only nontrivial case, and so the Theorem is established.

16.11.   REGULAR DOMAINS OF LOWER DIMENSIONS, STOKES' THEOREM FOR EXACT FORMS

So far we have defined regular domains $\overline{D}$ of dimension n, and proved Stokes' Theorem for exact n-forms alone. We were able, in this case, to exploit the fact that D is an open subset of M (by definition!) to conclude that the boundary ∂D is not only a regular orientable $(n-1)$ dimensional submanifold but also a closed subset of M. However we could not determine whether $\overline{D}$ being a regular domain implies that ∂D too is one such - the definition of lower dimensional regular domains is lacking! Now we take up these matters, in the course of establishing Stokes' Theorem for exact forms of degree $k \leq n-1$. Many of the steps will be simple repetitions of what we have already done, but in a lower dimension. When new points are involved, they will be explained.

We know that a regular submanifold D of dimension k can be locally described by locking coordinates; in any chart $(\mathcal{U}, \psi)$ adapted to D, out of the n coordinates $\boldsymbol{x} = (x^1, x^2, \ldots, x^n)$, the last $(n-k)$ get locked to zero: $x_\perp = \left(x^{k+1}, \ldots, x^n\right) = 0$ at points of D. The closure $\overline{D}$ of D can be again defined by the usual topological rule: it is the smallest closed subset of M containing D. However, as pointed out earlier, we must carefully notice that for $k \leq n-1$, D is not an open subset of M and not even the interior of $\overline{D}$. (An illustration of these remarks is an open curve $\gamma \subset M$ when $n \geq 2$). Now the boundary ∂D of D is again defined by

$$\partial D = \overline{D} \cap D' \cdot \tag{16.39}$$

It consists of just those points of $\overline{D}$ that are not in D. (Sometimes D may itself be closed, $D = D$; for example this happens if D is a smooth nonself intersecting closed loop in a plane, or $D = S^2 \subset M = \mathcal{R}^3$ etc. In such cases the boundary is empty, $\partial D = \phi$, and the always valid relation $D \cap \partial D = \phi$ is trivially obeyed). However, we cannot any longer conclude that ∂D is closed, since D' is not closed! We will turn to this aspect in a moment. To handle ∂D via local coordinates, and to combine the properties of "half Euclidean space" with the coordinate locking process, we now define subsets $\mathcal{R}^{n,k}$ and $H^{n,k}$ in $\mathcal{R}^n$ as follows:

$$\mathcal{R}^{n,k} = \left\{ \boldsymbol{x} = (x_\|, x_\perp) \in \mathcal{R}^n \middle| x_\| = (x^1, \ldots, x^k) \in \mathcal{R}^k, \right.$$
$$\left. x_\perp = (x^{k+1}, \ldots x^n) = 0 \right\} ; \tag{16.40a}$$

$$H^{n,k} = \left\{ \boldsymbol{x} = (x_\|, x_\perp) \in \mathcal{R}^{n,k} \middle| x^1 \leq 0, \tilde{x} = (x^2, \ldots, x^k) \in \mathcal{R}^{k-1} \right\} ; \tag{16.40b}$$

$$H^{n,k} \subset \mathcal{R}^{n,k} \subset \mathcal{R}^n \cdot \tag{16.40c}$$

These definitions amount to systematically ignoring the last $(n-k)$ coordinates $x^{k+1}, \ldots, x^n$, and adopting the earlier definition (16.15) but with the replacement $n \to k$.

Bases of open sets for $\mathcal{R}^{n,k}$ and $H^{n,k}$ are easily obtained by taking their intersections with n-dimensional open spheres in $\mathcal{R}^n$, ie., with

$$S_n(\boldsymbol{x}; \varepsilon) = \{ \boldsymbol{y} \in \mathcal{R}^n | (\boldsymbol{y} - \boldsymbol{x})^2 < \varepsilon^2 \} \cdot \tag{16.41}$$

For $\mathcal{R}^{n,k}$ we recover k-dimensional open spheres in $\mathcal{R}^k$, ie., in the subspace of the nonzero variables $x_{\|} = (x^1, \ldots, x^k)$:

$$(x_{\|}, 0) \in \mathcal{R}^{n,k} \quad : \quad S_k(x_{\|}; \varepsilon) = S_n((x_{\|}, 0); \varepsilon) \cap \mathcal{R}^{n,k}$$
$$= \left\{ y = (y_{\|}, 0) \in \mathcal{R}^{n,k} | (y_{\|} - x_{\|})^2 < \varepsilon^2 \right\} \cdot \tag{16.42}$$

For $H^{n,k}$ we get, as we would expect, two kinds of basic open sets; these follow the pattern of eqns. (16.16,17) with the replacement $n \to k$, and need not be written out in detail; we simply interpret $\tilde{x}$ as $(x^2, \ldots, x^k)$ in those equations.

We can now define what is meant by $\overline{D} \subset M$ being a k-dimensional regular domain. It must obey the following:

i) $\overline{D}$ is the closure of a regular orientable k-dimensional submanifold D in M;

ii) Each point $p \in \overline{D}$ must be of Type (1) or Type (2) as given below, *but not both*:

<u>Type (1) points</u> We can find a chart $(\mathcal{U}, \psi)$ adapted to D such that

$$p \in \mathcal{U}, \ \psi(\overline{D} \cap \mathcal{U}) = \text{open subset of } \mathcal{R}^{n,k} \cdot \tag{16.43a}$$

<u>Type (2) points</u> No such chart can be found, but we can find a chart $(\mathcal{U}, \psi)$ adapted to D such that

$$p \in \mathcal{U}, \ \psi(\overline{D} \cap \mathcal{U}) = \text{open subset of } H^{n,k} \cdot \tag{16.43b}$$

Now we can analyse these two mutually exclusive alternatives in the same manner as before when we had $k = n$, and we can see fairly easily that several consequences follows:

a) $p \in D \iff p$ is a Type (1) point $\cdot$

b) $p \in \partial D \iff p$ is a Type (2) point $\cdot$

c) If $p \in \partial D$ and the chart $(\mathcal{U}, \psi)$

realises eqn.(16.43b) above, then

$$\psi(p) = \boldsymbol{x}^{(p)} = \left(0, \tilde{x}^{(p)}, 0\right) \in \text{ boundary of } H^{n,k},$$

$$\psi(\partial D \cap \mathcal{U}) = \left\{ \boldsymbol{x} \in \psi(\overline{D} \cap \mathcal{U}) | x^1 = 0, \ x_\perp = 0, \ \left(\tilde{x} - \tilde{x}^{(p)}\right)^2 < \varepsilon^2 \right\}.$$

$$(16.44)$$

(Here we have assumed for simplicity that $\psi(\overline{D} \cap \mathcal{U})$ is a second kind basic open set in $H^{n,k}$).

d) Thus $\tilde{x} = (x^2, \dots, x^k)$ are local coordinates for ∂D,
while x^1 and $x_\perp = (x^{k+1}, \dots, x^n)$ are all locked to zero ·

e) ∂D is a regular, orientable $(k-1)$ dimensional submanifold in M ·

$$(16.45)$$

With this much we can repeat the previous proof of Stokes' Theorem, now for a closed k-form, replacing $x_\perp \to 0$, $n \to k$ in all previous steps:

$$\overline{D} = \text{ regular domain of dimension } k, \ \alpha \in C^{(k-1)}(M):$$

$$\int_D d\,\alpha = \int_{\partial D} \alpha, \qquad (16.46)$$

for an unambiguously defined choice of orientation on ∂D, determined by that on D.

We can supplement this result with an "integration by parts" formula for differential forms! Let $\alpha \in C^{(k_1)}(M)$, $\beta \in C^{(k_2)}(M)$, with $k_1 + k_2 = k - 1$. Then we have the exact k-form

$$d(\alpha \wedge \beta) = d\alpha \wedge \beta + (-1)^{k_1} \alpha \wedge d\beta \in C^{(k)}(M) \cdot \qquad (16.47)$$

Using $\alpha \wedge \beta$ in place of α in Stokes' Theorem (16.45) we find:

$$\int_D d\alpha \wedge \beta = (-1)^{k_1+1} \int_D \alpha \wedge d\beta + \int_{\partial D} \alpha \wedge \beta \cdot \qquad (16.48)$$

16.12. THE BOUNDARY OF A BOUNDARY - CARTAN'S LEMMA

Two questions remain: is ∂D a regular domain, and what is its boundary? As mentioned earlier, for $k \le n - 1$, D is no longer an open subset of M, so the closure of ∂D does not follow immediately from eqn.(16.39). However we can establish $\overline{\partial D} = \partial D$ by an alternative argument. Recall from Sections 5 and 6 that by definition a differentiable manifold obeys the Hausdorff separation axiom and the two axioms of countability. This -

as briefly mentioned in Section 6 - means that the operation of obtaining the closure $\overline{D}_0$ of any subset $D_0 \subset M$, by looking for the smallest closed subset in M containing D_0, coincides with the following operation: add to D_0 the limits of all sequences in D_0 which are convergent in the topology of M. Now let $\{p_j\}$, $j = 1, 2, \ldots$ be a convergent sequence of points each of which belongs to ∂D : $p_j \in \partial D$. Let the limit of this sequence be $p \in M$. Since $\partial D \subset \overline{D}$ and $\overline{D}$ is closed, we certainly have $p \in \overline{D}$. So either $p \in D$ or $p \in \partial D$. Suppose $p \in D$, so p is a Type (1) point in $\overline{D}$, and we can find a chart $(\mathcal{U}, \psi)$ realising eqn.(16.43a). So for some integer N we have $p_j \in \mathcal{U}$ for $j \geq N$. But then since $p_j \in \overline{D}$, this same chart shows that for $j \geq N$, p_j is a Type (1) point, hence $p_j \in D$, which contradicts $p_j \in \partial D$. We thus conclude that $p \in \partial D$, and this argument establishes the closure of the boundary:

$$\overline{\partial D} = \partial D \cdot \tag{16.49}$$

All in all then, $\overline{D}$ being a regular domain of dimension k has led to ∂D being a closed regular orientable submanifold of dimension $(k-1)$ in M.

But with this we see that ∂D fulfills all the conditions to be a regular domain of dimension $(k-1)$, with all its points being of Type (1) and none of Type (2)! This is clear from combining the statements (16.45c,d,e) with (16.49). So we arrive at the fundamental result

$$\partial \partial D = 0 , \tag{16.50}$$

whatever be the dimension k of D. Examples of this are easy to picture: just think of $S^1 \subset \mathcal{R}^2$ as the boundary of the unit disc, or of $S^2 \subset \mathcal{R}^3$ as the boundary of the unit sphere, etc. Equation (16.50) is called Cartan's lemma.

With this clear characterisation of the boundary ∂D of a regular domain D of dimension k, we define a *closed domain* to be a regular domain D *with vanishing boundary:* $\partial D = 0$. As an example, the total manifold M is a closed domain of dimension n. Then by Stoke's theorem, the integral of an exact k-form over a k-dimensional closed domain vanishes identically.

We can see that the result (16.50) is needed for consistency between Stokes' Theorem and the general idempotent property $dd = 0$, eqns. (9.25, 32), of exterior differentiation! For, with $\overline{D}$ a regular domain of dimension k, and any $\alpha \in C^{(k-2)}(M)$, a double application of Stokes' Theorem gives:

$$\int_{\partial \partial D} \alpha = \int_{\partial D} d\alpha = \int_D dd\alpha = 0 ,$$

ie $\int_{\partial \partial D} \alpha = 0$, all $\alpha \in C^{(k-2)}(M) \cdot \tag{16.51}$

There is thus a duality:

$$d\,d = 0 \longleftrightarrow \partial\,\partial = 0 \qquad (16.52)$$

between repeated exterior differentiation, and forming the boundary of a boundary.

16.13. A GLANCE AT DE RHAM COHOMOLOGY

We conclude this Section with a brief look at some further properties of closed and exact forms on M. As defined earlier in Section 11, eqns.(11.51), for each $k = 0, 1, \ldots, n$ the spaces $B^k(M)$, $Z^k(M)$ consist of all exact and all closed k-forms respectively on M. (We agree to regard $B^0(M)$ as trivial). Since exactness implies closedness, we have the inclusion relations (11.51) which we repeat here:

$$B^k(M) \subset Z^k(M) \subset C^{(k)}(M) \cdot \qquad (16.53)$$

These spaces have specific linearity properties. Constant linear combinations of forms in $B^k(M)$ or $Z^k(M)$ belong again to these same spaces, so each is a real linear vector space. In the case of $C^{(k)}(M)$ we can form linear combinations with *functions* on M as coefficients, and get new forms in $C^{(k)}(M)$.

Now we introduce an equivalence relation among closed forms of each degree k:

$$\alpha,\,\beta \in Z^k(M) \; : \; \alpha \sim \beta \Longleftrightarrow \alpha - \beta \in B^k(M) \cdot \qquad (16.54)$$

That is, two closed forms (of same degree) are declared equivalent if their difference is exact. It is easy to check that this is indeed an acceptable equivalence relation. The relation to Stokes' Theorem is that if α and β are equivalent k-forms and D is a regular submanifold of dimension k with no boundary, that is, a closed domain, then the integrals of α and β are equal:

$$\alpha - \beta \in B^k(M)\,, \quad \partial D \;=\; 0 \Longrightarrow$$
$$\int_D \alpha \;=\; \int_D \beta \qquad (16.55)$$

Since we are dealing here with a linear vector space $Z^k(M)$ and a subspace $B^k(M)$, the set of equivalence classes is simply the quotient vector space obtained by projecting $Z^k(M)$ with respect to $B^k(M)$. This carries a special symbol and name:

$$H^k(M) \;=\; Z^k(M)/B^k(M)$$
$$\;=\; k^{\text{th}} \text{de Rham Cohomology vector space of } M \cdot (16.56)$$

These spaces "measure" the obstruction to the passage from closed to exact forms, ie., to converting the local nature of the Poincaré Lemma in Section 11 to a global statement. The dimensions of these vector spaces are the so-called Betti numbers of M:

$$\dim \cdot H^k(M) \;=\; b^k$$

$$= \; k^{\text{th}} \text{Betti number of } M \;,\; k = 0, 1, \ldots, n \cdot \text{ (16.57)}$$

In relation to eqn.(16.55) we may say qualitatively that b^k is the number of independent k-dimensional regular submanifolds in M which have no boundary but not for a trivial reason, ie., are not themselves boundaries of $(k+1)$-dimensional submanifolds.

It should be evident that if two differentiable manifolds M, M' are diffeomorphic to one another, then they have the same Betti numbers. Actually these numbers have a much more elementary definition and have much wider invariance, ie., they are topological invariants and are equal for two homeomorphic spaces (being defined however in a different manner!).

Here are some facts worth quoting sans proof. For the spheres S^n, $n = 1, 2, \ldots$ as differentiable manifolds, we have:

$$
\begin{aligned}
H^0(S^n) \;&=\; Z^0(S^n) = \{\text{space of constant functions on } S^n\} = \mathcal{R} \;; \\
H^k(S^n) \;&=\; 0 \;,\; k = 1, 2, \ldots, \, n-1 \;; \\
H^n(S^n) \;&=\; \mathcal{R} \cdot
\end{aligned}
\tag{16.58}
$$

With this brief look at de Rham Cohomology, we conclude this Section.

17. Homotopy and Holonomy

17.1. INTRODUCTION

In this Section we turn to another global aspect of differentiable manifolds, more generally of topological spaces. This is the property of connectivity, conveyed by the term 'homotopy', at several levels. The object of interest could be a topological space, a differentiable manifold, a Lie group, a coset space, etc. For definiteness we may keep in mind a differentiable manifold; when we come to the case of groups, we will deal with Lie groups rather than topological groups in general.

The subject of homotopy is very vast. In our treatment we necessarily have to be selective in choosing the concepts and results to be described. We will often be content to give 'pictorial proofs' or just intuitive plausibility arguments, avoiding detail. A general feature that will emerge is that for every result valid for a general topological space, the corresponding result for groups is significantly simpler. However, rather than repeatedly interrupting the general development to point this out, we shall at first deal with a general topological space, and later take up Lie groups and their coset spaces.

For a topological space X the property of being *connected* has been defined in Section 5 - we must not be able to express X as the union of two disjoint open subsets. However, even if connected, the nature of this connectivity can be nontrivial and of various kinds. The concept of homotopy is a way to study this nature. The principal tool, to begin with, is the concept of a continuous loop in X, and its behaviour under continuous deformations. A loop is a continuous map of the circle $S^1 \subset \mathcal{R}^2$ into X. This is then followed up by higher dimensional generalisations of loops: continuous maps of spheres $S^n \subset \mathcal{R}^{n+1}$, $n = 2, 3, \ldots$, into X. The intrinsic connectivity properties of X are captured by a sequence of groups, the homotopy groups $\pi_n(X)$. The group $\pi_1(X)$ reflects properties at the loop level, and is the one we study in some detail.

Here is a listing of the topics dealt with in this Section. We begin with a few remarks about the lowest construct in the sequence $\pi_n(X)$, namely $\pi_0(X)$, which in general is not a group. Then we study the properties of continuous paths and loops in X, operations with them and homotopies (continuous deformations) connecting them. This leads to the concept of the first homotopy group, or the fundamental group, $\pi_1(X)$. Several aspects of this are taken up, including the ideas of simple and multiple connectivity, the homotopy type of a space, and contractible spaces. Turning to the higher homotopy groups $\pi_n(X)$, we describe briefly several convenient and easily picturisable ways of dealing with the spheres S^n - each is suited for a particular purpose, so familiarity with them all is useful. The definitions and some properties of the groups $\pi_n(X)$ are dealt with, though not in as much detail as with $\pi_1(X)$. At this point we turn to the case of Lie groups and their coset spaces. We recall without proof some basic facts about the global structure of Lie groups, extending the notion of Lie algebras and their relation to Lie groups as dealt with in Section 13. The idea of the universal covering group is brought in. This sets the stage for the study of the homotopy properties of Lie groups; at relevant places we point out the specific simplifications that occur precisely because we are concerned with a group and not a general topological space. Then we go on to a study of homotopy properties of coset spaces, and their relations to the properties of the groups themselves. Lastly we discuss briefly the idea of the holonomy group - this arises when we have a PFB carrying a connection. This is a nice illustration of the idea of the fundamental group combined with the Lie group acting as fibre and structure group in the bundle, when a connection is specified.

17.2. THE COMPONENTS OF A TOPOLOGICAL SPACE

Let X be a topological space. As we know from Section 5, a topology on X is the minimum structure needed to define continuity of functions, say from X to $\mathcal{R}$ or from $\mathcal{R}$ to X, of maps between two spaces X and Y, etc. (For $\mathcal{R}, \mathcal{R}^2, \ldots$ as always we have in mind their "usual topologies" - open spheres, intervals in case of $\mathcal{R}$, as a basis of open sets). We have recalled above the definition of X being connected. Conversely, X is disconnected if it is expressible as the union of two or more mutually disjoint open subsets. If so, carry the process far enough to ensure that each open subset in the union is itself connected, ie., not further decomposable in this way. The object $\pi_0(X)$ is then an enumeration of the various mutually disjoint but individually connected subsets of X. (This is a provisional definition, to be strengthened later). We can formally arrive at a definition of $\pi_0(X)$ by beginning with maps of a two-point set into X, but omit details. Suffice it to say that in general $\pi_0(X)$ has no group structure.

If X is connected, $\pi_0(X)$ is the trivial one-element set. This is indicated by writing $\pi_0(X) = 0$.

17.3. PATHS AND PATH-CONNECTEDNESS

We begin with the definition of a path in a given topological space X. (We have earlier used this, in the case of a differentiable manifold, in several contexts - as an integral curve of a vector field, to define geodesics, for integrating one-forms, etc.). A path $\gamma \subset X$ is a continuous map from the closed unit interval $[0, 1] \subset \mathcal{R}$ to X:

$$\gamma \; : \;\; s \in [0, 1] \to x(s) \in X \;,$$
$$x(0) = x_0, \;\; x(1) = x_1 \cdot \qquad\qquad (17.1)$$

(The range of the parameter for any path will always be $[0, 1]$, and this will not be mentioned repeatedly). So inverse images, under γ, of open sets in X must be open sets in $[0, 1]$; the latter are intersections of $[0, 1]$ with open sets in $\mathcal{R}$. The path γ runs from x_0 to x_1.

The space X is *path-connected* if any pair of points $x_0, x_1 \in X$ can be connected by a path γ. Intuitively, we can pass continuously from any point in X to any other "without ever leaving X". Path connectedness implies connectedness, as we see by the following easy argument. Suppose X is path-connected but not connected. Express it as the union of two nonempty open disjoint subsets X_1 and X_2:

$$X \; = \;\; X_1 \cup X_2 \;, \; X_{1,2} \neq \phi \;, \text{ open} \;;$$
$$X_1 \cap X_2 = \phi \cdot \qquad\qquad (17.2)$$

Take points $x_0 \in X_1$, $x_1 \in X_2$, and let the path γ connect them. Clearly $\gamma^{-1}[X_1]$ and $\gamma^{-1}[X_2]$ are nonempty open subsets of $[0,1]$; moreover they are disjoint because X_1 and X_2 are disjoint. Finally

$$[0,1] = \gamma^{-1}(X_1 \cup X_2) = \gamma^{-1}(X_1) \cup \gamma^{-1}(X_2) , \qquad (17.3)$$

which implies that $[0,1]$ is not connected. But $[0,1]$ *is* connected, hence the conclusion follows.

However, possibly surprisingly, the converse is not guaranteed: a connected topological space may not be path-connected! This means that path-connectedness is a stronger property than connectedness. The promised strengthening of the definition of $\pi_0(X)$ consists in the following: it is an enumeration of mutually disjoint individually path-connected, not merely connected, components of X. Hereafter, unless specified otherwise, we shall consider path-connected topological spaces; then $\pi_0(X) = 0$ and connectedness is ensured.

17.4.   OPERATIONS WITH PATHS-HOMOTOPIC EQUIVALENCE

We return to paths and natural operations with them. We should remark that at this stage the parametrisation of a path γ is carried along - we are not content merely with the image or 'trace' of the map γ as a subset of X. A path may also cross itself any number of times, indeed it may do any number of strange things - even "standing still now and then" - as long as it is continuous! A constant path is one where the point $x(s)$ is independent of s.

Given two paths γ_1, γ_2 running respectively from x_0 to x_1 and from x_1 to x_2 (the end of γ_1 equals the start of γ_2), we can compose them in that sequence to get a "product" path written as $\gamma_1 * \gamma_2$ running from x_0 to x_2:

$$
\begin{aligned}
\gamma_1 &= \{x(s)\}, \; \gamma_2 = \{x'(s)\} , \\
x(0) &= x_0, \; x(1) = x'(0) = x_1, \; x'(1) = x_2 : \\
\gamma_1 * \gamma_2 &= \{x''(s)\} , \\
x''(s) &= \begin{cases} x(2s), \; 0 \leq s \leq 1/2 \\ x'(2s-1), \; 1/2 \leq s \leq 1 \end{cases}
\end{aligned}
\qquad (17.4)
$$

We travel first along γ_1, then switch to γ_2, but in each stretch go "twice as fast as before" to maintain the parameter range $[0,1]$. The inverse to a path γ from x_0 to x_1 runs from x_1 back to x_0:

$$
\begin{aligned}
\gamma &= \{x(s)\} \quad \to \quad \gamma^{-1} = \{x^{-1}(s)\} , \\
x^{-1}(s) &= x(1-s) .
\end{aligned}
\qquad (17.5)
$$

It is easy to check that

$$(\gamma_1 * \gamma_2)^{-1} = \gamma_2^{-1} * \gamma_1^{-1} ,$$
$$(\gamma^{-1})^{-1} = \gamma , \tag{17.6}$$

so to this extent we can use familiar algebraic rules for these operations with paths.

Now we come to homotopic equivalence of paths. Two paths γ_1, γ_2 both running from x_0 to x_1 are homotopic to one another, or are homotopically equivalent, if one can be continuously deformed into the other. Formally we need a continuous map h from the square $[0,1] \times [0,1] \subset \mathcal{R}^2$ to X obeying the following:

$$\gamma_1 = \{x(s)\}, \gamma_2 = \{x'(s)\}, x(0) = x'(0) = x_0, x(1) = x'(1) = x_1 :$$
$$h : (s', s) \in [0,1] \times [0,1] \to h(s', s) \in X ,$$
$$h(s', 0) = x_0 , \; h(s', 1) = x_1 ,$$
$$h(0, s) = x(s) , \; h(1, s) = x'(s) \cdot \tag{17.7}$$

Thus as s' varies continuously from 0 to 1, we have a continuous family of paths $\{h(s', \cdot)\}$, always running from x_0 to x_1, and interpolating between γ_1 and γ_2 as shown in Figure 12:

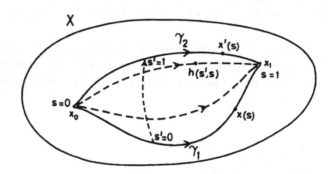

Figure 12. A homotopy connecting two paths illustrating Eqn.(17.7)

The map $h : [0,1] \times [0,1] \to X$ is then a homotopy connecting γ_1 to γ_2.

This idea of homotopic equivalence applies in general to continuous maps between topological spaces. Thus if f and g are two continuous maps from a topological space X to a topological space Y, they are homotopically equivalent if we have a continuous map $h : [0,1] \times X \to Y$ such that for each $s' \in [0,1]$, $h(s', \cdot)$ is a continuous map $X \to Y$, and this interpolates continuously between f at $s' = 0$ and g at $s' = 1$. Then f is continuously deformable to g.

Returning to paths between given end points x_0 and x_1, we indicate homotopic equivalence of γ_1 and γ_2 by $\gamma_1 \sim \gamma_2$. This is an equivalence relation (Section 2):

$$\gamma \sim \gamma \, ,$$
$$\gamma_1 \sim \gamma_2 \Rightarrow \gamma_2 \sim \gamma_1 \, ,$$
$$\gamma_1 \sim \gamma_2, \; \gamma_2 \sim \gamma_3 \Rightarrow \gamma_1 \sim \gamma_3 \, . \tag{17.8}$$

One can check these properties by playing with the relevant homotopies and their parametrisations to construct new ones. Then the set of all paths from x_0 to x_1 breaks up into mutually disjoint equivalence classes, the class containing γ being denoted by $[\gamma]$.

Monotonic reparametrisation of a path γ leads to a distinct but homotopically equivalent path γ'. It is instructive to construct this homotopy explicitly. We have a real continuous nondecreasing (and let us say differentiable) function $f(s)$ of the parameter s obeying

$$\frac{df(s)}{ds} \geq 0 \, , \; f(0) = 0 \, , \; f(1) = 1 \, , \tag{17.9}$$

and the new path γ' is defined in this way:

$$\gamma = \{x(s)\} \to \gamma' = \{x'(s)\} \, ,$$
$$x'(s) = x(f(s)) \cdot \tag{17.10}$$

Then one can check that the choice

$$h(s', s) = x(s + s'(f(s) - s)) \tag{17.11}$$

is just right to deform γ continuously to γ' as s' runs from 0 to 1. For each fixed s', moreover, the expression $s + s'(f(s) - s)$ is nondecreasing as a function of s and goes from 0 to 1 as well.

Now comes the link between the operations in eqns.(17.4,5) and the idea of homotopic equivalence, namely they are compatible with one another:

$$\gamma_1 \sim \gamma_1' \text{ from } x_0 \text{ to } x_1 \, , \; \gamma_2 \sim \gamma_2' \text{ from } x_1 \text{ to } x_2 \Rightarrow$$
$$\gamma_1 * \gamma_2 \sim \gamma_1' * \gamma_2' \text{ from } x_0 \text{ to } x_2 \, ;$$
$$\gamma_1^{-1} \sim \gamma_1'^{-1} \text{ from } x_1 \text{ to } x_0 \cdot \tag{17.12}$$

These are again easy to check by drawing pictures or by construction of the necessary homotopies. Therefore, always paying due attention to end

point requirements, in a consistent and unambiguous way one can define
products and inverses of classes of homotopically equivalent paths:

$$[\gamma_1][\gamma_2] = [\gamma_1 * \gamma_2] ,$$
$$[\gamma]^{-1} = [\gamma^{-1}] . \qquad (17.13)$$

As simple examples, if γ runs from x_0 to x_1, we can convince ourselves that

$$[\gamma * \gamma^{-1}] = [\text{ constant path at } x_0] ,$$
$$[\gamma^{-1} * \gamma] = [\text{ constant path at } x_1] . \qquad (17.14)$$

17.5. LOOPS AND BASED LOOPS

The path $\gamma : x_0$ to x_1 becomes a *loop* if the end points coincide: $x(1) = x(0) = x_0$. In explicit terms a loop is a continuous closed parametrised curve in X starting and ending at some point $x_0 \in X$. We can also view it as a continuous map of the circle S^1 into X, *based* at the starting point x_0. Here we are using the description of S^1 as the unit interval $[0,1]$ *with end points identified* - this will be generalised to higher dimensions later on.

Two loops γ and γ' need have no points in common. For a group structure to eventually emerge, however, we need to limit ourselves (for a while) to *based loops* all of which start and end at some given point $x_0 \in X$. Let us denote the collection of all such loops by $\mathcal{L}_{x_0}$.

The composition and inversion operations for based loops are specialisations of the earlier general definitions in eqns.(17.4,5); we must only set $x_2 = x_1 = x_0$ throughout. We then see that $\mathcal{L}_{x_0}$ is closed under both operations:

$$\alpha , \beta \in \mathcal{L}_{x_0} \Rightarrow \alpha^{-1}, \alpha * \beta \in \mathcal{L}_{x_0} . \qquad (17.15)$$

The constant loop (at x_0) may be denoted by α_0 and is its own inverse:

$$\alpha_0 = \alpha_0^{-1} = \{x(s) = x_0\} . \qquad (17.16)$$

It is tempting to suppose that these definitions allow us to make a group out of all loops belonging to $\mathcal{L}_{x_0}$, but this is not quite so : neither associativity nor inverses work properly. One problem is the retention of the parametrisation. For instance, $\alpha*(\beta*\gamma)$ and $(\alpha*\beta)*\gamma$ are generally different: $\alpha*(\beta*\gamma)$ runs along α for $0 \le s \le 1/2$, along β for $1/2 \le s \le 3/4$, and then along γ; while $(\alpha * \beta) * \gamma$ traverses α for $0 \le s \le 1/4$, β for $1/4 \le s \le 1/2$ and then γ. Then again, $\alpha * \alpha^{-1}$ and $\alpha^{-1} * \alpha$ are generally different, and neither of them is the constant loop α_0. We need to go one more step to reveal a group structure.

Homotopic equivalence of loops in $\mathcal{L}_{x_0}$ is again a specialisation of the general definition (17.7) for paths, with $x_1 = x_0$ throughout. We need only stress that in a homotopy, at each value of the interpolating parameter s' *we have a loop at x_0*. The class of loops at x_0 equivalent to $\alpha \in \mathcal{L}_{x_0}$ is naturally written as $[\alpha]$. The operations (17.15) on loops preserve homotopic equivalence : for α, α', β, $\beta' \in \mathcal{L}_{x_0}$,

$$\alpha \sim \alpha', \beta \sim \beta' \Rightarrow \alpha^{-1} \sim \alpha'^{-1}, \alpha * \beta \sim \alpha' * \beta' , \qquad (17.17)$$

and so (as in eqn.(17.13)) these operations are definable on the classes $[\alpha] \subset \mathcal{L}_{x_0}$.

In general, a loop $\alpha \in \mathcal{L}_{x_0}$ and its inverse α^{-1} are not homotopically equivalent: the sense of travel along a loop cannot be continuously reversed. For instance, if we take $X = \mathcal{R}^2 - \{\underline{0}\}$, a loop α going once counter clockwise around $\underline{0}$ has for its inverse α^{-1} a loop circling $\underline{0}$ once clockwise, and these cannot be bridged by a homotopy!

17.6.   THE FUNDAMENTAL (FIRST HOMOTOPY) GROUP $\pi_1(X;x_0)$

Armed with the division of $\mathcal{L}_{x_0}$ into equivalence classes $[\alpha]$, and eqn.(17.17) above, we arrive at a group. Namely, we can define multiplication and inverses for entire classes in a consistent and unambiguous way, echoing eqns.(17.13) for paths:

$$\begin{aligned} [\alpha], [\beta] &\subset \mathcal{L}_{x_0} : \\ [\alpha][\beta] &= [\alpha * \beta] \subset \mathcal{L}_{x_0} , \\ [\alpha]^{-1} &= [\alpha^{-1}] \subset \mathcal{L}_{x_0} . \end{aligned} \qquad (17.18)$$

The identity class is the one containing the constant loop α_0 of eqn.(17.16), namely $[\alpha_o]$. So this consists of all $\alpha \in \mathcal{L}_{x_0}$ which can be continuously deformed to the constant loop. As seen from eqns.(17.14) specialised to loops, for any $\alpha \in \mathcal{L}_{x_0}$ both $\alpha * \alpha^{-1}$ and $\alpha^{-1} * \alpha$ are homotopic to α_0, and this then shows that $[\alpha][\alpha^{-1}]$ is the class $[\alpha_0]$. We can similarly check associativity : while generally $\alpha * (\beta * \gamma) \neq (\alpha * \beta) * \gamma$, they *are* homotopically equivalent as only a reparametrisation is involved; so we get

$$\begin{aligned} \alpha * (\beta * \gamma) &\sim (\alpha * \beta) * \gamma , \\ [\alpha]([\beta][\gamma]) &= ([\alpha][\beta])[\gamma] \\ &= [\alpha][\beta][\gamma] . \end{aligned} \qquad (17.19)$$

This group is written $\pi_1(X;x_0)$ and is called the fundamental group, or the first homotopy group, of X at x_0. To the extent that it is nontrivial, there are loops based at x_0 not deformable to one another.

17.7. FUNDAMENTAL GROUPS AT DIFFERENT POINTS -
SIMPLE AND MULTIPLE CONNECTEDNESS

We now exploit the path-connectedness of X, $\pi_0(X) = 0$. Let x, y be two points of X, with corresponding fundamental groups $\pi_1(X; x), \pi_1(X; y)$. *The fact that x and y can be connected by a path helps us show that these two groups are isomorphic.* Indeed, let γ be a path from x to y, with γ^{-1} going from y to x. Then for every $\alpha \in \mathcal{L}_y$, we see easily that $\gamma * \alpha * \gamma^{-1} \in \mathcal{L}_x$, and also homotopic equivalence of loops is maintained. (Here the fact that $\gamma * (\alpha * \gamma^{-1})$ and $(\gamma * \alpha) * \gamma^{-1}$ are generally different does no harm, since by eqn. (17.19) they are homotopically equivalent, and that is all we need; so for simplicity we drop parentheses when composing three paths). So we have:

$$\alpha \in \mathcal{L}_y \;\;\Rightarrow\;\; \gamma * \alpha * \gamma^{-1} \in \mathcal{L}_x \; ;$$
$$\alpha \sim \beta \in \mathcal{L}_y \;\;\Rightarrow\;\; \gamma * \alpha * \gamma^{-1} \sim \gamma * \beta * \gamma^{-1} \in \mathcal{L}_x \cdot \qquad (17.20)$$

The required homotopy is easily constructed. Therefore there is an unambiguous class of loops $[\gamma * \alpha * \gamma^{-1}] \subset \mathcal{L}_x$ determined by each class $[\alpha] \subset \mathcal{L}_y$. Moreover each class in $\mathcal{L}_x$ does arise in this way - indeed the situation is

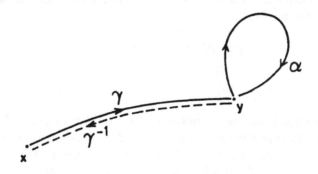

Figure 13. Transferring loops from y to x "along" γ

symmetric between $\mathcal{L}_x$ and $\mathcal{L}_y$ if γ is replaced by γ^{-1}! So we have a bijective mapping between $\pi_1(X; x)$ and $\pi_1(X; y)$, given by γ. One finally checks easily that composition of classes is respected, so we have an isomorphism. The dependence on γ means that in general this isomorphism is not natural or canonical. What is immediately evident, however, is that continuous deformation of γ leaves $\gamma * \alpha * \gamma^{-1}$ homotopic to itself: ·

$$\gamma_1 \sim \gamma_2 \text{ from } x \text{ to } y \;,\; \alpha \in \mathcal{L}_y \Rightarrow$$
$$\gamma_1 * \alpha * \gamma_1^{-1} \sim \gamma_2 * \alpha * \gamma_2^{-1} \in \mathcal{L}_x \cdot \qquad (17.21)$$

So the isomorphism between $\pi_1(X;x)$ and $\pi_1(X;y)$ depends only on the class $[\gamma]$, not on an individual path γ:

$$[\alpha] \in \pi_1(X;y) \underset{[\gamma^{-1}]}{\overset{[\gamma]}{\underset{\longleftarrow}{\longrightarrow}}} [\gamma * \alpha * \gamma^{-1}] \in \pi_1(X;x) \cdot \qquad (17.22)$$

We return soon to studying this $[\gamma]$-dependence, in particular the condition for no dependence at all.

The fundamental, or first homotopy, group $\pi_1(X)$ of the space X itself is now defined as that abstract group of which $\pi_1(X;x)$ for each $x \in X$ is an isomorphic copy. With this notion in hand, we can define what we mean by X being *simply* or *multiply* connected:

X simply connected $\iff \pi_1(X)$ trivial $\iff$ every $\alpha \in \mathcal{L}_x$ is

homotopic to constant $\alpha_0 \in \mathcal{L}_x$, for any $x \in X \iff$ any $\alpha, \beta \in \mathcal{L}_x$

are homotopic to one another, for any $x \in X$;   (17.23a)

X multiply connected $\iff \pi_1(X)$ nontrivial $\iff$ at every $x \in X$,

there are loops not homotopic to the constant loop$\cdot$ (17.23b)

The case of a trivial $\pi_1(X)$ (identity element only) is indicated by writing $\pi_1(X) = 0$. A nice consequence of X being simply connected is that it is then orientable - something good to know.

Here are some simple examples where the stated results are intuitively evident, or can be seen using simple pictures:

$$\pi_1(\mathcal{R}^n) = 0 , \qquad n \geq 1 ;$$
$$\pi_1(\mathcal{R}^2 - \{\underline{0}\}) \; = \; \pi_1(S^1) = \mathcal{Z} ;$$
$$\pi_1(S^n) = 0 , \qquad n \geq 2 ;$$
$$\pi_1(S^n/ \text{ antipodal points identified}) \; = \; \mathcal{Z}_2 = \text{two-element group, } n \geq 2 ;$$
$$\pi_1(SU(2)) = 0 ;$$
$$\pi_1(SO(3)) = \pi_1(SU(2)/\mathcal{Z}_2) \; = \; \pi_1(S^3/\mathcal{Z}_2) = \mathcal{Z}_2 \cdot \qquad (17.24)$$

So the circle S^1 is infinitely multiply connected: for each loop we can count the number of complete circuits taken, positively for counter clockwise and negatively for clockwise circuits. This gives the "winding number" of the loop, and two loops with the same winding number are homotopic to each other. Composition of two loops results in addition of their winding numbers.

In the examples listed above, $\pi_1(X)$ is either trivial or Abelian. Here are two examples with non-abelian fundamental groups.

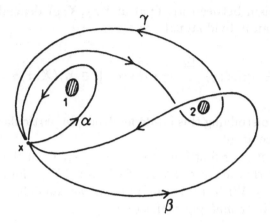

Figure 14. The "figure-eight" example - nonabelian fundamental group

(i) This is a famous and always quoted "figure eight" example. Take X to be $\mathcal{R}^2$ minus two points, or with two holes, as in Figure 14. For the three loops α, β, γ shown, we easily see the following relationships:

$$\alpha \not\sim \beta \not\sim \gamma \not\sim \alpha, \alpha * \gamma \sim \beta * \alpha$$

For elements of $\pi_1(X; x)$ this implies:

$$[\alpha][\gamma][\alpha]^{-1} \;=\; [\beta] \;,\; [\gamma] \neq [\beta] \tag{17.25}$$

which establishes its non-abelian nature: $[\alpha]$ and $[\gamma]$ *cannot* commute! What *is* the structure of $\pi_1(X)$ in this case? It can be shown that it is the infinite free group on two independent generators, their inverses, and the identity. Namely, one has the symbols a_1, a_2, a_1^{-1}, a_2^{-1} (and the identity), with *no* special simplifying algebraic relations among them; and each element of $\pi_1(X)$ is a string of arbitrary (finite) length, each entry being one of these symbols. Products and inverses are handled in the obvious ways. We interpret a_1 (respectively a_2) as one elementary anticlockwise circuit of the hole 1 (respectively 2) in Figure 14; thus $a_1 \sim [\alpha]$ and $a_2 \sim [\beta]$.

(ii) Our second example involves the group $SU(2)$. Let Q be the discrete eight element nonabelian "quaternion subgroup" consisting of the matrices $\{\pm 1, \pm i\,\sigma_1, \pm i\,\sigma_2, \pm i\,\sigma_3\}$. Take X to be the coset space $SU(2)/Q$. Precisely because Q is nonabelian, $\pi_1(X)$ turns out to be nonabelian as well, in fact $\pi_1(X) = Q$ itself. We will see this as a particular example of a general theorem to be proved later.

17.8.   PATH-DEPENDENCE OF ISOMORPHISM BETWEEN π_1' s

Let us return to the isomorphism (17.22) between the fundamental groups at any two points and ask: under what conditions does the dependence on $[\gamma]$ disappear? The basic result is that the necessary and sufficient condition is that $\pi_1(X)$ be Abelian. Then the isomorphisms (17.22) become canonical or natural. Indeed, we prove now that nontrivial dependence on $[\gamma]$, and $\pi_1(X)$ being nonabelian, imply each other.

(i) Isomorphism $[\gamma]$-dependent $\Rightarrow$ $\pi_1(X)$ nonabelian

By assumption, we have two paths γ_1, γ_2 from x to y, and an (at least one!) element $[\alpha] \in \pi_1(X;y)$, such that the two resulting elements in $\pi_1(X;x)$ are distinct:

$$\gamma_1, \gamma_2 : x \text{ to } y, \qquad \alpha \in \mathcal{L}_y :$$
$$[\gamma_1 * \alpha * \gamma_1^{-1}] \neq [\gamma_2 * \alpha * \gamma_2^{-1}] ,$$
$$\text{i.e., } \gamma_1 * \alpha * \gamma_1^{-1} \not\sim \gamma_2 * \alpha * \gamma_2^{-1} ,$$
$$\text{i.e., } \gamma_2^{-1} * \gamma_1 * \alpha \not\sim \alpha * \gamma_2^{-1} * \gamma_1 . \qquad (17.26)$$

But $\gamma_2^{-1} * \gamma_1 \in \mathcal{L}_y$, and the last result means $\pi_1(X;y)$ is nonabelian.

(ii) $\pi_1(X)$ nonabelian $\Rightarrow$ Isomorphism $[\gamma]$-dependent

Now we start with the assumption that we have two loops α, $\beta \in \mathcal{L}_y$ such that their products in two opposite orders are not homotopically equivalent:

$$\alpha, \beta \in \mathcal{L}_y : \quad \alpha * \beta \not\sim \beta * \alpha ,$$
$$\text{i.e.,} \quad \alpha \not\sim \beta * \alpha * \beta^{-1} . \qquad (17.27)$$

Now for any other $x \in X$, we can continuously deform β in this way: Choose some point z lying on β, as in Figure 15, and connect z to x by some path. Denote by γ_1 the path from x to y along the lower part of the

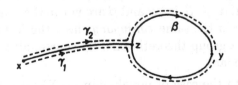

Figure 15.   From nonabelian π_1 to path-dependence of isomorphism

figure, and by γ_2 the one along the upper part, shown for clarity by dotted displaced lines. Then β is homotopically equivalent to the product $\gamma_1^{-1} * \gamma_2$ and eqn.(17.27) implies

$$\alpha \not\sim \gamma_1^{-1} * \gamma_2 * \alpha * \gamma_2^{-1} * \gamma_1 ,$$

$$\text{i.e.,} \quad \gamma_1 * \alpha * \gamma_1^{-1} \not\sim \gamma_2 * \alpha * \gamma_2^{-1} . \qquad (17.28)$$

This means that the isomorphisms between $\pi_1(X;x)$ and $\pi_1(X;y)$ established by $[\gamma_1]$ and by $[\gamma_2]$ have different effects on $[\alpha] \in \pi_1(X;y)$. To sum up, then:

$$\pi_1(X) \text{ Abelian} \quad \Leftrightarrow \quad \text{isomorphisms between } \pi_1(X;x)$$
$$\text{and } \pi_1(X;y) \text{ are canonical },$$
$$\pi_1(X) \text{ nonabelian} \quad \Leftrightarrow \quad \text{these isomorphisms are path-dependent} \cdot$$
$$(17.29)$$

So far x and y were any two points in X. Now suppose we take them to be the same. Then the path γ from x to y, used in eqns. (17.20,22) becomes a loop at x, so we are concerned with the relationship, in the sense of homotopy, between α and $\gamma * \alpha * \gamma^{-1}$ for $\alpha, \gamma \in \mathcal{L}_x$. According to eqn.(17.22), the equivalence class $[\gamma]$ of γ produces an automorphism of $\pi_1(X_1;x)$, indeed an inner automorphism:

$$[\alpha] \in \pi_1(X;x) \xrightarrow{[\gamma] \in \pi_1(X;x)} [\gamma * \alpha * \gamma^{-1}]$$
$$= [\gamma][\alpha][\gamma]^{-1} \in \pi_1(X;x) \cdot \qquad (17.30)$$

One can now easily see the following general result: if $\alpha, \beta \in \mathcal{L}_x$, the existence of another $\gamma \in \mathcal{L}_x$ such that $\alpha \sim \gamma * \beta * \gamma^{-1}$ is equivalent to $[\alpha]$ and $[\beta]$ being in the same conjugacy class as elements of the group $\pi_1(X;x)$. So even if $\alpha \not\sim \beta$, ie., α and β are not in the same *homotopy* class, $[\alpha]$ and $[\beta]$ can be in the same *conjugacy* class: the former is a homotopy notion, the latter a group theoretic one. Of course, all this can occur only if $\pi_1(X)$ is nonabelian.

Continuing with the case of nonabelian $\pi_1(X)$, we can analyse further the nature of the dependence of the isomorphism (17.22) on $[\gamma]$. Namely we can answer the question: if $[\gamma_1]$ and $[\gamma_2]$ lead to different isomorphisms between $\pi_1(X;x)$ and $\pi_1(X;y)$, to what extent can they differ? For any $[\alpha] \in \pi_1(X;y)$ the effects of transport to x via γ_1 and via γ_2 are:

$$[\gamma_1 * \alpha * \gamma_1^{-1}] \in \pi_1(X; x)$$

$[\gamma_1]$

$[\alpha] \in \pi_1(X; y)$

$[\gamma_2]$

$$[\gamma_2 * \alpha * \gamma_2^{-1}] \in \pi_1(X; x) \ ;$$

$$\begin{aligned}
\left[\gamma_2 * \alpha * \gamma_2^{-1}\right] &= \left[\beta * \left(\gamma_1 * \alpha * \gamma_1^{-1}\right) * \beta^{-1}\right] \\
&= [\beta]\left[\gamma_1 * \alpha * \gamma_1^{-1}\right][\beta]^{-1} \ , \\
\beta &= \gamma_2 * \gamma_1^{-1} \in \mathcal{L}_x \ .
\end{aligned}$$
$$\hspace{8cm}(17.31)$$

So if the elements $\left[\gamma_1 * \alpha * \gamma_1^{-1}\right]$, $\left[\gamma_2 * \alpha * \gamma_2^{-1}\right]$ in $\pi_1(X; x)$ differ, they are related by the inner automorphism generated by $[\beta] = \left[\gamma_2 * \gamma_1^{-1}\right] \in \pi_1(X; x)$. This means that as elements of $\pi_1(X; x)$ they belong to the same conjugacy class. In other words, when we link x and y by various homotopically inequivalent paths $\gamma_1, \gamma_2, \ldots$, entire conjugacy classes in $\pi_1(X; y)$ go over into entire conjugacy classes in $\pi_1(X; x)$ in an unambiguous manner. However individual members in a class may be shuffled around in a $[\gamma]$-dependent way - this is the extent to which there can be path-dependence in the isomorphisms (17.22).

17.9.   FREE HOMOTOPY OF GENERAL LOOPS

The definition of the group $\pi_1(X; x)$ has used loops and homotopies all based at $x \in X$. We can extend this notion of based homotopic equivalence to free homotopic equivalence for general loops. There are two ways of expressing this idea. Let α and β be two loops based respectively at x and y in X. Then the two definitions of α and β being freely homotopically equivalent are:

Definition (1) There is a path $\gamma = \{x(s')\}$ from x to y, and for each $s' \in [0, 1]$ a loop $\alpha(s') \in \mathcal{L}_{x(s')}$, such that $\alpha(s')$ changes continuously with s' and $\alpha(0) = \alpha$, $\alpha(1) = \beta$. This is depicted in Figure 16 :

Definition (2) There is a path $\gamma = \{x(s')\}$ from x to y such that $\alpha \sim \gamma * \beta * \gamma^{-1}$ in the sense of based homotopic equivalence.

By definition (2), then, any $\beta \in \mathcal{L}_y$ and $\gamma * \beta * \gamma^{-1} \in \mathcal{L}_x$ are *always* freely homotopic to one another.

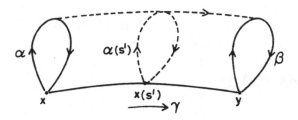

Figure 16.   First definition of free homotopic equivalence of loops

We can check the equivalence of these definitions.
Definition (1)$\Rightarrow$ Definition (2)
Both $\gamma = \{x(s')\}$ from x to y, and $\alpha(s') \in \mathcal{L}_{x(s')}$ for $0 \leq s' \leq 1$, are
given. We have to define a based homotopy connecting α to $\gamma * \beta * \gamma^{-1}$ at
x. Upto final fixing of the (second) parameter s, we construct it as follows:
at parameter value $s' \in [0,1]$, the interpolating loop $h(s', \cdot) \in \mathcal{L}_x$ is built
up of three pieces:

$$h(s', \cdot) = \{x \text{ to } x(s') \text{ along } \gamma\} * \alpha(s') * \{x(s') \text{ back to } x \text{ along } \gamma^{-1}\} \ .$$

It is easily seen that this obeys the required conditions at $s' = 0$ and $s' = 1$.
Definition (2) $\Rightarrow$ Definition (1) Again $\gamma = \{x(s')\}$ from x to y is given, as
well as a based homotopy $h(s', \cdot)$ connecting α and $\gamma * \beta * \gamma^{-1}$ at x. We have
to construct a loop $\alpha(s') \in \mathcal{L}_{x(s')}$ varying continuously for $s' \in [0,1]$,
with $\alpha(0) = \alpha$ and $\alpha(1) = \beta$. We define (upto final reparametrisation):

$$\alpha(s') = \{x(s') \text{ to } x \text{ along } \gamma^{-1}\} * h(s', \cdot) * \{x \text{ to } x(s') \text{ along } \gamma\} \ ,$$

and find from $h(0, \cdot) = \alpha$, $h(1, \cdot) = \gamma * \beta * \gamma^{-1}$ that $\alpha(0) = \alpha$, $\alpha(1) = \beta$ as
required.
When we take $x = y$ here, and compare the implications of based and
free homotopic equivalences, we are brought back to conjugacy classes in
$\pi_1(X; x)$! In any case, based homotopic equivalence is more restrictive than
free (even with $x = y$), so the latter may hold when the former does not.
Let us use definition (2), and note that now $\gamma \in \mathcal{L}_x$ is also a loop. Then

$\alpha, \beta \in \mathcal{L}_x$ are freely homotopic $\Leftrightarrow$ there is a $\gamma \in \mathcal{L}_x$ such that
$\alpha \sim \gamma * \beta * \gamma^{-1}$ in the sense of based homotopy $\Leftrightarrow$ $[\alpha], [\beta]$ are in
the same conjugacy class as elements of $\pi_1(X, x)$;
$\alpha, \beta \in \mathcal{L}_x$ are homotopic $\Leftrightarrow$ $[\alpha] = [\beta]$ as elements of $\pi_1(X; x)$.

$$(17.32)$$

So the differing implications of free and based homotopies are seen clearly; of course this is present only when $\pi_1(X)$ is nonabelian, otherwise conjugacy classes reduce to single group elements!

A nice example of this situation is provided by the "figure eight" described earlier. Referring to Figure 14, we see that the loops β and γ are *not* homotopically equivalent to each other because any homotopy must consist throughout of loops based at x. But if we lift this restriction, we can easily see that β and γ *are* freely homotopic to one another, and eqn.(17.25) confirms this.

17.10.   COMPARING FUNDAMENTAL GROUPS - HOMOTOPY TYPES - CONTRACTIBLE SPACES

Let X, Y be two topological spaces, each path connected. Are there ways to compare $\pi_1(X)$ and $\pi_1(Y)$, when are they isomorphic? Certainly if X and Y are homeomorphic to one another, ie., as topological spaces they are "the same", we expect the two fundamental groups to be isomorphic. But this already happens with a much weaker requirement - it is enough that X and Y be of the *same homotopy type*. To define this we need to use the notion of homotopic equivalence of continuous maps between topological spaces, which we have already mentioned earlier in this Section. Let us begin by expressing it via equations.

Two continuous maps $f_1 : X \to Y$, $f_2 : X \to Y$ are homotopic to one another, or are homotopically equivalent, $f_1 \sim f_2$, if there is a continuous map $h : [0,1] \times X \to Y$ obeying

$$s' \in [0,1] \, , \ x \in X \ \to \ h(s',x) \in Y \, ,$$
$$h(0,x) \ = \ f_1(x), \ h(1,x) = f_2(x) \cdot \qquad (17.33)$$

Then the set of all continuous maps $X \to Y$ splits up into disjoint homotopic equivalence classes, as $f_1 \sim f_2$ is an equivalence relation.

With this in hand, we say X and Y are of the *same homotopy type* if there exist continuous maps $f : X \to Y$, $g : Y \to X$ (acting in opposite directions!) such that

$$f \circ g \sim \mathcal{I}d_Y \, , \quad g \circ f \sim \mathcal{I}d_X \cdot \qquad (17.34)$$

If X and Y were homeomorphic spaces we could take $g = f^{-1}$, and both products would have been *equal* to the respective identity maps. What makes the notion of homotopy type weaker than that of homeomorphism is precisely that we only demand equivalences and not equalities in eqn. (17.34). So:

$$X \text{ homeomorphic to } Y \ \Rightarrow \ X \text{ and } Y \text{ are of the same homotopy}$$
$$\text{type, but not vice versa} \qquad (17.35)$$

Here is an illustration of the latter part of this statement. Take $X = \mathcal{R}^2 - \{\underline{0}\}$, the punctured plane, and $Y = S^1$. Clearly they are not homeomorphic spaces. However, using polar variables r, θ (with $r > 0$) if we set

$$f : (r, \theta) \in X \rightarrow \theta \in Y ,$$
$$g : \theta \in Y \rightarrow (1, \theta) \in X , \qquad (17.36)$$

we get:

$$f \circ g : \theta \in Y \rightarrow \theta \in Y, \ f \circ g = \mathcal{I}d_Y ;$$
$$g \circ f : (r, \theta) \in X \rightarrow (1, \theta) \in X, \ g \circ f \neq \mathcal{I}d_X \cdot \qquad (17.37)$$

But one can easily show that $g \circ f$ is continuously deformable to $\mathcal{I}d_X$, by gradually varying the radial coordinate. We can exhibit $h(s', x)$ of eqn. (17.33) explicitly:

$$s' \in [0, 1], \ (r, \theta) \ \in \ X :$$
$$h(s'; r, \theta) \ = \ (1 + (r - 1)s', \theta) \in X ;$$
$$h(0; r, \theta) \ = \ (1, \theta) ,$$
$$h(1; r, \theta) \ = \ (r, \theta) \cdot \qquad (17.38)$$

(The fact that the angle θ is not globally well defined causes no problems). So $\mathcal{R}^2 - \{\underline{0}\}$ and S^1 are of the same homotopy type, though not homeomorphic. And indeed, from eqn.(17.24), their fundamental groups are the same.

Here are some more examples of spaces of the same homotopy type: $\mathcal{R}^n$ for any n, and a single point; $\mathcal{R}^n$ and $\mathcal{R}^{n'}$ for any n and n'; the solid unit sphere minus the origin in any $\mathcal{R}^n$, $B^n - \{\underline{0}\}$, and the surface of B^n, namely S^{n-1}. (Both B^n and S^{n-1} will be described more fully later on when we study higher homotopy groups).

We leave it as an exercise to check that the property of being of the same homotopy type is an equivalence relation among topological spaces.

Now we proceed to establish the result we are after : if X and Y are of the same homotopy type, then $\pi_1(X)$ and $\pi_1(Y)$ are isomorphic groups. Let $x_0 \in X$ have image $y_0 = f(x_0) \in Y$, and in the reverse direction let $x'_0 = g(y_0) \in X$. From continuity of f we see that loops $\alpha, \beta, \ldots, \in \mathcal{L}_{x_0}$ are mapped to loops $\alpha', \beta', \ldots \in \mathcal{L}_{y_0}$ in such a way that composition, inversion and homotopic equivalence of loops are all preserved:

$$\alpha = \{x(s)\} \in \mathcal{L}_{x_0} \rightarrow \alpha' = f(\alpha) = \{y(s)\} \in \mathcal{L}_{y_0} ,$$
$$y(s) = f(x(s)) ;$$

$$f(\alpha * \beta) \;=\; f(\alpha) * f(\beta) \,,$$
$$f(\alpha^{-1}) \;=\; (f(\alpha))^{-1} \,,$$
$$\alpha \sim \beta \;\Rightarrow\; f(\alpha) \sim f(\beta) \,. \tag{17.39}$$

Therefore each equivalence class of loops in $\mathcal{L}_{x_0}$ is mapped into one equivalence class of loops in $\mathcal{L}_{y_0}$, preserving group operations: f gives us a group homomorphism from $\pi_1(X;x_0)$ to $\pi_1(Y;y_0)$. In the same way, g leads to a homomorphism from $\pi_1(Y;y_0)$ to $\pi_1(X;x_0')$ What we need to show now is that these homomorphisms are isomorphisms. The properties of f (or g) alone allow for the possibility that two or more elements of $\pi_1(X;x_0)$ (or $\pi_1(Y;y_0)$) get mapped to one element of $\pi_1(Y;y_0)$ (or $\pi_1(X;x_0')$). It is here that the requirements (17.34) come to our rescue. Suppose we take two loops α, $\beta \in \mathcal{L}_{x_0}$ such that their images in $\mathcal{L}_{y_0}$ under f are equivalent; then applying g to these images gives equivalent loops at x_0':

$$\alpha, \beta \in \mathcal{L}_{x_0}, f(\alpha) \sim f(\beta) \Rightarrow (g \circ f)(\alpha) \sim (g \circ f)(\beta) \in \mathcal{L}_{x_0'} \,. \tag{17.40}$$

But since $g \circ f$ can be continuously deformed to $\mathcal{I}d_X$, we get the equivalence of α and β themselves! This clinches the argument and proves the isomorphism of $\pi_1(X)$ and $\pi_1(Y)$:

$$X \text{ and } Y \text{ of same homotopy type } \Rightarrow$$
$$\pi_1(X) \text{ isomorphic to } \pi_1(Y) \tag{17.41}$$

So in particular, combined with (17.35), we see that for homeomorphic spaces the fundamental groups are isomorphic - the fundamental group is a *topological invariant*.

One can now define what is meant by a *contractible space* :

$$X \text{ is contractible } \iff X \text{ is of the same homotopy type as a single point}$$
$$\iff \mathcal{I}d_X \text{ is homotopic to a constant map} \tag{17.42}$$

The last statement here is just the latter part of the requirement (17.34). With this definition we can establish the triviality of $\pi_1(X)$ in this case:

$$X \text{ contractible} \Rightarrow X \text{ simply connected}, \pi_1(X) = 0, \text{ but not conversely} \tag{17.43}$$

The explicit proof in the forward direction is also easy. Let the homotopy connecting $\mathcal{I}d_X$ and a constant map be

$$h \;:\; s' \in [0,1], x \in X \to h(s',x) \in X \,,$$
$$h(0,x) = x \,, \quad h(1,x) = x_0 \in X \,. \tag{17.44}$$

Now take any loop $\alpha = \{x(s)\} \in \mathcal{L}_{x_0}$. By a two-step process exploiting h, we can construct a homotopy linking α to the constant loop $\alpha_0 \in \mathcal{L}_{x_0}$, eqn.(17.16). To begin, we notice that as s' varies from 0 to 1, $h(s', x_0)$ itself describes a loop in $\mathcal{L}_{x_0}$. Now the naturally constructed expression $h(s', x(s))$ describes, for s' fixed and s running from 0 to 1, a loop based at $h(s', x_0)$. On the other hand, $h(s''s', x_0)$ for $0 \le s'' \le 1$ gives us a path from x_0 to $h(s', x_0)$, with inverse going back to x_0. We can combine these paths and the previously mentioned loop at $h(s', x_0)$ in the manner of eqns.(17.20) and thus construct, for each s', a loop in $\mathcal{L}_{x_0}$. This however begins with α at $s' = 0$, varies continuously with s', and ends up with α_0 at $s' = 1$, so we are done. So any $\alpha \in \mathcal{L}_{x_0}$ is shrinkable to "zero", and $\pi_1(X)$ is trivial.

To show that the converse in (17.43) fails, we take the example $X = S^2$: every loop on S^2 is shrinkable to "zero", but as is intuitively clear, S^2 is not contractible and not of the same homotopy type as a single point. The map $\mathcal{I}d_{S^2}$ cannot be deformed to a constant map without cutting or tearing S^2!

Let us mention some simple examples of contractible spaces: $\mathcal{R}^n$ for any n; the unit interval $I = [0,1] \subset \mathcal{R}$; the higher dimensional "cube" $I \times I \times \ldots \times I(n \text{ factors}) \subset \mathcal{R}^n$; the solid unit sphere $B^n \subset \mathcal{R}^n$.

One can follow up (17.43) with the remark that all contractible spaces are of the same homotopy type, whatever their dimensions may be! This is because of the transitive property - being of the same homotopy type is an equivalence relation among topological spaces. We may also point out that the kind of region over which we were able to establish the Poincare Lemma in Section 11 - locally, a closed form is exact - is a contractible region. Another easy result is that products of contractible spaces are also contractible.

Lastly we state an important theorem relating to Principle Fibre Bundles, PFB's : if either the base or the structure group of a PFB is contractible, the bundle is trivial.

17.11.   THE HIGHER HOMOTOPY GROUPS $\pi_n(X)$ -INTRODUCTION

As we have mentioned at the beginning of this Section, the higher homotopy groups arise by replacing the circle S^1 by the spheres S^n, $n = 2, 3, \ldots$, and considering continuous maps $S^n \to X$. We dealt with S^1 in two ways: either as a unit circle drawn in the plane $\mathcal{R}^2$, centred at the origin; or as the unit interval $I = [0, 1] \subset \mathcal{R}$ with end points identified. For $n \ge 2$ too, it is good to be able to switch between different equivalent ways of handling S^n. We need to be able to picture S^n in a simple geometrical way, as well as to deal with it in a simple analytical manner to define group operations on maps nicely. We now give in brief these alternative versions of S^n and the relations among them.

17.12.   MODELS FOR THE SPHERES S^n

Since we have to deal interchangeably with vectors in the Euclidean spaces $\mathcal{R}^n$, $\mathcal{R}^{n+1}$ for general n, as a convenient and uniform notation we adopt the following:

$$\begin{aligned}
\boldsymbol{\xi} &= (\xi_1, \xi_2, \ldots, \xi_{n+1}) \in \mathcal{R}^{n+1} , \\
\hat{\boldsymbol{\xi}} &= \text{unit vector in } \mathcal{R}^{n+1} ; \\
\boldsymbol{s} &= (s_1, s_2, \ldots, s_n) \in \mathcal{R}^n , \\
\hat{\boldsymbol{s}} &= \text{unit vector in } \mathcal{R}^n .
\end{aligned} \tag{17.45}$$

We denote the Cartesian component with the largest magnitude by $m(\boldsymbol{\xi})$, $m(\boldsymbol{s})$:

$$\begin{aligned}
m(\boldsymbol{\xi}) &= \max(|\xi_a|, a = 1, 2, \ldots, n+1) , \\
m(\boldsymbol{s}) &= \max(|s_j|, j = 1, 2, \ldots, n) .
\end{aligned} \tag{17.46}$$

In most treatments of the higher homotopy groups, one introduces the n-dimensional unit "hyper cube" $I^n = [0,1] \times [0,1] \times \ldots \times [0,1](n \text{ factors})$ $\subset \mathcal{R}^n$, with the origin at one corner, and defines S^n in terms of it. However, for the sake of inversion symmetry, and to pass more easily between higher dimensional spheres and cubes all centred at the origin, we shall define the hyper cube to be of side two units, each Cartesian coordinate varying in $[-1, 1]$. So we define the (solid) unit spheres and cubes in $\mathcal{R}^{n+1}$, $\mathcal{R}^n$ as follows:

$$\begin{aligned}
B^{n+1} &= \left\{ \boldsymbol{\xi} \in \mathcal{R}^{n+1} \,\middle|\, |\boldsymbol{\xi}| \leq 1| \right\} , \\
I^{n+1} &= \left\{ \boldsymbol{\xi} \in \mathcal{R}^{n+1} \,\middle|\, m(\boldsymbol{\xi}) \leq 1 \right\} \\
&= \left\{ \boldsymbol{\xi} \in \mathcal{R}^{n+1} \,\middle|\, -1 \leq \xi_a \leq 1, \ a = 1, 2, \ldots, n+1 \right\} ; \\
B^n &= \left\{ \boldsymbol{s} \in \mathcal{R}^n \,\middle|\, |\boldsymbol{s}| \leq 1 \right\} , \\
I^n &= \left\{ \boldsymbol{s} \in \mathcal{R}^n \,\middle|\, m(\boldsymbol{s}) \leq 1 \right\} \\
&= \left\{ \boldsymbol{s} \in \mathcal{R}^n \,\middle|\, -1 \leq s_j \leq 1, j = 1, 2, \ldots, n \right\} .
\end{aligned} \tag{17.47}$$

It is quite easy to pass continuously between B^n and I^n as they are homeomorphic spaces:

$$\begin{aligned}
\boldsymbol{s} \in B^n \to \boldsymbol{s}' &= \frac{|\boldsymbol{s}|}{m(\boldsymbol{s})} \boldsymbol{s} \in I^n , \\
\boldsymbol{s}' \in I^n \to \boldsymbol{s} &= \frac{m(\boldsymbol{s}')}{|\boldsymbol{s}'|} \boldsymbol{s}' \in B^n ; \\
m(\boldsymbol{s}') = |\boldsymbol{s}|, \ m(\boldsymbol{s}) &= |\boldsymbol{s}|^2/|\boldsymbol{s}'| .
\end{aligned} \tag{17.48}$$

So directions are preserved and only the radial variables are changed in a simple manner. The points preserved under this correspondence are of the form

$$s'_j = s_j = \sigma\, \delta_{jj_0}\ ,\quad -1 \le \sigma \le 1\ ,\ \text{any fixed } j_0 \cdot \qquad (17.49)$$

Similar equations can be set up to pass between B^{n+1} and I^{n+1}.

Now the direct geometrical definitions of the n and $(n-1)$ dimensional spheres S^n, S^{n-1} are as the boundaries of B^{n+1} and B^n respectively:

$$\begin{aligned} S^n &= \partial\, B^{n+1} = \left\{\hat{\xi} \in \mathcal{R}^{n+1}\right\}\ , \\ S^{n-1} &= \partial\, B^n = \{\hat{s} \in \mathcal{R}^n\} \cdot \end{aligned} \qquad (17.50)$$

(From here, by the way, it follows that $\partial\, S^n = 0$). With the help of the mappings (17.48), as far as homotopy is concerned, we can regard these spheres equally well as boundaries of I^{n+1} and I^n respectively:

$$\begin{aligned} S^n = \partial B^{n+1} \sim \partial I^{n+1} &= \{\boldsymbol{\xi} \in \mathcal{R}^{n+1} | m(\boldsymbol{\xi}) = 1\}\ , \\ S^{n-1} = \partial B^n \sim \partial I^n &= \{\boldsymbol{s} \in \mathcal{R}^n | m(\boldsymbol{s}) = 1\} \cdot \end{aligned} \qquad (17.51)$$

(For $n = 2$, to say that $S^1 \sim \partial\, I^2$ is really like squaring the circle!) However, apart from these direct geometrical representations of the spheres S^n, S^{n-1} we can develop other representations using B^n and I^n for S^n (and B^{n-1}, I^{n-1} for S^{n-1}) as follows: Start with $S^n = \partial\, B^{n+1}$ and represent each $\hat{\xi}$ as an n-dimensional vector followed by the $(n+1)$ th component $\hat{\xi}_{n+1}$ parametrised by a "polar angle" θ:

$$S^n = \partial\, B^{n+1} = \left\{\hat{\xi} = (\hat{s}\sin\theta,\ \cos\theta) | \hat{s} \in S^{n-1},\ 0 \le \theta \le \pi\right\}\ , \qquad (17.52)$$

with the understanding that $\hat{s}$ is undefined at $\theta = 0$ or π. Here $\hat{s}$ plays exactly the role of the azimuth angle ϕ in the case of S^2. The "North" ("South") pole $\mathcal{N}(\mathcal{S})$ of S^n corresponds to $\theta = 0(\pi)$. The fact that the unit vector $\hat{s}$ corresponds (by eqn.(17.50)) to a point on S^{n-1} means that there are as many ways of approaching $\mathcal{N}$ or $\mathcal{S}$ (or indeed any other point) on S^n as there are directions in S^{n-1}. So the pair $(\hat{s}, \theta)$ is the natural generalisation of the usual spherical polar angles from S^2 to any S^n. Now we define a vector $\boldsymbol{s} \in \mathcal{R}^n$ of magnitude less than or equal to unity by

$$(\hat{s}, \theta) \in S^n \longrightarrow \boldsymbol{s} = \hat{s}\ \sin\theta/2 \cdot \qquad (17.53)$$

In this way, each point $(\hat{s}, \theta) \in S^n = \partial\, B^{n+1}$ gets mapped to a definite point of B^n, with the $\mathcal{N}$ pole of S^n going into the origin; except that as $\theta \to \pi$ and we approach the $\mathcal{S}$ pole, we get *all* points on the boundary of

B^n! Therefore we have this representation of S^n in addition to the previous more geometric one:

$$S^n \sim B^n = \{s \in \mathcal{R}^n \| |s| \leq 1\} \,,$$
$$N \in S^n \rightarrow s = 0 \,,$$
$$S \in S^n \rightarrow \text{all points of } \partial B^n, \text{ i.e., } |s| = 1 \cdot \qquad (17.54)$$

In other words, S^n can be pictured as B^n *with all boundary points identified to be the South pole S*. This is the generalisation of regarding S^1 as $I = [0, 1]$ with the two end-points identified. So the sphere S^2 is given by the unit *disk $B^2 \subset \mathcal{R}^2$ with all boundary points on its circumference identified*. One can then switch from B^n to I^n and present S^n also in this way:

$$S^n \sim I^n = \{s \in \mathcal{R}^n | m(s) \leq 1\} \,,$$
$$N \in S^n \rightarrow s = 0 \,,$$
$$S \in S^n \rightarrow \text{all points of } \partial I^n, \text{ i.e., } m(s) = 1 \cdot \qquad (17.55)$$

(The replacement for eqn.(17.53) is obtained by combining that equation with (17.47)). Now the sphere S^2 is depicted as the *square* $I^2 = [-1, 1] \times [-1, 1] \subset \mathcal{R}^2$ with all boundary points identified as representing the South pole S. The convenience of the representation (17.55) of S^n is that each coordinate s_j has an independent domain of variation, and this will be used presently.

17.13. DEFINITION AND PROPERTIES OF n-LOOPS AND $\pi_n(X; x_0)$

Now we turn to maps $S^n \rightarrow X$, a given (path-connected) topological space. An n-loop based at $x_0 \in X$ is a continuous map $\alpha : S^n \rightarrow X$ described thus:

$$\alpha : I^n \subset \mathcal{R}^n \rightarrow X :$$
$$s \in I^n \rightarrow x(s) \in X \,,$$
$$x(s)|_{m(s)=1} = x_0 \cdot \qquad (17.56)$$

Here we are using the model (17.55) for S^n. The "boundary condition" on α, which makes it a map based at x_0, says that the South pole $S \in S^n$ must always be taken to the given base point x_0. To compose two such n-loops, we use the same procedure as for ordinary loops with respect to the first parameter s_1 (adjusting for the range) and leave $s_2, \ldots, s_n$ untouched:

$$\alpha = \{x(s)\} \,, \quad \beta = \{x'(s)\} \rightarrow \alpha * \beta = \{x''(s)\} :$$
$$x''(s_1, s_2, \ldots, s_n) = \begin{cases} x(2s_1 + 1, s_2 \ldots, s_n) \,, & -1 \leq s_1 \leq 0 \\ x'(2s_1 - 1, s_2, \ldots, s_n) \,, & 0 \leq s_1 \leq 1 \end{cases} \cdot (17.57)$$

So, at each fixed $s_2, \ldots, s_n$, the two n-loops α and β are continuously glued together over $s_1 = 0$. We see that the boundary conditions of eqn.(17.56) are obeyed by $x''(s)$, so $\alpha * \beta$ is an n-loop based at x_0. The inverse of α again works with s_1 alone:

$$\alpha = \{x(s)\} \to \alpha^{-1} = \{x^{-1}(s)\} ,$$
$$x^{-1}(s) = x(-s_1, s_2, \ldots, s_n) \cdot \qquad (17.58)$$

The constant n-loop at x_0 is

$$\alpha_0 : x(s) = x_0 , \text{ all } s \in I^n \cdot \qquad (17.59)$$

We can see why it was convenient to work with the model (17.55) for S^n!

To arrive at a group structure, we need to define homotopies and homotopic equivalence among n-loops. This involves bringing in one more interpolating parameter $s' \in [0, 1]$. Two based n-loops $\alpha = \{x(s)\}$ and $\beta = \{x'(s)\}$ are homotopic to one another if we can find a continuous map $h : [0, 1] \times I^n \to X$ such that

$$h : s' \in [0, 1] , s \in I^n \to h(s', s) \in X ,$$
$$h(0, s) = x(s), h(1, s) = x'(s) ,$$
$$h(s', s)|_{m(s)=1} = x_0 \cdot \qquad (17.60)$$

So for each fixed s', $h(s', :)$ is an n-loop based at x_0; and as s' varies continuously from 0 to 1 we begin at α and end up at β. (One can now convince oneself that any change in the choice of coordinate to compose and invert n-loops in the manner of eqn.(17.57) leads to homotopically equivalent results). It is easy to see that homotopic equivalence among based n-loops is an equivalence relation, which moreover has the same properties (17.17) as in the case $n = 1$.

Thus by working with equivalence classes of n-loops based at x_0 and defining products and inverses exactly as before via eqn.(17.18), we arrive at the nth based homotopy group $\pi_n(X; x_0)$. The identity element is the equivalence class $[\alpha_0]$ of the constant n-loop α_0, and associativity and inverses work out properly.

17.14. $\pi_n(X; x_0)$ IS ABELIAN IF $n \geq 2$

For the first homotopy group $\pi_1(X; x_0)$ we have exhibited both Abelian and nonabelian examples, and looked at some specific features in the latter case. It is a striking result that *all the higher homotopy groups are always Abelian!* The proof is best conveyed by pictures, in which the first Cartesian coordinate of I^n is plotted along the ordinate and all the rest are compressed along the abcissa.

Let α, β be two n-loops based at x_0, and depict them as follows:

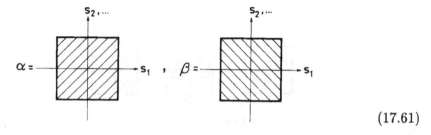

$$(17.61)$$

All the points which are mapped to the base x_0 are shown by a heavy "line". The definition (17.57) for composing α and β to get $\alpha * \beta$ amounts in pictures to the following:

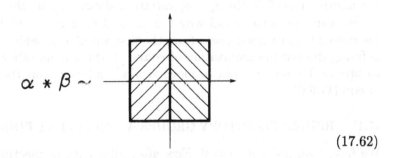

$$(17.62)$$

Each of the figures in (17.61) has been shrunk in the s_1 direction to half its original extent, and the two have then been pasted together. Now the central vertical "line" is naturally also shown as a heavy one. We now use the enormous flexibility given by the possibility of continuous deformation and carry out the follow sequence of transformations in the $s_1 - s_2$ plane at each fixed $s_3, \ldots, s_n$:

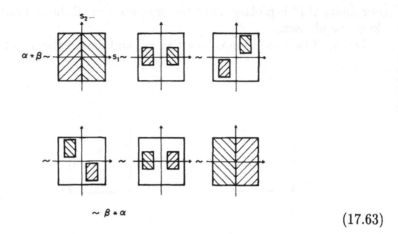

$$(17.63)$$

Here in the second to the fifth figures *all* points outside the two smaller rectangles but within the outer one are mapped to x_0. We can see that at every stage the proper boundary conditions - n-loop based at x_0- are obeyed. The convenience of the I^n-model for S^n is again evident: since the range for each s_j is $[-1, 1]$ independent of the rest, we could go through the above "dance" in the $s_1 - s_2$ variables alone, *keeping the rest fixed.*

We can also understand why the method does not work for $\pi_1(X; x_0)$ (as indeed it must not): apart from the first variable s_1 which is used up in defining the law of composition of α and β, there is no other variable left to provide leeway or room to move around and carry out the manoeuvers of eqn.(17.63)!

17.15.   HIGHER HOMOTOPY GROUPS AT DIFFERENT POINTS

We have assumed $\pi_0(X) = 0$. Now after all a path connecting two points is a one-dimensional object. So it may come initially as somewhat of a surprise that path-connectedness is enough to show that for any two points x, y $\in$ X, the nth homotopy groups $\pi_n(X; x)$ and $\pi_n(X; y)$, for any n, are isomorphic. We sketch the proof but remark in advance that what is really exploited is the truly enormous flexibility afforded by continuous deformations of maps maintaining homotopic equivalence.

We first supplement the definition (17.47) of the cube I^n by defining another cube of half the linear dimension, which we write as $I^n(1/2)$:

$$I^n(1/2) = \{s \ \in \ \mathcal{R}^n | m(s) \leq 1/2\} \subset I^n \cdot \qquad (17.64)$$

Here are some elementary geometrical relations connecting I^n and $I^n(1/2)$:

$$s \in I^n \Rightarrow s = s s^{(0)}, \ 0 \le s \le 1, \ s^{(0)} \in \partial I^n \ ;$$
$$s \, s^{(0)} \in I^n(1/2) \text{ for } 0 \le s \le 1/2 \ ,$$
$$s \, s^{(0)} \notin I^n(1/2), \ \in I^n \text{ for } 1/2 < s \le 1 \cdot \quad (17.65)$$

So $s^{(0)}$ fixes the direction and obeys $m(s^{(0)}) = 1$, while s is like a radial variable. Further,

$$s \in I^n(1/2) \ \Leftrightarrow \ 2 s \in I^n \ ,$$
$$s \in \partial I^n(1/2) \ \Leftrightarrow \ 2 s \in \partial I^n \cdot \quad (17.66)$$

Now take any two points $x, y \in X$ and let γ be a path connecting them, with γ^{-1} going the other way:

$$\gamma \ = \ \{c(s)\} \ , \ \gamma^{-1} = \{c(1-s)\} \ ,$$
$$c(0) \ = \ x \ , \ c(1) = y \cdot \quad (17.67)$$

Let $\alpha = \{x(s)\}$ be any n-loop based at x, so $[\alpha] \in \pi_n(X; x)$. We combine α and γ, an n-loop and a path, to define an n-loop α' based at y in this way:

$$\alpha' \ : \ s \in I^n \longrightarrow x'(s) \in X \ :$$
$$x'(s) \ = \ \begin{cases} x(2s), \ s \in I^n(1/2) \ ; \\ c(2 s - 1), \ s = s \, s^{(0)} \ , \ 1/2 < s \le 1 \ , \ s^{(0)} \in \partial I^n \cdot \end{cases}$$

$$(17.68)$$

What we have done here is to "compress" the n-loop α to the small cube $I^n(1/2)$ sitting within I^n; all over $\partial I^n(1/2)$ we have $x'(s) = x(2 s) = x$ as α is based at x; then from $\partial I^n(1/2)$ all the way out to ∂I^n, $x'(s)$ is independent of α and involves only the path γ. In fact beyond $\partial I^n(1/2)$, $x'(s)$ has only a "radial" dependence, the path γ being exploited to move continuously from x over $\partial I^n(1/2)$ to y over ∂I^n. So α' is indeed an n-loop based at y, though it is a somewhat degenerate or special one. We replace eqn.(17.20) by the notation

$$\alpha \to \alpha' = \gamma^*(\alpha) \quad (17.69)$$

and can depict the way α' has arisen from α in a pictorial manner:

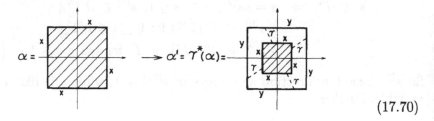

$$(17.70)$$

The values x, y reached over various boundary regions, and the way γ has been exploited, are also shown.

In a similar way one can use $(\gamma^{-1})^*$ to transfer n-loops at y to n-loops at x. One can see the following general features of these two maps by playing around with homotopies:

$$
\begin{aligned}
\gamma^*(\text{ any } \alpha \text{ at } x) &= \text{ some special } \alpha' \text{ at } y\ , \\
\gamma^*(\text{any } \beta \text{ in } [\alpha] \text{ at } x) &= \text{ some special } \beta' \text{ in } [\gamma^*(\alpha)] \text{ at } y; \\
(\gamma^{-1})^*(\text{ any } \alpha' \text{ at } y) &= \text{ some special } \alpha \text{ at } x\ , \\
(\gamma^{-1})^*(\text{ any } \beta' \text{ in } [\alpha'] \text{ at } y) &= \text{ some special } \alpha \text{ in } [(\gamma^{-1})^*(\alpha')] \text{ at } x \cdot
\end{aligned}
$$

$$(17.71)$$

However, because of the special way the maps γ^* , $(\gamma^{-1})^*$ are defined we must note that:

$$
\begin{aligned}
\text{general } \beta' \text{ in } [\gamma^*(\alpha)] \text{ at } y &\neq \gamma^*(\text{ some } \beta \text{ in } [\alpha] \text{ at } x)\ , \\
\text{general } \beta \text{ in } [(\gamma^{-1})^*(\alpha')] \text{ at } x &\neq (\gamma^{-1})^* (\text{some } \beta' \text{ in } [\alpha'] \text{ at } y) \cdot
\end{aligned}
$$

$$(17.72)$$

In a similar vein one can check that

$$
\begin{aligned}
(\gamma^{-1})^*(\gamma^*(\alpha)) &\sim \alpha, \text{ any } \alpha \text{ at } x\ ; \\
\gamma^*((\gamma^{-1})^*(\alpha')) &\sim \alpha'\ , \text{ any } \alpha' \text{ at } y \cdot
\end{aligned}
$$

$$(17.73)$$

All these properties enable us to make the following claim: γ^* establishes an unambiguous bijective (one-to-one, onto) correspondence between elements of $\pi_n(X; x)$ and $\pi_n(X; y)$, and $(\gamma^{-1})^*$ does so in the reverse direction; but in both cases this does not work at the level of *individual* n-loops:

$$[\alpha] \in \pi_n(X;x) : \gamma^*[\alpha] = [\gamma^*(\alpha)] \in \pi_n(X;y) ;$$
$$[\alpha'] \in \pi_n(X;y) : (\gamma^{-1})^*[\alpha'] = [(\gamma^{-1})^*(\alpha')] \in \pi_n(X;x) ;$$
$$(\gamma^{-1})^* \equiv (\gamma^*)^{-1} . \tag{17.74}$$

Now these correspondences can be shown to be isomorphisms between the two groups! We need only check the effects on the identity and on a general product. For the identity:

$$\alpha_0 : x(s) = x = \text{constant} \Rightarrow \gamma^*(\alpha_0) = \{x'(s)\} ,$$

$$x'(s) = \begin{cases} x , & s \in I^n(1/2) ; \\ c(2\,s-1) , & s = s\,s^{(0)} , 1/2 < s \le 1 , s^{(0)} \in \partial\,I^n . \end{cases} \tag{17.75}$$

We must find a homotopy $h(s', s)$ to deform this to the constant n-loop at y. We can do so because $x'(s)$ in (17.75) is purely "radial":

$$s = s\,s^{(0)} \in I^n , s^{(0)} \in \partial\,I^n , 0 \le s \le 1 :$$
$$x'(s) = x'(s\,s^{(0)}) = \tilde{c}(s) ,$$
$$\tilde{c}(s) = \begin{cases} x , & 0 \le s \le 1/2 ; \\ c(2\,s-1) , & 1/2 \le s \le 1 \end{cases} \tag{17.76}$$

So here $\tilde{c}(s)$ gives us another path $\tilde{\gamma}$ from x to y : for "half the time" it stays put at x, then it runs along γ at "double the speed" to reach y by $s = 1$! So $\tilde{\gamma}$ is just a reparametrised form of γ. If we now choose the homotopy as

$$h(s', s) = \tilde{c}(1 - (1 - s')(1 - s)), s = s\,s^{(0)} , s^{(0)} \in \partial\,I^n , \tag{17.77}$$

we see it has just the properties we want: it is continuous, and

$$h(0, s) = x'(s) ,$$
$$h(1, s) = \tilde{c}(1) = y . \tag{17.78}$$

So we have shown that

$$\gamma^* (\text{constant } n - \text{loop at } x) \sim \text{constant } n - \text{loop at } y . \tag{17.79}$$

As for products, experience tells us it is best to turn to pictures. Start with n-loops α, β based at x, compose them, then apply γ^*:

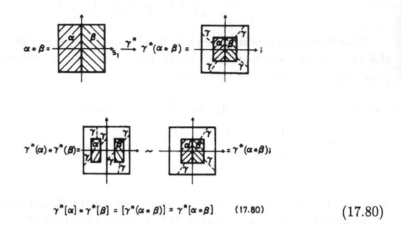

$$\gamma^*[\alpha] * \gamma^*[\beta] = [\gamma^*(\alpha * \beta)] = \gamma^*[\alpha * \beta] \qquad (17.80) \qquad\qquad (17.80)$$

So indeed we have an isomorphism between $\pi_n(X;x)$ and $\pi_n(X;y)$, dependent in general on γ.

However, exactly as at the $n = 1$ loop level, this isomorphism depends only on $[\gamma]$, being unchanged if γ is continuously deformed! So a more correct way to denote it would be:

$$\gamma \ : \ \text{path } x \to y, \ [\alpha] \ \in \ \pi_n(X;x) \longrightarrow$$
$$[\alpha'] \ = \ [\gamma]([\alpha]) = [\gamma^*(\alpha)] \ \in \ \pi_n(X;y) \ . \qquad (17.81)$$

One can now introduce the group $\pi_n(X)$, the nth homotopy group of X itself, as that abstract group (Abelian for $n \geq 2$) of which each $\pi_n(X;x)$ is an isomorphic copy.

Suppose as a special case of the above we take $y = x$. Then γ becomes a loop at x, $\gamma \in \mathcal{L}_x$, and $[\gamma] \in \pi_1(X;x)$. Then we see that the isomorphism (17.81) turns into an action of $\pi_1(X;x)$ on $\pi_n(X;x)$ by a family of automorphisms. (For $n \geq 2$, these cannot be characterized as inner automorphisms). If this action is trivial, then X is said to be n-simple.

If X is a contractible space, then of course each $\pi_n(X)$ is trivial.

A last statement we present sans proof is this: if X and Y are (path-connected) topological spaces of the same homotopy type, then $\pi_n(X)$ and $\pi_n(Y)$ are isomorphic groups.

Having made so much use of the spheres S^n, it is only fair that at least as examples we mention their own higher homotopy groups! These determinations are by no means trivial, neither are they complete; the situation is:

$$\pi_3(S^2) \;=\; \mathcal{Z} \;;$$

$$n \geq 3 : \pi_k(S^n) \;=\; \left\{ \begin{array}{l} 0 \,, \; 1 \leq k \leq n-1 \,, \\ \mathcal{Z} \,, \; k = n \cdot \end{array} \right. \tag{17.82}$$

We shall conclude our account of higher homotopy groups for general topological spaces X at this point, and forego an account of freely homotopic maps $S^n \to X$, their terminology, etc. It is time to turn now to Lie groups and their coset spaces.

17.16.   HOMOTOPY PROPERTIES OF LIE GROUPS - PRELIMINARIES

In several earlier Sections, in a limited way, we have touched upon global aspects of Lie groups and their coset spaces. In Section 13, we have seen that every (connected) Lie group G determines unambiguously its Lie algebra $\underline{G}$. In the reverse direction, we have given basically a local account of the exponential map leading from $\underline{G}$ to G. Later in Section 15 while considering the passage from linear representations of $\underline{G}$ to those of G, we have mentioned briefly the special role of the universal covering group $\overline{G}$ of G. The example of coset spaces G/H as instances of PFB's has been described in Section 14. We begin by supplementing all this with some more useful information, depending often on plausibility arguments. First some remarks on $\pi_0(G)$.

17.17.   PATH-CONNECTED COMPONENTS OF A LIE GROUP

Let G be a Lie group which may consist of several mutually disjoint pieces, each path connected and of some common dimension. Denote by G_0 the component containing the identity. It is easy to see that G_0 is an invariant subgroup of G. So we can pass to the quotient G/G_0, which is essentially an enumeration of the disjoint components of G *along with a group composition law*. Thus $\pi_0(G)$ turns out, in the first place, to be a group; and secondly it is just the above quotient:

$$\pi_0(G) = G/G_0 = \text{discrete group} \cdot \tag{17.83}$$

The fact that $\pi_0(G)$ is a group is the first example of a bonus we get because we are dealing with a group rather than a general topological space X. One can see easily that $\pi_0(G)$ is in general nonabelian. Indeed, as an example we can consider G to be the direct product of some G_0 and some discrete nonabelian group K, $G = G_0 \times K$, in which case $\pi_0(G) = K!$

A familiar example is provided by $G = 0(3)$, the group of all orthogonal rotations in three-dimensional space. Here $G_0 = S0(3)$, the subgroup of proper (unit determinant) rotations, and elements of G outside of G_0 are just those which involve once inversion through the origin (elements with determinant - 1). Then $\pi_0(0(3)) = 0(3)/S0(3) = \mathcal{Z}_2$, an abelian two-element group.

From here on, we shall always assume $\pi_0(G) = 0$, unless the contrary is stated explicitly.

17.18.   THE LIE ALGEBRA AND THE UNIVERSAL COVERING GROUP

We know from Section 13 that from a Lie group G we can pass to its unique associated Lie algebra $\underline{G}$ by studying the properties of left or right invariant vector fields on G. Defining $\underline{G}$ on its own as a Lie algebra - a real linear vector space with a Lie bracket operation subject to bilinearity, antisymmetry and the Jacobi identity - in the reverse direction $\underline{G}$ does not in general lead uniquely to G. There may exist several (connected) Lie groups $G, G_1, G_2, \ldots G_j, \ldots$ each possessing $\underline{G}$ as its Lie algebra. All these groups look exactly alike near the identity, but differ globally. Of them all, is there any unique one, which can be characterized in a nice way? There is, and it is the one *with a trivial fundamental group*. Write $\overline{G}$ for it; then we have the chain:

$$G, G_1, \ldots, G_j, \ldots \quad \longrightarrow \text{common Lie algebra } \underline{G} \longrightarrow$$
$$\text{unique } \overline{G}, \text{ a Lie group with } \pi_1(\overline{G}) = 0 \cdot$$

$$(17.84)$$

(So in fact $\overline{G}$ appears in the list on the left!). This $\overline{G}$ is called the *universal covering group* of each of $G, G_1, \ldots, G_j, \ldots$. So only $\pi_1(\overline{G}) = 0$, while $\pi_1(G$ or G_1 or $G_j \ldots$ other than $\overline{G}) \neq 0$.

How are each of $G, G_1, \ldots, G_j, \ldots$ related to $\overline{G}$? And how can we directly construct $\overline{G}$, given $G \neq \overline{G}$? It turns out that each of $G, G_1, \ldots G_j \ldots$ is the quotient (and therefore the coset space) of $\overline{G}$ with respect to a corresponding discrete invariant central subgroup $K, K_1, \ldots, K_j, \ldots$ in $\overline{G}$. The centre of $\overline{G}$ consists of all those elements which commute with all elements, and so of course among themselves; it is therefore abelian, which means each of $K, K_1, \ldots, K_j, \ldots$ is also abelian. (We can appreciate why these K's have to be discrete. All the groups $G, G_1, \ldots, \overline{G}$ have the same dimension, namely the dimension of $\underline{G}$, so we would have been in trouble if any K had a nonzero dimension!). So for each $G = \overline{G}/K$, there is a many to one homomorphism $\overline{G} \rightarrow G$, the multiplicity being the order of K.

The reconstruction of $\overline{G}$ from G is very interesting: an element of $\overline{G}$ is defined to be an element of G together with a path (upto homotopic equivalence) running from the identity of G upto that element. (There is some redundancy here since a path in G includes information on where it ends). The identity element, inverses and the composition law in $\overline{G}$ are easy to set up. It is also intuitively plausible that $\overline{G}$ is different from G precisely to the extent that $\pi_1(G)$ is nontrivial. One then finds that $\overline{G}$ is a simply connected Lie group, having the same Lie algebra, $\underline{G}$, as G itself; and $\overline{G}$ "covers" G as many times as the order of K.

We can now ask: what are the structures of the fundamental groups of the Lie groups $G, G_1 \ldots$, and how do they differ from one another? We state the answer at this point, with the promise that the proof will appear later as a special case of a more general result on the fundamental group of a coset space. Each $\pi_1(G_j)$ is a discrete abelian group, and is in fact the subgroup K_j of $\overline{G}$ involved in the quotienting:

$$\pi_1(G) = \pi_1(\overline{G}/K) = K \cdot \qquad (17.85)$$

This result should be very carefully distinguished from eqn. (17.83)!

Here are some familiar (and may be also not so familiar) examples of groups and their universal covers, with the degree or multiplicity of the covering also indicated:

Group	Universal covering group	Multiplicity
$U(1)$	$\mathcal{R}$	Infinite
$SO(3)$	$SU(2)$	Two
$SO(3,1)$	$SL(2,C)$	Two
$SO(n)$	$\mathrm{Spin}(n)$	Two
$SU(n)$	$SU(n)$	—
$USp(2n)$	$USp(2n)$	—
$SU(1,1) \simeq Sp(2,R) \simeq SL(2,R)$	$Sp(2,R)$	Infinite
$SU(3)/\mathcal{Z}_3$	$SU(3)$	Three

$$(17.86)$$

17.19.   THE FUNDAMENTAL GROUP $\pi_1(G)$, AND THE SECOND HOMOTOPY GROUP $\pi_2(G)$ IN THE COMPACT CASE

For any $g \in G$, the group $\pi_1(G; g)$ consists of equivalence classes of loops based at g, as a special case of the general definition. However, the existence of an isomorphism between any two such groups $\pi_1(G; g_1)$ and $\pi_1(G; g_2)$ follows "painlessly" by simply exploiting the fact that G is a group - there is no need for a path from g_1 to g_2. This is our second example of a bonus. (Indeed, unlike the case of a general topological space X where

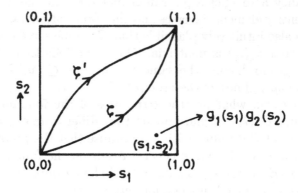

Figure 17.   Illustrating eqn.(17.88) of the text

we had to assume $\pi_0(X) = 0$ to establish the analogous result, here even path-connectedness of G is not needed!). For, left multiplication by $g_2\, g_1^{-1}$ translates each loop at g_1 to a loop at g_2 "in one swift step":

$$\alpha = \{g(s)\} \in \mathcal{L}_{g_1}, \ g(0) = g(1) = g_1 \Rightarrow$$
$$\alpha' = g_2\, g_1^{-1}\, \alpha \equiv \left\{ g_2\, g_1^{-1} g(s) \right\} \in \mathcal{L}_{g_2}. \qquad (17.87)$$

And clearly this mapping preserves homotopic equivalence, composition and inverses of loops. So the isomorphism of $\pi_1(G; g_1)$ and $\pi_1(G; g_2)$ is established. One also appreciates that it is natural or canonical - after all, what else could one do?

In fact one can see that the same translation idea works for all the higher homotopy groups, so $\pi_n(G; g_1)$ and $\pi_n(G; g_2)$ are isomorphic, any n. Again there is no need for any path from g_1 to g_2 or the rather elaborate manoeuvers we used in the general situation!

Having seen this, we can now restrict ourselves to $\pi_1(G; e)$ at the identity. Now we see the third bonus - this group is always abelian - a result due to Cartan, with an elegantly simple proof. We exploit to the full the existence of a composition law in G. Let $\alpha_1 = \{g_1(s)\}, \alpha_2 = \{g_2(s)\}$ be two loops based at e. We can take one element from each loop, multiply them, and so define a continuous map from the unit square in $\mathcal{R}^2$ to G:

$$(s_1, s_2) \in [0, 1] \times [0, 1] \longrightarrow g_1(s_1)g_2(s_2) \in G : \qquad (17.88)$$

This is shown in Figure 17.

All four corners of the square are mapped to $e \in G$. Now any continuous path $\mathcal{C}$ from the corner $(0,0)$ to the opposite corner $(1,1)$, lying totally within the square, determines a relation between s_1 and s_2 and leads to some loop at e:

$$g_1(s_1)\, g_2(s_2)\big|_{\text{along } C} \in \mathcal{L}_e \cdot \qquad (17.89)$$

Any other continuous path C', to which any C can surely be continuously deformed, then gives another loop at e homotopic to the former one. Now the path $(0,0)$ to $(1,0)$ to $(1,1)$ gives precisely the product $\alpha_1 * \alpha_2$, while the path $(0,0)$ to $(0,1)$ to $(1,1)$ gives the product $\alpha_2 * \alpha_1$. These are thus homotopically equivalent, hence the result:

$$\alpha_1 * \alpha_2 \sim \alpha_2 * \alpha_1 \Rightarrow \pi_1(G) \text{ Abelian} \qquad (17.90)$$

We follow this up with two comments. In combination with the first statement in eqn. (17.29), we confirm that the isomorphism between the fundamental groups at any two points of G is canonical. Secondly, our result is consistent with the (yet to be proved) statement (17.85), since we stated there that K is a *central* invariant (discrete) subgroup in $\overline{G}$.

After we discussed the nature of $\pi_0(G)$, we agreed to thereafter assume that it is trivial, ie., G is path-connected. In a similar way, having now seen that $\pi_1(G)$ is always discrete abelian, and more particularly that G can always be obtained from its simply connected universal covering group $\overline{G}$ as a quotient, we shall hereafter assume that G is already simply connected, $\pi_1(G) = 0$. If in any argument this is not initially so, we can always "raise ourselves up" to the level of $\overline{G}$, and carry on with the argument.

Turning to $\pi_2(G)$, we merely state an extremely important and significant theorem of Cartan which however refers to connected *compact* Lie groups only: it states that for such groups G, $\pi_2(G) = 0$. We may regard this too as a bonus, though a limited one, in the case of groups!

17.20. LIE GROUP COSET SPACES, THEIR CONNECTIVITIES AND FUNDAMENTAL GROUPS

We shall consider coset spaces G/H of Lie groups G (obeying $\pi_0(G) = \pi_1(G) = 0$) where the subgroup H could be of any one of three kinds:

(i) H discrete, so not a Lie group ;

(ii) H the component of a Lie subgroup connected to the identity ;

(iii) H a Lie subgroup with more than one

  connected component $\cdot$ $\qquad\qquad\qquad\qquad$ (17.91)

(Of course, in cases (ii) and (iii) we are concerned with connectivities by paths lying totally in H). As we have seen in Section 14, we can view G as a

PFB over G/H as base, with H as both typical fibre and structure group. (The present situation is however more general, since in Section 14 it was assumed that H is connected). Let us then generally write $M = G/H$ as the coset space. There is a natural projection $\pi : G \to M$ taking each $g \in G$ into its (left) coset $g H$. Depending on the above possibilities for the structure of H, each fibre too can be of three kinds - a discrete set of points; a single continuous connected component; or several disjoint components, each of some common positive dimension. In case (iii) above, let us denote the identity component of H by H_0; so by an application of eqn.(17.83), $\pi_0(H) = H/H_0$. In cases (i) and (ii) we take $H_0 = \{e\}$ and H respectively, so then H_0 is well-defined in all cases and $\pi_0(H) = H/H_0$ also in all cases. There is always a distinguished point $m_0 \in M$, the point representing the identity coset $e H : m_0 = \pi(e)$.

In spite of the possibility that H may be of any one of the above three types, we can quickly see that $\pi_0(G) = 0$ implies $\pi_0(M) = 0$ always. Any two points m_1, $m_2 \in M$ arise by projection π applied to any two group elements g_1, g_2 sitting in the fibres $\pi^{-1}(m_1)$, $\pi^{-1}(m_2)$. Since g_1 and g_2 can be connected by a path, applying π to the elements along the path gives us a path in M connecting m_1 and m_2!

Now we turn to the fundamental group $\pi_1(M)$. We can work at m_0 and examine loops based there. What we shall now prove (somewhat heuristically!) is that *because $\pi_1(G) = 0$*,

$$M = G/H : \pi_1(M) = \pi_0(H) = H/H_0 \cdot \qquad (17.92)$$

Let us list the disjoint components of H as H_0, H_1, $H_2, \ldots$:

$$H = \bigcup_{N=0,1,\ldots} H_N \cdot \qquad (17.93)$$

So the H_N are cosets of H with respect to H_0. Now the continuity of group operations and connectedness of each H_N imply in an obvious notation:

$$
\begin{aligned}
H_{N_1} H_{N_2} &= H_{\psi(N_1, N_2)} , \\
(H_N)^{-1} &= H_{\phi(N)} , \\
\psi(N_1, 0) &= N_1 , \; \psi(0, N_2) = N_2 , \\
\phi(0) &= \psi(N, \phi(N)) = \psi(\phi(N), N) = 0 , \text{ etc} \cdot \qquad (17.94)
\end{aligned}
$$

So the elements of H/H_0 are enumerated by $N = 0$, 1, 2, $\ldots$; the identity is $N = 0$; products are given by $\psi(\cdot, \cdot)$, and inverses by $\phi(\cdot)$.

Next, from any path $\Gamma \subset G$ we get by projection a path $\gamma \subset M$:

$$\Gamma = \{g(s)\} \subset G \xrightarrow{\pi} \gamma = \pi[\Gamma] = \{m(s) = \pi(g(s))\} \subset M \cdot \qquad (17.95)$$

If γ is to be a loop based at m_0, clearly Γ must begin and end in H:

$$\Gamma = \{g(s)\}, \ g(0) \text{ and } g(1) \ \in \ H \Rightarrow \gamma = \pi[\Gamma] \ \in \ \mathcal{L}_{m_0} \cdot \qquad (17.96)$$

Hereafter we shall consider only loops and homotopies based at m_0. The image γ is however unchanged by continuous right H action on Γ:

$$\begin{aligned} \Gamma' \ &= \ \{g'(s) = g(s) \, h(s), h(s) \ \in \ H_N \text{ for some fixed } N\} \subset G \\ &\xrightarrow{\pi} \pi[\Gamma'] = \pi[\Gamma] = \gamma \cdot \end{aligned} \qquad (17.97)$$

It is continuity of $h(s)$ as a function of s that obliges $h(s)$ to lie in some fixed connected component H_N of H throughout.

Now we argue that (17.96) can be reversed: every loop $\gamma \ \in \ \mathcal{L}_{m_0}$ can be lifted to paths $\Gamma \subset G$ starting and ending in H, with all the freedom expressed by eqn.(17.97). In fact, except in case (i) of eqn.(17.91), we always have the freedom of continuous changes in Γ keeping the projection γ fixed. The argument is the following. Every $\gamma \ \in \ \mathcal{L}_{m_0}$ is a map $[0,1] \to M$ starting and ending at m_0. It is this boundary condition $m(0) = m(1) = m_0$ that effectively converts $[0,1]$ into S^1, which is not contractible. If however we limit ourselves to $\text{Int}[0,1] = (0,1) = S^1$ minus one point (its "South" pole), we have a *contractible* space; and γ maps it into a contractible one-dimensional submanifold in M. One can now pass to the corresponding subbundle of G (as defined in Section 15), ie., essentially limit ourselves to the one-parameter set of fibres sitting on top of $m(s)$ for $0 < s < 1$. Then according to the result quoted earlier, this subbundle is trivial, and $\gamma \subset M$ (minus its end points) can always be lifted up to $\Gamma = \{g(s)\} \subset G$. Having done so, we may take the limits of Γ as $s \to 0$, 1 and conclude that by continuity $g(s)$ must tend in these limits to points in H.

A similar argument applies to any homotopy linking any two loops $\gamma, \ \gamma' \ \in \ \mathcal{L}_{m_0}$: it can also be lifted to a homotopy at the level of G. Let $\overline{m}$ be the homotopy linking γ and γ':

$$\begin{aligned} \gamma \ &= \ \{m(s)\}, \ \gamma' = \{m'(s)\} \, , \\ m(0) \ &= \ m'(0) = m(1) = m'(1) = m_0 \, ; \\ \overline{m} \ &: \quad [0,1] \times [0,1] \to M \ : \ (s', \, s) \to \overline{m}(s', \, s) \ \in \ M \, , \\ \overline{m}(0,s) \ &= \ m(s), \ \overline{m}(1,s) = m'(s) \, , \\ &\qquad \overline{m}(s', \, 0 \text{ or } 1) = m_0 \cdot \end{aligned} \qquad (17.98)$$

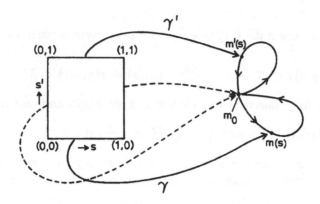

Figure 18. A homotopy between loops as a map : cylinder → M

If we depict this as in Figure 18, we see that the "side conditions" over $s = 0$ and $s = 1$ mean that $\overline{m}$ is a map from a cylinder to M.

Once again a cylinder is not contractible but by limiting ourselves to the interior in the variables, $(0,1) \times (0,1)$ we avoid the boundary condition and get a contractible region over which $\overline{m}$ can be lifted to G. Let $\overline{\Gamma}$ be such a lift (possessing all the freedom of right H action). Then by taking the appropriate limits we see that we have the following to accompany eqn.(17.98):

$$\overline{\Gamma} : [0,1] \times [0,1] \to G \quad : \quad (s',s) \to \overline{g}(s',s) \in G \; ,$$
$$\pi\left(\overline{g}(s',\ s)\right) \;=\; \overline{m}(s',\ s) \; ;$$
$$\overline{g}(s',\ 0 \text{ or } 1) \;\in\; H \cdot \qquad\qquad\qquad\qquad (17.99)$$

After this preparation we examine loops at $m_0 \in M$ and their behaviours. Let the lift Γ of $\gamma \in \mathcal{L}_{m_0}$ begin in H_{N_1} and end in H_{N_2}; then certainly if $N_1 \neq N_2$, at some stage Γ must venture into parts of G outside of H. Using the freedom (17.97) in the choice of Γ, we can arrange for at least one of N_1 and N_2 to be zero. For later convenience we pick $N_2 = 0$; then Γ begins at one of the components H_N of H, and ends in H_0. The residual freedom (17.97) is restricted to choosing $h(s) \in H_0$ throughout. This can be used to make Γ terminate at e; then $h(s)$ in (17.97) must obey $h(1) = e$.

We now establish a one-to-one and onto correspondence between $[\gamma] \in \pi_1(M; \, m_0)$ and elements of H/H_0; later we will see that this is an isomorphism. Let the lift Γ of $\gamma \in \mathcal{L}_{m_0}$ begin at $g(0) \in H_N$ (and end at $g(1) = e$). Any continuous variation of $g(0)$ staying within H_N, and maintaining continuity of Γ, leads to continuous deformation of γ. This is what motivates the result. So, take two loops γ, $\gamma' \in \mathcal{L}_{m_0}$, and let Γ, Γ' be lifts beginning in H_N, $H_{N'}$ respectively:

$$\begin{aligned}
\Gamma &= \{g(s)|g(0) = h \in H_N, \, g(1) = e\}, \, \gamma = \pi[\Gamma] \,; \\
\Gamma' &= \{g'(s)|g'(0) = h' \in H_{N'}, \, g'(1) = e\}, \, \gamma' = \pi[\Gamma'] \cdot
\end{aligned}$$
$$(17.100)$$

We will see that $\gamma' \sim \gamma \Leftrightarrow N' = N$.

$N' = N \Rightarrow \gamma' \sim \gamma$ Since H_N is a connected component of H, we can find a path Λ from h' to h, lying totally in H_N. Then $\Gamma'^{-1} * \Lambda * \Gamma$ is a loop in G based at e. Since (by assumption) $\pi_1(G) = 0$, this can be continuously shrunk to zero. Therefore Γ' is homotopic to $\Lambda * \Gamma$. As $\Lambda \subset H_N$, by suitable reparametrisation we find $\pi[\Lambda * \Gamma] \sim \pi[\Gamma] = \gamma$, while $\pi[\Gamma'] = \gamma'$. Any homotopy linking $\Lambda * \Gamma$ to Γ' gives upon projection a homotopy linking γ to γ', so $\gamma' \sim \gamma$.

$\gamma' \sim \gamma \Rightarrow N' = N$ Now let γ, γ' and a homotopy $\overline{m}$ linking them be given by eqn.(17.98). Let $\overline{\Gamma}$ be a lift of $\overline{m}$, following eqns. (17.99) and connecting Γ' and Γ of eqn.(17.100). We can use the freedom of right H action on $\overline{\Gamma}$ to supplement eqns.(17.99) with the following:

$$\begin{aligned}
\overline{g}(0,0) &= h \in H_N, \, \overline{g}(1,0) = h' \in H_{N'}, \\
\overline{g}(s',1) &= e \cdot
\end{aligned}$$
$$(17.101)$$

But $\overline{g}(s', 0)$ is continuous in s', so $N' = N$ follows.

To show that we have an isomorphism between $\pi_1(M; m_0)$ and H/H_0, take two loops γ_1, $\gamma_2 \in \mathcal{L}_{m_0}$; go to lifts Γ_1, Γ_2 respectively beginning at $h_1 \in H_{N_1}$, $h_2 \in H_{N_2}$ and both ending at e. Then $\gamma_1 * \gamma_2$ is obtainable by applying projection π to a suitably constructed path in G built up from Γ_1 and Γ_2 and ending at e. It is easy to see that this path should be constructed as follows: "shift" Γ_1 "rigidly" by multiplying the elements along it with h_2 on the right (so as to leave γ_1 intact) to get a path running from $h_1 \, h_2$ to h_2. Then follow Γ_2 from h_2 to e. This composite path begins at $h_1 \, h_2$ which lies in $H_{N_1} H_{N_2}$, so

$$[\gamma_1] \leftrightarrow N_1, \, [\gamma_2] \leftrightarrow N_2 \Rightarrow [\gamma_1 * \gamma_2] \leftrightarrow \psi(N_1, N_2) \cdot \qquad (17.102)$$

Similarly for inverses we can easily show that

$$[\gamma] \leftrightarrow N \Rightarrow [\gamma]^{-1} = [\gamma^{-1}] \leftrightarrow \phi(N) , \qquad (17.103)$$

and the isomorphism (17.92) is established.

We can now connect up with the example of the coset space $SU(2)/Q$ given earlier as having a nonabelian fundamental group, and also with the relation (17.85) for the fundamental group of a (connected) Lie group. In both cases we deal with coset spaces of a simply connected Lie group with respect to a discrete subgroup, case (i) of (17.91). Therefore H_0 is trivial, and the results stated earlier form a special case of the isomorphism (17.92), since $\pi_0(H) = H$.

17.21. THE SECOND HOMOTOPY GROUP OF A COSET SPACE - CASE OF COMPACT G

The last topic we consider relating to homotopy properties of Lie groups and coset spaces is the group $\pi_2(G/H)$ when G is compact. In addition to the easily arranged properties $\pi_0(G) = \pi_1(G) = 0$, now the compactness of G gives us also Cartan's theorem: $\pi_2(G) = 0$. Armed with all these properties of G, we have the result

$$M = G/H \; : \; \pi_2(M) = \pi_1(H_0) \; , \; H_0 = \text{identity component of } H \; .$$
$$(17.104)$$

The possible types of subgroups H are given again by eqn.(17.91).

We will see that the proof of this result is similar in spirit to that of eqn.(17.92), except that one deals with one higher dimension replacing S^1 by S^2. We adopt the following general notations for the present argument: γ, γ', γ_1, γ_2,... for maps $S^2 \to M$ based at m_0; Γ, Γ', Γ_1, Γ_2,... for suitably defined lifts of these to the level of G; and $\tilde{\gamma}$, $\tilde{\gamma}'$, $\tilde{\gamma}_1$, $\tilde{\gamma}_2$, ... for maps $S^1 \to H_0$. We model S^2 by the square $I^2 = [-1, \, 1] \times [-1, \, 1] \subset \mathcal{R}^2$, with *all* boundary points identified with the South pole $S \in S^2$. This is in line with eqn.(17.55). What we will use, of course, is that while S^2 is not contractible, $S^2 - S \sim \text{Int} \cdot I^2$ is contractible.

To begin, we examine the possibility of lifting a based map $\gamma : S^2 \to M$. Let us be given the map

$$\gamma \; : \; I^2 \to M \; : \; (s_1, \, s_2) \to m(s_1, \, s_2) \in M \; ,$$
$$m(s_1, \, s_2)|_{\partial \, I^2} = m_0 \; . \qquad (17.105)$$

Since $\text{Int} \cdot I^2 = (-1,1) \times (-1,1)$ is contractible, by considering the corresponding sub bundle of G with base $\gamma[\text{Int} \cdot I^2] \subset M$, we can go to a lift Γ with the following properties:

$$\Gamma \; : \; \text{Int} \cdot I^2 \to G \; : \; (s_1, \, s_2) \to g(s_1,s_2) \in G \; ,$$
$$\pi(g(s_1, \, s_2)) = m(s_1, \, s_2) \; . \qquad (17.106)$$

Such a lift Γ may be said to "represent" γ. As we approach points on the boundary of I^2, we see that $g(s_1, s_2)$ must approach elements of H which

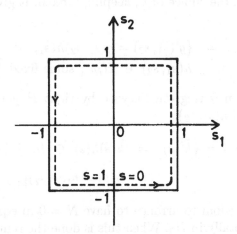

Figure 19. Parametrising ∂I^2 by $s \in [0,1]$

vary continuously over ∂I^2 but need not be constant:

$$g(s_1,\ s_2) \xrightarrow[(s_1,s_2) \to \partial I^2]{} \text{elements in } H \cdot \qquad (17.107)$$

Let us parametrise ∂I^2 by s running from 0 to 1 as shown by the dotted line in Figure 19, with the values $s = 0, 1$ corresponding to the same point $(s_1, s_2) = (0, -1)$:

So we can express eqn.(17.107) more precisely as follows: the boundary values of $g(s_1, s_2)$ determine a loop $\tilde{\gamma} \subset H$,

$$\tilde{\gamma} = \left\{ \tilde{h}(s) \in H_N \text{ , some fixed } N \right\} ,$$
$$\tilde{h}(s) = g(s_1,\ s_2)\big|_{(s_1,s_2) \to \partial\, I^2} , \; \tilde{h}(0) = \tilde{h}(1) \cdot \qquad (17.108)$$

As seen earlier, it is the continuity of $\tilde{h}(s)$ and connectedness of each H_N that leads to $\tilde{\gamma}$ lying wholly within some one component H_N of H. So the lift Γ acts as an intermediary in passing from γ to $\tilde{\gamma}$:

$$\gamma : S^2 \to M \xrightarrow{\text{lift}} \Gamma : S^2 - \mathcal{S} \to G \xrightarrow{\text{boundary values}} \tilde{\gamma} : S^1 \to H \cdot$$
$$(17.109)$$

We see that in general Γ is "multivalued" at the South pole of S^2, which is why it is not definable as a map $S^2 \to G$; but as there are as many ways of approaching $\mathcal{S}$ as directions in S^1, this multivaluedness gets expressed via the loop $\tilde{\gamma}$!

The freedom in the choice of Γ, keeping γ fixed, is given by continuous right H action:

$$\Gamma \to \Gamma' = \{g'(s_1, s_2) = g(s_1, s_2)h(s_1, s_2),$$
$$h(s_1, s_2) \in H_{N'} \text{ , some fixed } N'\} \cdot \qquad (17.110)$$

Then the change in $\tilde\gamma$ is given likewise by right H action involving the boundary values of $h(s_1, s_2)$:

$$\tilde\gamma \to \tilde\gamma' = \left\{ \tilde{h}'(s) = \tilde{h}(s)h(s) \in H_{\psi(N,N')} \, , \right.$$
$$\left. h(s) = h(s_1, s_2)\big|_{\partial I^2} \right\} \qquad (17.111)$$

We exploit this freedom to arrange to have $N = 0$ in eqn.(17.108), ie., for the loop $\tilde\gamma$ to be totally in H_0. When this is done the remaining freedom of transformation (17.110) can only use $h(s_1, s_2) \in H_0$. Finally, to arrange for $\tilde\gamma$ to be a loop based at $e \in H_0$, we constrain the lift Γ by one more condition : this involves a *rigid* change of the form of (17.110) using the constant element $h(s_1, s_2) = g(0, -1)^{-1}$. With all these conditions imposed, the properties of Γ and the freedom in its choice are given as follows:

$$\gamma = \{m(s_1, s_2)\} \subset M \to \Gamma = \{g(s_1, s_2)\} \subset G \to \tilde\gamma = \{\tilde{h}(s)\} \subset H_0 \, ,$$

$$\underset{(s_1, s_2) \to (0, -1)}{\text{Lt}} \qquad g(s_1, s_2) = \tilde{h}(0) = \tilde{h}(1) = e \, ;$$

$$\Gamma \to \Gamma' = \{g'(s_1, s_2)$$
$$= g(s_1, s_2)h(s_1, s_2)\}, \ h(s_1, s_2) \in H_0, h(0, -1) = e \Rightarrow$$
$$\gamma \to \gamma' = \gamma, \ \tilde\gamma \to \tilde\gamma'$$
$$= \left\{\tilde{h}'(s) = \tilde{h}(s)h(s), h(s) = h(s_1, s_2)\big|_{\partial I^2}\right\} \cdot \qquad (17.112)$$

With this setup we establish a series of four simple facts about the existence of various homotopies. We first list them to know where we are heading, then prove them one by one:

(i) If Γ_1 and Γ_2 are two lifts of a given γ, they lead to loops $\tilde\gamma_1$ and $\tilde\gamma_2$ which are equivalent, $\tilde\gamma_1 \sim \tilde\gamma_2$.

(ii) If $\gamma_1 \to \Gamma_1 \to \tilde\gamma_1$ and $\gamma_2 \to \Gamma_2 \to \tilde\gamma_2$ are two chains of maps, then $\gamma_1 \sim \gamma_2 \Rightarrow \tilde\gamma_1 \sim \tilde\gamma_2$.

(iii) Conversely, in (ii) above, $\tilde\gamma_1 \sim \tilde\gamma_2 \Rightarrow \gamma_1 \sim \gamma_2$. It is here that we use $\pi_2(G) = 0$.

(iv)Every loop $\tilde\gamma$ based at $e \in H_0$ can be obtained from some γ and lift Γ by the route (17.112). It is here that we use $\pi_1(G) = 0$.

Actually (i) is a particular case of (ii) when $\gamma_1 = \gamma_2 = \gamma$. What these results (to be proven presently) show are: each homotopically equivalent class of maps $[\gamma] \in \pi_2(M; m_0)$ determines uniquely a class $[\tilde{\gamma}] \in \pi_1(H_0; e)$ (results (i), (ii) above); this is injective (result (iii) above); and surjective (result (iv) above). After we prove these results, what will remain is the demonstration that we have an isomorphism.

Proof of (i) We will see that this is just a reinterpretation of the freedom (17.112) in going from γ to Γ. We have two lifts $\Gamma_1 = \{g_1(s_1, s_2)\}$, $\Gamma_2 = \{g_2(s_1, s_2)\}$ of γ obeying:

$$
\begin{aligned}
g_2(s_1, s_2) &= g_1(s_1, s_2) h(s_1, s_2), h(s_1, s_2) \in H_0, h(0, -1) = e \ ; \\
\tilde{\gamma}_1 &= \left\{ g_1(s_1, s_2)|_{\partial I^2} = \tilde{h}_1(s), \tilde{h}_1(0) = \tilde{h}_1(1) = e \right\} \ ; \\
\tilde{\gamma}_2 &= \left\{ g_2(s_1, s_2)|_{\partial I^2} = \tilde{h}_2(s), \tilde{h}_2(0) = \tilde{h}_2(1) = e \right\} \cdot \quad (17.113)
\end{aligned}
$$

So the link between $\tilde{\gamma}_1$ and $\tilde{\gamma}_2$ is this:

$$
\tilde{h}_2(s) = \tilde{h}_1(s)(h(s_1, s_2))_{\partial I^2} \cdot \quad (17.114)
$$

We now show that by a simple reparametrisation of the values of $h(s_1, s_2)$ over the square I^2, we can interpret it as a homotopy linking $\tilde{\gamma}_1$ and $\tilde{\gamma}_2$! Draw a continuously expanding family of squares within I^2, all sharing the common point $(0, -1)$, and of steadily increasing side $2\,s'$ where $0 \leq s' \leq 1$. For each fixed s', we let s run from 0 to 1 as we traverse the boundary of the square anticlockwise, starting and ending at $(0, -1)$. This is shown in Figure 20.

Then we rewrite the values of $h(s_1, s_2)$ over I^2 as $\tilde{h}(s', s)$, $0 \leq s', s \leq 1$:

$$
\begin{aligned}
h(s_1, s_2) &= \tilde{h}(s', s) \ , \\
\tilde{h}(s', 0 \text{ or } 1) &= \tilde{h}(0, s) = h(0, -1) = e \ , \\
\tilde{h}(1, s) &= (h(s_1, s_2))_{\partial I^2} \cdot \quad (17.115)
\end{aligned}
$$

If we now consider the product $\tilde{h}_1(s)\,\tilde{h}(s', s)$, for fixed s' and varying s we have a loop in H_0 based at e; and as s' varies continuously from 0 to 1, this product begins at $\tilde{h}_1(s)$ and ends, by (17.114), at $\tilde{h}_2(s)$.

So each based map $\gamma : S^2 \to M$ leads unambiguously to a definite equivalence class of loops $S^1 \to H_0$ based at e, independent of the lift used on the way.

Proof of (ii) Let $\gamma_1 = \{m_1(s_1, s_2)\}$ and $\gamma_2 = \{m_2(s_1, s_2)\}$ obey the necessary conditions. Let the homotopy connecting them be the following:

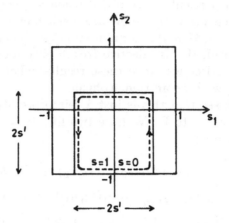

Figure 20. Reparametrising $h(s_1, s_2)$ to reveal a homotopy

$$[0,1] \times I^2 \to M \quad : \quad (s'; s_1, s_2) \to m(s'; s_1, s_2) \in M ,$$
$$m(0; s_1, s_2) = m_1(s_1, s_2), m(1; s_1, s_2) = m_2(s_1, s_2) ;$$

$$m(s'; s_1, s_2)\big|_{(s_1, s_2) \, \in \, \partial \, I^2} = m_0 . \tag{17.116}$$

Now a product of contractible spaces is contractible, so $[0,1] \times \text{Int} \cdot I^2$ is contractible. (For $[0,1]$, say with the variable x, the family of maps $x \to I_{s'}(x) = (1-s')x + \frac{s'}{2}$ is continuous in both s' and x, $I_{s'}(x) \in [0,1]$, $I_0(x) = x$ and $I_1(x) = 1/2$, establishing it is contractible). So for $s' \in [0,1]$ and $(s_1, s_2) \in \text{Int} \cdot I^2$ we can lift the above homotopy to the level of G:

$$[0,1] \times \text{Int} \cdot I^2 \to G \quad : \quad (s'; s_1, s_2) \to g(s'; s_1, s_2) \in G ,$$
$$\pi(g(s'; s_1, s_2)) = m(s'; s_1, s_2) ,$$
$$g(0; s_1, s_2) = g_1(s_1, s_2) = \text{a lift of } \gamma_1 ,$$
$$g(1; s_1, s_2) = g_2(s_1, s_2) = \text{a lift of } \gamma_2 ,$$
$$g(s'; s_1, s_2)\big|_{(s_1, s_2) \, \in \, \partial \, I^2} = \tilde{h}(s'; s) \in H_0 . \tag{17.117}$$

This $\tilde{h}(s'; s)$ interpolates continuously between $\tilde{\gamma}_1$ and $\tilde{\gamma}_2$ determined by the boundary values of $g_1(s_1, s_2)$ and $g_2(s_1, s_2)$ over ∂I^2, so we are done: $\gamma_1 \sim \gamma_2 \Rightarrow \tilde{\gamma}_1 \sim \tilde{\gamma}_2$.

So with (i) and (ii) proved, we have that each element of $\pi_2(M; m_0)$ unambiguously determines an element of $\pi_1(H_0; e)$.

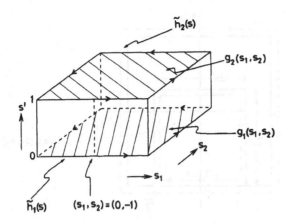

Figure 21.   Construction to exploit $\pi_2(G) = 0$

Proof of (iii) This is the converse of (ii). Given γ_1, γ_2 and respective lifts Γ_1, Γ_2 involving functions $g_1(s_1, s_2)$, $g_2(s_1, s_2)$, which lead via their boundary values $\tilde{h}_1(s)$, $\tilde{h}_2(s)$ over $\partial\, I^2$ to loops $\tilde{\gamma}_1$, $\tilde{\gamma}_2$ in H_0. Construct the rectangular box $[0, 1] \times I^2$ as shown in Figure 21.

Over the bottom I^2 face we "paste" the values of $g_1(s_1, s_2)$, and over the opposite top face those of $g_2(s_1, s_2)$; the perimeters of these two faces carry the values of $\tilde{h}_1(s)$, $\tilde{h}_2(s)$ "belonging to" $\tilde{\gamma}_1$, $\tilde{\gamma}_2$. Given the equivalence $\tilde{\gamma}_1 \sim \tilde{\gamma}_2$, over the vertical walls of the above box we lay out the homotopy linking them; so all points over these walls are mapped into H_0. The base point e is the image of all the points on the dotted vertical line above $(s_1, s_2) = (0, -1)$.

The set of six faces of the box amounts to an S^2 (essentially $\partial\, I^3$, eqn.(17.51)), so by the above procedure we have a continuous map $S^2 \to G$ (with vertical walls mapped into H_0, dotted vertical line to e). Now we use Cartan's Theorem $\pi_2(G) = 0$. This means we can extend this map continuously into the inside of the box, giving a map $[0, 1] \times I^2 \to G$, consistent with the values prescribed over the six faces. Now "read" this map layer by layer as s' steadily increases from bottom to top: the result is an interpolation from $g_1(s_1, s_2)$ to $g_2(s_1, s_2)$! Apply the projection π to this to get a homotopy linking γ_1 to γ_2. Hence the result.

Proof of (iv) Given any loop $\tilde{\gamma} = \{\tilde{h}(s)\}$ based at e in H_0, since $\pi_1(G) = 0$ we can find a homotopy $\{\tilde{g}(s'; s)\}$ sweeping through G and transforming $\tilde{\gamma}$ to the constant loop at e. (We may be unable to do this within H_0). We then use this homotopy to construct a map $\Gamma : \text{Int} \cdot I^2 \to G$ by a reparametrisation based on the same kind of argument as used in the proof

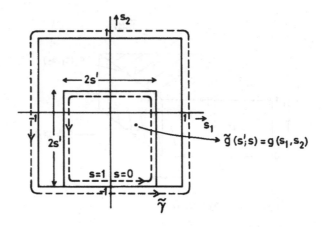

Figure 22.   Reconstructing Γ and γ from a $\tilde{\gamma}$

of (i) above:

$$\Gamma : (s_1, s_2) \ \in \ \text{Int} \cdot \ I^2 \to g(s_1, s_2) = \tilde{g}(s'; s) \ \in \ G \qquad (17.118)$$

The construction is shown in Figure 22.

Finally we apply the projection π to this Γ to get a map $\gamma : S^2 \to M$ which would have led to $\tilde{\gamma}$ in the first place.

So far then the existence of a bijective map $\pi_2(M; m_0) \to \pi_1(H_0; e)$ has been established. Now our task is to show that this is a group isomorphism. But at this point we switch to viewing Γ as the primary object; then γ is obtained as $\gamma = \pi \circ \Gamma$, and $\tilde{\gamma}$ is obtained by looking at the values of Γ as we approach $\partial\ I^2$. As the arguments of the last few pages show, *we lose nothing in the process!* The conditions on Γ, originally given in eqns. (17.106, 107), now are :

$$\Gamma \ : \ (s_1, s_2) \ \in \ \text{Int} \cdot \ I^2 \to g(s_1, s_2) \ \in \ G \ ,$$
$$g(s_1, s_2)\big|_{(s_1, s_2) \to \partial\ I^2} = \tilde{h}(s) \ \in \ H_0, \ \tilde{h}(0) = \tilde{h}(1) = e \ (17.119)$$

Then γ is automatically based at m_0, and $\tilde{\gamma}$ at e. Any continuous deformation of Γ induces continuous deformations of γ and $\tilde{\gamma}$, staying within their respective homotopy classes.

First we deal with the identity elements of the two groups. The constant map

$$\Gamma_0 : (s_1, s_2) \ \in \ \text{Int} \cdot \ I^2 \to g(s_1, s_2) = e \qquad (17.120)$$

obeys all boundary conditions; it leads on the one hand to a constant γ and on the other to a constant $\tilde{\gamma}$:

$$\Gamma_0 \to \gamma_0 = \{m(s_1, s_2) = m_0\}, \ \tilde{\gamma}_0 = \{\tilde{h}(s) = e\} \cdot \qquad (17.121)$$

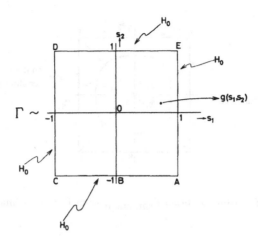

Figure 23.   Pictorial representation of Γ : $\tilde{\gamma}$ =image of BCDEAB

So the identity of $\pi_2(M; m_0)$ is taken correctly to the identity of $\pi_1(H_0; e)$.

Now we use the freedom in choice of Γ to put it into a specially convenient form. Here we see again the enormous flexibility given by the notion of homotopic equivalence - it is like kneading dough almost beyond recognition, yet remaining equivalent to itself! We must however note that so far we have *not defined* any composition law for maps Γ of the type (17.119). But this can now be done (after choosing Γ's of a suitable "canonical" form) so that after projection π we recover the (already defined) composition laws for γ's, and similarly for $\tilde{\gamma}$'s. Take any Γ obeying (17.119) and lay it out pictorially as in Figure 23.

Then continuously deform $g(s_1, s_2)$ as follows: draw a straight line from the centre O to the boundary point B (where $g(0, -1) = e$), and steadily rotate it clockwise while the end point moves on the boundary, until it reaches the position OA. All along keep "pushing" the values of $g(s_1, s_2)$ forward; while in the rear let the values of $g(s_1, s_2)$ along OB be "repeated" along each radial line all the way from OB through OC, OD, OE till OA. Call the resulting map $\Gamma_{\text{canonical}}$ given by $g'(s_1, s_2)$, depicted in Figure 24. All the values of $g(s_1, s_2)$ over Int $\cdot$ I^2 are now faithfully swept and compressed into the values of $g'(s_1, s_2)$ over the triangle OAB. Over the rest of I^2, $g'(s_1, s_2)$ has no angular dependence but only a "radial" one, and $g'(s_1, s_2) = e$ over the part $BCDEA$ of the boundary. (All this is of course better seen if we use Int $\cdot$ B^2 rather than Int $\cdot$ I^2, but that causes awkwardness when we want to compose these maps!). The string of elements $\tilde{h}(s)$ $\in$ H_0 defining the loop $\tilde{\gamma}$, originally laid out along ∂I^2, is now contained in the straight line stretch B to A or, what is homotopically

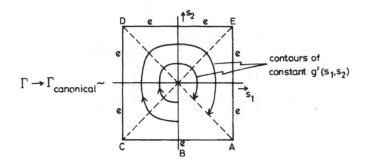

Figure 24. How to obtain $\Gamma_{canonical}$ from Γ : $\tilde{\gamma}$ $\sim$ image of CA

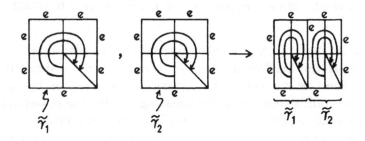

Figure 25. Composition of two canonical Γ's

equivalent, C to A. It is pictorially evident that $\Gamma_{canonical}$ is homotopic to Γ, and the changes induced in γ and $\tilde{\gamma}$ maintain them in their equivalence classes.

Now take two such $\Gamma_{canonical}$'s, reduce the width of each by half in the s_1 direction, and stand them side by side. The result is a new Γ which obeys all the conditions in eqn.(17.119); it is in general not canonical but is of course homotopically equivalent to one. The procedure is shown in Figure 25.

Now it is evident upon inspection that projection π applied to the composite figure gives the product of the two original γ's (up to reparametrisations); while the $\tilde{\gamma}$ of the result, read off from the bottom of the figure, is equivalent to the product of the individual $\tilde{\gamma}$'s. So we have proved the isomorphism (17.104).

It is useful to point out the following feature of this result. We saw that for a general topological space X, $\pi_2(X)$ is always abelian while $\pi_1(X)$ could be nonabelian. On the other hand, for a Lie group G, $\pi_1(G)$ is always abelian. Thus the isomorphism $\pi_2(G/H) = \pi_1(H_0)$, in which incidentally only H_0 is involved on the right, fits in beautifully with these general facts.

We conclude our discussion of homotopy properties of Lie groups and their coset spaces at this point. Further developments would involve the concepts of relative homotopies and exact homotopy sequences, leading to relations between $\pi_n(G/H)$ and $\pi_{n-1}(H)$ for general n, etc. Relative homotopy ideas are in fact strongly suggested by the structure of canonical Γ's we have been naturally led to above.

For the convenience of the reader and as a reminder we highlight once again in tabular form the special simplifications we have seen in the homotopy properties of Lie groups:

General topological space X	Case of a Lie group G or coset space G/H
$\pi_0(X)$ may not be a group	$\pi_0(G) = G/G_0$ = always a group
$\pi_0(X) = 0 \Rightarrow \pi_n(X;x)$ is "x-independent"	$\pi_n(G;g)$ is always "g-independent"
$\pi_1(X)$ may not be abelian	$\pi_1(G)$ is always abelian
$\pi_n(X)$ is abelian, $n \geq 2$	$\pi_2(G) = 0$ by Cartan's Theorem
	$\pi_0(G/H) = 0$ always
	$\pi_1(G/H) = \pi_0(H)$
	$\pi_2(G/H) = \pi_1(H_0)$

The precise conditions for the validity of some of the results on the right are not repeated here.

17.22. PATH DEPENDENCE OF PARALLEL TRANSPORT - THE HOLONOMY GROUP IN A *PFB*

A very instructive combination of what we have learnt about PFB's and connections on the one hand, and about homotopy on the other, is the concept of the holonomy group of a PFB. In Section 15 we have discussed the process by which a base space curve in a PFB can be horizontally lifted into the total space. This of course depends on the connection. We have also seen in Sections 10 and 15 how this leads to the notions of parallel transport and curvature.

Recall the constructions of Section 15. Given the PFB (P, π, M, G) and a connection ω, horizontal subspaces are defined at each point in P. Now if γ is a parametrised curve in M (cf. eqn.(15.93)):

$$\gamma \; : \; s \in [a,b] \subset \mathcal{R} \to m(s) \in M \;,$$

$$\gamma_* \left(\frac{d}{ds} \right) = u(s) \in T_{m(s)} M \;, \tag{17.122}$$

we can pass to horizontal lifts Γ lying in P and projecting on to γ (eqn. (15.95)):

$$\Gamma : s \in [a, b] \subset \mathcal{R} \;\rightarrow\; p(s) \in P \,,$$
$$\pi(p(s)) \;=\; m(s) \,,$$
$$\Gamma_* \left(\frac{d}{ds} \right) \;=\; \sigma_{p(s)}(u(s)) \in H_{p(s)} \,. \qquad (17.123)$$

As we have seen, a given $\gamma \subset M$ has many horizontal lifts $\Gamma \subset P$; each choice of initial point $p(a) \in \pi^{-1}(m(a))$ determines a corresponding one. The global action of G on P permutes these lifts among themselves:

$$g \in G \,, \Gamma \;=\; \{p(s)\} = \text{horizontal lift of } \gamma \Rightarrow$$
$$\Gamma' = \psi_g[\Gamma] \;=\; \{p'(s) = \psi_g(p(s))\} = \text{another}$$
$$\text{horizontal lift of } \gamma \,. \qquad (17.124)$$

This is the property of covariance under G action. In a local trivialization of the PFB over an open set $\mathcal{U} \subset M$, every Γ obeys a first order ordinary differential equation most simply expressed using an (unspecified) matrix representation of G:

$$m(s) \in \gamma \cap \mathcal{U} \,:\, p(s) \;=\; (m(s), \, g(s)) \,,$$
$$\frac{d}{ds} D(g(s)) \;=\; - A(m(s))(u(s)) \, D(g(s)) \,. \quad (17.125)$$

If we consider the fibres at the end points of γ, then "parallel transport along γ" maps each point $p(a) \in \pi^{-1}(m(a))$ to its "image" $p(b) \in \pi^{-1}(m(b))$ by travelling along the Γ passing through $p(a)$. This fibre to fibre mapping is dependent on both γ and ω.

The concept of holonomy is then essentially a study of the dependence of this map on the base space curve γ. Let us now assume $\pi_0(M) = 0$, so the properties to be studied are essentially the same at all points of M. Moreover we can limit ourselves to loops based at a chosen point $m_0 \in M$. Then the path dependence of parallel transport is naturally "measured" by means of group elements, since initial and final fibres coincide.

Let us then consider a loop $\alpha \in \mathcal{L}_{m_0}$ and for simplicity work in a local trivialization of P large enough to contain α. The solution to eqn.(17.125) is given by a path-ordered exponential:

$$D(g(s)) = P \left\{ \exp \left(- \int_0^s ds' A(m(s'))(u(s')) \right) \right\} D(g(0)) \,. \quad (17.126)$$

The meaning of the P symbol is that in the multiple integrals occurring in the series expansion of the exponential, the noncommuting factors of A

should always be arranged with "later" integration variables appearing to the left of "earlier" ones. We see that the dependence of the lift Γ on the initial point $g(0)$ is explicitly separated, and the prefactor is independent of $g(0)$. This is consistent with the covariance under G action, eqn.(17.124). At $s = 1$ we return to the starting point m_0 of α, and we are led to define a group element $h[\alpha] \in G$, a functional of α, by

$$D(h[\alpha]) = P\left\{\exp\left(-\int_0^1 ds\ A(m(s))(u(s))\right)\right\} . \qquad (17.127)$$

The integrand in the exponential is the value of the $\underline{G}$-valued one form A locally representing the connection ω, evaluated on the tangent vector to α. If we introduce local coordinates x^μ over $\mathcal{U} \subset M$ and a basis $\{T_a\}$ for $\underline{G}$, we have the more explicit expression

$$D(h[\alpha]) = P\left\{\exp\left(-\int_0^1 ds\ A_\mu^a(x(s))T_a\ \dot{x}^\mu(s)\right)\right\} . \qquad (17.128)$$

We now explore the properties of $h[\alpha]$.

The following are easily checked by direct calculations:

(i) $h[\alpha]$ is reparametrisation invariant ;

(ii) $h[\alpha_1 * \alpha_2] = h[\alpha_1]h[\alpha_2]$;

(iii) $\alpha_0 = $ constant loop $\to h[\alpha_0] = e$;

(iv) $h[\alpha^{-1}] = h[\alpha]^{-1} .$ (17.129)

Properties (i) and (ii) together lead to a significant remark. One reason why $\mathcal{L}_{m_0}$ does not have a group structure is because associativity fails: while the "traces" of $\alpha_1 * (\alpha_2 * \alpha_3)$ and $(\alpha_1 * \alpha_2) * \alpha_3$ coincide, their parametrisations differ. However property (i) of $h[\alpha]$ gets over this "problem" and we do have, with no ambiguity:

$$h[\alpha_1](h[\alpha_2]h[\alpha_3]) = (h[\alpha_1]h[\alpha_2])h[\alpha_3]$$
$$= h[\alpha_1 * (\alpha_2 * \alpha_3)] = h[(\alpha_1 * \alpha_2) * \alpha_3] . \qquad (17.130)$$

The set of group elements $h[\alpha] \in G$ for all $\alpha \in \mathcal{L}_{m_0}$ is then a subgroup of G. It is called the *full holonomy group* of the connection ω at $m_0 \in M$. We denote it by $\mathcal{H}_f(\omega; m_0)$:

$$\mathcal{H}_f(\omega; m_0) = \{h[\alpha] \in G | \alpha \in \mathcal{L}_{m_0}\} \subset G . \qquad (17.131)$$

One can convince oneself that for any two points m_1, m_2 in M, $\mathcal{H}_f(\omega; m_1)$ and $\mathcal{H}_f(\omega; m_2)$ are conjugate subgroups in G.

It is good to appreciate the significance of this definition. We know that $\mathcal{L}_{m_0}$ is *not* a group; to reach the group $\pi_1(M; m_0)$ we are obliged to ignore *all* differences between homotopically equivalent loops, and regard *all* elements of a class $[\alpha]$ as collectively defining *one* group element. The holonomy group $\mathcal{H}_f(\omega; m_0)$ (while dependent on ω) stands somewhere *in between* $\mathcal{L}_{m_0}$ on one side and $\pi_1(M; m_0)$ on the other! It is a group, but it *does not ignore* all differences between homotopically equivalent loops:

$$\alpha_1 \sim \alpha_2 \quad , \quad \text{i.e., } \alpha_1 * \alpha_2^{-1} \in [\alpha_0] \not\Rightarrow h[\alpha_1] = h[\alpha_2] \,,$$
$$\alpha \in [\alpha_0] \not\Rightarrow h[\alpha] = e \cdot \qquad (17.132)$$

However for a loop of the form $\alpha * \alpha^{-1}$, any $\alpha \in \mathcal{L}_{m_0}$, which *is* equivalent to α_0, we do have:

$$h[\alpha * \alpha^{-1}] = e \cdot \qquad (17.133)$$

This is consistent because we must realise that

$$\alpha \in [\alpha_0] \not\Rightarrow \alpha = \beta * \beta^{-1} \,, \text{ some } \beta \in \mathcal{L}_{m_0} \cdot \qquad (17.134)$$

We see that the passages $\mathcal{L}_{m_0} \to \mathcal{H}_f(\omega; m_0)$ and $\mathcal{H}_f(\omega; m_0) \to \pi_1(M; m_0)$ are both many to one. Of these, only $\mathcal{H}_f(\omega; m_0)$ depends on the connection ω:

$$\alpha \in \mathcal{L}_{m_0} \to h[\alpha] \in \mathcal{H}_f(\omega; m_0) \longrightarrow [\alpha] \in \pi_1(M; m_0) \cdot \quad (17.135)$$

The first map does not go so far as to obliterate all differences between homotopically equivalent loops. The extent to which $h[\alpha]$ changes when α is varied within its homotopy class is then of natural interest - it determines the many-to-oneness of the second map above! This leads to the definition of the restricted holonomy group at m_0. It is clear that within the equivalence class $[\alpha_0]$ of the constant loop we have

$$\alpha \in [\alpha_0] \Rightarrow \alpha^{-1} \in [\alpha_0] \,,$$
$$\alpha_1, \alpha_2 \in [\alpha_0] \Rightarrow \alpha_1 * \alpha_2 \in [\alpha_0] \cdot \qquad (17.136)$$

Based on this, the restricted holonomy group $\mathcal{H}_r(\omega; m_0)$ is defined as

$$\mathcal{H}_r(\omega; m_0) = \{h[\alpha] \in G | \alpha \in [\alpha_0]\} \subset \mathcal{H}_f(\omega; m_0) \subset G \cdot \quad (17.137)$$

In fact, $\mathcal{H}_r(\omega; m_0)$ is a normal subgroup of $\mathcal{H}_f(\omega; m_0)$.

What consequence does this have for the path dependence of $h[\gamma]$ for *general* paths γ? The definition is again given by eqn.(17.127). If $\gamma_1 \sim \gamma_2$ are two homotopically equivalent paths from m_1 to m_2, we have a one-parameter continuous family of paths $\gamma(s')$ from m_1 to m_2, $0 \leq s' \leq 1$, interpolating between γ_1 at $s' = 0$ and γ_2 at $s' = 1$. Then $h[\gamma(s')]$ can be set up for each s', and this interpolates continuously between $h[\gamma_1]$ and $h[\gamma_2]$ - so all we can say is that these two elements are path connected in G.

18. Concluding remarks and some references

In this set of notes, our main aim has been to motivate and explain intrinsic geometric ideas, notations and methods, having in mind someone who may have been earlier introduced to tensor calculus in an old-fashioned or traditional coordinate-based manner. To round out the material presented, some excursions into Lie group theory, integration of forms, fibre bundles, homotopy and holonomy have been included. As mentioned in the Introduction, to learn the new terminology and notations is like picking up a new language - one has to master the alphabet, then go on to words and phrases, and may be end up with the ability to write creative prose-even poetry! For some, Hermann Weyl's words in another context may be appropriate: "The gods have imposed upon me the yoke of a foreign tongue which was not sung at my cradle". For others who have been brought up from the start on a diet of the new methods, it would all come so much more easily and naturally.

Being a set of notes growing out of a set of lectures, and not a full-fledged book, there are some gaps, omissions of topics particular readers might have wished to find - for instance, the theory of characteristic classes of PFB's; simplicial cohomology and a fuller account of de Rham's theory; the development of the concept of orientability to include the notions of internal and external orientability of a submanifold in a differentiable manifold; the version of Frobenius' Theorem via differential forms; and many other items both minor and major. In answer we can do no better than recall with Chesterton -

"If something is worth doing, it is worth doing badly".

We conclude with a list of useful references drawn from a vast literature, to books and reviews and individual sections of books, which the interested reader can turn to for further enlightenment:

Acknowledgement

My sincere thanks to G.Marmo and G.Morandi for educating me in these matters over the years; to B.R.Iyer and C.V.Vishveshwara for remarkable patience; and to Mrs. Karunavathi for skillful typing of a difficult manuscript.

References

1. S. Chandrasekhar, "The Mathematical Theory of Black Holes", Oxford University Press, (1983), Chapter 1
2. Y.Choquet-Bruhat and C.De Witt-Morette, "Analysis, Manifolds and Physics", North-Holland (1989)
3. S.Coleman, "The Magnetic Monopole Fifty Years Later", Lectures at the 1981 International School of Subnuclear Physics "Ettore Majorana"
4. W.D.Curtis and F.R.Miller, "Differential Manifolds and Theoretical Physics", Academic Press, Inc., (1985)
5. Felsager, "Geometry, Particles and Fields", Odense University Press (1981)
6. M.Francaviglia, "Elements of Differential and Riemannian Geometry", Bibliopolis, Napoli (1988)
7. P.Goddard and D.I.Olive, "Magnetic monopoles in gauge field theories", Reports on Progress in Physics **41**, 1357 (1978)
8. C.J. Isham, "Modern Differential Geometry for Physicists", World Scientific Publishing Co. (P) Ltd., (1989)
9. A.A. Kirillov, "Elements of the Theory of Representations", Springer-Verlag, (1976), Sections 5 and 6
10. G.W.Mackey, "Mathematical Foundations of Quantum Mechanics", W.A.Benjamin, Inc., (1963), Chapter 1
11. N.D.Mermin, "The Topological Theory of Defects in Ordered Media", Reviews of Modern Physics **51**, 591 (1979)
12. G.Morandi, "The Role of Topology in Classical and Quantum Physics", Lecture Notes in Physics m7, Springer-Verlag (1992)
13. S.Mukhi and N.Mukunda, "Introduction to Topology, Differential Geometry and Group Theory for Physicists", Wiley Eastern Limited, New Delhi (1990)
14. L.S.Pontrjagin, "Topological Groups", 2nd edition, Gordon and Breach, New York (1966)
15. B.Schutz, "Geometrical methods of mathematical physics", Cambridge University Press, Cambridge (1988)
16. A. Trautman, "Fibre Bundles Associated with Space-Time", Reports on Mathematical Physics, **1**, 29 (1970)
17. A. Trautman, "Differential Geometry for Physicists", Bibliopolis, Napoli (1984)
18. Tulsi Dass, "Symmetries, Gauge Fields, Strings and Fundamental Interactions" - Vol. 1, Wiley Eastern Limited (1993), Chapters I to V
19. R.M.Wald, "General Relativity", University of Chicago Press (1984), Chapters 2 and 3, Appendices A, B and C

2. PROBLEMS ON GEOMETRICAL METHODS FOR PHYSICS

RAVI KULKARNI
Raman Research Institute
Bangalore 560 080, India

Present address:

Ameya Softech
1184/4, Fergusson College Road
Pune 411 005, India

Note to the reader

The problems are divided into sections.

1. Manifolds and smooth maps
2. Differential forms
3. Vector-fields and Lie derivatives
4. Miscellaneous problems
5. Frobenius' theorem
6. Connections and curvature
7. Lie groups and Lie algebras
8. Fibre bundles
9. Supplementary problems

The problems are followed by a section on hints and solutions to selected problems. I have not included any solutions to sections (3), (5) and (6) above since Prof. Mukunda's lecture notes cover all this material. Solutions to the supplementary problems are also not included since I hope that this will encourage the reader to explore the literature.
There are many excellent books available:

(1) 'Calculus on Manifolds' by Michael Spivak. This is a slim book and is introductory and is highly recommended. This book is a precursor to his series of five volumes called 'A Comprehensive Introduction to Differential Geometry'.

(2) 'Modern Differential Geometry for Physicists' by Chris Isham. An introductory book and is very clearly written. Has a brief discussion of universal bundles and other advanced topics.

(3) 'Applicable Differential Geometry' by M.Crampin and F.A.E.Pirani. Introductory. Has a section on Hamiltonian mechanics.

(4) 'Analysis, Manifolds and Physics' Part-II, by Y.Choquet-Bruhat and C.DeWitt-Morette. This book is arranged in the form of solved problems and contains a wealth of material. Advanced for the most part.

(5) 'Geometry Topology and Physics' by M.Nakahara. Ranges from introductory to advanced. Contains some applications to gauge fields (anomalies) and string theory.

(6) 'Differential forms in Algebraic Topology' by Raoul Bott and Loring Tu. An excellent book for Algebraic topology. Is written for mathematicians but parts of it should be fairly accessible.

This list above is not exhaustive of course and is but a small sample. Finally, do think about the problems before peeking at the solutions!

NOTATION

R :   Real numbers
R^n :   n-dimensional real Euclidean space
Z :   Integers
S^n :   The unit sphere in R^{n+1}
ϵ :   The volume form
C :   Complex numbers

Two notations are used for the interior product: $i_X\omega$ and $X \perp \omega$, with ω a k-form and X a vector-field.

1. Manifolds and Smooth Maps

(1) The circle S^1 is a smooth manifold.
(2) The torus in three dimensions is a smooth manifold.
(3) The x-y axes do not form a differential manifold.
(4) An example to show that there can be a global choice of frame on a manifold which cannot be covered by a single chart.
(5) A single chart cannot cover all of the sphere S^2.
(6) $GL(n, R)$ has the structure of a smooth manifold.

(7) Real projective space of n dimensions, RP^n, is defined as the space obtained by identifying antipodal points of the n-sphere S^n. RP^n is a smooth manifold. Describe local charts for RP^n.

(8) The following is a parametrization of the torus in R^3.

$$
\begin{aligned}
x &= (a + b\sin v)\cos u \\
y &= (a + b\sin v)\sin u \\
z &= b\cos v
\end{aligned}
$$

(9) As a manifold $SU(2)$ is S^3.

(10) As a manifold $SO(3)$ is RP^3.

(11) The differential structure of S^2 as a submanifold of R^3 coincides with the differential structure given by stereographic projection from the North and South poles.

(12) R^n and R^m are not diffeomorphic when $n \neq m$.

(13) $SL(2, R)$ is a smooth submanifold of $GL(2, R)$.

(14) Calculate the rank of the Jacobian matrix of the map $f : R^2 \to R^2$, $f(x, y) = (x, 0)$.

(15) An example of a smooth one-one map which is not a diffeomorphism.

(16) An example of two distinct differential structures on one manifold.

(17) $f : (-1, 1) \to R$, $f(u) = u/1 - u^2$. Is f a diffeomorphism?

(18) The composite of smooth maps is smooth.

(19) $f : R \to R^2$, $f(t) = (t^2, t^3)$ is smooth. Is it an embedding?

(20) $f : R^3 \to R^6$, $f(x, y, z) = (x^2, y^2, z^2, 2yz, 2zx, 2xy)$. The image of S^2 under this map is a two dimensional submanifold of R^6 (the Veronese surface).

(21) R/Z is diffeomorphic to S^1. $f : R \to R^2$, $f(t) = (\cos 2\pi t, \sin 2\pi t)$. Show that f defines a map $\bar{f}$ on the quotient R/Z. $\bar{f}$ is injective, its image is S^1. f is an immersion.

2. Differential Forms

(1) Calculate the wedge product of α and β

$$
\begin{aligned}
\alpha &= x\,dy \wedge dz + y\,dz \wedge dx + z\,dx \wedge dy \\
\beta &= x\,dx + y\,dy + z\,dz.
\end{aligned}
$$

(2) In R^3 with coordinates r, θ, ψ

$$
e_r = \frac{\partial}{\partial r}, \quad e_\theta = \frac{1}{r}\frac{\partial}{\partial \theta}, \quad e_\psi = \frac{1}{r\sin\theta}\frac{\partial}{\partial \psi}
$$

Find a basis of 1-forms dual to this.

(3) $\omega = x^2 dx + y dy$, $\alpha = x dx \wedge dy - y z dz \wedge dx$,
$\beta = xyz dx \wedge dy \wedge dz$

$$X = x\frac{\partial}{\partial x} + y^2\frac{\partial}{\partial y} + z\frac{\partial}{\partial z},$$

$$Y = \frac{\partial}{\partial x} + y\frac{\partial}{\partial z},$$

$$Z = 3xy\frac{\partial}{\partial y}$$

Compute $\omega(X)$, $\alpha(X, Y)$, $\beta(X, Y, Z)$.

(4) In R^3 with coordinates x, y, z calculate the exterior derivatives of
   (a) $x^3 y dx + y^2 z dz$
   (b) $9xy^2 z dx \wedge dy - 3xz dx \wedge dy - x dy \wedge dz$
   (c) $f dx \wedge dy + g dy \wedge dz$
   (d) $dx \wedge dy \wedge dz$

(5) If ω is a p-form and p is odd then $\omega \wedge \omega = 0$.

(6) Construct a form ω on R^5 such that $\omega \wedge \omega \neq 0$

(7) [Electromagnetic plane waves]
   Let $F = A \exp(ik.x)$, A a constant 2-form, k a constant 4-vector. Show that the source-free Maxwell equations for F can be written $k \wedge A = 0$ and $k \perp A = 0$. Show that k must be null. Show that there exists a 1-form l such that $A = k \wedge l$. Show that $l.k = 0$. Deduce the usual (in terms of E and B) electromagnetic plane wave equations from the above.

(8) [Continuation of (7)]
   $F = k \wedge l \exp(ik.x)$ is an electromagnetic plane wave. Assume $l = (0, \vec{l})$. Then the 1-form $-il \exp(ik.x)$ is a potential for F. Find a potential for $*F$ of the form $-im \exp(ik.x)$ where $m = (0, \vec{m})$. $\vec{l}$ and $\vec{m}$ are 3-space vectors.

(9) Show that

$$\phi^*(\omega_1 + \omega_2) = \phi^*\omega_1 + \phi^*\omega_2$$
$$\phi^*(f\omega) = (f.\phi)\phi^*\omega$$
$$\phi^*(\omega \wedge \alpha) = \phi^*\omega \wedge \phi^*\alpha$$
$$\phi^*(df) = d(fd\phi)$$

(10) $\alpha : [0, 2\pi] \to R^2, \alpha(u) = (\cos u, \sin u)$. Evaluate $\alpha^* dx, \alpha^* dy$.

(11) $\phi : M \to N$ is a smooth map. ω is a k-form. Show that $\phi^*(d\omega) = d(\phi^*\omega)$.

(12) [Laplace's equation].
   $\nabla^2 \phi = 0$ can be written as $d^* d\phi = 0$. (ϕ is a smooth function).

(13) α and β are k-forms. Show that $\alpha \wedge^* \beta = <\alpha, \beta> \epsilon$.

(14) α and β are p-forms. Then $\alpha \wedge^* \beta = \beta \wedge^* \alpha$.

(15) For a positive-definite, nondegenerate metric $^{**}\omega = (-1)^{(n-k)k}\omega$ where ω is a k-form in a dimensions. If the index of the metric is s, then $^{**}\omega = (-1)^{k(n-k)+s}\omega$.

(16) The exterior derivative in coordinate independent form: If ω is a 1-form, X and Y are vector-fields,

$$d\omega(X,Y) = X(\omega Y) - Y(\omega X) - \omega[X,Y]$$

Generalise to k-forms.

(17) Use this definition to show $d^2 = 0$.

(18) α is a 1-form on S^2. Assume that α is invariant under rotations, i.e., $s^*\alpha = \alpha$ for all $s \in SO(3)$. Then $\alpha = 0$.

(19) What are the n-forms ω on S^n such that $s^*\omega = \omega$ for all $s \in SO(n+1)$?

(20) If n is even then every n-form on RP^n vanishes at least at one point. If n is odd, there exist nowhere vanishing n-forms on RP^n.

3. Vector-Fields and Lie Derivatives

(1)

$$\begin{aligned}
V &= x^2\partial_x + y^2\partial_y + z^2\partial_z \\
\omega &= yzdx + xzdy + xydz \\
L_V\omega &= yz(2x + y + z)dx + xz(x + 2y + z)dy \\
&+ xy(x + y + 2z)dz .
\end{aligned}$$

(2) $V = ydx - xdy$ and $\omega = (x^2 + y^2)dx \wedge dy$. Then $L_V\omega = 0$. Give a geometrical interpretation.

(3) $\Omega = \rho dx_1\wedge,\ldots,\wedge dx^n$ is an n-dimensional space. V is a vector field.

$$L_V\Omega = (\rho\partial_a V^a\rho)dx^1 \wedge \ldots \wedge dx^n$$

(4) Write the Lie bracket of two vector-fields in terms of coordinates.

(5) Compute $[e_\theta, e_\psi]$

$$e_\theta = \frac{1}{r}\frac{\partial}{\partial\theta}, \ e_\phi = \frac{1}{r\sin\theta}\frac{\partial}{\partial\psi}$$

(6) The Lie bracket of two vector-fields is a vector-field.

(7) The Lie bracket satisfies the Jacobi identity.

(8) $L_X df = d(Xf)$.

(9) $(L_X Y)(f)$
$\quad L_X Y = -L_Y X$

(10) f is a smooth function, ω a p-form, V and W are vector-fields
   (a) $L_{fV}\omega = fL_V\omega + df \wedge (V \perp \omega)$
   (b) $L_V(L_W\omega) - L_W(L_V\omega) = L_{[V,W]}\omega$
   (c) $L_V(W \perp \omega) = L_VW \perp \omega + W \perp L_V\omega.$

(11) The Cartan formula. On differential forms $L_X = i_X d + d i_X.$

(12) Find a coordinate expression for $L_X T$ for an arbitrary tensor T.

(13) g is a Riemann metric. Vector-fields X satisfying $L_X g = 0$ are called Killing vector-fields. Write this condition in coordinates. What are the Killing vector fields for R^3 with its usual metric?

(14) The commutator of Killing vectors is a Killing vector.

4. Miscellaneous Problems

(1) Let $\omega = dp \wedge dq$. Given any smooth function H, define a vector-field X_H by

$$X_H \perp \omega = -dH$$

Show that the integral curves of X_H satisfy Hamilton's equations:

$$\dot{q} = \frac{\partial H}{\partial p}, \dot{p} = -\frac{\partial H}{\partial q}$$

(2) $i : S^2 \to R^3$ denotes the inclusion map. Let g be the usual Euclidean metric on R^3. Compute i^*g.

(3) RP^n is orientable if and only if n is odd.

(4) The sphere S^n is orientable.

(5) The Cartesian product of orientable manifolds is orientable.

(6) The Mobius strip is not orientable.

(7) Construct a smooth nowhere vanishing vector-field on S^3.

(8) Find a smooth 2-form on $R^3 - \{0\}$ which is closed but not exact (think of electromagnetic fields !).

(9) S^2 cannot have a Lorentz metric.

(10) There are three scalars that can be constructed from the electromagnetic field 2-form F

$$\frac{1}{2}F^{ab}F_{ab} = B^2 - E^2$$

$$\frac{1}{2}F^{ab*}F_{ab} = E.B$$

$$\frac{1}{2}{}^*F^{ab*}F_{ab} = E^2 - B^2$$

(11) Show that $F \wedge^* F$ is equal to $\frac{1}{2}F^{ab}F_{ab}$ and that $F \wedge F$ is equal to $\frac{1}{2}{}^*F^{ab}F_{ab}$.

(12) e^k is a 1-form. $e^{j_1 \cdots j_p}$ denotes $e^{j_1} \wedge \ldots \wedge e^{j_p}$. Show that $i_{e_j} * e^{j_1 \cdots j_p} =* e^{j_1 \cdots j_p j}$.

(13) g is a Riemann metric on N. $\psi : M \to N$ is a smooth regular map. Give an example to show that if g is semi-Riemannian then
(a) $\psi^* g$ need not be semi-Riemannian.
(b) $\psi^* g$ is semi-Riemannian of a different index than g.

5. Frobenius Theorem

(1) The distribution defined by $-x^2 dx^1 + x^1 dx^2 + dx^3$ does not satisfy the Frobenius integrability condition.

(2) What is the Frobenius integrability condition for the distribution (in R^3) $P_1 dx^1 + P_2 dx^2 + P_3 dx^3$? Interpret classically.

(3) The Frobenius integrability condition is automatically satisfied for any 1-dimensional distribution.

6. Connections and Curvature

(1) Deduce the relation between the Christoffel symbols and the connection coefficients in an arbitrary frame.

(2) Write down the components of the torsion tensor and the Riemann tensor in an arbitrary frame (in terms of the connection coefficients and the structure constants).

(3) For a torsion-free symmetric connection, show that the curvature satsifies the (cyclic) Bianchi identity.

$$R(U,V)W + R(V,W)U + R(W,U)V = 0$$

(4) Write the cyclic Bianchi identity in component form.

(5) For a torsion-free connection prove the validity of the (differential) Bianchi identity

$$(D_U R)(V,W)X + (D_V R)(W,U)X + (D_W R)(U,V)X = 0$$

Write this in component form.

(6) The Bianchi identities are vacuous on a 2-dimensional manifold.

(7) Use the Cartan structure equations to compute the connection and curvature of the metric

$$ds^2 = 2du dv - dx^2 - dy^2 - 2H(x,y,u)du^2$$

Show that the Einstein equations are $H_{xx} + H_{yy} = 0$.

(8) Show that Lagrange's equations for the Lagrangian $L = \frac{1}{2} g_{ab} \dot{q}^a \dot{q}^b$ are precisely the geodesic equations for the Levi-Civita connections of g_{ab}.

(9) D denotes the Levi-Civita connections. Show that D satisfies the Koszul formula

$$
\begin{aligned}
2 < D_V W, X > \; = \; & V < W, X > + W < X, V > \\
& - \; X < V, W > - < V, [W, X] > \\
& + \; < X, [V, W] > + < W, [X, V] >
\end{aligned}
$$

7. Lie Groups and Lie Algebras

(1) $\exp \begin{bmatrix} 0 & a \\ -a & 0 \end{bmatrix} = \begin{bmatrix} \cos a & \sin a \\ -\sin a & \cos a \end{bmatrix}$

(2) A and B are matrices. Give an example to show that $\exp(A + B)$ in general is not equal to $\exp A . \exp B$. When is it true that they are equal?

(3) M is a matrix. Show that $\det \exp M = \exp \operatorname{tr} M$.

(4) G is a topological group, H a subgroup of G.
   (a) If H is open, so is every coset gH
   (b) If H is open then H is closed.

(5) Show that R^3 with the multiplication law

$$
\begin{bmatrix} X_1 \\ X_2 \\ X_3 \end{bmatrix} \begin{bmatrix} Y_1 \\ Y_2 \\ Y_3 \end{bmatrix} = \begin{bmatrix} X_1 + Y_1 \\ X_2 + Y_2 \\ X_3 + Y_3 + X_1 Y_2 - X_2 Y_1 \end{bmatrix}
$$

is a Lie group. Calculate the structure constants of the Lie algebra with respect to some basis.

(6) $SO(n)/SO(n-1)$ is homeomorphic to S^{n-1} for $n \geq 2$.

(7) $SO(3)$ is not simply connected.

(8) If a form ω is left invariant, then so is $d\omega$.

(9) $f : G \to G, f(a) = a^{-1}$,
   (a) ω is left invariant if and only if $f^*\omega$ is right invariant.
   (b) If ω is a k-form on G_e then $f^*\omega = (-1)^k \omega$.
   (c) If ω is both left and right invariant then $d\omega = 0$.

(10) Compute the Lie algebras of $GL(n)$, $SL(n)$, $SO(n)$, $SU(n)$, $SP(n)$.

(11) The vector-fields

$$
\frac{\partial}{\partial \psi}, \cos \psi \cot \theta \frac{\partial}{\partial \psi} + \sin \psi \frac{\partial}{\partial \theta}, -\sin \psi \cot \theta \frac{\partial}{\partial \psi} + \cos \psi \frac{\partial}{\partial \theta}
$$

are Killing vectors on S^2. What Lie algebra do they generate?

(12) $X_1, \ldots, X_n$ are a basis for the Lie algebra of G. $\alpha^1, \ldots, \alpha^n$ are the Maurer-Cartan forms $(\alpha^i X_j = \delta_i^j)$.

Then

$$d\alpha^a = -\frac{1}{2} \sum f_{bc}^a \alpha^b \wedge \alpha^c$$

(The Maurer-Cartan structure equation) where $f^a{}_{bc}$ are the structure constants:

$$[X_a, X_b] = f_{ab}^c X_c.$$

(13) (continuation): The identity $d^2 \alpha^a = 0$ is equivalent to the Jacobi identity.

(14) Compute the Maurer-Cartan form for $SU(2)$.

(15) (In this problem and the next, α, β and γ are Lie algebra valued forms).

α is a p-form, β a q-form, γ an r-form.

(a) $[\alpha, \beta] = (-1)^{pq+1} [\beta, \alpha]$

(b) $(-1)^{pr} [\alpha, [\beta, \gamma]] + (-1)^{qp} [\beta, [\gamma, \alpha]] + (-1)^{qr} [\gamma, [\alpha, \beta]] = 0.$

(16) $[\alpha, \alpha] = 0$ if α is an even form. Construct an odd form β so that $[\beta, \beta] \neq 0$. If β is odd then $[[\beta, \beta], \beta] = 0.$

(17) In problem 7 of section (6), explicitly write out the connection and the curvature as Lie algebra valued forms.

8. Fibre Bundles

(1) Derive the classical transformation rules for contravariant and covariant vectors starting from the definitions of the tangent and cotangent bundles respectively.

(2) [Example of a fibre bundle] $\pi : U(1) \to U(1), \pi(e^{it}) = e^{int}, n \in Z$. The fibre is Z_n. This bundle is trivial when $n = 1$.

(Another example): $\pi : R \to U(1), \pi(t) = \exp(2\pi i t)$. The fibre is Z.

[Remark : Note that the fibres are discrete. These are examples of covering spaces.]

(3) The tangent bundle of a Lie group is trivial.

(4) A principal bundle $\pi : P \to M$ is trivial if and only if it admits a section.

(5) A vector bundle with m-dimensional fibres is trivial if and only if it admits m linearly independent sections at each point.

9. Supplementary Problems

(1) Find a matrix representation of the group of rigid motions in the plane (*i.e.*, the group of rotations plus translations).

(2) On any two dimensional manifold with a positive definite metric tensor g, there always exist local coordinates u,v such that g has the form

$$g = f(u, v)[du \otimes du + dv \otimes dv]$$

for some smooth function f.

Is an analogous theorem true if g is indefinite?

(3) Are GL(n), SO(n), SU(n) connected over R, over C?

(4) The Laplacian. Let $*$ denote the Hodge operator. Define $\delta = *d*$ (d is the exterior derivative). Show that the Laplacian acting on functions is δd. (Use a coordinate system.) Verify that $\delta\delta = 0$.

[The usual Laplacian acts on functions, i.e. on 0-forms. This can be generalised to a Laplacian acting on arbitrary forms:

$$\Delta := \delta d + d\delta$$

Verify that

$$\Delta d = d\Delta, \Delta\delta = \delta\Delta, \Delta* = *\Delta.$$

(5) Δ is the Laplacian. A function f is harmonic if $\Delta f = 0$. Prove that on a compact manifold the only harmonic functions are the constant functions.

(6) Let R_{ab} denote the Ricci tensor of a Riemann metric g_{ab}. Prove that if $R_{ab} = \lambda g_{ab}$ then λ must be a constant.

(7) Define $\phi : R^2 \to R^3$ by

$$\phi(u, v) = (2\cos u + v\sin\frac{u}{2}\cos u, 2\sin u + v\sin\frac{u}{2}\sin u, \cos\frac{u}{2})$$

Show that the image of ϕ is the Mobius strip in R^3.

(8) The m-dimensional sphere S^m is simply connected if $m \geq 2$.

(9) Let J be the $2n \times 2n$ matrix

$$J = \begin{bmatrix} 0 & I \\ -I & 0 \end{bmatrix}$$

where I is the unit $n \times n$ matrix. The symplectic group Sp(n) is defined to be the set of all $2n \times 2n$ matrices A such that $A^t J A = J.(A^t$ denotes the transpose of A). Prove that Sp(n) is a Lie group. Compute its dimension. Compute its Lie algebra.

(10) Does SO(3) have any normal subgroups?

(11) A smooth k-dimensional surface in R^n defined by a system of n-k equations is orientable.

(12) Prove that the connected component of the identity in a Lie group is a normal subgroup.

(13) A connected Lie group is generated by an arbitrarily small neighbourhood of the identity.

(14) Every Lie group is orientable.

(15) There exists a Riemann metric on any compact manifold. (Use partitions of unity.)

(16) A space purports to be 3-dimensional, with coordinates X,Y,Z and the metric
$$g = dX^2 + dY^2 + dZ^2 - (\tfrac{3}{13}dX + \tfrac{4}{13}dY + \tfrac{12}{13}dZ)^2$$
Show that it is really a two dimensional space. Find two new coordinates W and Z so that $g = dW^2 + dZ^2$.

(17) (a) What is the Riemann tensor in a 1-dimensional space?

(b) Express the Riemann tensor for a 2-dimensional space in terms of the metric and the Ricci scalar.

(c) Express the Riemann tensor for a 3-dimensional space in terms of the metric and the Ricci tensor.

(18) If X is a Killing vector prove that
$$X_{a;bc} = R_{dcba}X^d$$

(19) If X is a Killing vector field and Y is tangent to a geodesic then g(X,Y) is constant along the geodesic.

(20) On a Riemann manifold (M,g) show that the volume element
$$\Omega = \sqrt{\det g}\, dX^1 \wedge ... \wedge dX^n$$
is an invariant (i.e. for a different choice of local coordinates $Y^1, ...Y^n$, depending smoothly on the X^a, Ω has the form
$$\sqrt{\det g}\, dY^1 \wedge ... \wedge dY^n).$$

(21) Write the following expressions in index-free notation
- (a) $U_{a;b}U^a U^b$
- (b) $V^a_{;b}U^b - U^a_{;b}V^b$
- (c) $T_{ab;c}U^a V^b W^c$
- (d) $W^{a;b}V_{b;c}U^c$
- (d) $W^a_{;bc}U^b U^c + W^a_{;b}U^b_{;c}U^c - U^a_{;c}W^c_{;b}U^b.$

Hints and Solutions:

1. Manifolds and Smooth Maps

(1) The circle S^1 is a smooth manifold. Consider the circle in the x-y plane. Put two charts (U_1, φ_1) and (U_2, φ_2) on S^1 :

$$U_1 = S^1 - \{(0,1)\}, \varphi_1(x,y) = \frac{1}{1-y}x,\ y \neq 1$$

$$U_2 = S^1 - \{(0,-1)\}, \varphi_2(x,y) = \frac{1}{1+y}x,\ y \neq -1$$

U_1 is the circle minus the north pole, U_2 is the circle minus the south pole and φ_1 and φ_2 are stereographic projections from the north and south poles.

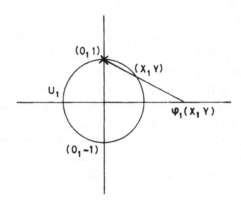

Then, a little calculation shows that

$$\varphi_2 \bullet \varphi_1^{-1} = \frac{1}{x^2+y^2}x$$

which is a smooth map, as is $\varphi_1 \bullet \varphi_2^{-1}$.
S^1 therefore is a smooth manifold.
A similar method works for any S^n. (Also, see problem 3).

(2) The torus in R^3 is a smooth manifold. The torus is the product of $S^1 \times S^1$, and a product of smooth manifolds is a smooth manifold.

(3) A useful way to show that a space is or is not a smooth manifold is to use the implicit function theorem (sometimes called the preimage theorem):
Let $f : R^n \to R^m$ be a smooth map, with $n > m$ and with derivative (Jacobian) f_*. Then for $p \in R^m$, $f^{-1}(p)$ is a smooth submanifold of R^n iff, the rank of f_* at all q in the preimage of p equals m. Further, the dimension of the submanifold is $n - m$. (The preimage of p in R^m is the set of all points q in R^n with $f(q) = p$).
The x-y axes in R^2 do not form a smooth manifold:

Define

$f : R \to R$ by $f(x,y) = xy$.

$f^{-1}(0)$ is the x-y axes.

$f_* = [y \ x]$. The rank of this 1×2 matrix is 1 for all points on the axes except for the origin. The x-y axes therefore do not form a smooth manifold.

This theorem can be used to show directly that S^n is a smooth manifold.

Define

$f : R^{n+1} \to R$ by

$f(x_1, ..., x_{n+1}) = x_1^2 + ...x_{n+1}^2 - 1$.

What is $f^{-1}(0)$? Use the theorem above.

(4) Examples : S^1, the torus, the cylinder, S^3 ..... Also see problem $H3$.

(5) If it did, S^2 would be homeomorphic to an open subset of R^2, but S^2 is compact.

(6) $GL(n, R)$ is homeomorphic to an open set in R^{n^2}.

Hint : Use the determinant map. $GL(n, \mathbf{R})$ can be described as the inverse image of an open set in R.

(7) Local charts for RP^2. (The general case is similar). The definition of RP^2 in the problem is equivalent to the following : RP^2 is the set of all lines through the origin in R^3. (Every line intersects S^2 in a pair of antipodal points and all points on a line are equivalent).

Let $[x, y, z]$ denote all nonzero multiples of (x, y, z). $[x, y, z]$ is thus a point of RP^2.

Define three charts on RP^2, $(U_i, \varphi_i), i = 1, 2, 3$ with $\varphi_i : U_i \to R^2$.

$$U_1 = \{[x, y, z], \ x \neq 0\}, \ \varphi_1[x, y, z] = \left(\frac{y}{x}, \frac{z}{x}\right)$$

$$U_2 = \{[x, y, z], \ y \neq 0\}, \ \varphi_2[x, y, z] = \left(\frac{x}{y}, \frac{z}{y}\right)$$

$$U_3 = \{[x, y, z], \ z \neq 0\}, \ \varphi_3[x, y, z] = \left(\frac{x}{z}, \frac{y}{z}\right)$$

Clearly, the U_i cover RP^2, and the φ_i are homeomorphisms. Check,

$$\varphi_1^{-1}(a, b) = [1, a, b]$$
$$\varphi_2^{-1}(a, b) = [a, 1, b]$$
$$\varphi_3^{-1}(a, b) = [a, b, 1]$$

And finally, $\varphi_2 \bullet \varphi_1^{-1}(a, b) = \varphi_2(1, a, b) = \left(\dfrac{1}{a}, \dfrac{b}{a}\right)$ defined on the domain $a \neq 0$.

So, $\varphi_2 \bullet \varphi_1^{-1}$, is smooth .... etc., etc.

(9) $SU(2)$ is the group of all 2×2 complex matrices A satisfying $A^{-1} = A^\dagger$ and $\det A = 1$.

If $\begin{bmatrix} a & b \\ c & d \end{bmatrix} \in SU(2)$, the two conditions above imply $c = -\bar{b}$ and $d = \bar{a}$ and $a\bar{a} + b\bar{b} = 1$.

If $a = x_1 + ix_2$ and $d = x_3 + ix_4$, then the last condition reads $x_1^2 + x_2^2 + x_3^2 + x_4^2 = 1$. And this is the equation of the sphere S^3 in 4-dimensions.

(10) There is a 2 to 1 homomorphism from $SU(2)$ to $SO(3)$ which carries matrices differing in an overall sign to the same matrix in $SO(3)$. (See chapter 41 of Misner, Thorne and Wheeler 'Gravitation' for details). Now, $SU(2)$ has topology S^3 and recall the definition of RP^3 from problem 7.

(12) They are not even homeomorphic! For example, to show R^1 is not homeomorphic to R^2, remove a point from R^1. This disconnects R^1 but does not disconnect R^2. In general, removing an $(m-1)$-dimensional plane from R^m disconnects R^m.

(13) $SL(2, R)$ is the set of all 2×2 real matrices A satisfying $\det A = 1$. We know that $GL(2, R)$ is an open set in R^{n^2}. So, an $SL(2, R)$ matrix can be thought of as a point in R^4. Let $A = \begin{bmatrix} a & b \\ c & d \end{bmatrix}$ be an $SL(2,R)$ matrix thought of as the point (a, b, c, d) in R^4. Define $f : R^4 \to R$ by
$f(a, b, c, d) = ad - bc - 1$.
What is $f^{-1}(0)$? Use the theorem of problem 3. [This also shows that $SL(2, R)$ is a *closed* submanifold of $GL(2, R)$. Why ?].

(15) $f:R \to R$, $f(x) = x^3$. What is its inverse? Is it differentiable everywhere ?

(16) Take M to be R with the chart $(R, \alpha), \alpha(x) = x$. Take N to be R with the chart $R, \beta), \beta = x^{1/3}$. These two differential structures are inequivalent : $\beta \bullet \alpha^{-1}$ is not smooth.

(21) $\bar{f}$ is defined on the quotient R/Z if all the integers get mapped to the same point in R^2.

2. Differential Forms

(1) $(x^2 + y^2 + z^2)\, dx \wedge dy \wedge dz$

(2) $e^r = dr,\ e^\theta = rd\theta,\ e^\psi = r\sin\theta d\psi$

(3) $\omega(X) = x^3 + y^3$

$\alpha(X, Y) = -xy^2 - yz^2 + xy^2z$

$\beta(X, Y, Z) = xyz(3xyz - 3x^2y^2)$

(4) a) $x^3\, dx \wedge dy + 2yzdy \wedge dz$

 b) $(9xy^2 - 3x - 1)\, dx \wedge dy \wedge dz$

 c) $(\partial f/\partial z + \partial g/\partial x)\, dx \wedge dy \wedge dz$

 d) 0

(5) $\alpha^* dx = -\sin u du,\ \alpha^* dy = \cos u du$

(18) Hint : every 1-form field on S^2 must vanish at least one point.

(20) RP^n is S^n with antipodal points identified. On S^n (for any n) there is always a smooth nowhere vanishing n-form (the volume form):

$$\omega = \frac{1}{\Sigma(x_i)^2}(x_1 dx_2 \wedge ... \wedge dx_{n+1} \wedge dx_1 \ + \ .....$$

$$+ \ dx_{n+1} \wedge dx_1 ... \wedge dx_n)$$

This will produce a well-defined n-form on RP^n if it is invariant under the involution $(x_1, ..., x_{n+1}) \mapsto (-x_1, ..., -x_{n+1})$. Inspection shows that ω is invariant under this involution only if n is odd. Thus, for odd n, there is a nowhere vanishing n-form on RP^n. Now complete the argument to show that there cannot exist a nowhere vanishing n-form on RP^n for even n.

4. Miscellaneous Problems

(1) Let $c(t)$ be an integral curve to X_H. That is $dc/dt = X_H$. Expressed as a vector-field in the p-q plane,

$$X_H = \frac{dq}{dt}\left(\frac{\partial}{\partial q}\right) + \frac{dp}{dt}\left(\frac{\partial}{\partial p}\right) \equiv \dot{q}\frac{\partial}{\partial q} + \dot{p}\frac{\partial}{\partial p}.$$

A little calculation shows that if $\omega = dp \wedge dq$ then

$$X_H \perp \omega = \dot{p}dq - \dot{q}dp \ = \ -dH$$

$$= \ -\frac{\partial H}{\partial p}dp - \frac{\partial H}{\partial q}dq$$

Comparing coefficients, Hamilton's equations follow.

(2) It is the usual metric on S^2.

(3) See problem B.20.

(4) Problem B.20 provides a nowhere vanishing volume form on S^n.

(5) Each manifold has a nowhere vanishing volume form since it is orientable. Take their wedge product.

(6) Hint : Show that there cannot be a nowhere vanishing volume form on the Mobius strip. The Mobius strip can be thought of as a rectangle with the left and right edges identified after a twist. Put $x - y$ coordinates on the rectangle. Traversing the rectangle from the left edge to the right edge changes y to $-y$ (because of the twist). Finally, remember that any volume form on the Mobius strip must be of the form $f(x, y)\mathrm{d}x \wedge \mathrm{d}y$.

(7) Hint : Think of S^3 as sitting in R^4 and remember that the tangent vector at any point is perpendicular to the radius vector to that point. (This also shows that all odd-dimensional spheres admit a nowhere vanishing vector-field).

(8) Hint 1 : Can you find a 2-form on S^2 which is closed but not exact?
Hint 2 : The electromagnetic field is (as you know) described by a 2-form F. What is F corresponding to a point charge q sitting at the origin in R^3? Why is this F closed but not exact?

(9) A manifold admits a Lorentz metric *iff* it admits a smooth nowhere vanishing vector-field. We prove this one way first.Suppose M admits a smooth nowhere vanishing vector-field X. Now every manifold always admits a smooth Riemann, (*i.e.*, positive definite) metric. (Manifolds are always assumed to be paracompact. They thus admit partitions of unity, and these can be used to patch up locally defined Riemann metrics. See some diferential geometry book for details). Call this Riemann metric g. Use this metric to make X have unit length and also lower the index on X using the g metric. Then

$$h_{ab} = g_{ab} - 2X_aX_b$$

is a Lorentz metric with signature $+ + + -$ and with X a timelike vector-field. [Proof: Choose an orthonormal basis (w.r.t. g) for M to be X, e^1, e^2, e^3. Then $g = X \otimes X + e^1 \otimes e^1 + e^2 \otimes e^2 + e^3 \otimes e^3$ and the statement above follows]. The converse: Let M have a Lorentz metric. Then (roughly speaking; see Barrett O'Neill, 'Semi-Riemannian Geometry', Chapter 5, proposition 37 for details) the null cones of the metric vary smoothly (because the metric is smooth) so it is possible to make a choice of a vector in each null-cone to produce a smooth vector-field. Finally, S^2 does not admit a Lorentz metric because it does not admit a smooth nowhere vanishing vector-field. (A compact manifold admits a nowhere vanishing vector-field *iff* its Euler characteristic is zero; a noncompact manifold always admits such a vector-field. See some topology book for details).

7. Lie Groups and Lie Algebras

(3) If M is diagonal or diagonalizable, the statement is trivial to verify. If M is not diagonalizable, it can still be reduced to Jordan normal form. The Jordan normal form exhibits M as a direct sum of blocks of the following form:

$$J\lambda = \begin{bmatrix} \lambda & 1 & & & 0 \\ & \lambda & 1 & & \\ & & \ddots & & \\ & & & \lambda & 1 \\ 0 & & & & \lambda \end{bmatrix}$$

verify the equality $\det \exp M = \exp \operatorname{tr} M$ for such a block.
(Hint: J_λ is the sum of a diagonal matrix and a nilpotent matrix and these commute with each other).

(4(b)) Let H be an open subgroup. G is the union of H and all its cosets gH. Since all the cosets are open, their complement H must be closed. (Assuming G is connected).

(6) This is a special case of a more general result (which is easy to prove). Let G be a group which acts transitively on a space X. Let H be a subgroup of G which fixes a point of X. Then X is homeomorphic to the coset space G/H.

(8) d commutes with pull-backs.

(9) [Following Spivak]
Let R_g and L_g denote right and left translations respectively. Thus, $R_g(h) = gh$ and $L_g(h) = hg$, for elements g and h of the Lie group G.
(a) Let ω be left invariant (*i.e.*, $L_g^*\omega = \omega$) and let $f : G \to G$ be given by $f(a) = a^{-1}$. Clearly $f \bullet R_g = L_{g^{-1}} \bullet f$
therefore, $R_g^* f^* = f^* L_{g^{-1}}^*$
If ω is left invariant

$$\begin{aligned} R_g^*(f^*\omega) &= f^* L_{g^{-1}}^*(\omega) \\ &= f^*\omega \end{aligned}$$

and so $f^*\omega$ is right invariant.
(b) If ω is a k-form on G_e (the tangent space to the identity) then $f^*(\omega) = (-1)^k \omega$. It suffices to prove this for $k = 1$. (For the general case follows on taking wedge products of basic 1-forms). Now, for any

$X \in G_e$, the action of $f^*\omega$ on X is given by $f^*\omega(X) = \omega(f_{*e}X)$. So it suffices to prove that $f_{*e}X = -X$. Now X is the tangent vector at $t = 0$ of the curve $t \to \exp tX$. So $f_{*e}X$ is the tangent vector to the curve $t \to (\exp tX)^{-1} = \exp(-tX)$. But this tangent vector is $-X$.

(c) Let ω be both left and right invariant. Consider $\omega_e \epsilon G_e$. By (b) above

$$f^*(\omega_e) = (-1)^k \omega_e.$$

Since ω and $f^*\omega$ are both left and right invariant this equation is true anywhere on G. Thus,

$$f^*(\omega) = (-1)^k \omega$$

But $d\omega$ is also left and right invariant (why?).
therefore $f^*(d\omega) = (-1)^{k+1}d\omega$
But $f^*(d\omega) = d(f^*\omega) = (-1)^k d\omega$ and therefore $d\omega = 0$.

[REMARK: This is an important result since it relates de Rham co-homology of Lie groups to bi-invariant fields on the group].

(14) The Maurer-Cartan form for SU(2).
    The Maurer-Cartan form is a Lie algebra valued 1-form on SU(2) and is computed by calculating $A^{-1}dA$ for $A \in$ SU(2). We choose a parametrization for SU(2) as follows:
    Choose the axis of rotation to be described by a unit vector n pasametrized by two angles α and β.

$$n = (\sin \beta \cos \alpha, \sin \beta \sin \alpha, \cos \beta), \quad 0 \le \alpha \le 2\pi$$
$$0 < \beta < \pi.$$

If the rotation is through an angle θ about this axis, recall that the SU(2) matrix describing this rotation is

$$A = \cos \frac{\theta}{2} \cdot 1 - i \sin \frac{\theta}{2} \sigma \cdot n$$

where $\sigma \cdot n$ means $n_1\sigma_1 + n_2\sigma_2 + n_3\sigma_3$, and the σ_i are the Pauli matrices

$$\sigma_1 = \begin{bmatrix} 0 & 1 \\ 1 & 0 \end{bmatrix}, \quad \sigma_2 = \begin{bmatrix} 0 & i \\ -i & 0 \end{bmatrix}, \quad \sigma_3 = \begin{bmatrix} 1 & 0 \\ 0 & -1 \end{bmatrix}$$

write out the matrix A and calculate dA, *i.e.*, take the exterior derivative of each entry of this matrix). Finally calculate the matrix $A^{-1}dA$. This is the Maurer-Cartan form. It is of the form

$$\omega_1\sigma_1 + \omega_2\sigma_2 + \omega_3\sigma_3$$

with

$$\omega_1 = -\sin\beta\cos\alpha d\theta - \cos\beta\cos\alpha\sin\frac{\theta}{2}d\beta + \sin\frac{\theta}{2}\sin\alpha\sin\beta d\alpha$$

$$\omega_2 = -\sin\alpha\sin\beta d\theta - \sin\alpha\sin\frac{\theta}{2}\cos\beta d\beta - \cos\alpha\sin\beta\sin\frac{\theta}{2}d\alpha$$

$$\omega_3 = -\cos\beta d\theta + \sin\frac{\theta}{2}\sin\beta d\beta.$$

The ω_i are the left-invariant forms on SU(2). Calculating the Maurer-Cartan form $A^{-1}dA$ provides all the left invariant 1-forms on a group.

[REMARK: It is now easy to write down an invariant measure on SU(2) : it is simply $\omega_1 \wedge \omega_2 \wedge \omega_3$].

(15) The notation here needs to be clearly understood. It is best to discuss it in more generality.

Let E and F be vector spaces. It is clear how to define p-forms on E with values in F. For example, a 2-form on E with values in F is a bilinear map $\omega : E \times E \to F$ with $\omega(X,Y) = -\omega(Y,X)$ for $X,Y \in F$. Think of ordinary k-forms for which the vector space F is just R.

Now suppose one is given a product structure of F. This is a bilinear map $\varphi : F \times F \to F$. Then one define the wedge product of forms on E with values in F using this map φ, just as one uses ordinary multiplication when F is R for ordinary k-forms. This wedge product is denoted $\wedge_\varphi$.

For example, if α and β are 1-forms on E with values in F (and $X,Y \in E$) then

$$(\alpha \wedge_\varphi \beta)(X,Y) = \varphi(\alpha(X),\ \beta(Y)) - \varphi(\alpha(Y),\ \beta(X)).$$

(Think again of ordinary, real-valued forms: the right hand side would have been $\alpha(X)\beta(Y) - \alpha(Y)\beta(X)$).

Now let F be a Lie algebra. On a Lie algebra we have a natural product structure namely the Lie bracket :

$$\varphi(U,V) = [U,V] = U, V \in F.$$

In this case $\alpha \wedge_\varphi \beta$ is denoted $[\alpha,\beta]$. Note now for instance that if α is a 1-form, it is no longer true that $\alpha \wedge_\varphi \alpha = 0$! In fact

$$\begin{aligned}(\alpha \wedge_\varphi \alpha)(X,Y) &\equiv [\alpha,\alpha](X,Y) = [\alpha(X),\alpha(Y)] - [\alpha(Y),\alpha(X)]\\ &= 2[\alpha(X),\alpha(Y)].\end{aligned}$$

To tackle the given problem examine some special cases first. Suppose α and β are Lie algebra valued 1-forms. Then it is easy to check that $[\alpha, \beta] = [\beta, \alpha]$:

$$[\alpha, \beta](X, Y) = [\alpha(X), \beta(Y)] - [\alpha(Y), \beta(X)]$$

and calculating $[\beta, \alpha](X, Y)$ gives the same result. The general result can be proved by putting in all the right alternating symbols and doing it will do the reader's soul much good.

8. Fibre Bundles

(3) Pick a basis $X_{1e}, \cdots, X_{ne}$ for G_e (the tangent space to G at the identity e). Let $X_1, \cdots, X_n$ be the left invariant vector fields on G which coincide with the chosen basis at the identity. Then $X_1, \cdots, X_n$ are linearly independent everywhere (why?). But if the tangent bundle admits n independent sections it is trivial.

(4) If the bundle is trivial it clearly admits a section: pick any $g \in G$ (G is the structure group) and define a section by

$$X \longmapsto (X, g).(X \epsilon M).$$

Conversely, let S a section. Pick $p \epsilon P$. Then $S(\pi(P))$ is back in the total space P (in the fibre over $\pi(P)$). Since G acts transitively and freely on the fibres, there is a unique element $g_p \epsilon G$ such that $S(\pi(P)) \cdot g_p = P$. Now define the map $P \to M \times G$ by $P \longmapsto (\pi(P), g_p)$. This is clearly an isomorphism of bundles. P therefore is trivial.

(5) If the vector bundle admits n linearly independent sections then the associated principal bundle of frames is trivial since it admits a section. But then the vector bundle is also trivial since it has the same set of transition functions as its frame bundle.

3. TETRADS, THE NEWMAN–PENROSE FORMALISM AND SPINORS

S.V.DHURANDHAR

Inter-University Center for Astronomy & Astrophysics
Post Bag No.4, Ganeshkhind
PUNE 411 007, India

1. Introduction

The usual method of solution of problems in General Relativity was to use a local coordinate basis to suit a given problem. However, it has been found useful to employ non-coordinate basis techniques in some problems. This is the tetrad formalism which consists of setting up four linearly independent vector fields called a tetrad basis at each point of a region of spacetime. The relevant equations are written in this basis and if the tetrad is aligned according to the symmetries of the spacetime an easier set of equations may ensue which could be amenable to solution.

The Newman-Penrose (NP) approach consists of using complex null tetrads to treat certain types of problems. The germ of the idea arose from Hermann Bondi. He suggested that to study electromagnetic or gravitational radiation in curved spacetimes one should analyse the fields along null directions, since they propagate along those directions. Newman and Penrose made this idea concrete in their formalism. This approach has turned out to be particularly useful for investigating massless fields. They also showed that their formalism is completely equivalent to the SL(2, C) spinor approach.

The method turns out to be particularly powerful when the spacetime is of an algebraically special type: The Weyl tensor of a spacetime determines a set of four null eigen-vectors called the principal null directions of the Weyl tensor. If they are all different the spacetime is called algebraically general otherwise it is algebraically special, *i.e.*, atleast two of the principal null directions coincide. The coincident null direction is called the repeated principal null direction (r.p.n.d.) of the Weyl tensor. If one aligns one of the real null vectors of the null tetrad along the r.p.n.d. then the spin coefficients occuring in the NP equations coincide with certain invariants (optical scalars) of the congruence generated by the r.p.n.d. and the NP equations normally simplify often resulting in a solution.

We present a simple illustrative example of Maxwell equations in flat spacetime but in polar coordinates. The usual solution in terms of vector spherical harmonics is quite cumbersome but in the NP formalism the field variables decouple and the solution comes out easily. In curved spacetime the equations are more strongly coupled due to the presence of the Riemann tensor and the NP formalism can be successfully applied in certain situations to yield a solution.

The NP formalism has found application in several areas in general relativity. It has been used effectively to deal with the asymptotic properties of spacetimes e.g. the BMS group, conformal infinity etc. Attempt has been made via the NP formalism to relate the asymptotic properties of the gravitational field to the motion of a localised source. The wave equation in Kerr geometry has been solved using the formalism. Recently, the formalism has been applied to study the responses of certain gravity wave detectors, the Weber bars and laser interferometers. The angular functions in the responses are the spin weighted spherical harmonics appearing in the NP formalism.

In these lectures I will begin with the tetrad formalism. Then I will introduce null tetrads, spin coefficients and discuss the NP formalism. Then I will go to the applications, Maxwell's equations, optical scalars etc. Finally I will consider spinors, the spinorial approach to the NP formalism and applications.

2. The Minkowski Space and Lorentz Transformations

I have chosen to begin with the Minkowski space since the notion of tetrads can easily be introduced in it. The transition to curved spacetimes can be made with little difficulty, since the tangent space at each point in a spacetime is a Minkowski space. This is also a convenient starting point for $SL(2, C)$ spinors.

A Minkowski space M is a 4-dimensional vector space over $\mathcal{R}$, the field of real numbers, endowed with

1. bilinear inner product with signature $(+, -, -, -)$,
2. an orientation,
3. a time orientation.

I will explain the above terms in the matter that follows. A tetrad is a set of basis vectors of M, i.e., a set of four linearly independent vectors (e_0, e_1, e_2, e_3) or in short e_a, $a = 0, 1, 2, 3$. Any vector $A \epsilon M$ can be written as a linear combination of the basis vectors:

$$A = A^0 e_0 + A^1 e_1 + A^2 e_2 + A^3 e_3 = A^a e_a \qquad (2.1)$$

where the 'Einstein's summation convention' has been used. A^a are called the components of A in the tetrad $\{e_a\}$.

Let $f_a, a = 0, 1, 2, 3$ be another tetrad then,

$$f_a = L_a^b e_b \qquad (2.2)$$

where L_a^b is a 4×4 matrix. Since L connects one basis to another basis the matrix L is non-singular and the $\det(L)$ is nonzero.

We say that the tetrads $\{e_a\}$ and $\{f_a\}$ have the same *orientation* if $\det(L)$ is positive. If $\det(L)$ is negative they have opposite orientation. It is easy to verify that *having the same orientation* is an equivalence relation on the set of tetrads which partitions the tetrads into two disjoint classes. We choose one of these classes and call this class as the class of *positively oriented* tetrads or *proper* tetrads. This choice makes M oriented.

The inner product denoted by a dot $(\cdot)$ maps a pair of vectors of M into a real number in a bilinear fashion. The Lorentzian signature $(+, -, -, -)$ means that there exist tetrads satisfying the conditions,

$$e_a.e_b = \eta_{ab},$$

where,

$$\eta_{ab} = \begin{pmatrix} 1 & 0 & 0 & 0 \\ 0 & -1 & 0 & 0 \\ 0 & 0 & -1 & 0 \\ 0 & 0 & 0 & -1 \end{pmatrix}. \qquad (2.3)$$

Such tetrads are called *orthonormal* tetrads.

Let $A, B \epsilon M$, then, $A = A^a e_a$, $B = B^b e_b$; the inner product can be written in terms of the components as,

$$A.B = A^a e_a.B^b e_b = A^a B^b e_a.e_b = A^a B^b \eta_{ab}. \qquad (2.4)$$

The *Lorentz norm* of a vector $A \epsilon M$ is defined as,

$$A.A = \eta_{ab} A^a A^b. \qquad (2.5)$$

The vectors in M fall into three classes according as their norm is positive, negative or zero. A is timelike if $A.A > 0$, A is null if $A.A = 0$, A is spacelike if $A.A < 0$.

The orthonormal tetrad as defined above has e_0 timelike and e_1, e_2, e_3 spacelike. In fact, it follows from Sylvester's theorem in linear algebra that every orthonormal tetrad in M must consist of one timelike vector and three spacelike vectors.

The timelike vectors can be shown to fall into two disjoint classes, say, F and P. These are defined by the conditions that the inner product of any two vectors belonging to one class, say, F (or P) is positive. One of these classes, say F we call the set of *future timelike* vectors. The other class P then consists of *past timelike* vectors. This choice of F and P makes M *time oriented*. Normally, we fix F (or P) from thermodynamical considerations.

An orthonormal tetrad $\{e_a\}$ is said to be *orthochronous* if $e_0 \epsilon F$.

A *proper orthochronous* tetrad is said to be *restricted*.

Although we have not said anything about space orientation (the left or right handedness) of a tetrad, it gets fixed once we fix the orientation and the time orientation.

A linear map $L : M \to M$ which preserves the inner product is called a *Lorentz* transformation.

Let L be a Lorentz transformation and $\{e_a\}$ be an orthonormal tetrad. Then L can be realised in a matrix form,

$$L(e_a) = L_a^c e_c \tag{2.6}$$

L_a^c is the matrix of L in the tetrad basis $\{e_a\}$.

Let $A, B \epsilon M$ and under L get mapped to C, D respectively. Then,

$$C^c = L_a^c A^a, \qquad D^d = L_b^d B^b. \tag{2.7}$$

The invariance of inner product implies $A.B = C.D$, *i.e.*,

$$\eta_{cd} C^c D^d = \eta_{cd} L_a^c L_b^d A^a B^b = \eta_{ab} A^a B^b \tag{2.8}$$

Since A, B are arbitrary vectors we get the relation,

$$\eta_{cd} L_a^c L_b^d = \eta_{ab} \tag{2.9}$$

Taking determinants on both sides of this equation gives,

$$\det(L) = \pm 1 \tag{2.10}$$

Clearly, since inner products are preserved under Lorentz transformations, orthonormal tetrads are mapped to orthonormal tetrads; and the converse is also true that, any transformation which maps orthonormal tetrads to orthonormal tetrads is a Lorentz transformation. If $\det(L) = 1$ then the orientation of the tetrad is preserved; if a Lorentz transformation preserves the time orientation as well, it is said to be *restricted*. A restricted Lorentz transformation carries a restricted tetrad to a restricted tetrad and conversely.

3. Tetrads in Curved Spacetimes

Let M be a spacetime manifold endowed with a metric g. Then the tangent space at each point is a Minkowski space and considerations of the last section apply at each point of the spacetime. We assume that the connection is Riemannian (no torsion) satisfying,

$$\nabla g = 0. \tag{3.1}$$

Consider a chart U of M with coordinates $x^i, i = 0, 1, 2, 3$. We will restrict our attention to this region. To each point of this region we assign a tetrad $\{e_a(x^i)\}$. We have now a tetrad *field* on U. We will assume that each vector field $e_a(x^i)$ is smooth so that the tetrads are chosen in a smooth way. In the coordinate basis we write,

$$e_a(x) = e_a^i(x)\frac{\partial}{\partial x^i} \tag{3.2}$$

where the symbol x stands for the dependence of a quantity on a spacetime point in M. For each a, e_a^i are the components of e_a in the coordinate basis $\frac{\partial}{\partial x^i}$. The $e_a^i(x)$ at each point x are 16 numbers which form a nonsingular matrix.

If g_{ij} be the components of g in the coordinate basis then we define the following,
   (i) the covariant $e_{ai} = g_{ij}e_a^j$ and,
   (ii) e_i^b via the equations,

$$e_i^b e_a^i = \delta_a^b. \tag{3.3}$$

An orthonormal tetrad field can be constructed, since the metric g defines an inner product at each point of M. For $\{e_a^i(x)\}$ to be an orthonormal tetrad at each x we require,

$$g_{ij}e_a^i e_b^j = \eta_{ab}, \tag{3.4}$$

where η_{ab} is defined as in the last section. It is also useful to have η^{ab} which is just the inverse of the matrix η_{ab}. Thus,

$$\eta^{ab}\eta_{bc} = \delta_c^a. \tag{3.5}$$

Given a vector field V, it can be expanded either in the coordinate basis or the tetrad basis. Thus,

$$V = V^i\frac{\partial}{\partial x^i}, \tag{3.6a}$$

$$V = V^a e_a. \tag{3.6b}$$

V^i are the coordinate basis components and V^a are the tetrad components. We further obtain relations between the two: Expanding e_a in the coordinate basis, using equations (3.6a,b) and equating components, we obtain,

$$V^i = V^a e_a^i. \tag{3.7a}$$

The opposite relation is easily obtained on multiplying equation (3.7a) by e_i^b.

$$V^a = V^i e_i^a. \tag{3.7b}$$

The advantage we have in constructing tetrad components V^a is that, they are *scalars* under coordinate transformations. The idea is to project relevant quantities on a tetrad basis and consider the equations satisfied by them. Hopefully, these equations will be simpler if the tetrad is chosen judiciously.

We can raise and lower tetrad indices just like coordinate indices. Here the η_{ab} plays the role of g_{ij}. For instance,

$$V^a = \eta^{ab} V_b, \qquad V_a = \eta_{ab} V^b. \tag{3.8}$$

More generally, we can obtain tetrad components of any tensor:

$$T_{ab} = e_a^i e_b^j T_{ij}, \tag{3.9a}$$

and switch back to the coordinate basis components,

$$T_{ij} = e_i^a e_j^b T_{ab}. \tag{3.9b}$$

The extension to higher rank tensors is obvious.

Example: The Schwarzschild Metric

$$ds^2 = (1 - \frac{2m}{r})dt^2 - (1 - \frac{2m}{r})^{-1}dr^2 - r^2(d\theta^2 + \sin^2\theta d\phi^2) \tag{3.10}$$

An orthonormal tetrad field on the region $r > 2m$:

$$e_t = (1 - \frac{2m}{r})^{-\frac{1}{2}}\frac{\partial}{\partial t}$$

$$e_r = (1 - \frac{2m}{r})^{\frac{1}{2}}\frac{\partial}{\partial r} \tag{3.11}$$

$$e_\theta = \frac{1}{r}\frac{\partial}{\partial \theta}$$

$$e_\phi = \frac{1}{r\sin\theta}\frac{\partial}{\partial \phi}$$

This tetrad field corresponds to static observers of the Schwarzschild spacetime. The worldline of such an observer has r, θ, ϕ constant. The 4-velocity vector of this observer is precisely e_t. If P is the 4- momentum of a test-particle then $P_t = P.e_t$ is the energy of the particle as measured by a static observer.

4. Directional Derivatives and Ricci Rotation Coefficients

Suppose we have a scalar field ϕ, say, the electrostatic potential defined over a region of $\mathcal{R}^3$ the electric field component in a direction of the unit vector $\bar{n}$ is given by, $\bar{n}.\nabla\phi$ (disregarding the minus sign); it is the directional derivative of ϕ in the direction of $\bar{n}$. This concept can be generalised to curved spacetimes.

Let ϕ be smooth scalar field defined over a region of M. Then the directional derivative of ϕ in the direction of e_a is just,

$$e_a(\phi) = e_a^i \frac{\partial \phi}{\partial x^i} = \phi_{,a} \tag{4.1}$$

Observe that any vector field defines a directional derivative, in particular, so do each of the vector fields constituting a tetrad.

Now, consider a vector field $A = A^a e_a = A_a e^a$ and take the directional derivative of a component scalar field A_a in the direction of e_b, $A_{a,b}$. What is $A_{a,b}$?

$$
\begin{aligned}
A_{a,b} &= e_b^i \frac{\partial}{\partial x^i} A_a \\
&= e_b^i \frac{\partial}{\partial x^i} (e_a^k A_k) \\
&= e_b^i (e_a^k A_k)_{;i} \\
&= e_b^i e_{a;i}^k A_k + e_b^i e_a^k A_{k;i} \\
&= e_b^i e_{a;i}^k e_{ck} A^c + e_b^i A_{k;i} e_a^k \\
&= \gamma_{cab} A^c + A_{a;b} \tag{4.2}
\end{aligned}
$$

$$\text{where, } \gamma_{cab} = e_c^k e_{ak;i} e_b^i \tag{4.3}$$

$$\text{and } A_{a;b} = e_a^k A_{k;i} e_b^i. \tag{4.4}$$

γ_{cab} are called the *Ricci rotation coefficients*. The name stems from the following:

Parallely drag e_a along the integral curve of e_b and take its scalar product with e_c. This is γ_{cab}. It describes the rotation of e_a, when dragged along e_b with respect to e_c.

We also observe that,

$$
\begin{aligned}
A_{a;b} &= A_{a,b} - \gamma_{cab}A^c \\
&= A_{a,b} - \gamma^c{}_{ab}A_c
\end{aligned}
\tag{4.5}
$$

where we define,

$$
\gamma^c{}_{ab} = \eta^{cd}\gamma_{dab}.
\tag{4.6}
$$

This formula is like the usual one of the covariant derivative of a covariant vector. This *is* the formula for the covariant derivative of A but in the *tetrad basis*. The γ's are precisely the connection coefficients in the tetrad basis:

$$
\gamma_{cab} = e_c . \nabla_{e_b} e_a.
\tag{4.7}
$$

It can be easily shown that the γ's are antisymmetric in the first two indices, *i.e.*,

$$
\gamma_{abc} = -\gamma_{bac}.
\tag{4.8}
$$

Hence there are 24 independent γ's; there are six combinations in the first pair of indices multiplied by four of the last index.

In the absence of torsion we have a simple formula which relates the rotation coefficients to the structure constants $C^c{}_{ab}$ of a tetrad field. The Lie bracket between any two tetrad vector fields can be expanded on the tetrad basis itself:

$$
[e_a, e_b] = C^c{}_{ab}e_c,
\tag{4.9}
$$

$$
\text{then, } C^c{}_{ab} = \gamma^c{}_{ba} - \gamma^c{}_{ab}.
\tag{4.10}
$$

This formula can be used effectively to calculate the γ's.

5. Null Tetrads and Spin Coefficients

The germ of the idea arose from Hermann Bondi who said that to study electromagnetic or gravitational radiation one must analyse the propagation of the fields along null directions. Newman and Penrose made the idea concrete. They introduced null tetrads. This approach is particularly useful in the study of massless fields since they propagate along null directions.

We introduce a set of four linearly independent null vector fields on a region of spacetime which satisfy certain 'orthogonality' conditions. As in the case of orthonormal tetrads the matrix of scalar products between the null vector fields is constant; many of the considerations of the previous sections hold when this is so.

We call the vector fields $l, n, m, \bar{m}$. At a point, l and n are two future directed null vectors, m a complex null vector and $\bar{m}$ the complex conjugate of m. The pairwise scalar products between the vectors are as follows:

$$
l.n = 1, \qquad m.\bar{m} = -1,
\tag{5.1}
$$

and all other scalar products zero. If we label the vectors in the following way:

$$e_0 = l, \quad e_1 = n, \quad e_2 = m, \quad e_3 = \bar{m},$$

the scalar product matrix is,

$$\eta_{ab} = \begin{pmatrix} 0 & 1 & 0 & 0 \\ 1 & 0 & 0 & 0 \\ 0 & 0 & 0 & -1 \\ 0 & 0 & -1 & 0 \end{pmatrix}. \qquad (5.2)$$

The vector m is made up of two unit spacelike vectors a and b, which satisfy the conditions,

$$m = \frac{1}{\sqrt{2}}(a + ib); \quad a.a = b.b = -1, \quad a.b = 0. \qquad (5.3)$$

Example of a null tetrad: Consider Minkowski space and a Cartesian coordinate system. Then a null tetrad in the Cartesian basis is,

$$l^i = \frac{1}{\sqrt{2}}(1,0,0,1), \quad n^i = \frac{1}{\sqrt{2}}(1,0,0,-1), \quad m^i = \frac{1}{\sqrt{2}}(0,1,i,0). \quad (5.4)$$

Note that this *not* the only null tetrad that can be defined on Minkowski space. In fact, a Lorentz transformation acting on the given null tetrad will produce another null tetrad since scalar products are preserved by Lorentz transformations. A six parameter family of such tetrads exists corresponding to the six parameters of the Lorentz group.

The complex null vector is not so bizarre as it looks. Consider a monochromatic plane electromagnetic wave travelling in the z-direction and align the null tetrad so that, $m = \frac{1}{\sqrt{2}}(e_x + ie_y)$ (as in equation (5.4)). Then the projections of the electric and magnetic fields on m are simply the components of one type of *circular* polarisation. The projections of the fields on $\bar{m}$ correspond to the opposite circular polarisation.

6. Null Tetrad Geometry and Null Rotations

We consider a null tetrad at a given point in the spacetime. Therefore without loss of generality we may restrict ourselves to the Minkowski space.

For visualising the null tetrad, let us for the time being, suppress one space dimension of the Minkowski space, say, the z dimension. We are now left with the coordinates t, x, y. The light cone is given by the equation,

$$t^2 - x^2 - y^2 = 0. \qquad (6.1)$$

Given a vector A the vectors (t, x, y) orthogonal to A obey the linear equation,

$$A^t t - A^x x - A^y y = 0 \qquad (6.2)$$

and lie in a plane, say, Π. For example if A^t is nonzero and $A^x = A^y = 0$ the vectors orthogonal to A clearly lie in the (x, y) plane. But, now if one tilts A from the t-axis the plane Π tilts *towards* A. This is the consequence of the indefinite metric. If A is timelike, the plane is *spacelike*, *i.e.*, it consists of only spacelike vectors. If one tilts A until it lies on the lightcone the plane tilts 'upwards' until it is tangent to the lightcone and A *lies* in it (see figure (1)). A is at the same time tangent and normal to the plane. This is consistent with $A.A = 0$; a null vector is orthogonal to itself. Π now consists of all spacelike vectors except for A, which is null, and its multiples. The plane Π is called *null*. If one tilts A still further it becomes spacelike and Π becomes timelike consisting of timelike, null and spacelike vectors; the plane now slices the lightcone. All these statements obtained from visual intuition can be rigorously proved using Schwarz inequalities etc.

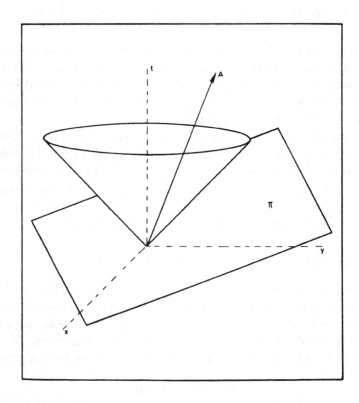

The transition to the full 4−dimensional spacetime can be made in an obvious way. The 2−dimesional plane gets replaced by a 3−dimensional hyperplane but the rest of the discussion remains the same. This intuition can be used to visualise the null tetrad.

We can get a null tetrad by the following prescription:

Choose l anywhere on the future lightcone which automatically sets $l.l = 0$. There are 3 degrees of freedom for choice of l. n has to be chosen again on the future lightcone taking care that it is not a multiple of l. n should be chosen to have a different spatial direction from that of l. Clearly, then $l.n \neq 0$, in fact since l and n are both future timelike $l.n > 0$. By multiplying n by a suitable scalar we can make $l.n = 1$. There are 2 degrees of freedom in choosing n. Now m remains to be chosen. m is determined if a and b are given. We observe that a and b should be orthogonal to both l and n. Let Π and Π' be the null hyperplanes orthogonal to l and n respectively. Then $\Pi \cap \Pi'$ is a spacelike 2-plane which must contain a and b. Choose a anywhere in $\Pi \cap \Pi'$. b gets fixed since $a.b = 0$. There is 1 degree of freedom for choosing a, a rotation in the 2-plane $\Pi \cap \Pi'$. The null tetrad is now fully constructed. The total number of degrees of freedom of constructing the null tetrad are 6, corresponding to the 6 parameter Lorentz group.

Since a Lorentz transformation preserves scalar products it maps a null tetrad to another null tetrad. If the Lorentz transformation is restricted, the future directedness of l and n is preserved and the space orientation is also preseved. Also if one begins with a null tetrad and applies all possible Lorentz transformations to it one produces all the null tetrads. The 6 degrees of freedom in the choice of the null tetrad then correspond to the 6 parameters of the Lorentz group. These transformations of the null tetrad are called *null rotations*. The null rotations help in simplifying the equations in the null tetrad formalism. The alignment of the tetrads to suit a particular situation is very crucial in obtaining solutions.

A simple example of a null rotation is a boost in the (l, n) plane. It has the effect of multiplying l by a scalar α. The n then gets multiplied by $\frac{1}{\alpha}$ to preserve the condition $l.n = 1$; m remains unchanged. Physically, we may imagine a wave of a massless field (e.g. electromagnetic) whose wave vector is l. The multiplying of l by α is equivalent to changing the frequency of the wave or Doppler shifting the wave.

7. Spin Coefficients and Weyl Scalars

Consider a smooth null tetrad field on a region of a spacetime M (the region could extend to include the entire spacetime). The Ricci coefficients of rotations for a null tetrad field are called *spin coefficients*. We label the tetrad vectors as above and the spin coefficients are denoted by γ_{abc}, where a, b, c

take the values $0, 1, 2, 3$. There are special symbols in the NP formalism for denoting γ's or their combinations based on geometrical significance.

$$
\begin{aligned}
\kappa &= \gamma_{200} & \rho &= \gamma_{200} & \epsilon &= 1/2(\gamma_{100} + \gamma_{230}) \\
\sigma &= \gamma_{202} & \mu &= \gamma_{132} & \gamma &= 1/2(\gamma_{101} + \gamma_{231}) \\
\lambda &= \gamma_{133} & \tau &= \gamma_{201} & \alpha &= 1/2(\gamma_{103} + \gamma_{233}) \\
\nu &= \gamma_{131} & \pi &= \gamma_{130} & \beta &= 1/2(\gamma_{102} + \gamma_{232})
\end{aligned}
\tag{7.1}
$$

There are 12 complex spin coefficients, corresponding to the 24 real γ's in case of real tetrad fields.

In the NP formalism the directional derivatives in the directions of the tetrad vectors are represented by special symbols:

$$
D = l^i \frac{\partial}{\partial x^i}, \qquad \Delta = n^i \frac{\partial}{\partial x^i}, \qquad \delta = m^i \frac{\partial}{\partial x^i}, \qquad \bar{\delta} = \bar{m}^i \frac{\partial}{\partial x^i}. \tag{7.2}
$$

The spin coefficients have useful geometrical properties. For example, if $\kappa = 0$ then the congruence of l (integral curves of the vector field l) are geodesic. If in addition $\nu = 0$ then the n congruence is geodetic, etc. A judicious choice of the null tetrad field therefore can simplify the resulting equations by making some of the coefficients vanish.

Other quantities which are important are the *Weyl scalars* particularly in the source free regions of a spacetime. It is known that the Riemann tensor can be written as a sum of two terms: the Weyl tensor, and a term involving the Ricci tensor. In the absence of matter the Ricci tensor vanishes and the Riemann tensor is the same as the Weyl tensor. The Weyl tensor possesses all the symmetries of the Riemann tensor and in addition satisfies,

$$
g^{jl} C_{ijkl} = 0 \tag{7.3}
$$

The Weyl tensor C_{ijkl} has 10 independent components. In the NP formalism there are 5 complex scalars – the *Weyl scalars* – obtained by projecting the Weyl tensor on the null tetrad. Thus,

$$
\begin{aligned}
\Psi_0 &= -C_{ijkl} l^i m^j l^k m^l \\
\Psi_1 &= -C_{ijkl} l^i n^j l^k m^l \\
\Psi_2 &= -C_{ijkl} l^i m^j \bar{m}^k n^l \\
\Psi_3 &= -C_{ijkl} l^i n^j \bar{m}^k n^l \\
\Psi_4 &= -C_{ijkl} n^i \bar{m}^j n^k \bar{m}^l.
\end{aligned}
\tag{7.4}
$$

To complete the story the Ricci tensor is projected on to the null tetrad and the resulting scalars are denoted by Φs. We then have:

$$\Phi_{00} = -\frac{1}{2}R_{ij}l^i l^j, \Phi_{22} = -\frac{1}{2}R_{ij}n^i n^j, \Phi_{02} = -\frac{1}{2}R_{ij}m^i m^j,$$

$$\Phi_{20} = -\frac{1}{2}R_{ij}\bar{m}^i \bar{m}^j, \Phi_{10} = -\frac{1}{2}R_{ij}l^i \bar{m}^j$$

$$\Phi_{01} = -\frac{1}{2}R_{ij}l^i m^j, \Phi_{12} = -\frac{1}{2}R_{ij}n^i m^j, \Phi_{21} = -\frac{1}{2}R_{ij}n^i \bar{m}^j,$$

$$\Phi_{11} = -\frac{1}{4}R_{ij}(l^i n^j + m^i \bar{m}^j). \tag{7.5}$$

and the scalar curvature R is given in terms of $\Lambda = -\frac{1}{24}R$. The Einstein equations can now be written in terms of the quantities defined above. One then obtains 18 complex equations. We do not list them here and do not pursue this point any further. Instead we go over to the Maxwell equations where the power of the formalism can be seen in the elegant way the equations decouple.

8. The Maxwell Equations in the NP Formalism

If F_{ij} is the electromagnetic field tensor then the source-free Maxwell equations are,

$$F_{[ij;k]} = 0 \qquad g^{ik}F_{ij;k} = 0. \tag{8.1}$$

In the tetrad basis the i, j, k are replaced by a, b, c where projections are taken on the tetrad basis.

In the NP formalism the 6 independent components of the F_{ij} are replaced by 3 complex scalars called Teukolsky scalars,

$$\phi_0 = F_{ij}l^i m^j$$

$$\phi_1 = \frac{1}{2}F_{ij}(l^i n^j + \bar{m}^i m^j)$$

$$\phi_2 = F_{ij}\bar{m}^i n^j. \tag{8.2}$$

The Maxwell equations can readily be put in terms of the ϕ_s, the spin coefficients and the directional derivatives. They take the following form,

$$D\phi_1 - \bar{\delta}\phi_0 = (\pi - 2\alpha)\phi_0 + 2\rho\phi_1 - \kappa\phi_2$$
$$D\phi_2 - \bar{\delta}\phi_1 = -\lambda\phi_0 + 2\pi\phi_1 + (\rho - 2\epsilon)\phi_2$$
$$\delta\phi_1 - \Delta\phi_0 = (\mu - 2\gamma)\phi_0 + 2\tau\phi_1 - \sigma\phi_2$$
$$\delta\phi_2 - \Delta\phi_1 = -\nu\phi_0 + 2\mu\phi_1 + (\tau - 2\beta)\phi_2. \tag{8.3}$$

Although the equations may look cumbersome they can take a simple form in a number of cases with judicious choice of a null tetrad field. We consider the very simple case of the flat spacetime where the solution is required in polar coordinates. The method is less cumbersome than the usual method of vector spherical harmonics. Note that the method is applicable to more complex situations.

Example: Maxwell's equations in flat spacetime.
Polar coordinates: (t, r, θ, ϕ)
The null tetrad:

$$l^i = (1, 1, 0, 0), \quad n^i = \frac{1}{2}(1, -1, 0, 0), \quad m^i = \frac{1}{r\sqrt{2}}(0, 0, 1, \frac{i}{\sin\theta}) \quad (8.4)$$

The directional derivatives:

$$D = \partial_t + \partial_r, \quad \Delta = \frac{1}{2}(\partial_t - \partial_r), \quad \delta = \frac{1}{r\sqrt{2}}(\partial_\theta + \frac{i}{\sin\theta}\partial_\phi) \quad (8.5)$$

The nonvanishing spin coefficients:

$$\rho = -\frac{1}{r}, \quad \beta = -\alpha = \frac{\cot\theta}{2\sqrt{2}r}, \quad \mu = -\frac{1}{2r} \quad (8.6)$$

The Maxwell equations:

$$(\partial_t + \partial_r + \frac{2}{r})\phi_1 - \frac{1}{r\sqrt{2}}(\partial_\theta - \frac{i}{\sin\theta}\partial_\phi + \cot\theta)\phi_0 = 0$$

$$(\partial_t + \partial_r + \frac{1}{r})\phi_2 - \frac{1}{r\sqrt{2}}(\partial_\theta - \frac{i}{\sin\theta}\partial_\phi)\phi_1 = 0$$

$$\frac{1}{r\sqrt{2}}(\partial_\theta - \frac{i}{\sin\theta}\partial_\phi + \cot\theta)\phi_2 - \frac{1}{2}(\partial_t - \partial_r - \frac{2}{r})\phi_0 = 0$$

$$\frac{1}{r\sqrt{2}}(\partial_\theta + \frac{i}{\sin\theta}\partial_\phi)\phi_1 - \frac{1}{2}(\partial_t - \partial_r - \frac{1}{r})\phi_0 = 0. \quad (8.7)$$

From the above equations one can easily obtain decoupled equations for the field quantities ϕ_s. For example the decoupled equation for ϕ_0 is obtained from the first and the last equations in (8.7). We can operate on the first equation with a suitable operator and eliminate ϕ_1 to obtain a second order equation for ϕ_0. Thus,

$$[(\partial_t + \partial_r + \frac{2}{r})r(\partial_t - \partial_r - \frac{1}{r}) - \frac{1}{r}(\partial_\theta + \frac{i}{\sin\theta}\partial_\phi)(\partial_\theta - \frac{i}{\sin\theta}\partial_\phi + \cot\theta)]\phi_0 = 0. \quad (8.8)$$

Decoupled equations for ϕ_1 and ϕ_2 can be similarly obtained. The Maxwell tensor is easily computed from the ϕ_s. The reverse relation is,

$$F_{ij} = \phi_0(\bar{m}_i n_j - n_i\bar{m}_j) + \phi_1(n_i l_j + m_i\bar{m}_j) + \phi_2(l_i m_j - m_i l_j) + c.c. \quad (8.9)$$

9. The Optical Scalars, Propagation of Shadows

If l^i a vector field, then the family of integral curves $x^i(\lambda)$ of l^i are called the congruence of l^i. The congruence $x^i(\lambda)$ is generated by integrating the differential equations,

$$\frac{dx^i}{d\lambda} = l^i. \tag{9.1}$$

If the curves $x^i(\lambda)$ are null geodesics then they satisfy,

$$l^i l_i = 0, \qquad l^i{}_{;k} l^k = 0. \tag{9.2}$$

Physically, the congruence could represent light rays. We can study the properties of such light rays by the shadows cast on a screen by objects inserted in their path. If the screen is held not too far from the object, the image is determined by the irreducible tensors $l_{i;k}$ can be decomposed into by the Lorentz group. The optical behaviour is given by three scalar fields called the *optical scalars* constructed from $l_{i;k}$.

The *Ehlers-Sachs* theorem brings out the relationship between the object and the shadow in terms of the optical scalars. Let a small plane circular disc be interposed in the path of the light rays so that the rays are perpendicular to it. Then the shadow on a nearby screen, also held perpendicular to the rays, is elliptical. If the screen is at a distance $\delta\lambda$ from the disc then the shadow is expanded, sheared and rotated with respect to the disc by the amounts $\theta\,\delta\lambda, \omega\,\delta\lambda, |\sigma|\,\delta\lambda$, respectively where,

$$\theta = \frac{1}{2} l^i{}_{;i}, \qquad \omega = \left[\frac{1}{2} l_{[i,k]} l^{i;k}\right]^{\frac{1}{2}}, \qquad |\sigma| = \left[\frac{1}{2} l_{(i;k)} l^{i;k} - \theta^2\right]^{\frac{1}{2}} \tag{9.3}$$

The quantities θ, ω and σ are the expansion, twist and shear respectively of the congruence l^i.

Proof: Let u^i be the 4-velocity of the frame in which the disc and the screen are at rest. Consider the spacelike hyperplane orthogonal to u^i. The projection of l^i on this hyperplane is the 'space' direction of the rays as seen by the observer whose 4-velocity is u^i. Choose n^i in the 2-plane determined by u^i and l^i satisfying the usual conditions of being future null and $l^i n_i = 1$. The projection of n^i in the hyperplane is a vector whose direction is opposite to the space direction of the rays as seen by the observer u^i. Consequently m^i lies in a plane parallel to the plane of the disc and screen. There is one degree of freedom of rotation for m^i about the space direction of the rays. We may fix m^i arbitrarily but orthogonal to the space direction of the rays. This specifies the null tetrad.

Consider two neighbouring rays (null geodesics whose tangent vector is l^i); the relative positions of these curves is given by a connecting vector

ζ^i which connects points of equal λ of the l^i congruence. The connecting vector ζ^i satisfies the conditions $\zeta^i u_i = 0$ and $\zeta^i l_i = 0$. This may be seen as follows:

We choose the parametrisation of the l^i congruence so that the rays have the same value of the affine parameter at the object. Hence $\zeta^i u_i = 0$. The rays leave the disc simultaneously. But the rays are orthogonal to the disc:

$$\zeta^i(\delta_i^k - u^k u_i)l_k = 0 \tag{9.4}$$

Using $\zeta^i u_i = 0$ we get the condition $\zeta^i l_i = 0$.

Therefore, ζ^i lies in the plane determined by m^i,

$$\zeta^i = \bar{\zeta} m^i + \zeta \bar{m}^i \tag{9.5}$$

By definition, the Lie derivative of the connecting vector along the l^i congruence must vanish:

$$\mathcal{L}_l \zeta^i = 0, \qquad \zeta^i{}_{;k} l^k = l^i{}_{;k} \zeta^k \tag{9.6}$$

Consider,

$$(l_i \zeta^i)_{;k} l^k \quad = l_{i;k} l^k \zeta^i + l_i(\zeta^i{}_{;k} l^k) \quad = \quad 0, \tag{9.7}$$

since l^i is geodesic and a vector of constant(zero) length.

$l^i \zeta_i$ is constant along the rays with the constant being zero. Let m^i be parallely transported along the rays then,

$$m^i{}_{;k} l^k = 0 \tag{9.8}$$

and equation (9.5) holds along the rays. Contracting equation (9.5) with m_i, differentiating along l^i and using equation (9.6) we get after some algebra,

$$-\frac{d\zeta}{d\lambda} = \bar{\zeta}\sigma + \zeta\rho \tag{9.9}$$

Therefore the rays define a mapping from the object to the image by, $\zeta \to \zeta + \delta\zeta$ where $\delta\zeta = \frac{d\zeta}{d\lambda}\delta\lambda$. Then the vector of the shadow ζ' is given by,

$$\zeta' = \zeta + \delta\zeta = \zeta(1 - \rho\delta\lambda) - \bar{\zeta}\sigma\delta\lambda \tag{9.10}$$

Let $\zeta = e^{i\theta}$ trace a unit circle, say the rim of a disc, then,

$$\zeta' = (1 - \rho\delta\lambda)e^{i\theta} - \sigma\delta\lambda e^{-i\theta} \tag{9.11}$$

If we work to a linear order in $\delta\lambda$ then ζ' describes an ellipse as θ ranges from 0 to 2π. The stationary values of $\zeta'\bar{\zeta}'$ are, $1 - (\rho + \bar{\rho} \pm |\sigma|)\delta\lambda$. The area of the ellipse is obtained by multiplying these two values and π. To the first order in $\delta\lambda$ the area is,

$$A = \pi[1 - (\rho + \bar{\rho})\delta\lambda]. \tag{9.12}$$

The linear expansion θ is the square root of the ratio of A to the area of the unit circle. Thus to the first order in $\delta\lambda$ we have,

$$\theta = 1 - \frac{1}{2}(\rho + \bar{\rho})\delta\lambda, \tag{9.13a}$$

$$\text{shear} = \frac{1 - \frac{1}{2}(\rho + \bar{\rho} + |\sigma|)\delta\lambda}{1 - \frac{1}{2}(\rho + \bar{\rho} - |\sigma|)\delta\lambda}$$

$$= 1 + |\sigma|\delta\lambda, \tag{9.13b}$$

$$\text{twist} = \langle arg(\frac{\zeta'}{\zeta})\rangle_{average} = \text{Im}(\rho)\delta\lambda. \tag{9.13c}$$

where $\text{Im}(\rho)$ is the imaginary part of ρ. This completes the proof of the Ehlers-Sachs theorem. The quantities expansion, shear and twist are illustrated in figure (2).

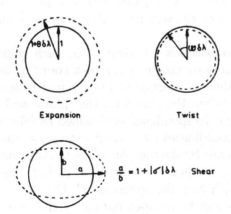

Expansion   Twist

$$\frac{a}{b} = 1 + |\sigma|\delta\lambda \quad \text{Shear}$$

10. Spinors

So far we had represented each vector of the Minkowski space by an ordered set of 4 real numbers. Alternatively, we could do the same with complex numbers. A real vector can be equally well represented by a 2×2 Hermitian matrix. In particular we would like to represent null vectors in this way and obtain a coordinatisation of the null cone. This naturally leads to the concept of a spinor. A spinor, basically, at a spacetime point is an ordered pair of complex numbers corresponding to a restricted tetrad at the point subject to a specified group of transformations. An interesting aspect of this transformation law is that the spinor flips sign when the basis in the tangent space is rotated through 2π. Spinors arise naturally in the quantum theory but have also proved to be very useful in the classical scenario. For example, Witten's proof of the positivity of mass conjecture employed spinorial techniques. Ashtekar's variables are spinorial in nature.

We shall first consider spinors in Minkowski space and later when we discuss spinor analysis we will go over to curved spacetimes. We will start by assigning complex coordinates to the null cone.

At first consider just the "null directions". A general null vector with components (t, x, y, z) satisfies

$$x^2 + y^2 + z^2 = t^2 \qquad (10.1)$$

Since we are only considering null directions we can take any representative vector for a given null direction; $t = 1$ slice of the null cone. On this slice the null vector components satisfy,

$$x^2 + y^2 + z^2 = 1 \qquad (10.2)$$

This is an equation of a sphere of unit radius and is called the *Riemann sphere* which we denote by S. Physically, if a point source emits an electromagnetic wave then the wavefront after say one second is an example of such a sphere.

We now assign complex coordinates to each point on the Riemann sphere. This amounts to assigning complex coordinates to null directions. We use the so called *stereographic projection* to establish a one to one correspondence between the points on the sphere and the complex plane. Geometrically, the correspondence is obtained as follows:

Choose polar coordinates : $x = \sin\theta \cos\varphi$, $y = \sin\theta \sin\varphi$, $z = \cos\theta$, and let the (x, y) plane be the complex plane $\mathcal{C}$. Any point $P' \in \mathcal{C}$ is mapped on to the sphere by joining P' to the point $(0, 0, 1)$, the North pole, N, by a straight line which cuts the sphere at P. Conversely, any point, except N, from the sphere can be mapped onto $\mathcal{C}$ by the inverse mapping. This is shown in figure (3).

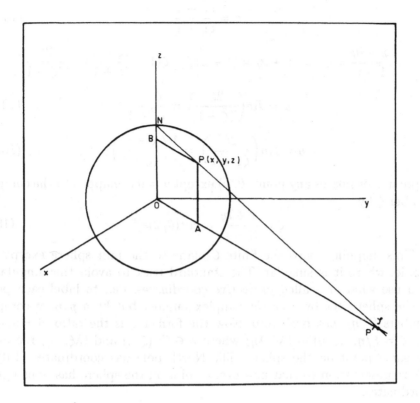

The following relations obtain:

$$P' : \zeta = x' + iy' \rightarrow P : (x, y, z)$$

$$\zeta = OP' = \alpha OA = \alpha(x + iy)$$

$$\text{where, } \alpha = \frac{OP'}{OA}.$$

Triangles NOP' and NBP are similar. Thus

$$\alpha = \frac{OP'}{OA} = \frac{OP'}{BP} = \frac{ON}{BN} = \frac{1}{1-z}$$

$$\zeta = \frac{x + iy}{1 - z}$$

The inverse mapping is given by

$$\zeta\bar{\zeta} = \frac{x^2 + y^2}{(1-z)^2} = \frac{1-z^2}{(1-z)^2} = \frac{1+z}{1-z}$$

$$z = \frac{\zeta\bar{\zeta} - 1}{\zeta\bar{\zeta} + 1} \tag{10.3a}$$

$$\frac{x + iy}{1 - z} = \zeta \;\Rightarrow\; x + iy = (1 - z)\zeta = \zeta(1 - \frac{\zeta\bar{\zeta} - 1}{\zeta\bar{\zeta} + 1}) = \frac{2\zeta}{\zeta\bar{\zeta} + 1}$$

$$x = Re\left(\frac{2\zeta}{\zeta\bar{\zeta} + 1}\right) = \frac{\zeta + \bar{\zeta}}{\zeta\bar{\zeta} + 1} \tag{10.3b}$$

$$y = Im\left(\frac{2\zeta}{\zeta\bar{\zeta} + 1}\right) = \frac{1}{i}\left(\frac{\zeta - \bar{\zeta}}{\zeta\bar{\zeta} + 1}\right) \tag{10.3c}$$

In polar coordinates any point (θ, ϕ) except $\theta = 0$ is mapped to the complex number ζ by,

$$\zeta = \frac{x + iy}{1 - z} = \cot(\theta/2)e^{i\phi} \tag{10.4}$$

This mapping maps the finite C-plane to the unit sphere except the N-pole, where it is singular. The standard trick to avoid this singularity is to use what are called *projective coordinates*, *i.e.*, to label each point on the sphere not by a *single* complex number but by a *pair* of complex numbers (ξ, η), not both zero. Now the former ζ is the ratio of ξ and η, *i.e.*, $\zeta = \xi/\eta$, $(\xi, \eta) \sim (\lambda\xi, \lambda\eta)$ where $\lambda \in C$; (ξ, η) and $(\lambda\xi, \lambda\eta)$ represent the same point on the sphere. The North pole has coordinates $(1,0)$ in this representation so that now every point on the sphere has nonsingular coordinates.

11. Null vectors in terms of the projective coordinates

Consider a point (x, y, z) in S and along with $t = 1$, we have the 4-vector $(1, x, y, z)$. This is a null vector and can be represented in terms of (ξ, η) : Using the relation $\zeta = \frac{\xi}{\eta}$ and equations (10.3) we obtain,

$$t = 1, \quad x = \frac{\xi\bar{\eta} + \bar{\xi}\eta}{\xi\bar{\xi} + \eta\bar{\eta}}, \quad y = \frac{\xi\bar{\eta} - \bar{\xi}\eta}{\xi\bar{\xi} + \eta\bar{\eta}}, \quad z = \frac{\xi\bar{\xi} - \bar{\eta}\eta}{\xi\bar{\xi} + \eta\bar{\eta}}, \tag{11.1}$$

In order to get rid of denominators, we slice not by $t = 1$ but by $t = \xi\bar{\xi} + \eta\bar{\eta}$, . The point P on S becomes R where $OR = OP(\xi\bar{\xi} + \eta\bar{\eta})$:

$$t = \frac{1}{\sqrt{2}}(\xi\bar{\xi} + \eta\bar{\eta})$$

$$x = \frac{1}{\sqrt{2}}(\xi\bar{\eta} + \eta\bar{\xi})$$

$$y = \frac{1}{\sqrt{2}}(\xi\bar{\eta} - \eta\bar{\xi})$$

$$z = \frac{1}{\sqrt{2}}(\xi\bar{\xi} - \eta\bar{\eta}) \tag{11.2}$$

or in matrix form,

$$\begin{bmatrix} \xi\bar{\xi} & \xi\bar{\eta} \\ \bar{\xi}\eta & \eta\bar{\eta} \end{bmatrix} = \frac{1}{\sqrt{2}} \begin{bmatrix} t+z & x+iy \\ x-iy & t-z \end{bmatrix} \tag{11.3}$$

This is a Hermitian matrix.

Since the row vectors are proportional to each other the determinant of the matrix on the left hand side of equation (11.3) is zero. This implies that (t, x, y, z) are components of a null vector. Thus the 2 complex numbers ξ and η can be used to represent a null vector. One writes these as a pair,

$$\begin{bmatrix} \xi \\ \eta \end{bmatrix} \in \mathcal{C}^2$$

It is convenient in case of transformations to use an index notation for the pair $(\xi, \eta) \cdot \rightarrow (\xi^0, \xi^1)$. Thus:

$$\xi^A = \begin{bmatrix} \xi^0 \\ \xi^1 \end{bmatrix}, \quad A = 0, 1. \tag{11.4}$$

12. SL(2,$\mathcal{C}$) Group of Transformations

Consider a pair of complex numbers; to this pair there corresponds a future directed null vector given through the equation (11.3). Now consider a restricted Lorentz transformation acting on the null vector. It produces another future directed null vector. But to this null vector there must, in general, correspond another pair of complex numbers. In this way a Lorentz transformation forces a transformation on pairs of complex numbers, *i.e.*, on $\mathcal{C}^2$. This transformation is linear and can be represented by a 2×2 matrix of complex numbers L_B^A which satisfies certain conditions.

$$L_B^A = \begin{bmatrix} \alpha & \beta \\ \gamma & \delta \end{bmatrix}, \quad \alpha, \beta, \gamma, \delta \in \mathcal{C}$$

The condition imposed is $\det[L] = 1$. Such matrices form a group under multiplication denoted by SL(2,$\mathcal{C}$) – *special linear group of 2×2 matrices over complex numbers*. By a simple counting argument, it has six free real parameters corresponding to those of the Lorentz group. For a Lorentz transformation acting on Minkowski space, there are strictly speaking two transformations $\pm L_B^A \in$ SL(2,$\mathcal{C}$) but this sign ambiguity may be resolved by choosing a path connected to the identity transformation. There is more discussion about this in section 18.

Definition: A spinor ξ^A of rank 1 is complex vector $\in C^2$ subject to transformations belonging to SL(2,C).

$$\zeta^A = L_B^A \xi^B, \quad \text{where} \quad L_B^A \in \text{SL}(2,C) \tag{12.1}$$

Remember, that the L_B^A corresponds to a Lorentz transformation on the Minkowski space. These are two equations in complex numbers. Clearly the identical content of these equations is present in their complex conjugates.

Definition: The complex conjugate of ξ^A say $\bar{\xi}^{A'}$ transforming according to the complex conjugate of the equation (12.1) is called a *primed* spinor of rank 1:

$$\bar{\zeta}^{A'} = \bar{L}_{B'}^{A'} \bar{\xi}^{B'}. \tag{12.2}$$

If we call $\bar{\xi}^{A'} = \eta^{A'}$ and $\bar{\zeta}^{A'} = \kappa^{A'}$, then the transformation law is

$$\kappa^{A'} = \bar{L}_{B'}^{A'} \eta^{B'} \tag{12.3}$$

where $\bar{L}_{B'}^{A'}$ is the conjugate transpose of L_B^A given by,

$$\bar{L}_{B'}^{A'} = \begin{bmatrix} \bar{\alpha} & \bar{\gamma} \\ \bar{\beta} & \bar{\delta} \end{bmatrix} = \bar{L}. \tag{12.4}$$

We can write these equations in the matrix form:

$$\begin{bmatrix} \zeta^0 \\ \zeta^1 \end{bmatrix} = \begin{bmatrix} \alpha & \beta \\ \gamma & \delta \end{bmatrix} \begin{bmatrix} \xi^0 \\ \xi^1 \end{bmatrix}$$

The complex conjugate of this equation is,

$$\begin{bmatrix} \bar{\zeta}^{0'} & \bar{\zeta}^{1'} \end{bmatrix} = \begin{bmatrix} \bar{\xi}^{0'} & \bar{\xi}^{1'} \end{bmatrix} \begin{bmatrix} \bar{\alpha} & \bar{\gamma} \\ \bar{\beta} & \bar{\delta} \end{bmatrix}$$

Under a spin transformation L a spinor with components ξ, η goes to,

$$\begin{bmatrix} \xi \\ \eta \end{bmatrix} \to L \begin{bmatrix} \xi \\ \eta \end{bmatrix}, \tag{12.5a}$$

and its complex conjugate goes to,

$$\begin{bmatrix} \bar{\xi} & \bar{\eta} \end{bmatrix} \to \begin{bmatrix} \bar{\xi} & \bar{\eta} \end{bmatrix} \bar{L}. \tag{12.5b}$$

Consider the product,

$$\begin{bmatrix} \xi \\ \eta \end{bmatrix} \begin{bmatrix} \bar{\xi} & \bar{\eta} \end{bmatrix} \to L \begin{bmatrix} \xi \\ \eta \end{bmatrix} \begin{bmatrix} \bar{\xi} & \bar{\eta} \end{bmatrix} \bar{L},$$

or

$$\begin{bmatrix} \xi\bar{\xi} & \xi\bar{\eta} \\ \xi\eta & \eta\bar{\eta} \end{bmatrix} \rightarrow L \begin{bmatrix} \xi\bar{\xi} & \xi\bar{\eta} \\ \xi\eta & \eta\bar{\eta} \end{bmatrix} \bar{L}.$$

Transforming back to 4-vector components (equation (11.3)),

$$\begin{bmatrix} \tilde{t}+\tilde{z} & \tilde{x}+i\tilde{y} \\ \tilde{x}-i\tilde{y} & \tilde{t}-\tilde{z} \end{bmatrix} = L \begin{bmatrix} t+z & x+iy \\ x-iy & t-z \end{bmatrix} \bar{L}. \tag{12.6}$$

This last step follows since the RHS of (12.6) is Hermitian (This follows from the fact that if H is Hermitian then $LH\bar{L}$ is Hermitian). Let $\tilde{H} = LH\bar{L}$, then,

$$\det(\tilde{H}) = \det(L)\det(H)\det(\bar{L}) = \det(H)$$

since $\det(L) = \det(\bar{L}) = 1$. Therefore,

$$\tilde{t}^2 - \tilde{x}^2 - \tilde{y}^2 - \tilde{z}^2 = t^2 - x^2 - y^2 - z^2 \tag{12.7}$$

for every vector (t,x,y,z) and L_B^A induces a Lorentz transformation by the above operation. We note that this Lorentz transformation is restricted.

We give some examples of L_B^A in simple cases:

(a) A space rotation by the Euler angles (ϕ,θ,ψ). We follow the Goldstein convention. Then the L matrix is,

$$L = \begin{bmatrix} \cos\frac{\theta}{2}e^{-i\frac{(\phi+\psi)}{2}} & i\sin\frac{\theta}{2}e^{i\frac{(\phi-\psi)}{2}} \\ i\sin\frac{\theta}{2}e^{-i\frac{(\phi-\psi)}{2}} & \cos\frac{\theta}{2}e^{i\frac{(\phi+\psi)}{2}} \end{bmatrix} \tag{12.8a}$$

(b) A boost in the z-direction with velocity v. The L matrix is,

$$L = \begin{bmatrix} w^{\frac{1}{2}} & 0 \\ 0 & w^{-\frac{1}{2}} \end{bmatrix} \tag{12.8b}$$

where, $w = \sqrt{\frac{1-v}{1+v}}$.

13. Spinor Algebra

One can add and multiply rank 1 spinors by complex numbers. They form a 2−dimensional vector space over $\mathcal{C}$. The primed and unprimed spinors give rise to different vector spaces which are however isomorphic. For example,

$$\zeta^A = \lambda\xi^A + \mu\eta^A, \qquad \lambda,\mu \in \mathcal{C} \tag{13.1}$$

is a first rank unprimed spinor if ξ^A and η^A are unprimed first rank spinors.

ϵ-spinor: This spinor plays the role of the metric in spinor algebra. Since we have not yet defined higher rank spinors we will for the moment treat it as a symbol with four components. It is also the Levi-Civita symbol:

$$\epsilon_{AB} = \begin{bmatrix} 0 & 1 \\ -1 & 0 \end{bmatrix}$$

i.e., $\epsilon_{00} = \epsilon_{11} = 0, \epsilon_{01} = -\epsilon_{10} = 1$. We can also define upper index, lower index and primed ϵ- spinors, thus,

$$\epsilon^{AB} = \begin{bmatrix} 0 & 1 \\ -1 & 0 \end{bmatrix}, \epsilon_{A'B'} = \begin{bmatrix} 0 & 1 \\ -1 & 0 \end{bmatrix}, \epsilon^{A'B'} = \begin{bmatrix} 0 & 1 \\ -1 & 0 \end{bmatrix}. \qquad (13.2)$$

Given two spinors ξ^A and η^B we can form their scalar product with the ϵ_{AB},

$$\epsilon_{AB}\xi^A\eta^B = \xi^0\eta^1 - \xi^1\eta^0 = \begin{vmatrix} \xi^0 & \xi^1 \\ \eta^0 & \eta^1 \end{vmatrix}. \qquad (13.3)$$

The scalar product is invariant under a SL(2, C) transformation: Consider an SL(2,C) transformation acting on ξ^A and η^A,

$$\tilde{\xi}^A = L_B^A\xi^B, \qquad \tilde{\eta}^A = L_B^A\eta^B.$$

then,

$$\begin{aligned} \epsilon_{AB}\tilde{\xi}^A\tilde{\eta}^B &= \epsilon_{AB}L_C^A L_D^B\xi^C\eta^D \\ &= (\det L)\epsilon_{CD}\xi^C\eta^D \\ &= \epsilon_{CD}\xi^C\eta^D. \end{aligned} \qquad (13.4)$$

Thus, ϵ_{AB} acts like a metric 2-spinor.
The upper and lower indexed ϵ's are inverses of each other:

$$\epsilon^{AC}\epsilon_{BC} = \delta_B^A. \qquad (13.5)$$

It can be used to raise and lower spinor indices. Thus,

$$\xi_A = \xi^B\epsilon_{BA}, \quad \xi^A = \epsilon^{AB}\xi_B. \qquad (13.6)$$

Remark: Since ϵ_{AB} is anti-symmetric one has to be careful about the order of indices.
Note that

$$\xi_A = \xi^B\epsilon_{BA} = -\xi^B\epsilon_{AB}.$$

Written explicitly, these equations imply

$$\xi_0 = -\xi^1, \quad \xi_1 = \xi^0.$$

Transformation law for ξ_A : We can obtain the transformation law for ξ_A from the transformation law for ξ^A. Let,

$$\tilde{\xi}_A = \ell_A^B \xi_B \tag{13.7}$$

where ℓ_A^B must be determined from the two equations,

$$\tilde{\xi}_A = \tilde{\xi}^B \epsilon_{BA} = L_C^B \xi^C \epsilon_{BA} = L_C^B \epsilon^{CD} \xi_D \epsilon_{BA}, \tag{13.8}$$

$$\text{and } \tilde{\xi}_A = \ell_A^D \xi_D. \tag{13.9}$$

From these two equations we obtain

$$\ell_A^D = L_C^B \epsilon^{CD} \epsilon_{BA} \tag{13.10}$$

Multiplying (13.10) by L_F^A gives,

$$L_F^A \ell_A^D = L_F^A L_C^B \epsilon^{CD} \epsilon_{BA} = \epsilon^{CD} \epsilon_{CF} = \delta_F^D. \tag{13.11}$$

Therefore, ℓ is the inverse of L and ξ_A transforms according to the inverse of L. Analogous to the upper indexed spinors there are spinors which transform according to the complex conjugate of equation (13.7).

$$\tilde{\eta}_{A'} = \bar{\ell}_{A'}^{B'} \eta_{B'} \tag{13.12}$$

Altogether we have four types of first rank spinors.

Penrose see-saw: $\xi^A \eta_A = -\xi_A \eta^A$.
This result follows directly from the antisymmetry of ϵ_{AB}.

$$\begin{aligned} \xi^A \eta_A &= \xi^A \eta^B \epsilon_{BA} \\ &= -\xi^A \epsilon_{AB} \eta^B \\ &= -\xi_B \eta^B. \end{aligned} \tag{13.13}$$

It follows from (13.13) that,

$$\xi^A \xi_A = 0 \tag{13.14}$$

The ϵ-spinor satisfies the following relations:

1. $\epsilon_{A[B} \epsilon_{CD]} = 0$ (Jacobi Identity).
2. $\epsilon_{AB} L_C^A L_D^B = \epsilon_{CD}$ (spinor transformation law).
3. $\epsilon^{AC} \epsilon_{BC} = \delta_B^A$ (inverses).

Spin Dyad

Let ξ^A be a spinor. Consider a spinor η^A such that $\xi_A\eta^A = 1$. The spinors are then linearly independent because then any other spinor ζ^A can be written as a linear combination of them. Suppose we write,

$$\zeta^A = \alpha\xi^A + \beta\eta^A \tag{13.15}$$

then there are solutions for α and β. Taking scalar products of (13.15) with ξ_A and η_A we can solve for α and β. Thus,

$$\alpha = -\eta_A\zeta^A \quad , \qquad \beta = \xi_A\zeta^A \tag{13.16}$$

The pair of spinors $(\xi^A, \quad \eta^A)$ is called a *spin dyad*.

Given a spinor ξ^A, does there exist a η^A such that the pair forms a dyad? The equation $\xi_A\eta^A = 1$ can be written as follows:

$$\epsilon_{AB}\xi^A\eta^B = 1 \tag{13.17}$$

that is,

$$\xi^0\eta^1 - \xi^1\eta^0 = 1.$$

This is just one complex equation for two complex numbers η^0 and η^1. Hence not only does η^A exist but there is one complex degree of freedom too. This freedom is seen as follows: Consider $\hat{\eta}^A = \eta^A + \lambda\xi^A$, then, $\xi_A\hat{\eta}^A = \xi_A\eta^A + \lambda\xi_A\xi^A = 1$. Conversely let $\xi_A\eta^A = \xi_A\hat{\eta}^A = 1$. Set $\zeta^A = \hat{\eta}^A - \eta^A$, then $\xi_A\zeta^A = 0$. This implies that $\zeta^A = \lambda\xi^A$ where $\lambda \in C$. Hence if (ξ^A, η^A) is a spin dyad then $(\xi^A, \hat{\eta}^A)$ is also a spin dyad if and only if $\hat{\eta}^A = \eta^A + \lambda\xi^A$.

Higher rank spinors:

Starting from the first rank spinors it is easy to extend the notion to higher rank spinors. The definition is analogous to tensors which are multilinear mappings over the tangent space and its dual.

In C^2 space fix a basis. In this basis ξ^A are the components of a rank 1 spinor. Under a change of basis $\xi^A \to \tilde{\xi}^A$, where $\tilde{\xi}^A = L_B^A\xi^B$. Consider a quantity $W_{C'}^{AB}$ which transforms as,

$$\tilde{W}_{C'}^{AB} = L_D^A L_E^B \bar{\ell}_{C'}^{F'} W_{F'}^{DE} \tag{13.18}$$

This is a rank 3 spinor with two unprimed upper indices and one lower primed index. Spinors of arbitrary rank, primed or unprimed, upper indexed or lower indexed can be defined in the obvious way as illustrated in the case of the third rank spinor $W_{C'}^{AB}$.

We observe that ϵ_{AB} is a 2nd rank spinor since

$$\epsilon_{AB} = L_A^C L_B^D \epsilon_{CD} \tag{13.19}$$

If $\overline{W^{AA'}} = W^{AA'}$ for a 2-spinor then W is said to be *real* or *Hermitian*. Such a spinor can be associated with real vector in Minkowski space as we shall see in what follows.

14. Connection between tensors and spinors

As seen in §11 we can associate a null vector with a spinor of rank 1 by the correspondence, $\xi^A \to k^\mu$.

$$\begin{bmatrix} \xi^0 \bar{\xi}^{0'} & \xi^0 \bar{\xi}^{1'} \\ \xi^1 \bar{\xi}^{0'} & \xi^1 \bar{\xi}^{1'} \end{bmatrix} = \frac{1}{\sqrt{2}} \begin{bmatrix} k^0 + k^3 & k^1 + ik^2 \\ k^1 - ik^2 & k^0 - k^3 \end{bmatrix}. \tag{14.1}$$

Sometimes, this relation is written more simply as,

$$k^\mu \equiv \xi^A \bar{\xi}^{A'}. \tag{14.2}$$

Clearly, the 2-spinor $\xi^A \bar{\xi}^{A'}$ is Hermitian or real. An obvious extension to this is that if $\overline{W^{AA'}} = W^{AA'}$ is Hermitian then we can associate a real vector w^μ (not necessarily null) by the correspondence:

$$\begin{bmatrix} W^{00'} & W^{01'} \\ W^{10'} & W^{11'} \end{bmatrix} = \frac{1}{\sqrt{2}} \begin{bmatrix} w^0 + w^3 & w^1 + iw^2 \\ w^1 - iw^2 & w^0 - w^3 \end{bmatrix}. \tag{14.3}$$

This is possible since $W^{00'}$ and $W^{11'}$ are real while $\overline{W^{10'}} = W^{01'}$. We write equation (14.3) in an index notation:

$$W^{AA'} = \sigma_\mu^{AA'} w^\mu, \tag{14.4}$$

where we have introduced symbols $\sigma_\mu^{AA'}$ called the Van der Waarden symbols,

$$\sigma_0^{AA'} = \frac{1}{\sqrt{2}} \begin{bmatrix} 1 & 0 \\ 0 & 1 \end{bmatrix}, \qquad \sigma_1^{AA'} = \frac{1}{\sqrt{2}} \begin{bmatrix} 0 & 1 \\ 1 & 0 \end{bmatrix}$$

$$\sigma_2^{AA'} = \frac{1}{\sqrt{2}} \begin{bmatrix} 0 & i \\ -i & 0 \end{bmatrix}, \qquad \sigma_3^{AA'} = \frac{1}{\sqrt{2}} \begin{bmatrix} 1 & 0 \\ 0 & -1 \end{bmatrix}. \tag{14.5}$$

Remark: Note that, except for the factor of $\frac{1}{\sqrt{2}}$ for $\mu = 1, 2$ and 3 these are just Pauli matrices and for $\mu = 0$ it is an identity matrix.

The inverse relation to equation (14.4) exists and is written as,

$$w^\mu = \sigma^\mu_{AA'} W^{AA'}. \tag{14.6}$$

The σ's have the following properties:

1. $\sigma^\mu_{AA'} \sigma_\nu^{AA'} = \delta^\mu_\nu.$

2. $\sigma^{\mu}_{AA'}\sigma^{BB'}_{\mu} = \delta^{B}_{A}\delta^{B'}_{A'}$.

3. Each σ^{μ} is a Hermitian 2×2 matrix.

The σ's therefore give a mapping of tensors to spinors. A tensor of rank n is mapped to a Hermitian spinor of rank $2n$ with n primed and n unprimed indices. Moreover the σ's give an isomorphism between tensors and this special class of spinors. Thus the operations on tensors are merely special cases of operations on spinors in which only certain spinors and certain types of operations are considered. On the other hand, the contraction of a spinor on a single pair of indices has no straightforward analogue in the tensor world. From this point of view, spinor algebra is richer than the usual tensor algebra.

For example, with a third rank tensor, say $t^{\mu}_{\nu\lambda}$ we associate a spinor of rank six in the following manner:

$$t^{\mu}_{\nu\lambda} = \sigma^{\mu}_{AA'}\sigma^{BB'}_{\nu}\sigma^{CC'}_{\lambda}T^{AA'}_{BB'CC'} \tag{14.7}$$

The extension of this rule to tensors of various types is obvious.

Remarks:

1. The order relative to the primed and the unprimed indices can be interchanged.
2. The properties listed above can be taken to be definitions of the σ's.
3. The Pauli matrix representation which we have chosen for the σ's is not unique.

15. Geometrical Picture of a First Rank Spinor

For a vector we already have a geometrical picture: a *directed line segment* or an *arrow*. This gives an excellent geometrical picture of a vector. In a similar fashion we wish to associate a geometrical picture with a spinor ξ^{A}. Our picture will be some structure in the Minkowski vector space.

Essential requirement: The picture must be independent of the coordinates used or independent of components of the spinor. (ξ^{0}, ξ^{1}) can be considered as components of ξ^{A} in some basis. If we make a change of basis by a SL(2,$\mathcal{C}$) passive transformation, only the components of the spinor should change and not the picture. A similar situation holds for a vector. The components of a given vector in two bases connected by a transformation are in general different but the picture remains the same. The corresponding picture we will associate with a rank 1 spinor is a *flag*.

Let ξ^{A} be a spinor then $k^{\mu} \equiv \xi^{A}\bar{\xi}^{A'}$ is the null vector determined by this spinor. However, it is not sufficient to just associate k^{μ}, because k^{μ} is determined by a whole family of rank 1 spinors – ξ^{A} and those that differ from ξ^A by a phase factor, *i.e.*, if $\zeta^A = e^{i\theta}\xi^A$ then $\xi^A\bar{\xi}^{A'} = \zeta^A\bar{\zeta}^{A'} = k^\mu$. Both ζ^A and ξ^A produce the same null vector. To take care of this redundancy in the phase factor it is necessary to associate a richer structure — that of a half-plane. A first rank spinor also determines a 2-form and hence a 2-plane. We proceed as follows:

Let η^A be such that (ξ^A, η^A) is a dyad; *i.e.*, select η^A such that $\xi_A\eta^A = 1$. Consider the 2nd rank spinor

$$W^{AA'} = \xi^A\bar{\eta}^{A'} + \eta^A\bar{\xi}^{A'} \tag{15.1}$$

It is clear that $\overline{W^{AA'}} = W^{AA'}$ and hence W is real. Therefore $W^{AA'}$ corresponds to a real vector w^μ by

$$\begin{bmatrix} W^{00'} & W^{01'} \\ W^{10'} & W^{11'} \end{bmatrix} = \frac{1}{\sqrt{2}}\begin{bmatrix} w^0 + w^3 & w^1 + iw^2 \\ w^1 - iw^2 & w^0 - w^3 \end{bmatrix}. \tag{15.2}$$

Note that w^μ satisfies the following conditions:

1. w^μ is real,
2. $k^\mu w_\mu = 0$,
3. $w_\mu w^\mu = -2$, which means w^μ is spacelike.

But due to the freedom of the choice of the spin dyad in which ξ^A is one of the members, the other spinor η^A is not unique. We have seen that a $\hat{\eta}^A$ related to η^A through $\hat{\eta}^A = \eta^A + \lambda\xi^A$ also produces a spin dyad along with ξ^A. This freedom produces a family of w^μ as λ varies over $\mathcal{C}$.

$$\begin{aligned} \hat{w}^\mu &= \xi^A\bar{\hat{\eta}}^{A'} + \bar{\xi}^{A'}\hat{\eta}^A \\ &= w^\mu + 2\text{Re}(\lambda)k^\mu \end{aligned} \tag{15.3}$$

We restrict $\text{Re}(\lambda)$ to be positive and this gives rise to a half plane – a 2-plane spanned by w^μ and k^μ. This is the flag.

To summarise, a first rank spinor is pictured as a flag which consists of

(i) flag pole k^μ and
(ii) a flag-plane which is a 2-plane spanned by k^μ and w^μ.

The entire structure is also called a *null flag*.

The effect of changing the phase of a spinor $\xi^A \to \xi^A e^{i\theta}$ rotates the flag-plane by an angle 2θ. Since the dyad condition $\xi_A\eta^A = 1$ must be maintained $\eta^A \to \eta^A e^{-i\theta}$. Thus,

$$w^\mu = \xi^A\bar{\eta}^{A'} + \bar{\xi}^{A'}\eta^A \to \xi^A\bar{\eta}^{A'}e^{2i\theta} + \bar{\xi}^{A'}\eta^A e^{-2i\theta} \tag{15.4}$$

The new w^μ vector is changed to $\cos 2\theta w^\mu + \sin 2\theta v^\mu$ where the vector $v^\mu = i(\xi^A\bar{\eta}^{A'} - \bar{\xi}^{A'}\eta^A)$. Thus the effect of multiplying ξ^A by a phase factor is to rotate w^μ in the (w^μ, v^μ) plane.

We note that the flag returns to its initial orientation when the phase θ reaches π. This means that ξ^A and $-\xi^A$ have the same geometrical picture. This property is crucial to the nature of a spinor.

16. Dyad Formalism

Analogous to a tetrad in Minkowski space, here we have a spin dyad (ξ^A, η^A) satisfying the condition $\xi_A \eta^A = 1$. It is convenient to rename the dyad as,

$$\begin{aligned}
\zeta_{(0)A} &= \xi_A \\
\zeta_{(1)A} &= \eta_A
\end{aligned} \tag{16.1}$$

Then we have the relations,

$$\zeta_{(0)A}\zeta_{(1)}^A = 1, \quad \zeta_{(0)A}\zeta_{(0)}^A = 0, \quad \zeta_{(1)A}\zeta_{(1)}^A = 0, \quad \zeta_{(1)A}\zeta_{(0)}^A = -1. \tag{16.2}$$

More compactly we may write,

$$\zeta_{(a)A}\zeta_{(b)}^A = \epsilon_{(a)(b)} \quad \text{where} \quad \epsilon_{(a)(b)} = \begin{bmatrix} 0 & 1 \\ -1 & 0 \end{bmatrix}.$$

Under a SL(2,$\mathcal{C}$) transformation, since scalar products are preserved, a dyad is mapped to another dyad and conversely. Hence dyad to dyad transformations correspond to Lorentz transformations in the Minkowski space.

There is a natural relation between spin dyads and null tetrads. A null tetrad $(l^\mu, n^\mu, m^\mu, \bar{m}^\mu)$ can be associated with a spin dyad by the following identification:

$$l^\mu = \zeta_{(0)}^A \bar{\zeta}_{(0)}^{A'}, \qquad n^\mu = \zeta_{(1)}^A \bar{\zeta}_{(1)}^{A'}$$

$$m^\mu = \zeta_{(0)}^A \bar{\zeta}_{(1)}^{A'}, \qquad \bar{m}^\mu = \zeta_{(1)}^A \bar{\zeta}_{(0)}^{A'} \tag{16.3}$$

For a spin-dyad $\zeta_{(a)}^A$ the following identities are true:

1. $\epsilon_{AB}\zeta_{(a)}^A \zeta_{(b)}^B = \epsilon_{(a)(b)}$.
2. $\epsilon^{(a)(b)}\zeta_{(a)}^A \zeta_{(b)}^B = \epsilon^{AB}$, where the upper indexed ϵ is defined through the relation $\epsilon^{(a)(c)}\epsilon_{(b)(c)} = \delta_{(b)}^{(a)}$.
3. $\zeta_{(a)A}\zeta^{(b)A} = \delta_{(a)}^{(b)}$, where $\zeta_A^{(a)} = \epsilon^{(a)(b)}\zeta_{(b)A}$.

Since $\zeta_{(a)}^A$ is a basis we can expand an arbitrary spinor κ^A in it:

$$\kappa_{(a)} = \kappa_A \zeta_{(a)}^A. \tag{16.4}$$

Observe that $\zeta_B^{(a)}\kappa_{(a)} = \zeta_B^{(a)}\kappa_A\zeta_{(a)}^A = \kappa_A\delta_B^A = \kappa_B$. In other words

$$\kappa_B = \kappa_{(0)}\zeta_B^{(0)} + \kappa_{(1)}\zeta_B^{(1)}. \qquad (16.5)$$

The Van der Waarden symbols $\sigma_{AA'}^{(a)}$ can be expressed in terms of the null tetrad (we enclose the tetrad index in brackets):

$$\sigma_{AA'}^{(0)} = \frac{1}{\sqrt{2}}\begin{bmatrix} 1 & 0 \\ 0 & 1 \end{bmatrix}, \quad \sigma_{AA'}^{(1)} = \frac{1}{\sqrt{2}}\begin{bmatrix} 0 & 1 \\ 1 & 0 \end{bmatrix}$$

$$\sigma_{AA'}^{(2)} = \frac{1}{\sqrt{2}}\begin{bmatrix} 0 & i \\ -i & 0 \end{bmatrix}, \quad \sigma_{AA'}^{(3)} = \frac{1}{\sqrt{2}}\begin{bmatrix} 1 & 0 \\ 0 & -1 \end{bmatrix} \qquad (16.6)$$

More compactly one can write

$$\sigma_{AA'}^{(a)} = \begin{bmatrix} l^{(a)} & m^{(a)} \\ \bar{m}^{(a)} & n^{(a)} \end{bmatrix}, \qquad (16.7)$$

where

$$l^{(a)} = \frac{1}{\sqrt{2}}(1,0,0,1) \quad m^{(a)} = \frac{1}{\sqrt{2}}(0,1,-i,0)$$

$$n^{(a)} = \frac{1}{\sqrt{2}}(1,0,0,-1) \quad \bar{m}^{(a)} = \frac{1}{\sqrt{2}}(0,1,i,0). \qquad (16.8)$$

Clearly, the vectors $l^{(a)}, n^{(a)}, m^{(a)}$ constitute a null tetrad in Minkowski space.

Finally, if $e_{(a)}^\mu$ is an orthonormal tetrad then we can define a new set of σ's by,

$$\sigma_{AA'}^\mu = e_{(a)}^\mu \sigma_{AA'}^{(a)} = \begin{bmatrix} l^\mu & m^\mu \\ \bar{m}^\mu & n^\mu \end{bmatrix}. \qquad (16.9)$$

In a given spacetime there may exist a special null tetrad field dictated by the symmetries of the spacetime. Identifying the tangent space with the Minkowski space we may choose the σ's to be given by the above formula (16.9). The null tetrad vectors relate in the following manner:

$$l^{(a)} = e_\mu^{(a)}l^\mu \quad n^{(a)} = e_\mu^{(a)}n^\mu \quad m^{(a)} = e_\mu^{(a)}m^\mu. \qquad (16.10)$$

17. The Application of Spinor Algebra to Petrov Classification

Given a spacetime $(\mathcal{M}, g_{ab})$ we can classify it by the algebraic properties of the Weyl tensor C_{abcd} associated with the metric. Many of the well known spacetimes have special type of Weyl tensors. This is useful for studying electromagnetic or gravitational radiation. If the Weyl tensor is of a special type then it is possible to choose a null tetrad field aligned along certain directions – the repeated principal null directions (r.p.n.d.) of the Weyl tensor – in which the equations generally decouple and simplify. In this section we will discuss the algebraic classification of the Weyl tensor at each point of the spacetime so that spinor algebra suffices. We fix our attention on a point of a spacetime and look at its tangent space.

The first task is to write C_{abcd} in its spinor equivalent form. Since C_{abcd} is a 4th rank tensor the corresponding spinor will be of rank 8. But due to the inherent symmetries of the Weyl tensor (in four dimensions C_{abcd} has only ten independent components) the spinor equivalent of it, is particularly simple,

$$C_{abcd} = \psi_{ABCD}\epsilon_{W'X'}\epsilon_{Y'Z'} + \bar{\psi}_{W'X'Y'Z'}\epsilon_{AB}\epsilon_{CD} \qquad (17.1)$$

where ψ_{ABCD} is a totally symmetric spinor and contains all the information of the Weyl tensor. It is straight forward although tedious algebra to derive equation (17.1). We do not do so here. Total symmetry implies,

$$\psi_{ABCD} = \psi_{(ABCD)}. \qquad (17.2)$$

The round brackets denote total symmetrisation on the indices enclosed within the brackets. ψ_{ABCD} has five independent complex components corresponding to the ten real independent components of the Weyl tensor.

The Weyl spinor can be factored into four first rank spinors. The analysis that follows is generally applicable to a totally symmetric spinor of any rank where the spinor factors into first rank spinors, the number of factors being equal to the rank of the original spinor. We begin with the expression,

$$Q(z) = \psi_{ABCD}\zeta^A\zeta^B\zeta^C\zeta^D, \qquad (17.3)$$

$$\text{where,} \quad \zeta^A = \begin{bmatrix} 1 \\ z \end{bmatrix} \qquad z \in \mathcal{C}.$$

Observe that $Q(z)$ is a quartic in z. There is an advantage in working over a complex field $\mathcal{C}$ since it is algebraically closed. Because of this property $Q(z)$ can be factored into linear factors:

$$\begin{aligned} Q(z) &= (\alpha_0 + \alpha_1 z)(\beta_0 + \beta_1 z)(\gamma_0 + \gamma_1 z)(\delta_0 + \delta_1 z) \\ &= (\alpha_A\zeta^A)(\beta_B\zeta^B)(\gamma_C\zeta^C)(\delta_D\zeta^D) \\ &= \alpha_{(A}\beta_B\gamma_C\delta_{D)}\zeta^A\zeta^B\zeta^C\zeta^D \end{aligned} \qquad (17.4)$$

The last step follows because the product, $\alpha_A\beta_B\gamma_C\delta_D$ is totally symmetric. The equation (17.4) leads to,

$$\left(\psi_{ABCD} - \alpha_{(A}\beta_B\gamma_C\delta_{D)}\right)\zeta^A\zeta^B\zeta^C\zeta^D = 0 \qquad (17.5)$$

Since z is arbitrary, so is ζ^A (upto a complex scalar factor) and further, using the total symmetry of the Weyl spinor we can set the expression within the brackets of equation (17.5) equal to zero.

$$\psi_{ABCD} = \alpha_{(A}\beta_B\gamma_C\delta_{D)}. \qquad (17.6)$$

The spinors α_A, β_B, γ_C, δ_D are called principal spinors. Each of the spinors is determined upto a complex scalar factor. Therefore the principal spinors determine 4 null directions called *principal null directions* of the Weyl spinor or tensor. Whether these directions are distinct or some or all of them coincide determines the algebraic properties of the spacetime or the gravitational field. This motivates the following classification for spacetimes:

Definition: The Weyl spinor ψ_{ABCD} is said to be algebraically general if all its four principal null directions are distinct. Otherwise it is said to be algebraically special.

Several possibilities exist when the Weyl spinor is algebraically special; two directions can coincide with the other two remaining distinct or two, two can coincide pairwise and so on. There is a classification due to Petrov and Pirani which includes all these possibilities. The following table summarises the partitioning and the Petrov type:

Partition	Petrov type	Form of ψ_{ABCD}	Algebraic type
[1111]	I	$\alpha_{(A}\beta_B\gamma_C\delta_{D)}$	General
[211]	II	$\alpha_{(A}\alpha_B\gamma_C\delta_{D)}$	Special
[22]	D	$\alpha_{(A}\alpha_B\beta_C\beta_{D)}$	Special
[31]	III	$\alpha_{(A}\alpha_B\alpha_C\beta_{D)}$	Special
[4]	N	$\alpha_{(A}\alpha_B\alpha_C\alpha_{D)}$	Special
—	O	$\psi_{ABCD} \equiv 0$	Conformally flat

As remarked before, any totally symmetric spinor can be split up as above with the number of principal null directions equal to the rank of the spinor. We consider the example of the electromagnetic field which is simpler than the gravitational field treated above. The electromagnetic field is described by a symmetric second rank spinor.

Example: The electromagnetic field.

Analogous to the Weyl tensor, the electromagnetic field strength tensor F_{ab} can be expressed in terms of spinors as follows:

$$F_{ab} \equiv \phi_{AB}\epsilon_{W'X'} + \bar{\phi}_{W'X'}\epsilon_{AB}. \tag{17.7}$$

Here ϕ_{AB} is the symmetric spinor which contains all the information in F_{ab}. ϕ_{00}, ϕ_{01}, ϕ_{11} are its independent components (they are precisely the ϕ_0, ϕ_1, ϕ_2 – the Teukolsky scalars of section 8). Since the ϕ_{AB} is complex they correspond to six real quantities F_{ab} or $\bar{E}$ and $\bar{B}$. Since $\phi_{AB} = \phi_{(AB)}$ we can apply the foregoing analysis for the Weyl tensor to the electromagnetic spinor. Thus the electromagnetic spinor factors into two rank 1 spinors,

$$\phi_{AB} = \alpha_{(A}\beta_{B)}. \tag{17.8}$$

The two principal null directions are determined by α_A and β_A. There are two cases to consider: $\alpha_A \neq \beta_A$ and $\alpha_A = \beta_A$. The table below describes the algebraic classification of electromagnetic fields.

Partition	Form of ϕ_{AB}	Algebraic type
[11]	$\alpha_{(A}\beta_{B)}$	General
[2]	$\alpha_A\alpha_B$	Special

Examples of algebraically special electromagnetic fields are a wave in free space or more generally a radiation field.

The corresponding analysis with tensors is much more laborious. For the gravitational field the principal null directions k^a satisfy the eigenvalue equation,

$$C_{abc[d}k_{f]}k^c = 0 \tag{17.9}$$

This equation has to be solved to yield the principal null directions, which happens to be quite tedious.

An important application of Petrov classification is the *Sachs peeling off theorem*. We notice that there is increasing specialisation as one moves down the table of classification suggesting an hierarchy. This hierarchy has physical significance which is described in Sach's theorem concerning retarded multipole gravitational fields of localised sources.

For a localised source, the vacuum Riemann tensor (Weyl tensor) of the retarded multipole field has the form:

$$C_{abcd} = \frac{N_{abcd}}{r} + \frac{III_{abcd}}{r^2} + \frac{II_{abcd}}{r^3} + \frac{I_{abcd}}{r^4} + \frac{I'_{abcd}}{r^5} + O(r^{-6}). \qquad (17.10)$$

The derivation of the above equation needs considerable effort. The tensors N_{abcd} etc. appearing in equation (17.10) belong to the corresponding Petrov type. We observe that very far away from the source the first term dominates since it goes as $\frac{1}{r}$. All the four principal null directions coincide as the Weyl tensor is of type N. As one moves towards the source the second term becomes appreciable so that the Weyl tensor is of type III. Now we have three principal null directions coincident while one has peeled off. Therefore, the principal null directions peel off one after another as one moves towards the source starting from infinity, until very close to the source all terms are important where the Weyl tensor is algebraically general.

18. Spin Structure and Global Considerations

It is sufficient here to consider the group of rotations in Euclidean 3-space denoted by SO(3) because it is topologically the nontrivial part of the restricted Lorentz group. A restricted Lorentz transformation can be uniquely written as a product of a rotation and a boost. The boost part is topologically trivial having the topology of $\mathcal{R}^3$ and hence the topological properties of the restricted Lorentz group are essentially that of SO(3).

Let us consider in some detail the topological structure of SO(3). Any rotation $R(\hat{n}, \theta)$ where $\hat{n}$ is the unit vector along the axis of rotation and θ the angle of rotation, can be represented by the vector $\theta\hat{n}$, where $0 \leq \theta \leq \pi$. This is a solid sphere of radius π. However, the diametrically opposite points on the surface of the sphere correspond to the same rotation, i.e., $R(-\hat{n}, \pi) = R(\hat{n}, \pi)$, i.e., if one rotates an object by $R(-\hat{n}, \pi)$ or $R(\hat{n}, \pi)$ it comes back to the same orientation. This means that the diametrically opposite points on the surface of the sphere have to be *identified* in order to get the topology of SO(3).

The topological property of SO(3) of interest to us is that it is not simply connected. A topological space is said to be simply connected if every closed loop in it can be continuously shrunk to a point. If we consider any diameter of the solid sphere representing SO(3), then this is a closed loop because diametrically oppposite points are indentified. But it cannot be continuously deformed into a point. Hence SO(3) is not simply connected. It is however doubly connected, i.e., there are just two classes of loops: one class in which all the loops can be continuously shrunk to a point; and another class in which none of the loops can be shrunk to a point but can however be continuously deformed into each other. A natural group structure can be endowed on the set of equivalence classes; in this case the group has two elements and is denoted by Z_2.

In general the group is denoted by π_1; we say $\pi_1(SO(3)) = Z_2$.

If we consider a continuous rotation of an object about some axis by 2π, then the object comes back to its initial orientation. In $SO(3)$ this gives a closed loop but this loop cannot be shrunk to a point. But if we rotate an object through 4π, then the object returns to its original orientation and we get a closed loop in the other class which can be continuously deformed into a point or into a state of no rotation. This is quite counter intuitive but can be illustrated – by the well known Dirac scissors problem.

We observed that when we rotate the flag plane of the spinor by 2π the spinor changes sign. If we however rotate the flag plane by 4π the spinor returns to itself. We observe that spinors are sensitive to this non-simply-connectedness of $SO(3)$ while vectors are not. The spinors keep track of the nature of the closed loops those which can be shrunk to a point and those which cannot. They keep track of the orientation of the object with respect to other fixed objects. This is in fact illustrated by the Dirac scissor problem in which the scissor which is rotated is attached by strings to a fixed object such as a chair. MTW call this the orientation-entanglement relation.

What is the relation of the restricted Lorentz group to the $SL(2,\mathcal{C})$ group? The concept involved here is that of universal covering spaces. Let X be a connected space then we can construct its universal covering space as follows. Take a fixed point $x_0 \in X$ and consider all paths from x_0 to $x \in X$. The paths fall into equivalence classes according as they can or cannot be continuously deformed into each other. For a given $x \in X$ all the equivalence classes of paths from x_0 to x can be considered as copies of the point x. If we let x vary over X all these copies of all points of X produce a new topological space U which is assigned the obvious topology through the projection map from U to X; the coarsest topology which makes the projection map continuous. It can be shown that U is simply connected and is independent of the choice of x_0. U is called the *universal covering space* of X. If X is not simply connected then U basically 'unwraps' X into a bigger space. In our case of $SO(3)$ or the restricted Lorentz group, there are just two equivalence classes of paths and the universal covering space is a two fold covering or unwrapping. For every restricted Lorentz transformation there are two transformations $\pm L_B^A \in SL(2,\mathcal{C})$. In this way $SL(2,\mathcal{C})$ is the universal covering space, a twofold covering of $SO(3)$.

In the following sections we will be concerned with spinor fields defined over curved spacetimes. Hence we will briefly mention the kind of problems encountered when we go over from spinors at a given point in spacetime to spin structure being defined globally on a spacetime $\mathcal{M}$ and the conditions to be imposed on it. The topology of $\mathcal{M}$ plays an important role.

As seen earlier a spinor is represented by a null flag in Minkowski space. Hence a spinor at a spacetime point is represented by a null flag in the tangent space at the point. A spinor field therefore generates a field of null flags over the spacetime. Since a null flag is associated with the future null cone there must exist a continuous choice of future null cones all over $\mathcal{M}$ for a consistent definition of null flags. This is precisely the definition of a time-oriented manifold. Thus $\mathcal{M}$ should be *time-orientable*. Secondly, we have also seen that multiplying a spinor by a phase factor rotates the null flag in certain sense. There should be a continuous choice of this sense of rotation of the null flags. The condition on $\mathcal{M}$ is that it should be *spacetime-orientable*. However, both these conditions on $\mathcal{M}$ athough necessary are not sufficient to permit a spin structure. Basically, we need to keep track of the sign of a spinor not only if we move it around a given point of $\mathcal{M}$ but also from point to point of $\mathcal{M}$. It is found that it is just the topology of $\mathcal{M}$ which guarantees the existence and uniqueness of a spin structure. If $\mathcal{M}$ possesses trivial topology the spin structure exists and is unique, but in nontrivial cases this may not be so. Several problems may arise if $\mathcal{M}$ has nontrivial topology. Even if $\mathcal{M}$ is simply connected a spinor structure may not exist. If $\mathcal{M}$ is not simply connected different inequivalent spinor structures can exist or none can exist. Examples of different possible cases and criteria for spinor structures to exist on manifolds have been given by Geroch, Milnor, Clarke (see bibliography).

19. Spinor Analysis

Our aim here is to define the differentiation of spinors. Hence we need to define a parallel transport law for spinors. Just as there is no natural way of identifying tangent spaces at different points in a spacetime there is no natural way of identifying spinor spaces. However, the Riemannian connection can be used to extend the notion of parallel transport to spinors. The parallel transport of a 2-component spinor can be defined along a curve by requiring that the null flag is parallely transported and that the sign of the spinor does not change discontinuously. Once parallel transport has been defined the covariant derivative is obtained easily. The rule for covariant differentiation can then in an obvious manner be extended to higher rank spinors.

We assume that all the conditions necessary for the existence of a spin structure on $\mathcal{M}$ are satisfied and there do exist spinor fields on $\mathcal{M}$. Let U be a chart on $\mathcal{M}$ with coordinate functions x^α. A spinor field on U is an assignment of a spinor to each point $p \in U$. Since p has coordinates $x^\alpha(p)$ the spinor field becomes a function of coordinates x^α. For example, we may have a third rank spinor field: $W_B^{AA'}(x^\alpha)$.

Definition: A spinor field is said to be smooth if each of its component functions are C^∞. For example, if ξ^A is a smooth spinor field on U then each component $\xi^A(x^\alpha)$ is a smooth function from $\mathcal{R}^4 \longrightarrow \mathcal{C}$.

The Van der Waarden symbols.
In flat space the Van der Wardeen symbols gave a mapping from spin space to Minkowski space; in curved spacetime the Minkowski space is replaced by the tangent space. A set of σ's can be constructed as follows:

Choose a smooth orthonormal restricted tetrad field $e_{(a)}^\mu(x^\alpha)$ on U. Define the σ's in this tetrad basis exactly as we had defined on Minkowski space. Thus,

$$\sigma_{AA'}^{(0)} = \frac{1}{\sqrt{2}} \begin{bmatrix} 1 & 0 \\ 0 & 1 \end{bmatrix}, \qquad \sigma_{AA'}^{(1)} = \frac{1}{\sqrt{2}} \begin{bmatrix} 0 & 1 \\ 1 & 0 \end{bmatrix},$$

$$\sigma_{AA'}^{(2)} = \frac{1}{\sqrt{2}} \begin{bmatrix} 0 & -i \\ i & 0 \end{bmatrix}, \qquad \sigma_{AA'}^{(3)} = \frac{1}{\sqrt{2}} \begin{bmatrix} 1 & 0 \\ 0 & -1 \end{bmatrix} \qquad (19.1)$$

The σ's in the local coordinate frame are obtained through,

$$\sigma_{AA'}^\mu(x^\alpha) = e_{(a)}^\mu(x^\alpha)\sigma_{AA'}^{(a)}. \qquad (19.2)$$

Observe that the σ's, in a coordinate basis, are in general functions of the coordinates. Clearly there is considerable latitude in the choice of the σ's. At each point there are six degrees of freedom of the restricted Lorentz transformations which carry restricted tetrads to restricted tetrads. But in the choice of the tetrad field, barring smoothness there is no other restriction. Other relations satisfied by the σ's are:

(a) $\sigma_\mu^{AA'} = e_\mu^{(a)} \sigma_{(a)}^{AA'}$,

(b) $\sigma_\mu^{AA'} \sigma_\nu^{BB'} \epsilon_{AB} \epsilon_{A'B'} = g_{\mu\nu}$,

(c) $\sigma_{AA'}^\mu = [\ell^\mu \quad m^\mu \bar{m}^\mu \quad n^\mu]$, where $\ell^\mu = e_{(a)}^\mu \ell^{(a)}$, etc.

We now define the covariant derivative of a spinor. To do this we require the spinor affine connection coefficients. They are defined through the requirement that the ϵ_{AB} and the σ's are covariantly constant, i.e.,

$$\epsilon_{AB;\mu} = 0 \qquad , \qquad \sigma_{AA';\nu}^\mu = 0. \qquad (19.3)$$

We define the covariant derivative of a spinor analogous to that of the vector. For first rank spinors:

$$\xi^A{}_{;\mu} = \xi^A{}_{,\mu} + \Gamma_{\mu B}^A \xi^B \qquad (19.4a)$$

$$\xi_{A;\mu} = \xi_{A,\mu} - \Gamma^B_{\mu A}\xi_B \qquad (19.4b)$$

$$\xi^{A'}{}_{;\mu} = \xi^{A'}{}_{,\mu} + \bar{\Gamma}^{A'}_{\mu B'}\xi^{B'} \qquad (19.4c)$$

$$\xi_{A';\mu} = \xi_{A',\mu} - \bar{\Gamma}^{B'}_{\mu A'}\xi_{B'} \qquad (19.4d)$$

The definition is extended in an obvious way analogous to tensors to higher rank spinors and composite objects having spinor and tensor indices. For example,

$$T^\mu_{AA';\nu} = T^\mu_{AA',\nu} + \Gamma^\mu_{\nu\lambda}T^\lambda_{AA'} - \Gamma^B_{\nu A}T^\mu_{BA'} - \bar{\Gamma}^{B'}_{\nu A'}T^\mu_{AB'} \qquad (19.5)$$

The Γs are obtained from equations (19.3). Some amount of algebra leads to the following expression for them,

$$\Gamma^C_{\mu B} = \frac{1}{2}\sigma^{CY'}_\nu(\sigma^\lambda_{BY'}\Gamma^\nu_{\mu\lambda} + \partial_\mu\sigma^\nu_{BY'}). \qquad (19.6)$$

$\bar{\Gamma}$ is the complex conjugate of Γ.

Besides the semicolon notation for the covariant derivative the notation with ∇ is also used. Thus,

$$\xi^A{}_{;\mu} \equiv \nabla_\mu\xi^A \equiv \nabla_{BB'}\xi^A \qquad (19.7)$$

where in the extreme right of equation (19.7) we have multiplied by σ, i.e., $\nabla_{BB'} \equiv \sigma^\mu_{BB'}\nabla_\mu$.

It can be shown that the above definition of parallel transport satisfies the conditions mentioned at the beginning of the section. For a first rank spinor, parallel transport implies that the null flag is parallely propagated.

20. Spin Dyads and Spin Coefficients

We have seen that the concept of the null tetrad emerges most naturally from the spin dyad. We will see further here that this is also true for spin coefficients. In fact the entire NP formalism is completely equivalent to the spinor formulation.

For a spin dyad $\zeta^A_{(a)}$,

$$\nabla_\mu\zeta^A_{(a)} = \partial_\mu\zeta^A_{(a)} + \Gamma^A_{\mu C}\zeta^C_{(a)} \qquad (20.1a)$$

$$\nabla_\mu\zeta_{(a)A} = \partial_\mu\zeta_{(a)A} - \Gamma^C_{\mu A}\zeta_{(a)C} \qquad (20.1b)$$

Suppose we contract with $\zeta^A_{(b)}$ then we get a vector:

$$\zeta^A_{(b)}\nabla_\mu\zeta^A_{(a)} = \Gamma_{(a)(b)\mu}. \qquad (20.2)$$

We can replace the vector index μ by two spinor indices, say CD', with the help of equation (19.7). Multiplying equation (20.2) by $\sigma^\mu_{CD'}$, we obtain,

$$\zeta^A_{(b)}\nabla_{CD'}\zeta_{(a)A} = \Gamma_{(a)(b)CD'}. \tag{20.3}$$

Spin Coefficients:

The spin coefficients $\Gamma_{(a)(b)(c)(d')}$ for a spin dyad field $\zeta^A_{(a)}$ are given by the following relation:

$$\zeta^C_{(c)}\zeta^{D'}_{(d')}\zeta^A_{(b)}\nabla_{CD'}\zeta_{(a)A} = \Gamma_{(a)(b)(c)(d')} \tag{20.4}$$

We assert the following: The spin coefficients are symmetric in (a) and (b). *i.e.*,

$$\Gamma_{(a)(b)(c)(d')} = \Gamma_{(b)(a)(c)(d')} \tag{20.5}$$

Proof: We have from equation (20.3),

$$\Gamma_{(a)(b)CD'} = \zeta^F_{(b)}\nabla_{CD'}\zeta_{(a)F}$$

Let us start with the identity,

$$\nabla_{CD'}(\zeta_{(a)F}\zeta^F_{(b)}) = 0$$

Expanding,

$$\zeta_{(a)F}\nabla_{CD'}\zeta^F_{(b)} + \zeta^F_{(b)}\nabla_{CD'}\zeta_{(a)F} = 0.$$

The second term on the left hand side is $\Gamma_{(a)(b)CD'}$. Thus,

$$\begin{aligned}
\Gamma_{(a)(b)CD'} &= -\zeta_{(a)F}\nabla_{CD'}\zeta^F_{(b)} \\
&= -\zeta^X_{(a)}\epsilon_{XF}\nabla_{CD'}\zeta^F_{(b)} \\
&= -\zeta^X_{(a)}\nabla_{CD'}(\epsilon_{XF}\zeta^F_{(b)}) \\
&= -\zeta^X_{(a)}\nabla_{CD'}\zeta_{(b)X}.
\end{aligned}$$

Multiplying both sides by $\zeta^C_{(c)}\bar{\zeta}^{D'}_{(d')}$, we obtain the required result,

$$\Gamma_{(a)(b)(c)(d')} = \Gamma_{(b)(a)(c)(d')}.$$

There are 12 independent spin coefficients in view of the symmetry of the first two indices. The indices $(c)(d')$ take 2 values each, *i.e.*, 2×2. The indices $(a)(b)$ together take only 3 independent values 00, 01, 11. Below we tabulate the spin coefficients. Note that these are the same as those obtained from the null tetrad.

$(a)(b) \rightarrow$ $(c)(d') \downarrow$	00	01 10	11
$00'$	κ	ϵ	π
$10'$	ρ	α	λ
$01'$	σ	β	μ
$11'$	τ	γ	ν

Directional derivatives

We now complete the section by discussing directional derivatives. The simplest case is for a smooth scalar field, say, ϕ.

The directional derivative of ϕ in the direction (AX') is given by,

$$\partial_{AX'}\phi = \sigma^\mu_{AX'}\partial\phi = \phi_{,AX'} \qquad (20.6)$$

The operator matrix $\partial_{AX'}$ is written below in its explicit form,

$$\begin{bmatrix} \partial_{00'} & \partial_{01'} \\ \partial_{10'} & \partial_{00'} \end{bmatrix} = \frac{1}{\sqrt{2}} \begin{bmatrix} \frac{\partial}{\partial x^0} - \frac{\partial}{\partial x^3} & -\frac{\partial}{\partial x^1} + i\frac{\partial}{\partial x^2} \\ -\frac{\partial}{\partial x^1} - i\frac{\partial}{\partial x^2} & \frac{\partial}{\partial x^0} + \frac{\partial}{\partial x^3} \end{bmatrix} \qquad (20.7)$$

For the contravariant directional derivative $\partial^{AX'}$ the correspondance is just the inverse of the matrix on the R.H.S. of equation (20.7).

For spinor fields of arbitrary rank, results analogous to tensors follow. To illustrate, consider a rank 1 spinor field ξ^A. The results can be extended to higher rank spinor fields in an obvious manner. Consider a dyad component of the spinor ξ^A:

$$\xi_{(a)} = \zeta^A_{(a)}\xi_A.$$

Now

$$\begin{aligned} \xi_{(a)|BC'} &= \zeta^A_{(a)}\nabla_{BC'}\xi_A \\ &= \nabla_{BC'}\left(\zeta^A_{(a)}\xi_A\right) - \xi_A\nabla_{BC'}\zeta^A_{(a)} \\ &= \xi_{(a),BC'} - \xi_A\nabla_{BC'}\epsilon^{AD}\zeta_{(a)D} \\ &= \xi_{(a),BC'} - \xi_A\epsilon^{(b)(d)}\zeta^A_{(b)}\zeta^D_{(d)}\nabla_{BC'}\zeta_{(a)D} \\ &= \xi_{(a),BC'} - \xi_A\epsilon^{(b)(d)}\zeta^A_{(b)}\Gamma_{(a)(d)BC'} \\ &= \xi_{(a),BC'} - \xi_A\zeta^A_{(b)}\Gamma^{(b)}_{(a)BC'} \qquad (20.8) \end{aligned}$$

This completes the tools required for spinor analysis.

21.　Conclusion

In these lectures I have more or less covered the tetrad formalism begin-ning with tetrads in Minkowski space, Lorentz transformations, rotation coefficients. I have then introduced null tetrads, spin coefficients and then made a transition to curved spacetimes. The NP formalism is discussed and it is shown how natural the spinor approach is in the NP formalism. That the null tetrad is intimately connected with the spin dyad and the spin coefficients easily follows. The spinorial methods make the algebraic classification of spacetimes almost trivial.

In these lectures I have tried to adopt a logical and simple intuitive approach. The topics covered here have been discussed extensively in the literature. I have provided a few references in the bibliography to which the interested reader can refer to. References 1-4, are general references to all topics covered in the lectures. Reference 5, is the original paper on NP formalism. Reference 6 is for Spinors. References 7-9, discuss existence of spinor structure on manifolds. Several applications have been left out in these lectures due to the paucity of time but the idea in these lectures was to give the reader an introduction and basic tools which will hopefully help in further work in the field.

References

1.　S. Chandrasekhar, *The Mathematical Theory of Blackholes*, Oxford University Press, (1983)
2.　V.P.Frolov, *The Newman-Penrose Method in the Theory of General Relativity*, in problems in the General Theory of Relativity and Theory of Group Representations, Ed. N.G.Basov, Consultants Bureau, NY (1979)
3.　F.A.E.Pirani, *Lectures on General Relativity* in: Brandeis Summer Institute in The-oretical Physics, Vol. 1 (1964)
4.　R.M.Wald, *General Relativity*, The University of Chicago Press, (1984)
5.　E.T.Newman and R.Penrose, *J. Math. Phys.*, **3**, 566 (1962)
6.　R.Penrose and W.Rindler, *Spinors and Spacetime*, Vol. 1, Cambridge University Press, (1987)
7.　J.W.Milnor, *Spin structures on manifolds*, L'enseignement math., **9**, 198 (1963)
8.　R.P.Geroch, *Spinor structures on spacetimes in General Relativity I and II.*
J. Math. Phys., **9**, 1739 (1968)
J. Math. Phys., **11**, 343 (1970)
9.　C.J.Clarke, *Gen. Rel. and Grav.*, **2**, 43 (1971)

4. PROBLEMS ON TETRADS, THE NEWMAN–PENROSE FORMALISM AND SPINORS

SAI IYER
Physical Research Laboratory
Navarangpura
Ahmedabad 380 009, India

Problems

Convention: i, j etc., are tensor indices and (a), (b) etc., are tetrad-basis indices.

A, B etc., and A', B' etc., are spinor indices of the two kinds.

The metric signature is $(+, -, -, -)$.

1. Let V be an n-dimensional vector space and let g be a metric on V. Show that

   a) One can always find an orthonormal basis $v_1, \ldots, v_n$ of V, *i.e.*, a basis such that

   $$g(v_i, v_j) = \pm \delta_{ij}$$

   (Hint: Use induction.)

   (b) Show that the signature of g is independent of the choice of the orthonormal basis.

2. Show that

   $$e^{(b)}{}_i e_{(a)}{}^i = \delta^{(b)}{}_{(a)}.$$

3. Show that

   $$e_{(a)i} e^{(a)}{}_j = g_{ij}.$$

4. Show that if T_{ij} is symmetric (antisymmetric), so is $T_{(a)(b)}$.

5. With the help of $\lambda_{(a)(b)(c)}$, defined by

   $$\lambda_{(a)(b)(c)} = e_{(b)i,j} [e_{(a)}{}^i e_{(c)}{}^j - e_{(a)}{}^j e_{(c)}{}^i],$$

   establish that Christoffel symbols are not needed to evaluate $\gamma_{(a)(b)(c)}$.

331

6. Establish
$$A_{(a)|(b)} = A_{(a),(b)} - \eta^{(n)(m)}\gamma_{(n)(a)(b)}A_{(m)}.$$

7. The connection coefficients $w^l{}_{jk}$ are related to the connection forms $w^l{}_j$ of a basis e_k by
$$w^l{}_j(e_k) = w^l{}_{jk}.$$

The covariant derivative ∇ is given by
$$(\nabla_U V)^j = U(V^j) + w^j{}_k(U)V^k.$$

In particular,
$$(\nabla_k V)^j = V^j{}_{,k} + w^j{}_{ik}V^i,$$

where
$$\nabla_k \equiv \nabla_{e_k} \quad \text{and} \quad V^j{}_{,k} \equiv e_k(V^j).$$

(a) Starting from
$$\boldsymbol{R(X,Y)} = \nabla_X\nabla_Y - \nabla_Y\nabla_X - \nabla_{[X,Y]},$$

show that the components of Riemann on a basis e_k are given by
$$R^j{}_{lnm} = w^j{}_{lm,n} - w^j{}_{ln,m} + w^j{}_{kn}w^k{}_{lm} - w^j{}_{km}w^k{}_{ln} - C^k{}_{nm}w^j{}_{lk},$$

where
$$[e_i, e_j] = C^k{}_{ij}e_k.$$

(b) Show that, for vanishing torsion,
$$C^i{}_{jk} = w^i{}_{kj} - w^i{}_{jk}.$$

(c) Prove that, if the derivative operator is compatible with the metric,
$$g_{ij,k} = w_{jik} + w_{ijk}$$

and hence
$$w_{ijk} = \tfrac{1}{2}(g_{ij,k} + g_{ik,j} - g_{jk,i} + C_{ikj} + C_{jik} + C_{kij}).$$

(d) Show that in a coordinate basis the $w^i{}_{jk}$ (usually called $\Gamma^i{}_{jk}$) satisfy $w^i{}_{jk} = w^i{}_{kj}$, and that the expressions in parts (a) and (c) reduce to the usual expressions for the Riemann tensor and Christoffel symbols.

(e) In a tetrad basis ($g_{(a)(b)}$ = constant), prove that the $\omega_{(a)(b)(c)}$ (usually denoted $\gamma_{(a)(b)(c)}$) satisfy $\omega_{(a)(b)(c)} = -\omega_{(b)(a)(c)}$, and that

$$
\begin{aligned}
R_{(a)(b)(c)(d)} &= -\gamma_{(a)(b)(c),(d)} + \gamma_{(a)(b)(d),(c)} \\
&\quad + \gamma_{(b)(a)(f)}[\gamma_{(c)}{}^{(f)}{}_{(d)} - \gamma_{(d)}{}^{(f)}{}_{(c)}] \\
&\quad + \gamma_{(f)(a)(c)}\gamma_{(b)}{}^{(f)}{}_{(d)} \\
&\quad - \gamma_{(f)(a)(d)}\gamma_{(b)}{}^{(f)}{}_{(c)}.
\end{aligned}
$$

(f) Using components of the tetrad basis vectors on a coordinate basis, show

$$
\gamma_{(c)(a)(b)} = e_{(c)}{}^{k} e_{(a)k;i} e_{(b)}{}^{i}.
$$

8. In Kaluza-Klein theory spacetime is assumed to be five dimensional. *Notation:* The metric tensor in 5D is $\hat{g}_{ij}$. A caret symbol over any geometrical object indicates that it is constructed using the 5D metric. Careted indices refer to 5 dimensions; uncareted ones to 4. y denotes the additional spatial coordinate. The line element is given by

$$
ds^2 = \hat{g}_{ij}(x, y)dx^i dx^j = g_{ij}(x)dx^i dx^j - (dy + kA_i(x)dx^i)^2.
$$

Here $0 \le y \le L$ and k is a constant. We introduce the 'horizontal lift basis' given by the one-forms

$$
\hat{\theta}^i = dx^i \qquad \text{and} \qquad \hat{\theta}^5 = dy + kA_i(x)dx^i.
$$

Show the following:

a) The components of the metric tensor are

$$
\hat{g}_{ij} = \begin{pmatrix} g_{ij} & 0 \\ 0 & -1 \end{pmatrix}.
$$

b) The basis vectors dual to $\hat{\theta}^i$ are

$$
\hat{e}_i = \partial_i - kA_i(x)\partial_y \qquad \text{and} \qquad \hat{e}_5 = \partial_y.
$$

c) The commutators of the basis vectors are given by

$$
[\hat{e}_i, \hat{e}_j] = -kF_{ij}(x)\partial_y \qquad \text{and} \qquad [\hat{e}_i, \hat{e}_5] = 0,
$$

where $F_{ij}(x) = \partial_i A_j(x) - \partial_j A_i(x)$.

d) The non-vanishing connection coefficients are given by

$$
\begin{aligned}
\hat{\Gamma}_{ijl} &= \tfrac{1}{2}\{g_{ij,l} + g_{il,j} - g_{jl,i}\}, \qquad \hat{\Gamma}_{ij5} = \hat{\Gamma}_{i5j} = \tfrac{1}{2}kF_{ij}, \\
\hat{\Gamma}_{5ij} &= -\tfrac{1}{2}kF_{ij}.
\end{aligned}
$$

e)
$$\hat{R}^i{}_{jlm} = R^i{}_{jlm} - \tfrac{1}{4}(k^2 F^i{}_m F_{jl} - k^2 F^i{}_l F_{jm} - 2k^2 F^i{}_j F_{lm}),$$
$$\hat{R}^i{}_{5j5} = -\tfrac{1}{4}k^2 F^i{}_l F^l{}_j,$$

where $R^i{}_{jlm}$ is constructed from the 4D metric g_{ij}.

f)
$$\hat{R}^{ij}{}_{ij} = R + \tfrac{3}{4}k^2 F^{ij} F_{ij} \qquad \text{and} \qquad \hat{R}^{i5}{}_{i5} = -\tfrac{1}{4}k^2 F^{ij} F_{ij},$$

where $R = R^{ij}{}_{ij}$.

g)
$$\hat{R} = R + \tfrac{1}{4}k^2 F^{ij}{}_{ij},$$

where $\hat{R} = \hat{R}^{ij}{}_{ij}$.

9. Show that if $(\boldsymbol{l}, \boldsymbol{n}, \boldsymbol{m}, \bar{\boldsymbol{m}})$ is a null tetrad, then
$$g_{ij} = l_i n_j + n_i l_j - m_i \bar{m}_j - \bar{m}_i m_j.$$

10. *Schwarzschild spacetime in the Newman-Penrose formalism.*

   a) Obtain the radial null geodesics for the Schwarzschild metric.

   b) From the null vectors representing these geodesics, form the real null vectors

$$l^i = (l^t, l^r, l^\theta, l^\phi) = \frac{1}{\Delta}(r^2, +\Delta, 0, 0) \quad \text{and} \quad n^i = \frac{1}{2r^2}(r^2, -\Delta, 0, 0),$$

   where $\Delta = r^2 - 2Mr$. Show that these vectors, along with the complex null vector

$$m^i = \frac{1}{r\sqrt{2}}(0, 0, 1, i \csc \theta)$$

   and its complex conjugate constitute a null tetrad satisfying the standard 'ortho-normality' conditions.

   c) Show that the only non-vanishing spin coefficients are

$$\rho = -\frac{1}{r}, \qquad \beta = -\alpha = \frac{1}{2\sqrt{2}}\frac{\cot \theta}{r},$$
$$\mu = -\frac{r - 2M}{2r^2} \qquad \text{and} \qquad \gamma = \frac{M}{2r^2}.$$

   d) Compute the Weyl scalars and show that only $\Psi_2 = -M/r^3$ is non-vanishing.

   e) Does the vanishing of the other Weyl scalars follow from general principles?

11. Prove the following

a) $\epsilon^{AC}\epsilon_{BC} = \delta^A_B$,   b) $\epsilon_{A[B}\epsilon_{CD]} = 0$,

c) $\xi_{AB} - \xi_{BA} = \epsilon_{AB}\xi_C{}^C$,

d) If $\phi_A\eta^A = 1$, $\phi_A\eta_B - \phi_B\eta_A = \epsilon_{AB}$,

e) $\epsilon_{AB}L^A{}_C L^B{}_D = (\det L)\epsilon_{CD}$.

12. For the spin dyad $\zeta_{(a)}{}^A$, show

a) $\epsilon_{AB}\zeta_{(a)}{}^A\zeta_{(b)}{}^B = \epsilon_{(a)(b)}$,   b) $\epsilon^{(a)(b)}\zeta_{(a)}{}^A\zeta_{(b)}{}^B = \epsilon^{AB}$

and   c) $\zeta_{(a)A}\zeta^{(b)A} = -\zeta_{(a)}{}^A\zeta^{(b)}{}_A = \delta^{(b)}_{(a)}$.

13. Show that

$$\psi_{AB...JK}\phi^K = 0 \Leftrightarrow \psi_{AB...JK} = \lambda_{AB...J}\phi_K \text{ for some } \lambda_{AB...J}.$$

14. Show that every spinor is equivalent to a completely symmetric spinor of the same rank modulo products of ϵ's by spinors of lower rank.

15.   a) Show that for a real tensor T_{ij},

$$\tfrac{1}{2}(T_{AA'BB'} - T_{BB'AA'}) = \phi_{AB}\epsilon_{A'B'} + \bar{\phi}_{A'B'}\epsilon_{AB},$$

where $T_{AA'BB'}$ is the spinorial tensor corresponding to T_{ij} and ϕ_{AB} is symmetric.

b) Specialize the above formula for a Maxwell field F_{ij}.

16. Let $B_{ijkl} = B_{[ij][kl]} = B_{klij}$. (The Riemann and Levi-Civita tensors have these symmetries.)

a) Show that the spinor equivalent of B_{ijkl} satisfies

$$\begin{aligned}
B_{AW'BX'CY'DZ'} = {} & B_{ABCD}\epsilon_{W'X'}\epsilon_{Y'Z'} + \bar{B}_{W'X'Y'Z'}\epsilon_{AB}\epsilon_{CD} \\
& + C_{ABY'Z'}\epsilon_{CD}\epsilon_{W'X'} + C_{CDW'X'}\epsilon_{AB}\epsilon_{Y'Z'},
\end{aligned}$$

where

$$B_{ABCD} = \tfrac{1}{4}B_{AP'B}{}^{P'}{}_{CQ'D}{}^{Q'} = B_{(AB)(CD)} = B_{CDAB}$$

and

$$C_{ABY'Z'} = \tfrac{1}{4}B_{AP'B}{}^{P'}{}_{GY'}{}^G{}_{Z'} = C_{(AB)(Y'Z')} = \bar{C}_{ABY'Z'}.$$

b) Show that

$$
\begin{aligned}
B_{AW'BX'CY'DZ'} &= A_{ABCD}\epsilon_{W'X'}\epsilon_{Y'Z'} + \epsilon_{AB}\epsilon_{CD}\bar{A}_{W'X'Y'Z'} \\
&\quad + \tfrac{1}{6}(\epsilon_{AD}\epsilon_{BC} + \epsilon_{AC}\epsilon_{BD})\epsilon_{W'X'}\epsilon_{Y'Z'}B \\
&\quad + C_{ABY'Z'}\epsilon_{CD}\epsilon_{W'X'} + C_{CDW'X'}\epsilon_{AB}\epsilon_{Y'Z'} \\
&\quad + \tfrac{1}{6}(\epsilon_{W'Z'}\epsilon_{X'Y'} + \epsilon_{W'Y'}\epsilon_{X'Z'})\epsilon_{AB}\epsilon_{CD}\bar{B},
\end{aligned}
$$

where

$$
A_{ABCD} = B_{(ABCD)} \quad \text{and} \quad B = B_{GH}{}^{GH}.
$$

17. Show that if F_{ij} is null, there exists a real null vector ξ^i such that

$$
F_{ij}\xi^j = F^*_{ij}\xi^j = 0, \text{ where } F^*_{ij} = \tfrac{1}{2}\epsilon_{ij}{}^{kl}F_{kl}.
$$

18. Prove that if $D\xi^A = 0$, both the flagpole and the flagplane determined by ξ^A are parallelly propagated.

19. Prove

$$
\Gamma_a{}^B{}_A = \tfrac{1}{2}\sigma_b{}^{BA'}(\sigma^c{}_{AA'}\Gamma^b{}_{ac} + \partial_a\sigma^b{}_{AA'}).
$$

20. Prove Friedman's lemma

$$
\Gamma_{(a)(b)CD'} = \tfrac{1}{2}\epsilon^{(k')(f')}\zeta_{(a)}{}^E\bar{\zeta}_{(f')}{}^{F'}[\zeta_{(b)E}\bar{\zeta}_{(k')F'}]_{;CD'}.
$$

21. *Notation:* In this problem greek indices run from 0 to 3, and lowercase latin ones from 1 to 3. The spinor indices follow the usual convention. Show that the Dirac equation in 4-component form,

$$
\gamma^\mu\partial_\mu\psi + im\psi = 0,
$$

is equivalent to

$$
\sigma^\mu{}_{AB'}\partial_\mu P^A + \frac{im}{\sqrt{2}}\bar{Q}_{B'} = 0 \quad \text{and} \quad \sigma^\mu{}_{AB'}\partial_\mu Q^A + \frac{im}{\sqrt{2}}\bar{P}_{B'} = 0.
$$

22. a) Show that in a vacuum spacetime, $(R_{ij} = 0)$, the Bianchi identity takes the form

$$
\nabla^{AA'}\Psi_{ABCD} = 0.
$$

 b) Show that in the current-free case, $(J^i = 0)$, Maxwell's equations become

$$
\nabla^{AA'}\phi_{AB} = 0.
$$

Solutions

1. a) If V is 1-dimensional, any non-zero vector, v, forms the required basis. v is normalized by dividing it by $|g(v, v)|^{-1/2}$. Assume that the theorem is true when V is k-dimensional. Now, let S be a k-dimensional subspace of a vector space V of $(k + 1)$ dimensions. By the induction hypothesis, there exists an orthonormal basis $\{v_1,...,v_k\}$ for S. For $w \notin S$, let

$$z = w - \sum_{i}^{k} c_i v_i,$$

where $c_i = g(w, v_i)/g(v_i, v_i)$. For every v_i, $i = 1 \ldots k$,

$$\begin{aligned} g(z, v_i) &= g(w - \sum_{j}^{k} c_j v_j, v_i) = g(w, v_i) - \sum_{j}^{k} c_j g(v_j, v_i) \\ &= g(w, v_i) - c_i g(v_i, v_i) = 0. \end{aligned}$$

The normalized z and $\{v_1,...,v_k\}$ form the required basis for V.

b) In one basis, let

$$g(x, x) = (x^1)^2 + (x^2)^2 + \cdots + (x^p)^2 - (x^{p+1})^2 - \cdots - (x^n)^2, \quad (i)$$

while in another basis, let

$$g(y, y) = (y^1)^2 + (y^2)^2 + \cdots + (y^q)^2 - (y^{q+1})^2 - \cdots - (y^n)^2, \quad (ii)$$

with $q < p$. According to (i), for any vector w with $w^{p+1} = \cdots = w^n = 0$, $g(w, w) \geq 0$. These vectors constitute a p-dimensional subspace, S_1, of V. Similarly, from (ii), for any non-zero vector w with $w^1 = \cdots = w^q = 0$, $g(w, w) < 0$. These conditions determine an $(n - q)$-dimensional subspace, S_2, of V. Now,

$$\dim(S_1) + \dim(S_2) = p + n - q = n + (p - q) > n,$$

which means that $S_1 \cap S_2 \neq 0$, i.e., S_1 and S_2 have non-zero vectors in common. For such a vector, w, $g(w, w) > 0$ by (i), but $g(w, w) < 0$ by (ii). A similar argument rules out $q > p$. The signature is $p - (n - p) = 2p - n$.

2.

$$e^{(b)}{}_i e_{(a)}{}^i = \eta^{(c)(b)} e_{(c)i} e_{(a)}{}^i = \eta^{(c)(b)} \eta_{(c)(a)} = \delta^{(b)}{}_{(a)}$$

3.

$$e_{(a)i}e^{(a)}{}_j = g_{ik}e_{(a)}{}^k e^{(a)}{}_j = g_{ik}\delta^k{}_j = g_{ij}.$$

4.

$$T_{(a)(b)} = e_{(a)}{}^i e_{(b)}{}^j T_{ij} = e_{(a)}{}^j e_{(b)}{}^i T_{ji} = e_{(b)}{}^i e_{(a)}{}^j (\pm T_{ij}) = \pm T_{(b)(a)}.$$

5.

$$
\begin{aligned}
\lambda_{(a)(b)(c)} &= e_{(b)i,j}[e_{(a)}{}^i e_{(c)}{}^j - e_{(a)}{}^j e_{(c)}{}^i] \\
&= e_{(b)i,j}e_{(a)}{}^i e_{(c)}{}^j - e_{(b)i,j}e_{(a)}{}^j e_{(c)}{}^i \\
&= e_{(b)i,j}e_{(a)}{}^i e_{(c)}{}^j - e_{(b)j,i}e_{(a)}{}^i e_{(c)}{}^j \\
&= [e_{(b)i,j} - e_{(b)j,i}]e_{(a)}{}^i e_{(c)}{}^j.
\end{aligned}
$$

In the absence of torsion, the ordinary derivatives may be replaced by covariant derivatives to give

$$\lambda_{(a)(b)(c)} = [e_{(b)i;j} - e_{(b)j;i}]e_{(a)}{}^i e_{(c)}{}^j = \gamma_{(a)(b)(c)} - \gamma_{(c)(b)(a)},$$

from which we obtain

$$\gamma_{(a)(b)(c)} = \tfrac{1}{2}[\lambda_{(a)(b)(c)} + \lambda_{(c)(a)(b)} - \lambda_{(b)(c)(a)}].$$

As the λ's involve only ordinary derivatives, we see that Christoffel symbols are not needed to evaluate $\gamma_{(a)(b)(c)}$.

6.

$$
\begin{aligned}
A_{(a),(b)} &= e_{(b)}{}^i \frac{\partial}{\partial x^i} A_{(a)} = e_{(b)}{}^i \frac{\partial}{\partial x^i} e_{(a)}{}^j A_j \\
&= e_{(b)}{}^i \nabla_{\partial_i}[e_{(a)}{}^j A_j] = e_{(b)}{}^i [e_{(a)}{}^j A_{j;i} + A_k e_{(a)}{}^k{}_{;i}] \\
&= A_{(a)|(b)} + e_{(a)k;i}e_{(b)}{}^i e_{(c)}{}^k A^{(c)} \\
&= A_{(a)|(b)} + \gamma_{(c)(a)(b)} A^{(c)} \\
&= A_{(a)|(b)} + \eta^{(n)(m)} \gamma_{(n)(a)(b)} A_{(m)}.
\end{aligned}
$$

7. a)

$$
\begin{aligned}
R^j{}_{lnm}e_j &= R(e_n, e_m)e_l \\
&= \nabla_n(\nabla_m e_l) - \nabla_m(\nabla_n e_l) - \nabla_{[e_n, e_m]}e_l \\
&= \nabla_n(\omega^k{}_{lm}e_k) - \nabla_m(\omega^k{}_{ln}e_k) - C^k{}_{nm}\nabla_k e_l \\
&= \omega^k{}_{lm,n}e_k + \omega^k{}_{lm}\omega^j{}_{kn}e_j - \omega^k{}_{ln,m}e_k - \omega^k{}_{ln}\omega^j{}_{km}e_j \\
&\quad - C^k{}_{nm}\omega^j{}_{lk}e_j.
\end{aligned}
$$

Renaming the dummy index k to j in the first and third terms, we deduce

$$R^j{}_{lnm} = \omega^j{}_{lm,n} - \omega^j{}_{ln,m} + \omega^j{}_{kn}\omega^k{}_{lm} - \omega^j{}_{km}\omega^k{}_{ln} - C^k{}_{nm}\omega^j{}_{lk}.$$

b) For vanishing torsion

$$\nabla_X Y - \nabla_Y X = [X, Y].$$

Applying this to basis vectors, we obtain

$$\nabla_j e_k - \nabla_k e_j = [e_j, e_k],$$

and hence,

$$C^i{}_{jk} = \omega^i{}_{kj} - \omega^i{}_{jk}.$$

c)

$$\nabla_k g_{ij} = 0 \Rightarrow g_{ij,k} - g_{lj}\omega^l{}_{ik} - g_{il}\omega^l{}_{jk} = 0.$$

So $g_{ij,k} = \omega_{jik} + \omega_{ijk}$. Using this relation, we find

$$\begin{aligned}
g_{ij,k} + g_{ik,j} - g_{jk,i} &= \omega_{ijk} + \omega_{ikj} - (\omega_{jki} - \omega_{jik}) - (\omega_{kji} - \omega_{kij}) \\
&= 2\omega_{ijk} - C_{ikj} - C_{jik} - C_{kij}.
\end{aligned}$$

Thus we establish

$$\omega_{ijk} = \tfrac{1}{2}(g_{ij,k} + g_{ik,j} - g_{jk,i} + C_{ikj} + C_{jik} + C_{kij}).$$

d) In a coordinate basis, the basis vectors commute, thus making $C^i{}_{jk} = 0$. Using part (b), we infer from this that $\omega^i{}_{jk} = \omega^i{}_{kj}$. With the vanishing of $C^i{}_{jk}$, the expressions in parts (a) and (c) obviously reduce to the usual expressions.

e) As the components of the metric, $g_{(a)(b)}$, are constant, from the first result of part (c) it follows that $\omega_{(a)(b)(c)} = -\omega_{(b)(a)(c)}$. Using this in the expression for the Riemann obtained in part (a), it follows that

$$\begin{aligned}
R_{(a)(b)(c)(d)} &= \gamma_{(a)(b)(d),(c)} - \gamma_{(a)(b)(c),(d)} + \gamma_{(a)(f)(c)}\gamma^{(f)}{}_{(b)(d)} \\
&\quad - \gamma_{(a)(f)(d)}\gamma^{(f)}{}_{(b)(c)} - C^{(f)}{}_{(c)(d)}\gamma_{(a)(b)(f)} \\
&= -\gamma_{(a)(b)(c),(d)} + \gamma_{(a)(b)(d),(c)} \\
&\quad + \gamma_{(b)(a)(f)}[\gamma_{(c)}{}^{(f)}{}_{(d)} - \gamma_{(d)}{}^{(f)}{}_{(c)}] \\
&\quad + \gamma_{(f)(a)(c)}\gamma_{(b)}{}^{(f)}{}_{(d)} - \gamma_{(f)(a)(d)}\gamma_{(b)}{}^{(f)}{}_{(c)}.
\end{aligned}$$

f) From the definition of $\gamma^{(d)}{}_{(a)(b)}$, $\nabla_{(b)}e_{(a)} = \gamma^{(d)}{}_{(a)(b)}e_{(d)}$, we get

$$\gamma^{(c)}{}_{(a)(b)} = \langle e^{(c)}, \nabla_{(b)}e_{(a)} \rangle = e^{(c)k}e_{(b)}{}^i \nabla_i e_{(a)k}.$$

The desired result is obtained by lowering the index (c).

8. a) The components can be read off directly from the line element given above.

b) We verify that the conditions of duality are satisfied.

$$\langle \hat{e}_i, \hat{\theta}^j \rangle = \langle \partial_i, dx^j \rangle - kA_i(x)\langle \partial_y, dx^j \rangle = \delta_i^j.$$

$$\langle \hat{e}_i, \hat{\theta}^5 \rangle = \langle \partial_i, kA_j dx^j \rangle + \langle -kA_i\partial_y, dy \rangle = kA_j\delta_i^j - kA_i = 0.$$

Also, clearly,

$$\langle \hat{e}_5, \hat{\theta}^j \rangle = 0 \quad \text{and} \quad \langle \hat{e}_5, \hat{\theta}^5 \rangle = 1.$$

c)

$$
\begin{aligned}
[\hat{e}_i, \hat{e}_j] &= [\partial_i, -kA_j\partial_y] + [-kA_i\partial_y, \partial_j] \\
&= -k(\partial_i A_j)\partial_y - kA_j\partial_i\partial_y + kA_j\partial_y\partial_i \\
&\quad -kA_i\partial_y\partial_j + k(\partial_j A_i)\partial_y + kA_i\partial_j\partial_y \\
&= -kF_{ij}\partial_y.
\end{aligned}
$$

$$[\hat{e}_i, \hat{e}_5] = [\partial_i, \partial_y] - kA_i(x)[\partial_y, \partial_y] = 0.$$

d) The results of part (c) show that the only non-vanishing structure constants are $\hat{C}^5{}_{ij} = -\hat{C}_{5ij} = -kF_{ij}$. The results required in this part are obtained by substituting these $\hat{C}^i{}_{\hat{j}\hat{k}}$, and the form of the metric given in part (a), in the expression for the connection coefficients given in part (c) of Prob. 6.

e) We use the result of Prob. 6, part (a). Apart from the terms involving only (i, j, l, m) (which constitute $R^i{}_{jlm}$), we have terms involving the index 5:

$$
\hat{\Gamma}^i{}_{5l}\hat{\Gamma}^5{}_{jm} - \hat{\Gamma}^i{}_{5m}\hat{\Gamma}^5{}_{jl} - \hat{C}^5{}_{lm}\hat{\Gamma}^i{}_{j5} = \\
\tfrac{1}{4}k^2 F^i{}_l F_{jm} - \tfrac{1}{4}k^2 F^i{}_m F_{jl} + \tfrac{1}{2}k^2 F^i{}_j F_{lm}.
$$

Hence,

$$\hat{R}^i{}_{jlm} = R^i{}_{jlm} - \tfrac{1}{4}(k^2 F^i{}_m F_{jl} - k^2 F^i{}_l F_{jm} - 2k^2 F^i{}_j F_{lm}).$$

In evaluating $\hat{R}^i_{5j5}$, we note that the only non-vanishing term is

$$-\hat{\Gamma}^i{}_{l5}\hat{\Gamma}^l{}_{5j} = -\tfrac{1}{4}k^2 F^i{}_l F^l{}_j.$$

f) Raising j and contracting on the pairs (i, l) and (j, m), we get

$$\hat{R}^{ij}{}_{ij} = R^{ij}{}_{ij} - \tfrac{1}{4}(k^2 F^i{}_j F^j{}_i - k^2 F^i{}_i F^j{}_j - 2k^2 F^{ij} F_{ij})$$

$$= R - \tfrac{1}{4}k^2(F^{ij} F_{ji} - 2F^{ij} F_{ij}) = R + \tfrac{3}{4}k^2 F^{ij} F_{ij}.$$

In a similar manner,

$$\hat{R}^{i5}{}_{i5} = -\hat{R}^i{}_{5i5} = \tfrac{1}{4}k^2 F^i{}_j F^j{}_i = -\tfrac{1}{4}k^2 F^{ij} F_{ij}.$$

g)

$$\hat{R} = \hat{R}^{i\hat{j}}{}_{i\hat{j}} = \hat{R}^{ij}{}_{ij} + \hat{R}^{i5}{}_{i5} + \hat{R}^{5i}{}_{5i} = \hat{R}^{ij}{}_{ij} + 2\hat{R}^{i5}{}_{i5} = R + \tfrac{1}{4}k^2 F^{ij} F_{ij}.$$

9. The metric coefficients are determined by contracting the metric with pairs of basis vectors. The orthonormality conditions imposed on the null tetrad imply

$$g(l, l) = g(n, n) = g(m, m) = g(\bar{m}, \bar{m}) = 0,$$

$$g(l, m) = g(l, \bar{m}) = g(n, m) = g(n, \bar{m}) = 0,$$

$$g(l, n) = 1 \quad \text{and} \quad g(m, \bar{m}) = -1.$$

10. a) As shown in Chandrasekhar's book (sections 19 and 20), the null geodesics satisfy the equation

$$\left(\frac{dr}{d\tau}\right)^2 + \frac{L^2}{r^2}\left(1 - \frac{2M}{r}\right) = E^2,$$

where

$$E = p_t = \left(1 - \frac{2M}{r}\right)\frac{dt}{d\tau}$$

and

$$L = p_\phi = r^2\frac{d\phi}{d\tau}.$$

For radial null geodesics, $L = 0$, and the equations reduce to

$$\frac{dr}{d\tau} = \pm E \quad \text{and} \quad \left(1 - \frac{2M}{r}\right)\frac{dt}{d\tau} = E,$$

or

$$\frac{dr}{dt} = \pm\left(1 - \frac{2M}{r}\right) = \pm\frac{\Delta}{r^2}.$$

The tangent vectors associated with these geodesics are

$$\frac{dt}{d\tau} = \frac{r^2}{\Delta}E, \quad \frac{dr}{d\tau} = \pm E, \quad \frac{d\theta}{d\tau} = 0 \quad \text{and} \quad \frac{d\phi}{d\tau} = 0,$$

where the θ equation is a result of the motion being confined to the invariant plane characterized by $\theta = \pi/2$.

b) Note that n^i, the vector corresponding to the negative sign for $dr/d\tau$, has been multiplied by $\Delta/(2r^2)$ precisely to satisfy the orthonormality conditions.

$$l \cdot l = g_{ij}l^i l^j = \frac{\Delta}{r^2}\left(\frac{r^2}{\Delta}\right)^2 + \left(-\frac{r^2}{\Delta}\right) = 0.$$

The relation $n \cdot n = 0$ follows similarly.

$$l \cdot n = \frac{\Delta}{r^2} \cdot \frac{r^2}{\Delta} \cdot \frac{1}{2} + \left(-\frac{r^2}{\Delta}\right) \cdot 1 \cdot \left(-\frac{\Delta}{2r^2}\right) = 1.$$

From the form of the vectors, it is obvious that

$$l \cdot m = l \cdot \bar{m} = n \cdot m = n \cdot \bar{m} = 0.$$

Finally,

$$m \cdot \bar{m} = (-r^2)\frac{1}{2r^2} + (-r^2 \sin^2 \theta)\frac{\operatorname{cosec}^2 \theta}{2r^2} = -1.$$

c) Knowing the basis vectors and the corresponding covariant vectors [1] [Chapter 3, eq. 285], we can calculate the $\lambda_{(a)(b)(c)}$ defined in Prob. 4. The only non-vanishing λ-symbols (apart from the ones obtained using the antisymmetry of the λ-symbols on the first and third indices, and complex conjugation which corresponds to replacing the index 3 by 4 and vice versa) are

$$\lambda_{122} = -\frac{M}{r^2}, \quad \lambda_{243} = -\frac{r - 2M}{2r^2}, \quad \lambda_{341} = -\frac{1}{r}$$

$$\text{and } \lambda_{334} = \frac{\cot \theta}{r\sqrt{2}}.$$

Using these, with the help of the expressions for the spin coefficients in terms of the λ-symbols, given in the solution to Prob. 4, we obtain the required results. As an example, we show the derivation of ρ:

$$\rho = \gamma_{314} = \tfrac{1}{2}[\lambda_{314} + \lambda_{431} - \lambda_{143}] = \tfrac{1}{2}[0 - 1/r - 1/r] = -1/r,$$

where $\lambda_{431} = \bar{\lambda}_{341}$ and $\lambda_{143} = -\lambda_{341}$.

d) The Weyl scalars are computed in a straightforward way using the standard definition of the scalars [1] [Chapter 1, eq. 294] and the components of the Riemann tensor [1] [Chapter 3, eq. 76].

e) The vanishing of κ, σ, λ and ν implies, by the Goldberg-Sachs theorem, that the Schwarzschild spacetime is of Petrov type-D, and that Ψ_0, Ψ_1, Ψ_3 and Ψ_4 vanish.

11. a) Proof by inspection.

b) Each of the indices can take only two distinct values, but the antisymmetrized part vanishes unless each of the three indices is different.

c)

$$0 = \epsilon_{A[B}\epsilon_{CD]} = \epsilon_{AB}\epsilon_{CD} + \epsilon_{AC}\epsilon_{DB} + \epsilon_{AD}\epsilon_{BC}.$$

Contracting this relation with an arbitrary spinor ξ^{CD}, we get

$$\epsilon_{AB}\xi_C{}^C - \xi^{CD}\epsilon_{CA}\epsilon_{DB} + \xi^{CD}\epsilon_{CB}\epsilon_{DA} = 0,$$

on simplifying and rearranging which, we obtain the desired result.

d) If ξ^{AB} in part (c) is a product of two 1-spinors (i.e., $\xi^{AB} = \phi^A\eta^B$), we have

$$\phi_A\eta_B - \phi_B\eta_A = \epsilon_{AB}\phi_C\eta^C = \epsilon_{AB}.$$

e) This can be shown by considering the four choices for the pair of indices CD and noting that $\det L = L^0{}_0 L^1{}_1 - L^1{}_0 L^0{}_1$.

12. Let $\zeta_{(0)}{}^A = o^A$ and $\zeta_{(1)}{}^A = \iota^A$. The condition of orthonormality is

$$\epsilon_{AB}o^A\iota^B = o_B\iota^B = -o^A\iota_A = 1.$$

a)

$$\epsilon_{AB}\zeta_{(a)}{}^A\zeta_{(b)}{}^B = \zeta_{(a)B}\zeta_{(b)}{}^B = \epsilon_{(a)(b)},$$

using the orthonormality condition.

b)

$$\epsilon^{(a)(b)}\zeta_{(a)}{}^A\zeta_{(b)}{}^B = \zeta_{(0)}{}^A\zeta_{(1)}{}^B - \zeta_{(1)}{}^A\zeta_{(0)}{}^B = o^A\iota^B - o^B\iota^A = \epsilon^{AB},$$

using Prob. 3(d).

c) The dyad indices are raised and lowered by $\epsilon^{(a)(b)}$ and $\epsilon_{(a)(b)}$:

$$\zeta^{(b)A}\epsilon_{(b)(a)} = \zeta_{(a)}{}^A \qquad \text{and} \qquad \epsilon^{(a)(b)}\zeta_{(b)}{}^A = \zeta^{(a)A}.$$

So

$$\zeta_{(a)A}\zeta^{(b)A} = \epsilon^{(b)(c)}\zeta_{(a)A}\zeta_{(c)}{}^A = \epsilon^{(b)(c)}\epsilon_{(a)(c)} = \delta^{(b)}_{(a)},$$

where the results of part (a) and Prob. 3(a) have been used. Also,

$$\zeta_{(a)A}\zeta^{(b)A} = \epsilon^{AC}\epsilon_{BA}\zeta_{(a)}{}^B\zeta^{(b)}{}_C = -\epsilon^{CA}\epsilon_{BA}\zeta_{(a)}{}^B\zeta^{(b)}{}_C = -\zeta_{(a)}{}^C\zeta^{(b)}{}_C.$$

13. Contracting the expression in Prob. 3(b) with $\psi^{AB...JK}\phi^L$ and proceeding as in 3(c), we infer

$$\psi_{AB...JK}\phi_L - \psi_{AB...JL}\phi_K = \epsilon_{KL}\psi_{AB...JM}\phi^M.$$

Hence,

$$\psi_{AB...JM}\phi^M = 0 \Leftrightarrow \psi_{AB...JK} = \lambda_{AB...J}\phi_K \text{ for some } \lambda_{AB...J}.$$

14. We denote the equivalence by $\cong$. We first prove a preliminary result. If $\phi_{AB...K}$ and $\chi_{AB...K}$ are two p-spinors, and if

$$\lambda^A\phi_{AB...K} \cong \lambda^A\chi_{AB...K}$$

for arbitrary λ^A, then

$$\phi_{AB...K} \cong \chi_{AB...K}.$$

Taking λ^A successively to be the members κ^A and μ^A of a basis, and forming the appropriate combination, we see that

$$(\kappa_L\mu^A - \mu_L\kappa^A)(\phi_{AB...K} - \chi_{AB...K}) \cong 0,$$

i.e.,

$$\delta^A_L(\phi_{AB...K} - \chi_{AB...K}) \cong 0,$$

which proves the result. The proof of the main result is by induction. The result of Prob. 3(c) can be rewritten as

$$\xi_{AB} = \xi_{(AB)} + \tfrac{1}{2}\epsilon_{AB}\xi_C{}^C.$$

Hence,

$$\xi_{AB} \cong \xi_{(AB)}.$$

We assume, as the induction hypothesis, that for any $(p-1)$-spinor,

$$\psi_{B...K} \cong \psi_{(B...K)}.$$

Now consider a p-spinor $\phi_{AB...K}$. By first symmetrizing ϕ on $(p-1)$ indices and then on the p-th index, we may write

$$\phi_{(AB...K)} = \tfrac{1}{p}(\underbrace{\phi_{A(BC...K)} + \phi_{B(AC...K)} + \cdots + \phi_{K(AB...J)}}_{p \text{ terms}}).$$

Any two terms within the parentheses differ by the exchange of only one pair of indices, and are therefore $\cong$, e.g.,

$$\phi_{A(BC...K)} - \phi_{B(AC...K)} = -\epsilon_{AB}\phi^M{}_{(MC...K)} \cong 0.$$

So, replacing each of those terms by the first one,

$$\phi_{(AB...K)} \cong \phi_{A(BC...K)}.$$

Contracting with an arbitrary spinor λ^A,

$$\lambda^A \phi_{(AB...K)} \cong \lambda^A \phi_{A(BC...K)}.$$

By our inductive hypothesis, the $(p-1)$-spinor on the right satisfies

$$\lambda^A \phi_{A(BC...K)} \cong \lambda^A \phi_{ABC...K},$$

and by the preliminary result proved above,

$$\phi_{A(BC...K)} \cong \phi_{ABC...K}.$$

Hence,

$$\phi_{ABC...K} \cong \phi_{(ABC...K)}.$$

15.   a)

$$\begin{aligned}
\tfrac{1}{2}(T_{AA'BB'} - T_{BB'AA'}) &= \tfrac{1}{2}(T_{AA'BB'} - T_{BA'AB'} \\
&\quad + T_{BA'AB'} - T_{BB'AA'}) \\
&= \tfrac{1}{2}(\epsilon_{AB} T_{CA'}{}^C{}_{B'} + \epsilon_{A'B'} T_{BC'A}{}^{C'}).
\end{aligned}$$

Defining ϕ_{AB} by

$$\phi_{AB} = \tfrac{1}{2} T_{BC'A}{}^{C'},$$

we have

$$\tfrac{1}{2}(T_{AA'BB'} - T_{BB'AA'}) = \phi_{AB}\epsilon_{A'B'} + \bar{\phi}_{A'B'}\epsilon_{AB},$$

where the reality of T_{ij} implies $\tfrac{1}{2}T_{CA'}{}^C{}_{B'} = \bar{\phi}_{A'B'}$. The obvious antisymmetry of the above expression along with the antisymmetry of ϵ_{AB} and $\epsilon_{A'B'}$ requires that ϕ_{AB} be symmetric.

b) For a Maxwell field, $F_{ij} = F_{[ij]}$. So

$$F_{ij} \leftrightarrow F_{AA'BB'} = \phi_{AB}\epsilon_{A'B'} + \bar{\phi}_{A'B'}\epsilon_{AB}.$$

16.   a) As B_{ijkl} is antisymmetric in two pairs of indices, the results of Prob. 14 may be applied to each pair. This produces the required result. The form and symmetries of B_{ABCD} and $C_{ABY'Z'}$ follow directly from those of ϕ in Prob. 14. The reality of $C_{ABY'Z'}$ is a consequence of the reality of B_{ijkl} and the fact that $C_{ABY'Z'}$ has an equal number of primed and unprimed indices.

b) We first write B_{ABCD} in terms of its totally antisymmetric part (using the symmetries of B_{ABCD} to simplify the expression):

$$
\begin{aligned}
B_{ABCD} &= \tfrac{1}{3}(B_{ABCD} + B_{ACBD} + B_{ADBC}) \\
&\quad + \tfrac{1}{3}(B_{ABCD} - B_{ACBD}) + \tfrac{1}{3}(B_{ABCD} - B_{ADBC}) \\
&= B_{(ABCD)} + \tfrac{1}{3}\epsilon_{BC}B_{AH}{}^H{}_D + \tfrac{1}{3}\epsilon_{BD}B_{AH}{}^H{}_C.
\end{aligned}
$$

But, using the 'see-saw' property and the symmetries of B_{ABCD}, we may show

$$
B_{AH}{}^H{}_D = -B_A{}^H{}_{HD} = -B_{DH}{}^H{}_A,
$$

from which it follows that

$$
B_{AH}{}^H{}_D = \tfrac{1}{2}(B_{AH}{}^H{}_D - B_{DH}{}^H{}_A) = \tfrac{1}{2}\epsilon_{AD}B_{GH}{}^{GH}
$$

and

$$
B_{ABCD} = B_{(ABCD)} + \tfrac{1}{6}(\epsilon_{BC}\epsilon_{AD} + \epsilon_{BD}\epsilon_{AC})B.
$$

Substituting this in the expression for $B_{AW'BX'CY'DZ'}$ found in part (a), the required relation is easily established.

17. Let $F_{ij} \leftrightarrow F_{AX'BY'}$ with

$$
F_{AX'BY'} = \epsilon_{AB}\bar{\phi}_{X'Y'} + \epsilon_{X'Y'}\phi_{AB}.
$$

As F_{ij} is null, $\phi_{AB} = \alpha_A\alpha_B$ for some α_A. The null vector we require is the one constructed from α_A, viz.,

$$
\xi^a = \sigma^a{}_{AX'}\xi^{AX'}, \quad \text{where } \xi^{AX'} = \alpha^A\bar{\alpha}^{X'}
$$

We prove the spinor form of the identity $F_{ij}\xi^j = 0$.

$$
\begin{aligned}
F_{AX'BY'}\xi^{BY'} &= (\epsilon_{AB}\bar{\phi}_{X'Y'} + \epsilon_{X'Y'}\phi_{AB})\xi^{BY'} \\
&= (\epsilon_{AB}\bar{\alpha}_{X'}\bar{\alpha}_{Y'} + \epsilon_{X'Y'}\alpha_A\alpha_B)\alpha^B\bar{\alpha}^{Y'} \\
&= 0.
\end{aligned}
$$

The identity $F_{ij}^*\xi^j = 0$ is proved similarly, using the fact that $F_{ij}^* \leftrightarrow i(\epsilon_{AB}\bar{\phi}_{X'Y'} - \epsilon_{X'Y'}\phi_{AB})$ [?] [Section 3.4].

18. Flagpole:

$$
D\xi^a = D(\sigma^a{}_{BX'}\xi^B\bar{\xi}^{X'}) = 0,
$$

where the Leibnitz property and the condition $D\sigma^a{}_{BX'} = 0$ have been used.

Flagplane:

Let (ξ^A, η^A) form a basis. $D(\xi_A \eta^A) = 0$ if and only if $\xi_A D\eta^A = 0$, whence $D\eta^A = \gamma \xi^A$ for some γ.

$$Dw^a \equiv D(\sigma^a{}_{BX'}[\xi^B \bar{\eta}^{X'} + \eta^B \bar{\xi}^{X'}]) = (\gamma + \bar{\gamma})\xi^a.$$

Hence $DF_{ab} \equiv 2D(\xi_{[a} w_{b]}) = 0$.

19. From

$$0 = \nabla_a \epsilon_{AB} = \epsilon_{AB,a} - \Gamma_a{}^C{}_A \epsilon_{CB} - \Gamma_a{}^C{}_B \epsilon_{AC} = -\Gamma_{aBA} + \Gamma_{aAB},$$

we deduce

$$\Gamma_{aAB} = \Gamma_{aBA}.$$

Also

$$0 = \nabla_a \sigma^b{}_{AA'} = \partial_a \sigma^b{}_{AA'} + \Gamma^b{}_{ac}\sigma^c{}_{AA'} - \Gamma_a{}^C{}_A \sigma^b{}_{CA'} - \bar{\Gamma}_a{}^{C'}{}_{A'}\sigma^b{}_{AC'}.$$

Rearranging terms, we have

$$\Gamma_a{}^C{}_A \sigma^b{}_{CA'} + \bar{\Gamma}_a{}^{C'}{}_{A'}\sigma^b{}_{AC'} = \partial_a \sigma^b{}_{AA'} + \sigma^c{}_{AA'}\Gamma^b{}_{ac}.$$

Multiplying by $\sigma_b{}^{BB'}$ results in

$$\Gamma_a{}^B{}_A \delta^{B'}_{A'} + \bar{\Gamma}_a{}^{B'}{}_{A'}\delta^B_A = \sigma_b{}^{BB'}(\partial_a \sigma^b{}_{AA'} + \sigma^c{}_{AA'}\Gamma^b{}_{ac}).$$

Contract on A', B', noting $\delta^{A'}_{A'} = 2$ and $\bar{\Gamma}_a{}^{A'}{}_{A'} = \epsilon^{A'E'}\bar{\Gamma}_{aE'A'} = 0$. The result is

$$\Gamma_a{}^B{}_A = \tfrac{1}{2}\sigma_b{}^{BA'}(\sigma^c{}_{AA'}\Gamma^b{}_{ac} + \partial_a \sigma^b{}_{AA'}).$$

20. The spin coefficients are defined by

$$\Gamma_{(a)(b)(c)(d')} = [\zeta_{(a)F}]_{;CD'}\zeta_{(b)}{}^F \zeta_{(c)}{}^C \zeta_{(d')}{}^{D'},$$

or, more briefly,

$$\Gamma_{(a)(b)CD'} = [\zeta_{(a)F}]_{;CD'}\zeta_{(b)}{}^F.$$

Contracting this with $\zeta^{(b)}{}_E$ and using the dyad relations of Prob. 11 and the symmetry of Γ on its first pair of indices, we obtain

$$[\zeta_{(a)E}]_{;CD'} = -\zeta^{(b)}{}_E \Gamma_{(b)(a)CD'} = \zeta_{(b)E}\Gamma^{(b)}{}_{(a)CD'}.$$

With the help of the Leibnitz rule and the results of Prob. 11, it is seen that

$$\tfrac{1}{2}\epsilon^{(k')(f')}\zeta_{(a)}{}^{E}\bar\zeta_{(f')}{}^{F'}[\zeta_{(b)E}\bar\zeta_{(k')F'}]_{;CD'}$$

$$= \tfrac{1}{2}\epsilon^{(k')(f')}\left\{\zeta_{(a)}{}^{E}\bar\zeta_{(f')}{}^{F'}\zeta_{(b)E}[\bar\zeta_{(k')F'}]_{;CD'}+\right.$$

$$\left.\zeta_{(a)}{}^{E}\bar\zeta_{(f')}{}^{F'}\bar\zeta_{(k')F'}[\zeta_{(b)E}]_{;CD'}\right\}$$

$$= \tfrac{1}{2}\epsilon^{(k')(f')}\left\{-\epsilon_{(a)(b)}\bar\zeta_{(f')}{}^{F'}\bar\Gamma^{(d')}{}_{(k')CD'}\bar\zeta_{(d')F'}+\right.$$

$$\left.\epsilon_{(k')(f')}\zeta_{(a)}{}^{E}\Gamma^{(d)}{}_{(b)CD'}\zeta_{(d)E}\right\}$$

$$= \tfrac{1}{2}\epsilon^{(k')(f')}\left\{-\epsilon_{(a)(b)}\delta^{(d')}_{(f')}\bar\Gamma_{(d')(k')CD'}+\epsilon_{(k')(f')}\delta^{(d)}_{(a)}\Gamma_{(d)(b)CD'}\right\}$$

$$= \tfrac{1}{2}\epsilon^{(k')(f')}\left\{-\epsilon_{(a)(b)}\bar\Gamma_{(k')(f')CD'}+\epsilon_{(k')(f')}\Gamma_{(a)(b)CD'}\right\}$$

$$= \tfrac{1}{2}\epsilon^{(k')(f')}\epsilon_{(k')(f')}\Gamma_{(a)(b)CD'} = \Gamma_{(a)(b)CD'}.$$

21. The γ matrices are given by

$$\gamma^0 = \begin{bmatrix} 0 & 1 \\ 1 & 0 \end{bmatrix} \quad \text{and} \quad \gamma^i = \begin{bmatrix} 0 & -\sigma^i \\ \sigma^i & 0 \end{bmatrix},$$

where the σ^i are the Pauli matrices. Setting

$$\psi = \begin{pmatrix} P^A \\ \bar Q_{B'} \end{pmatrix},$$

the Dirac equation becomes

$$\begin{bmatrix} 0 & 1 \\ 1 & 0 \end{bmatrix}\begin{bmatrix} \partial_0 P^A \\ \partial_0 \bar Q_{B'} \end{bmatrix} + \begin{bmatrix} 0 & -\sigma^i \\ \sigma^i & 0 \end{bmatrix}\begin{bmatrix} \partial_i P^A \\ \partial_i \bar Q_{B'} \end{bmatrix} + im\begin{bmatrix} P^A \\ \bar Q_{B'} \end{bmatrix} = 0,$$

i.e.,

$$\partial_0 \bar Q_{B'} - \sigma^i \partial_i \bar Q_{B'} + im P^A = 0$$

and

$$\partial_0 P^A + \sigma^i \partial_i P^A + im\bar Q_{B'} = 0.$$

Noting that $\sqrt{2}\sigma^\mu{}_{AB'} \equiv (1, \sigma^i)$, we see that the second equation in the above set is equivalent to

$$\sigma^\mu{}_{AB'}\partial_\mu P^A + \frac{im}{\sqrt{2}}\bar Q_{B'} = 0.$$

We now show that the other spinor equation is equivalent to the first of the equations in the above set. We have

$$\sqrt{2}\sigma^\mu{}_{AB'}\partial_\mu Q^A + im\bar P^{C'}\epsilon_{C'B'} = 0.$$

The complex conjugate of this equation is

$$\sqrt{2}\sigma^\mu{}_{BA'}\partial_\mu\bar{Q}^{A'} - imP^C\epsilon_{CB} = 0,$$

where the fact that $\sigma^\mu{}_{AB'}$ is Hermitian has been used. We multiply this equation by ϵ^{DB}, producing

$$\sqrt{2}\sigma^{\mu D}{}_{A'}\partial_\mu\bar{Q}^{A'} - imP^C\epsilon^{DB}\epsilon_{CB} = 0.$$

As $\epsilon^{DB}\epsilon_{CB} = \delta^D_C$, with the help of the Penrose 'see-saw', we have

$$\sqrt{2}\sigma^{\mu DA'}\partial_\mu\bar{Q}_{A'} + imP^D = 0.$$

But

$$\sigma^{\mu DA'} = \epsilon^{DA}\epsilon^{A'B'}\sigma^\mu{}_{AB'},$$

or, in matrix notation,

$$\begin{bmatrix} \sigma^{\mu 00'} & \sigma^{\mu 01'} \\ \sigma^{\mu 10'} & \sigma^{\mu 11'} \end{bmatrix} = [\epsilon][\sigma^\mu][\epsilon]^T$$

$$= \begin{bmatrix} 0 & 1 \\ -1 & 0 \end{bmatrix}\begin{bmatrix} \sigma^\mu{}_{00'} & \sigma^\mu{}_{01'} \\ \sigma^\mu{}_{10'} & \sigma^\mu{}_{11'} \end{bmatrix}\begin{bmatrix} 0 & -1 \\ 1 & 0 \end{bmatrix}$$

$$= \begin{bmatrix} \sigma^\mu{}_{11'} & -\sigma^\mu{}_{10'} \\ -\sigma^\mu{}_{01'} & \sigma^\mu{}_{00'} \end{bmatrix}.$$

So

$$\sigma^{0DA'} = \sigma^0{}_{DA'} \quad \text{and} \quad \sigma^{iDA'} = -\sigma^i{}_{DA'}.$$

Hence,

$$\partial_0\bar{Q}_{A'} - \sigma^i\partial_i\bar{Q}_{A'} + imP^D = 0.$$

22. a) Noting that in the expression for the spinor equivalent for the Riemann tensor (see Prob. 15, part (b)), $C_{ABY'Z'}$ is completely determined by the trace-free Ricci tensor and that $B = R/4$ (see [?] [Section 13.2], we find that in this case, $C_{ABY'Z'}$ and B are zero. The expression for the Riemann tensor becomes

$$R_{AW'BX'CY'DZ'} = \Psi_{ABCD}\epsilon_{W'X'}\epsilon_{Y'Z'} + \epsilon_{AB}\epsilon_{CD}\bar{\Psi}_{W'X'Y'Z'},$$

where $\Psi_{ABCD} = \Psi_{(ABCD)}$. As in Prob. 16, the right dual is given by

$$R^*_{abcd} \leftrightarrow i(\epsilon_{AB}\epsilon_{CD}\bar{\Psi}_{W'X'Y'Z'} - \epsilon_{W'X'}\epsilon_{Y'Z'}\Psi_{ABCD}).$$

Writing the Bianchi identities in the form $\nabla^d R^*_{abcd} = 0$ and taking the spinor equivalent $(\nabla^{DZ'} R^*_{AW'BX'CY'DZ'} = 0)$, we obtain on symmetrizing (AB),

$$0 = \nabla^D{}_{Y'} \Psi_{ABCD},$$

or, on rearranging and renaming the indices (note symmetry of Ψ_{ABCD}),

$$\nabla^{AA'} \Psi_{ABCD} = 0.$$

b) In the current-free case, Maxwell's equations are

$$\nabla^a F_{ab} = 0 \qquad \text{and} \qquad \nabla^a F^*_{ab} = 0.$$

Their spinor equivalents are, respectively,

$$\nabla^{AA'} (\epsilon_{AB} \bar{\phi}_{A'B'} + \phi_{AB} \epsilon_{A'B'}) = 0$$

and

$$\nabla^{AA'} (\epsilon_{AB} \bar{\phi}_{A'B'} - \phi_{AB} \epsilon_{A'B'}) = 0.$$

Subtracting the second equation from the first, we obtain the required result.

References

1. Chandrasekhar S, 1983, *The Mathematical Theory of Black Holes*, (Clarendon:Oxford); Sections 4, 5, 6, 7, 19, 20, 21, 102c, 102d.
2. Pirani F A E, 1965, *Introduction to Gravitational Radiation Theory* in *Lectures on General Relativity*, Brandeis Summer Institute on Theoretical Physics, 1964, vol 1 (Prentice-Hall:New Jersey); Secs. 3.2, 3.3, 3.4, 3.6, 3.7, 3.8.
3. Toms D J, 1984, *Kaluza-Klein Theoreies* in *An Introduction to Kaluza-Klein Theories*, edited by Lee H C, (World Scientific:Singapore)
4. Wald R M, 1984, *General Relativity*, (University of Chicago:Chicago); Chapter 2.

5.   ASPECTS OF QUANTUM FIELD THEORY

T.PADMANABHAN
Inter-University Center for Astronomy & Astrophysics
Post Bag No.4, Ganeshkhind
Pune 411 007, India

1. General Introduction

These lectures concentrate on a series of topics in quantum field theory
which, in my opinion, are becoming increasingly relevant to the students of
general relativity and gravity. Since there exists several formal textbooks
in quantum field theory, it is probably worthwhile to explain how these
lectures differ from standard text books and what exactly their scope is.

For most part of the lectures I have chosen topics which are not discussed
in adequate details in standard textbooks. Even while dealing with standard
material I have tried to concentrate on subtleties and questions of technique
which are not usually emphasised. This is done because it is precisely these
aspects of quantum field theory which become relevant in the study of
quantum fields in curved spacetimes and in other topics in the interface of
gravity and quantum field theory.

The lectures are divided into five parts. Part 2 is a fairly comprehensive and self-contained introduction to the concept and application of path
integrals. No previous acquaintance with the subject is assumed though
familiarity with conventional quantum mechanics (at the level of a first
course) is required. The emphasis is on using path integrals as a technique
for studying non-perturbative aspects of quantum theory. Several important concepts in field theory are illustrated in the conceptually simpler
environment of quantum mechanics so as to make the transition in the latter parts 3 and 4 easier. The discussion of path integrals based on Jacobi
action and its connection with an infinite system of harmonic oscillators
is new and (as far as the author known) has not been emphasised before.
This connection allows one to proceed logically from the path integral for
a relativistic particle to the concept of a quantum field. Part 3 clarifies this

connection and introduces the scalar field to describe a relativistic spinless particle. Possible generalization to other fields are briefly mentioned.

At this juncture one could take different routes to proceed further. I have omitted the discussion of conventional topics like canonical quantization, perturbative study of interactions etc. etc. There are two reasons for this conscious choice. First of all, many of these concepts are fairly useless in the context in which gravitational field plays a crucial role. The conceptual machinery behind this approach – which has been so successful in quantum electrodynamics and electroweak unification – fails to provide us with a clear direction to proceed further. Personally, I consider perturbative renormalizability as an overemphasised trick which needs to be replaced by sounder and more fundamental concepts if progress has to be achieved in combining quantum theory with gravity. Since these lectures are primarily intended for relativists I have not bothered to include historically relevant topics like perturbation theory. Secondly there exists excellent text books which discuss perturbation methods in quantum field theory, Feynman rules etc. and an interested reader will have no difficulty in learning these topics.

Instead of covering these subjects, I have devoted part 4 to a detailed discussion of the concept of effective action. The basic idea of effective action is explained using a quantum mechanical toy model and generalized to the study of a scalar field with arbitrary self interaction. The renormalizability (or otherwise) of a scalar field with self interaction is discussed in the context of finiteness of effective potential. This also allows the introduction of "running coupling constant" without having to go through the detailed discussion of Feynman rules etc. I have also included in part 4 an extensive discussion of Schwinger's proper time method applied to the evaluation of effective Lagrangian and pair creation in external fields. These are illustrated in the context of creation of scalar particles by an externally specified electromagnetic field from different points of view.

Part 5 discusses a series of selected examples from the study of quantum field theory in non-trivial backgrounds. The intimate connection between the choice of harmonic oscillators to describe the field and the concept of a field is illustrated by working out the ground state of the scalar field in $(1+1)$ dimension in two different coordinate systems. This is followed by a discussion of particle creation in several external gravitational fields. Particle creation in an expanding universe is studied by techniques similar to those used in part 4; other cases like Schwarzschild metric etc. are discussed in a unified manner using a semiclassical propagator.

Since the lectures were intended to be of pedagogical nature, I have kept citations to original literature to a minimum. The suggestions for further reading given at the end might help the reader to delve into the original literature if he so desires.

2. The Path Integral

2.1. INTRODUCTION

This part is devoted to a detailed discussion of path integral techniques. Section 2, 3 and 4 introduce the basic ideas and defines the path integral. The rigorous definition of path integral by analytic continuation to Euclidean time is covered in section 5 and various techniques using the path integral is illustrated in section 7. Section 8 and 9 discuss the system of harmonic oscillators using path integrals, paving the way for quantum field theory. The last two sections contain a discussion of path integrals based on Jacobi action and its relation with harmonic oscillators.

2.2. AMPLITUDES FROM 'SUM OVER PATHS'

In classical mechanics, the laws governing the motion of a particle in a potential $V(x)$ can be obtained from the principle of least action. This principle states that the trajectory followed by a particle in travelling from (t_1, x_1) to (t_2, x_2) will be the one which makes the 'action'

$$A[x(t)] \equiv \int_{t_1}^{t_2} dt L(\dot{x}, x) = \int_{t_1}^{t_2} dt (\frac{1}{2}m\dot{x}^2 - V(x)) \tag{1}$$

an extremum. This extremum path can be found as follows: Consider any two paths $x(t)$ and $y(t)$ connecting the events $\mathcal{P}1$ and $\mathcal{P}2$. We can always write $y(t)$ as $x(t) + \epsilon f(t)$ where ϵ is an adjustable 'book-keeping' parameter. Since both $x(t)$ and $y(t)$ connect the same events it is clear that the function $f(t)$ vanishes at l_1 and l_2. We can now compute the difference ΔA between the value of the actions $A[x(t)]$ and $A[y(t)]$ for the two paths. This difference, will depend on ϵ and can be expanded as a Taylor series in ϵ. The action will be an extremum for a path $x(t)$ if the difference ΔA has no linear term in ϵ. From (1) it is clear that

$$\begin{aligned} \Delta A &\equiv A[x(t) + \epsilon f(t)] - A[x(t)] \\ &= -\epsilon \int_{t_1}^{t_2} dt \left(m\frac{d^2x}{dt^2} + V'(x) \right) f(t) + \mathcal{O}(\epsilon^2). \end{aligned} \tag{2}$$

If the linear term has to vanish for arbitrary $f(t)$, then we must have

$$m\frac{d^2x}{dt^2} + V'(x) = 0 \tag{3}$$

which determines the extremum path. The solution to this differential equation connecting the events $\mathcal{P}1$ and $\mathcal{P}2$ gives the classical trajectory of the particle. We will denote this classical path by $x_c(t)$ and the corresponding value for the action, $A(x_c)$ by A_c.

The action, in general, assigns a real number to a path $x(t)$ and is called a 'functional' of $x(t)$. The action in (1) is a very special kind of functional in the sense that it can be expressed as an integral over a local lagrangian $L(\dot{x}, x)$. To calculate the action for a particular path $x(t)$, we will first evaluate the integrand $L(\dot{x}(t), x(t)) = L(t)$ for this path and then integrate the resulting function over t. The action in (1) is defined only for those paths $x(t)$ for which this procedure can be carried out in an unambiguous way; in particular the integrand $L(t)$ should be a single-valued function of t. This, in turn, implies that the function $x(t)$ should be single-valued. Paths like the one in Figure 1 are not allowed as valid arguments for the

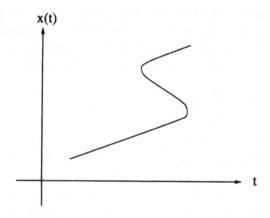

action functional.

The classical description of dynamics, outlined above, depends crucially on the existence of well defined trajectories for motion. To characterize a path at any instant of time, it is necessary to specify both the position and velocity of the particle at that instant of time. Since uncertainty principle forbids such a simultaneous specification of position and momentum the above description needs to be modified in quantum mechanics.

A suitable modification can be arrived at by considering the results of standard two-slit interference experiment with, say, electrons. These experiments suggest that the electrons do not follow a definite trajectory in travelling from the electron gun to the screen. Instead, we must associate with each path connecting the electron gun and any particular point on the screen, a probability amplitude $\mathcal{A}(\text{path})$. The net probability amplitude $K(2; 1)$ for the particle to go from the event $\mathcal{P}1$ to the event $\mathcal{P}2$, is obtained by adding up the amplitudes for all the paths connecting the events:

$$K(2;1) \equiv K(t_2, x_2; t_1, x_1) = \sum_{\text{paths}} A(\text{path}) \qquad (4)$$

The addition of the *amplitudes* allows for the quantum mechanical interference between the paths. (In the case of the two-slit experiment, for example, we will add the amplitudes for paths through hole-1 and hole-2; this will lead to the correct interference pattern.). The *probability* for any process, of course, is obtained by taking the square of the modulus of the amplitude.

The quantity $K(t_2, x_2; t_1, x_1)$ contains the full dynamical information about the quantum mechanical system. Given $K(t_2, x_2; t_1, x_1)$ and the initial amplitude $\psi(t_1, x_1)$ for the particle to be found at x_1, we can compute the wave function $\psi(t, x)$ at any later time by the usual rules for combining the amplitudes:

$$\psi(t, x) = \int dx_1 K(t, x; t_1, x_1) \psi(t_1, x_1) \qquad (5)$$

Therefore the specification of (i) A and (ii) the rule for evaluating the sum, in (4), will provide a complete quantum mechanical description of the system.

Since $K(t_2, x_2; t_1, x_1)$ contains the complete dynamical information of a quantum mechanical system, it is obvious that we will not be able to *derive* the rules for its computation from fundamental considerations. We have to content ourselves by *motivating* a possible choice for A and the rule for computing the sum in (4).

Since we do not expect any one path to be more probable than the other it seems reasonable to demand that the *probability* for any particular path $|A(\text{path})|^2$ must be independent of the path. In other words, A should have the form

$$A = \exp i\Lambda(\text{path}) \qquad (6)$$

where Λ is real and we have ignored an overall normalization constant. In the classical limit, however, we would like the classical path x_c – obtained by extremising the action – to contribute dominantly to the sum in (4). This can be achieved most easily by taking $\Lambda(\text{path}) = [A(\text{path})/\hbar]$. Then the Kernel becomes

$$K(t_2, x_2; t_1, x_1) = \sum_{\text{all x(t)}} \exp i \frac{A[x(t)]}{\hbar}. \qquad (7)$$

In the limit of $\hbar$ going to zero, the phase of A oscillates rapidly and the contributions from different paths are mostly cancelled out; the only ones that survive are those for which A is an extremum, viz. the classical paths.

This choice in (7) thus provides a natural explanation for the validity of principle of least action in the classical theory.

Since the action functional A is well defined only for single-valued functions $x(t)$, the sum in (7) may also be restricted to such functions. This imposes an important constraint on $K(t_2, x_2; t_1, x_1)$. Consider three instants of time (t_1, t_2, t_3) such that $t_1 < t_2 < t_3$. Since the paths are single-valued, the path which connects the event $\mathcal{P}1$ to the event $\mathcal{P}3$ must cross the $t = t_2$ line at some single co-ordinate x_2. Hence the usual law of combining probability amplitudes allows us to write

$$K(3;1) = \int dx_2 K(t_3, x_3; t_2, x_2) K(t_2, x_2; t_1, x_1). \qquad (8)$$

which is a constraint on the normalization of K.

The behaviour of the amplitude $K(t_2, x_2; t_1, x_1)$ under time reversal, $t_1 \leftrightarrow t_2$, allows us to put another constraint on the Kernel. Assuming that the prescription for summing over paths does not single out a direction of time, and noticing that the action functional changes sign under time reversal, we get

$$K(t_2, x_2; t_1, x_1)^* = K(t_1, x_2; t_2, x_2) \qquad (9)$$

Thus time reversal is equivalent to complex conjugation of the amplitude, which is a general feature of quantum theory. It is easy to show that equations (8) and (9) together guarantee that the normalization of wave functions are preserved under time evolution.

2.3. SUM OVER PATHS FOR QUADRATIC ACTIONS

We are now in a position to work out the form of $K(t_2, x_2; t_1, x_1)$ for a particularly important class of systems. These are the systems described by an action which is at most quadratic in x and $\dot{x}$; that is, for actions in the form

$$A[x(t)] = \int (B(t)\dot{x}^2 + C(t)x^2 + M(t)x)dt \qquad (10)$$

A more general form for a quadratic action

$$A[x(t)] = \int [a(t)\dot{x}^2 + b(t)\dot{x} + c(t)x\dot{x} + d(t)x^2 + e(t)x + f(t)]dt \qquad (11)$$

can be reduced to the form in (10) by suitable partial integrations. To evaluate (7) for such an action we proceed as follows: We write an arbitrary path $x(t)$ as $x_c(t) + q(t)$ where $q(t)$ denotes the deviation from the classical path. Since all the paths are between two specified end points, it follows that $q(t_1) = q(t_2) = 0$. We can now write

$$K(t_2, x_2; t_1, x_1) = \sum_{\text{all x(t)}} \exp \frac{i}{\hbar} A[x(t)] = \sum_{\text{all q(t)}} \exp \frac{i}{\hbar} A[x_c(t) + q(t)] \quad (12)$$

But since A has only terms which are at most quadratic, $A[x_c(t) + q(t)]$ has the form

$$A[x_c(t) + q(t)] = A[x_c(t)] + L[x_c, q] + Q[q; t_1, t_2] \quad (13)$$

in which L is linear in q (and x_c) while Q is quadratic in q. (The Q cannot depend on x_c but it can depend on (t_1, t_2) because these appear as the limits of t-integration.) But since x_c is an extremum (classical) path, the linear term must identically vanish; $L = 0$. Therefore

$$
\begin{aligned}
K(t_2, x_2; t_1, x_1) &= \sum_{\text{all}} q(t) \exp \frac{i}{\hbar} A[x_c(t) + q(t)] \\
&= \exp \frac{i}{\hbar} A_c \left(\sum_{\text{all}} q(t) \exp \frac{i}{\hbar} Q(t_1, t_2; q(t)) \right). \quad (14)
\end{aligned}
$$

The expression inside bracket is some function of t_1 and t_2 alone. Calling this quantity $N(t_1, t_2)$, we can write the form of the Kernel to be

$$K(t_2, x_2; t_1, x_1) = N(t_1, t_2) \exp \frac{i}{\hbar} A_c(t_2, x_2; t_1, x_1) \quad (15)$$

We see that the x-dependence of the Kernel is only through the classical action A_c. We emphasize that the above result is *exact* for systems with quadratic actions.

So far we have not specified the exact prescription for calculating the sum over paths. To determine the value of N we need to specify the rule for summing over the paths. In the case of quadratic actions, a natural definition exists allowing us to express N as a determinant of a differential operator. This is achieved as follows: For actions in the form of (10) the quantity Q can be expressed as

$$
\begin{aligned}
Q &= \int_{t_1}^{t_3} dt [B\dot{q}^2 + Cq^2] \\
&= [B q \dot{q}]_{t_1}^{t_2} - \int_{t_1}^{t_2} \left[q(\frac{d}{dt} B \frac{d}{dt} - C)q \right] dt \\
&= -\int_{t_1}^{t_2} \left[q(\frac{d}{dt} B \frac{d}{dt} - C)q \right] dt \equiv -\int_{t_1}^{t_2} dt \, q(t) \hat{D} q. \quad (16)
\end{aligned}
$$

In arriving at the last line we have used the fact that q vanishes at the endpoints and defined an operator

$$\hat{D} = (\frac{d}{dt}B\frac{d}{dt} - C) \tag{17}$$

[One may worry that the vanishing of q does not ensure the vanishing of $q\dot{q}$ for certain paths; it turns out that these paths form a set of zero measure in the sum over paths.] In all cases of physical interest this operator will possess a complete set of orthonormal eigenfunctions $\{f_n(t)\}$ with the eigenvalues $\{\lambda_n\}$, satisfying the same boundary conditions as q. That is, there will exist a complete set of functions satisfying the conditions

$$\hat{D}f_n = \lambda_n f_n; \int_{t_1}^{t_2} dt f_n f_m = \delta_{nm}; f_n(t_1) = f_n(t_m) = 0. \tag{18}$$

We can now expand any $q(t)$ in terms of the functions $\{f_n\}$

$$q(t) = \sum_n c_n f_n \tag{19}$$

obtaining a set of numbers $\{c_n\}$. This set of numbers completely characterize the function $q(t)$. The quantity $Q[q(t)]$ which was a *functional* of the path $q(t)$ can now be expressed as a *function* of the numbers $\{c_n\}$'s as above equation (21):

$$
\begin{aligned}
Q[q(t)] &= -\int q\hat{D}q dt = -\int (\sum_n c_n f_n)\hat{D}(\sum_m c_m f_m)dt \\
&= -\sum_{nm} c_n c_m \int f_n f_m \lambda_m dt = -\sum_{nm} \lambda_n c_n c_m \delta_{nm} = -\sum_n \lambda_n c_n^2 \\
&= Q[c_1, c_2, ..]
\end{aligned}
\tag{20}
$$

Therefore, it seems reasonable to define the sum over all functions $q(t)$ as equivalent to an integration over the set of $\{c_n\}$'s. That is, we would like to make the replacement

$$\sum_{\text{all } q(t)} \to \int_{-\infty}^{+\infty} \prod_n \frac{dc_n}{M_n} \tag{21}$$

where M_n is a measure which determines the weightage to be given to the n-th eigenmode. In general, we could have made M_n's explicit functions of c_n's. *In making the above choice, we have decided that the weightage given to each path depends only on how 'wiggly' each path is and not on the explicit shape of the path.* We can now write

$$N = \sum_{\text{all } q(t)} \exp \frac{i}{\hbar} Q[q(t)] = \int_{-\infty}^{+\infty} \prod_n \frac{dc_n}{M_n} \exp -\frac{i}{\hbar} \sum_n \lambda_n c_n^2$$

$$= \prod_n \left[\int_{-\infty}^{+\infty} \frac{dc_n}{M_n} \exp -\frac{i}{\hbar} \lambda_n c_n^2 \right] \tag{22}$$

We now face a mathematical difficulty. The integrals over c_n in the above expression does not exist because the integrand oscillates for large c_n if all the λ_n's are real. It is necessary to give an extra prescription which will allow us to interpret these integrals.

We can give meaning to this integral if we assume each of the λ_n's have an infinitesimal negative imaginary part. That is we replace λ_n by $(\lambda_n - i\epsilon)$ and set ϵ to zero at the end of the calculations. In this case,

$$I_n = \int_{-\infty}^{+\infty} \frac{dc_n}{M_n} \exp -\frac{i}{\hbar} \lambda_n c_n^2 \equiv \lim_{\epsilon \to 0} \int_{-\infty}^{+\infty} \frac{dc_n}{M_n} \exp -\frac{i}{\hbar} (\lambda_n - i\epsilon) c_n^2$$

$$= \lim_{\epsilon \to 0} \frac{1}{M_n} \left(\frac{i\pi\hbar}{(\lambda_n - i\epsilon)} \right)^{\frac{1}{2}} = \frac{1}{M_n} \left(\frac{i\pi\hbar}{\lambda_n} \right)^{\frac{1}{2}} \tag{23}$$

With this definition of the integrals, we get

$$N = \prod_n \frac{(i\pi\hbar)^{\frac{1}{2}}}{M_n} \lambda_n^{-\frac{1}{2}} \tag{24}$$

The normalization constant M_n was not specified so far. We have to choose it in such a manner that the resulting Kernel satisfy our conditions (8) and (9). To do this correctly, we will work out the expression for N in the special case of a free particle using (8) and (9). Comparing this result with (24), we can determine M_n.

Since the extremum path for a free particle is a straight line, the classical action for the free particle will be

$$A_c = \left(\frac{m}{2} \right) \frac{(x_2 - x_1)^2}{t_2 - t_1} \tag{25}$$

giving

$$K(t_2, x_2; t_1, x_1) = N(t_2 - t_1) \exp \frac{i}{\hbar} \left(\frac{m}{2} \right) \frac{(x_2 - x_1)^2}{t_2 - t_1}$$

$$\equiv N(T) \exp \frac{i}{\hbar} \left(\frac{m}{2} \right) \frac{(x_2 - x_1)^2}{T} \tag{26}$$

We have set $N(t_2, t_1) = N(t_2 - t_1) = N(T)$ using the time translation invariance of the system. We shall now determine $N(T)$ using (8) and (9). Substituting (26) into (8) we get

$$K(x_3 t_3; x_1 t_1) = N(t_3 - t_1) \exp \frac{im}{2\hbar} \frac{(x_3 - x_1)^2}{(t_3 - t_1)}$$

$$= N(t_3 - t_2)N(t_2 - t_1) \int_{-\infty}^{+\infty} dx_2 \exp \frac{im}{2\hbar} \left[\frac{(x_3 - x_2)^2}{t_3 - t_2} + \frac{(x_2 - x_1)^2}{t_2 - t_1} \right]$$
(27)

Working out the integral, we can write this condition in the form

$$N(t_3 - t_1) = N(t_3 - t_2)N(t_2 - t_1) \left(\frac{2\pi i\hbar}{m} \right)^{1/2} \frac{(t_3 - t_2)^{1/2}(t_2 - t_1)^{1/2}}{(t_3 - t_1)^{1/2}}.$$
(28)

If we now put $(t_2 - t_1) = \alpha$, $(t_3 - t_2) = \beta$ and

$$M(z) \equiv N(z) \left(\frac{2\pi i\hbar z}{m} \right)^{1/2}$$
(29)

the above relation reduces to the form

$$M(\alpha + \beta) = M(\alpha)M(\beta).$$
(30)

This equation has the general solution

$$M(z) = \exp(kz)$$
(31)

where k is some constant. Therefore $N(T)$ must be of the form

$$N(T) = e^{kT} \left(\frac{m}{2\pi i\hbar T} \right)^{1/2}.$$
(32)

We now use the condition (9), that $K(x_2 t_2; x_1 t_1) = K^*(x_2 t_1; x_1 t_2)$. This will give

$$\exp(k^* T) = \exp(-kT)$$
(33)

implying that k is purely imaginary; $k = (i/\hbar)\mu$ with real μ. Therefore, the Kernel can be written as

$$K(x_2 T; x_1, 0) = \left(\frac{m}{2\pi i\hbar T} \right)^{1/2} \exp \frac{i}{\hbar} \left[\frac{m}{2} \frac{(x_2 - x_1)^2}{T} + \mu T \right]$$
(34)

We see that the quantity μ is only an additive constant to the original lagrangian. The expression in (34) is what we would have obtained if we had taken the free particle lagrangian to be $(\frac{1}{2}m\dot{x}^2+\mu)$ rather than $(\frac{1}{2}m\dot{x}^2)$. Therefore, we can set $\mu = 0$ without any loss of generality. The free-particle-Kernel can be then taken to be

$$K(x_2 t_2; x_1 t_1) = \left[\frac{m}{2\pi\, i\hbar(t_2 - t_1)}\right]^{1/2} \exp\frac{i}{\hbar}\left[\frac{m}{2}\frac{(x_2 - x_1)^2}{(t_2 - t_1)}\right]. \quad (35)$$

with the normalization constant

$$N(T) = \left[\frac{m}{2\pi\, i\hbar T}\right]^{1/2}. \quad (36)$$

Let us now work out the expression for $N(T)$ for a free particle from (24). The differential operator $\hat{D}$ for a particle of mass m

$$\hat{D} = \frac{m}{2}\frac{d^2}{dt^2} \quad (37)$$

has the eigenvalues

$$\lambda_{n0} \equiv -\frac{m\pi^2 n^2}{2T^2} \quad (38)$$

for a complete set of eigenfunctions which vanish at $t = 0, T$. Substituting this expression into (24), we get

$$N = \prod_n \left(\frac{2\hbar}{i\pi m}\right)^{\frac{1}{2}}\left(\frac{T}{M_n n}\right) \quad (39)$$

Comparing (36) and (39) we see that M_n's should be chosen to satisfy the condition:

$$\prod_n \left(\frac{2\hbar}{i\pi m}\right)^{\frac{1}{2}}\left(\frac{T}{M_n n}\right) = \left(\frac{m}{2\pi i\hbar T}\right)^{\frac{1}{2}} \quad (40)$$

We shall take this relation to be the 'definition' of M_n in the following sense: We will, hereafter, write the normalization for an *arbitrary* quadratic lagrangian as

$$\begin{aligned}
N &= \prod_n \frac{(i\pi\hbar)^{\frac{1}{2}}}{M_n}\lambda_n^{-\frac{1}{2}} = \prod_n \frac{(i\pi\hbar)^{\frac{1}{2}}}{M_n}\left(\frac{\lambda_{n0}}{\lambda_n}\right)^{\frac{1}{2}}\lambda_{n0}^{-\frac{1}{2}} \\
&= N_{\text{free-particle}}(T)\prod_n \left(\frac{\lambda_{n0}}{\lambda_n}\right)^{\frac{1}{2}} \\
&= \left(\frac{m}{2\pi i\hbar T}\right)^{\frac{1}{2}}\prod_n \left(-\frac{m\pi^2}{2T^2}\right)^{\frac{1}{2}}\left(\frac{n^2}{\lambda_n}\right)^{\frac{1}{2}} \quad (41)
\end{aligned}$$

This expression can be computed if λ_n's are determined from $\hat{D}$. All reference to the weightage M_n has now disappeared.

It can be shown, from the study of the Sturm-Liouville problem for the operator $\hat{D}$ that, $\lambda_n \propto n^2$ for *large* n for all systems. (For a free particle, $\lambda_n \propto n^2$ for *all* n.) Though we never bothered to display M_n explicitly, it should be clear from (24) that M_n should scale as $M_n \propto n^{-1}$ for large n to ensure convergence of the product. Since the weightage for each path is $M_n^{-1} \propto n$, it follows that the paths which wiggle more are given higher weightage in the sum over paths.

As an example of the use of the above formula, let us evaluate the N for a harmonic oscillator. The operator $\hat{D}$ will be

$$\hat{D} = \frac{m}{2}\left(\frac{d^2}{dt^2} + \omega^2\right) \tag{42}$$

which has the eigenvalues

$$\lambda_n = -\frac{m}{2}\left(\frac{n^2\pi^2}{T^2} - \omega^2\right) \tag{43}$$

for eigenfunctions which vanish at $t = 0, T$. From (41), we get

$$
\begin{aligned}
N(T) &= \left(\frac{m}{2\pi i\hbar T}\right)^{\frac{1}{2}} \prod_n \left(-\frac{m\pi^2}{2T^2}\right)^{\frac{1}{2}} \left(\frac{n^2}{\lambda_n}\right)^{\frac{1}{2}} \\
&= \left(\frac{m}{2\pi i\hbar T}\right)^{\frac{1}{2}} \prod_n \left(1 - \frac{\omega^2 T^2}{n^2\pi^2}\right)^{-\frac{1}{2}}
\end{aligned}
\tag{44}
$$

Using the relation

$$\left(\frac{\omega T}{\sin \omega T}\right)^{\frac{1}{2}} = \prod_n \left(1 - \frac{\omega^2 T^2}{n^2\pi^2}\right)^{-\frac{1}{2}} \tag{45}$$

we find that

$$N(T) = \left(\frac{m}{2\pi i\hbar T}\right)^{\frac{1}{2}} \left(\frac{\omega T}{\sin \omega T}\right)^{\frac{1}{2}} \tag{46}$$

The expression for $N(T)$ is conventionally written in a somewhat different form. Noticing that

$$\prod_n \lambda_n^{-\frac{1}{2}} = \left[\prod_n \lambda_n\right]^{-\frac{1}{2}} = (\det D)^{-\frac{1}{2}} \tag{47}$$

where the determinant of an operator is defined as the product over its eigenvalues we can write

$$N \equiv \int \mathcal{D}q \, \exp\left[-\frac{i}{\hbar}\int q\hat{D}q dt\right] = N_0(\frac{\det D}{\det D_0})^{-\frac{1}{2}} \qquad (48)$$

where N_0 and D_0 refer to the free particle expressions and the curly-D in the integration symbol is a reminder of the particular choice made for defining the summation over paths ("path integral"). Even though both determinants may be individually divergent, their ratio will turn out to be finite in several physically interesting situations. Textbooks often quote this result as

$$N = \int \mathcal{D}q \, \exp\left[-\frac{i}{\hbar}\int q\hat{D}q dt\right] = (\det D)^{-\frac{1}{2}} \qquad (49)$$

where it is implicitly assumed that the divergences in the right hand side are handled by dividing out the corresponding expression for the free-particle case. We will adopt this notation when no confusion will arise.

2.4. PATH INTEGRAL WITH EXTERNAL SOURCE

There is an extension of the above result which is repeatedly used in field theory. Let us consider the path integral for the action

$$A = -\int(x\hat{D}x + J(t)x)dt \qquad (50)$$

where $J(t)$ is some externally specified function. This action, of course, is quadratic and we already know how to evaluate the path integral. But, in doing that, we will have to expand $x(t)$ as $\bar{x}_c(t) + q(t)$ where $\bar{x}_c$ is the classical solution obtained from A. Often, it is convenient to treat $J(t)$ as a separate entity and expand $x(t)$ as $x_c(t) + q(t)$ where $x_c(t)$ is the classical solution to the *original* action – i.e., the one with $J = 0$. It is easy to see that N will now become, instead of (49), the expression

$$N[t_2, t_1; J(t)] = \int \mathcal{D}q \, \exp\left[-\frac{i}{\hbar}\int(q\hat{D}q + J(t)q)dt\right] \qquad (51)$$

We can evaluate this expression by following exactly the same procedure as before; we expand $q(t)$ in terms of the eigenfunctions $\{f_n\}$ of the operator $\hat{D}$ and evaluate the sum over paths as a product over a set of integrals. The only difference is that, for the I_n's in (23), we now get

$$\begin{aligned}
I_n &= \lim_{\epsilon \to 0} \int_{-\infty}^{+\infty} \frac{dc_n}{M_n} \exp -\frac{i}{\hbar}\left[(\lambda_n - i\epsilon)c_n^2 + J_n c_n\right] \\
&= \lim_{\epsilon \to 0} \frac{1}{M_n}\left(\frac{i\pi\hbar}{(\lambda_n - i\epsilon)}\right)^{\frac{1}{2}} \exp \frac{i}{4\hbar}\frac{J_n^2}{(\lambda_n - i\epsilon)} \qquad (52)
\end{aligned}$$

where

$$J_n = \int_{t_1}^{t_2} dt\, J(t) f_n(t) \tag{53}$$

Therefore

$$N = \left(\prod_n \frac{(i\pi\hbar)^{\frac{1}{2}}}{M_n} (\lambda_n - i\epsilon)^{-\frac{1}{2}} \right) \left(\exp \frac{i}{4\hbar} \sum_n \frac{J_n^2}{(\lambda_n - i\epsilon)} \right) \tag{54}$$

with the understanding that ϵ should be set equal to zero at the end of the calculations.

In most applications we will require the value of this expression in the limit of $t_1 \to -\infty, t_2 \to +\infty$. The result can then be recast in a more useful form as

$$N = (\det D)^{-\frac{1}{2}} \exp \frac{i}{4\hbar} \int dt \int dt'\, J(t) G(t,t') J(t') \tag{55}$$

where the function $G(t,t')$, defined as

$$G(t,t') \equiv \sum_n \frac{f_n(t) f_n(t')}{\lambda_n - i\epsilon} \tag{56}$$

is the Green function for the operator $(\hat{D} - i\epsilon)$. It satisfies the differential equation

$$\begin{aligned} (\hat{D}_t - i\epsilon) G(t,t') &= (\hat{D}_t - i\epsilon) \sum_n \frac{f_n(t) f_n(t')}{\lambda_n - i\epsilon} \\ &= \sum_n f_n(t) f_n(t') = \delta(t - t') \end{aligned} \tag{57}$$

Our final result can be stated as

$$\begin{aligned} &\int \mathcal{D}q \, \exp\left[-\frac{i}{\hbar} \int (q\hat{D}q + J(t)q) dt \right] \\ &= (\det D)^{-\frac{1}{2}} \exp \frac{i}{4\hbar} \int dt \int dt'\, J(t) G(t,t') J(t') \end{aligned} \tag{58}$$

We will use this result extensively in the later sections.

The $i\epsilon$ in the definition of the Green function is quite crucial. To see this, let us evaluate $G(t)$ for a harmonic oscillator. We need to solve the equation

$$(\hat{D} - i\epsilon) G(t) = \frac{m}{2} \left(\frac{d^2}{dt^2} + \omega^2 - i\epsilon \right) G(t) = \delta(t) \tag{59}$$

which can be easily done in the Fourier space. Writing

$$G(t) = \int_{-\infty}^{+\infty} \frac{d\nu}{2\pi} G(\nu) e^{-i\nu t} \tag{60}$$

we find that $G(\nu)$ satisfies the equation

$$\frac{m}{2}[\omega^2 - i\epsilon - \nu^2]G(\nu) = 1. \tag{61}$$

Therefore,

$$G(t) = -\frac{2}{m}\int_{-\infty}^{+\infty}\frac{d\nu}{2\pi}\frac{e^{-i\nu t}}{\nu^2 - (\omega^2 - i\epsilon)} \tag{62}$$

The importance of $i\epsilon$ can be seen at this stage. If it were not present, the integrand will have poles on the real axis and hence the integral will not exist. To give meaning to such an integral one has to specify the path of integration in the complex plane and the results will depend crucially on the path chosen. The existence of $i\epsilon$ give an unambiguous value to the integral by shifting the poles away from the real axis. The poles are now located at $\nu = \pm\omega(1 - i\epsilon)$, infinitesimally away from the real axis. For $t > 0$, we close the contour on the lower half plane and obtain the contribution from the pole at $(\omega - i\epsilon)$; for $t < 0$ we close the contour on the upper half plane and the pole at $(-\omega + i\epsilon)$ contributes. We thus obtain

$$G(t) = \frac{i}{m\omega}[\theta(t)e^{-i\omega t} + \theta(-t)e^{+i\omega t}] = \frac{i}{m\omega}e^{-i\omega|t|}. \tag{63}$$

The final result for the harmonic oscillator can be stated as,

$$\begin{aligned}
N &= (\det D)^{-1/2}\exp\frac{i}{4\hbar}\int dt dt'\, J(t)G(t,t')J(t')\\
&= (\det D)^{-1/2}\exp -\frac{i}{\hbar}\frac{1}{2m}\int_{-\infty}^{+\infty}\frac{d\nu}{2\pi}\frac{|J(\nu)|^2}{\nu^2 - \omega^2 + i\epsilon}
\end{aligned} \tag{64}$$

where we have used the fact that $J^*(\nu) = J(-\nu)$ for real $J(t)$.

Even though this Green function was obtained as a solution to the harmonic oscillator operator, it is quite different from the usual Green functions defined in the classical theory of the oscillator. In classical mechanics, the equation for a forced harmonic oscillator

$$\frac{m}{2}\left(\frac{d^2}{dt^2} + \omega^2\right)q(t) = J(t) \tag{65}$$

is solved by expressing $q(t)$ as

$$q(t) = \int G_R(t - t')J(t')dt' \tag{66}$$

where $G_R(t)$ is the classical Green function. This object has the following Fourier representation:

$$G_R(t) = -\frac{2}{m}\int_{-\infty}^{+\infty}\frac{d\nu}{2\pi}\frac{e^{-i\nu t}}{\nu^2 - (\omega - i\epsilon)^2} \tag{67}$$

Both the poles of the integrand are now in the lower half plane. Therefore, the integral is zero for $t < 0$ and is a real quantity for $t > 0$:

$$G_R(t) = \frac{2}{m\omega}\theta(t)\sin\omega t. \tag{68}$$

This 'retarded Green function' propagates the effect of the source $J(t)$ only 'forward in time'. In other words, q at some time $t = t_0$ is only influenced by the behaviour of $J(t)$ for $t < t_0$. On the other hand, our $G(t)$ propagates the effects of $J(t)$ both forward and backward in time. Thus these functions are mathematically quite different; the position of $i\epsilon$ factor is quite crucial.

2.5. THE EUCLIDEAN TIME

We have made one important assumption in arriving at the expressions quoted above which needs to be highlighted and discussed. We needed to interpret the integrals which appear in the definition of sum over paths in a specific manner, by attributing a small imaginary part to all the eigenvalues. This is equivalent to considering the original operator $\hat{D}$ as the limit

$$\hat{D} \equiv \lim_{\epsilon \to 0}(\hat{D} - i\epsilon) \tag{69}$$

This procedure, called the '$i\epsilon$-prescription' is just one of the many ways of making sense out of an ill-defined integral. It is possible to devise other modifications of the operator $\hat{D}$ – and corresponding limiting procedures – to give meaning to the integral. There is no assurance, a priori, that all these procedures will lead to the same final result.

One such important alternative procedure, which is extensively used, is based on analytically continuing the expressions into complex-t plane. Let us introduce a variable $\tau \equiv it$ (so that $t = -i\tau$) in the action. Under this substitution, the quantity

$$\exp\frac{i}{\hbar}Q = \exp\frac{i}{\hbar}\int_{t_1}^{t_2} dt(B(t)\dot{q}^2 + C(t)q^2) \tag{70}$$

becomes

$$\exp\left(\frac{i}{\hbar}Q\right) = \exp\left(-\frac{Q_E}{\hbar}\right) = \exp-\frac{1}{\hbar}\int_{\tau_1}^{\tau_2} d\tau\left(B_E(\tau)\left(\frac{dq}{d\tau}\right)^2 - C_E(\tau)q^2\right) \tag{71}$$

where $B_E(\tau) \equiv B(t = -i\tau)$ etc. *We will assume that the original action is such that (i) $B_E(\tau)$ and $C_E(\tau)$ are real (ii) $B_E(\tau) > 0$ and (iii) $C_E(\tau) < 0$.* Then the argument of the exponent in (71) is negative definite for all *real* paths $q(\tau)$. [This set of paths, of course, is different from the set of paths obtained by substituting $t = -i\tau$ in the original set of paths; in general, if $q(t)$ is a real function, $q_E(\tau) = q(t = -i\tau)$ will not be real.] Let us now consider the sum

$$N_E(\tau_2, \tau_1) \equiv \sum_{\text{all real } q(\tau)} \exp -\frac{1}{\hbar} \int_{\tau_1}^{\tau_2} d\tau \left(B_E \left(\frac{dq}{d\tau} \right)^2 - C_E\, q^2 \right) \qquad (72)$$

which, by an analysis similar to the one performed before, can be reduced to the form

$$N_E(\tau_2, \tau_1) = \prod_n \left(\int_{-\infty}^{+\infty} \frac{dc_n}{M_n} \exp \left(-\frac{1}{\hbar} \lambda_n c_n^2 \right) \right) \qquad (73)$$

where λ_n are the eigenvalues of the operator $\hat{D}_E$ appearing in the eigenvalue equation

$$\hat{D}_E f_n = -\left[\frac{d}{d\tau} \left(B_E \frac{d}{d\tau} \right) + C_E \right] f_n = \lambda_n f_n.$$

Expressing λ_n as

$$\begin{aligned} \lambda_n &= \lambda_n \int_{\tau_1}^{\tau_2} d\tau f_n^2 = -\int_{\tau_1}^{\tau_2} f_n \left[\frac{d}{d\tau} \left(B_E \frac{d}{d\tau} \right) + C_E \right] f_n d\tau \\ &= \int_{\tau_1}^{\tau_2} d\tau \left[B_E \left(\frac{df_n}{d\tau} \right)^2 - C_E f_n^2 \right] \end{aligned} \qquad (74)$$

and noticing that $B_E > 0$ and $C_E < 0$, we find that λ_n is positive definite. Therefore the integrals in (73) are well-defined, leading to

$$N_E(\tau_2, \tau_1) = \prod_n \frac{(\pi\hbar)^{1/2}}{M_n} \left(\frac{1}{\lambda_n} \right)^{1/2} = (\det D_E)^{-1/2}. \qquad (75)$$

In arriving at the last expression we have made the implicit assumption that the determinants are regularized in the usual manner by dividing out the free particle contribution. We shall now *define* the original expression $N(t_2, t_1)$ as the analytic continuation of $N_E(\tau_2, \tau_1)$:

$$N(t_2, t_1) \equiv N_E(\tau_2 = i\,t_2; \tau_1 = i\,t_1). \qquad (76)$$

This procedure may be summarized as follows: (i) From the original expression $Q[q(t)]$ obtain $Q_E[q(\tau)]$ by analytically continuing from t to τ. (ii) Check that B_E, C_E are real and $B_E > 0$ and $C_E < 0$. (iii) Evaluate the sum over paths for Q_E, by summing over all real $q(\tau)$. (iv) Analytically continue back to t; this is *defined* to be the value of the original sum over paths. It should be emphasized that this method works only for those actions for which the condition (ii) above is satisfied. The quantity τ is called the 'Euclidean time' and other variables like A_E, G_E etc. are called 'Euclidean action', 'Euclidean Green function' etc.

The above idea can be easily extended to path integrals with an external $J(t)$. Instead of (58), we will now get

$$\int \mathcal{D}q \, \exp\left[-\frac{1}{\hbar}\int (q\hat{D}_E q + J_E(t)q)dt\right]$$
$$= (\det \, D_E)^{-\frac{1}{2}} \exp\frac{1}{4\hbar}\int dt \int dt' J_E(t)G_E(t,t')J_E(t') \qquad (77)$$

where G_E is the Green function for the operator D_E:

$$\hat{D}_E G_E = \delta(\tau) \qquad (78)$$

This Green function will be well defined even without any additional $i\epsilon$ prescriptions.

As an example, let us find $G_E(\tau)$ for a harmonic oscillator. This function satisfies the equation

$$\hat{D}_E G_E(\tau) = -\frac{m}{2}\left(\frac{d^2}{d\tau^2} - \omega^2\right)G_E(\tau) = \delta(\tau) \qquad (79)$$

which can again be solved using the Fourier space. Writing

$$G(\tau) = \int_{-\infty}^{+\infty}\frac{d\nu}{2\pi}G(\nu)e^{-i\nu\tau} \qquad (80)$$

we find that $G(\nu)$ satisfies the equation

$$\frac{m}{2}[\omega^2 + \nu^2]G(\nu) = 1. \qquad (81)$$

Therefore,

$$G(\tau) = \frac{2}{m}\int_{-\infty}^{+\infty}\frac{d\nu}{2\pi}\frac{e^{-i\nu\tau}}{\nu^2 + \omega^2} \qquad (82)$$

This integral is perfectly well-defined and can be easily worked out to give

$$G_E(\tau) = \frac{1}{m\omega}e^{-\omega|\tau|} \qquad (83)$$

We see that the analytic continuation of (77), with the above expression for G_E correctly reproduces (58). Thus for this simple system the Green function defined by the $i\epsilon$ prescription and the one defined by analytic continuation from imaginary time are identical.

2.6. PATH INTEGRALS FROM TIME SLICING

The procedure described above to define the sum over paths works only for quadratic actions for which an operator $\hat{D}$ can be defined. We will now provide a more general definition which will work for any action in the form (1). Let us divide the time interval $T \equiv t_f - t_i$ into J equal divisions, each of size $\Delta t \equiv= J^{-1}(t_f - t_i)$. Let $t_K = t_i + K\Delta t$ with $K = 0, 1, 2, ...J$, so that $t_0 = t_i$ and $t_J = t_f$. By using (8) repeatedly, we can write

$$K(t_f, x_f; t_i, x_i) = \int_{-\infty}^{+\infty} \left(\prod_{M=1}^{M=J-1} dx_M \right) \left[\prod_{M=0}^{M=J-1} K(t_{M+1}, x_{M+1}; t_M, x_M) \right]$$
(84)

We now consider the limit of the above expression with $J \to \infty, \Delta t \to 0$ with $J\Delta t = (t_f - t_i)$ remaining finite. Each of the Kernels appearing in (84) will then represent the amplitude of propagation between two events which are infinitesimally separated in time:

$$
\begin{aligned}
K(t_{M+1}, x_{M+1}, t_M, x_M) &= K(t_M + \Delta t, x_{M+1}; t_M, x_M) \\
&= \sum_{\text{paths}} \exp \frac{i}{\hbar} \int_{t_M}^{t_M + \Delta t} dt \left(\frac{1}{2}m\dot{x}^2 - V(x) \right) \\
&= \sum_{\text{paths}} \exp \frac{i}{\hbar} \left(\frac{1}{2}m\frac{(\Delta x)^2}{\Delta t} - V(x)\Delta t \right) \quad (85)
\end{aligned}
$$

with $\Delta x = x_{M+1} - x_M$. We notice that in the limit of $\Delta t \to 0$ the kinetic energy term will dominate over the potential energy if 'wiggly' paths contribute most to the sum. Therefore, in this limit, we can replace the Kernel by a free particle Kernel with the potential energy providing an extra phase factor. That is,

$$\lim_{\Delta t \to 0} K(t_M + \Delta t, x_{M+1}, t_M, x_M) = \lim_{\Delta t \to 0} \left(\frac{m}{2\pi i\hbar \Delta t} \right)^{\frac{1}{2}} \exp \frac{i}{\hbar} A_0 \quad (86)$$

where

$$A_0 = \left(\frac{1}{2}m\frac{(x_{M+1} - x_M)^2}{\Delta t} - V(x_M)\Delta t \right) \quad (87)$$

Substituting (87) into (84) we get the required expression for the Kernel:

$$
\begin{aligned}
K(t_f, x_f; t_i, x_i) &= \lim_{\Delta t \to 0} \lim_{J \to \infty} \int_{-\infty}^{+\infty} \left(\prod_{M=1}^{M=J-1} dx_M \right) \left(\frac{m}{2\pi i\hbar \Delta t} \right)^{\frac{J}{2}} \\
&\quad \exp \frac{i}{\hbar} \sum_{M=0}^{M=J-1} \left(\frac{1}{2}m\frac{(x_{M+1} - x_M)^2}{\Delta t} - V(x_M)\Delta t \right) \quad (88)
\end{aligned}
$$

This expression provides a definition for the sum over paths for all actions in the form (1). Though formally correct, it is not of much use in the actual computation of Kernels. The integrals involved in (88), can be evaluated in a closed, simple form only for quadratic actions for which – it can be shown that – (88), and (15) give the same result. For non-quadratic actions, the conventional approach to quantum theory – based on operators and eigenstates – turns out to be much more convenient. In fact, the physical meaning of several expressions derived earlier becomes clearer when the Kernel is connected up with the more conventional description. We shall now examine these connections.

2.7. KERNELS AND GROUND-STATE EXPECTATION VALUES

In the conventional approch to quantum mechanics using the Heisenberg picture the description will be in terms of the position and momentum operators $\hat{x}$ and $\hat{p}$. Let $|x, t>$ be the eigenstate of the operator $\hat{x}(t)$ with eigenvalue x. The Kernel – which represents the probability amplitude for a particle to propagate from (t_1, x_1) to (t_2, x_2) – can be expressed, in a more conventional notation, as the matrix element:

$$K(t_2, x_2; t_1, x_1) = < x_2, t_2|t_1, x_1 > = < x_2, 0| \exp -\frac{i}{\hbar}\hat{H}(t_2 - t_1)|0, x_1 > .$$
$$(89)$$

where $\hat{H}$ is the Hamiltonian for the system. This relation allows one to represent the Kernel in terms of the energy eigenstates of the system, provided the hamiltonian is independent of time. We have

$$
\begin{aligned}
K(T, x_2; 0, x_1) &= < x_2, 0| \exp -\frac{i}{\hbar}HT|0, x_1 > \\
&= \sum_{n,m} < x_2|E_n >< E_n| \exp -\frac{i}{\hbar}HT|E_m >< E_m|x_1 > \\
&= \sum_n \psi_n(x_2)\psi_n^*(x_1) \exp -\frac{i}{\hbar}E_n T
\end{aligned}
$$
$$(90)$$

where $\psi_n(x) = < x|E_n >$ is the n-th energy eigenfunction of the system under consideration.

In physical applications, we often require the limiting form

$$
\begin{aligned}
W(T; x_2, x_1) &\equiv \lim_{t_2 \to +\infty} \lim_{t_1 \to -\infty} K(x_2 t_2; x_1 t_1) \\
&= \lim_{T \to \infty} K(x_2 T; x_1 0)
\end{aligned}
$$
$$(91)$$

This cannot be directly ascertained from (90) because the exponent oscillates. However, we can give meaning to this limit if we first transform

(90), to the imaginary time $\tau_1 = it_1$ and $\tau_2 = it_2$ and consider the limit $(\tau_2 - \tau_1) \to \infty$. We find that

$$
\begin{aligned}
W_E(T; x_2, x_1) &= \lim_{\tau_2 \to \infty} \lim_{\tau_1 \to -\infty} K_E(x_2\tau_2; x_1\tau_1) \\
&\cong \psi_0(x_2)\psi_0(x_1) \exp[-\frac{E_0}{\hbar}(\tau_2 - \tau_1)]
\end{aligned}
\tag{92}
$$

where the zero-subscript denotes the lowest energy state. (Note that $\psi_0^* = \psi_0$). From (92), we see that only the ground state contributes in this infinite time limit. We may now *define* the limit in (91), as the analytic continuation of (92), getting

$$
W(T; x_2, x_1) = \lim_{T \to \infty} K(x_2 T; x_1 0) \approx \psi_0(x_2)\psi_0(x_1) \exp(-i\frac{E_0 T}{\hbar})
\tag{93}
$$

This expression allows one to determine the ground state energy of the system from the Kernel in a simple manner. We see that

$$
W_E(T; 0, 0) \approx (\text{constant}) \exp(-\frac{E_0 T}{\hbar})
\tag{94}
$$

giving

$$
E_0 = \lim_{T \to \infty} \left(-\frac{\hbar}{T} \ln W_E(T; 0, 0) \right)
\tag{95}
$$

The Kernel can also be used to study the effect of external perturbations on the system. Let us suppose that the system was in the ground state in the asymptotic past ($t_1 \approx -\infty$). At some time $t = -T$ we switch on an external time dependent disturbance $\lambda(t)$ affecting the system. Finally at $t = +T$ we switch off the perturbation. Because of the time-dependence, we no longer have stationary energy eigenstates for the system. In fact, the system is likely to have absorbed energy from the perturbation and would have ended up at some excited state at $t_2 = +\infty$; the probability for it to be found in the ground state at $t_2 = +\infty$ will be less than one. This probability can be computed from the Kernel. Consider the amplitude

$$
\begin{aligned}
\mathcal{P} &= \lim_{t_2 \to \infty} \lim_{t_1 \to -\infty} K(t_2 x_2; t_1 x_1; \lambda(t)) = \lim_{t_2 \to \infty} \lim_{t_1 \to -\infty} < t_2 x_2 | t_1 x_1 > \\
&= \lim_{t_2 \to \infty} \lim_{t_1 \to -\infty} \left[\int_{-\infty}^{+\infty} dx dx' < t_2, x_2 | T, x > \right. \\
&\quad \times \left. < T, x | -T, x' > < -T, x' | t_1 x_1 > \right]
\end{aligned}
\tag{96}
$$

Since $\lambda = 0$ during $t_2 > t > T$ and $-T > t > t_1$, matrix elements in these intervals can be expressed in terms of the energy eigenstates of the original system:

$$\lim_{t_2 \to \infty} \; < \; t_2, x_2 | T, x > \cong \psi_0(x_2)\psi_0(x) \exp -i\frac{E_0}{\hbar}(t_2 - T)$$

$$\lim_{t_1 \to -\infty} \; < \; -T, x' | t_1, x_1 > \cong \psi_0(x')\psi_0(x_1) \exp -i\frac{E_0}{\hbar}(-T - t_1) \quad (97)$$

Therefore (setting $\hbar = 1$ for simplicity)

$$
\begin{aligned}
\mathcal{P} \;\cong\; & \left[\psi_0(x_2)\psi_0(x_1)e^{-iE_0(t_2 - t_1)} \right] \int_{-\infty}^{+\infty} dx\,dx' (\psi_0(x)e^{+iE_0 T}) \\
\times \; & < T, x | x', -T > (\psi_0(x')e^{iE_0 T}) \\
\cong\; & \lim_{(t_2 - t_1) \to \infty} K(t_2, x_2; t_1 x_1; \lambda = 0) \int_{-\infty}^{+\infty} dx\,dx' [\psi_0(x, T)]^* \\
\times \; & < T, x | x', -T > [\psi_0(x, -T)] \quad (98)
\end{aligned}
$$

where $\psi_0(x, T)$ represents the ground state wave function at time T etc. The quantity

$$W = \int_{-\infty}^{+\infty} dx\,dx' [\psi_0(x, T)]^* < x, T | x', -T > [\psi_0(x, -T)] \quad (99)$$

represents the amplitude for the system to remain in the ground state in the asymptotic future if it started out in the ground state in the asymptotic past [usually called the "vacuum to vacuum" amplitude]. From (98), we find that this amplitude is given by the limit:

$$W = \lim_{t_2 \to \infty} \lim_{t_1 \to -\infty} \frac{K(t_2, x_2; t_1; \lambda(t))}{K(t_2, x_2; t_1, x_1; 0)} \quad (100)$$

This result can be further simplified by noticing that the x_2 and x_1 dependences cancel out in the ratio in (100) so that we can set $x_2 = x_1 = 0$, getting

$$W = \lim_{t_1 \to \infty} \lim_{t_1 \to -\infty} \frac{K(t_2, 0; t_1, 0; \lambda(t))}{K(t_2, 0; t_1, 0; 0)}. \quad (101)$$

Thus the vacuum-vacuum amplitude can be found from the Kernel by a simple limiting procedure.

The importance of W emerges from the fact that it contains useful information about the excitation to other levels as well. If W_n denote the amplitude for the system to be found in the n-th excited state at $t_2 = \infty$, then $|W_n|^2$ can be usually approximated as a Poisson distribution:

$$|W_n|^2 = \frac{\mu^n}{n!} e^{-\mu} \tag{102}$$

where $\mu = -\ln |W_0|^2$. Thus, W_0 contains full information about the system if the transition probabilities to different levels are independent of each other, validating (102). In this case, μ denotes the mean level to which the system is excited: $\mu = <n>$. The mean energy absorbed by the system from the driving source is $(E_n \mu)$.

In the above calculation we have not specified the nature of the coupling between $\lambda(t)$ and the original system. In principle, this could be arbitrary; in practice, however, we will be able to calculate $K[\lambda(t)]$-needed to compute W- only if the coupling is through the coefficients of a quadratic action. The simplest of such situations correspond to the addition of a linear coupling to an external source $\lambda(t) = J(t)$:

$$A_{\text{add}} = \int J(t) q(t) dt \tag{103}$$

to the original quadratic action. We have already discussed this situation in section (2.3). In this case W is easily computed. We get:

$$W = \exp \frac{i}{4\hbar} \int_{-\infty}^{+\infty} dt \int_{-\infty}^{+\infty} dt' J(t)\, G(t,t')\, J(t'). \tag{104}$$

As an example of the evaluation of W, let us consider the case of harmonic oscillator. Writing

$$R = \int_{-\infty}^{+\infty} dt\, dt'\, J(t)\, G(t,t') J(t') = -\frac{2}{m} \int_{-\infty}^{+\infty} \frac{d\nu}{2\pi} \frac{|J(\nu)|^2}{\nu^2 - \omega^2 + i\epsilon} \tag{105}$$

we are interested in the probability $|W|^2$ for which only the imaginary part of R contributes. Since

$$\frac{1}{x + i\epsilon} = \hat{P}\frac{1}{x} - i\pi\delta(x) \tag{106}$$

where $\hat{P}$ denotes the principle value of the integral, we get

$$\text{Im}\, R = \frac{1}{m} \int_{-\infty}^{+\infty} d\nu |J(\nu)|^2 \delta(\nu^2 - \omega^2) = \frac{1}{m\omega} |J(+\omega)|^2 \tag{107}$$

[We have used the fact that $|J(\omega)|^2 = |J(-\omega)|^2$ for real $J(t)$.] Therefore, the probability for a harmonic oscillator to remain in the ground state even after the action of a perturbation $J(t)$ is

$$
\begin{aligned}
|W|^2 &= |\exp \frac{i}{4\hbar} R|^2 = \exp\left(-\frac{1}{2\hbar} \text{Im}\, R\right) \\
&= \exp\left[-\frac{1}{(\hbar\omega)} \cdot \frac{1}{2} \frac{|J(\omega)|^2}{m}\right] = \exp\left(-\frac{\mathcal{E}}{\hbar\omega}\right) \tag{108}
\end{aligned}
$$

This result has a very simple interpretation. Note that only the power $|J(\omega)|^2$ at the resonance frequency $\nu = \omega$ causes the transitions. According to the discussion following (102), $(\mathcal{E}_0/\hbar\omega)$ denotes the mean level $< n >$ to which the system is excited and $\mathcal{E}_0 =< n > \hbar\omega$ is the mean energy absorbed by the system. In fact, ϵ is the total amount of energy absorbed by a *classical* oscillator when driven by $J(t)$. This can be most easily seen by writing the oscillator equation

$$m(\ddot{x} + \omega^2 x) = -J(t) \tag{109}$$

as

$$\dot{z} + i\omega z = -J(t) \tag{110}$$

where

$$z(t) = m(\dot{x} - i\omega x) \tag{111}$$

Solving (110) we get

$$z(t) = -e^{i\omega t} \int_{-\infty}^{t} J(t')e^{+i\omega t'}\, dt \tag{112}$$

from which it is easy to see that

$$\text{(Energy absorbed)} \quad = \quad \mathcal{E} = \frac{1}{2}m(\dot{x}^2 + \omega^2 x^2)|_{t=\infty}$$

$$= \quad \frac{1}{2m}\left\{|z|^2\right\}_{t=\infty} = \frac{1}{2m}|J(\omega)|^2 \tag{113}$$

In fact, for the harmonic oscillator, the probability for transition to the n-th energy level given by (102), turns out to be exact.

Another case of interest in which the external perturbation can be handled is the "adiabatic case". This is the situation in which the perturbation $\lambda(t)$ varies slowly compared to the intrinsic time scales of the system. In that case, the ground state evolves in time adiabatically, as

$$\psi_0(x,t) = \psi_0(x,0)\exp -\frac{i}{\hbar}\int_0^t E_0(\lambda(t))dt \tag{114}$$

where $E_0(\lambda)$ is the ground state energy of the hamiltonian calculated by treating λ as some given, time-independent parameter. In this case, it is easy to see that

$$W = \exp -\frac{i}{\hbar}\int_{-\infty}^{+\infty} E_0(\lambda(t))dt \tag{115}$$

Lastly, we will establish an important connection between matrix elements of the form $< x_2, t_2|x(t)x(t')|x_1, t_1 >$ and the Kernel. Consider the quantity

$$K[x_2, t_2; x_1, t_1; J(t)] = \int \mathcal{D}x(t)\exp\left[\frac{i}{\hbar}A[x(t)] + \frac{i}{\hbar}\int J(t)x(t)dt\right] \tag{116}$$

where A is some *arbitrary* action functional. By taking the functional derivative of this expression with respect to $J(t)$ two times, we can write,

$$\left(\frac{\hbar}{i}\frac{\delta}{\delta J(t)}\right)\left(\frac{\hbar}{i}\right)\frac{\delta}{\delta J(t')}K(x_2t_2;x_1t_1;J(t)) = \int \mathcal{D}x\, x(t)x(t')e^{\frac{i}{\hbar}[A+\int Jxdt]}$$

$$(117)$$

Setting $J = 0$, we get

$$\int \mathcal{D}x\, x(t)x(t')\exp\frac{i}{\hbar}A = \left[\frac{\hbar}{i}\frac{\delta}{\delta J(t)}\frac{\hbar}{i}\frac{\delta}{\delta J(t')}K(x_2t_2;x_1t_1;J)\right]_{J=0} \quad (118)$$

The expression on the left hand can be expressed using the Kernel:

$$\int \mathcal{D}x\, x(t)x(t')e^{\frac{i}{\hbar}A}$$

$$= \int_{-\infty}^{+\infty} dx \int_{-\infty}^{+\infty} dx'\, K(x_2,t_2;x,t)x\, K(x,t;x',t')x'\, K(x',t';x_1t_1)$$

$$= \int_{-\infty}^{+\infty} dx \int_{-\infty}^{+\infty} dx' <x_2,t_2|x,t> x <x,t|x',t'> x' <x',t'|x_1t_1>$$

$$= <x_2,t_2|x(t)x(t')|x_1,t_1>$$

$$(119)$$

Therefore, we get the relation.

$$<x_2,t_2|x(t)x(t')|x_1,t_1> = \left[\frac{\hbar}{i}\frac{\delta}{\delta J(t)}\cdot\frac{\hbar}{i}\frac{\delta}{\delta J(t')}K(x_2,t_2;x_1,t_1;J)\right]_{J=0}.$$

$$(120)$$

This relation shows that the matrix elements of a string of co-ordinate operators at different times can be evaluated as a functional derivative of the Kernel. It is clear that this method can be generalized to give

$$F(x_2,t_2;x_1t_1;t,t',t'',\cdots) \equiv <x_2t_2|x(t)x(t')x(t'')\cdots|x_1t_1>$$

$$= \left[\frac{\hbar}{i}\frac{\delta}{\delta J(t)}\cdot\frac{\hbar}{i}\frac{\delta}{\delta J(t')}\cdot\frac{\hbar}{i}\frac{\delta}{\delta J(t'')}\cdots K[J]\right]_{J=0}.$$

$$(121)$$

In this sense, $K[J]$ may be considered the "generating function" for the matrix elements $<x_2,t_2|x(t)x(t')x(t'')\cdots|x_1t_1>$.

We will usually use this result in the limit $t_2 \to \infty$, $t_1 \to -\infty$ with $x_1 = x_2 = 0$. Writing $K[J(t)] = K(0,\infty;0,-\infty;J(t))$ we have

$$<0,\infty|x(t)x(t')|0,-\infty> = \left[\frac{\hbar}{i}\frac{\delta}{\delta J(t)}\cdot\frac{\hbar}{i}\frac{\delta}{\delta J(t')}\cdot K[J(t)]\right]_{J=0} \quad (122)$$

In this limit, (119), also simplifies because only ground states contribute in $< x_2, t_2|x, t >$ and $< x', t'|x_1, t_1 >$. We get, by analysis similar to that which led to (98),

$$< 0, \infty|x(t)x(t')|0, -\infty > \cong < 0, \infty|0, -\infty >$$
$$\int_{-\infty}^{+\infty} dx \int_{-\infty}^{+\infty} dx' \psi_0(x, t)K(x, t; x', t')x'\psi_0(x', t') \qquad (123)$$

where $\psi_0(x, t) = \psi_0(x) \exp(-iE_0 t)$ etc. Therefore,

$$\frac{< 0, \infty|x(t)x(t')|0, -\infty >}{< 0, \infty|0, -\infty >}$$
$$= \int_{-\infty}^{+\infty} dx \int_{-\infty}^{+\infty} dx' [\psi_0(x, t)x]^* K(x, t; x', t')[x'\psi_0(x', t')] \qquad (124)$$

which may be interpreted as the amplitude for the system to be in a state described by the wavefunction

$$f(x, t) = x\psi_0(x) \exp(-iE_0 t) \qquad (125)$$

from time t to t'.

There is one small complication regarding the above formulas which needs to be taken care of. The evaluation given above assumes that $t > t'$. If $t < t'$ the same results can be obtained if we use $< x(t')x(t) >$ rather than $< x(t)x(t') >$. It is usual, therefore, to write these results by replacing $< x_2 t_2|x(t)x(t')|x_1 t_1 >$ by a "time-ordered" product $< x_2, t_2|T(x(t)x(t'))|x_1, t_1 >$ where we define:

$$T(x(t)x(t')) = \begin{cases} x(t)x(t') & \text{for } t \geq t' \\ x(t')x(t) & \text{for } t' \geq t. \end{cases} \qquad (126)$$

Everything derived so far is valid for arbitrary actions. These results, however, take particularly simple form for quadratic actions, for which

$$K[J] = K[0] \exp \frac{i}{4\hbar} \int_{-\infty}^{+\infty} J(t)G(t, t')J(t')dtdt'. \qquad (127)$$

Using (122), we get

$$\frac{< 0, \infty|T(x(t)x(t'))|0, -\infty >}{< 0, \infty|0, -\infty >} = \frac{\hbar}{2i}G(t, t') \equiv \mathcal{G}(t, t') \qquad (128)$$

In other words, the Green function can be expressed as the matrix element of time-ordered product of operators. [The factor (1/2) was due to our definition of $\hat{D}$ in a somewhat non-standard manner].

For the harmonic oscillator we have already computed $G(t, t')$ earlier. The expression in the right hand side of (124) has a simple interpretation in this case. We note that the first excited state $(n = 1)$ for a harmonic oscillator has the wavefunction

$$\psi_1(x, t) = \left(\frac{2m\omega}{\hbar} \right)^{1/2} x\psi_0(x, t)e^{-i\omega t} \qquad (129)$$

so that $f(x, t)$ in (125) can be written as

$$f(x, t) = \left(\frac{\hbar}{2m\omega} \right)^{1/2} e^{i\omega t}\psi_1(x) \qquad (130)$$

Since the Kernel propagates $\psi_1(x, t)$ unchanged, (124), implies

$$\mathcal{G}(t, t') = \left(\frac{\hbar}{2\omega m} \right) \exp -i\omega(t - t') \qquad (131)$$

which, of course, agrees with the expression for $(\hbar G/2i)$ if $t > t'$. Thus, the Green function contains the information about the first excited state of the system.

2.8. HARMONIC OSCILLATORS

The systems which we have considered so far have Hamiltonians of the form

$$\hat{H}(\hat{p}, \hat{x}) = \frac{\hat{p}^2}{2m} + V(\hat{x}) \qquad (132)$$

in which $\hat{p}$ and $\hat{x}$ appear quite asymmetrically. If we now impose an additional constraint on the Hamiltonian in (132), that it should be symmetric under the interchange of position and momentum coordinates, we are forced to choose $V(x) \propto x^2$. The constant of proportionality must be positive definite to ensure lower bound for the Hamiltonian. With suitable scaling, we can write such a Hamiltonian as

$$\begin{aligned} \hat{H}(\hat{p}, \hat{x}) &= \frac{\hat{p}^2}{2m} + \frac{1}{2}m\omega^2\hat{x}^2 \\ &= \frac{1}{2}\hbar\omega(\hat{P}^2 + \hat{Q}^2) \end{aligned} \qquad (133)$$

where we have defined the dimensionless variables

$$\hat{P} = \frac{\hat{p}}{\sqrt{m\hbar\omega}}; \quad \hat{Q} = \sqrt{\frac{m\omega}{\hbar}}\hat{x}; \quad [\hat{Q}, \hat{P}] = \frac{1}{\hbar}[\hat{x}, \hat{p}] = i \qquad (134)$$

In quantum theory, we are interested in the eigenvalues and eigenvectors of $\hat{H}$. The eigenvalues can be easily found. We rewrite the Hamiltonian as

$$
\begin{aligned}
\frac{\hat{H}}{\hbar\omega} &= \frac{1}{2}(\hat{P}^2 + \hat{Q}^2) = \frac{1}{\sqrt{2}}(\hat{Q} - i\hat{P})\frac{1}{\sqrt{2}}(\hat{Q} + i\hat{P}) - \frac{i}{2}[\hat{Q}, \hat{P}] \\
&\equiv \hat{a}^\dagger \hat{a} + \frac{1}{2} \equiv \hat{n} + \frac{1}{2}
\end{aligned}
\tag{135}
$$

where

$$
\hat{a} = \frac{1}{\sqrt{2}}(\hat{Q} + i\hat{P}); \ \hat{a}^\dagger = \frac{1}{\sqrt{2}}(\hat{Q} - i\hat{P}); \ \hat{n} = \hat{a}^\dagger \hat{a}. \tag{136}
$$

From $[\hat{Q}, \hat{P}] = i$, it follows that

$$
[\hat{a}, \hat{a}^\dagger] = 1 \tag{137}
$$

Let $|n >$ be the eigenstates of $\hat{n}$ with eigenvalue n. It is then easy to see that $\hat{a}^\dagger |n >$ and $a|n >$ are also eigenvectors of $\hat{n}$ with eigenvalues $(n + 1)$ and $(n - 1)$ respectively. This fact, added to the condition that $< n|\hat{n}|n >=< n|a^\dagger a|n >= n < n|n >\geq 0$ implies that $n = 0, 1, 2 \cdots$.

[Alternatively, one may argue as follows: The set of complex analytic functions form a Hilbert space with the norm

$$
< g|f >= \int \frac{dz d\bar{z}}{2\pi i} e^{-z\bar{z}} \bar{g}(z) f(\bar{z}). \tag{138}
$$

The commutator (137) can be implemented in this space with the realization

$$
\hat{a} \to \frac{\partial}{\partial \bar{z}}; \qquad a^\dagger \to \bar{z} \tag{139}
$$

We again see that the operator

$$
(a^\dagger a) = \bar{z}\frac{\partial}{\partial \bar{z}} \tag{140}
$$

has integral eigenvalues].

From (135), it follows that the hamiltonian has equally spaced energy eigenvalues

$$
E_n = \hbar\omega(n + \frac{1}{2}); \ n = 0, 1, 2 \cdots \tag{141}
$$

The eigenstates of the hamiltonian $|n >$ are labelled by an integer. We normalize them in such a way that

$$
< n|n >= 1; \ \hat{a}|n >= \sqrt{n}|n - 1 >; \ \hat{a}^\dagger |n >= \sqrt{n+1}|n + 1 > . \tag{142}
$$

The operators $\hat{a}^\dagger$, $\hat{a}$ and $\hat{n}$ are called creation, annihilation and number operators respectively.

The dynamics of the system described by (132) can be studied in either in Schrodinger picture or in Heisenberg picture. In Schrodinger picture, $\hat{a}$ and $\hat{a}^\dagger$ have the representations

$$\hat{a} = \frac{1}{\sqrt{2}}\left(i(-i)\frac{\partial}{\partial Q} + Q\right) = \frac{1}{\sqrt{2}}\left(\frac{\partial}{\partial Q} + Q\right)$$
$$\hat{a}^\dagger = \frac{1}{\sqrt{2}}\left((-i)(-i)\frac{\partial}{\partial Q} + Q\right) = \frac{1}{\sqrt{2}}\left(-\frac{\partial}{\partial Q} + Q\right) \tag{143}$$

The $n = 0$, ground state $\psi_0(Q)$, satisfies the condition

$$\hat{a}\psi_0 = \frac{1}{\sqrt{2}}\left(\frac{\partial\psi_0}{\partial Q} + Q\psi\right) = 0 \tag{144}$$

with $< \psi_0|\psi_0 >= 1$. Integrating (144) and normalising we find that

$$\psi_0(Q) = \frac{1}{\sqrt{2\pi}}\exp\left(-\frac{1}{2}Q^2\right) \tag{145}$$

which in more familar variables $x = (\hbar/m\omega)^{1/2}Q$, becomes:

$$\psi_0(x) = \left(\frac{m\omega}{\pi\hbar}\right)^{1/4}\exp\left(-\frac{m\omega}{2\hbar}x^2\right) \tag{146}$$

All excited states can be found from the ground state by operating with $\hat{a}^\dagger$ and normalising. Since the ground state has energy $\frac{1}{2}\hbar\omega$, the time evolution of ψ_0 is described by

$$\psi_0(t, x) = \left(\frac{m\omega}{\pi\hbar}\right)^{1/4}\exp\left(-\frac{i\hbar\omega}{2}t - \frac{m\omega}{2\hbar}x^2\right) \tag{147}$$

In the Heisenberg picture, we have to solve the equations of motion for the operator $\hat{a}(t)$; since

$$i\hbar\dot{a} = [\hat{a}, \hat{H}] = \hbar\omega[\hat{a}, \hat{a}^\dagger a] = \hbar\omega a \tag{148}$$

we find

$$\hat{a}(t) = \hat{a}(0)e^{-i\omega t} \equiv \hat{a}e^{-i\omega t} \tag{149}$$

and similarly

$$\hat{a}^\dagger(t) = \hat{a}^\dagger(0)e^{+i\omega t} \equiv \hat{a}^\dagger e^{i\omega t} \tag{150}$$

where we have condensed the notation by writing $\hat{a}(0) = \hat{a}$ etc. From these relations we find that

$$
\begin{aligned}
\hat{P}(t) &= \frac{i}{\sqrt{2}}(\hat{a}^\dagger(t) - \hat{a}(t)) = -\frac{i}{\sqrt{2}}\left[ae^{-i\omega t} - a^\dagger e^{i\omega t}\right] \\
\hat{Q}(t) &= \frac{1}{\sqrt{2}}(\hat{a}^\dagger(t) + \hat{a}(t)) = \frac{1}{\sqrt{2}}\left[ae^{-i\omega t} + a^\dagger e^{i\omega t}\right]
\end{aligned}
\tag{151}
$$

Equivalently,

$$
x(t) = \sqrt{\frac{\hbar}{2m\omega}}\left[a\,e^{-i\omega t} + a^\dagger e^{i\omega t}\right]
\tag{152}
$$

and $\hat{p}(t) = m\dot{x}(t)$. These relations completely solve the problem. Note that $\hat{Q}$ and $\hat{x}$ are Hermitian.

As an example of a calculation with these operators, let us compute the quantity $< E_0|\hat{x}(t')x(t)|E_0 >$, where $|E_0 >$ is the ground state. Using (152) and noting that $\hat{a}|E_0 >= 0$, we get

$$
< E_0|\hat{x}(t')\hat{x}(t)|E_0 >= \frac{\hbar}{2m\omega}e^{-i\omega(t'-t)} = \mathcal{G}
\tag{153}
$$

which is proportional to the Green function (for $t' > t$) we have seen several times before. Repeating the calculation for $t < t'$ and combining the results, we get

$$
< E_0|T(\hat{x}(t')\hat{x}(t))|E_0 >= \frac{\hbar}{2m\omega}\left[\theta(t'-t)e^{-i\omega(t'-t)} + \theta(t-t')e^{i\omega(t'-t)}\right]
\tag{154}
$$

where $T(\ )$ is the time-ordering operator introduced earlier.

The path integral representation of the same system has already been covered in the earlier discussion. Since the action corresponding to (132) is quadratic, the system allows exact solution.

We shall now extend the above analysis to a system of several harmonic oscillators.

2.9. INFINITE NUMBER HARMONIC OSCILLATORS

Consider a bunch of N harmonic oscillators with the co-ordinate variables $\{q_1(t), q_2(t) \cdots q_k(t), \cdots q_N(t)\}$. [We change the notation from $x(t)$ to $q(t)$ to emphasize the fact that these degrees of freedom have nothing to do with the (x, y, z) co-ordinates of physical space]. For the sake of convenience, we will take the mass, m, of each degree of freedom, to be unity. The frequencies will, in general, be different; let ω_k be the frequency of the k-th oscillator. Since the oscillators do not interact with each other, everything we have developed so far can be trivially extended. We will quickly summarize these generalizations.

The Hamiltonian is now the sum of the individual hamiltonians:

$$H = \sum_{k=1}^{N} \frac{1}{2}(p_k^2 + \omega_k^2 q_k^2) \tag{155}$$

Therefore, the energy eigenstates of the system are labelled by a set of N integers $(n_1, n_2 \cdots n_k, \cdots n_N)$. This state, denoted by $|\{n_k\} >$ corresponds to the situation in which the first oscillator is in the state labelled by $n_1, \cdots$ the k th oscillator is in the state labelled by $n_k \cdots$ and the N'th oscillator is in the state n_N. The wave function corresponding to this state will be

$$\Psi[q_1, q_2 \cdots q_k, \cdots q_N; t] \equiv \Psi[\{q_k\}; t] = \prod_{k=1}^{N} \Psi_{n_k}(q_k, t) \tag{156}$$

corresponding to the energy eigenvalue

$$E[\{n_k\}] = \sum_{k=1}^{N} \hbar\omega_k(n_k + \frac{1}{2}). \tag{157}$$

For example, the lowest energy state will be the one with all n_k's set to zero. This "ground-state" has the wave function

$$\Psi_0[\{q_k\}] = \prod_{k=1}^{N} \psi_0(q_k, t) = \left\{\prod_{k=1}^{N} \left(\frac{\omega_k}{\pi\hbar}\right)^{1/4}\right\} \exp(-iE_0 t - \frac{1}{2\hbar}\sum_{k=1}^{N}\omega_k q_k^2) \tag{158}$$

with the ground state energy

$$E_0 = \sum_{k=1}^{N} \frac{1}{2}\hbar\omega_k \tag{159}$$

Each oscillator has its own creation and annihilation operator $\hat{a}_k^\dagger, \hat{a}_k^\dagger$. Excited states can be constructed by operating repeatedly by $\hat{a}_k^\dagger$. Note that $\hat{a}_k^\dagger$ changes only the integer corresponding to the kth oscillator:

$$\hat{a}_k^\dagger |n_1, n_2 \cdots, n_k, \cdots n_N > = \sqrt{n_k + 1}|n_1, n_2, \cdots n_k + 1, \cdots n_N > . \tag{160}$$

The results derived earlier using path integrals for the harmonic oscillator can also be extended easily for $N-$dimensional systems. Since the action

$$A = \sum_{k=1}^{N} \int dt \frac{1}{2}(\dot{q}_k^2 - \omega_k^2 q_k^2) \tag{161}$$

is a sum of individual actions, the path integral Kernel becomes

$$K\left[\{q_k\}_F, t_2; \{q_k\}_I, t_1\right] = \left\{\prod_{k=1}^{N}\left(\frac{\omega_k}{2\pi i\hbar \sin\omega_k T}\right)^{1/2}\right\} \exp\frac{i}{\hbar}A_c \qquad (162)$$

where $\{q_k\}_F$ stands for the final values of all the coordinates $q_k : \{q_1^F, q_2^F \cdots q_N^F\}$ etc. This Kernel represents the probability amplitude for the system to propagate from an initial state to a final state, such that first oscillator co-ordinate changes from q_1^I to q_1^F, second from q_2^I to q_2^F, etc. etc.

We can also generalize the results obtained in the presence of external sources $J(t)$ to the $N-$dimensional system. Since there are $N-$oscillators we will add $N-$external source functions $[J_1(t), J_2(t) \cdots J_k(t) \cdots J_N(t)]$ by adding to the action the term

$$A_{\text{add}} = \sum_{k=1}^{N}\int dt q_k(t) J_k(t). \qquad (163)$$

The transition amplitudes computed earlier now generalizes to

$$K[0,\infty; 0-\infty; J_k(t)] = \left\{\prod_{k=1}^{N}(\det D_k)^{-1/2}\right\} \exp-\frac{i}{2\hbar}W[J_k] \qquad (164)$$

with

$$\begin{aligned}
W[J] &= \sum_{k=1}^{N}\int_{-\infty}^{+\infty} dt dt' J_k(t) G_k(t,t') J_k(t')\\
&= \sum_{k=1}^{N}\int \frac{d\nu}{(2\pi)}\frac{|J_k(\nu)|^2}{\nu^2 - (\omega_k^2 - i\epsilon)}\\
&= \sum_{k=1}^{N}\int \frac{d\nu}{(2\pi)}J_k^*(\nu)G_k(\nu)J_k(\nu) \qquad (165)
\end{aligned}$$

where $J_k(\nu)$ is the Fourier transform of $J_k(t)$ and $G_k(\nu)$ is proportional to the Fourier transform of the Green function for the k'th oscillator:

$$G_k(\nu) = \frac{1}{\nu^2 - (\omega_k^2 - i\epsilon)}. \qquad (166)$$

The Green function for each oscillator, of course, can be expressed as the expectation value of coordinate operators, *i.e.*,

$$G_k(t,t') = <E_0|T(q_k(t)q_k(t'))|E_0>. \qquad (167)$$

It is more convenient to write this in a somewhat more general form

$$G_{kp}(t,t') = <E_0|T(q_k(t)q_p(t'))|E_0> = \delta_{kp}G_k(t,t') \qquad (168)$$

With a view to future applications in mind, we want to reexpress the above formulas in a different manner. Let us first consider the role of the label 'k' in the above analysis. We can think of k as labelling the positive lattice points in a line – i.e., one-dimensional space. In other words, we consider the interval $[0, \infty]$ in the real line and pick out from this continuum of points the first N lattice points $k = 1, 2 \cdots N$. To each of these points, we associate a harmonic oscillator q_k with frequency ω_k.

This picture suggests an immediate, and useful, extension of our formalism. We need not confine ourselves to the positive side of real axis or to the lattice points. Let us associate with each real value of a variable $k[-\infty < k < \infty]$ an oscillator q_k with frequency ω_k. We now have an uncountably infinite number oscillators labelled by a continuous index k. [To be precise, we should now use a notation $q(k,t)$ rather than $q_k(t)$; but we will not bother to do this.]

We can take over all the previous results to this continuum case in a formal sense. For example, the ground state wave function of (158) becomes,

$$\Psi_0[q_k;t] = \left\{\prod_{allk}\left(\frac{\omega_k}{\pi\hbar}\right)^{1/4}\right\} \exp\left[-iE_0t - \frac{1}{2\hbar}\sum_{all\,k}\omega_k q_k^2\right]$$

$$= \exp - \int_{-\infty}^{+\infty}\frac{dk}{2\pi}\left\{i\frac{\hbar\omega_k}{2} - \frac{1}{2}\ln\left(\frac{\omega_k}{\hbar\pi}\right)\right\} \qquad (169)$$

For this expression to be rigorously meaningful, the integral in the exponent should converge. This will put severe constraints on the nature of the function ω_k; in fact, for most of the systems which we consider, ω_k will increase with k, for large k. The convergence condition will be badly violated in this case and expressions like (169) need to interpreted very carefully. We will say more about it later.

There are, however, other results which carry over neatly to the continuum case. For example, the exponent of (164) becomes

$$W = \int_{-\infty}^{+\infty}\frac{dk}{2\pi}\int_{-\infty}^{+\infty}\frac{d\nu}{2\pi}J_k(\nu)G_k(\nu)J_k(\nu) \qquad (170)$$

This expression suggests another obvious modification. We note that ν and k appear on the same footing in W. The variable ν corresponds to t on Fourier transforming; in a similar manner, we may introduce a Fourier conjugate variable for k. Let us call this, one-dimensional, real, variable x.

Writing

$$J(t;x) \equiv \int_{-\infty}^{+\infty} \frac{d\nu}{2\pi} \int_{-\infty}^{+\infty} \frac{dk}{2\pi} J_k(\nu) e^{-i\nu t + ikx}$$

$$G(t;x) \equiv \int_{-\infty}^{+\infty} \frac{d\nu}{2\pi} \int_{-\infty}^{+\infty} \frac{dk}{2\pi} G_k(\nu) e^{-i\nu t + ikx}$$

$$= \int_{-\infty}^{+\infty} \frac{d\nu dk}{(2\pi)^2} \frac{e^{-i\nu t + ikx}}{\nu^2 - (\omega_k^2 - i\epsilon)}. \tag{171}$$

We can put W in the form

$$W = \int_{-\infty}^{+\infty} dt dx \int_{-\infty}^{+\infty} dt' dx' J(t;x) G(t - t'; x - x') J(t';x') \tag{172}$$

Instead of working with the function $J_k(\nu)$ or $J_k(t)$, we can work with the function $J(t,x)$. All the features of the system are contained in the Green function $G_k(\nu)$ or -equivalently – in $G(t;x)$.

The k-space (and its Fourier conjugate x-space) we have introduced is purely a mathematical construct at this stage. We have merely attached, to each point in the real line $R^{(1)}$- labelled by k – one harmonic oscillator. Quite clearly, we can generalize this concept to a $D-$dimensional k-space, labelled by a $D-$dimensional vector $\mathbf{k} = (k_1, k_2, \cdots k_D)$. To each point, in this space, we associate an oscillator $q_\mathbf{k}$. The k- integrations in previous formulas involve the volume element $[dk_1 \cdots dk_D/(2\pi)^D] = [d\mathbf{k}/(2\pi)^D]$. Corresponding to this k-space, we have the Fourier conjugate $\mathbf{x}$- space which is again $D-$dimensional.

All the previous expressions can be easily generalized. For example, (172) will become

$$W = \int_{-\infty}^{+\infty} dt d\mathbf{x} \int_{-\infty}^{+\infty} dt' d\mathbf{x}' J(t;\mathbf{x}) G(t - t'; \mathbf{x} - \mathbf{x}') J(t';\mathbf{x}') \tag{173}$$

with

$$G(t;\mathbf{x}) = \int_{-\infty}^{+\infty} \frac{d\nu d\mathbf{k}}{(2\pi)^{D+1}} \frac{e^{-i\nu t + i\mathbf{k}.\mathbf{k}}}{\nu^2 - \omega_\mathbf{k}^2 + i\epsilon} \tag{174}$$

and similar expressions for $J(t;\mathbf{x})$ etc.

The original Green function for each oscillator we started with $G_k(t, t')$, could be expressed as the expectation value $< E_0|(q_k(t) q_k(t'))|E_0 >$. The quantity $G(t,\mathbf{x})$ can also be expressed in a similar fashion with suitably defined operators. Note that, for $t > t'$,

$$G(t - t'; \mathbf{x} - \mathbf{x}')$$

$$= \int \frac{d\mathbf{k}}{(2\pi)^D} \int \frac{d\mathbf{p}}{(2\pi)^D} G_{kp}(t-t')e^{i\mathbf{k}.\mathbf{x}-i\mathbf{p}.\mathbf{x}'}$$

$$= \int \frac{d\mathbf{k}}{(2\pi)^D} \int \frac{d\mathbf{p}}{(2\pi)^D} < E_0|q_{\mathbf{k}}(t)q_{\mathbf{p}}(t')|E_0 > e^{i\mathbf{k}.\mathbf{x}-i\mathbf{p}.\mathbf{x}'}$$

$$= \int \frac{d\mathbf{k}}{(2\pi)^D} \int \frac{d\mathbf{p}}{(2\pi)^D} < E_0|(q_k(t)e^{i\mathbf{k}.\mathbf{x}})(q_p(t')e^{i\mathbf{p}.\mathbf{x}'})^\dagger|E_0 > \quad (175)$$

In arriving at the last expression we have used the fact that $q_k(t)$'s are Hermitian; *i.e.*, $q_k^\dagger = q_k$. Let us now define an operator

$$\hat{\phi}(t,\mathbf{x}) \equiv \hat{\phi}_{\mathbf{x}}(t) \equiv \int \frac{d\mathbf{k}}{(2\pi)^D} \hat{q}_{\mathbf{k}}(t)e^{i\mathbf{k}.\mathbf{x}} \quad (176)$$

Then we can write

$$G(t-t';\mathbf{x}-\mathbf{x}') = < E_0|\hat{\phi}(t,\mathbf{x})\hat{\phi}^\dagger(t',\mathbf{x}')|E_0 >; \, t > t'. \quad (177)$$

We can take care of the condition $t > t'$ by putting a time- ordering operator. Then we finally get

$$G(t-t';\mathbf{x}-\mathbf{x}') = < E_0|T(\hat{\phi}(t,\mathbf{x})\hat{\phi}^\dagger(t',\mathbf{x}'))|E_0 > \quad (178)$$

expressing the Green function in the $(\mathbf{x},t)$ coordinates in terms of the ground state expectation value of the set of operators $\hat{\phi}_{\mathbf{x}}(t)$. Note that we have associated with each point $\mathbf{x}$, this operator $\hat{\phi}_{\mathbf{x}}(t)$.

Since we have come far away from the simple harmonic oscillator with one degree of freedom, it is worthwhile to take stock what we have done. These are the crucial steps of involved:

1. Consider a $D-$dimensional Cartesian space in which each point is labelled by a $D-$dimensional vector $\mathbf{k}$.

2. We associate with each point in this abstract $\mathbf{k}$ dimensional space, a harmonic oscillator of unit mass and real, positive, frequency $\omega_{\mathbf{k}}$. Let $\hat{q}_{\mathbf{k}}(t)$ be the (Heisenberg picture) operator characterizing the $\mathbf{k}$ th oscillator.

3. We introduce next another $D-$dimensional space which is Fourier conjugate to the $\mathbf{k}$-space. The points in this space are labelled by the $D-$dimensional vector $\mathbf{x}$. Physical variables in these two spaces are related by Fourier transform.

4. The Kernel in the presence of external sources $J_{\mathbf{k}}(t)$ can be written as

$$K[J] = \exp -\frac{i}{2\hbar}W \quad (179)$$

with

$$
\begin{aligned}
W[J] &= \int \frac{d\mathbf{k}}{(2\pi)^D} \int_{-\infty}^{+\infty} dt dt' J_{\mathbf{k}}(t) G_{\mathbf{k}}(t,t') J_{\mathbf{k}}(t') \\
&= \int d\mathbf{x} dt \int d\mathbf{x}' dt' \, J(t;\mathbf{x}) G(t-t';\mathbf{x}-\mathbf{x}') J(t';\mathbf{x}')
\end{aligned} \quad (180)
$$

where

$$
\begin{aligned}
J(t;\mathbf{x}) &= \int \frac{d\mathbf{k}}{(2\pi)^D} J_{\mathbf{k}}(t) e^{i\mathbf{k}.\mathbf{x}} = \int \frac{d\mathbf{k} d\nu}{(2\pi)^{D+1}} J_{\mathbf{k}}(\nu) e^{i\mathbf{k}.\mathbf{x}-i\nu t} \\
G(t;\mathbf{x}) &= \int \frac{d\mathbf{k}}{(2\pi)^D} G_{\mathbf{k}}(t) e^{i\mathbf{k}.\mathbf{x}} = \int \frac{d\mathbf{k} d\nu}{(2\pi)^{D+1}} \frac{e^{i\mathbf{k}.\mathbf{x}-i\nu t}}{\nu^2 - \omega_{\mathbf{k}}^2 + i\epsilon}
\end{aligned} \quad (181)
$$

5. The properties of the system is contained in the function $G(t;\mathbf{x})$ which – in turn – depends only on the frequency of the various oscillators, i.e., the function $\omega(\mathbf{k}) = \omega_{\mathbf{k}}$.

6. To each point in $\mathbf{x}$-space associate an operator $\hat{\phi}_{\mathbf{x}}(t) = \hat{\phi}(t;\mathbf{x})$ given by

$$
\hat{\phi}(t;\mathbf{x}) = \int \frac{d\mathbf{k}}{(2\pi)^D} \hat{q}_{\mathbf{k}}(t) e^{i\mathbf{k}.\mathbf{x}} \quad (182)
$$

The Green function can be then expressed as

$$
G(t-t';\mathbf{x}-\mathbf{x}') = <E_0|T(\hat{\phi}(T;\mathbf{x})\hat{\phi}^\dagger(t;\mathbf{x}))|E_0> \quad (183)
$$

where $|E_0>$ is the state in which all the harmonic oscillators are in the respective ground state.

The above analysis was done using normal time co-ordinate and hence contain exponents which oscillate. It is, of course, possible to carry out the same analysis in the Euclidean sector. It is easy to see that we will then obtain the expression

$$
K[J] = \exp \frac{1}{2\hbar} W \quad (184)
$$

with

$$
W = \int_{-\infty}^{+\infty} d\tau d\mathbf{x} \int_{-\infty}^{+\infty} d\tau' d\mathbf{x}' J(\tau;\mathbf{x}) G(\tau-\tau';\mathbf{x}-\mathbf{x}') J(\tau';\mathbf{x}') \quad (185)
$$

where

$$
G(\tau;\mathbf{x}) = \int \frac{d\nu d\mathbf{k}}{(2\pi)^{D+1}} \frac{e^{-i\nu\tau+i\mathbf{k}.\mathbf{x}}}{\nu^2 + \omega_k^2} = \int \frac{d\nu d\mathbf{k}}{(2\pi)^{D+1}} \frac{e^{i(\mathbf{k}.\mathbf{x}+\nu\tau)}}{\nu^2 + \omega_k^2} \quad (186)
$$

This expression has an interesting connection with the Laplace transform of the free-particle propagator. The Euclidean propagator for a free-particle in N−dimensions is

$$K(\mathbf{x}; \tau) = \left(\frac{m}{2\pi\hbar\tau}\right)^{N/2} \exp -\frac{1}{\hbar}\frac{m|\mathbf{x}|^2}{2\tau} \tag{187}$$

where $\mathbf{x} = \mathbf{x_2} - \mathbf{x_1}$ and $\tau = \tau_2 - \tau_1$. The Laplace transform of this expression,

$$F(\mathbf{x}; \lambda) = \int_0^\infty d\tau e^{-\lambda\tau} K(\mathbf{x}; \tau) \tag{188}$$

can be evaluated easily by writing K as

$$K(\mathbf{x}; \tau) = \int \frac{d\mathbf{k}}{(2\pi)^N} \exp(i\mathbf{k}.\mathbf{x} - \frac{\hbar\tau}{2m}k^2) \tag{189}$$

and doing the τ integration first. This gives,

$$
\begin{aligned}
F(\mathbf{x}; \lambda) &= \int \frac{d\mathbf{k}}{(2\pi)^N} e^{i\mathbf{k}.\mathbf{x}} \int_0^\infty d\tau e^{-\tau(\lambda + \frac{\hbar k^2}{2m})} \\
&= \int \frac{d\mathbf{k}}{(2\pi)^N} e^{i\mathbf{k}.\mathbf{x}} \frac{1}{(\lambda + \hbar k^2/2m)} \\
&= \left(\frac{2m}{\hbar}\right) \int \frac{d\mathbf{k}}{(2\pi)^N} \frac{e^{i\mathbf{k}.\mathbf{x}}}{(\mathbf{k}^2 + \mu^2)}
\end{aligned} \tag{190}
$$

where we have defined $\mu^2 = (2m\lambda/\hbar)$. Let us separate out of the N−dimensional integral $[d\mathbf{k}] = [dk_1 dk_2 \cdots dk_N]$ the N-th integral and write

$$F(x_1, x_2 \cdots x_N; \lambda) \equiv F(\mathbf{x}, x_N; \lambda) = \left(\frac{2m}{\hbar}\right) \int \frac{d\mathbf{k}.dk_N}{(2\pi)^N} \frac{e^{i(\mathbf{k}.\mathbf{x} + k_N x_N)}}{(k_N^2 + \mathbf{k}^2 + \mu^2)} \tag{191}$$

in which $\mathbf{x}$ and $\mathbf{k}$ stand for $(N - 1)$ dimensional vectors. This expression is essentially the same as $G(\tau; \mathbf{x})$ if we identify $N = D + 1$; $x_N = \tau$; $k_N = \nu$ and choose the frequencies of the harmonic oscillators to be given by

$$\omega^2(\mathbf{k}) = \mathbf{k}^2 + \mu^2 \tag{192}$$

We shall later show that μ^2 is essentially the energy of a free particle. This gives us the important identification between: (1) one free particle in N−dimensions with energy μ^2 and (2) an infinite number of oscillators in an $(N - 1)$ dimensional space with the frequency relation $\omega^2(\mathbf{k}) = \mathbf{k}^2 + \mu^2$. As we shall see, this result is of fundamental significance.

2.10. PATH INTEGRALS WITH JACOBI ACTION

We shall now consider a different description of path integral Kernel, which turns out to be extremely important. Let us begin by observing that the action in classical mechanics can also be written in the form

$$
\begin{aligned}
A[\mathbf{x}(t), \mathbf{p}(t)] &= \int_0^T dt[\mathbf{p}.\dot{\mathbf{x}} - H(\mathbf{p}, \mathbf{x})] \\
&= \int_0^T dt[\mathbf{p}.\dot{\mathbf{x}} - \frac{\mathbf{p}^2}{2m} - V(\mathbf{x})].
\end{aligned}
\tag{193}
$$

To facilitate future use, we are considering a theory in a N−dimensional space; the position $\mathbf{x}$ and momentum $\mathbf{p}$ are N−dimensional vectors. If we vary $\mathbf{p}$ and $\mathbf{x}$ independently in the above expression we get

$$
\delta A = \int_0^T dt \left[(\dot{\mathbf{x}} - \frac{\mathbf{P}}{m}).\delta\mathbf{p} - (\dot{\mathbf{p}} + \nabla V).\delta\mathbf{x} \right] + \mathbf{p}.\delta\mathbf{x}|_0^T
\tag{194}
$$

We confine our attention to variations for which $\delta\mathbf{x} = 0$ at $t = 0, T$ but $\delta\mathbf{p}$ is entirely arbitrary. This gives,

$$
\mathbf{p} = m\dot{\mathbf{x}}; \dot{\mathbf{p}} = -\nabla V
\tag{195}
$$

which are the Hamilton's equations. We can now attempt to write the path integral using (193) in the form

$$
K(\mathbf{x_2}, \mathbf{x_1}; T) = \sum_{\text{allx}} \sum_{\text{allp}} \exp \frac{i}{\hbar} \int_0^T dt(\mathbf{p}.\dot{\mathbf{x}} - H(\mathbf{p}, \mathbf{x}))
\tag{196}
$$

where the sum is over *all* functions $\mathbf{p}(t)$ but only those $\mathbf{x}(t)$ which has the correct boundary values. The sum over all p can be performed by slicing the time axis into small intervals, in a manner identical to what was done earlier. This will lead to an expression for the Kernel as the sum over all $\mathbf{x}$ of some amplitude; this amplitude turns out to be the usual one with the lagrangian form of the action.

We will, however, proceed in a somewhat different way in calculating (196). Instead of summing over $\mathbf{x}$ and $\mathbf{p}$, we will first (i) sum over all $\mathbf{x}(t)$ (satisfying the boundary conditions) for a given value of $H(\mathbf{p}, \mathbf{x}) \equiv E$ and then (ii) sum over all values of E. That is, we replace (196) by,

$$
\begin{aligned}
K(\mathbf{x_2}, \mathbf{x_1}; T) &= \sum_{\text{all E}} \sum_{\text{all x}} \exp \frac{i}{\hbar} \left[\int_0^T dt(\mathbf{p}.\dot{\mathbf{x}} - E) \right] \\
&= \sum_{\text{all E}} \sum_{\text{all x}} \exp \frac{i}{\hbar} \left[\int_0^T dt \{2m(E - V(\mathbf{x}))\}^{1/2} |\dot{\mathbf{x}}| - ET \right] \\
&= \sum_{\text{all E}} \exp \left(-\frac{iET}{\hbar} \right) \left[\sum_{\text{all x}} \exp \frac{i}{\hbar} \int_0^T dt \sqrt{2m(E - V(\mathbf{x}))\dot{\mathbf{x}}^2} \right]
\end{aligned}
\tag{197}
$$

The 'sum over all E', is just an integration over the parameter E with some weightage $g(E)$ [if needed]. Assuming the Hamiltonian is bounded from below we can normalise the Hamiltonian so that $E \geq 0$. Then we can write,

$$
\begin{aligned}
K(\mathbf{x_2}, \mathbf{x_1}; T) &= \int_0^\infty dE g(E) e^{-\frac{i}{\hbar} ET} G(\mathbf{x_2}, \mathbf{x_1}; E) \\
&\equiv \int_0^\infty dE e^{-\frac{i}{\hbar} ET} B(\mathbf{x_2}, \mathbf{x_1}; E)
\end{aligned}
\tag{198}
$$

where

$$
G(\mathbf{x_2}, \mathbf{x_1}; E) = \sum_{\text{all } \mathbf{x}} \exp \frac{i}{\hbar} \int_0^T dt \sqrt{2m(E - V\mathbf{x}))\dot{\mathbf{x}}^2}
\tag{199}
$$

Relabelling t by $s = (t/T)$, we get

$$
G(\mathbf{x_2}, \mathbf{x_1}; E) = \sum_{\text{all} \mathbf{x}} \exp \frac{i}{\hbar} \int_0^1 ds \sqrt{2m(E - V)|\frac{d\mathbf{x}}{ds}|^2}
\tag{200}
$$

In this form, the paths are parametrised so that $\mathbf{x}(0) = \mathbf{x_1}$ and $\mathbf{x}(1) = \mathbf{x_2}$.

This expression offers an interesting interpretation. By inverting the Fourier transform in (198), we can write.

$$
B = g(E) G(\mathbf{x_2}, \mathbf{x_1}; E) = \int_0^\infty dT e^{\frac{i}{\hbar} ET} K(\mathbf{x_2}, \mathbf{x_1}; T)
\tag{201}
$$

[Strictly speaking, the Fourier integrals go over the range $(-\infty, +\infty)$. However, $K(T)$ vanishes for $T < 0$ and $B(E)$ vanishes for $E < 0$. We will not bother to indicate this fact explicitly everytime]. Since $K(\mathbf{x_2}, \mathbf{x_1}; T)$ gives the amplitude for propagation from $\mathbf{x_1}$ to $\mathbf{x_2}$ in a time interval T it is natural to interpret B as the amplitude for propagation between these two points with energy E. This interpretation is also borne out by the fact that argument of the exponent in (200) is what is called the Jacobi action capable of describing paths of particles with definite energy.

Notice that we have also obtained something much more useful: we have provided an interpretation for the 'sum over paths' appearing in (200)! Since the Jacobi action has a square root in it, none of our previous definitions of 'sum over paths' will work in this case. We can now take (201) as defining (200). That is we take

$$
\sum_{\text{all } \mathbf{x}} g(E) \exp \frac{i}{\hbar} \int_0^1 ds \sqrt{2m(E - V)|\frac{d\mathbf{x}}{ds}|^2}
$$

$$
= \sum_{\text{all } \mathbf{x}} \exp \frac{i}{\hbar} \int_0^1 ds \sqrt{2m(E - V)|\dot{\mathbf{x}}|^2}
$$

$$= \int_0^\infty dT e^{\frac{i}{\hbar}ET} \int \mathcal{D}x(t) \exp \frac{i}{\hbar} \int_0^T dt \left[\frac{1}{2}m\dot{x}^2 - V \right] \qquad (202)$$

In arriving at the second expression we have redefined the measure in "sum over paths" by absorbing the $g(E)$ factor.

There is one crucial point in the above definition which needs to be mentioned. The Jacobi action, defined as,

$$A_{\text{Jacobi}} = \int_0^T dt \sqrt{2m(E - V(\mathbf{x}))|\dot{\mathbf{x}}|^2} \qquad (203)$$

has the property of being "reparametrisation invariant" under 'time relabelling'. This is clear from the fact that, on performing the transformation $t \to \tau = \tau(t)$ where

$$t = \int_0^T N(\tau')d\tau' \qquad (204)$$

the integrand does not change:

$$\int dt \sqrt{2m(E - V)|\dot{\mathbf{x}}|^2} = \int N d\tau \sqrt{2m(E - V)N^{-2}|\mathbf{x}_\tau|^2}$$

$$= \int d\tau \sqrt{2m(E - V)|\frac{d\mathbf{x}}{d\tau}|^2}. \qquad (205)$$

Therefore two different paths $\mathbf{x}(t)$ and $\mathbf{x}(t(\tau)) = \mathbf{x}'(\tau)$ will give the same value to the action, even though the functional form of $\mathbf{x}(t)$ and $\mathbf{x}'(\tau)$ may be quite different. Obviously, we will get an infinite value for G, if we count all these paths are different. Therefore, if the sum over paths in (200) should be well-defined, we must remove this 'reparametrisation invariance' by choosing a definite parametrisation. This is precisely what is achieved by the rescaling $t \to \tau = t/T$ in the definition of (200).

The classical equations of motion are invariant even if A is replaced by $-A$. If we had used the negative of Jacobi action in (197), then we would have obtained, in place of (200) and (201), the relations:

$$G(\mathbf{x_2}, \mathbf{x_1}; E) = \sum_{\text{all}\mathbf{x}} \exp -\frac{i}{\hbar} \int_0^1 ds \sqrt{2m(E - V)|\frac{d\mathbf{x}}{ds}|^2}$$

$$B(\mathbf{x_2}, \mathbf{x_1}; E) = \int_0^\infty dT e^{-\frac{i}{\hbar}ET} K(\mathbf{x_2}, \mathbf{x_1}; T) \qquad (206)$$

Let us now consider the Euclidean analogue of this result. With the lagrangian form of the action, we could tackle the oscillating exponents by analytically continuing in t through the substitution $\tau = it$. This procedure converts the quantity

$$iA = i \int_0^T dt \left(\frac{1}{2} m \dot{x}^2 - V \right) = - \int_0^{\tau_0} d\tau \left(\frac{1}{2} m \left(\frac{dx}{d\tau} \right)^2 + V \right) \tag{207}$$

to a negative definite expression (we assume $V > 0$). But if we change the parameter s in (200) to $\bar{\eta} = is$ we will get a *positive* definite expression in the exponent

$$i \int ds \sqrt{2m(E-V)|\frac{dx}{ds}|^2} = \int d\bar{\eta} \sqrt{2m(-E+V)|\frac{dx}{d\bar{\eta}}|^2} \tag{208}$$

for all $E < 0$. The proper change to make is not $is = \bar{\eta}$ but $\eta = -is$. Then, we get, for $E < 0$,

$$i \int ds \sqrt{2m(E-V)\left(\frac{dx}{ds}\right)^2} = - \int d\eta \sqrt{2m(|E|+V)\left(\frac{dx}{ds}\right)^2} \tag{209}$$

In Euclidean space (202), becomes

$$\sum_{\text{all } x} \exp -\frac{1}{\hbar} \int_0^1 d\eta \sqrt{2m(|E|+V)|\dot{x}|^2}$$

$$= \int_0^\infty d\tau e^{-\frac{|E|\tau}{\hbar}} \int \mathcal{D}x \exp -\frac{1}{\hbar} \int_0^\tau \left(\frac{1}{2}m\dot{x}^2 + V\right)d\tau \tag{210}$$

Let us evaluate this expression for a free particle in $N-$dimensions. The Euclidean free particle Kernel in $N-$dimension is

$$K(x;\tau) = \int \mathcal{D}x \exp -\frac{1}{\hbar} \int_0^\tau \frac{1}{2} m|\dot{x}|^2 d\tau$$

$$= \left(\frac{m}{2\pi\hbar\tau} \right)^{\frac{N}{2}} \exp -\frac{1}{\hbar} \frac{m|x|^2}{2\tau}; x = x_2 - x_1 \tag{211}$$

Therefore, calling $|E| = \lambda$,

$$B(x;\lambda) = \int_0^\infty d\tau e^{-\frac{\lambda\tau}{\hbar}} \left(\frac{m}{2\pi\hbar\tau} \right)^{N/2} \exp -\frac{1}{\hbar} \frac{m|x|^2}{2\tau} \tag{212}$$

Writing

$$\left(\frac{m}{2\pi\hbar\tau} \right)^{N/2} \exp -\frac{1}{\hbar} \frac{m|x|^2}{2\tau} = \int \frac{dk}{(2\pi)^N} e^{ik.x - \frac{\hbar k^2}{2m}\tau} \tag{213}$$

and doing the τ-integration first, we get

$$
\begin{aligned}
B(\mathbf{x};\lambda) &= \int_0^\infty d\tau e^{-\frac{\lambda\tau}{\hbar}} \int \frac{d\mathbf{k}}{(2\pi)^N} e^{i\mathbf{k}\cdot\mathbf{x} - \frac{\hbar k^2}{2m}\tau} \\
&= \int \frac{d\mathbf{k}}{(2\pi)^N} e^{i\mathbf{k}\cdot\mathbf{x}} \int_0^\infty d\tau e^{-\frac{\tau}{\hbar}(\lambda + \frac{\hbar^2 k^2}{2m})} \\
&= \int \frac{d\mathbf{k}}{(2\pi)^N} e^{i\mathbf{k}\cdot\mathbf{x}} \left[\frac{1}{\hbar}\left(\lambda + \frac{\hbar^2 k^2}{2m}\right)\right]^{-1}
\end{aligned}
\tag{214}
$$

This can be rewritten in the form

$$
B(\mathbf{x};\lambda) = \left(\frac{2m}{\hbar}\right) \int \frac{d\mathbf{k}}{(2\pi)^N} \frac{e^{i\mathbf{k}\cdot\mathbf{x}}}{(\mu^2 + |\mathbf{k}|^2)}
\tag{215}
$$

where $\mu^2 = (2m\lambda/\hbar^2)$. This form is strikingly similar to the Euclidean Green function we derived earlier for the $D-$dimensional harmonic oscillator system. We found that,

$$
G_{\mathrm{Eu}}(\mathbf{x};\tau) = \int \frac{d\nu d\mathbf{k}}{(2\pi)^{D+1}} \frac{e^{i\mathbf{k}\cdot\mathbf{x} + i\nu\tau}}{\nu^2 + \omega^2(\mathbf{k})}
\tag{216}
$$

The identification between B and G_{Eu} follows if we choose the frequencies of the harmonic oscillators to be

$$
\omega^2(\mathbf{k}) = \mathbf{k}^2 + \mu^2
\tag{217}
$$

and $N = D + 1$. Then

$$
\begin{aligned}
G_{\mathrm{Eu}}(\mathbf{x},\nu) &= \int \frac{d\nu d\mathbf{k}}{(2\pi)^{D+1}} \frac{e^{i\mathbf{k}\cdot\mathbf{x} + i\nu\tau}}{\nu^2 + \mathbf{k}^2 + \mu^2} \\
&= \int \frac{d\mathbf{p}}{(2\pi)^N} \frac{e^{i\mathbf{p}\cdot\mathbf{x}}}{\mathbf{p}^2 + \mu^2} = G_{\mathrm{Eu}}(\mathbf{x}); N = D + 1
\end{aligned}
\tag{218}
$$

where the $(D+1)$ dimensional vectors $\mathbf{p}$ and $\mathbf{x}$ have the components $(\mathbf{k},\nu)$ and $(\mathbf{x},\tau)$. Comparing (218), and (215), we see that

$$
B(\mathbf{x};\lambda) = \frac{2m}{\hbar} G_{\mathrm{Eu}}(\mathbf{x})
\tag{219}
$$

To make the identification complete, we will choose $m = (1/2)$ and set $\hbar = 1$. [This will make $\mu^2 = (2m\lambda/\hbar^2) = \lambda = |E|$]. Then we can write

$$
\begin{aligned}
B(\mathbf{x};\mu^2) &= \int_0^\infty d\tau e^{-\mu^2\tau} K(\mathbf{x};\tau) \\
&= \int_0^\infty d\tau e^{-\mu^2\tau} \int \mathcal{D}x \exp - \int_0^\tau d\tau \left[\frac{1}{4}\dot{\mathbf{x}}^2\right] \\
&= G_{\mathrm{Eu}}(\mathbf{x}) = \int \frac{d\mathbf{k}}{(2\pi)^N} \frac{e^{i\mathbf{k}\cdot\mathbf{x}}}{\mathbf{k}^2 + \mu^2}.
\end{aligned}
\tag{220}
$$

This is a remarkable result! The $B(\mathbf{x}; \mu^2)$ represent the amplitude for a free particle in N-dimensional space to propagate from $\mathbf{x}_1$ to $\mathbf{x}_2$ with energy μ^2. The $G_{\mathrm{Eu}}(\mathbf{x})$ is the Green function for a system with infinite number of harmonic oscillators labelled by a $(N - 1)$ dimensional vector $\mathbf{k}$), with a particular dispersion relation $\omega^2(\mathbf{k}) = k^2 + \mu^2$. The above result, therefore, expresses an equivalence between a free particle in $N-$ dimensions and a system of infinite number of oscillators in $(N - 1)$ dimensions.

2.11. RIGOROUS EVALUATION OF THE JACOBI PATH INTEGRAL

In the discussion above, we defined the path integral over the Jacobi action by connecting it up with the more conventional path integral which we had already defined rigorously earlier. In doing so, we have bypassed the need for defining the measure for the Jacobi integral from first principles.

It is, however, interesting to consider the question of defining the Jacobi path integral from the first principles. This analysis will allow us to explore an alternative means of defining path integrals.

We will work directly in the Euclidean sector of $D-$dimensions. Since we are primarily interested in the issues of principle, regarding the measure for the path integral it is enough for us to consider the path integral for a free particle. We have to, therefore, evaluate

$$
\begin{aligned}
\mathcal{G}(\mathbf{x}_2, \mathbf{x}_1; E) &= \sum_{\text{all } \mathbf{x}(t)} \exp \frac{i}{\hbar} \int_0^1 ds \sqrt{2mE} \left| \left(\frac{d\mathbf{x}}{ds}\right)^2 \right|^{1/2} \\
&= \sum_{\text{all } \mathbf{x}(t)} \exp i\mu_0 \int_0^1 ds \left| \left(\frac{d\mathbf{x}}{ds}\right)^2 \right|^{1/2}
\end{aligned} \tag{221}
$$

where we have defined $\mu_0^2 = (2mE/\hbar^2)$ as before. We notice that the quantity

$$
l(\mathbf{x}_2, \mathbf{x}_1) = \int_0^1 ds \left| \left(\frac{d\mathbf{x}}{ds}\right)^2 \right|^{1/2} \tag{222}
$$

is just the length of the curve $\mathbf{x}(s)$, connecting $\mathbf{x}(0) = \mathbf{x}_1$ and $\mathbf{x}(1) = \mathbf{x}_2$. We will, therefore, consider the path integral

$$
\mathcal{G}_E(\mathbf{x}_2, \mathbf{x}_1; \mu_0) = \sum_{\text{all } \mathbf{x}(t)} \exp -\mu_0 \, l[\mathbf{x}(t)] \tag{223}
$$

in the Euclidean sector, where l is the length of the path.

This quantity can be defined through the following limiting procedure: Consider a lattice of points in a $D-$dimensional lattice with a uniform lattice spacing of ϵ. We will work out $\mathcal{G}_E$ in the lattice and will then take the limit of $\epsilon \to 0$ with suitable measure $M(\epsilon)$. To obtain a finite answer, we also have to treat μ_0 (which is the only parameter in the problem) as different for different lattice spacings; *i.e.*, $\mu = \mu(\epsilon)$ in a specific manner. We will reserve the symbol μ_0 with a subscript, for the parameter in the continuum limit. Thus we have

$$\mathcal{G}(\mathbf{x_2}, \mathbf{x_1}; \mu_0) = \lim_{\epsilon \to 0} [M(\epsilon)\mathcal{G}(\mathbf{x_2}, \mathbf{x_1}; \mu(\epsilon))] \qquad (224)$$

In a lattice with spacing of ϵ, (223) can be evaluated in a straightforward manner. Because of the translation invariance of the problem, $\mathcal{G}_E$ can only depend on $\mathbf{x_2} - \mathbf{x_1}$; so we can set $\mathbf{x_1} = 0$ and call $\mathbf{x_2} = \epsilon\mathbf{R}$ where $\mathbf{R}$ is a $D-$dimensional vector with integral components: $\mathbf{R} = (n_1, n_2, n_3 \cdots n_D)$. Let $C(N, \mathbf{R})$ be the number of paths of length $N\epsilon$ connecting the origin to the lattice point $\epsilon\mathbf{R}$. Since all the paths contribute a term $\exp -\mu(\epsilon)(N\epsilon)$ to (223), we get,

$$\mathcal{G}_E(\mathbf{R}; \epsilon) = \sum_{N=0}^{\infty} C(N; \mathbf{R}) \exp -\mu(\epsilon) N\epsilon \qquad (225)$$

It can be shown from elementary 'combinotrics', that $C(N; \mathbf{R})$ are determined by the generating function

$$F^N \equiv \left[e^{ik_1} + e^{ik_2} + \cdots e^{ik_D} + e^{-ik_1} + \cdots e^{-ik_D} \right]^N = \sum_{\mathbf{R}} C(N; \mathbf{R}) e^{i\mathbf{k} \cdot \mathbf{R}} \qquad (226)$$

Therefore,

$$\sum_{\mathbf{R}} e^{i\mathbf{k} \cdot \mathbf{R}} \mathcal{G}_E(\mathbf{R}; \epsilon) = \sum_{N=0}^{\infty} \sum_{\mathbf{R}} c(N; \mathbf{R}) e^{i\mathbf{k} \cdot \mathbf{R}} \exp -\mu(\epsilon) N\epsilon$$

$$= \sum_{N=0}^{\infty} e^{-\mu(\epsilon)\epsilon N} F^N = \sum_{N=0}^{\infty} \left[F e^{-\mu(\epsilon)\epsilon} \right]^N$$

$$= \left[1 - F e^{-\mu(\epsilon)\epsilon} \right]^{-1} \qquad (227)$$

Inverting the Fourier transform, we get

$$\mathcal{G}_E(\mathbf{R}; \epsilon) = \int \frac{d^D\mathbf{k}}{(2\pi)^D} \frac{e^{-i\mathbf{k} \cdot \mathbf{R}}}{(1 - e^{-\mu(\epsilon)\epsilon} F)}$$

$$= \int \frac{d^D\mathbf{k}}{(2\pi)^D} \frac{e^{-i\mathbf{k} \cdot \mathbf{R}}}{(1 - 2e^{-\mu(\epsilon)\epsilon} \sum_{j=1}^{D} \cos k_j)} \qquad (228)$$

Converting to the physical length scales $\mathbf{x} = \epsilon\mathbf{R}$ and $\mathbf{p} = \epsilon^{-1}\mathbf{k}$ we get

$$\mathcal{G}_E(\mathbf{x}; \epsilon) = \int \frac{\epsilon^D d^D\mathbf{p}}{(2\pi)^D} \frac{e^{-i\mathbf{p} \cdot \mathbf{x}}}{(1 - 2e^{-\mu(\epsilon)\epsilon} \sum_{j=1}^{D} \cos p_j \epsilon)} \qquad (229)$$

We are now ready to take the limit of zero lattice spacing. As $\epsilon \to 0$, the denominator of the integrand becomes

$$
1 - 2e^{-\epsilon\mu(\epsilon)}(D - \frac{1}{2}\epsilon^2|\mathbf{p}|^2) = 1 - 2De^{-\epsilon\mu(\epsilon)} + \epsilon^2 e^{-\epsilon\mu(\epsilon)}|\mathbf{p}|^2
$$

$$
= \epsilon^2 e^{-\epsilon\mu(\epsilon)} \left[|\mathbf{p}|^2 + \frac{1 - 2De^{-\epsilon\mu(\epsilon)}}{\epsilon^2 e^{-\epsilon\mu(\epsilon)}} \right] \tag{230}
$$

so that we will get, for small ϵ,

$$
\mathcal{G}_E(\mathbf{x}; \epsilon) \simeq \int \frac{d^D\mathbf{p}}{(2\pi)^D} \frac{A(\epsilon)e^{-i\mathbf{p}\cdot\mathbf{x}}}{|\mathbf{p}|^2 + B(\epsilon)} \tag{231}
$$

where

$$
\begin{aligned}
A(\epsilon) &= \epsilon^{D-2}e^{\epsilon\mu(\epsilon)} \\
B(\epsilon) &= \frac{1}{\epsilon^2}\left[e^{\epsilon\mu(\epsilon)} - 2D\right]
\end{aligned} \tag{232}
$$

The continuum theory has to be defined in the limit of $\epsilon \to 0$ with some measure $M(\epsilon)$; that is we want to obtain

$$
\mathcal{G}_E(\mathbf{x}; \mu_0)|_{\text{continuum}} = \lim_{\epsilon\to 0} \{M(\epsilon)\mathcal{G}_E(\mathbf{x}; \epsilon)\} \tag{233}
$$

The choice of the measure is dictated by the requirement that the right hand side should be finite in this limit. It is easy to see that, we need to demand

$$
\lim_{\epsilon\to 0} \left[\frac{1}{\epsilon^2}\left(e^{\epsilon\mu(\epsilon)} - 2D\right) \right] = \mu_0^2 \tag{234}
$$

and

$$
\lim_{\epsilon\to 0} \left[M(\epsilon)\epsilon^{D-2}e^{\epsilon\mu(\epsilon)} \right] = 1 \tag{235}
$$

The first condition implies that, near $\epsilon \approx 0$,

$$
\mu(\epsilon) \approx \frac{\ln 2D}{\epsilon} + \frac{\mu_0^2}{2D}\epsilon^2 \approx \frac{\ln 2D}{\epsilon} \tag{236}
$$

The second condition (235), allows us to determine the measure as

$$
M(\epsilon) = \frac{1}{2D}\frac{1}{\epsilon^{D-2}} \tag{237}
$$

With this choice, we get

$$
\lim_{\epsilon\to 0} \mathcal{G}_E(\mathbf{x}; \epsilon)M(\epsilon) = \int \frac{d^D\mathbf{p}}{(2\pi)^D} \frac{e^{-i\mathbf{p}\cdot\mathbf{x}}}{|\mathbf{p}|^2 + \mu_0^2} \tag{238}
$$

which is the continuum Green function we have computed earlier. This analysis gives a rigorous meaning to the Jacobi path integral.

The measure in (237) has a simple interpretation. Since μ scales with energy as $\mu \propto E^{1/2}$, (236) shows that ϵ scales as $\epsilon \propto E^{-1/2}$; combining this with (237) we get $M(\epsilon) \propto \epsilon^{-(D-2)} \propto E^{\frac{D}{2}-1}$. This is precisely the scaling of density of states $g(E)$ for a D-dimensional system with $E \propto |\mathbf{p}|^2$. Thus the measure merely keeps count of the density of states between E and $E + dE$.

3.   The Concept of Fields

3.1. INTRODUCTION

The purpose of this short section is to present the material discussed in section 2 in the context of quantum field theory. In fact, much of the motivation for the discussion in the last part originates from this connection, which we will now explore. Section (3.2) establishes the connection between the path integral for a relativistic particle and the concept of a quantum field. Some general properties of quantum fields are discussed in sections (3.3) and (3.4).

3.2. PATH INTEGRAL FOR A RELATIVISTIC PARTICLE

Consider a free particle of mass m moving in accordance with the laws of special relativity. Its world line $x^i(s)$[with $i = 0, 1, 2, 3$ and signature $+ - - -$] satisfies the equation $(d^2x^i/d\tau^2) = 0$. This equation can be obtained from varying several different actions of which the following two are of primary importance : (i) The quadratic action

$$A_{\text{quad}} = \frac{m}{4} \int \dot{x}^i \dot{x}_i ds \qquad (1)$$

and (ii) the square-root action :

$$A_{\text{sq}} = -m \int \sqrt{\dot{x}^i \dot{x}_i} ds \qquad (2)$$

[The multiplicative constant in front is not determined by the classical equations of motion but is chosen for future convenience]. While the two actions lead to the same equations of motion, they differ in several other properties. It is usual to use equation 2 in classical relativity since it gives the correct expression for the energy and momentum.

Let us now consider how one can obtain a quantum theory for the relativistic particle. Following the philosophy of path integrals one would like to construct the amplitude for a particle to propagate from the event y^i at $s = 0$ to the event x^i at $s = \tau$:

$$K(x^i, \tau; y^i, 0) = \sum_{\text{allx}^i(s)} \exp i \, A[x(s)] \qquad (3)$$

where A is a suitable action. Several, highly non-trivial, problems arise at this stage:

To begin with, let us consider the possible physical meaning we will attribute to $K(x^i, \tau; y^i, 0)$. At first sight one might think of K as providing the probability amplitude for a particle to propagate from y^i to x^i in a proper time interval τ. However, such an interpretation has some strange features : To begin with, the proper time lapse τ is not a physically relevant parameter in the problem; what we are really interested in is the probability amplitude for the particle to propagate from y^i to x^i *irrespective of the elapsed proper time*. In other words, we have to integrate over τ with a suitable weightage factor.

The suitable weightage factor is easy to obtain for the action in equation (1). Since the energy of the particle in the rest frame is m and since τ denotes the time in the rest frame, a world line with a lapse factor of τ should have a weightage of $\exp(-im\tau)$. Evaluating the quadratic path integral in equation (1) and incorporating the weightage factor we get

$$
\begin{aligned}
G(x, y) &= \int_0^\infty d\tau e^{-im\tau} K(x, \tau; y, 0) \\
&= \int_0^\infty d\tau e^{-im\tau} \cdot \left(\frac{m}{4\pi\tau i}\right)^{1/2} \left(\frac{mi}{4\pi\tau}\right)^{3/2} \exp\left[\frac{im(x-y)^2}{4\tau}\right] \\
&= i \int_0^\infty \frac{d\tau}{\tau^2} \left(\frac{m}{4\pi}\right)^2 \exp \, im\left[\frac{(x-y)^2}{4\tau} - \tau\right] \qquad (4)
\end{aligned}
$$

This integral can be expressed in terms of Hankel functions. However, we have evaluated this integral in a different context in section (2.10). [see equation $(\cdots)$]. Using the relation

$$\left(\frac{m}{4\pi\tau i}\right)^2 \exp \frac{im}{4} \frac{(x-y)^2}{\tau} = \int \frac{d^4k}{(2\pi)^4} \exp\left(ikx - \frac{1}{m}k^2\tau\right) \qquad (5)$$

and performing the τ integral, it is easy to show that

$$i \int_0^\infty \frac{d\tau}{\tau^2} \left(\frac{m}{4\pi}\right)^2 \exp im\left[\frac{(x-y)^2}{4\tau} - \tau\right] = mG(x, y) \qquad (6)$$

where $G(x, y)$ is as

$$G(x,y) = \int \frac{d^4k}{(2\pi)^4} G(k) e^{-ik(x-y)} \equiv \int \frac{d^4k}{(2\pi)^4} \frac{e^{-ik(x-y)}}{k^2 - m^2 + i\epsilon} \qquad (7)$$

The situation is more complicated if we try to use the square root action. But note that this action is identical to the Jacobi action discussed in section (2.10) with $E = m_0, m = (m_0/2)$ and $V = 0$. We saw that such actions will lead to divergent amplitudes because of reparametrisation invariance. In fact, the study of Jacobi action showed that we can choose a specific parametrisation and interpret the sum over paths by the rule :

$$\sum_{\text{path}} \exp{-\frac{i}{\hbar} \int_0^1 d\eta\, m_0 \sqrt{\dot{x}_i \dot{x}^i}} = \int_0^\infty d\tau\, e^{-im_0\tau} \int \mathcal{D}x \, \exp{\frac{i}{\hbar} \frac{m_0}{4} \int_0^\tau \dot{x}^2 ds} \qquad (8)$$

This is precisely the connection between the two different path integrals. Thus both action functionals, when correctly interpreted, lead to the same propagator G. There are, however, several interpretational problems related to our path integral which we shall now discuss.

3.3. FIELDS AND OSCILLATORS

The propagation amplitude for a free relativistic particle, as we have seen, can be defined in terms of the path integral and action functional. To this extent, relativistic and non-relativistic particles behave in a similar manner. Unfortunately, this similarity is superficial. Closer inspection shows that there are serious conceptual differences in the two cases which needs to be taken into account.

To begin with, note that there is no assurance that x^i is in the future lightcone of y^i or even that $x^0 > y^0$. There will be non-zero amplitude for a particle to propagate outside the lightcone or even to go 'backward' in time. The second feature arises from the fact that we are now treating all the coordinates (x^0, x^1, x^2, x^3) as the *dependent* variables and s as the independent variable in evaluating the path integral. There is no reason for the final value of time (x^0) to be greater than the initial value of time (y^0) just as there is no reason for the final value of any other coordinate to have a definite relation with the initial value. This creates serious problems of interpretation. One immediate consequence of this fact is that the propagation amplitude will *not* obey the 'transitivity rule' in time:

$$G(x^0, \mathbf{x}; y^0, \mathbf{y}) \neq \int_{-\infty}^{+\infty} dz^0 G(x^0, \mathbf{x}; z^0, \mathbf{z}) G(z^0, \mathbf{z}; y^0, \mathbf{y}) \qquad (9)$$

This implies that one cannot introduce a conserved probability density and current unlike in non-relativistic mechanics. We cannot study the quantum theory of a relativistic particle in terms of a wave function $\psi(x^0, \mathbf{x})$ such that $G(x', x)$ propagates $\psi(x^0, \mathbf{x})$ from x^i to x'^i.

There is a fundamental reason for this difficulty. To see this reason most clearly, consider the paths which contribute to the amplitude. Even when $x^0 > y^0$, the amplitude will pick up contributions from paths like YABX shown in Figure 2. Consider now an intermediate time t such that $x^0 > t > y^0$. From the figure it is clear that the relativistic particle is located at three different locations 1, 2 and 3 at this instant!. One can, of course, draw other paths which will cut the t line at arbitrarily large number of points. In other words, the propagation amplitude takes into account configurations containing arbitrarily large number of particles at intermediate times. *We can no longer consider the quantum theory of the relativistic particle as describing the dynamics of a single particle at all times.*

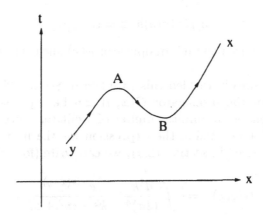

The above fact is of crucial importance. To accommodate this aspect, one can use two different (but, of course, related) physical pictures. In the first picture, one interprets the part of the trajectory which is going "backward in time" [like the part AB in Figure 2] as an "anti particle"going "forward in time". Further, we shall assume that particle-antiparticle pairs can be created and annihilated out of the vacuum repeatedly. In such a picture, the propagation of particle from y to x in figure 2 will be interpreted through the following sequence of events: (i) A particle propagates from Y to A; (ii) a particle-antiparticle pair is created out of the vacuum at B; (iii) the antiparticle created at B annihilates with the (original) particle; (iv) the particle created at B propagates to X. Notice that we are forced into such a description because the path integral takes contribution from the paths like the one in figure 2.

The second (and more useful) picture for interpreting the situation is as follows: Notice that the above description stresses the fact that we can no longer talk about the propagation of a *particular* particle from y to x. All we can do is to study the amplitude for *a* particle to disappear at y^i and *a* particle to reappear at x^i. Let us denote by $|0>$ a quantum state with no particles. A quantum state $|x^i>$ with a particle at some location x^i can always be obtained from $|0>$ by the action of some suitable operator $\hat{\phi}(x^i)$; *i.e.*, we write $|x^i> = \hat{\phi}(x^i)|0>$. [In fact, this defines the operator $\hat{\phi}(x^i)$]. The amplitude that a particle at y^i will end up at x^i is given by

$$\mathcal{P} = < x^i|y^i> = < 0|\phi^\dagger(x^i)\phi(y^i)|0> = < 0|\phi(x^i)\phi(y^i)|0> \qquad (10)$$

[For the sake of simplicity, we have assumed that ϕ in hermitian; we have also dropped the caret from $\hat{\phi}$ with the understanding that ϕ denotes an operator]. Since $\mathcal{P}$ is also given by a path integral expression, we must have the fundamental relation

$$< 0|\phi(x)\phi(y)|0> = G(x,y) \qquad (11)$$

In other words, we need to find an operator $\phi(x)$ such that this relation is satisfied.

But, we have already tackled this problem in Section 2! We showed in section (2.10) that the propagator $G(x,y)$ can be expressed in terms of the Green function for an infinite number of oscillators with the dispersion relation $\omega^2 = \mathbf{k}^2 + m^2$. Using the expression for the harmonic oscillator Green function derived in section (2.9), we can write (for $x^0 > y^0$)

$$\begin{aligned} G(x,y) &= \int \frac{d^4k}{(2\pi)^4} \frac{e^{-ik(x-y)}}{k^2 - m^2 + i\epsilon} \\ &= \langle E_0|\phi(x^0,\mathbf{x})\phi(y^0,\mathbf{y})|E_0\rangle \end{aligned} \qquad (12)$$

where the operator ϕ can be expressed in the form

$$\hat{\phi}(t,\mathbf{x}) = \int \hat{q}_k(t)e^{i\mathbf{k}\mathbf{x}} \frac{d^3\mathbf{k}}{(2\pi)^3} \qquad (13)$$

with $\hat{q}_k(t)$ obeying the (Heisenberg picture) equations of motion of a harmonic oscillator

$$\left(\frac{d^2}{dt^2} + \omega_k^2\right)\hat{q}_k = 0; \quad \omega_k^2 = \mathbf{k}^2 + m^2 \qquad (14)$$

and $|E_0 >$ representing the ground state of the oscillators. This relation is the cornerstone of quantum field theory: The amplitude $G(x, y)$ for a relativistic free particle to propagate from y^i to x^i can be expressed as the ground state expectation value of a 'field' $\hat{\phi}(t, \mathbf{x})$ which can be constructed from a bunch of oscillators $\hat{q}_\mathbf{k}(t)$. Since $G(x, y)$ is the central quantity we are interested in, we could equally well study the dynamics of $\hat{\phi}(t, \mathbf{x})$. This, in turn, is equivalent to studying a system of harmonic oscillators $\{q_k\}$ which we have already done in Part 2. For the sake of completeness we shall summarise the key results:

(1) To begin with, it is easy to verify that $\hat{\phi}$ itself satisfies the equation of motion

$$(\partial_i \partial^i + m^2)\hat{\phi}(t, \mathbf{x}) = 0 \tag{15}$$

which is fully relativistically invariant. Similarly, using the relation

$$q_\mathbf{k}(t) = \int \phi(t, \mathbf{x}) e^{-i\mathbf{k} \cdot \mathbf{x}} d^3\mathbf{x} \tag{16}$$

in the action for the harmonic oscillators

$$A = \int dt \int \frac{d^3\mathbf{k}}{(2\pi)^3} \; \frac{1}{2}(|\dot{q}_\mathbf{k}|^2 - (\mathbf{k}^2 + m^2)|q_\mathbf{k}|^2) \tag{17}$$

we can find the action for the field $\phi(t, \mathbf{x})$. We find that

$$A = \int dt \int d^3\mathbf{x} \frac{1}{2}(\partial_i \phi \partial^i \phi - m^2 \phi^2) \tag{18}$$

Where $\partial_i \phi = (\partial \phi / \partial x^i)$ etc. Quite clearly, this action is also Lorentz invariant.

(2) Let us next consider the energy eigenstates of the system. Since the energy eigenstates of the k-th oscillator is labelled by an integer $n_\mathbf{k}$, the general energy eigenstate is described by a set of integers $\{n_{\mathbf{k}_1}, n_{\mathbf{k}_2}, \cdots \text{etc.}\}$. This state will have the energy

$$\begin{aligned} E &= \sum_\mathbf{k} \omega_\mathbf{k}(n_\mathbf{k} + \frac{1}{2}) = \sum_\mathbf{k} \sqrt{\mathbf{k}^2 + m^2}(n_\mathbf{k} + \frac{1}{2}) \\ &= E_0 + \sum_\mathbf{k} n_\mathbf{k} \sqrt{\mathbf{k}^2 + m^2} \end{aligned} \tag{19}$$

where $E_0 = \sum_\mathbf{k}(\omega_k/2)$ is the energy of the ground state $|0, 0, \dots >$ which has all $n_\mathbf{k} = 0$. Since the energy of *one* relativistic particle with momentum $\mathbf{k}$ is $\omega_\mathbf{k} = \sqrt{k^2 + m^2}$, we can interpret $|\{n_\mathbf{k}\} >$ as the state containing $n_{\mathbf{k}_1}$ particles with momentum $\mathbf{k}_1$ and energy $\sqrt{\mathbf{k}_1^2 + m^2}$, $n_{\mathbf{k}_2}$ particles with momentum $\mathbf{k}_2$ and energy $\sqrt{\mathbf{k}_2^2 + m^2}$.... etc. As an example, consider the state $|x^i > \equiv \phi(t, \mathbf{x})|0 >$ we introduced earlier. Using the results of section (2.8) and noting that $|0 >$ has to be identified with ground state of the oscillators $|E_0 >$, we find

$$
\begin{aligned}
|x^i > &= \phi(t, \mathbf{x})|0 >= \int \frac{d^3\mathbf{k}}{(2\pi)^3} e^{i\mathbf{k} \cdot \mathbf{x}} \hat{q}_{\mathbf{k}}(t)|E_0 > \\
&= \int \frac{d^3\mathbf{k}}{(2\pi)^3} \frac{1}{\sqrt{2\omega_{\mathbf{k}}}} e^{i(\mathbf{k} \cdot \mathbf{x} - \omega_{\mathbf{k}} t)}|0, 0, ...1_{\mathbf{k}}, 0, 0.... > \quad (20)
\end{aligned}
$$

This state is clearly a superposition of 1-particle states with different momentum $\mathbf{k}$. This is the closest to the concept of a "particle located at x^i" which is possible in relativistic field theory.

(3) The ground state ("vacuum") of the quantum field has several peculiarities which need to be stressed. To begin with, note that this state is an eigenstate of the number operator $n_{\mathbf{k}} = a_{\mathbf{k}}^\dagger a_{\mathbf{k}}$ with eigenvalue zero for all $\mathbf{k}$ [This is why we think of ground state as a state with no particles or a "vacuum state"]. But this state has non-trivial dynamical features. For example, it has infinite amount of energy :

$$
E_0 = \sum_{\mathbf{k}} \frac{1}{2}\sqrt{\mathbf{k}^2 + m^2} = \int \frac{d^3\mathbf{k}}{(2\pi)^3} \frac{1}{2}\sqrt{\mathbf{k}^2 + m^2} = \lim_{k \to \infty}[k^4] \quad (21)
$$

No satisfactory interpretation of this feature is available at present, though several mathematical procedures which will allow one to systematically subtract out E_0 from observable effects can be devised.

The ground state also contains quantum fluctuations in the field $\phi(\mathbf{x}, t)$ which can lead to nontrivial effects. To see this, we can use the 'coordinate' representation of the ground state. This will be discussed in the next section.

The discussion so far can be summarised as follows: The propagation amplitude for a free relativistic particle can be interpreted either directly in terms of path integral or in terms of the ground state expectation value related to the field operator $\phi(x)$. While they lead to the same $G(x, y)$, these approaches are conceptually very different. It turns out that the description in terms of harmonic oscillators and fields is far more general than the approach based on path integral for a relativistic particle. In particular, it is quite easy to discuss particles with nonzero spin in a Lorentz invariant manner using the field approach. One can easily construct spinor, vector or tensor fields [all of which can be decomposed into harmonic oscillators] which could represent spin-1/2, spin-1 and higher spin particles. The dynamical equations for these fields can be obtained from suitable action functionals for the fields themselves.

Interaction between particles can be represented by suitable coupling between fields in the action functional. For example one of the simplest ways of including an interaction term for a scalar field is to modify $m^2\phi^2$ to a more general function $V(\phi)$ which we will discuss in the next part.

4. The Technique of Effective Action

4.1. INTRODUCTION

We have developed the technique of path integral in section 2 and the basic concepts of quantum field theory in section 3. In this section, we shall combine these two concepts to develop an approximation technique which will allow one to study the behaviour of a quantum field in a given external background. Such an approximation is particularly useful in studying gravitational interactions. Since we do not have a complete theory of quantum gravity, considerable amount of attention has been focussed in the study of quantum field theory in a given background gravitational field. The techniques developed in this part has special relevance to such studies which will be developed in section 5.

In section (4.2) we shall illustrate the basic idea using a quantum mechanical example followed by that of a scalar field. The concept of renormalization so central in the study of quantum field theory is introduced in the context of a self interacting scalar field in sections (4.3) and (4.4). The last three sections (4.5), (4.6) and (4.7) develop the Euler-Heisenberg effective action for the electromagnetic field and illustrate the phenomena of pair creation in an external electric field from different points of view.

4.2. THE CONCEPT OF EFFECTIVE ACTION

Let us consider a theory which describes the interaction between two systems having the dynamical variables Q and q. [This notation is purely formal; the symbol Q, for example, could describe a set of variables, like the components of a vector field. The detailed nature of these variables is not of importance at this stage.] The action functional for the system, $A[Q, q]$ will then depend on both the variables, possibly in a fairly complicated way. The full theory can be constructed from the exact Kernel

$$K(Q_2, q_2; Q_1, q_1; t_2, t_1) = \int \mathcal{D}Q \int \mathcal{D}q \exp \frac{i}{\hbar} A[Q, q] \qquad (1)$$

which is quite often impossible to evaluate. It would be, therefore, useful to have some approximate ways of handling the situation.

The nature of approximation which one should use in evaluating (1) depends on the physical situation. Different contexts will require different approaches and one should not consider any one technique to be of universal applicability. The 'effective action' method is one of the many approximation schemes available for handling (1). This method is of value in the following context: It may turn out that, we are interested in a physical situation in which one of the variables, say, Q, behaves nearly classically while the other variable is fully quantum mechanical. In that case, we can attack the problem in the following manner:

Let us suppose that we can do the path integral over q in (1) exactly for some given $Q(t)$. That is, we could evaluate the quantity

$$F[Q(t); q_2, q_1; t_2, t_1] \equiv \exp \frac{i}{\hbar} W = \int \mathcal{D}q \exp \frac{i}{\hbar} A[Q(t), q] \qquad (2)$$

treating $Q(t)$ as some specified function of time. If we could now do

$$K = \int \mathcal{D}Q \exp \frac{i}{\hbar} W[Q] \qquad (3)$$

exactly, we could have completely solved the problem. Since this is not possible, we will evaluate (3) by invoking the fact that Q is almost classical. This means that most of the contribution to (3) comes from nearly classical paths satisfying the condition

$$\frac{\delta W}{\delta Q} = 0 \qquad (4)$$

It is often quite easy to evaluate (3) in this approximation and thereby obtain an approximate solution to our problem. In fact, quite often, we will be content with obtaining the solutions to (4), and will not even bother to calculate (3) in this approximation. Equation (4), of course, will contain some of the effects of the quantum fluctuations of q on Q, and is often called the 'semiclassical equation'. The quantity W is called the 'effective action'. It is also convenient to define an 'effective lagrangian' through the relation

$$W = \int L_{\text{eff}} dt \qquad (5)$$

There is, however, one minor complication in the above formalism. The way we have defined our expressions, the quantities K and W depends on the boundary conditions (t_2, q_2, t_1, q_1). We would prefer to have an effective action which is completely independent of the q-degree of freedom. The most natural way of achieving this is to integrate out the effect of q for *all times* by considering the limit $t_2 \to +\infty, t_1 \to -\infty$ in our definition of the effective action. We will also assume, as is usual, that $Q(t)$ vanishes asymptotically. From our discussion in section 2 we know that, in this limit, the Kernel essentially represents the amplitude for the system to go from the ground state in infinite past to the ground state in the infinite future. Using the results of section (2.7), we can write

$$F(q_2, q_1; +\infty, -\infty) \equiv \exp \frac{i}{\hbar} W[Q(t)] = N(q_2, q_1) < E_0, +\infty| -\infty, E_0 >_{Q(t)}$$
(6)

where $< E_0, +\infty| -\infty, E_0 >_{Q(t)}$ stands for the vacuum to vacuum amplitude in the presence of the external source $Q(t)$ and $N(q, q_2)$ is a normalization factor, independent of $Q(t)$. Taking logarithms we get

$$W[Q(t)] = -i\hbar \ln < E_0, +\infty| -\infty, E_0 >_{Q(t)} +(\text{constant})$$
(7)

Since the constant term is independent of Q it will not contribute in the equation (4). Therefore, for the purposes of our calculation we may take the the effective action to be defined by the relation

$$W[Q(t)] \equiv -i\hbar \ln < E_0, +\infty| -\infty, E_0 >_{Q(t)}$$
(8)

in which all reference to the quantum mode is eliminated. Note that $|E_0 >$ is the ground state of the original system; that is, the ground state with $Q = 0$.

This discussion also highlights an important feature of the effective action. We have seen in section 2 that an external perturbation can cause transitions in a system from ground state to excited state. In other words, the probability for the system to be in the ground state in the infinite future (even though it started in the ground state in the infinite past) could be less than unity. This implies that our effective action W_0 need not be a real quantity ! If we use this W directly in (4) we have no assurance that our solution Q will be real. The imaginary part of W contains information about the rate of transitions induced in the q-system by the presence of $Q(t)$; or – in the context of field theory – the rate of production of particles from the vacuum. The semiclassical equation is of very doubtful validity if these excitations drain away too much energy from the Q- mode. Thus we must confine ourselves to the situations in which

$$\text{Im } W \ll Re \ W$$
(9)

In that case, we can modify the semiclassical equations to read

$$\frac{\delta Re \ (W_0)}{\delta Q} = 0$$
(10)

In most practical situations, (9) will automatically arise because of another reason. Notice that the success of the entire scheme depends on our ability to evaluate the first path integral in (2). This task is far from easy, especially because we need this expression for an arbitrary $Q(t)$. Quite often, one evaluates this expression by assuming that the time variation of $Q(t)$ is slow compared to time scale over which the quantum variable q fluctuates. [Once (4) is solved we can explicitly verify whether the solution to (4) which we are interested in satisfies this assumption or not. This acts as a reasonable test on the reliability of the theory.] In such a case, the characteristic frequencies of the q-mode will be much higher than the frequency at which Q-mode is evolving and hence there will be very little transfer of energy from Q to q. The real part of W will dominate.

The above discussion allows an alternative picture of the effective action which is very useful. Let us suppose that $Q(t)$ varies slowly enough for the adiabatic approximation to be valid. We then know – from our discussion in section 2 – that the 'vacuum to vacuum' amplitude is given by [see (99) of section 2].

$$\lim_{t_2 \to \infty} \lim_{t_1 \to -\infty} F(q_2, q_1; t_2, t_1) = W = (\text{const}). \exp -\frac{i}{\hbar} \int_{-\infty}^{+\infty} E_0(Q)dt. \quad (11)$$

This expression allows us to identify the effective lagrangian as the ground state energy of the q-mode in the presence of Q:

$$L_{\text{eff}} = -E_0(Q) \quad (12)$$

This result, which is valid when the time dependence of Q is completely ignored in the calculation of E_0, provides an alternative means of computation of the effective lagrangian if the Q dependence of the ground state energy can be ascertained.

The transitions to the higher states, indicated by the existence of an imaginary part to W_0, can also be discussed in terms of the above relation. The W_0 can become complex only if L_{eff} and hence E_0 becomes complex. The appearance of an imaginary part to the ground state energy indicates an exponential decay probability for this state with some half life. This is precisely what we expect if transitions to higher states are possible.

The above discussion may suggest that whenever Q varies slowly enough the real part of W – or, equivalently, the real part of L_{eff} – will give the dominant contribution. If that is the case, we should get no imaginary part to W when the time variation of Q is highly suppressed by treating Q as an adiabatically varying parameter. This is usually true but one must make sure that a ground state exists for the range of Q values considered in the problem. As a simple example, consider the action

$$A[Q, q] = \int dt \left(\frac{1}{2}\dot{Q}^2 + \frac{1}{2}\dot{q}^2 - \frac{1}{2}(\omega^2 - Q^2)q^2 \right) \tag{13}$$

We see that q behaves as a harmonic oscillator with the effective frequency

$$\omega_{\text{eff}} = \sqrt{\omega^2 - Q^2} \tag{14}$$

It is possible to arrange matters so that Q becomes larger than ω in the course of the evolution even though Q vanished in the asymptotic past and was increasing arbitrarily slowly. If this happens, no vacuum state will exist for the q-mode and our calculation will lead to an imaginary part for the effective action. So, in general, the existence of an imaginary part to the effective action may either be due to transitions to higher states or due to the non-existence of the ground state. In the course of our discussion we will come across examples for both the situations.

We have so far considered the situation in which the action describes two different physical systems which are interacting. The idea of effective action can also be used in a different context. Consider a system described by a single dynamical variable, say, $Q(t)$. Let us suppose that we are interested in a situation in which the behaviour of the system is nearly classical with small quantum fluctuations around the classical solution. We would like to estimate the effects of small quantum fluctuations around the classical behaviour. For this we can proceed in the following manner:

We expand the action $A[Q]$ as a Taylor series in $q \equiv (Q - Q_c)$, where Q_c is the classical solution which we are interested in, retaining up to quadratic terms in the deviation $(Q - Q_c)$. We will then get

$$
\begin{aligned}
A[Q] &= A[Q_c + q] = A_c + \frac{1}{2} \left(\frac{\delta^2 A}{\delta Q^2} \right)_{Q=Q_c} q^2 \\
&= A_c[Q_c] + A_{\text{add}}(Q_c, q)
\end{aligned} \tag{15}
$$

[The linear term will vanish because Q_c is a classical solution.] The action in (15), can be interpreted as describing the coupling between a nearly classical mode Q_c and the quantum fluctuations q. The effect of quantum fluctuations on Q_c can therefore be studied by using an effective action $A_{\text{eff}}[Q_c]$ which is obtained by integrating out q in (15). We define

$$
\begin{aligned}
\exp \frac{i}{\hbar} A_{\text{eff}}[Q_c] &= \int \mathcal{D}q \exp \frac{i}{\hbar} A[Q_c + q] \\
&= \exp \frac{i}{\hbar} A_c[Q_c] \cdot \int \mathcal{D}q \exp \frac{i}{\hbar} A_{\text{add}}[Q_c, q] \\
&= \exp \frac{i}{\hbar} [A_c[Q_c] + W_{\text{corr}}[Q_c]] \tag{16}
\end{aligned}
$$

where the 'correction' $W_{\text{corr}}[Q_c]$ to the classical action $A_c[Q_c]$ is defined by

$$\exp \frac{i}{\hbar} W_{\text{corr}}[Q_c] = \int \mathcal{D}q \exp \frac{i}{\hbar} A_{\text{add}}(Q_c, q). \tag{17}$$

This expression is exactly in the form of path integrals we have considered earlier. The right hand side describes the 'vacuum to vacuum' amplitude for a system characterised by q, in the presence of Q_c. If $Q_c(t)$ is varying adiabatically, then we can write

$$L_{\text{eff}} = L_c + L_{\text{corr}} = L_c - E_0(Q_c) \tag{18}$$

where $E_0(Q_c)$ is the ground state energy of the quantum fluctuations q in the background of Q_c.

If L_c has the form

$$L_c = \frac{1}{2}\dot{Q}^2 - V(Q) \tag{19}$$

then (18) corrects the potential $V(Q)$ to the value

$$V_{\text{eff}} = V(Q) + E_0(Q) \tag{20}$$

In this – quantum mechanical – case, E_0 is just the ground state energy of the harmonic oscillator

$$E_0(Q) = \frac{1}{2}\hbar \left[\frac{\partial^2 V}{\partial Q^2}\right]^{1/2}_{Q=Q_c} \tag{21}$$

so that the corrected "effective" potential is

$$V_{\text{eff}}(Q) = V(Q) + \frac{1}{2}\left[\frac{\partial^2 V}{\partial Q^2}\right]^{1/2} \tag{22}$$

The situation becomes more interesting when we apply these ideas to a field. Consider a scalar field Φ governed by the action

$$A[\Phi] = \frac{1}{2}\int d^D x\, dt [\Phi^i \Phi_i - V(\Phi)] \tag{23}$$

where $V(\Phi)$ is a potential describing the self interaction of the scalar field and D is the dimension of space we are working in. [For usual field theory $D = 3$]. Let us suppose that we are interested in studying the effect of quantum fluctuations around some classical solution $\Phi = \Phi_c$. This solution will be taken to be either constant or adiabatically varying so that we can ignore its derivatives. In the spirit of the discussion in the previous section, we will expand Φ around Φ_c as

$$\Phi = \Phi_c + \phi \tag{24}$$

and retain terms upto quadratic order in ϕ. The Lagrangian then becomes

$$L_{\text{total}} = L_0(\Phi_c) + \frac{1}{2}(\phi^i \phi_i - m^2 \phi^2) = L_0(\Phi_c) + L_{\text{corr}} \tag{25}$$

where

$$m^2 = V''(\Phi_c) \tag{26}$$

The correction term L_{corr} represents a scalar field with effective mass $m^2(\Phi_c)$. The effective Lagrangian and potential will be, therefore,

$$L_{\text{eff}} = L_0 - E_0(m^2); \quad V_{\text{eff}} = V + E_0(m^2) \tag{27}$$

where $E_0(m^2)$ is the ground state energy of a scalar field theory with mass m.

$$E_0 = \frac{1}{2}\hbar \int \frac{d^D k}{(2\pi)^D}(k^2 + m^2)^{1/2} \tag{28}$$

Since this expression is badly divergent for $D \geq 1$, we need to consider methods for making sense out of this expression. We will address ourselves to this question of 'renormalisation' in the next section. Before that, we will first cast this expression in a more manageable form.

It is convenient, as usual, to work in the Euclidean sector. In Lorentzian space, $L_{\text{corr}} = -E_0$; but the L_{corr} in Euclidean sector differ by a sign from that in Lorentzian space. So, in the Euclidean sector we need to calculate

$$L_{\text{corr}}^{(\text{Euclidean})} = +E_0(m^2) = \frac{1}{2} \int \frac{d^D k}{(2\pi)^D}(\mathbf{k}^2 + m^2)^{1/2} \equiv L_c \tag{29}$$

where $\mathbf{k}$ is a D−dimensional vector. We begin our manipulations by calculating

$$\begin{aligned}
\frac{\partial L_c}{\partial m^2} &= \frac{1}{4} \int \frac{d^D k}{(2\pi)^D}\frac{1}{(\mathbf{k}^2 + m^2)^{1/2}} \\
&= \frac{1}{4} \int \frac{d^D k}{(2\pi)^D}\cdot\frac{2}{\sqrt{\pi}} \int_0^\infty d\lambda\, e^{-\lambda^2(\mathbf{k}^2 + m^2)} \\
&= \frac{1}{4} \int \frac{d^D k}{(2\pi)^D} \int_0^\infty \frac{ds}{(2\pi s)^{1/2}}e^{-\frac{1}{2}s(\mathbf{k}^2 + m^2)} \tag{30}
\end{aligned}$$

We will now use a little trick to eliminate the $s^{-1/2}$ factor. We introduce a variable p and rewrite this factor as another integral

$$\frac{1}{(2\pi s)^{1/2}} = \int_{-\infty}^{+\infty} \frac{dp}{2\pi} e^{-\frac{1}{2}sp^2} \tag{31}$$

Then we get

$$\frac{\partial L_c}{\partial m^2} = \frac{1}{4} \int \frac{d^D k}{(2\pi)^D} \int_0^\infty ds \int_{-\infty}^{+\infty} \frac{dp}{2\pi} e^{-\frac{1}{2}s(k^2+p^2+m^2)} \tag{32}$$

We can now combine the $\mathbf{k}$ and p integrations into a $(D+1)$ dimensional integration over the vector $\mathbf{q} = (\mathbf{k}, p)$. Then

$$
\begin{aligned}
\frac{\partial L_c}{\partial m^2} &= \frac{1}{4} \int \frac{d^{D+1}q}{(2\pi)^{D+1}} \int_0^\infty ds\, e^{-\frac{1}{2}(q^2+m^2)} \\
&= \frac{1}{4} \int_0^\infty ds\, e^{-\frac{1}{2}sm^2} \int \frac{d^{D+1}q}{(2\pi)^{D+1}} e^{-\frac{1}{2}sq^2} \\
&= \frac{1}{4} \int_0^\infty \frac{ds}{(2\pi s)^{\frac{1}{2}(D+1)}} e^{-\frac{1}{2}m^2 s}
\end{aligned} \tag{33}
$$

Integrating this expression with respect to m^2, we get

$$L_c = -\frac{1}{2} \int_0^\infty \frac{ds}{s(2\pi s)^{\frac{1}{2}(D+1)}} e^{-\frac{1}{2}m^2 s} \tag{34}$$

We have omitted an integration constant which is independent of m^2. As it stands (34) is also divergent at $s = 0$; however, in this form the divergences are easy to isolate and handle.

There is another way of deriving (34) which is more straightforward (though it hides the physical meaning of L_{eff}) and is quite useful. We begin by noticing that the effect of quantum fluctuations ϕ which we are interested in are contained in the Kernel

$$K \equiv \exp - \int dx_E\, L_{\text{corr}} = \int \mathcal{D}\phi \exp - \int dx\phi \hat{D}\phi = (\det \hat{D})^{-1/2} \tag{35}$$

where D is the Euclidean space operator

$$\hat{D} = -\frac{1}{2}(\partial_a \partial^a - m^2) \tag{36}$$

in which $\partial_a \partial^a$ denotes the $(D+1)$ dimensional D'Alembertian [containing D-space and 1 Euclidean time]. We will now write this determinant as

$$\det D = \exp[Tr \ln D] \tag{37}$$

so that the Kernel becomes

$$(\det D)^{-\frac{1}{2}} = \exp -\frac{1}{2} Tr \ln D$$

$$= \exp -\frac{1}{2} \int dx_E < x| \ln D|x > \equiv \exp - \int dx_E \, L_{\text{corr}} \quad (38)$$

In arriving at the last expression, we have used some basis vectors $|x >$ to evaluate the trace. We will now use the integral representation for the logarithm,

$$\ln F = \int_0^\infty \frac{ds}{s} e^{-Fs} \quad (39)$$

to get

$$L_{\text{corr}} = \frac{1}{2} < x| \ln D|x > = -\frac{1}{2} \int_0^\infty \frac{ds}{s} < x| \exp -sD|x >$$

$$= -\frac{1}{2} \int_0^\infty \frac{ds}{s} K(x, x; s) \quad (40)$$

where the quantity

$$K(x, y; s) = < x|e^{-sD}|y > \quad (41)$$

is just the Euclidean path integral Kernel for a *quantum mechanical* particle with the hamiltonian D.

This result is of very general validity and should be emphasized. It shows that if the Euclidean action coupling two systems has the form

$$A_{\text{corr}}[\Phi, \phi] = \int \phi \hat{D}_\Phi \phi \quad (42)$$

where $\hat{D}_\Phi$ is an operator depending on Φ , then the correction term in effective lagrangian is given by

$$L_{\text{corr}} = -\frac{1}{2} \int_0^\infty \frac{ds}{s} K(x, x; s) \quad (43)$$

where $K(x, y; s)$ represents the propagation Kernel for some fictitious quantum *mechanical* particle described by the hamiltonian

$$\hat{h} = \hat{D}_\Phi \quad (44)$$

In other words, we have reduced the problem involving a path integral over *fields* to a problem involving quantum *mechanical* Kernel.

In this particular case, the hamiltonian is

$$h = D = \frac{1}{2}(-\partial_a \partial^a + m^2) = -\frac{1}{2}\left(\frac{d^2}{d\tau^2} + \nabla^2\right) + \frac{1}{2}m^2 \quad (45)$$

We can evaluate this Kernel easily. The lagrangian corresponding to this hamiltonian is

$$l = +\frac{1}{2}\left((\frac{d\tau}{ds})^2 + |\frac{d\mathbf{x}}{ds}|^2\right) - \frac{1}{2}m^2 \tag{46}$$

which represents a free particle in $(D+1)$ dimensional space with a constant background potential $(m^2/2)$. [Note that m^2 is treated as a constant in the adiabatic limit] The Kernel K we are after is the one for a free particle:

$$K(x,x;s) = \left(\frac{1}{2\pi s}\right)^{\frac{D+1}{2}} \exp -\frac{1}{2}m^2 s \tag{47}$$

We thus get the expression for the effective lagrangian to be

$$L_{\text{eff}} = -\frac{1}{2}\int_0^\infty \frac{ds}{s}\left(\frac{1}{2\pi s}\right)^{(D+1)/2} . \exp\left(-\frac{1}{2}m^2 s\right) \tag{48}$$

which agrees with the previous result. [Note the way in which i-factors disappeared in the Kernel. In arriving at the last two expressions we have proceeded as follows: The quantity $< x'|\exp -iTD|x >$ with $D = -\frac{1}{2}\partial_a\partial^a + \frac{1}{2}m^2$ is a proper Schrodinger Kernel with D as hamiltonian and T as time. Therefore

$$K(T;x,x) = \left(\frac{1}{2\pi iT}\right)^{\frac{1}{2}(D+1)} \exp -\frac{i}{2}m^2 T \tag{49}$$

changing to $iT = s$ leads to our expression above].

4.3. RENORMALISATION OF THE EFFECTIVE LAGRANGIAN

The effective potentials we have derived are badly divergent and cannot be interpreted as they stand. Physical meaning can be attached to these expressions only after the divergent terms are isolated and reabsorbed in some sensible fashion. We will now discuss when and how this can be achieved.

To see what is involved let us evaluate the effective potential for the quantum mechanical case, corresponding to $D = 0$, using the above formula. We find that in $D = 0$ we have

$$L_{\text{corr}} = -\frac{1}{2}\left(\frac{1}{2\pi}\right)^{1/2}\int_0^\infty \frac{ds}{s^{3/2}}\exp(-\frac{1}{2}m^2 s) \tag{50}$$

This integral is divergent at $s = 0$! But since we are studying a quantum mechanical problem we know that this divergence must be completely spurious; and this is indeed the case. This divergence arises because we used an integral representation for $\ln D$ which is mildly divergent at the origin.

That integral representation makes sense only when it is used to calculate the *difference* between the logarithm of two operators.

This analysis also shows how to avoid the divergence in this case; we actually only need the difference $L(m^2) - L(m = 0)$ which is finite. The easiest way to evaluate this expression is to do the integral from some non-zero lower limit Λ and then consider the limit of the expression as Λ tends to zero. Performing one integration by parts, we can write

$$L_{corr} = -\frac{1}{2}\left(\frac{1}{2\pi}\right)^{1/2}\left\{\lim_{\Lambda\to 0}\frac{1}{\Lambda^{1/2}}\right\} + \frac{m^2}{2}\left(\frac{1}{2\pi}\right)^{1/2}\int_0^\infty \frac{ds}{s^{1/2}}e^{-\frac{1}{2}m^2 s}$$

$$\equiv L(m = 0) + \frac{m^2}{2}\left(\frac{1}{2\pi}\right)^{1/2}\left(\frac{1}{2}m^2\right)^{-1/2}\sqrt{\pi} = L_0 + \frac{1}{2}m \quad (51)$$

where L_0 is an infinite constant. Except for this unimportant – though infinite – constant, this is precisely the ground state energy of the harmonic oscillator we derived earlier.

The situation becomes much more complicated in field theory which corresponds to the $D = 3$ case. Our expression for L_{eff} becomes

$$L_{corr} = -\frac{1}{8\pi^2}\int_0^\infty \frac{ds}{s^3}e^{-\frac{1}{2}m^2 s} = -\frac{1}{8\pi^2}I(p) = V_{eff} \quad (52)$$

with $p = \frac{1}{2}m^2 = \frac{1}{2}V''(\phi)$. The divergence near the origin is now quadratic. We will again evaluate this integral with the lower limit set to some small value Λ and then consider the limit of this small cutoff parameter going to zero. We only need to retain the leading terms which will dominate in this limit. With this aim in our mind let us first calculate $I(p)$. By repeated partial integration, we get:

$$I = \int_\Lambda^\infty \frac{ds}{s^3}e^{-ps} = \left[e^{-ps}\left(\frac{s^{-2}}{-2}\right)\right]_\Lambda^\infty - \int_\Lambda^\infty (-p)e^{-ps}\left(\frac{s^{-2}}{-2}\right)ds$$

$$= \frac{1}{2}\Lambda^{-2} - \frac{1}{2}p\int_\Lambda^\infty \frac{e^{-ps}}{s^2}ds = \frac{1}{2\Lambda^2} - \frac{p}{2\Lambda} - \frac{p^2}{2}\ln\Lambda + \frac{p^3}{2}\int_0^\infty e^{-ps}\ln s\, ds$$

$$= \frac{1}{2}\left[\frac{1}{\Lambda^2} - \frac{p}{\Lambda} - p^2\ln\Lambda\right] + \frac{1}{2}p^2\int_0^\infty e^{-x}\ln(\frac{x}{p}).dx$$

$$= \frac{1}{2}\left[\frac{1}{\Lambda^2} - \frac{p}{\Lambda} - p^2\ln\Lambda\right] - \frac{1}{2}p^2\ln p - \frac{1}{2}\gamma p^2 \quad (53)$$

where

$$\gamma \equiv -\int_0^\infty e^{-x}\ln x\, dx \quad (54)$$

is the Euler's constant.

We are supposed to take the limit of Λ going to zero in this expression. We see that the last two terms involving $p^2 \ln p$ and p^2 are finite. The term in the square bracket diverges as Λ tends to zero; there are quadratic, linear and logarithmically divergent terms. Of these, the quadratic term can be dropped because it is just an infinite constant; this situation is analogous to the $D = 0$ quantum mechanical case. But the next two terms $\Lambda^{-1} p$ and $p^2 \ln \Lambda$ cannot be dropped because they depend on p as well. We must think up some way of interpreting this.

For an arbitrary $V(\phi)$, it is impossible to make any sense out of this expression. This is a major problem in quantum field theory for which no one has found a solution; it probably suggests that the entire formulation of field theory is wrong. But no one has succeeded in providing a viable alternative either.

In such a pathetic situation, we are forced to confine our attention to those $V(\phi)$ in which something can be salvaged. This procedure, called "renormalisation" proceeds as follows:

Let us suppose that $V = V(\phi; \lambda_1, \lambda_2, \cdots \lambda_N)$ where λ_i are a set of constants determining the form of the function. The quantities $\Lambda^{-1} p$ and $p^2 \ln \Lambda$ will also be some functions of ϕ and the constants λ_i. Now suppose we are lucky enough to have potential for which the quantity $(\Lambda^{-1} p + p^2 \ln \Lambda)$ has the same form as our original $V(\phi)$ with a different set of constants λ_i'. Then we can absorb the divergent terms into these constants and reinterpret the theory.

Let us see when this will work. It is obvious that non-polynomial form of $V(\phi)$ will not satisfy our criteria. So let us assume that $V(\phi)$ is an n-th degree polynomial in ϕ with n coefficients $\lambda_1, \lambda_2 \cdots \lambda_n$.

$$V(\phi) = \lambda_1 \phi + \lambda_2 \phi^2 + \cdots \lambda_n \phi^n = \sum_{k=1}^{n} \lambda_k \phi^k \qquad (55)$$

Then $p = (V''/2)$ will be a polynomial of $(n-2)$th degree and p^2 will be polynomial with $2(n-2)$th degree. If this expression is not to have terms originally not present then we must have

$$2(n - 2) \leq n \quad \text{i.e.,} \quad n \leq 4. \qquad (56)$$

Thus if $V(\phi)$ is a polynomial of quartic degree or less we can reinterpret our theory.

As an example, let us consider the case in which $V(\phi)$ has a quartic and quadratic terms. That is

$$V(\phi) = \frac{1}{2}m^2\phi^2 + \frac{\lambda}{4!}\phi^4; \quad p = \frac{1}{2}V'' = \frac{1}{2}(m^2 + \frac{\lambda}{2}\phi^2) \qquad (57)$$

In I, we will drop the first term and rewrite the logarithmic term as

$$-\frac{1}{2}\gamma p^2 - \frac{1}{2}p^2 \ln \Lambda - \frac{1}{2}p^2 \ln p = -\frac{1}{2}p^2 \ln \Lambda\mu - \frac{1}{2}p^2 \ln\left(\frac{p}{\mu}\right) \quad (58)$$

where μ is an arbitrary finite constant introduced to keep the argument of logarithms dimensionless. Then, we have

$$
\begin{aligned}
I = & -\frac{1}{2\Lambda}\frac{1}{2}(m^2 + \frac{\lambda}{2}\phi^2) - (\frac{1}{2})\ (\frac{1}{4})(m^2 + \frac{\lambda}{2}\phi^2)^2 \ln \Lambda\mu \\
& - (\frac{1}{2})\ (\frac{1}{4})(m^2 + \frac{\lambda}{2}\phi^2)^2 \ln \frac{1}{2}(m^2 + \frac{\lambda}{2}\phi^2)\frac{1}{\mu}
\end{aligned} \quad (59)
$$

We will rearrange this expression dropping infinite constants and absorbing divergent coefficients into $\ln \Lambda, \Lambda^{-1}$ etc. This will allow us to write

$$
\begin{aligned}
I = & -\frac{\lambda}{8\Lambda}\phi^2 - \left[\frac{\lambda^2}{32}\phi^4 + \frac{1}{8}\lambda m^2 \phi^2\right] \ln \Lambda\mu - \\
& \frac{1}{8}(m^2 + \frac{\lambda}{2}\phi^2)^2 \ln(m^2 + \frac{\lambda}{2}\phi^2)\frac{1}{2\mu} \\
= & -\phi^2 \left(\frac{\lambda}{8\Lambda} + \frac{1}{8}\lambda m^2 \ln \Lambda\mu\right) - \phi^4 \left(\frac{\lambda^2}{32} \ln \Lambda\mu\right) + I_{\text{finite}}(\phi; \mu) \quad (60)
\end{aligned}
$$

Adding the correction $(-I/8\pi^2)$ to the original $V(\phi)$ we get the effective potential:

$$
\begin{aligned}
V = & \frac{1}{2}m^2\phi^2 + \frac{\lambda}{4!}\phi^4 - \frac{1}{8\pi^2}I \\
= & \frac{1}{2}a\phi^2 + \frac{b}{4}\phi^4 + V_{\text{finite}}(\phi, \mu)
\end{aligned} \quad (61)
$$

where

$$
\begin{aligned}
a = & m^2 + \frac{\lambda}{32\pi^2}\left(\frac{1}{\Lambda} + m^2 \ln \Lambda\mu\right) \\
b = & \lambda + \frac{3\lambda^2}{32\pi^2} \ln \Lambda\mu
\end{aligned} \quad (62)
$$

and

$$V_{\text{finite}} = \frac{1}{64\pi^2}\left(m^2 + \frac{\lambda}{2}\phi^2\right)^2 \ln \frac{1}{2\mu}\left(m^2 + \frac{\lambda}{2}\phi^2\right). \quad (63)$$

Let us analyse this expression. Our original potential had two constants m and λ, which were the coefficients of ϕ^2 and ϕ^4. In $V_{\text{eff}}(\phi)$ these are replaced by two other constants a and b which are functions of m, λ, and an arbitrary finite parameter μ. In addition, it also contains divergent terms involving Λ. We shall now describe a procedure by which V_{eff} can be interpreted.

4.4. 'RUNNING' COUPLING CONSTANTS

We shall, to begin with, pretend corrections to m^2 and λ are 'small', [even though the corrections are divergent when $\Lambda \to 0$]. Then, retaining upto first order accuracy in these corrections, we can replace m_0^2 and λ_0 by m^2 and λ in V_{finite}. Then we are left with

$$V_{\text{eff}} = \frac{1}{2}m^2\phi^2 + \frac{1}{4!}\lambda\phi^4 + \frac{1}{64\pi^2}\left(m^2 + \frac{\lambda}{2}\phi^2\right)^2 \ln\frac{1}{2\mu}\left(m^2 + \frac{\lambda}{2}\phi^2\right) \quad (64)$$

Next we notice that the physical values of m and λ are actually determined by comparing the theory with some observation; say, scattering cross sections measured at some energy E. Thus what is physically meaningful are the operationally defined parameters

$$m^2 = \left(\frac{d^2V}{d\phi^2}\right)_{\phi=0} \quad ; \qquad \lambda = \left(\frac{d^4V}{d\phi^2}\right)_{\phi=0} . \quad (65)$$

In the absence of any quantum corrections, we will have these relations reducing to identities $m^2 = m^2$ and $\lambda = \lambda$. However, when there is a finite correction to the classical potential we will get, instead, relations like

$$m^2 = m^2 + C_1(m^2, \lambda; \mu); \qquad \lambda = \lambda + C_2(m^2, \lambda; \mu) \quad (66)$$

These equations can be inverted to express m^2 and λ in terms of μ. Substituting these values back into V_{eff}, we can express it as

$$V_{\text{eff}} = V_{\text{eff}}(\phi; m_{\text{phy}}(\mu), \lambda_{\text{phy}}(\mu), \mu). \quad (67)$$

It may seem that we are still not out of woods because V_{eff} depends on the arbitrary scale μ. However, this is really not the case. If μ is changed to some value μ' then it is possible to change m_{phy} and λ_{phy} to some m'_{phy} and λ'_{phy} such that

$$V_{\text{eff}}(\phi; m'_{\text{phy}}, \lambda'_{\text{phy}}, \mu') = V_{\text{eff}}(\phi; m_{\text{phy}}, \lambda_{\text{phy}}, \mu). \quad (68)$$

In other words, m_{phy} and λ_{phy} are not constants but change when μ is changed.

We shall demonstrate the above results for the case with $m^2 = 0$, for which

$$V_{\text{eff}} = \frac{\lambda}{4!}\phi^4 + \frac{\lambda^2}{(16\pi)^2}\phi^4 \ln\frac{\lambda\phi^2}{4\mu} \quad (69)$$

It is clear that $V''_{\text{eff}}(\phi = 0) = 0$ making m_{phy} zero. To define λ we cannot use the previous definition because $(d^4 V/d\phi^4)$ diverges at $\phi = 0$. However, we can define

$$\lambda = \left(\frac{d^4 V}{d\phi^4}\right)_{\phi=M} \tag{70}$$

where M is an arbitrary scale. This gives

$$\lambda = \lambda + \left(\frac{5}{8\pi}\lambda\right)^2 + \frac{24}{(16\pi)^2}\lambda^2 \ln \frac{\lambda M^2}{4\mu}. \tag{71}$$

allowing us to express $(4\mu/\lambda)$ in terms of M

$$\ln \frac{\lambda M^2}{4\mu} = -\frac{25}{6} \tag{72}$$

Substituting back into (69) we get

$$V_{\text{eff}} = \frac{\lambda}{4!}\phi^4 + \frac{\lambda^2}{(16\pi)^2}\phi^4 \left[\ln \frac{\phi^2}{M^2} - \frac{25}{6}\right] \tag{73}$$

[The constant $(25/6)$, of course, can be reabsorbed into $\ln M^2$]. In this expression, we have traded off the μ dependence for the M-dependence which is still arbitrary. If we now change M to M', then we can retain the form of V_{eff} by changing λ to λ', such that

$$\lambda' = \lambda + \frac{3\lambda^2}{16\pi^2} \ln \frac{M'}{M} \tag{74}$$

Under $M \to M', \lambda \to \lambda'$ transformations, V_{eff} is invariant: $V_{\text{eff}}(\lambda', M') = V(\lambda, M) + \mathcal{O}(\lambda^3)$.

The physical content of the theory is expressed by (74) which shows how the coupling constant λ depends on the energy scale M at which it is defined. An equivalent form of this relation is

$$M\frac{\partial \lambda}{\partial M} = \frac{3\lambda^2}{16\pi^2} \tag{75}$$

which could have also been obtained from (74); note that $\mu \propto M^2$. Equations like (75) are called 'renormalisation group' equations. The modern interpretation of field theory draws heavily on this formalism.

4.5. EFFECTIVE ACTION IN ELECTRODYNAMICS

The formalism developed in the previous two sections can be applied to the study of two extremely important problems: The calculation of effective action for gravitational and electromagnetic fields due to their coupling with, say, a charged scalar field. We shall study the case of the electromagnetic field in the remaining sections of this part and take up the gravitational field in section 5.

The calculation of the effective action for the electromagnetic field allows us to determine the quantum correction to the classical Maxwell equations. Besides, it also illustrates several important conceptual issues in the formalism and allows us to understand the renormalization procedures in quantum electrodynamics. We shall provide a straightforward derivation of the electromagnetic effective lagrangian from the ground state energy in this section. A more powerful and formal technique based on the Schwinger's proper time method will be presented in the section (4.6). The divergences in the effective action and their renormalization is studied in section (4.7).

Consider a system described by the lagrangian density $L(A_i, \phi)$ where $A_i(x)$ is a vector potential describing the electromagnetic field and ϕ is a charged (complex) scalar field interacting with the electromagnetic field. The full quantum theory is described by the Kernel

$$K = \int \mathcal{D}A_i \mathcal{D}\phi \exp\left[i \int L dt \, d\mathbf{x}\right] \tag{76}$$

in which we have set $\hbar = 1$ for convenience. The effective action A_{eff} (and the effective lagrangian L_{eff}) for electrodynamics can be obtained by integrating over the scalar field:

$$\begin{aligned} \exp\left(iA_{\text{eff}}\right) &= \exp\left[i \int dt \, d\mathbf{x} L_{\text{eff}}(A_i)\right] \\ &= \int \mathcal{D}\phi \exp\left[i \int dt \, d\mathbf{x} L(A_i, \phi)\right]. \end{aligned} \tag{77}$$

Thus we need to evaluate the path integral over ϕ in a given background electromagnetic field.

As usual, this is an impossibly difficult task if $A_i(x)$ is an arbitrary background field. To make progress we will assume that $A_i(x)$ varies slowly with x so that we can write

$$A_i(x) \cong -\frac{1}{2}F_{ik}x^k + O((\partial F)x^2) \tag{78}$$

where F_{ik} are treated as constant. This corresponds to assuming that the background potential describes a constant electromagnetic field F_{ik}, or – more precisely – the field ϕ varies much more rapidly compared to the background electromagnetic field. Thus we will compute, in the adiabatic approximation:

$$\exp\left[i\,A_{\text{eff}}(F)\right] = \exp\left[i \int dt \, d\mathbf{x} L_{\text{eff}}(F)\right]$$

$$= \int \mathcal{D}\phi \exp\left[i \int dt\, d\mathbf{x}\, L\left[A_i = -1/2 F_{ik} x^k, \phi\right]\right]. \quad (79)$$

We have seen earlier that, in the adiabatic limit we are considering, L_{eff} is the negative of the ground state energy of the system. Thus if we compute the ground state energy $E_0(F)$ of a scalar field ϕ in a given background F_{ik}, then we can determine $L_{\text{eff}}(F) = -E_0(F)$.

This task is particularly easy if the background field satisfies the conditions $\mathbf{E}.\mathbf{B} = 0$ and $\mathbf{B}^2 - \mathbf{E}^2 > 0$. In such a case, the field can be expressed as purely magnetic in some Lorentz frame. Let $\mathbf{B} = (0, B, 0)$; we choose the gauge such that $A^i = (0, 0, 0, -Bx)$. The Klein-Gordon equation

$$[(i\partial_\mu - qA_\mu)^2 - m^2]\phi = 0 \quad (80)$$

can now be separated by taking

$$\phi(t, \mathbf{x}) = f(x) \exp i(k_y y + k_z z - \omega t). \quad (81)$$

where $f(x)$ satisfies the equation

$$\frac{d^2 f}{dx^2} + [\omega^2 - (qBx - k_z)^2]f = (m^2 + k_y^2)f \quad (82)$$

This can be rewritten as

$$-\frac{d^2 f}{d\xi^2} + q^2 B^2 \xi^2 f = \epsilon f \quad (83)$$

where

$$\xi = x - \frac{k_z}{qB}; \qquad \epsilon = \omega^2 - m^2 - k_y^2 \quad (84)$$

Equation (83) is that of a harmonic oscillator with mass $(1/2)$ and frequency $2(qB)$. So, if $f(x)$ has to be bounded for large x, the energy ϵ must be quantised:

$$\epsilon_n = 2(qB)(n + \frac{1}{2}) = \omega^2 - (m^2 + k_y^2) \quad (85)$$

Therefore the allowed set of frequencies is

$$\omega_n = \left[m^2 + k_y^2 + 2qB(n + \frac{1}{2})\right]^{1/2} \quad (86)$$

The ground state energy per mode is $2(\omega_n/2) = \omega_n$ because the complex scalar field has twice as many degrees of freedom as a real scalar field. The total ground state energy is given by the sum over all modes k_y and n. The weightage factor for the discrete sum over n, in a magnetic field is obtained by the correspondence:

$$\frac{dk_x}{2\pi} \frac{dk_y}{2\pi} \to \sum_n \left(\frac{qB}{2\pi}\right) \frac{dk_y}{2\pi} \tag{87}$$

Hence, the ground state energy is

$$E_0 = \sum_{n=0}^{\infty} \left(\frac{qB}{2\pi}\right) \int_{-\infty}^{+\infty} \frac{dk_y}{(2\pi)} \left[(k_y^2 + m^2) + 2qB(n + \frac{1}{2})\right]^{1/2} = -L_{\text{eff}} \tag{88}$$

This expression, as usual, is divergent. To separate out a finite part we will proceed as follows: Consider the quantity

$$I \equiv -\left(\frac{2\pi}{qB}\right) \frac{\partial^2 E_0}{\partial(m^2)^2} = \left(\frac{2\pi}{qB}\right) \frac{\partial^2 L_{\text{eff}}}{\partial(m^2)^2}. \tag{89}$$

which can be evaluated in the following manner:

$$
\begin{aligned}
I &= +\frac{1}{4} \sum_{n=0}^{\infty} \int_{-\infty}^{+\infty} \frac{1}{2\pi} \frac{dk_y}{\left[k_y^2 + m^2 + 2qB(n + \frac{1}{2})\right]^{3/2}} \\
&= +\frac{1}{8\pi} \sum_{n=0}^{\infty} \frac{1}{[m^2 + 2qB(n + \frac{1}{2})]} .2 = -\frac{1}{4\pi} \sum_{n=0}^{\infty} \int_0^{\infty} d\eta e^{-\eta(m^2 + 2qB(n+\frac{1}{2}))} \\
&= +\frac{1}{4\pi} \int_0^{\infty} d\eta e^{-\eta m^2} . e^{-qB\eta} . \frac{1}{1 - e^{-2qB\eta}} \\
&= +\frac{1}{4\pi} \int_0^{\infty} d\eta \frac{e^{-\eta m^2}}{e^{qB\eta} - e^{-qB\eta}} = +\frac{1}{8\pi} \int_0^{\infty} d\eta \frac{e^{-\eta m^2}}{\sinh qB\eta} = \left(\frac{2\pi}{qB}\right) \frac{\partial^2 L_{\text{eff}}}{\partial(m^2)^2}
\end{aligned}
\tag{90}
$$

The L_{eff} can be determined by integrating the expression twice with respect to m^2. We get

$$L_{\text{eff}} = \frac{qB}{(4\pi)^2} \int_0^{\infty} \frac{d\eta}{\eta^2} \frac{e^{-\eta m^2}}{\sinh qB\eta} = \int_0^{\infty} \frac{d\eta}{(4\pi)^2} . \frac{e^{-\eta m^2}}{\eta^3} . \frac{qB\eta}{\sinh qB\eta} \tag{91}$$

This – and the subsequent expressions – has a divergence at the lower limit of integrtation. This divergence can be removed by subtracting the contribution with $E = B = 0$; we will ignore this problem right now and will take it up later. The integration with respect to m^2 also produces a term like $(c_1 m^2 + c_2)$ with two (divergent) integration constants c_1 and c_2. We have not displayed this term here; this divergence is also connected with the "renormalisation" of L_{eff} and will be discussed later.

If the L_{eff} has to be Lorentz and gauge invariant then it can only depend on the quantities $(E^2 - B^2)$ and $\mathbf{E}.\mathbf{B}$. We will define two constants a and b by the relation

$$a^2 - b^2 = E^2 - B^2; \qquad ab = \mathbf{E}.\mathbf{B} \tag{92}$$

Then $L_{\text{eff}} = L_{\text{eff}}(a, b)$. In the case of pure magnetic field we are considering $a = 0$ and $b = B$. Therefore, the L_{eff} can be written in a manifestly invariant way as:

$$L_{\text{eff}} = \int_0^\infty \frac{d\eta}{(4\pi)^2} \cdot \frac{e^{-\eta m^2}}{\eta^3} \cdot \frac{qb\eta}{\sinh qb\eta} \tag{93}$$

Because this form is Lorentz invariant, it must be valid in any frame in which $E^2 - B^2 < 0$ and $\mathbf{E}.\mathbf{B} = 0$. In all such cases,

$$L_{\text{eff}} = \int_0^\infty \frac{d\eta}{(4\pi)^2} \frac{e^{-\eta m^2}}{\eta^3} \frac{q\eta\sqrt{B^2 - E^2}}{\sinh q\eta\sqrt{B^2 - E^2}}. \tag{94}$$

The L_{eff} for a pure electric field can be determined from this expression if we analytically continue the expression even for $B^2 < E^2$. We will find, for $B = 0$,

$$L_{\text{eff}} = \int_0^\infty \frac{d\eta}{(4\pi)^2} \frac{e^{-\eta m^2}}{\eta^3} \frac{q\eta E}{\sin q\eta E} \tag{95}$$

The same result can be obtained by noticing that a and b are invariant under the transformation $E \to iB, B \to -iE$. Therefore, $L_{\text{eff}}(a, b)$ must also be invariant under these transformations: $L_{\text{eff}}(E, B) = L_{\text{eff}}(iB, -iE)$. This allows us to get (95) from (91).

We will now consider the general case with arbitrary $\mathbf{E}$ and $\mathbf{B}$ for which a and b are not simultaneously zero. It is well known that by choosing our Lorentz frame suitably, we can make E and B parallel, say along the y-axis. We will describe this field $[\mathbf{E} = (0, E, 0); \mathbf{B} = (0, B, 0)]$ in the gauge $A_i = [-Ey, 0, 0, -Bx]$. The Klein-Gordon equation becomes

$$[(i\partial_\mu - qA_\mu)^2 - m^2]\phi$$
$$= \left[\left(i\frac{\partial}{\partial t} + qEy\right)^2 + \frac{\partial^2}{\partial x^2} + \frac{\partial^2}{\partial y^2} - \left(i\frac{\partial}{\partial z} + qBx\right)^2 - m^2\right]\phi = 0 \tag{96}$$

Separating the variables by assuming

$$\phi(t, \mathbf{x}) = f(x, y) \exp -i(\omega t - k_z z) \tag{97}$$

we get

$$\left[\left(\frac{\partial^2}{\partial x^2} + \frac{\partial^2}{\partial y^2}\right) + (\omega + qEy)^2 - (k_z - qBx)^2\right] f = m^2 f \qquad (98)$$

which separates out into x and y modes. Writing

$$f(x,y) = g(x)Q(y) \qquad (99)$$

where $g(x)$ satisfies the harmonic oscillator equation

$$\frac{d^2g}{dx^2} - (k_z - qBx)^2 g = -2qB(n + \frac{1}{2})g \qquad (100)$$

we get

$$\frac{d^2Q}{dy^2} + (\omega + qEy)^2 Q = \left[m^2 + 2qB(n + \frac{1}{2})\right] Q \qquad (101)$$

Changing to the dimensionless variable

$$\eta = \sqrt{qE}y + \frac{\omega}{\sqrt{qE}} \qquad (102)$$

we obtain

$$\frac{d^2Q}{d\eta^2} + \eta^2 Q = \frac{1}{qE}\left(m^2 + 2qB(n + \frac{1}{2})\right) Q. \qquad (103)$$

To proceed further, we use a trick due to Landau. The above expression shows that, the only dimensionless combination which occurs in the presence of electric field is $\tau = (qE)^{-1}(m^2 + qB(2n + 1))$. Thus, purely from dimensional considerations, we expect the ground state energy to have the form

$$E_0 = \sum_{n=0}^{\infty}(2qB)G(\tau) \qquad (104)$$

where G is a function to be determined. Introducing the Laplace transform F of G, by the relation

$$G(\tau) = \int_0^{\infty} F(k)e^{-k\tau}dk \qquad (105)$$

we can write

$$L_{\text{eff}} = (2qB)\sum_{n=0}^{\infty}\int_0^{\infty} dk F(k) \exp\left[-\frac{k}{qE}(m^2 + qB(2n + 1))\right] \qquad (106)$$

Summing the geometric series, we obtain

$$
\begin{aligned}
L_{\text{eff}} &= 2(qB)(qE)\int_0^\infty ds\, F(qEs)e^{-sm^2}e^{-qBs}\cdot\frac{1}{1-e^{-2qBs}}\\
&= 2(qB)(qE)\int_0^\infty ds\,\frac{F(qEs)e^{-sm^2}}{e^{qBs}-e^{-qBs}}\\
&= (qB)(qE)\int_0^\infty ds\,\frac{F(qEs)}{\sinh qBs}e^{-m^2s}i
\end{aligned}
$$

We now determine F by using the fact that L_{eff} must be invariant under the transformation $E \to iB, B \to -iE$. This means that

$$
L_{\text{eff}} = (qB)(qE)\int_0^\infty dse^{-m^2s}\frac{F(iqBs)}{-\sinh(iqEs)}
$$

Comparing the two expressions and using the uniqueness of the Laplace transform with respect to m^2, we get

$$
\frac{F(qEs)}{\sinh qBs} = -\frac{F(iqBs)}{\sinh(iqEs)} \tag{107}
$$

Or, equivalently,

$$
F(qEs)\sin qEs = F(iqBs)\sin(iqBs) \tag{108}
$$

Since each side depends only on either E or B alone, each side must be a constant independent of E and B. Therefore

$$
F(qEs)\sin qEs = F(iqBs)\sin(iqBs) = \text{constant} = A(s) \tag{109}
$$

giving

$$
L_{\text{eff}} = (qB)(qE)\int_0^\infty ds\,\frac{e^{-m^2s}A(s)}{\sin qEs \sinh qBs} \tag{110}
$$

The $A(s)$ can be determined by comparing this expression with, say, (91) in the limit of $E \to 0$. We have

$$
\begin{aligned}
L_{\text{eff}}(E=0,B) &= qB\int_0^\infty \frac{ds}{s}e^{-m^2s}\cdot\frac{A(s)}{\sinh qBs}\\
&= qB\int_0^\infty \frac{ds}{(4\pi)^2s^2}e^{-m^2s}\frac{1}{\sinh qBs} \tag{111}
\end{aligned}
$$

implying

$$
A(s) = \frac{1}{(4\pi)^2s} \tag{112}
$$

Thus we arrive at the final answer

$$L_{\text{eff}} = \int_0^\infty \frac{ds}{(4\pi)^2} \frac{e^{-m^2 s}}{s^3} \left(\frac{qEs}{\sin qEs} \right) \left(\frac{qBs}{\sinh qBs} \right) \qquad (113)$$

In the situation we are considering $\mathbf{E}$ and $\mathbf{B}$ are parallel making $a^2 - b^2 = E^2 - B^2$ and $ab = \mathbf{E}.\mathbf{B} = EB$. Therefore $E = a$ and $B = b$. Thus our result can be written in a manifestly invariant form as

$$L_{\text{eff}}(a, b) = \int_0^\infty \frac{ds}{(4\pi)^2} \frac{e^{-m^2 s}}{s^3} \left(\frac{qas}{\sin qas} \right) \left(\frac{qbs}{\sinh qbs} \right) \qquad (114)$$

This result will be now valid in any gauge or frames with a and b determined in terms of $(\mathbf{E}^2 - \mathbf{B}^2)$ and $(\mathbf{E}.\mathbf{B})$.

The integral, as it stands, is ill-defined for two different reasons. (i) The sine function has poles along the path of integration at $qas = n\pi; n = 1, 2, ...$ (ii) The integral diverges at $s = 0$. The second problem is related to renormalisation and will be taken up in the next section while the first problem can be tackled in the following way:

The integral is evaluated by going around each of the poles by a small semicircle in the upper half plane. This choice of upper half plane is suggested by the general principle in field theory that m^2 should be treated as the limit of $(m^2 - i\epsilon)$. In (104), this is equivalent to treating qE as limit $(qE + i\epsilon)$, changing $\sin qas$ to $\sin(qa + i\epsilon)s$. This makes the contour go above the poles. Equivalently, we can rotate the contour of integration in L_{eff} to the imaginary axis and express it in the alternative form:

$$L_{\text{eff}} = -\int_0^\infty \frac{ds}{(4\pi)^2} \frac{e^{-i(m^2 - i\epsilon)s}}{s^3} \left(\frac{qas}{\sinh qas} \right) \left(\frac{qbs}{\sin qbs} \right) \qquad (115)$$

This expression is sometimes easier to handle; it should be supplemented by the rule that poles along the real axis should be ignored by going below the axis.

The occurrence of the poles along the real axis and our $i\epsilon$-prescription has the following important consequence: It shows that L_{eff} has an imaginary part if a is non-zero. From (115) we get

$$\text{Im}\,(L_{\text{eff}}) = \int_0^\infty \frac{ds}{(4\pi)^2} \left(\frac{\sin m^2 s}{s^3} \right) \left(\frac{qas}{\sinh qas} \right) \left(\frac{qbs}{\sin qbs} \right) \qquad (116)$$

and

$$\text{Re}\,(L_{\text{eff}}) = -\int_0^\infty \frac{ds}{(4\pi)^2} \left(\frac{\cos m^2 s}{s^3} \right) \left(\frac{qas}{\sinh qas} \right) \left(\frac{qbs}{\sin qbs} \right) \qquad (117)$$

The expression in (116) can be evaluated by standard contour integration techniques. However, we can also calculate it from (114) directly; this calculation will explicitly show the origin of $\text{Im}\,(L_{\text{eff}})$. In (114),

$$L_{\text{eff}}(E) = \int_0^\infty \frac{ds}{(4\pi)^2}\frac{e^{-m^2 s}}{s^2}\left(\frac{qa}{\sin qas}\right)\left(\frac{qbs}{\sinh qbs}\right) \tag{118}$$

the poles at $s = s_n = (n\pi/qa)$ are to be avoided by going around small semicircles of radius ϵ in upper half plane. The n-th pole contributes to this semicircle the quantity

$$
\begin{aligned}
I_n &= \int_{\theta=\pi}^{\theta=0} \frac{(\epsilon e^{i\theta}id\theta)}{(4\pi)^2 s_n^2}e^{-m^2 s_n}\cdot\frac{qa}{\cos(n\pi).\epsilon e^{i\theta}}\left(\frac{qbs_n}{\sinh qbs_n}\right)\\
&= i(-1)^{n+1}\cdot\frac{(qa)^2}{16\pi^3}\left[\frac{1}{n^2}\exp\left(-\frac{m^2\pi}{qa}n\right)\right]\left(\frac{qbs_n}{\sinh qbs_n}\right) \tag{119}
\end{aligned}
$$

So the total contribution to $\text{Im}\,L_{\text{eff}}$ is:

$$\text{Im}\,L_{\text{eff}} = \sum_{n=1}^\infty (-1)^{n+1}\cdot\frac{1}{2}\frac{(qa)^2}{(2\pi)^3}\frac{1}{n^2}\exp\left(-\frac{m^2\pi}{qa}n\right)\cdot\left(\frac{qbs_n}{\sinh qbs_n}\right) \tag{120}$$

It is now clear that $(\text{Im}\,L_{\text{eff}})$ arises because of non-zero a, i.e., whenever (i) there is an electric field in the direction of magnetic field or (ii) if $\mathbf{E}$ is perpendicular to $\mathbf{B}$, but $E^2 > B^2$. (In this case, we can go to a frame in which the field is purely electric). For a purely electric field, the imaginary part is

$$\text{Im}\,L_{\text{eff}} = \sum_{n=1}^\infty \frac{1}{2}\frac{(qE)^2}{(2\pi)^3}\frac{(-1)^{n+1}}{n^2}\exp\left(-\frac{\pi m^2}{qE}n\right) \tag{121}$$

Note that this expression is non-analytic in q; perturbation in powers of q will not produce this result.

4.6. EFFECTIVE LAGRANGIAN FROM PATH INTEGRAL

The above analysis relied heavily on the facts that: (i) the energy levels in a magnetic field are well known and (ii) the gauge and lorentz invariance of the theory puts severe restrictions of the form of L_{eff}. This method, therefore, is of only very limited validity. A more formal way of deriving this result will be to use the proper time representation for L_{eff} discussed in section (4.2). Since this gives a general formalism for handling arbitrary time dependence of the electric field, we will discuss this method next.

This method can produce both the Green's function and the effective lagrangian in a single stroke. The results quoted here will also be relevant for comparing the quantum theory in an arbitrary, time dependent, electric field background with quantum theory in an expanding universe. The central quantity in this description is the Kernel:

$$K(x, y; s) = < x | e^{i\frac{s}{2}[(i\partial - qA)^2 - m^2 + i\epsilon]} | y > \tag{122}$$

We saw in section (3.2) that the effective lagrangian L_{eff} and the propagator $G(x', x)$ can be calculated from this Kernel by the relations

$$L_{\text{eff}} = -i \int_0^\infty \frac{ds}{s} K(x, x; s) \tag{123}$$

and

$$G(x', x) = \int_0^\infty ds K(x', x; s). \tag{124}$$

In the context of a scalar field interacting with an electromagnetic field, we can write the kernel in the form

$$K(x, y; s) = < x | e^{ish} | y > \tag{125}$$

with the 'Hamiltonian'

$$h = \frac{1}{2}(i\partial - qA)^2 - \frac{m^2}{2} + i\epsilon \tag{126}$$

We will first consider an electric field along z-axis, which has an *arbitrary time dependence*; *i.e.*, $\mathbf{E} = E(t)\,\hat{\mathbf{z}}, \mathbf{B} = 0$. The gauge is chosen such that $A^\mu = (0; 0, 0, A(t))$[so that $A_\nu = (0; 0, 0, -A(t))$; $E(t) = -A'(t)$]. Using the translational invariance along the spatial coordinates, we can write

$$
\begin{aligned}
K(x^0, y^0; \mathbf{x}, \mathbf{x}; s) &= \int \frac{d^3\mathbf{p}}{(2\pi)^3} < x^0 | \exp \frac{is}{2}[(i\partial_t)^2 - p_\perp^2 - (p_z - qA(t))^2 - \\
& \quad m^2 + i\epsilon] | y^0 > \\
&= \int \frac{d^3\mathbf{p}}{(2\pi)^3} e^{-\frac{is}{2}(p_\perp^2 + m^2 - i\epsilon)} < x^0 | \exp \frac{is}{2}[-\frac{\partial^2}{\partial t^2} - \\
& \quad (p_z - qA(t))^2] | y^0 > \\
&= \int \frac{d^3\mathbf{p}}{(2\pi)^3} \mathcal{G}(x^0, y^0; s) \exp\left[-(is/2)(p_\perp^2 + m^2 - i\epsilon)\right]
\end{aligned}
\tag{127}
$$

where $\mathcal{G}(t, t'; s)$ is the propagator for the one-dimensional quantum mechanical problem with the Hamiltonian

$$H = -\frac{1}{2}\frac{\partial^2}{\partial t^2} - \frac{1}{2}(p_z - qA(t))^2 \tag{128}$$

Let us now apply this formalism for the case of a uniform electric field for which the potential is $A = -Et$. Then

$$H = -\frac{1}{2}\frac{\partial^2}{\partial t^2} - \frac{1}{2}(p_z + qEt)^2 = -\frac{1}{2}\frac{\partial^2}{\partial \rho^2} - \frac{1}{2}q^2E^2\rho^2 \qquad (129)$$

where $\rho = t + (p_z/qE)$. This is a Harmonic oscillator with mass $m = 1$ and *imaginary* frequency (iqE) ("inverted oscillator"). Since the path integral Kernel for this problem is well-known we can immediately write down the coincidence limit for the propagator:

$$\begin{aligned}\mathcal{G}(t,t;s) &= \left[\frac{qE}{(2\pi i \sinh qEs)}\right]^{1/2} \exp\left[-\frac{qE}{2i}\frac{2(\cosh qEs - 1)}{\sinh qEs}\left(t + \frac{p_z}{qE}\right)^2\right]\\ &= \left[\frac{qE}{2\pi i \sinh qEs}\right]^{1/2} \exp i\frac{qE}{\sinh qEs}(\cosh qEs - 1).\left(t + \frac{p_z}{qE}\right)^2\end{aligned}$$
$$(130)$$

Doing the p_x, p_y and ω integrations, we are left with

$$K = \frac{qE}{(2\pi)^2}.\left(\frac{1}{2is}\right).\frac{e^{-\frac{is}{2}(m^2-i\epsilon)}}{\sinh(qEs/2)} = \frac{1}{(2\pi)^2 is}.\frac{(qE/s)}{\sinh(qEs/2)}.e^{-\frac{i}{2}(m^2-i\epsilon)s} \qquad (131)$$

Giving

$$\begin{aligned}L_{\text{eff}} &= -i\int_0^\infty \frac{ds}{s}.\frac{qE}{(2\pi)^2.(2is)}.\frac{e^{-i\frac{s}{2}(m^2-i\epsilon)}}{\sinh(qEs/2)}\\ &= -\frac{1}{4}\int_0^\infty \frac{ds}{(2\pi)^2}\frac{1}{s^2}\frac{qE}{\sinh qEs}e^{-i(m^2-i\epsilon)s}\\ &= -\int_0^\infty \frac{ds}{4\pi^2}.\frac{1}{s^2}.\frac{qE}{\sinh qEs}.e^{-i(m^2-i\epsilon)s}.\end{aligned}$$
$$(132)$$

In this approach it is clear that the imaginary part arises because of the imaginary frequency (inverted nature) of the harmonic oscillator. This point is brought out more vividly by the corresponding calculation for the constant magnetic field. Magnetic fields, in general, give bounded Hamiltonians. For example, consider the case with $A^\mu = (0; A(z), 0, 0)$ giving $B_y = (-\partial A/\partial z)$. Then,

$$\begin{aligned}K &= \int \frac{d^2p_\perp d\omega}{(2\pi)^3} < e^{\frac{is}{2}[\omega^2 - p_y^2 - (p_x - qA)^2 + \partial_z^2 - m^2 + i\epsilon]} >\\ &= \int \frac{d^2p_\perp d\omega}{(2\pi)^3}e^{+\frac{is}{2}(\omega^2 - p_y^2 - m^2 + i\epsilon)}\mathcal{G}(z,z;s)\end{aligned}$$
$$(133)$$

where the effective Hamiltonian will be now

$$H = -\frac{1}{2}\frac{\partial}{\partial z^2} + \frac{1}{2}(p_x - qA(z))^2 \tag{134}$$

which has a potential bounded from below. Let us apply this equation to a uniform magnetic field; $A = -Bz$. Then

$$H = -\frac{1}{2}\frac{\partial^2}{\partial z^2} + \frac{1}{2}(p_x + qBz)^2 = -\frac{1}{2}\frac{\partial^2}{\partial \rho^2} + \frac{1}{2}q^2 B^2 \rho^2 \tag{135}$$

where $\rho = z + (p_x/aB)$. This is a Harmonic oscillator with mass $m = 1$ and *real* frequency (qB). Therefore

$$
\begin{aligned}
\mathcal{G}(z, z; s) &= \left[\frac{qB}{(2\pi i \sin qBs)}\right]^{1/2} \exp\left[-\frac{qB}{2i}\frac{2(\cos qBs - 1)}{\sin qBs}\left(z + \frac{p_x}{qB}\right)^2\right] \\
&= \left[\frac{qB}{2\pi i \sin qBs}\right]^{1/2} \exp\left[i\frac{qB}{\sin qBs}(\cos qBs - 1)\cdot\left(z + \frac{p_x}{qB}\right)^2\right]
\end{aligned}
\tag{136}
$$

Doing the p_x, p_y and ω integrations, we are left with

$$K = \frac{qB}{(2\pi)^2}\left(\frac{1}{2is}\right)\cdot\frac{e^{-i\frac{s}{2}(m^2 - i\epsilon)}}{\sin(qBs/2)} = \frac{1}{(2\pi)^2 is}\cdot\frac{(qB/s)}{\sin(qBs/2)}\cdot e^{-i\frac{s}{2}(m^2 - i\epsilon)} \tag{137}$$

Giving

$$
\begin{aligned}
L_{\text{eff}} &= -i\int_0^\infty \frac{ds}{s}\cdot\frac{qB}{(2\pi)^2\cdot(2is)}\cdot\frac{e^{-i\frac{s}{2}(m^2 - i\epsilon)}}{\sin(qBs/2)} \\
&= -\frac{1}{4}\int_0^\infty \frac{ds}{(2\pi)^2}\frac{1}{s^2}\frac{qB}{\sin qBs/2}e^{-i(m^2 - i\epsilon)s} \\
&= -\int_0^\infty \frac{ds}{4\pi^2}\cdot\frac{1}{s^2}\cdot\frac{qB}{\sin qBs/2}\cdot e^{-i(m^2 - i\epsilon)s}.
\end{aligned}
\tag{138}
$$

As it stands, the integrand has poles due to the $\sin(qBs/2)$ in the denominator. However, notice that the proper definition of harmonic oscillator path integral involves the prescription: $\omega = \lim_{\epsilon\to 0}(\omega - i\epsilon)$. Therefore in the Kernel the factor $\sin qBs$ should be interpreted as the limit of the expression $\sin qBs(1 - i\epsilon)$. So the poles are actually at

$$s_n = \pm\frac{2n\pi}{qB}(1 + i\epsilon) \tag{139}$$

We can now transform the integral to one along the imaginary axis. Because of the $\exp -is(m^2/2)$ factor the contour should be closed in the lower half plane. Then we get

$$
L_{\text{eff}} = -i \int_0^\infty \frac{ds}{s^2} K(s) \quad = \quad \int_0^\infty \frac{dy}{y^2} \frac{ie^{-\frac{m^2}{2}y}}{\sinh\left(\frac{qBy}{2}\right)} \cdot \frac{(qB/2)}{(2\pi)^2 i}
$$

$$
= \int_0^\infty \frac{dy}{y^2} \frac{e^{-\frac{m^2}{2}y}}{\sinh\left(\frac{qBy}{2}\right)} \cdot \frac{1}{(2\pi)^2} \cdot \left(\frac{qB}{2}\right) \quad (140)
$$

This expression, which is the same as (111), is real showing that the constant magnetic field does not create particles. We shall now discuss the renormalisation of L_{eff}.

4.7. RENORMALISATION OF THE EFFECTIVE ACTION

We have seen earlier that the real and imaginary parts of the effective lagrangian lead to different class of phenomenon. Since the Kernel is

$$
\begin{aligned}
K_{\text{total}} &= \exp i[L_0(F) + L_{\text{eff}}(F)] \\
&= \exp i[L_0(F) + \operatorname{Re} L_{\text{eff}}(F)] \exp(-\operatorname{Im} L_{\text{eff}}) \\
&= \; <0, +\infty | 0, -\infty > \quad (141)
\end{aligned}
$$

we may interpret $\operatorname{Re}(L_{\text{eff}})$ as a correction to the original lagrangian for the electromagnetic field

$$
L_0(F) = \frac{1}{8\pi}(E^2 - B^2) \quad (142)
$$

The $(\operatorname{Im}(L_{\text{eff}}))$ is related to the probability for the system to make transitions from ground state to the excited state. In this particular case the excited state will be the one with the quanta of the scalar field present. We may, therefore, interpret, $2\operatorname{Im}(L_{\text{eff}})$ as the probability per unit volume per unit time for production of scalar particles. In this section, we shall discuss the effects due to $\operatorname{Re}(L_{\text{eff}})$.

The first point to note about $\operatorname{Re}(L_{\text{eff}})$ is that it is divergent near $s = 0$. In fact, $\operatorname{Re}(L_{\text{eff}})$ is divergent even when $\mathbf{E} = \mathbf{B} = 0$. This divergence – in accordance with the discussion we had before – must be spurious and can be removed by simply subtracting out the value for $\mathbf{E} = \mathbf{B} = 0$. Thus we modify (117) to

$$
\operatorname{Re} L_{\text{eff}} \equiv R = -\int_0^\infty \frac{ds}{(4\pi)^2} \frac{\cos m^2 s}{s^3} \left[\frac{q^2 abs^2}{\sin qbs \sinh qas} - 1 \right] \quad (143)
$$

Since the subtracted term is a constant independent of $\mathbf{E}$ and $\mathbf{B}$, the equations of motion are unaffected. The expression R is still logarithmically divergent near $s = 0$, since the quantity in the square brackets behaves as $[-\frac{1}{6}q^2s^2(a^2 - b^2)]$ near $s = 0$. But notice that this divergent term is proportional to $(a^2 - b^2) = \mathbf{E}^2 - \mathbf{B}^2$, which is the original – uncorrected – lagrangian. This opens up the possibility that we can reabsorb the divergence by redefining the field strengths, charges, etc. This can be done as follows: Let us first write

$$L_{\text{total}} = L_0 + L_{\text{eff}} = (L_0 + L_c) + (L_{\text{eff}} - L_c) \qquad (144)$$

where

$$
\begin{aligned}
L_c &= -\frac{1}{(4\pi)^2} \int_0^\infty \frac{ds}{s^3} \cos m^2 s \left[-\frac{1}{6}(qs)^2(a^2 - b^2) \right] \\
&= \frac{q^2}{6(4\pi)^2} \int_0^\infty \frac{ds}{s} \cos m^2 s.(a^2 - b^2) \equiv \frac{Z}{8\pi}(a^2 - b^2) = \frac{Z}{8\pi}(\mathbf{E}^2 - \mathbf{B}^2)
\end{aligned}
$$

$$(145)$$

with Z being a formally divergent quantity. With this trick, we can separate out the finite and divergent quantities in L_{total} and write

$$L_{\text{div}} = L_0 + L_c = \frac{1}{8\pi}(\mathbf{E}^2 - \mathbf{B}^2) + \frac{Z}{8\pi}(\mathbf{E}^2 - \mathbf{B}^2) = \frac{1}{8\pi}(1 + Z)(\mathbf{E}^2 - \mathbf{B}^2)$$

$$(146)$$

and

$$
\begin{aligned}
L_{\text{finite}} &\equiv L_{\text{eff}} - L_c \\
&= -\frac{1}{(4\pi)^2} \int_0^\infty \frac{ds}{s^3} \cos m^2 s \\
&\quad \times \left[\frac{q^2 s^2 ab}{\sin(qsb)\sinh(qsa)} - 1 + \frac{1}{6}q^2 s^2(a^2 - b^2) \right]
\end{aligned}
\qquad (147)
$$

The quantity L_{finite} is perfectly well-defined and finite. [The leading term coming from the square bracket, near $s = 0$ is proportional to s^3 and hence L_{finite} is finite near $s = 0$.] So all the divergences are in the first term $(L_0 + L_c) = (1 + Z)L_0$. We shall now redefine all our field strengths and charges by the rule

$$
\begin{aligned}
\mathbf{E}_{\text{phy}} &= (1 + Z)^{1/2}\mathbf{E}; \\
\mathbf{B}_{\text{phy}} &= (1 + Z)^{1/2}\mathbf{B}; \\
q_{\text{phy}} &= (1 + Z)^{-1/2}q
\end{aligned}
\qquad (148)
$$

This is, of course, same as scaling a and b by $(1+Z)^{1/2}$ leaving $(q_{\mathrm{phy}}E_{\mathrm{phy}}) = qE$ invariant. Since only the products qa, qb appear in L_{finite}, it can also be expressed in terms of $(q_{\mathrm{phy}}E_{\mathrm{phy}})$. Thus it is possible to redefine the variables in our theory, thereby absorbing the divergent quantities. The remaining expression L_{finite} is well-defined and possesses a Taylor expansion in q^2. Using this expansion, one can calculate corrections to the electromagnetic lagrangian in an order-by-order manner.

5. Quantum Theory in Curved Space – Selected Examples

In this last section, we shall consider the applications of the formalism derived so far to some important research problems. All these problems deal with the special effects which arise when one studies quantum field theory in a non-trivial background or with non-trivial boundary conditions. In section (5.1), we shall consider a phenomenon called the Casimir effect which illustrates the effect of boundary conditions on the concept of vacuum state. Section (5.2) discusses the by now famous examples of the thermal nature of the vacuum fluctuations as seen by an accelerated observer. Sections (5.3) and (5.4) study pair creation in a time dependent background and finally section (5.5) provides a unified description of the thermal effects seen in black hole space, deSitter spacetime and Rindler frames. The discussion in this part is, quite naturally, somewhat more advanced than that in the previous sections. However, it is still self contained and only uses techniques developed so far.

5.1. CASIMIR EFFECT

Consider two plane, parallel, conducting plates located with a separation L in between. It is experimentally observed that they attract each other with a force given by

$$F = -\frac{\pi^2}{240}\left(\frac{\hbar c}{L^4}\right) \tag{1}$$

It is possible to derive this result in several equivalent ways. For our purpose, it is best to consider it as arising from the fact that the insertion of the capacitor plates modifies the vacuum functional. The action for the electromagnetic field can be decomposed into harmonic oscillators by using some suitable set of mode functions. In the flat space-time with R^4 topology it is usual to take these mode functions to be plane waves of the form $\exp(ikx)$. This will lead to a vacuum functional of the usual form. Suppose we now introduce two conducting plates in the space-time. We can no longer use the mode functions exp*(ikx)* because they do not vanish on the location of the conductors. Instead we use some other suitable set of functions (like, say, sin(kx) etc.) ensuring the vanishing of mode functions on the plates. The vacuum functional now calculated will be quite different. *In other words, the vacuum state depends on the choice of mode functions— or, equivalently on the choice of the 'harmonic oscillators'. These choices, in turn, are dictated by the boundary conditions of the problem.*

The mathematical description of this phenomenon is quite straightforward. Since, in the later sections, we will be using the example of a scalar field in (1 + 1) dimensions, we will briefly illustrate the above phenomenon in this context. The action for a scalar field ϕ in (1 + 1) dimensions will be

$$A = \frac{1}{2} \int dT dX \left[\left(\frac{\partial \phi}{\partial T} \right)^2 - \left(\frac{\partial \phi}{\partial X} \right)^2 \right]. \tag{2}$$

If we expand the field in terms of the plane waves exp(ikx) then the action reduces to that for a sum of harmonic oscillators;

$$A = \frac{1}{2} \int \frac{dK}{(2\pi)} \int dT \left(|\dot{q}_k|^2 - \omega_k^2 |q_k|^2 \right) \tag{3}$$

where

$$\phi(X,T) = \int \frac{dK}{(2\pi)} q_k(T) e^{iKX}. \tag{4}$$

The ground state wavefunctional can be expressed in terms of the field in the form

$$
\begin{aligned}
\Psi\left[\phi(X),0\right] &= N \exp\left(-\frac{1}{2} \int_0^\infty \frac{dK}{(2\pi)} |K| |q_k|^2 \right) \\
&= N \exp\left[-\int dX dY \nabla\phi(X)\nabla\phi(Y)\mathcal{G}(X,Y) \right] \tag{5}
\end{aligned}
$$

where $\mathcal{G}$ is the green's function,

$$\mathcal{G}(X,Y) = \frac{1}{2} \int \frac{dK}{(2\pi)} \frac{\exp iK(X-Y)}{|K|} \tag{6}$$

If there are two conductors at $x = 0$ and at $x = L$, then we will expand the field in terms of the mode functions sin($n\pi x/L$) where n is an integer. The wave functional can again be calculated in terms of the field. It can be expressed in exactly the form as (5) but with a different Green's function. We find:

$$\mathcal{G}'(X,Y) = \frac{1}{2} \sum_{n=1}^{\infty} \left(\frac{L}{n\pi} \right) \exp\left[\left(\frac{in\pi}{L} \right) (X-Y) \right]. \tag{7}$$

Since the vacuum functionals are different, so are the fluctuation patterns and the vacuum expectation values of operators. In particular, calculations show that the $\langle T_{ik} \rangle$ calculated from (6) and from (7) are different. From (6) we get the result

$$E = \frac{1}{2} \int_{-\infty}^{+\infty} \frac{LdK}{(2\pi)} |K| = \frac{1}{2} \int_{0}^{\infty} dn \left(\frac{n\pi}{L} \right) \tag{8}$$

while from (6) we get

$$E' = \frac{1}{2} \sum_{n=1}^{\infty} \left(\frac{n\pi}{L} \right) \tag{9}$$

These two quantities differ by a finite amount. If we decide to regularize the $\langle T_{ik} \rangle$ in the presence of the plates—given by (9)—by merely subtracting the value in the absence of the plates, then we get the finite remainder:

$$\Delta E = - \left(\frac{\pi}{4L} \right) \tag{10}$$

(To arrive at the above expression we have used the following simple regularization procedure. In defining the difference between (8) and (9) we have used the limit

$$\lim_{\lambda \to 0} \left(\int_{0}^{\infty} ne^{-\lambda n} dn - \sum_{n=0}^{\infty} ne^{-\lambda n} \right) = \frac{1}{2} \tag{11}$$

which can be derived by straightforward calculation). Similar calculation can be performed for electromagnetic field in $(3 + 1)$ dimensions. In that case the corresponding result is:

$$\left(\frac{\Delta E}{\text{area}} \right) = - \left(\frac{\pi^2}{720} \right) \left(\frac{\hbar c}{a^3} \right). \tag{12}$$

This finite remainder can exactly account for the observed Casimir effect. In other words, it seems very reasonable—at least in this context—to compute $\langle T_{ik} \rangle$ using two different vacuum functionals made of different mode functions and subtract one from the other to obtain a finite remainder.

It is also important to realize that this finite residual quantity must contribute to the gravitational attraction. To see this, consider the following thought experiment: Two parallel capacitor plates A and B are kept at a distance L apart. A mass M is attached to each plate through the pulley arrangement. As usual we will assume the plates to be weightless etc. (These details are given only for the sake of visualization; our argument is independent of these details.) The plates were kept in the position by external forces for $t < 0$ and were let of at $t = 0$. Because of the Casimir effect, the plates will feel mutual attractive force and will start moving towards each other. At a short time later, the masses would have acquired some kinetic energy. This kinetic energy comes from the change in the Casimir energy between the plates. (The Ca simir energy depends on the plate separation which changes when the plates come closer.) If $\langle 0|T_{ik}|0\rangle_C$ denotes the Casimir energy of the vacuum and t_{ik}^M is the stress-energy of the masses, then we have, from energy conservation:

$$\left[\langle 0|T_k^i|0\rangle + t_k^i(M)\right]_{;i} = 0 \qquad (13)$$

However, we know that,

$$t_k^i(M)_{;i} \neq 0 \qquad (14)$$

since the masses are acted upon by external forces.

Now consider a region X far away from our Casimir plates. The gravitational field due to our setup is measured at X. If the Casimir energy $\langle 0|T_{ik}|0\rangle_C$ does not contribute to gravity, then the only source of gravity in our arrangement is M. Then Einstein's equations will read as:

$$G_{ik} = R_{ik} - \frac{1}{2}g_{ik}R = -8\pi G t_{ik}(M). \qquad (15)$$

This is blatantly wrong because G_{ik} has zero divergence while $t_{ik}(M)$ does not. We are forced to conclude that $\langle 0|T_{ik}|0\rangle_C$ does contribute to gravity and that (15) must be modified to

$$G_{ik} = -8\pi G\left[t_{ik}(M) + \langle 0|T_{ik}0\rangle_C\right]. \qquad (16)$$

It therefore follows that, in the absence of M, that is, if we take the limit of $(M \to 0)$, $\langle 0|T_{ik}|0\rangle_C$ should lead to observable gravitational effects.

The above example is extremely important and should be taken seriously. It shows that the finite parts of the expectation value T_{ik}, computed by subtracting one divergent quantity from another, must act as a source of gravity. If it does not, we run into contradictions and even perpetual motion. In this particular case the two divergent values for $\langle T_{ik}\rangle$ are obtained by using two different sets of mode functions in the flat space-time. We shall now consider similar effects which arise in the noninertial frames.

5.2. VACUUM FLUCTUATIONS IN THE RINDLER FRAME

To illustrate the concepts involved, we will use a scalar field in a $(1 + 1)$ dimensional spacetime and indicate the generalizations to four dimensions whenever needed. Consider the two-dimensional Minkowski space-time with

the line element:
$$ds^2 = dT^2 - dX^2. \tag{17}$$

The complete manifold is covered by the range $(-\infty < T < +\infty, -\infty < X < +\infty)$. We now introduce two sets of coordinate patches, (x, t) and (x', t') on the regions $X > T$(" Right ", R) and $-X > T$ ("Left ", L) by the transformations:

$$X = g^{-1}e^{gx} \cosh\ gt; \quad T = g^{-1}e^{gx} \sinh\ gt \quad \text{(in R)} \tag{18}$$

$$X = -g^{-1}e^{gx'} \cosh\ gt'; \quad T = -g^{-1}e^{gx'} \sinh\ gt' \quad \text{(in L)}. \tag{19}$$

All the coordinates $(x, t), (x', t')$ vary from $(-\infty, +\infty)$. The metric (17) in terms of (x, t) [or(x', t')] has the form

$$ds^2 = e^{2gx}(dt^2 - dx^2). \tag{20}$$

It can be shown that (x, t) corresponds to the proper coordinate system of a uniformly accelerated observer in the region R, t being the proper time of his clocks. For an observer, completely confined to R, the surfaces $t = $ constant provide a set of spacelike hypersurfaces. In the region R, one can introduce two Killing vector fields:

$$\xi_R^i = e^{-gx}(1, 0) \tag{21}$$

and

$$\xi_M^i = e^{-gx}(\cosh\ gt, \sinh\ gt). \tag{22}$$

The ξ_R^i leads to translation in the t-coordinate while ξ_M^i corresponds to translations in T-coordinate ; the latter has components $(1, 0)$ in the inertial frame.

Consider a scalar field $\phi(X, T) = \phi'(x', t')$, described by the generally covariant action

$$
\begin{aligned}
A &= \frac{1}{2} \int d^2x \sqrt{-g} g^{ik} \partial_i \phi \partial_k \phi \\
&= \frac{1}{2} \int_{-\infty}^{+\infty} dT \int_{-\infty}^{+\infty} dX \left[\left(\frac{\partial \phi}{\partial T} \right)^2 - \left(\frac{\partial \phi}{\partial X} \right)^2 \right].
\end{aligned} \tag{23}
$$

In the region R, the action can be written in terms of x and t in the same form. (This is because in 2−dimension, $\sqrt{-g} g^{ik} = \eta^{ik}$ for (20)):

$$A_R = \frac{1}{2} \int_{-\infty}^{+\infty} dt \int_{-\infty}^{+\infty} dx \left[\left(\frac{\partial \phi}{\partial t} \right)^2 - \left(\frac{\partial \phi}{\partial x} \right)^2 \right]. \tag{24}$$

We shall quantize this field in the Schrödinger picture by decomposing the field into harmonic oscillator modes. Consider a field configuration $\phi(X)$ on the $T = 0$ hypersurface, expanded as,

$$\phi(X) = \int_{-\infty}^{+\infty} \frac{dK}{2\pi} q_K e^{iKX} \tag{25}$$

The hypersurface $T = 0$ is covered completely by $(t = 0, x)$ for $X > 0$ and $(t' = 0, x')$ for $X < 0$. In R and L the field can be decomposed as,

$$\phi(X > 0) = \phi(x) = \int_{-\infty}^{+\infty} \frac{dk}{2\pi} a_k e^{ikx} \tag{26}$$

$$\phi(X < 0) = \phi(x') = \int_{-\infty}^{+\infty} \frac{dk}{2\pi} b_k e^{ikx'}. \tag{27}$$

Using the relations (25), (26) and (27), we can express q_k in terms of a_k and b_k. After some simple algebra, we get

$$q_K = \int_{-\infty}^{+\infty} \phi(X) e^{-iKX} dX = \int_{-\infty}^{+\infty} \frac{dk}{2\pi} \left[a_k f(k, -K) + b_k f(k, +K) \right] \tag{28}$$

where the function $f(k, K)$ is defined by

$$f(k, K) = \int_{-\infty}^{+\infty} dx \exp \left[gx + i \left(kx + \left(\frac{K}{g} \right) e^{gx} \right) \right]. \tag{29}$$

This function can be expressed in term of the gamma function of imaginary argument; but we will not need its explicit form.

The vacuum state in the Minkowski frame is described by the functional

$$\begin{aligned}
\Psi \left[\phi(X), 0 \right] = \Psi[(q_K)] &= \prod_K \left(\frac{\omega_K}{\pi} \right)^{1/4} \exp \left(-\frac{1}{2} \omega_K |q_K|^2 \right) \\
&= N \exp \left[-\frac{1}{2} \int_0^\infty \frac{dK}{2\pi} |K| |q_K|^2 \right]. \tag{30}
\end{aligned}$$

Using (28) we can express this wave function in terms of a_k's and b_k's . A detailed but straightforward calculation gives,

$$\Psi[a_k, b_k] = N \exp \left[-\frac{1}{2} \int_0^\infty \frac{dk}{2\pi} (P(k)(|a_k|^2 + |b_k|^2) - Q(k)(a_k^* b_k + a_k b_k^*)) \right] \tag{31}$$

with

$$P(k) = \coth \left(\frac{\pi \omega_k}{g} \right), \quad Q(k) = \csc \left(\frac{\pi \omega_k}{g} \right); \quad \omega_k = |k|. \tag{32}$$

An observer confined to R will have his observables made out of $a_k's$. Let $\mathcal{O}(a_k)$ be any such observable. The expectation value of $\mathcal{O}$ (at $T = t = 0$) in the state Ψ is given by

$$\langle \mathcal{O} \rangle = \int \prod_k da_k \int \prod_k db_k \Psi^*(a_k, b_k) \mathcal{O} \Psi(a_k, b_k)$$

$$= \int \prod_k da_k \rho(a_k, a_k) \mathcal{O}(a_k) = \mathrm{Tr}(\rho \mathcal{O}) \tag{33}$$

where

$$\rho(a'_k, a_k) \equiv \int \prod_k db_k \Psi^*(a'_k, b_k) \Psi a_k, b_k)$$

$$= N \exp\left[-\frac{1}{2} \int_{-\infty}^{+\infty} \frac{dk}{2\pi} \frac{\omega_k}{4} \left((a_k - a'_k)^2 \coth\left(\frac{\omega_k}{2T}\right) \right. \right.$$

$$\left. \left. + (a_k + a'_k)^2 \tanh\left(\frac{\omega_k}{2T}\right) \right) \right] \tag{34}$$

is a thermal density matrix corresponding to the temperature $T = (g/2\pi)$. This is a well known result, showing the thermal nature of the vacuum state (30) when expressed in terms of the Rindler mode functions.

The two examples studied so far shows that the concept of vacuum state in an external background is conceptually non-trivial. Indeed we have emphasized in section 2 and 3 that the concept of particle (and also the concept of vacuum state) is inextricably linked with the decomposition of a quantum field into oscillators. In the flat spacetimes with R^4 topology and inertial coordinate system, there exists a very natural decomposition of quantum fields as harmonic oscillators. This natural decomposition no longer exists when we use non-inertial coordinate systems or non-standard boundary conditions. The Casimir effect and Rindler effect discussed in the last two sections exhibit this feature in a simpler manner. We shall see more complicated examples of the same as we go along.

5.3. PAIR CREATION IN ELECTRIC FIELD AND EXPANDING UNIVERSE

There is a formal correspondence between pair creation in a time dependent electric field and pair creation in an expanding Friedmann universe. This can be seen as follows: Consider, for example, the action for a scalar field Φ

$$A = -\int d^4x \sqrt{-g} \frac{1}{2} \Phi \left[\partial_i \partial^i + m^2 + \frac{1}{6}R \right] \Phi \tag{35}$$

in the Friedmann spacetime with the line element

$$ds^2 = a^2(t)(dt^2 - d\mathbf{r}^2) \tag{36}$$

[This action is conformally invariant in the limit of m going to zero. This fact makes our analysis easy; however, the results are valid even for non-conformal coupling]. Writing Φ as (ϕ/a) and exploiting the conformal flatness of the metric, we can reduce the action to the form

$$A = -\frac{1}{2} \int d^4x \phi \left[\partial_i \partial^i_{\text{flat}} + m^2 a^2(t) \right] \phi \tag{37}$$

To study the pair creation, we can again use the effective lagrangian method. The Kernel we need is

$$
\begin{aligned}
K(x,y;s) &= \; < x|e^{-is\frac{1}{2}[\partial_i \partial^i + m^2 a^2(t) - i\epsilon]}|y > \\
&= \int \frac{d^3p}{(2\pi)^3} < t|e^{-is\frac{1}{2}[\partial_t^2 + p^2 + m^2 a^2(t) - i\epsilon]}|t' > \\
&= \int \frac{d^3p}{(2\pi)^3} e^{-is\frac{1}{2}(p^2 - i\epsilon)} \mathcal{G}(t,t;s) \tag{38}
\end{aligned}
$$

where $\mathcal{G}$ is the propagator for the quantum mechanical Hamiltonian

$$H = -\frac{1}{2}\frac{\partial^2}{\partial t^2} - \frac{1}{2}m^2 a^2(t) \tag{39}$$

Comparing this expression with the corresponding one for the electric field we can make the identification: $m^2 a^2(t) \Leftrightarrow (p_z - qA(t))^2$. Thus there exists an one-to-one correspondence between time dependent electric fields and expanding Friedmann universes as far as the quantisation of an external scalar field is concerned.

As an example, consider the case of constant electric field. The analogue in cosmology will be a universe with the conformal factor:

$$a^2(t) = \frac{1}{m^2}(p_z + qEt)^2 \equiv \alpha^2(t + t_0)^2; \; \alpha = \left(\frac{qE}{m} \right) \tag{40}$$

In the more familiar coordinate sytem with

$$ds^2 = d\tau^2 - a^2(\tau)\mathbf{dr}^2 \tag{41}$$

this corresponds to the expansion law

$$a(\tau) = (2\alpha\tau)^{1/2} \propto \tau^{\frac{1}{2}} \tag{42}$$

This corresponds to a radiation-dominated universe. Similar correspondences can be established in other cases which allows one to translate the results in one physical situation to another.

5.4. QUANTUM THEORY IN A MILNE UNIVERSE

We shall now take up the analogy between gauge and coordinate invariance. To do this, one requires some region of spacetime manifold which can be represented conveniently in two different co-ordinate systems: one system in which the metric is static and another in which it depends only on time. The simplest choice happens to be the upper quarter of the flat spacetime. In this 'top-quarter' of the Minkowski spacetime (i.e the region $T > |X|$ which we will call ('U'), the line element can be expressed in two different ways:

$$
\begin{aligned}
ds^2 &= dT^2 - dX^2 - dY^2 - dZ^2 \\
&= d\rho^2 - g^2\rho^2 dx^2 - dY^2 - dZ^2 \\
&= e^{2gt}(dt^2 - dx^2) - dY^2 - dZ^2
\end{aligned}
\tag{43}
$$

by the transformation $gX = e^{gt}\sinh gx$ and $gT = e^{gt}\cosh gx$; $g\rho = e^{gt}$. The intermediate form of the transformation shows that the metric belongs to the class of anisotropically expanding cosmological solutions. Because of this similarity, we will call this co-ordinate system the ' Milne Universe.' Since the 'static gauge' now is just the inertial co-ordinates, we only have to work out the quantum theory in the Milne universe. We want to study the evolution of a quantum field along the hypersurfaces defined by constant-t (in the Milne coordinates) and compare it with the conventional Minkowski quantisation. Since the metric in Milne co-ordinates depend only on t, the Klein-Gordon equation

$$
\frac{1}{\sqrt{-g}}\partial_i(\sqrt{-g}g^{ik}\partial_k\phi) - m^2\phi = 0
\tag{44}
$$

can be separated as

$$
\phi(\mathbf{x}, t) = \sum_{\mathbf{x}}\left\{a_k f_k(t)e^{i\mathbf{k}\cdot\mathbf{x}} + h.c\right\} = \sum_{\mathbf{k}}(\phi_k^{(+)} + h.c)
\tag{45}
$$

This equation has the two linearly independent solutions which may be taken to be $H_{ip}^{(1)}(\rho)$ and $H_{ip}^{(2)}(\rho)$ where $H_\mu(z)$ is the Hankel function. We write

$$
\begin{aligned}
f(t) &= c_1 H_{ip}^{(1)}(\rho) + c_2 H_{ip}^{(2)}(\rho) \\
&= c_1(J_\nu + iN_\nu) + c_2(J_\nu - iN_\nu) \\
&= (c_1 + c_2)J_\nu(\rho) + i(c_1 - c_2)N_\nu(\rho) \\
&\equiv b_1 J_\nu(\rho) + ib_2 N_\nu(\rho)
\end{aligned}
\tag{46}
$$

where $\nu = ip$ and J_ν and N_ν are the Bessel functions (see eg., Gradshteyn and Ryzhik, 1965). We are interested in the limits $t \to \pm\infty$. From the properties of the Bessel functions, it is easy to see that

$$\lim_{t\to-\infty} f_k(t) \cong \left\{ (b_1 + ib_2 \cot \nu\pi) \frac{\rho^\nu}{2^\nu} \frac{1}{\Gamma(1+\nu)} - ib_2 \csc \nu\pi \cdot \frac{\rho^{-\nu}}{2^{-\nu}} \frac{1}{\Gamma(1-\nu)} \right\} \tag{47}$$

Since $\rho^{\pm\nu} \simeq \exp(\pm g\nu t) = \exp(\pm i|k_x|t)$ (in U) and we want f to go as $\exp(-i\omega t)$ for the positive frequency mode, only the second term is admissible. Therefore the positive frequency modes in the infinite past are the ones obtained by the condition

$$b_1 = -ib_2 \frac{\cos ip\pi}{\sin ip\pi} = -ib_2 \frac{\cosh p\pi}{i\sin \rho\pi} = -b_2 \coth \pi p \tag{48}$$

We should take $f_k(t)$ to be

$$f_k(t) = ib_2 \csc \nu\pi. \ J_{-\nu} = -\frac{b_2}{\sinh p\pi} J_{-\nu}. \tag{49}$$

The value of b_2 is fixed by the normalisation condition:

$$i(f^* \dot{f} - f \dot{f}^*) = (2\pi)^{-3}. \tag{50}$$

Straightforward calculation gives,

$$|b_2|^2 = \left(\frac{1}{2\pi}\right)^3 \frac{\pi(\sinh p\pi)}{2g} = \left(\frac{1}{2\pi}\right)^3 \left(\frac{\pi}{2g}\right) (\sinh p\pi) \tag{51}$$

so that

$$|b_1|^2 = |b_2|^2 \coth^2 \pi p = \left(\frac{1}{2\pi}\right)^3 \left(\frac{\pi}{2g}\right) \frac{\cosh^2 p\pi}{\sinh p\pi}. \tag{52}$$

We know now that, the solution which behaves as $e^{-i\omega t}$ near $t \to -\infty$ in U, is

$$f(t) = -\frac{b_2}{\sinh p\pi} J_{-\nu}(\rho)$$
$$= -\left(\frac{1}{2\pi}\right)^{3/2} \left(\frac{\pi}{2g}\right)^{1/2} \frac{J_{-\nu}(\rho)}{\sinh^{1/2} p\pi}. \tag{53}$$

It is clear from the asymptotic form of the equation for f that we will not get $\exp(\pm i\omega t)$ in the infinite future. Therefore the positive frequency mode has to be identified by the WKB analysis, as in the case of electromagnetic field. This analysis shows that the proper mode is the one which behaves as

$\exp(-i\rho)$ in the infinite future. Since $H_\nu^{(2)}$ behaves as $\exp(-i\rho)$ near large ρ we can set $c_1 = 0$ and take the solution to be

$$g(t) = c_2 H_\nu^{(2)}(\rho) \tag{54}$$

To normalise this solution, we will again use the condition

$$W = i(g^* \dot{g} - g\dot{g}^*) = (2\pi)^{-3} \tag{55}$$

This gives

$$|c_2|^2 = \left(\frac{1}{2\pi}\right)^3 \left(\frac{\pi}{4g}\right) e^{+p\pi} \tag{56}$$

We can now express the positive frequency solution of the infinite past in terms of the positive and negative frequency solutions of the infinite future and identify the Bogoliubov coefficients. Using the identities

$$e^{i\nu\pi} H_\nu^{(1)} = \frac{i}{\sin \pi\nu} J_\nu - \frac{i}{\sin \pi\nu} e^{i\nu\pi} J_{-\nu}$$

$$e^{-i\nu\pi} H_\nu^{(2)} = -\frac{i}{\sin \nu\pi} J_\nu + \frac{i}{\sin \pi\nu} e^{-i\nu\pi} J_{-\nu} \tag{57}$$

and

$$e^{i\nu\pi} H_\nu^{(2)} + e^{-i\nu\pi} H_\nu^{(2)} = 2J_{-\nu} \tag{58}$$

it is easy to show that

$$f(t) = \frac{1}{\sqrt{2}} \left(\frac{1}{\sinh \pi p}\right)^{1/2} \left\{ e^{-\pi p/2} g^*(t) + e^{\pi p/2} g(t) \right\} \tag{59}$$

This corresponds to the Bogoliubov coefficients

$$\alpha = \frac{1}{\sqrt{2}} \left(\frac{1}{\sinh \pi p}\right)^{1/2} e^{\pi p/2}; \quad \beta = \frac{1}{\sqrt{2}} \left(\frac{1}{\sinh \pi p}\right)^{1/2} e^{-\pi p/2} \tag{60}$$

We see that

$$\alpha^2 - \beta^2 = \frac{1}{2} \frac{(e^{\pi p} - e^{-\pi p})}{\sinh \pi p} = 1 \tag{61}$$

as it should. The number density of created particles is

$$\beta^2 = -\frac{1}{2} \frac{2e^{-\pi p}}{e^{\pi p} - e^{-\pi p}} = \frac{1}{(e^{2\pi p} - 1)} = \frac{1}{e^{\frac{2\pi}{g}|k_x|} - 1} \tag{62}$$

which corresponds to a thermal spectrum of particles in the longitudinal momentum with the temperature $(g/2\pi)$.

Similar results can be obtained in a different context which is well-known in literature. Investigations in the study of particle production by expanding Friedmann universes have shown that, in a spatially flat model with the expansion law $a(t) \propto t$ a thermal spectrum of particles is produced at late times. Interestingly enough, the analysis is valid in 2−dimensions as well in which case the spacetime is just the $T - X$ sector of the Milne universe. Our analysis shows that the other two dimensions merely go for a ride.

Even though (62) corresponds to a temperature of $(g/2\pi)$, the result is very different from the standard result obtained in Rindler frame in section (5.2) for two reasons: (i) We are working in the upper and lower quarters, while the Rindler co-ordinates exist only in the right and left quarters. This makes the entire situation quite different. (ii) There is no 'particle creation' in the Rindler co-ordinates (τ', ρ, y, z). The Rindler mode functions behave as $\exp \pm i\omega\tau'$ for all times. The conventional result only says that these mode functions are connected to the Minkowski modes by a Bogoliubov transformation with off-diagonal term which leads to a result similar to that in (62) . In contrast, we are now working with a non-static background; the positive frequency mode in the infinite past *does* get mixed up with positive *and* negative frequency modes of the infinite future.

5.5. SPACETIME MANIFOLD IN SINGULAR GAUGES

We shall next consider the gravitational analogue of the effects discussed in section (4.7). It turns out that the 'thermal' effects in certain spacetime provide this analogy. Consider a patch of spacetime, which, in suitable coordinate system, has the line element,

$$
\begin{aligned}
ds^2 &= +B(r)dt^2 - B^{-1}(r)dr^2 - r^2(d\theta^2 + \sin^2\theta d\phi^2) \\
&\equiv +B(r)dt^2 - B^{-1}(r)dr^2 - dL^2
\end{aligned}
\tag{63}
$$

or

$$
\begin{aligned}
ds^2 &= B(x)dt^2 - B^{-1}(x)dx^2 - dy^2 - dz^2 \\
&\equiv B(x)dt^2 - B^{-1}(x)dx^2 - dL^2
\end{aligned}
\tag{64}
$$

Co-ordinate systems of the form (63) can be introduced in parts of Schwarzschild and de Sitter spacetimes while the choice $[B(x) = 1 + 2gx]$ in (64) represents a uniformly accelerated frame (Rindler frame) in flat spacetime. We will be concerned basically with the structure of the metric in the $r-t$ or $x-t$ plane. Since this structure is essentially the same in both (63) and (64) we shall work throughout with (63); the results are extendible to (64) in a straight forward manner.

The exponent of the Kernel $K(x', x; s)$ will now contain the integral

$$\mathcal{A} = \int_0^s d\tau g_{ik} \dot{x}^i \dot{x}^k = \int_0^s d\tau \left[B\dot{t}^2 - B^{-1}\dot{x}^2 + ... \right] \qquad (65)$$

Quite obviously we will run into problems if B vanishes along the path of integration. From the nature of our metric it is easy to see that the surfaces on which B vanishes are null surfaces corresponding to infinite redshift ('horizons').

To study the effect of horizons, let us proceed in the following manner: Suppose that at some $r = r_0 (> 0)$, $B(r)$ vanishes, $B'(r)$ finite and nonzero. Then near $r = r_0$, we can expand $B(r)$ as,

$$\begin{aligned} B(r) &= B'(r_0)(r - r_0) + \mathcal{O}[(r - r_0)^2] \\ &\equiv R(r_0)(r - r_0) \end{aligned} \qquad (66)$$

As long as the points 1 and 2 (between which the transition amplitude is calculated) are in the same side of the horizon, [i.e., both are at $r > r_0$ or both at $r < r_0$] the integral in the action is well defined and real. But if the points are located at two sides of the horizon then the integral does not exist due to the divergence of $B^{-1}(r)$ at $r = r_0$.

Let us first review briefly the conventional derivation of thermal effects using path integrals, say, in the context of Schwarzschild black hole. Given the co-ordinate system of (63), in some region R, we first verify that there is no *physical* singularity at the horizon. Having done that, we extend the geodesics into the past and future and arrive at two further regions of the manifold not originally covered by the co-ordinate system in (63). Let us label these regions as F and P. It is now possible to show that the probability for a particle with energy E to be lost from the region R (i.e., probability for propagation from $\mathcal{P}$ to $\mathcal{P}'$) in related to the probability for a particle with energy E to be gained by the region R, (i.e., probability for propagation from $\mathcal{P}'$ to $\mathcal{P}$)by the equation

$$P(\text{loss}) = P(\text{gain}) \exp{-\beta E} \qquad (67)$$

This is equivalent to assuming that the region R is bathed in radiation at temperature β^{-1}.

The above result can be interpreted differently, so as to bring out the connection with the case of electromagnetic field. This is most easily done by considering the semiclassical approximation to the path integral propagator, expressed in the saddle point approximation, as:

$$\mathcal{G}(x_2, t_2; x_1, t_1) = \mathcal{G}(2, 1) = N \exp{iA(2, 1)} \qquad (68)$$

where A is the action functional satisfying the classical Hamilton-Jacobi equation. For a particle of mass m, moving in our spacetime the Hamilton-Jacobi equation will be:

$$g^{ik}(\partial_i A)(\partial_k A) - m^2 = 0 \qquad (69)$$

The solution to this equation can be represented as

$$A = -Et + J\theta + A_r(r) \qquad (70)$$

with,

$$A_r(r) = \pm \int^r dr\, B^{-1}(r) \left[E^2 - B(r)(m^2 + J^2/r^2)\right]^{1/2} \qquad (71)$$

The sign ambiguity of the square-root is related to the "outgoing" $[(\partial A/\partial r) > 0]$ or "ingoing" $[(\partial A/\partial r) < 0]$ nature of the particle.

Thus, in order to obtain the probability amplitude in (68) for crossing the horizon, (i.e., when 1 and 2 are on two sides of the horizon), we have to give some extra prescription for evaluating the integral. Since the surface $B = 0$ is null (just like $x = \pm t$ in the electrodynamic case) we may carry out the calculation in the Euclidean space or – equivalently – use the $i\epsilon$ prescription to specify the contour over which the integral has to be performed around $r = r_0$. The usual $i\epsilon$ prescription can be easily shown to imply that we should take the contour for defining the integral to be an infinitesimal semi-circle above the pole at $r = r_0$. Thus, the contour is along the real line from, say, r_1 ($0 < r_1 < r_0$) to $(r_0 - \epsilon)$ and from $(r_0 + \epsilon)$ to, say, $r_2(r_2 > r_0)$. From $(r_0 - \epsilon)$ to $(r_0 + \epsilon)$ we go along a semicircle of radius ϵ in the upper complex plane.

Consider an outgoing particle $[(\partial A/\partial r) > 0]$ at $r = r_1 < r_0$. What is the amplitude for it to cross the horizon? Clearly, the contribution to A in the range $(r_1, r_0 - \epsilon)$ and $(r_0 + \epsilon, r_2)$ is real. Therefore,

$$A(\text{outgoing}) = -\int_{r_0-\epsilon}^{r_0+\epsilon} (dr/B(r))[E^2 - B(m^2 + J^2/r^2)]^{1/2} + (\text{real part}) \quad (72)$$

[The minus sign corresponds to the initial condition that $(\partial A/\partial r) > 0$ at $r = r_1 < r_0$. For the sake of definiteness we have assumed R in (66) to be positive, so that $B < 0$, at $r < r_0$. For the cases with $R < 0$, the answer has to be modified by a sign change.] Evaluating the integral, in the limit of $(\epsilon \to 0)$, we get

$$
\begin{aligned}
A(\text{outgoing}) &= -[E/R(r_0)](-i\pi) + (\text{real part}) \\
&= [i\pi E/R(r_0)] + (\text{real part}) \qquad (73)
\end{aligned}
$$

Now consider an ingoing particle $[(\partial A/\partial r) < 0]$ at $r = r_2 > r_0$. The corresponding action is,

$$
\begin{aligned}
A(\text{ingoing}) &= -\int_{r_0+\epsilon}^{r_0-\epsilon} (dr/B(r)).[E^2 - B(m^2 + J^2/r^2)]^2 + (\text{real part}) \\
&= [E/R(r_0)](+i\pi) + (\text{real part}) \\
&= [-i\pi E/R(r_0)] + (\text{real part})
\end{aligned}
\tag{74}
$$

Taking the modulus to obtain the probability, we get,

$$
P(\text{outgoing}) = N \exp[-2\pi E/R(r_0)]
\tag{75}
$$

and

$$
P(\text{ingoing}) = N \exp[+2\pi E/R(r_0)]
\tag{76}
$$

so that

$$
P(\text{out}) = \exp[-4\pi E/R(r_0)].P(\text{in})
\tag{77}
$$

This result shows that it is more likely for a particular region to gain particles than lose them. If one tries to do a consistent quantum field theory in this region, one has to introduce source terms at the singular boundaries. Further, the exponential dependence on the energy allows one to give a 'thermal' interpretation to this result. In a system with temperature β^{-1} then the absorption and emission probabilities are related by

$$
P\,[\text{emission}] = \exp(-\beta E)P\,[\text{absorption}]
\tag{78}
$$

Comparing (77) and (78) we identify the temperature of the horizon in terms of $R(r_0)$. Equation (72) is based on the assumption that $R > 0$. [see the comment after (72)]. For $R < 0$ there will be a change of sign in this equation. Incorporating both the cases, we can write the general formula for horizon temperature to be

$$
\beta^{-1} = |R|/4\pi
\tag{79}
$$

For the Schwarzschild black hole,

$$
B(r) = (1 - 2M/r) \approx (1/2M)(r - 2M) + \mathcal{O}[(r - 2M)^2]
\tag{80}
$$

giving $R = (2M)^{-1}$, and the temperature:

$$
\beta^{-1} = |R|/4\pi = 1/8\pi M
\tag{81}
$$

[The following point is worth noting regarding the derivation of the thermal effect in the case of a Schwarzschild black hole: The regularisation procedure which is adopted above is equivalent to replacing M by $(M-i\epsilon)$, where M is the mass of the black hole. This is identical to the regularisation procedure which would have been adopted in standard field theory if one is dealing with particles of mass M. Probably this result has no deep significance, but it certainly appears as an interesting coincidence.]. For the De Sitter spacetime,

$$B(r) = (1 - H^2 r^2) = 2H(H^{-1} - r) = -2H(r - H^{-1}) \tag{82}$$

giving

$$\beta^{-1} = |R|/4\pi = H/2\pi \tag{83}$$

Similarly for a metric of the uniformly accelerated frame

$$B(x) = (1 + 2gx) = 2g[x + (2g)^{-1}] \tag{84}$$

and

$$\beta^{-1} = (g/2\pi) \tag{85}$$

The formula can be used for more complicated metrics as well, and gives the same results as obtained by more detailed methods.

The above analysis is *not* intended to be a derivation of the thermal effects; rather, it is an *interpretation* of results derived by more rigorous methods. This interpretation, however, has the advantage that it allows one to obtain the thermal effects by invoking a simple prescription for handling the integrals across the horizon and emphasizes the role played by the singular gauge.

The Rindler frame discussed above is ususally considered to be part of field-free region, *i.e.*, it represents flat spacetime in a curvilinear co-ordinate system. Our earlier discussion on the pure gauge potential suggests that this aspect needs to be looked at closely, especially if Euclidean continuations are used to interpret the theory. In fact, it has been pointed out by Christensen and Duff that the Euler characteristic of the Euclidean sector – obtained by analytically continuing in the Rindler time co-ordinate – is different from that of standard (Euclidean) space. The difference arises precisely due to the nature of the singularities along the light cone in the Rindler gauge.

6. QUANTUM FIELD THEORY METHODS:

DIRAC EQUATION AND PERTURBATION THEORY

URJIT YAJNIK
Physics Department
Indian Institute of Technology
Powai, Mumbai 400 076, India

Dirac Equation

1. Lorentz Group and its Representations

1.1. $SO(3)$ AND $SU(2)$

In order to understand relativistic particles and their spin, we need to understand the Lorentz group. We begin with basic tools for handling real and complex rotations, the latter to be defined in the following. It is sufficient to work with real rotations in three dimensions and complex rotations in two complex dimensions. The connection to the Lorentz group will appear later. We are familiar with rotations in 3 dimensions, e.g.,

$$\begin{pmatrix} \cos\theta & -\sin\theta & 0 \\ \sin\theta & \cos\theta & 0 \\ 0 & 0 & 1 \end{pmatrix}$$

represents rotations about the z axis,

$$\begin{pmatrix} \cos\phi & 0 & \sin\phi \\ 0 & 1 & 0 \\ +\sin\phi & 0 & \cos\phi \end{pmatrix}$$

rotations about the y axis etc., and products of such as well. These keep the magnitude of vectors invariant, *i.e.*, for R a rotation matrix, if

$$x'^i = R^i_j x^j$$

447

then

$$\sum_i x'^{i2} = \sum_j x^{j2}$$

This requires that they have the property $R^T R =$ identity. Such matrices are called *orthogonal*. Rotations have the further property that $\det R = 1$. This more restricted class is called *special orthogonal*. The important algebraic property of rotations is that they form a group. This group is designated $SO(3)$. Rotations of n dimensional vectors constitute groups designated by $SO(n)$.

When the angles are small, we get for example,

$$R_{\hat{z}}(\theta) = \begin{pmatrix} 1 & -\theta & 0 \\ +\theta & 1 & 0 \\ 0 & 0 & 1 \end{pmatrix} = 1 + \theta \begin{pmatrix} 0 & -1 & 0 \\ 1 & 0 & 0 \\ 0 & 0 & 0 \end{pmatrix}$$

1 is the identity matrix and θ is an infinitesimal. It turns out that even when θ is not small one can write

$$R_{\hat{z}}(\theta) = 1 + \sum_1^\infty \frac{(\theta L_z)^n}{n!} \equiv \exp(L_z \theta)$$

Where L_z is the matrix explicitly written in the previous step, and $L_z^n = 1$ if $n = 0$ and $L_z \times L_z \times \cdots n$ times otherwise.

- *Exercise*: Calculate L_z^2, L_z^3 and L_z^4 and prove the above series expansion.

L_z is referred to as the *generator* of z rotations, and L_x, L_y are likewise given by

$$L_x = \begin{pmatrix} 0 & 0 & 0 \\ 0 & 0 & -1 \\ 0 & 1 & 0 \end{pmatrix}$$

$$L_y = \begin{pmatrix} 0 & 0 & +1 \\ 0 & 0 & 0 \\ -1 & 0 & 0 \end{pmatrix}$$

Note that these are the generators of *active* rotations. For *passive* rotations, where not the vector but the coordinate system is being rotated, the generators are negative of these.

In the representation above, the generators are real and skew symmetric. Define the hermitian matrices $J_{x,\,y,\,z} = iL_{x,\,y,\,z}$. Then for z rotations we get

$$R_{\hat{z}}(\theta) = \exp(-iJ_z\theta)$$

and more generally

$$R_{\hat{n}}(\theta_1, \theta_2, \theta_3) = \exp(-i\vec{J} \cdot \vec{\theta})$$

The J's satisfy the antisymmetric algebra

$$[J_x, J_y] = iJ_z$$

and cyclic permutations $x \to y \to z$ Or,

$$[J_i, J_j] = i\epsilon_{ijk}J_k$$

It turns out that knowing the exponential forms of R_z etc. in terms of the generators along with the algebra satisfied by the latter is sufficient for obtaining matrices for arbitrary finite rotations. This is the subject of Lie group theory.

The algebra obtained above can be thought of as abstract relations. In which case we can find sets of matrices of dimensions larger than 3 satisfying the same algebra. These are called *representations* of higher dimensions. In quantum mechanics we learn about representations of $SO(3)$, characterised by the j in the relation

$$\sum_i J_i^2 = j(j+1)$$

Each positive integer value of j gives an independent representation of rotation matrices of dimension $2j+1$. The basis of the vector space on which the representation acts is labelled by the eigenvalues m of J_3. $J_\pm \equiv J_x \pm iJ_y$ act as raising and lowering operators. All of these consequences can be derived directly from the above algebra to be satisfied by the generators. Details can be found in any textbook on quantum mechanics.

$SU(2)$: This is the group of unitary matrices with determinant $+1$, that leave magnitudes of 2−dimensional complex vectors invariant:

$$Z_1'\bar{Z}_1' + Z_2'\bar{Z}_2' = Z_1\bar{Z}_1 + Z_2\bar{Z}_2$$

Amusing fact is that the generators of $SU(2)$ are three in number, S_1, S_2, S_3 and satisfy

$$[S_i, S_j] = i\epsilon_{ijk}S_k$$

Direct algebraic proof is given in Ryder[1]. This is the connection between $SO(3)$ and $SU(2)$. The groups however differ in their global aspects. See Schiff[2]. There is a two-to-one mapping from $SU(2)$ to $SO(3)$. Thus one realisation of above algebra is the one already discussed previously. But this one is essentially real aside from overall i factor. $SU(2)$, a complex group, permits a strictly complex representation of lower dimensionality:

$$S_1 = \frac{1}{2}\sigma^1 \qquad\qquad S_2 = \frac{1}{2}\sigma^2 \qquad\qquad S_3 = \frac{1}{2}\sigma^3$$

where $\sigma's$ are the Pauli matrices

$$\sigma^1 = \begin{pmatrix} 0 & 1 \\ 1 & 0 \end{pmatrix}, \quad \sigma^2 = \begin{pmatrix} 0 & -i \\ i & 0 \end{pmatrix}, \quad \sigma^3 = \begin{pmatrix} 1 & 0 \\ 0 & -1 \end{pmatrix}$$

This representation has $\sum S_i^2 = s(s+1) = \frac{1}{2} \times \frac{3}{2}$. Other representations with half-integral values of s can be found from tensor products of this representation. One can also be sure that there are no more representations of the above algebra. This follows from the algebraic proof given in quantum mechanics where one learns that the eigenvalues of S_3 must be separated by integers, and for each eigenvalue $+m_s$, $-m_s$ has also to occur, so that $s = 0, \frac{1}{2}, 1, \frac{3}{2} \ldots$ are all the possibilities.

This short review of these two groups prepares us for the Lorentz group.

1.2. LORENTZ GROUP

The transformations (remember $c = 1$)

$$x' = \frac{x + vt}{\sqrt{1 - v^2}} \qquad\qquad t' = \frac{t + vx}{\sqrt{1 - v^2}}$$

and generalisations thereof are known to leave invariant the four-dimensional "distance" or interval

$$t'^2 - \sum_i x'^{i2} = t^2 - \sum_i x^{i2}$$

Together with ordinary rotations, already discussed, the group of these transformations is called $SO(3,1)$ rather than $SO(4)$ due to the different signs in the metric.

We can write above transformations in a suggestive form by letting

$$\beta \equiv v \qquad\qquad \text{and} \qquad\qquad \gamma \equiv (1 - \beta^2)^{-1/2}$$

and introducing α:

$$\cosh \alpha \equiv \gamma \qquad\qquad \text{and} \qquad\qquad \sinh \alpha \equiv \beta\gamma$$

— *Exercise*: Check that this is allowed.

α is called "rapidity" parameter. So "boost" in x direction looks

$$\begin{pmatrix} x' \\ t' \end{pmatrix} = \begin{pmatrix} \cosh \alpha & \sinh \alpha \\ \sinh \alpha & \cosh \alpha \end{pmatrix} \begin{pmatrix} x \\ t \end{pmatrix}$$

Aside from the appearance of hyperbolic functions instead of trigonometric ones, note the absence of opposite signs. It is easy to deduce generators:

$$
K_x = \begin{array}{c} \\ t \\ x \\ y \\ z \end{array}
\begin{array}{cccc} t & x & y & z \\ \end{array}
\left(\begin{array}{cccc}
0 & 1 & 0 & 0 \\
1 & 0 & 0 & 0 \\
0 & 0 & 0 & 0 \\
0 & 0 & 0 & 0
\end{array} \right),
$$

$$
K_y = \left(\begin{array}{cccc}
0 & 0 & 1 & 0 \\
0 & 0 & 0 & 0 \\
1 & 0 & 0 & 0 \\
0 & 0 & 0 & 0
\end{array} \right)
\quad \text{and} \quad
K_z = \left(\begin{array}{cccc}
0 & 0 & 0 & 1 \\
0 & 0 & 0 & 0 \\
0 & 0 & 0 & 0 \\
1 & 0 & 0 & 0
\end{array} \right).
$$

Algebra of K's:

$$
K_x K_y - K_y K_x =
$$

$$
\left(\begin{array}{cccc}
0 & 1 & 0 & 0 \\
1 & 0 & 0 & 0 \\
0 & 0 & 0 & 0 \\
0 & 0 & 0 & 0
\end{array} \right)
\left(\begin{array}{cccc}
0 & 0 & 1 & 0 \\
0 & 0 & 0 & 0 \\
1 & 0 & 0 & 0 \\
0 & 0 & 0 & 0
\end{array} \right)
-
\left(\begin{array}{cccc}
0 & 0 & 1 & 0 \\
0 & 0 & 0 & 0 \\
1 & 0 & 0 & 0 \\
0 & 0 & 0 & 0
\end{array} \right)
\left(\begin{array}{cccc}
0 & 1 & 0 & 0 \\
1 & 0 & 0 & 0 \\
0 & 0 & 0 & 0 \\
0 & 0 & 0 & 0
\end{array} \right)
$$

$$
= \left(\begin{array}{cccc}
0 & 0 & 0 & 0 \\
0 & 0 & 1 & 0 \\
0 & 0 & 0 & 0 \\
0 & 0 & 0 & 0
\end{array} \right)
-
\left(\begin{array}{cccc}
0 & 0 & 0 & 0 \\
0 & 0 & 0 & 0 \\
0 & 1 & 0 & 0 \\
0 & 0 & 0 & 0
\end{array} \right)
$$

$$
= -i J_z
$$

— *Exercise*: Check the rest similarly:

$$
[J_i, J_j] = i\epsilon_{ijk} J_k
$$

$$
[K_i, K_j] = i\epsilon_{ijk} J_k
$$

$$
[K_i, J_j] = i\epsilon_{ijk} K_k
$$

This algebra seems asymmetric between space and time. This is a result of how the generators are labelled. The notation that makes this transparent and generalises to any number of dimensions is M_{xy} instead of J_z, M_{zt} instead of K_z etc., specifiying the *plane* of rotation. *Axis* of rotation is an idea specific to three dimensions. In general, for the real skew symmetric generators of $SO(n)$, the reader can check that

$$[M_{ab}, M_{cd}] = 0 \qquad\qquad \text{if} \qquad a \neq c \neq d \neq b$$

and

$$[M_{ab}, M_{bc}] = -M_{ac}$$

This means that if the planes are unrelated, the commutator vanishes and if they share an axis, the resulting rotation is in the plane of the remaining two axes.

The Weyl trick: How do we get representations of the full Lorentz group? $SO(3)$ is a subgroup but K's get mixed in. Let

$$A_i = \frac{1}{2}(J_i + iK_i)$$

$$B_i = \frac{1}{2}(J_i - iK_i)$$

– *Exercise:* Then check that

$$\begin{aligned}
[A_i, A_j] &= i\epsilon_{ijk}A_k \\
[B_i, B_j] &= i\epsilon_{ijk}B_k \\
[A_i, B_i] &= 0
\end{aligned}$$

A_i, B_i are hermitian and so we have two disjoint $SU(2)$'s. In symbols, we have $SO(3,1) \simeq SU(2) \otimes SU(2)$. The representations of Lorentz Groups can now be classified by the representations of $SU(2)_A$ and $SU(2)_B$. The largest eigenvalues of A_3, B_3, to be denoted s_A and s_A, specify the representation. Basis vectors are labelled by m_A m_B. The spin of a particle species can be identified by studying properties under rotation in the rest frame. Since $\vec{J} = \vec{A} + \vec{B}$, spin of the system is given by $s_A + s_B$. A typical element of $SO(3,1)$ is now written

$$U_{(A,B)} = \exp\left(-i\theta_i^A A_i - i\theta_i^B B_i\right)$$

which can be obtained from the standard form

$$U(\theta, \xi) = \exp\left(-i\theta_i J_i - \xi_i K_i\right)$$

by defining

$$\theta_i^A = \theta_i - i\xi_i \qquad \theta_i^B = \theta_i + i\xi_i$$

Since K_i are hermitian, the K term in the exponent is antihermitian, or, in the previous line with appearance of i in front of the hermitian generators, the parameters are complex. Thus "U" is not unitary. The group theoretic reasons for this and implications thereof are discussed in text-books[1],[3],[4]. I will provide an example later.

2. The Electron and the Dirac Equation

2.1. DEDUCING THE DIRAC EQUATION

Suppose we didn't know the Dirac equation and wanted the equation satisfied by spin-$\frac{1}{2}$ particles. We know that the spin of a representation, J value, is $A + B$ (added as angular momenta). If we want $J = \frac{1}{2}$, we must have $A = \frac{1}{2}$ and $B = 0$ or $A = 0$ and $B = \frac{1}{2}$. In compact notation, either the representation $(\frac{1}{2}, 0)$ or the representation $(0, \frac{1}{2})$. For $(\frac{1}{2}, 0)$, $A = \frac{1}{2}$ and $B = 0$, so A_i can be chosen to be the Pauli matrices (times half) $\frac{1}{2}\sigma^i$. Substituting this in the general form of $U(a, b)$ obtained previously, we get for $(\frac{1}{2}, 0)$,

$$U_{(\frac{1}{2},0)} = \exp(-i(\theta_i - i\xi_i)\frac{1}{2}\sigma^i)$$

which for pure boosts $\quad \rightarrow \quad \exp(-\frac{1}{2}\xi_i\sigma^i)$

$$= \cosh\frac{|\vec{\xi}|}{2} - \sinh\frac{|\vec{\xi}|}{2}\hat{\xi}\cdot\vec{\sigma}$$

Similarly, for $(0, \frac{1}{2})$, $A_i = 0$ and $B_i = \frac{1}{2}\sigma^i$ so that for pure boosts,

$$U_{(0,\frac{1}{2})} = \cosh\frac{|\vec{\xi}|}{2} + \sinh\frac{|\vec{\xi}|}{2}\hat{\xi}\cdot\vec{\sigma}$$

Note the sign change.

Now it turns out, neither $(\frac{1}{2}, 0)$ nor $(0, \frac{1}{2})$ is adequate to describe spin-$\frac{1}{2}$ particles if parity is a good quantum number. This is because under parity, $K_i \rightarrow -K_i$ but $J_i \rightarrow J_i$ so that $A_i \leftrightarrow B_i$ and as a result, $(\frac{1}{2}, 0) \leftrightarrow (0, \frac{1}{2})$. One therefore needs to build the reducible representation $(\frac{1}{2}, 0) \oplus (0, \frac{1}{2})$. In matrix form, the reducible representation is written as

$$U = \begin{pmatrix} U_{(\frac{1}{2},0)} & \vdots & O \\ \cdots & \cdots & \cdots \\ O & \vdots & U_{(0,\frac{1}{2})} \end{pmatrix}$$

Let us begin with states with $J_3 = \pm\frac{1}{2}$ in the rest frame and then boost these standard states to required momentum. In the present representation,

$$J_3 = \begin{pmatrix} \frac{1}{2}\sigma^3 & \vdots & O \\ \cdots & \cdots & \cdots \\ O & \vdots & \frac{1}{2}\sigma^3 \end{pmatrix}$$

Its eigenvectors can be built out of those of σ^3. We make the following choice

$$\begin{pmatrix} 1 \\ 0 \\ 1 \\ 0 \end{pmatrix}, \qquad \begin{pmatrix} 0 \\ 1 \\ 0 \\ 1 \end{pmatrix}, \qquad \begin{pmatrix} 1 \\ 0 \\ -1 \\ 0 \end{pmatrix}, \qquad \begin{pmatrix} 0 \\ 1 \\ 0 \\ -1 \end{pmatrix}$$

The first and third have $J_3 = \frac{1}{2}$ and the second and fourth have $J_3 = -\frac{1}{2}$ and they constitute a linearly independent set. To distinguish between the members of each degenerate pair we want a matrix condition. We observe that if we define

$$\beta = \begin{pmatrix} 0 & \vdots & 1 \\ \cdots & \cdots & \cdots \\ 1 & \vdots & 0 \end{pmatrix}$$

then

$$\beta \begin{pmatrix} 1 \\ 0 \\ 1 \\ 0 \end{pmatrix} = \begin{pmatrix} 1 \\ 0 \\ 1 \\ 0 \end{pmatrix}, \qquad \text{and,} \qquad \beta \begin{pmatrix} 1 \\ 0 \\ -1 \\ 0 \end{pmatrix} = - \begin{pmatrix} 1 \\ 0 \\ -1 \\ 0 \end{pmatrix}$$

And similarly for the second and the fourth. We designate the above vectors

$$u(+,0) \qquad v(+,0) \qquad u(-,0) \qquad v(-,0)$$

With u, v to designate eigenvalues of β and $\pm$ designating the eigenvalues of J_3. The argument 0 designates the rest frame.

 — *Exercise*: What is the general choice for the eigenvectors of J_3? (Can you find β for the general case?)

Starting with the standard basis defined in the rest frame, we prescribe the basis in arbitrary frames by Lorentz boosting. In terms of the reducible representation specified above we define

$$u(\pm,\vec{p}) = N_p U_u(\pm,\vec{0}) \quad \text{and} \quad v(\pm,\vec{p}) = N_p U_v(\pm,\vec{0})$$

where N_p is normalisation to be determined later. To obtain an explicit expression for these, note that with the usual notation $\gamma = (1 - \beta^2)^{-1/2}$ etc., ($\beta \equiv v/c$, not to be confused with the matrix defined above)

$$\cosh\xi = \gamma = \frac{p^0}{m} \equiv \frac{\omega}{m} \qquad \sinh\xi = \gamma\beta = \frac{|\vec{p}|}{m}$$

so that

$$\cosh\frac{\xi}{2} = \sqrt{\frac{\omega + m}{2m}} \quad \text{and} \quad \sinh\frac{\xi}{2} = \sqrt{\frac{\omega - m}{2m}}$$

Finally, $\hat{\xi} \equiv \hat{p}$

— *Exercise*: Write out the required explicit forms of u, v in terms of the physical boost parameters ω, p^i.

The Dirac equation can now be shown to be the generalisation to arbitrary frames of the statement that in the rest frame, u, v can be characterised as eigenvectors of β. We can see that

$$(U\beta U^{-1} - I)u(+, \vec{p}) = 0$$

Consider

$$\Gamma(\vec{p}) \equiv U\beta U^{-1}$$

$$= \begin{pmatrix} \exp(-\tfrac{1}{2}\xi_i\sigma^i) & \vdots & 0 \\ \cdots & \cdots & \cdots \\ 0 & \vdots & \exp(\tfrac{1}{2}\xi_i\sigma^i) \end{pmatrix}$$

$$\times \begin{pmatrix} 0 & \vdots & 1 \\ \cdots & \cdots & \cdots \\ 1 & \vdots & 0 \end{pmatrix}$$

$$\times \begin{pmatrix} \exp(\tfrac{1}{2}\xi_i\sigma^i) & \vdots & 0 \\ \cdots & \cdots & \cdots \\ 0 & \vdots & \exp(-\tfrac{1}{2}\xi_i\sigma^i) \end{pmatrix}$$

(recall $U^{-1} \neq U^\dagger$)

$$= \begin{pmatrix} \exp(-\tfrac{1}{2}\xi_i\sigma^i) & \vdots & 0 \\ \cdots & \cdots & \cdots \\ 0 & \vdots & \exp(\tfrac{1}{2}\xi_i\sigma^i) \end{pmatrix}$$

$$\times \begin{pmatrix} 0 & \vdots & \exp(-\tfrac{1}{2}\xi_i\sigma^i) \\ \cdots & \cdots & \cdots \\ \exp(\tfrac{1}{2}\xi_i\sigma^i) & \vdots & 0 \end{pmatrix}$$

$$= \begin{pmatrix} 0 & \vdots & \exp(-\xi_i\sigma^i) \\ \cdots & \cdots & \cdots \\ \exp(\xi_i\sigma^i) & \vdots & 0 \end{pmatrix}$$

$$= \begin{pmatrix} 0 & \vdots & \frac{\omega}{m} - \frac{\vec{p}\cdot\vec{\sigma}}{m} \\ \cdots & \cdots & \cdots \\ \frac{\omega}{m} + \frac{\vec{p}\cdot\vec{\sigma}}{m} & \vdots & 0 \end{pmatrix}$$

Now define

$$\gamma^0 \quad = \quad \beta$$

$$\gamma^i \quad = \quad \begin{pmatrix} 0 & \vdots & \sigma^i \\ \cdots & \cdots & \cdots \\ -\sigma^i & \vdots & 0 \end{pmatrix}$$

Then our statement above becomes

$$(\gamma^0 p^0 - \vec{\gamma}\cdot\vec{p} - m)u(+,\vec{p}) = (\gamma^\mu p_\mu - m)u(+,\vec{p}) = 0$$

It then follows that

$$(i\gamma^\mu \partial_\mu - m)e^{-ix\cdot p}u(+,\vec{p}) = 0$$

The expression in the first brackets is the Dirac differential operator. The same equation holds for $u(-,\vec{p})$. For the $v(\pm,\vec{p})$ we have

$$(\gamma^\mu p_\mu + m)v(\pm,\vec{p}) = v(\pm,\vec{p})$$

so that

$$(i\gamma^\mu \partial_\mu - m)e^{ix\cdot p}v(\pm,\vec{p}) = v(\pm,\vec{p})$$

It is necessary to insert $\exp(+ix\cdot p)$ in order to get the same differential equation as the u's. Thus we may conclude that a general linear combination

$$\psi(x) = \sum_{\vec{p},\pm}\left\{ c_{\vec{p},\sigma}e^{-ix\cdot p}u(\sigma,\vec{p}) + d^\dagger_{\vec{p},\sigma}e^{ix\cdot p}v(\sigma,\vec{p})\right\}$$

solves the Dirac equation. Here σ takes the values $\pm$ and the c's and the $d^\dagger$'s are expansion coefficients.

— *Exercise*: Show that if ψ satisfies the Dirac equation then

$$(i\gamma^\mu \partial_\mu + m)(i\gamma^\mu \partial_\mu - m)\psi \quad = \quad -(\partial^\mu \partial_\mu + m^2)\psi \quad = \quad 0.$$

That is, each component of the spinor satisfies the Klein-Gordon equation.

We have explicitly constructed the spinorial functions describing spin-1/2 particles. They are then seen to obey the Dirac equation. These basis functions labelled by mode number (and spin) are also often called mode functions to distinguish them from momentum eigenstates of nonrelativistic wave mechanics. The procedure also illustrates in principle how to construct mode functions for particles of arbitrary spin. For most purposes, the equations satisfied by these mode functions are not needed. As in the exercise above, even in the general case, each component independently must always satisfy the Klein-Gordon equation. The coupled first order equations only serve as constraints that identify the spin content of the representation. Calculations of relativistic scattering amplitudes require the knowledge of the free propagator for particle of each species and the Lorentz scalar interaction terms which enter the Lagrangian. Both of these can be determined from the knowledge of the free mode functions[8]. In particular the interaction terms can be constructed by proper contraction of all group representation indices between the mode functions of the particle species concerned.

2.2. γ-MATRICES

The Dirac equation introduces into physics the fascinating γ-matrices, an efficient machinery for dealing with the massive spin-1/2 particles. The γ-matrices satisfy the *anticommutation* algebra

$$\{\gamma^\mu, \gamma^\nu\} = 2\eta^{\mu\nu} \mathbf{1}$$

Where $\{a, b\} \equiv ab + ba$ is the standard notation for the anticommuting bracket, and $\eta^{\mu\nu}$ is the metric. The matrices we have obtained in the preceeding subsection have the further property that

$$\gamma^{0\dagger} = \gamma^0 \qquad \text{whereas} \qquad \gamma^{i\dagger} = \gamma^0 \gamma^i \gamma^0$$

The right hand side of the above relation contains the spacetime metric, the left hand side is quadratic in the γs. In this sense the γ-matrices are a square-root of the Minkowskian metric. Similar matrices can be defined in arbitrary number of dimensions and with Euclidean or Minkowskian signature of the metric. An example we already know is the Pauli matrices with respect to 3−dimensional space. Algebras of this kind are called Clifford algebras.

The γ-matrices are not a closed set under multiplication even after the inclusion of the identity, as for example the Pauli matrices are. An important new matrix called γ^5 is obtained through

$$\gamma^5 = i\gamma^0\gamma^1\gamma^2\gamma^3 = \begin{pmatrix} -1 & \vdots & 0 \\ \cdots & \cdots & \cdots \\ 0 & \vdots & 1 \end{pmatrix}$$

It has the properties

$$\{\gamma^\mu, \gamma^5\} = 0,$$

along with

$$\gamma^{5\dagger} = \gamma^5 \qquad \text{and} \qquad (\gamma^5)^2 = 1$$

The γ^μ *generate* an algebra of 16 independent matrices in all, including the identity. Products such as $\psi^\dagger \Gamma \psi$ (with Γ standing for one of the 16 matrices), which are bilinear in ψ turn out to have definite Lorentz transformation properties. We have to abandon the discussion of their uses due to lack of time.

We conclude with the remark that the algebra of the γ's is general, not specific to the representation given here. The matrices obtained by similarity transformations of those above,

$$\gamma'^\mu = A\gamma^\mu A^{-1}$$

where A are arbitrary complex matrices are just as good a representation. Several different representations are in use depending upon the context. The one obtained above is called the chiral representation.

Why was it necessary to invent the γ-matrices? We can deal with higher spins such as 1 (photons for example) and 2 (gravitons in flat space) using second or higher rank tensors. It happens that all the tensor representations of $SO(3,1)$ or of $SO(n)$ are real and can be written as subspaces of $GL(n, R)$ or repeated tensor products of the same with itself. Here the symbol $GL(n, R)$ refers to the *General Linear Group in n Real dimensions*. This is simply the set of all possible $n \times n$ real matrices. The spinor representation that has been necessitated by the existence of the fermions is intrinsically complex. It cannot be constructed out of the real representations. The most convenient and compact way of dealing with it turns out to be to treat it as a subspace of $GL(4, C)$, C referring to the complex numbers. That the dimension of the coplex matrices also turns out to be 4 is an accident of four dimensions. In dimensions other than four, the complex dimension of the GL group is related in an intricate way with the dimension of the real space. There is no space here to go into further detail. Systematic accounts can be found in Georgi[4] or old classics such as Cartan[5].

2.3. ORTHOGONALITY AND NORMALISATION

A consequence of the fact that boosts U are not unitary is that the complex 'magnitude' $u^\dagger u$ of the vectors is not left invariant. It turns out however that $u^\dagger \gamma^0 u$ does remain invariant. Because of this, one defines a Dirac conjugate $\bar{u} \equiv u^\dagger \gamma^0$, a dual vector more handy than the Hermitian conjugate $u^\dagger$. Consider

$$\bar{u}(\sigma', \vec{p})u(\sigma, \vec{p}) = u^\dagger(\sigma', \vec{0})U\gamma^0 Uu(\sigma, \vec{0})N_{p'} N_p$$

Now

$$
\gamma^0 U = \begin{pmatrix} 0 & \vdots & 1 \\ \cdots & \cdots & \cdots \\ 1 & \vdots & 0 \end{pmatrix} \begin{pmatrix} e^{-\frac{1}{2}\xi_i\sigma^i} & \vdots & 0 \\ \cdots & \cdots & \cdots \\ 0 & \vdots & e^{\frac{1}{2}\xi_i\sigma^i} \end{pmatrix}
$$

$$
= \begin{pmatrix} e^{\frac{1}{2}\xi_i\sigma^i} & \vdots & 0 \\ \cdots & \cdots & \cdots \\ 0 & \vdots & e^{-\frac{1}{2}\xi_i\sigma^i} \end{pmatrix} \begin{pmatrix} 0 & \vdots & 1 \\ \cdots & \cdots & \cdots \\ 1 & \vdots & 0 \end{pmatrix}
$$

$$
= U^{-1}\gamma^0
$$

So

$$
\bar{u}(\sigma',\vec{p})u(\sigma,\vec{p}) = N_{p'}N_p u^\dagger(\sigma',\vec{0})u(\sigma,\vec{0})
$$
$$
= N_p^2\delta_{\sigma'\sigma}
$$

So this is a Lorentz scalar. Similarly

$$
\bar{v}(\sigma',\vec{p})v(\sigma,\vec{p}) = -N_p^2\delta_{\sigma'\sigma}
$$

There are two conventions for normalisation

$$
\bar{u}(\sigma',\vec{p})u(\sigma,\vec{p}) = \delta_{\sigma'\sigma} \quad \text{OR} \quad \bar{u}(\sigma',\vec{p})u(\sigma,\vec{p}) = \frac{m}{\omega}\delta_{\sigma'\sigma}
$$

The first is Lorentz invariant. But the second has the advantage of providing a more physical normalisation for creation and destruction operators in the quantum theory, to which we pass next.

2.4. QUANTIZATION

Klein and Jordan had shown that a consistent quantum theory of many identical bosons could be obtained by canonical quantisation applied to the Klein-Gordon field. (see Pauli[6] and Wentzel[7] for early accounts). Jordan and Wigner showed that to get the same for a system of Dirac particles, one had to use anticommutators instead of commutators[6][7]. The exclusion principle is then automatically built in. Accordingly, one needs to require

$$
\{\psi_a(\vec{x},t),\psi_b^\dagger(\vec{x}',t)\} = \delta^3(\vec{x},\vec{x}')\delta_{ab}
$$

a, b are spinor indices. Imposing this condition makes the coefficients $c_{\vec{p},\sigma}$, $d_{\vec{p},\sigma}$ introduced in sec. 2.2 into operators. The reader can verify on his or her own or consult a textbook to verify that the conditions on these coefficients become

$$\{c_{\vec{p},\sigma}, c^{\dagger}_{\vec{p}'\sigma'}\} = \delta^3(\vec{p},\vec{p}')\delta_{\sigma\sigma'}$$
$$\{d_{\vec{p},\sigma}, d^{\dagger}_{\vec{p}'\sigma'}\} = \delta^3(\vec{p},\vec{p}')\delta_{\sigma\sigma'}$$

and all brackets of the following form vanish

$$\{c,d\} = \{c,d^{\dagger}\} = 0$$

To prove this one needs the following result

- *Exercise*: Prove the spin sums

$$\sum_{\sigma} u_a(\sigma,\vec{p})\bar{u}_b(\sigma,\vec{p}) = \frac{(\gamma_{\mu}p^{\mu}+m)_{ab}}{2\omega}$$

$$\sum_{\sigma} v_a(\sigma,\vec{p})\bar{v}_b(\sigma,\vec{p}) = \frac{(\gamma_{\mu}p^{\mu}-m)_{ab}}{2\omega}$$

- *Exercise*: Check that had N_p been different, anticommutators of the c's and the d's would have to be normalised differently to retain the canonical quantization condition.
- *Exercise*: Write a Lagrangian that will give the Dirac equation and make $\psi^{\dagger}$ the conjugate variable.

2.5. PHYSICAL INTERPRETATION

$$(i\gamma^{\mu}\frac{\partial}{\partial x^{\mu}} - m)\psi = 0$$

$$\Rightarrow \quad \psi^{\dagger}(-i\gamma^{\mu\dagger}\frac{\overleftarrow{\partial}}{\partial x^{\mu}} - m) = 0$$

$$\Rightarrow \quad \bar{\psi}(i\gamma^{\mu}\frac{\overleftarrow{\partial}}{\partial x^{\mu}} + m) = 0$$

From which we can show

$$\partial_{\mu}(\bar{\psi}\gamma^{\mu}\psi) = 0$$

Hence by Gauss theorem

$$A \equiv \int d^3x\, \bar{\psi}\gamma^0\psi = \int d^3x\, \psi^{\dagger}\psi$$

is conserved in every Lorentz frame. Also, the density $\bar{\psi}\gamma^0\psi$ is positive definite. When Dirac invented the equation, he thought this fact was its prime advantage. This was because ψ was meant to be a single-particle

probability amplitude wave. The first relativistic equation was written by
Schrödinger who proposed

$$(-\frac{\partial^2}{\partial t^2} + \vec{\nabla}^2 - m^2)\phi(\vec{x}, t) = 0$$

This is more commonly known as Klein-Gordan equation. This was in
keeping with $p^{0^2} - \vec{p}^2 - m^2 = 0$ and the implementation $p^0 \rightarrow i\partial/\partial t$,
$p^i \rightarrow -i\partial/\partial x^i$. But there were two problems: 1) solutions with negative
energy, (i.e., eigenvalue of $i\partial/\partial t$ exist, and 2) the density whose integral is
conserved is not positive definite:

$$\rho = i(\phi^*\dot{\phi} - \dot{\phi}^*\phi)$$

Thus the Dirac theory appeared to be an advance. In Dirac's theory negative energies persisted but he proposed stability against indefinite transitions to negative energy states by using fermi statistics, Dirac sea and hole
theory.

The fact that has subsequently become clear is the interpretation first
advanced by Heisenberg and Pauli, wherein ϕ, ψ are operator valued space-
time fields. $i\partial^\mu$ is not the p^μ operator. p^μ, x^μ are only c-members. $i\partial/\partial x^\mu$
give spacetime-translations, brought about by the Hamiltonian H, or the
momenta P^i, distinct from mode labels p^μ.

There are several approaches to relativistic quantum theory, but if one
uses spacetime fields, the many-particle theory with quantized fields and
not the wave mechanics is the correct Relativistic Quantum Mechanics.

3. Interaction Picture and the S-matrix

3.1. INTERACTIONS AMONG (OTHERWISE) FREE PARTICLES

Interactions among particles result in a change in their momenta, and at
high energies, change in the species of the particles, e.g.,

$$^4\text{He}^{++} + \text{Au} \quad \rightarrow {}^4\text{He}^{++} + \text{Au} \quad \text{(Rutherford expteriment)}$$
$$p + e^- \qquad \rightarrow n + \nu_e \qquad\qquad \text{(inverse } \beta \text{ decay)}$$

or decays :

$$\pi^+ \quad \rightarrow \quad \mu^+ + \bar{\nu}_\mu$$
$$\pi^0 \quad \rightarrow \qquad 2\gamma$$

It is convenient to think of otherwise free particles that interact briefly
and result in the final product that is again free. Such transitions can be
represented by interaction terms of the form

$$a^\dagger_{p_2\sigma_2} b^\dagger_{p_2\sigma_2} c_{p_3\sigma_3} d_{p_4\sigma_4}$$

where the letters of the alphabet designate different particle species, and
the subscripts label momentum and spin of single particle states. Acting
on a state with free c and d particles it connects the latter with a state of
free a and b provided the various momenta and spins match. On physical
grounds we need to construct terms such that 1) energy and momentum
are conserved and 2) various charges are conserved and discrete symmetries are obeyed. A further requirement is Lorentz covariance of the final
answer, since different observers must agree about the process. A skeletal
expression such as the one above can not guarantee all this. Which is where
the construct of spacetime field operators with definite Lorentz covariant
properties helps. Let the interaction piece of H be $\int \mathcal{H} d^3 x$. As we shall see
later, for Lorentz invariance, we need that

$$[\mathcal{H}(x), \mathcal{H}(y)] = 0 \quad \text{for} \quad (x - y)^\mu (x - y)_\mu \text{ spacelike}$$

It turns out that this can be achieved if $\mathcal{H}$ is a product of local fields
and their derivatives and the Lorentz indices on the fields are properly
contracted to make $\mathcal{H}$ a Lorentz scalar. Typical $\mathcal{H}$ are : (g, λ etc. are real
constants)

$\quad g\phi^3, \; \lambda\phi^4, \; \sigma\phi^6$

with ϕ a scalar, real for ϕ^3 possibly complex for others

$\quad g\bar{\psi}\psi\bar{\psi}\psi, \qquad\qquad \psi$ a fermion

$\quad g\phi\bar{\psi}\psi, \; g\partial_\mu\phi\bar{\psi}\gamma^\mu\psi$

$\quad eA_\mu\bar{\psi}\gamma^\mu\psi \qquad\qquad A_\mu$ a vector

If we expand individual fields in terms of their modes, we get a summation of terms whose operator parts look like the skeletal example written
above. We now proceed to calculating the effects of such $\mathcal{H}$ treated as
perturbation to the free Hamiltonian. There are many good texts on the
subject. Good references for beginners are Lee[9] and Lurié[10] to name but
two.

3.2. IN, OUT STATES AND THE INTERACTION PICTURE

Calculations in quantum mechanics are done in either of the equivalent
'picture's:

Schrödinger: States undergo time evolution, operators are time independent

$$i\frac{\partial}{\partial t}|\alpha, t\rangle_S \;\; = \;\; H_S|\alpha, t\rangle_S$$

$$i\frac{d}{dt}H_S \;\; = \;\; 0$$

Here α labels the state.

Heisenberg: States are time dependent, operators undergo dynamical evolution

$$i\frac{\partial}{\partial t}|\alpha\rangle_H = 0$$

$$i\frac{d}{dt}\mathcal{O}_H = -[H_H, \mathcal{O}_H(t)]$$

for any operator $\mathcal{O}$. Choose

$$|\alpha, t = 0\rangle_S = |\alpha\rangle_H \quad \text{and} \quad \mathcal{O}_H(0) = \mathcal{O}_S$$

Then the two pictures are related through

$$|\alpha\rangle_S = e^{-iHt}|\alpha\rangle_H$$
$$\mathcal{O}_H = e^{iHt}\mathcal{O}_S e^{-iHt}$$

and H_S same as H_H.

In situations where interactions come "on" for short times, a hybrid picture is preferable. Write

$$H = H_0 + V$$

where eigenvalues and eigenstates of H_0 should be known exactly. Consider a Schrödinger picture state

$$|\psi\rangle = \sum_n c_n(t)|n, t\rangle$$

$$\text{where} \quad H_0|n, t\rangle = E_n|n, t\rangle,$$

$$\textit{i.e.,} \quad |n, t\rangle = e^{-iE_n t}|n, 0\rangle$$

$$\text{then} \quad i\frac{\partial}{\partial t}|\psi\rangle = (H_0 + V)|\psi\rangle$$

$$\Rightarrow \quad \dot{c}_n(t) = \sum_m c_m(t)\langle n, 0|V|m, 0\rangle e^{i(E_n - E_m)t}$$

$$= \sum_m c_m(t)\langle n, 0|e^{iH_0 t}V e^{-iH_0 t}|m, 0\rangle$$

Define

$$V_I(t) = e^{iH_0 t} V_S e^{-iH_0 t}$$

I stands for interaction picture. The interpretation is that V_I is the operator whose matrix elements give the instantaneous rate at which the amplitude of occupation of a particular state n is changing. Define correspondingly

$$|\psi\rangle_I = e^{iH_0 t}|\psi\rangle_S$$

And for a general operator $\mathcal{O}$,

$$\frac{d}{dt}\mathcal{O}_I = i[H_0, \mathcal{O}_I]$$

The important property of the I-picture can then be proved by the reader:

– *Exercise*: Show that $i\dfrac{\partial}{\partial t}|\psi\rangle_I = V_I|\psi\rangle_I$

Interaction picture proves to be very convenient in field theory which is done in the Heisenberg picture. In the absence of interaction, $V = 0$, I-picture reduces to the H-picture. However, the relation of I-picture directly to H-picture looks complicated:

$$|\psi\rangle_I = e^{iH_0t}e^{-iHt}|\psi\rangle_H$$

Of course, matrix elements have to be the same, calculated in any picture.

3.3. EVOLUTION OPERATOR

For a scattering process, consider the H-picture states in the Fock space of the all the particles involved in the interaction. We distinguish the basis before the interaction, called the "in" basis from that after the interaction, called the "out" basis. We denote the basis vectors $|\psi_\alpha^{in}(t)\rangle$ and $|\psi_\alpha^{out}(t)\rangle$. α denotes all possible quantum numbers required to specify the basis. Although the bases are isomorphic the two are not identical at all finite times due to interaction. The bases $\{|\psi_\alpha^{out}(\infty)\rangle\}$ and $\{|\psi_\alpha^{in}(-\infty)\rangle\}$ differ at most by an overall phase, which would be unimportant to observations. But in general the two are mapped one onto the other by a unitary operator, involving the interaction Hamiltonian which is assumed to be operative for a brief period. For further discussion of the assumptions involved and their implications see for instance Lee[9] and Itzykson and Zuber[3].

We seek amplitudes of the form

$$\langle\psi_\beta^{out}(t)|\psi_\alpha^{in}(t)\rangle$$

The H-picture $|\psi^{in}\rangle$ is just as well an I-picture state at $t = -\infty$. We introduce an operator that will evolve it as an I-picture state

$$|\psi_\alpha^{in}(t)\rangle_I \equiv U(t, -\infty)|\psi_\alpha^{in}\rangle$$

where U is the appropriate operator. From the preceeding exercise it follows that

$$i\frac{d}{dt}U(t, -\infty) = V_I(t)U(t, -\infty)$$

To conserve probability U ought to be unitary, which can be checked; since V_I is Hermitian, from the preceeding equation we get

$$-i\dot{U}^\dagger = U^\dagger V_I$$

$$\Rightarrow \quad i\frac{d}{dt}(UU^\dagger) = 0$$

So $UU^\dagger$ is a constant, and $U(t, -\infty) = 1$; hence the result follows.

The desired amplitude is then

$$\langle \psi^{out} \ (t) \ _\beta | \psi^{in}_\alpha(t) \rangle$$

$$= \langle \psi^{out}_\beta(\infty) | U^\dagger(t, \infty) U(t, -\infty) | \psi^{in}_\alpha(-\infty) \rangle$$

$$= \langle \psi_\beta | U(\infty, -\infty) | \psi_\alpha \rangle$$

where both ψ_α and ψ_β are taken to be eigenstates of the free Hamiltonian ignoring the overall phase difference between 'in' and 'out'.

— *Exercise*: Prove the last equality involving the U's.

The S-matrix is defined to be

$$S \equiv \lim_{\substack{t \to \infty \\ t' \to -\infty}} U(t, t')$$

And

$$S_{\beta\alpha} = \langle \psi_\beta | S | \psi_\alpha \rangle$$

which is seen to be the required matrix element.

Using the differential equation satisfied by $U(t, -\infty)$ we can obtain an expansion for $U(\infty, -\infty)$. First convert to the integral equation

$$U(t, t_0) = 1 - i \int_{t_0}^t V_I(t') \, U(t', t_0) \, dt'$$

which is equivalent and takes account of the initial condition. Then, upon iterating,

$$U^{(0)}(t, t_0) = 1$$

$$U^{(1)}(t, t_0) = -i \int_{t_0}^t dt_1 V_I(t_1)$$

$$U^{(2)}(t, t_0) = (-i)^2 \int_{t_0}^t dt_1 \int_{t_0}^{t_1} dt_2 V_I(t_1) V_I(t_2)$$

$$\cdots$$

$$U^{(n)}(t, t_0) = (-i)^n \int_{t_0}^t dt_1 \ldots \int_{t_0}^{t_{n-1}} dt_n V_I(t_1) \ldots V_I(t_n)$$

where $\sum_n U^{(n)}$ gives n^{th} order approximation to U. Recast in a more elegant form:

First,

$$\int_{t_0}^{t} dt_1 \int_{t_0}^{t_1} dt_2 V_I(t_1)V_I(t_2) = \int_{t_0}^{t} dt_2 \int_{t_0}^{t_2} dt_1 V_I(t_2)V_I(t_1)$$

by a change of variables. Now,

$$\int_{t_0}^{t} dt_2 \int_{t_0}^{t_2} dt_1 = \int_{t_0}^{t} dt_2 \int_{t_0}^{t} dt_1 \theta(t_2 - t_1)$$

$$= \int_{t_0}^{t} dt_1 \int_{t_1}^{t} dt_2$$

in the second step exchanging $\int dt_1$ and $\int dt_2$ and using up the step function θ. So

$$\int_{t_0}^{t} dt_1 \int_{t_0}^{t_1} dt_2 V_I(t_1)V_I(t_2) = \frac{1}{2}\int_{t_0}^{t} dt_1 \int_{t_0}^{t_1} dt_2 V_I(t_1)V_I(t_2)$$

$$+ \frac{1}{2}\int_{t_0}^{t} dt_1 \int_{t_1}^{t} dt_2 V_I(t_2)V_I(t_1)$$

Both t_1 and t_2 integrations range from t_0 to t but the order of the operators is different depending on $t_1 <$ or $> t_2$. Hence define

$$T\{V_I(t_1)V_I(t_2)\} \equiv \theta(t_1 - t_2)V_I(t_1)V_I(t_2)$$
$$+ \theta(t_2 - t_1)V_I(t_2)V_I(t_1)$$

called the time ordered product, introduced by Dyson. Then rewrite

$$\int_{t_0}^{t} dt_1 \int_{t_0}^{t_1} dt_2 V_I(t_1)V_I(t_2) = \frac{1}{2}\int_{t_0}^{t} dt_1 \int_{t_0}^{t} dt_2 T\{V_I(t_1)V_I(t_2)\}$$

It can be shown similarly that

$$\int_{t_0}^{t} dt_1 \dots \int_{t_0}^{t_{n-1}} dt_n V_I(t_1) \quad \dots \quad V_I(t_n)$$

$$= \frac{1}{n!}\int_{t_0}^{t} dt_1 \quad \dots \quad \int_{t_0}^{t} dt_n T\{V_I(t_1) \dots V_I(t_n)\}$$

So

$$U(t, t_0) = 1 + \sum_{n=1}^{\infty} \frac{(-i)^n}{n!}\int_{t_0}^{t} dt_1 \dots \int_{t_0}^{t} dt_n T\{V_I(t_1) \dots V_I(t_n)\}$$

$$\equiv T\exp\left\{-i\int_{t_0}^{t} V_I(t')dt'\right\}$$

The second is a convenient notation for the full expansion above it.

This allows us to calculate the S-matrix to any desired order in the interaction. While evaluating the matrix elements, a further fact needs to be kept in mind. We know that the free Hamiltonian needs to be normal ordered to avoid infinite energy of the ground state. The same prescription needs to be applied to the interacting part of the Hamiltonian V. If this is not done we once again encounter spurious infinities, as can be checked directly.

3.4. COVARIANCE

In the Hamiltonian formulation of dynamics, the time is specific to a particular reference frame and so are the canonical momenta so that in this formulation, Lorentz invariance, even if present is not obvious. Thus the formalism above seems to obscure Lorentz invariance. We shall verify that the latter is nevertheless very much present. First of all $V(t)$ can be written as

$$V(t) = \int \mathcal{H}(\vec{x}, t) \, d^3 x$$

In the absence of derivative coupling (involving $\dot{\phi}$ terms) $\mathcal{H}$ is the same as $-\mathcal{L}_{int}$, the interaction part of the Lagrangian density, and is a Lorentz scalar. Thus,

$$U(\infty, -\infty) = 1 + \sum_1^\infty \frac{(-i)^n}{n!} \int d^4 x_1 \ldots d^4 x_n \, T\{\mathcal{H}_I(x_1) \ldots \mathcal{H}_I(x_n)\}$$

Which has a greater chance of being Lorentz invariant. The T-product however does not seem Lorentz invariant due to the presence of the θ-function. It is, with further proviso on $\mathcal{H}$. $\mathcal{H}$ is Hermitian and therefore an observable. Causality requires that

$$[\mathcal{H}(x), \mathcal{H}(x')] = 0 \qquad \text{for } (x' - x)^\mu (x' - x)_\mu < 0$$

with this natural requirement we can show the T-product to be L-invariant.

Consider two spacetime points $(t_a, \vec{x}_a)$ and $(t_b, \vec{x}_b)$. Under a boost by speed v in the x direction, we find

$$\theta(t_a - t_b) \to \theta(\gamma t_a' - \gamma t_b' + \gamma v x_a' - \gamma v x_b')$$

Working directly in the primed frame, we would have written $\theta(t_a' - t_b')$ so the arguments of the two step functions don't match. But note that if $(x_a - x_b)^\mu (x_a - x_b)_\mu > 0$, i.e., the interval is timelike, the sign of $t_a' - t_b'$ has to be the same as that before the transformation, so the meaning of both the

θ-functions is the same. On the other hand, for the interval spacelike, the relative sign between the arguments can be negative. But this is precisely the case when the $\mathcal{H}$'s commute and the ordering of operators is no longer of any significance.

3.5. EXISTENCE OF S

For S to exist, the double limit $\lim_{\substack{t \to \infty \\ t' \to -\infty}} U(t, t')$ must exist and V should switch off in the same limits. The latter requirement is satisfied in non-relativistic scattering if the range of the potential is limited. But in relativisitic field theory it leads to intricate issues and sometimes signals phenomena that cannot be described in this formalism. In some of the cases field renormalisation cures the problem, in other cases infrared divergences have to be handled by making explicit some additional physical requirements. But in the case of quarks and gluons which are in principle massless and possess strong self and mutual coupling, no S can exist. The free particle basis for expressing the S-matrix is provided only by the bound states, nucleons and mesons, and not the supposed constituents.

There can be other cases where the S-matrix may not exist, as in the following example[3] where two isomorphic Hilbert spaces are not mappable onto each other by a unitary transformation.

Consider a 1-dimensional lattice of N spins. Let states be specified by the eigenvalues of $\prod_i^N \sigma_3^{(i)}$. The ground state $|\Omega\rangle$ may be taken to be that with all the spins down, and characterised by

$$\prod_i^N \sigma_-^{(i)} |-\tfrac{1}{2}, -\tfrac{1}{2} \cdots -\tfrac{1}{2}\rangle = 0$$

σ_-'s denoting the appropriate lowering operators. Make a change to new operators

$$\tau_2 = \sigma_2, \quad \tau_1 = \cos\theta\sigma_1 + \sin\theta\sigma_3, \quad \tau_3 = -\sin\theta\sigma_1 + \cos\theta\sigma_3$$

This change can be expressed by the unitary transformation

$$\tau_a^{(i)} = [\exp(i\tfrac{\theta}{2}\sigma_2^{(i)})] \, \sigma_a^{(i)} \, [\exp(-i\tfrac{\theta}{2}\sigma_2^{(i)})]$$

The states are similarly related, so that

$$|\Omega\rangle_\tau = \prod_i^N \exp(i\tfrac{\theta}{2}\sigma_2^{(i)})|\Omega\rangle$$

In the limit of infinite number of degrees of freedom however, the transformation does not exist because

$$\langle \Omega | \Omega \rangle_\tau \;=\; (\cos \frac{\theta}{2})^N \qquad \overset{N \to \infty}{\longrightarrow} \; 0$$

and the same is true of inner product between any two states from the two different Hilbert spaces because an infinite number of $\cos \theta/2$ or $\sin \theta/2$ factors will appear in every case.

- *Exercise:* Check the above calculation using $2i\sigma_2 = \sigma_+ - \sigma_-$.

4. Rates and cross-sections

The probability for the reaction $\alpha \to \beta$ is

$$P(\alpha \to \beta) \;=\; |S_{\beta\alpha}|^2$$

But S is of the form

$$S = 1 + (2\pi)^4 \, i \, \delta^4(P_\beta - P_\alpha)\mathcal{M}$$

where 1 corresponds to the possibility of no interaction. The remaining piece is imaginary and singular. We know that any reasonable way of calculating transitions will give energy momentum conservation so we write it in the form above. In the next section we shall see that this is indeed justified. In finding P, we ignore the 1. But we still get $(\delta^4(P_\beta P_\alpha))^2$ which needs interpreting. Roughly speaking, since we have two δ's of the same argument, one of them is '$\delta(0)$'. Consider

$$\delta^4\left(\sum_i p_i\right)\Big|_{\sum p=0} = \frac{1}{(2\pi)^4} \int d^4x \, e^{-ix(\sum p_i)}\Big|_{\sum p=0} = \frac{1}{(2\pi)^4} \int d^4x$$

So it will be interpreted as the total spacetime volume. But this is infinite. We have to start in a box of finite volume and then let $V \to \infty$ after making sure it cancels.

In a box, states are normalized differently

$$\langle \vec{p_1}, \sigma_1 | \vec{p_2}, \sigma_2 \rangle = \delta^3(\vec{p_1}, \vec{p_2})\delta_{\sigma_1\sigma_2}$$

While

$$\langle \vec{p_1}, \sigma_1 | \vec{p_2}, \sigma_2 \rangle^{\text{box}} = \delta_{\vec{p_1},\vec{p_2}}\delta_{\sigma_1\sigma_2}$$

Since

$$\int d^3p \;\overset{\text{box}}{\longrightarrow}\; \frac{(2\pi)^3}{V} \sum_{\vec{p}},$$

the corresponding

$$\delta^3(\vec{p}_1, \vec{p}_2) \xrightarrow{\text{box}} \frac{V}{(2\pi)^3} \delta_{\vec{p}_1, \vec{p}_2}$$

Thus

$$\langle \vec{p}_1 | \vec{p}_2 \rangle^{\text{box}} = [\frac{V}{(2\pi)^3}]^{-1} \langle \vec{p}_1 | \vec{p}_2 \rangle$$

So

$$S_{\beta\alpha}^{\text{box}} = [\frac{V}{(2\pi)^3}]^{-(N_\alpha + N_\beta)/2} S_{\beta\alpha}$$

Where N_α, N_β are numbers of particles in the two states.

Also, we calculate the differential

$$P\, d\beta \qquad \text{where} \qquad d\beta \equiv \prod_i^{N_\beta} d^3 p_i$$

which in the box is

$$d\beta^{\text{box}} = [\frac{V}{(2\pi)^3}]^{N_\beta} d\beta$$

So if we first do everything in a box and re-express in the continuum language,

$$P(\alpha \to \beta) d\beta = (2\pi)^4 \, \delta^4(\sum p_\beta - \sum p_\alpha) VT |\mathcal{M}_{\beta\alpha}|^2 [\frac{V}{(2\pi)^3}]^{-(N_\alpha + N_\beta)}$$
$$\times [\frac{V}{(2\pi)^3}]^{N_\beta} d\beta$$

Where VT represents the (4-dim) box volume. Hence the rate

$$d\Gamma(\alpha \to \beta) = (2\pi)^4 \delta^4(\sum p_\beta - \sum p_\alpha) V [\frac{V}{(2\pi)^3}]^{-N_\alpha}$$
$$|\mathcal{M}_{\beta\alpha}|^2 \, d\beta$$

N_α is usually 1 or 2. 3 is difficult to arrange and rare in nature. For single particle decay, we calculate rate

$$d\Gamma(\alpha \to \beta) = (2\pi)^4 \delta^4(\sum p_\beta - p_\alpha) \times (2\pi)^3 |\mathcal{M}_{\beta\alpha}|^2 d\beta$$

For a collision, we calculate rate per unit flux, also known as the differential cross-section. This gets rid of the extra V. The flux is $\Phi_\alpha \propto u_\alpha/V$ where u_α is relative speed of the particles. For a fixed target experiment, $u_\alpha = u_{\text{incident}}$. Then

$$d\sigma(\alpha \to \beta) = \frac{d\Gamma}{\Phi_\alpha}$$
$$= (2\pi)^4 \delta^4(\sum p_\beta - \sum p_\alpha)(2\pi)^6 \frac{|\mathcal{M}_{\alpha\beta}|^2}{u_\alpha} d\beta$$

The cross-section can be cast in a manifestly Lorentz invariant form, a demonstration we shall skip. It may also be noted that the normalisation $\langle \vec{p} | \vec{p}' \rangle = \delta^3(\vec{p}, \vec{p}')$ is not Lorentz invariant. Some authors prefer $\langle \vec{p} | \vec{p}' \rangle = (2\pi)^3 2p^0 \delta^3(\vec{p}, \vec{p}')$. With corresponding changes in $d\beta$ and flux expressions, final answer should remain the same. We now need a method for calculating $\mathcal{M}$.

5. Perturbation expansion and the Feynman rules (examples of Yukawa theory)

5.1. EVALUATING MATRIX ELEMENTS

To calculate $\mathcal{M}_{\alpha\beta}$, we need to evaluate things like

$$\int d^4x_1 d^4x_2 \langle 0| \prod_\beta a_\beta T\{: \mathcal{H}_I(x_1) :: \mathcal{H}_I(x_2) :\} \prod_\alpha a_\alpha^\dagger |0\rangle$$

We shall do this in a specific example and see the general rules. Consider

$$\mathcal{L} = \frac{1}{2}\partial_\mu\phi\partial^\mu\phi - \frac{1}{2}m^2\phi^2 + \bar{\psi}(i\not{\partial} - M)\psi - g\phi\bar{\psi}\psi$$

So

$$H_0 = \frac{1}{2}(\dot{\phi}^2 + |\vec{\nabla}\phi|^2 + m^2\phi^2) + \bar{\psi}(i\gamma^0\dot{\psi} + i\gamma^i\nabla_i\psi + M\psi)$$

and

$$V = g\phi\bar{\psi}\psi$$

In this theory a scalar can emit fermion-antifermion pair. Alternatively, a fermion (or antifermion) can emit a scalar and continue as a fermion (or antifermion). When the emitted scalar is absorbed by another fermion, there is an effective interaction between the two fermions. This is a simplified version of the Yukawa theory of nucleonic forces.

We need V in the interaction picture, *i.e.*, as a functional,

$$V_I = V[\phi_I, \psi_I, \bar{\psi}_I]$$

But the ϕ_I, ψ_I undergo evolution through H_0 so their mode expansion is identical to the free field expansion

$$\phi_I(\vec{x}, t) = \int \frac{d^3k}{(2\pi)^{3/2}} \{a_{\vec{k}} \frac{e^{-ikx}}{\sqrt{2w_k}} + a_{\vec{k}}^\dagger \frac{e^{ikx}}{\sqrt{2w_k}}\}$$

$$\psi_I(x) = \int \frac{d^3k}{(2\pi)^{3/2}} \sum_\sigma \{b_{\vec{k},\sigma} u(\vec{k}, \sigma)e^{-ikx} + c_{\vec{k},\sigma}^\dagger v(\vec{k}, \sigma)e^{ikx}\}$$

This is the advantage of the interaction picture. Consider evaluating the second order term

$$\frac{(-i)^2 g^2}{2} \int d^4 x_1 d^4 x_2 T\{: \phi(x_1)\bar{\psi}(x_1)\psi(x_1) :: \phi(x_2)\bar{\psi}(x_2)\psi(x_2) :\}$$

between the states $|\vec{p}; (\vec{k}, \frac{1}{2})\rangle$ and $|\vec{p}'; (\vec{k}, \frac{1}{2})\rangle$ where $\vec{p}$ refers to ϕ and $\vec{k}$ to the spinor, created by $b^\dagger_{\vec{k},\sigma}$. (To distinguish the antiparticle created by $c^\dagger_{\vec{k},\sigma}$ we need further notation, but we don't need it for the present example). For evaluating

$$\langle 0 | a_{\vec{p}'} b_{\vec{k}, \frac{1}{2}} T\{: \phi(x_1)\bar{\psi}(x_1)\psi(x_1) :: \phi(x_2)\bar{\psi}(x_2)\psi(x_2) :\} a^\dagger_{\vec{p}} b^\dagger_{\vec{k} \frac{1}{2}} | 0 \rangle$$

the strategy is to take all destruction operators towards the right so that when they reach $|0\rangle$ they give zero, but along the way generate c-numbers from commutators or anticommutators. This process by which two field operators are made to yield a c-number is referred to as the contraction between the two. The fact that each $\mathcal{H}_I$ term is normal ordered prevents contractions within the same $\mathcal{H}_I$. A general formula giving the vacuum expectation value of the time ordered product of normal ordered expressions in terms of c-number functions and delta-functions is the content of Wick's theorem. Our example will provide a specific case of the general result, and will also demonstrate how the latter is proved.

The contractions of the ϕ's are independent of those of ψ's and vice versa so we can consider each case separately. We introduce the shorthand notation $\phi_1 \equiv \phi(x_1)$ and denote by ϕ^{des} and ϕ^{cr} the parts of ϕ containing the destruction operators and the creation operators respectively.

$$\langle 0 | a_{\vec{p}'} T\{\phi(x_1)\phi(x_2)\} a^\dagger_{\vec{p}} | 0 \rangle$$

$$= \theta(t_1 - t_2)\langle 0 | a_{\vec{p}'} (\phi_1^{\mathrm{des}} + \phi_1^{\mathrm{cr}})(\phi_2^{\mathrm{des}} + \phi_2^{\mathrm{cr}}) a^\dagger_{\vec{p}} | 0 \rangle$$

$$+ \theta(t_2 - t_1)\langle 0 | a_{\vec{p}'} (\phi_2^{\mathrm{des}} + \phi_2^{\mathrm{cr}})(\phi_1^{\mathrm{des}} + \phi_1^{\mathrm{cr}}) a^\dagger_{\vec{p}} | 0 \rangle$$

$$= \theta(t_1 - t_2)\{\langle 0 | a_{\vec{p}'} \phi_1^{\mathrm{des}} \phi_2^{\mathrm{cr}} a^\dagger_{\vec{p}} | 0 \rangle + \langle 0 | a_{\vec{p}'} \phi_1^{\mathrm{cr}} \phi_2^{\mathrm{des}} a^\dagger_{\vec{p}} | 0 \rangle\}$$

$$+ \theta(t_2 - t_1)\{\langle 0 | a_{\vec{p}'} \phi_2^{\mathrm{des}} \phi_1^{\mathrm{cr}} a^\dagger_{\vec{p}} | 0 \rangle + \langle 0 | a_{\vec{p}'} \phi_2^{\mathrm{cr}} \phi_1^{\mathrm{des}} a^\dagger_{\vec{p}} | 0 \rangle\}$$

$$= \langle 0 | a_{\vec{p}'} \phi_1^{\mathrm{cr}} \phi_2^{\mathrm{des}} a^\dagger_{\vec{p}} | 0 \rangle + \langle 0 | a_{\vec{p}'} \phi_2^{\mathrm{cr}} \phi_1^{\mathrm{des}} a^\dagger_{\vec{p}} | 0 \rangle$$

$$+ \langle 0 | a_{\vec{p}'} a^\dagger_{\vec{p}} | 0 \rangle \{\theta(t_1 - t_2)[\phi_1^{\mathrm{des}}, \phi_2^{\mathrm{cr}}] + \theta(t_2 - t_1)[\phi_2^{\mathrm{des}}, \phi_1^{\mathrm{cr}}]\}$$

$$= [a_{\vec{p}'}, \phi_1^{\mathrm{cr}}][\phi_2^{\mathrm{des}}, a^\dagger_{\vec{p}}] + [a_{\vec{p}'}, \phi_2^{\mathrm{cr}}][\phi_1^{\mathrm{des}}, a^\dagger_{\vec{p}}] + \delta_{\vec{p}, \vec{p}'} \langle 0 | T\{\phi(x_1)\phi(x_2)\} | 0 \rangle$$

Diagrammatically, this can be written as

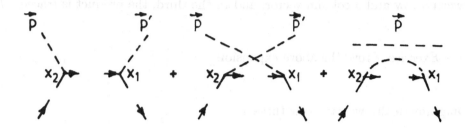

Here each dashed line represents a factor from the preceeding line. The incomplete pieces of solid line represent uncontracted fermionic parts and can be ignored for the moment.   A factor such as $[\phi_2^{\text{des}}, a_{\vec{p}}^\dagger]$ represents an *incoming* scalar disappearing at vertex. It has the value $\exp(-ipx)/(2\pi)^{3/2}\sqrt{2\omega_2}$. Similarly the *outgoing* lines, whose value can also be easily found. In addition we have the expression

$$\langle 0|T\{\phi(x_1)\phi(x_2)\}|0\rangle$$

represented by a line originating at a vertex and terminating at another. This *internal* line is the famous Feynman propagator, first proposed by E. C. G. Stueckelberg. Its value we shall record later. It can be shown that this expression is a Green function of the Klein-Gordon equation with mixed boundary conditions – it propagates positive frequency mode functions $\sim \exp(-i\omega t)$ forward in time and negative frequency mode functions $\sim \exp(+i\omega t)$ *backward* in time. In the old wavefunction interpretation negative frquency solutions meant negative *energy* particles. By resorting to Dirac's hole theory (for fermions) Feynman guessed that negative frequency solutions needed to be propagated backward in time. He also argued that a theory which permitted pair creation needed such a propagator for consistency. The systematic derivation given here (sec. 4.3 and present) is due to Dyson and Wick.

– *Exercise*: Prove by direct computation that the propagator above is given by the expression listed in the Feynman rules (sec. 5.2) below.

For each of the bosonic terms obtained above, there are three possiblities for fermions

$$\{b_{\vec{k}'\frac{1}{2}}, \bar{\psi}_1^{\text{cr}}\}\langle 0|T\{\psi(x_1)\bar{\psi}(x_2)\}|0\rangle\{\psi_2^{\text{des}}, b_{\vec{k}\frac{1}{2}}^\dagger\}$$

$$+\{b_{\vec{k}'\frac{1}{2}}, \bar{\psi}_2^{\text{cr}}\}\langle 0|T\{\psi(x_2)\bar{\psi}(x_1)\}|0\rangle\{\psi_1^{\text{des}}, b_{\vec{k}\frac{1}{2}}^\dagger\}$$

$$+\{b_{\vec{k}'\frac{1}{2}}, b_{\vec{k}\frac{1}{2}}^\dagger\}\text{Tr}\left[\langle 0|T\{\psi(x_2)\bar{\psi}(x_1)\}|0\rangle\langle 0|T\{\psi(x_1)\bar{\psi}(x_2)\}|0\rangle\right]$$

Here the vacuum expectation value expressions are matrix expressions for the fermionic propagator. In the first two terms these are sandwitched between a row and a column vector, and in the third, the product is traced.

— *Exercise*: Prove the above expansion.

Diagramatically we can show these as

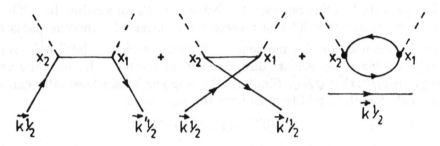

Putting together the bosonic and the fermionic calculations, we get the following nine diagrams.

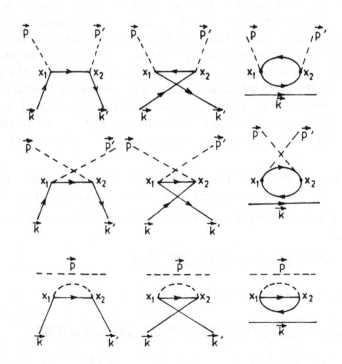

5.2. FEYNMAN RULES

To obtain the term corresponding to a given diagram, we have to assign the following factors to each kind of line.

	incoming boson	$\dfrac{1}{2\pi^{3/2}}\dfrac{e^{-ip\cdot z}}{\sqrt{2\omega_p}}$
	outgoing boson	$\dfrac{1}{2\pi^{3/2}}\dfrac{e^{ip'\cdot z}}{\sqrt{2\omega_p'}}$
	incoming electron	$u(\vec{k},\sigma)\dfrac{e^{-ik\cdot z}}{2\pi^{3/2}}$
	outgoing electron	$\bar{u}(\vec{k}',\sigma)\dfrac{e^{ik'\cdot z}}{2\pi^{3/2}}$
	electron propagator	$i\displaystyle\int\dfrac{d^4q}{(2\pi)^4}e^{-iq(z_1-z_2)}\dfrac{q_\mu\gamma^\mu+M}{q^2-M^2+i\epsilon}$

Other factors not appearing in the present example are

	incoming positron	$\dfrac{\bar{v}(\vec{k},\sigma)e^{-ik\cdot z}}{2\pi^{3/2}}$
	outgoing positron	$v(\vec{k}',\sigma)\dfrac{e^{ik'\cdot z}}{2\pi^{3/2}}$
	boson propagator	$i\displaystyle\int\dfrac{d^4q}{(2\pi)^4}\dfrac{e^{-iq(z_1-z_2)}}{q^2-M^2+i\epsilon}$

In our example we can see that some of the diagrams contain distinct pieces not connected to each other. They are called *disconnected* diagrams. In practice, one does not draw all the diagrams including the disconnected ones, but only the connected ones. This is because the subdiagrams of a disconnected diagram either correspond to particles that undergo no interaction and hence are discarded along with the "$\delta_{\alpha\beta}$" in $S_{\alpha\beta}$, or they are diagrams corresponding to a different scattering process than the one under consideration and are also perhaps of some other order in the perturbative expansion. Also, note several diagrams get repeated, drawn differently. This results from taking all vertices in all possible orders. We need to draw only one representative diagram. The repetition cancles the $\frac{1}{n!}$ in front.

<u>Momentum space rules:</u> For a given connected diagram in x-space, we have $\int d^4x$ for every $\mathcal{H}(x)$. Once every external line has been replaced by the wavefunction factor and internal line with a propagator, the d^4x integrals can all be trivially carried out. At a vertex with two external and two internal lines, such as that in the diagram below, we get

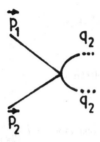

$$\int d^4x_1 e^{-ip_1 \cdot x_1} e^{-ip_2 \cdot x_1} \times \int \frac{d^4q_1}{(2\pi)^4} \frac{e^{-iq_1(x_1-x_r)}}{q_1^2 - m^2 + i\epsilon} \times \int \frac{d^4q_2}{(2\pi)^4} \frac{e^{-iq_2(x_1-x_s)}}{q_2^2 - m^2 + i\epsilon}$$

Here x_r, x_s are locations of some other vertices and we have not displayed factors or spinors which do not involve x_i. This gives

$$\int \frac{d^4q_1}{(2\pi)^4} \frac{d^4q_2}{(2\pi)^4} (2\pi)^4 \delta^4 (p_1 + p_2 + q_1 + q_2) \times \frac{1}{q_1^2 - m^2 + i\epsilon} \times \frac{1}{q_2^2 - m^2 + i\epsilon}$$

Thus the d^4x at every vertex simply gives conservation of energy momentum flowing through that vertex.

The equivalent *momentum space* rules then say that

1. For external lines leave out factors $e^{ip \cdot x}$ of coordinate space rules.
2. Leave out $e^{iq \cdot x}$ in propagators
3. Put four-momentum conserving δ^4 at every vertex and leave out the $\int d^4x$ operations.
4. Integrate over all internal momenta.

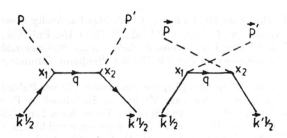

It is easy to check that in doing 4, one always picks up an overall $\delta^4(\sum_\beta p - \sum_\alpha p)$ balancing the total incoming and outgoing four momentum. This δ^4 is the one we extracted in anticipation while defining $\mathcal{M}_{\beta\alpha}$. $\mathcal{M}_{\beta\alpha}$ is then obtained after integrating the remaining internal momenta.

We can now return to our example and illustrate these comments. Firstly we ignore the disconnected diagrams. Of the remaining, there are two distinct diagrams, each of which appears twice. They are shown above. Leaving out $1/2!$, we get for the diagram on the left

$$(-i\,g)^2 \int d^4x_1 \int d^4x_2 \frac{e^{-ip\cdot x_1}}{(2\pi)^{\frac{3}{2}}\sqrt{2wp}} \frac{u(\vec{k},\tfrac{1}{2})e^{-ik\cdot x_1}}{(2\pi)^{\frac{3}{2}}}$$

$$\times i \int \frac{d^4q}{(2\pi)^4} e^{-iq(x_1-x_2)} \frac{q_\mu\gamma^\mu + M}{q^2 - M^2 + i\epsilon} \times \frac{e^{ip'\cdot x_2}}{(2\pi)^{\frac{3}{2}}\sqrt{2wp'}} \frac{\bar{u}(\vec{k}',\tfrac{1}{2})e^{-ik'\cdot x_2}}{(2\pi)^{\frac{3}{2}}}$$

$$= \frac{(-ig)^2(i)}{(2\pi)^6} \int \frac{d^4q}{(2\pi)^4} (2\pi)^4\delta^4(p+k+q)(2\pi)^4\delta^4(p'+k'+q)$$

$$\times \frac{\bar{u}(\vec{k}',\tfrac{1}{2})(q_\mu\gamma^\mu + M)u(\vec{k},\tfrac{1}{2})}{\sqrt{2\omega'_p}\sqrt{2\omega_p}(q^2 - M^2 + i\epsilon)}$$

$$= i(2\pi)^4\delta^4(p+k-p'-k') \times \frac{(ig)^2}{(2\pi)^6} \frac{\bar{u}(\vec{k}',\tfrac{1}{2})(\gamma^\mu(p_\mu + k_\mu) + M)u(\vec{k},\tfrac{1}{2})}{2\sqrt{\omega'_p\omega_p}((p+k)^2 - M^2 + i\epsilon)}$$

From this, one contribution $\mathcal{M}^{(1)}_{\beta\alpha}$ to $\mathcal{M}$ can be read off. The second contribution $\mathcal{M}^{(2)}_{\beta\alpha}$ comes from the diagram on the right. We can see that it can be easily obtained from $\mathcal{M}^{(1)}$ by interchanging p with p' but leaving k and k' where they are. There remains now the rather forbidding task of obtaining $|\mathcal{M}^{(1)} + \mathcal{M}^{(2)}|^2$, which also involves taking traces of products of Dirac matrices. We shall not take this up here.

References

1. Ryder L. H., *Quantum Field Theory*, Cambridge University Press, (1985)
2. Schiff L. I., *Quantum Mechanics*, 3rd Ed., McGraw-Hill Pub. Co., (1968)
3. Itzytkson C. and Zuber J-B., *Quantum Field Theory*, McGraw-Hill Pub. Co., (1980)
4. Georgi H., *Lie Algebras for Particle Physics*, Benjamin-Cummings Publishing Co., (1982)
5. Cartan E., *Theory of Spinors* (English translation), Dover Publishers
6. Pauli W., *Principles of Quantum Mechanics*, Translated by P. Achuthan and K. Venkatesan, Allied Publishers and Springer-Verlag India Ltd., (1980)
7. Wentzel G., *Quantum Theory of Fields*, Interscience Publishers, (1949)
8. Weinberg S., *Phys. Rev.* **133**, 1318 (1964); **134**, 882 (1964).
9. Lee T. D., *Particle Physics and Introduction to Field Theory*, Harwood Academic Publishers, (1982)
10. Lurié D., *Particles and Fields*, Interscience Publishers, (1968)

For Lie Group theory refer also to the recently published lectures:

11. N. Mukunda in *Introduction to Topologfy, Differential Geometry and Group Theory for Physicists* by S. Mukhi and N. Mukunda, Wiley Eastern Ltd., (1990)

7. RELATIVISTIC COSMOLOGY

J.V.NARLIKAR

Inter-University Center for Astronomy & Astrophysics
Post Bag 4, Ganeshkhind
Pune 411 007, India

The subject of cosmology is an admixture of imaginative ideas, intuitive predictions and hard scientific facts. This has made cosmology a case of three distinct cultures; that of astronomers, who look at the universe and find hard data, relativists – who build models of universe that range from simple to esoteric ones, and the particle physicists who can test their theories of very high energy physics only in the cosmic laboratory that was there at the very onset of the universe. This culture can well be compared with the British culture, where one has three classes: the working class, the professionals and the aristrocrats.

This course will try to give certain glimpses of cosmology in these three fields.

1. Large Scale Structure of the Universe

1.1. DISTANCE SCALE

We progressively increase our distance scale as we look into distant objects and there are several orders of magnitude involved in this increment. A few typical steps on the cosmic distance ladder are:

    a) Sun's radius : 7×10^{10} cms.
    b) Interstellar distance : 3×10^{18} cms.
    c) Diameter of the Galaxy (Milky way) : 10^{23} cms.
    d) Intergalactic distance : 10^{24} cms.
    e) Size of a cluster : 10^{25} cms.
    f) Size of a supercluster : 10^{26} cms.
    g) The Hubble Radius : 10^{28} cms.

The physics may vary from one distance scale to another.

1.2. DISCRETE SOURCES

Looking at the distribution of the discrete sources certain evidence of in-homogenity can be observed. Thus galaxies are clumped in hierarchical structures like groups, clusters, superclusters, etc. In the late 80's on anal-ysis of the deep sky surveys it was found that if we divide the space in lattice-like structures there are regions devoid of galaxies whose sizes often extended upto the volumes of superclusters. These empty regions are called "voids".

So, it is found that matter was not distributed evenly, at least, at the distance scale of superclusters and there is a certain degree of 'clumpiness' involved in the matter distribution.

1.3. RADIATION BACKGROUNDS

Other than matter there is yet another component in this universe which can tell us about the origin and the evolution of the large scale structure of the universe, and that is radiation.

The electro-magnetic radiation comes in a wide spectrum whose forms in a descending order of their wavelengths are: radio, microwave, infra-red, optical, ultra-violet, x-rays and gamma rays. In all of these wavelength ranges it has been possible to observe a diffuse background, which may or may not be traceable to particular discrete sources of energy. Considering the observed energy densities of this diffuse background radiation in the above different ranges,

Radio	$\rightarrow$	$10^{-18}\text{erg cm}^{-3}$
Microwave	$\rightarrow$	$4 \times 10^{-13}\text{erg cm}^{-3}$
Infra-red	$\rightarrow$	$4 \times 10^{-14}\text{erg cm}^{-3}$
Optical	$\rightarrow$	$3.5 \times 10^{-15}\text{erg cm}^{-3}$
Ultra-voilet	$\rightarrow$	$10^{-17}\text{erg cm}^{-3}$
X-rays	$\rightarrow$	$10^{-16}\text{erg cm}^{-3}$
Gamma rays	$\leq$	$2 \times 10^{-17}\text{erg cm}^{-3}$

We find the dominant part that stands out from the rest is in microwaves.

Unlike the distribution of matter density, the background radiation is quite homogenous, reaching its peak in the microwave region. Many ob-servations were made to look for patchiness over varying angular scales of this microwave background. However, its temperature was found to have a smoothness of the order of $\frac{\Delta T}{T} < \alpha \times 10^{-5}$ where, $1 \leq \alpha \leq 10$ over $\theta \leq 30'$. This statement depends upon wavelength and the above estimate is an upper limit on the inhomogeneity of the microwave background.

If we make an overall survey of the cosmic microwave backgound radiation then it can be found that as measured from the rest frame of the solar
system it does not have a perfect spherical symmetry : a small amount
of dipole anisotropy can be observed. This dipole anisotropy helps us to
understand the kinematics of our Galaxy and the local group of galaxies.
It was calculated that our Galaxy is moving in a specific direction with a
velocity of $550 - 600$ kms^{-1} relative to the radiation background.

1.4. HUBBLE'S LAW

In 1929 Edwin Hubble observed the distance and the velocity of recession
(from redshifts) of different galaxies and gave a relation between the speeds
of recession (v) and the inter-galactic distances (D):

$$cz = v = H_0 D. \tag{1}$$

Here redshift is the quantity which the astronomers really measure, its mag-
nitude z being given by the formula $z = \Delta\lambda/\lambda$ where $\Delta\lambda$ is the observed
increase over the 'rest' wavelength λ. (See Fig. 1). Distance can be calculated by measuring the apparent brightness. Hubble and Humason first
found this type of relation and gave the value of H_0 as 530 kms^{-1}. Mpc^{-1},

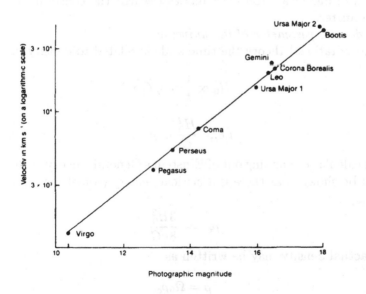

Figure 1. The velocity distance relation obtained by Hubble in 1929

(i) *Magnitude of H_0* : These measurements turned out to be overestimates. Now, many later researchers have tried to calculate the Hubble constant, H_0, and have come up with different answers, due to the uncertainity in determining the actual distance of the galaxies.
Tammann and Sandage have taken a sample of relatively nearby galaxies and given the value of H_0 as 50 kms^{-1}Mpc^{-1} while Van den Bergh and de Vaucoueulrs have calculated the value as 100 kms^{-1}Mpc^{-1} for a more distant sample. This divergence reflects the continuing uncertainty of estimates of extragalactic distances. So, at present the value of the Hubble constant is denoted by $H_0 = 100$kms^{-1}Mpc$^{-1} \times h_0$. where h_0 is a scale factor, $\frac{1}{2} \leq h_0 \leq 1$.

(ii) *The Rubin-Ford Effect* : In 1975, Rubin and Ford found that there is a dipole anisotropy in the above Hubble velocity flow. They showed that instead of observing the galaxies from a cosmological rest frame we are moving with a velocity of around 500 kms^{-1} in a specified direction relative to that frame. However, there is a discrepancy still present; the anisotropy of the Hubble flow does not seem to match the anisotropy in the cosmic microwave background either in magnitude or in direction.

(iii) *The inhomogenity of H_0* : It was observed that H_0 (h_0) tends to increase with local distance. Calculated with respect to the local group of galaxies it gives the value of $h_0 \simeq \frac{1}{2}$. But, when we look beyond, the value of h_0 tends to unity. This can be explained by a peculiar motion of our local group of galaxies towards the centre of the Virgo Supercluster.

(iv) *The density parameter of the universe*
In a gravitational theory the time scale is related to density ρ,

$$H_0 \propto \frac{1}{t} \propto \sqrt{G\rho}$$

$$\text{i.e.,} \quad \frac{H_0^2}{G} \propto \rho \quad . \tag{2}$$

From calculations arising out of Einstein's General Theory of Relativity it can be shown that there is a critical density (sometimes ρ_c is called $\rho_{closure}$)

$$\rho_c = \frac{3H_0^2}{8\pi G}. \tag{3}$$

The actual density may be written as

$$\rho = \Omega_0 \rho_c, \tag{4}$$

where Ω_0, the density parameter is a dimensionless quantity, whose value depends, theoretically upon the model we choose for the universe.

Observationally we may try to compare the actual density with the theoretically predicted value. Estimates of luminous matter density in the universe tell us that $\Omega_0 \leq 0.2$. Further, also taking into consideration the motion of matter relative to the cosmological rest frame we get $\Omega_0 \leq 0.12$.

(v) *Dark matter* : It seems that ρ_{actual} may not be equal to $\rho_{\text{luminous matter}}$. Dynamical considerations of 'bound' objects indicate the presence of gravitating, nonluminous matter the so called dark matter.

The presence of dark matter is indicated by the flat rotation curves obtained for galaxies. A rotation curve is the plot of the radial velocity and the radial distance of a test particle in the gravitational potential of a galaxy. Considering our galaxy, which is thought to be spiral shaped, it can be shown by simple Keplerian dynamics that

$$v = \sqrt{\frac{GM}{R}} \propto \frac{1}{\sqrt{R}}. \tag{5}$$

But considering the motion of the hydrogen clouds which are the 'test particles' over here, we find that instead of the velocity dropping after reaching a maximum, it attains a constant value as we go further away from the galaxy (See Fig 2). This flat rotation curve extends far beyond the luminous extent of the galaxy.

The question of dark matter also arises when we consider the galaxy cluster velocities. If we consider the thermodynamics of the cluster and take its kinetic energy as $T = \sum \frac{1}{2} m_i v_i^2$, and potential energy as; $\Phi = - \sum_{i, j} \frac{m_i m_j}{r_{ij}}$, then by the Virial Theorem we expect to find

$$2T + \Phi = 0. \tag{6}$$

Actually, the velocities come out to be higher than allowed by (6). This suggests that the potential energy must be higher than that computed for luminous systems thereby indicating presence of unaccounted mass. Theoreticians have said that the value of Ω_0 can go as high as unity, but they could not succeed in explaining the result by this effect alone.

2. Models of the Universe

2.1. WEYL'S POSTULATE

Considering the non-static models of the universe, we can come up with two situations, first where the world lines of galaxies criss-cross each other in a haphazard manner (See Fig. 3a) wherein there is no order and where two world lines intersect we have colliding galaxies and large random motions.

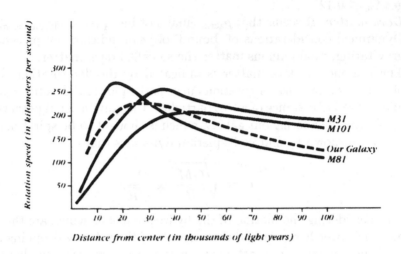

The Arms and the Nucleus

Figure 2.   The flat rotation curves of a few galaxies

Thus, finding a mathematically consistent model of the universe becomes very complex. Thanks to the finding of Hubble (where he made the observation that every galaxy is moving radially apart from all others) the world lines of galaxies are nearly well ordered (See Fig. 3b). Each line can be specified by 3 parameters x^μ, $\mu = 1, 2, 3$. Expressed in a mathematical language, this result is better known as Weyl's postulate:

"The world lines of galaxies form a 3-bundle of non-intersecting geodesics orthogonal to a series of spacelike hypersurfaces".

Thus, $x^o = constant$ is a typical spacelike hypersurface orthogonal to a typical world line given by: $x^\mu = $ constant. It may happen that all the conditions of the Weyl postulate are true for the universe except that of orthogonality in the case of a spinning universe.

Let the metric in this case be given by the tensor g_{ik}. The orthogonality condition tells us

$$g_{0\mu} = 0.$$

Now, $x^\mu = $ constant is a geodesic. Therefore we expect that the geodesic equations

$$\frac{d^2 x^i}{ds^2} + \Gamma^i_{kl} \frac{dx^k}{ds} \frac{dx^l}{ds} = 0 \tag{7}$$

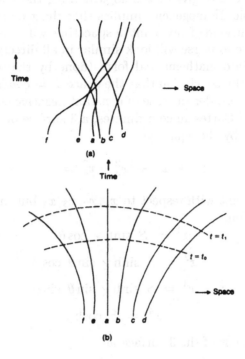

Figure 3. (a) An example of highly random motion. The worldlines criss-cross, interact and change directions arbitrarily.
(b) In contrast to (a) here the motion is streamlined.

are satisfied for x^μ = constant. This implies

$$\Gamma^\mu_{0\,0} = 0. \qquad \mu = 1, 2, 3,$$

$$i.e., \quad \frac{\partial g_{00}}{\partial x^\mu} = 0, \qquad g_{00} = f(x^0). \tag{8}$$

By a suitable transformation we can make $g_{00} = 1$, so that line element will become:

$$\begin{aligned} ds^2 &= (dx^0)^2 + g_{\mu\nu} dx^\mu dx^\nu. \\ &= c^2\, dt^2 + g_{\mu\nu}\, dx^\mu dx^\nu \end{aligned} \tag{9}$$

It is easily seen that the spacelike hypersurfaces in Weyl's postulate are the surfaces of simultaneity with respect to the cosmic time, $t = x^0/c$.

2.2. THE COSMOLOGICAL PRINCIPLE

Now, for doing a further simplification in deriving a model for the universe, we take help of another assumption, called the Cosmological Principle;

which says that, at any given cosmological time, the universe is homogeneous and isotropic. Homogeneity implies that the geometrical property of the local neighbourhood of any point in spacetime will look similar whereas, isotropy means the universe will look similar in all directions at any point. Translating this into mathematical form (done by the method of Killing Vectors) leads to the conclusion that the space $t = constant$ has constant curvature. Let us consider the case of constant negative curvature as an example. In terms of Cartesian co-ordinates, a 3 surface of constant negative curvature is given by the equation.

$$x_1^2 + x_2^2 + x_3^2 - x_4^2 = S^2$$

where S is a constant with respect to x_1, x_2, x_3, x_4 but may depend on t.

The substitution,

$$x^1 = S \sinh \chi \, \cos \theta$$

$$x^2 = S \sinh \chi \, \sin \theta \, \cos \phi$$

$$x^3 = S \sinh \chi \, \sin \theta \, \sin \phi$$

$$x^4 = S \cosh \chi$$

gives the line element of the 3-surface as

$$d\sigma^2 = S^2 \left[\frac{dr^2}{1 + r^2} + r^2 (d\theta^2 + \sin^2 \theta d\phi^2) \right]. \qquad (10)$$

The cases of zero or constant positive curvature can be introduced in this equation by rewriting as:

$$d\sigma^2 = S^2 \left[\frac{dr^2}{1 - kr^2} + r^2 (d\theta^2 + \sin^2 \theta d\phi^2) \right]$$

where k = 0 implies zero curvature,

k = 1 implies (+ve) curvature,

k = −1 implies (−ve) curvature.

Thus the line element for spacetime becomes

$$ds^2 = c^2 dt^2 - S^2 \left[\frac{dr^2}{1 - kr^2} + r^2 (d\theta^2 + \sin^2 \theta d\phi^2) \right]. \qquad (11)$$

$S(t)$ gives us curvature as a function of time. This line element is known as the Robertson – Walker line element as it was discovered independently by H. P. Robertson and A. G. Walker.

If the homogenity exists both in space and time; the Cosmological Principle becomes 'perfect' and time-like Killing motions are also included and we then deal with a more restricted type of model, which uses the de Sitter metric.

The steady state cosmology came from the Perfect Cosmological Priciple (PCP). Its line element is

$$ds^2 = c^2 dt^2 - e^{2Hot}\left[dr^2 + r^2(d\theta^2 + \sin^2\theta d\phi^2)\right], \qquad (12)$$

Thus the PCP tells us the full line element purely from the symmetry considerations.

2.3. THE ENERGY TENSOR

The Weyl postulate and the cosmological principle do not tell us about the rate of expansion of the universe given by the quantity $S(t)$; at the same time they also fail to answer our question about wheather the 3-space is closed or open. To deal with this problem we need a dynamical theory, such as given by Einstein's General relativity.

Considering Einstein's questions:

$$R_k^i - \frac{1}{2} g_k^i R = -\kappa T_k^i \quad \text{where} \quad \kappa = \frac{8\pi G}{c^4} \qquad (13)$$

and the Robertson – Walker line element:

$$ds^2 = c^2 dt^2 - S^2(t)\left[\frac{dr^2}{1 - kr^2} + r^2(d\theta^2 + \sin^2\theta d\phi^2)\right]$$

we can get two sets of equations:

$$\frac{2\ddot{S}}{S} + \frac{\dot{S}^2 + kc^2}{S^2} = -\frac{8\pi G}{c^4} T_1^1 \qquad (14)$$

$$\text{and,} \quad \frac{\dot{S}^2 + kc^2}{S^2} = \frac{8\pi G}{3c^4} T_0^0 \qquad (15)$$

The same equation (14) holds if T_1^1 is replaced by T_2^2 or T_3^3. Thus we write

$$T_1^1 = T_2^2 = T_3^3 = -p \text{ (pressure)},$$

$$\text{and } T_0^0 = u \text{ (energy density)}; \qquad (16)$$

and ultimately we can arrive at the equation, $T_{k;i}^i = 0$, i.e.,

$$\frac{d}{dS}(uS^3) + 3pS^2 = 0. \qquad (17)$$

This is the conservation equation for matter/energy. We next consider two cases of (16).

(i) *Dust approximation*: The Weyl postulate debars the galaxies from having a random motion, and then we would have a typical velocity vector
of a galaxy given by:

$$u^i = (1,0,0,0).$$ (18)

In a smooth dust approximation a velocity field like the above represents an orderly motion with no pressure. Thus, we have in this case
the system of galaxies behaving like dust, with $p = 0$, $u = \rho c^2$.
In reality practice, galaxies do not follow Weyl's postulate strictly, and
the velocity vector does not behave as given by equation (18). The
typical velocity for galaxies in clusters are found to be of the order of
≤ 1000 kms^{-1}. Considering this departure from streamlined motion,
we would arrive at a non-zero value of 'p' of the order of

$$p = \frac{v^2}{c^2}u \simeq 10^{-5}\,u$$

Thus, it is quite justified if we ignore the 'p' term in the present epoch,
in comparison with u.
From the energy conservation principle, we can write,

$$\rho \propto \frac{1}{S^3}.$$ (19)

Notice, however, that if S were changing, then the geodesic motion
requires the random speed to drop off as S^{-1}. Thus in an expanding
universe the random motions were larger in the past and pressures may
have been stronger.

(ii) *Relativistic approximation*: Going to the limit when all particles were
moving with speeds comparable to c, we get another simple case.
Under relativistic conditions, we can write,

$$p = \frac{1}{3}\,u.$$

and putting this in equation (17) we get,

$$u \propto \frac{1}{S^4}.$$ (20)

In other words, for small values of S radiation dominates whereas for
large values of S, dust dominates. Denoting the present value of S by
S_0, we can estimate the epoch when the transition took place from
the radition dominated phase to the dust dominated phase. Since
$\rho_0 c^2/u_0 \sim 10^3$, and ρ/uS = constant we see that at $S \sim 10^{-3}S_0$,

there was a transition from a radiation dominated universe to a matter dominated one.

We will first consider the matter dominated models or, mathematically $T_1^1 = 0$ and, $T_0^0 = \rho_0\, c^2 S_0^3/S^3$.

This simplication for giving a model of the universe was first proposed by A. Friedman. These models ignore any contribution of electromagnetic radiation to T_k^i and suppose that the matter in the universe can be approximated as dust. We shall consider the radiation dominated phase in the next chapter.

2.4. THE FRIEDMAN MODELS

We consider the two equations obtained from (14), (15) for dust:

$$2\frac{\ddot{S}}{S} + \frac{\dot{S}^2 + k}{S^2} = 0 \tag{21}$$

$$\frac{\dot{S}^2 + k}{S^2} = \frac{8\pi G \rho_0}{3}\frac{S_0^3}{S^3} \tag{22}$$

Henceforth we shall take $c = 1$ unless the value of c is explicitly needed.

(i) *Euclidean Sections; (k = 0)* : Of the three Robertson-Walker models, this is the simplest case and is known as Einstein-de Sitter model. It was given by Einstein and de Sitter in a joint paper in 1932. Considering equation (2) we get the solution as

$$S \propto t^{\frac{2}{3}}, \quad \dot{S}/S = 2/3t \equiv H(t). \tag{23}$$

The density comes out as,

$$\rho = \frac{3H^2}{8\pi G} \equiv \rho_c = \text{closure density.} \tag{24}$$

ρ_c is a critical threshold in the sense that (as we shall see later) for $\rho > \rho_c$ we get a closed universe, while if $\rho < \rho_c$ we are dealing with an open universe. Putting $t = t_o$ for the present epoch we get:

$$\begin{aligned} t_0 &= \tfrac{2}{3H_0} = 6.6 \times 10^9\; h_0^{-1}(\text{yrs}) \\ \text{and } \rho_c &= 2 \times 10^{-29} h_0^2\; (gm - cm^{-3}). \end{aligned} \tag{25}$$

(ii) *Closed Sections; (k = 1)* : Topologically the universe in this model is "closed", *i.e.*, finite but unbounded in its spatial extent. For such a model the equations (21), (22) take the form.

$$\frac{2\ddot{S}}{S} + \frac{\dot{S}^2}{S^2} = 0 \tag{26}$$

and,

$$\frac{\dot{S}^2}{S^2} - \frac{8\pi G \rho_0 S_0^3}{3S^3} = 0 \tag{27}$$

It is convenient to introduce a new parameter $q(t)$ through the relation:

$$\frac{\ddot{S}}{S} = -q(t) [H(t)]^2, \quad H(t) = \frac{\dot{S}}{S}. \tag{28}$$

This parameter $q(t)$, which is dimensionless is called the "deceleration parameter".

Now, substituting the values of $\ddot{S}/S$ we get,

$$\frac{1}{S^2} = (2q - 1)H^2 \tag{29}$$

and,

$$\rho = \left(\frac{3H^2}{4\pi G}\right) q. \tag{30}$$

Now, for the present epoch,

$$\rho_0 = \left(\frac{3H_0^2}{4\pi G}\right) q_0 \equiv \rho_c \, \Omega_0 \tag{31}$$

and ultimately we get,

$$\Omega_0 = 2q_0. \tag{32}$$

Further, since the left hand side of equation (29) is always positive, we get,

$$q > \frac{1}{2} \text{ and thus } \Omega_0 > 1. \tag{33}$$

Thus the closed model has a density exceeding the previously defined closure density.

(iii) *Open sections; (k = −1)* : Here the space is open and unbounded. The field equations will become,

$$\frac{1}{S^2} = (1 - 2q)H^2 \Rightarrow q < \frac{1}{2}, \quad \Omega < 1. \tag{34}$$

The density remains

$$\rho_0 = \left(\frac{3H_0^2}{4\pi G}\right) q_0 < \rho_c. \tag{35}$$

So, it is observed that three cases may arise depending on the value of the deceleration parameter:

$$\text{if } k \qquad = \qquad 1; \quad q > \frac{1}{2}; \quad \rho > \rho_c,$$

$$\text{if } k = -1; \; a < \tfrac{1}{2}; \; \rho < \rho_c,$$

$$\text{if } k \quad = \quad 0; \; \rho = \rho_c.$$

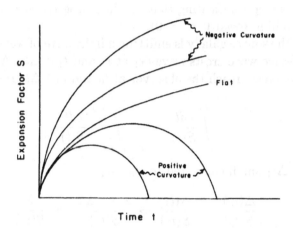

Figure 4.   The three curves describe three types of Friedman models with positive, negative and zero curvature

Fig. 4 illustrates the modes of expansion of the three types of models. Notice that all the models imply that the universe had a beginning a finite time ago. Since the Friedman models are frequently used to interpret cosmological observations, we will now derive some of the observable quantities in these models.

2.5. THE RED SHIFT, LUMINOSITY DISTANCE AND HUBBLE'S LAW

(i) *The red shift* : Consider the propagation of null rays in the Robertson Walker line elements given by.

$$ds^2 = c^2\, dt^2 - S^2(t) \left[\frac{dr^2}{1 - kr^2} + r^2(d\theta^2 + \sin^2\theta d\phi^2) \right].$$

Suppose, our observer is at $r = 0$ and receives the signal at t_0 from a source galaxy G_1 at co-ordinates (r_1, θ_1, ϕ_1) and the time of emission of signal of light rays was t_1. Now, from the general theory of relativity we know that light travels along null geodesics. The geodesic property implies the following: light follows the path of $\theta = $ constant $= \theta_1$ and $\phi = $ constant $= \phi_1$. Therefore, we can relate the radial co-ordinate r_1 of the galaxy G_1 to t_1 by the relation:

$$\int_{t_1}^{t_0} \frac{cdt}{S(t)} = -\int_{r_1}^{0} \frac{dr}{\sqrt{1 - kr^2}}, \tag{36}$$

the negative sign indicating that as time progresses, r decreases (the ray is travelling towards $r = 0$).

Suppose, the source galaxy is emitting a light wave of wavelength λ and two successive wave crests leave G_1 at t_1 and $t_1 + \Delta t_1$. Assuming that these wave crests reach the observer at t_0 and $t_0 + \Delta t_0$ respectively, we have

$$\int_{t_1}^{t_0} \frac{cdt}{S(t)} = \int_{t_1 + \Delta t_1}^{t_0 + \Delta t_0} \frac{cdt}{S(t)}. \tag{37}$$

For Δt_0, Δt_1 small compared to $|t_0 - t_1|$,

$$\frac{\Delta(t_0)}{S(t_0)} = \frac{\Delta(t_1)}{S(t_1)} \Rightarrow \frac{\lambda + \Delta\lambda}{S(t_0)} = \frac{\lambda}{S(t_1)}. \tag{38}$$

This equation implies that a wave of length λ from G_1 comes to the observer as a wave of length $\lambda + \Delta\lambda$. The fractional increase $\Delta\lambda/\lambda$ is denoted by z and is called the redshift. We have

$$1 + z = S(t_0)/S(t_1). \tag{39}$$

Therefore, red-shift is nothing but the increase in the scale factor. So, the scale factor was less in the past, if the spectra of all galaxies appear redshifted. Hence the words 'Expanding Universe'.

It must be kept in mind that the red-shift we are talking about is not the Doppler red shift because, then we would have observed blue shifts also which have not yet been seen.

(ii) *Hubble's Law:* Now, returning to the equation (36) for nearby galaxies, we will approximate the integrals by Taylor expansion,

Thus we can write:

$$\int_{0}^{r_1} \frac{dr}{\sqrt{1 - kr^2}} \simeq r_1,$$

$$\text{and} \int_{t_1}^{t_0} \simeq \frac{c(t_0 - t_1)}{S(t_0)}.$$

Since we are considering $S(t)$ to be nearly constant in a small interval,

$$S(t_1) = S(t_0) - (t_0 - t_1)\,\dot{S}(t_0)$$

$$\frac{S(t_1)}{S(t_0)} = 1 - (t_0 - t_1)\,\frac{\dot{S}(t_0)}{S(t_0)}$$

or,

$$\frac{1}{1+z} = 1 - (t_0 - t_1)\frac{\dot{S}(t_0}{S(t_0)}$$

Expanding binomially.

$$1 - z \approx 1 - (t_0 - t_1)H_0,$$
$$i.e., \quad z = (t_0 - t_1)\,H_0.$$

Hence,

$$r_1 = \frac{c(t_0 - t_1)}{S(t_0)} \rightarrow r_1 S(t_0) = \frac{cz}{H_0}.$$

Now, as per the line element, the spatial element of distance is given by $Sdr/\sqrt{1 - kr^2}$ and so the distance of G_1 from the observer at $r = 0$ will be given under our present assumptions by

$$D \approx r_1\,S(t_0).$$

Therefore, we have,

$$cz = H_0 D. \tag{40}$$

This relation is known as Hubble's law.

(iii) *The luminosity distance :* Let us now consider a non- Euclidean effect. If we have a source of light G_1 radiating a total quantity of energy L, and our space is Euclidean, then the amount of light energy received over a unit area, in unit time, at a distance D is,

$$l = \frac{L}{4\pi D^2}.$$

In the Robertson-Walker geometry the surface area $= 4\pi r_1^2 S^2(t_0)$. Therefore,

$$l = \frac{L}{4\pi r_1^2 S^2(t_0)}.$$

In this relation, two effects are neglected which we now include.

(i) When we are talking about flux, the concept of unit time appears. In an expanding universe time gets elongated as per formula (38). So, to include this effect we must write

$$l = \frac{L}{4\pi r_1^2 S^2(t_0).(1+z)}$$

where $1+z$ is the correction factor.

(ii) The frequency, of each photon received by us gets reduced by a factor of $1+z$:

$$\nu_{received} = \frac{\nu_{emitted}}{1+z}.$$

Hence, the corresponding energy is reduced by the factor $(1+z)$ so that

$$l = \frac{L}{4\pi r_1^2 S^2(t_0)(1+z)^2} \equiv \frac{L}{4\pi D^2} \text{ (say)}. \tag{41}$$

Comparing the above formula with the Euclidean case, the 'luminosity distance' is defined by

$$D = r_1 S(t_0)(1+z). \tag{42}$$

r_1 is found, after some calculations to be

$$r_1 = \frac{\sqrt{2q_0-1}}{q_0^2(1+z)} \left[q_0 z + (1-q_0)(1-\sqrt{1+2zq_0}) \right] \tag{43}$$

Therefore,

$$D = \frac{c}{H_0 q_0^2} \left[q_0 z + (q_0-1)(\sqrt{1+2zq_0}-1) \right] \tag{44}$$

If we take, $q_0 = 1$, then

$$D = \frac{c}{H_0} z. \tag{45}$$

which in our familiar Hubble's formula. Therefore, for this particular model ($q_0 = 1$) we get, $D \propto z$. In general, however, the $D-z$ relation is not linear as shown in the Fig. 5.

2.6. HORIZONS

There are two kinds of horizons in cosmology. The particle horizon limits our observations of the past while the event horizon limits our ability to communicate in the future.

THE SYNTHESIS OF HELIUM AND OTHER NUCLEI

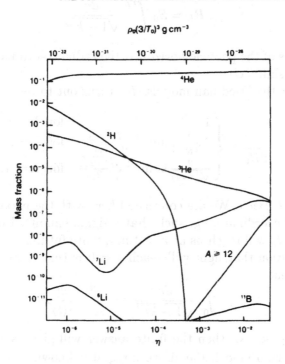

Figure 5.   A plot giving nuclear abundances of light elements as functions of baryon density in the universe

(i) *The particle horizon:* This typically arises in cosmological models like the Friedman models which imply that the universe had a beginning a finite time ago.

Consider an observer at $r = 0$, $t = t_0$ receiving signals from the distant galaxies. From (36) we see that the maximum value of R.H.S. is attained when $r = r_L$ where,

$$\int_0^{r_L} \frac{dr}{\sqrt{1 - kr^2}} = \int_0^{t_0} \frac{dt}{S(t)}. \tag{46}$$

This means that for $r > r_L$ the signal cannot reach the observer, provided the integral on the right hand side converges, as happens for almost all Friedman models. The surface $r = r_L$ defines the 'particle horizon'. Anything inside the particle horizon is conncected with the observer causally. Note that r_L is the coordinate distance. The metric radius of the particle horizon is given by

$$R_L = S_0 \int_0^{r_L} \frac{dr}{\sqrt{1 - kr^2}}. \tag{47}$$

The radius of the particle horizon is the radial co-ordinate of a galaxy whose redshift$= \infty$.

Finally for the Friedman models, R_L turns out to be

$$\frac{c}{2H_0} \times \begin{cases} 1 & \text{for } k = 0, \\ \frac{2}{\sqrt{2q_0-1}} \sin^{-1} \sqrt{\frac{2q_0-1}{2q_0}} & \text{for } k = 1, \\ \frac{2}{\sqrt{1-2q_0}} \sinh^{-1} \sqrt{\frac{1-2q_0}{2q_0}} & \text{for } k = -1. \end{cases}$$

(ii) *The event horizon:* We are concerned here with the maximum value of the radial coordinate, r_E, such that a signal emmitted by a galaxy at $r < r_E$ at t_0 will reach us at $r = 0$ in a finite future.

The condition that light will reach $r = 0$ is that there exists a finite t_F such that

$$\int_0^r \frac{dr}{\sqrt{1 - kr^2}} = \int_{t_0}^{t_F} \frac{cdt}{S(t)}.$$

If, $\int_{t_0}^{\infty} \frac{dt}{S(t)} < \infty$, then the finite answer will give us a limit of r_E. In a Friedman model, the above integral is known to take an infinite value. Thus there is no event horizon. But, in the de-Sitter model, $S(t) \propto \exp(Ht)$ and so there exists an 'event horizon'.

If we take $k = 0$, $S \propto \exp Ht$, then the event horizon has a finite radius:

$$R_E \equiv S_0 r_E = \frac{c}{H}. \tag{48}$$

Also, in the de-Sitter model there is no particle horizon.

2.7. SINGULARITY

The Friedman models have a spacetime singularity at $S = 0$ when all physical description breaks down and the geometrical invariants of spacetime structure diverge. This epoch is often called the 'big bang' and it is usual to start the cosmic time clock from this instant.

However, as we approach this $t = 0$ epoch, we must take note of the fact that the universe was radiation dominated and hence the dust models discussed here are not physically appropriate to describe the physical phenomena. We shall next consider the radiation dominated phase.

3. The early Universe

The 'early universe' refers to the state of the universe close to its origin when it was radiation dominated. The details of the nature of the universe at its early epoch was first discussed by George Gamow and his younger colleagues Alpher and Herman in the late 1940s.

Let us suppose that the radiation was electromagnetic in nature and in thermodynamic equilibrium with the photon energy density given by

$$\rho_\gamma = aT^4 , \qquad a = \text{radiation constant.} \tag{49}$$

Then, after ignoring the kc^2/S^2 terms we can write the field equation (15) as

$$\frac{\dot{S}^2}{S} = \frac{8\pi GaT^4}{3c^2}. \tag{50}$$

When we solve this equation, then we will find that the curvature term kc^2/S^2 is indeed negligible for sufficiently small S. To see this first note that

$$\rho_\gamma \propto \frac{1}{S^4} \tag{51}$$

so that $T = A/S$, $A = $ constant. Substituting into (15) we find that the first term goes as $\frac{1}{S^4}$ whereas the curvature term goes as $\frac{1}{S^2}$. Therefore, for small S, we can justify the omission of the latter term.

Solving the differential equations, we get,

$$S = A(\frac{3c^2}{32\pi Ga})^{-\frac{1}{4}} t^{\frac{1}{2}}. \tag{52}$$

Thus we find that the scale factor increases as $\sqrt{t}$, and

$$T = (\frac{3c^2}{32\pi Ga})^{1/4} t^{-\frac{1}{2}} . \tag{53}$$

This relation gives the temperature of the universe at a time 't' after the big-bang. It is interesting that the coefficient of $t^{-1/2}$ uses c, G, a that can all be determined from the laboratory experiments. It is found that, putting in the values of these constants leads to the relation

$$T_{\text{kelvin}} = 1.52 \times 10^{10} t^{-\frac{1}{2}}_{\text{sec}}. \tag{54}$$

Thus, 1 second after the big-bang the temperature of the universe was $1.52 \times 10^{10} K$. This figure is slightly altered if we take into account other particle species besides the photons. Now, the question arises, at such a high temperature what was the universe made of? We have to consider relativistic particles, other than radiation and include them in the energy-momentum tensor term in the Einstein equations.

From our knowledge of the strong and weak interactions, it can be said that, the particles that could have been present were,

$$\gamma,\ p,\ e,\ \bar{p},\ \bar{e},\ n,\ \bar{n},\ \nu_e,\ \nu_\mu,\ \bar{\nu}_e,\ \bar{\nu}_\mu, ...,\ \pi^+,\ \pi^-,\ \pi^0,\ \text{etc.}$$

We have to consider the universe as a mixture of these particles, which are moving very fast and randomly thereby colliding with each other. This scenario is far from Weyl's postulate ! There is a large scale random motion indicating that the pressure term which we have neglected previously (dust model) is important. At the temperature mentioned some of the above particles will be relativistic. Let us now consider the thermodynamic properties of these particles.

3.1. THE DISTRIBUTION FUNCTIONS

Assuming ideal gas approximation and thermodynamic equilibrium it is possible to write down the distribution function for any given species of particles. Let us use the symbol A to denote the typical species ($A = 1, 2, ...$)$n_A(P)dP$ denotes the number density of species A in the momentum range $(P, P + dP)$, where,

$$n_A(P)dP = \frac{g_A}{2\pi^2\hbar^3}P^2\left[\exp(\frac{E_A(P) - \mu_A}{kT} \pm 1)\right]^{-1}. \tag{55}$$

where, T= temperature of the distribution ; g_A= number of spin states of the species A; k= Boltzmann constant ; μ_A = chemical potential and

$$E_A{}^2 = c^2p^2 + m_A{}^2c^4. \tag{56}$$

As we are concentrating on a relatively small region of space, we can consider the space to be locally flat and we can use special theory of relativity instead of the general theory. Now, the total number of particles is given by

$$N_A = \int\limits_0^\infty n_A dP, \tag{57}$$

Energy density,

$$\rho_A = \int E_A n_A dP. \tag{58}$$

pressure,

$$p_A = \frac{1}{3}\int \frac{p^2}{E_A}n_A dP. \tag{59}$$

and entropy:

$$S_A = \frac{p_A + \rho_A}{T}. \tag{60}$$

In equation (55) the $(+)ve$ sign is for fermions, $e.g.$, protons and electrons and the $(-)ve$ sign is for bosons $e.g.$, γ, π^+, π^-. As we are working under the ideal gas approximation we assume that between two collisions a particle is acted on by no force, $i.e.$, the particle executes free motion between collisions. Initially, let us put $\mu_\gamma = 0$, since,

1. Photons can be emitted or, absorbed in any number, so their number is a free quantity, reconciled by the fact : $\mu_\gamma = 0$.
2. Normally the total number density of particles is $<<$ the photon number density, so we can ignore the chemical potential of the particles.

$$
\begin{aligned}
g_A \text{ the number of spin states} \quad &= \quad 2 \text{ for electron} \\
&= \quad 1 \text{ for neutrino} \\
&= \quad 2 \text{ for photon}
\end{aligned}
$$

For photons, the thermodynamic quantities are:

$$N_\gamma = \frac{2.404}{\pi^2} \left(\frac{kT}{c\hbar}\right)^3,$$

$$\rho_\gamma = \frac{\pi^2 (kT)^4}{15(c\hbar)^3} = 3p_\gamma,$$

$$S_\gamma = \frac{4\pi^2 k}{45} \left(\frac{kT}{c\hbar}\right)^3. \tag{61}$$

We can arrive at a simplified picture for particles in the High Temperature Approximation (HTA) (or, *The relativistic Approximation*)

(a) *High temperature approximation*: Here the kinetic temperature satisfies the condition

$$T >> T_A \equiv m_a c^2 / k. \tag{62}$$

We make two rules regarding the determination of the thermodynamic property of the particles:

i. For bosons, multiply the photon values by $\frac{g_A}{2}$.

ii. For fermions, multiply the photon values by $\frac{3g_A}{8}$ for N_A and, multiply the photon values by $\frac{7g_A}{16}$ for ρ_A, S_A. Thus the effective spin state number g for computing total energy of a family of relativistic particles is obtained by adding to the total spin state number g_b of bosons 7/8 times the total spin state number g_f of fermions.

So, at the age of 1 sec, of the universe (temperature $\simeq 10^{10}K$) $e^{\pm}$ were the only massive particles left to be relativistic.

(b) *Low temperature approximation (LTA)*: In this case we have

$$T \ll T_A$$

$$N_A = \frac{g_A}{h}\left(\frac{m_A kT}{2\pi}\right)^{\frac{3}{2}} \exp\left(-\frac{T_A}{T}\right)$$

$$\rho_A = m_A N_A \quad ; \quad p_A = N_A kT.$$

$$S_A = \frac{m_A N_A}{T}c^2. \tag{63}$$

As T goes below T_A, the exponential function drops, and the contribution of the particle to the thermodynamic properties becomes unimportant. Considering the electron-electron interaction in the HTA the average inter-electron distance is given by.

$$\langle r \rangle \simeq N_e^{-\frac{1}{3}} \simeq \frac{c\hbar}{kT}$$

Thus the average Coulomb interaction energy.

$$\langle\frac{e^2}{r}\rangle = (\frac{e^2}{c\hbar})kT \ll kT, \tag{64}$$

since,

$$\frac{e^2}{c\hbar} = \frac{1}{137} \ll 1.$$

Thus we are justified in treating the electron gas as free.

3.2. THE BEHAVIOUR OF ENTROPY

If we consider a co-moving volume the proper volume will be $S^3\times$ co-ordinate volume. Therefore entropy in a unit co-moving volume $= S^3s$. Now we can show that the universe is expanding in an adiabatic fashion and that

$$S^3s = \text{constant},$$

$$i.e., \quad \frac{d}{dt}\left(S^3\frac{p+\rho}{T}\right) = 0. \tag{65}$$

To see this, first note that the conservation of energy implies

$$\frac{d}{ds}(\rho S^3) + 3pS^2 = 0. \tag{66}$$

Rewriting (64) with help of (65) we need to show that

$$0 = \frac{d}{dt}\left(\frac{S^3 p}{T}\right) + \frac{1}{T}\frac{d}{dt}(S^3 \rho) + S^3 \rho \frac{d}{dt}\left(\frac{1}{T}\right)$$

$$= \frac{d}{dt}\left(\frac{S^3 p}{T}\right) - \frac{3pS^2}{T}\dot{S} + S^3 \rho \frac{d}{dt}\frac{1}{T};$$

$$\text{i.e.,} \quad \frac{dp}{dt} = \frac{(p+\rho)}{T}. \tag{67}$$

The result can be easily established by going back to the definitions of p, ρ, T etc. in the relations (55-60). Hence we will use the fact, that,

$$\sigma = \frac{S^3(p+\rho)}{T}. \tag{68}$$

is constant in the expanding universe. In the high temperature approximation

$$p, \rho \propto T^4$$

$$\Rightarrow \sigma \propto S^3 T^3 = \text{constant.}$$

$$\Rightarrow S \propto 1/T. \tag{69}$$

If we have a mixture of relativistic and non-relativistic particles, then this guiding result is often useful.

At the temperatures $\leq 10^{12}K$ the particles that have become non - relativistic are: p, n, $\mu^{\pm}$, $\pi^{\pm}$, π^0. So, these particles are not important in the dynamics of the universe. The particles remaining relativistic at these temperatures are:

$$\gamma, \nu_e, \nu_\mu, \bar{\nu}_e, \bar{\nu}_\mu, \text{ and } e^{\pm}$$

The neutrinos need a special mention as this phase happens to be crucial in determining the extent of their survival.

3.3. THE DECOUPLING OF NEUTRINOS

As the universe starts cooling, it expands and the neutrino being a weakly interacting particle, there is a competition between two processes, the reaction rate of neutrinos and the rate of expansion of the universe. If it happens that the reaction rate of neutrinos falls below the expansion rate, the neutrinos will decouple from the rest of the particles. It is an important exercise to find the temperature when this happens.

The reaction cross-section of a typical leptonic reaction involving neutrinos is of the order of

$$\Sigma = \mathcal{G}^2 \hbar^{-4}(kT)^4 c^{-4},$$

$$\mathcal{G} = \text{weak interaction constant} = 1.4 \times 10^{-49} \text{erg.cm}^{-3} \qquad (70)$$

Now, the number density of the participating $e^{\pm} \sim (\frac{kT}{c\hbar})^3$ (since, these particles are relativistic at this temperature). The number density of muons $\mu^{\pm}$ on the other hand is given by $\sim T^{3/2} \exp(-\frac{T_\mu}{T})$ where, the exponential term arises due to low temperature approximation. Notice that the muons are non-relativistic because of their comparatively larger masses. Thus the typical neutrino reaction rate becomes

$$\eta = \mathcal{G}^2 \hbar^{-7} c^{-6} kT^5 \exp(-\frac{T_\mu}{T}). \qquad (71)$$

We must now consider the rate at which a typical volume expands. According to the field equations

$$H^2 = \frac{\dot{S}^2}{S} = \frac{8\pi G}{3c^2} u \approx \frac{16\pi^3 G}{90\hbar^3 c^5} (kT)^4. \qquad (72)$$

Thus, the ratio of the reaction rate to expansion rate given by,

$$
\begin{aligned}
\frac{\eta}{H} &\sim \quad G^{-1/2} \hbar^{-11/2} \mathcal{G}^2 c^{-7/2} (KT)^4 \exp(-\frac{T_\mu}{T}) \\
&\sim \quad (\frac{T}{10^{10}K})^3 \exp\left(-\frac{10^{12}K}{T}\right) \\
&\sim \quad T_{10}{}^3 \exp(-\frac{1}{T_{12}}),
\end{aligned}
\qquad (73)
$$

where T_n is the temperature expressed in units of 10^n K.

As T decreases, the exponential term becomes dominant, and a stage comes when $\eta/H << 1$, and at this temperature the neutrinos decouple from leptons.

Earlier, when the calculation was done using the simple weak interaction theory and the Feynman – Gellmann cross-section formula it was found that the decoupling temperature was $\sim 10^{11} K$. Later, when the Electro-weak theory came about with the introduction of neutral current, the temperature was reduced to $\sim 10^{10} K$. This is because by opening additional channels, the Electro-weak theory keeps the neutrinos interacting for a longer period.

Now, the neutrinos are not in thermal equilibrium, so, when they are decoupled their distribution function is determined by looking at each neutrino. The momentum and energy of each neutrino scale down with expansion as $1/S$. Therefore, if we take each neutrino in the original distribution and scale it down, then we will see that the temperature also falls off as $1/S$. So, the neutrino temperature falls off as for rest of the matter.

But if the neutrinos were massive $p \propto \frac{1}{S}$ but $E \not\propto \frac{1}{S}$ since, $E^2 = c^2 p^2 + m^2 c^4$. Thus the temperature no longer scales scales as $1/S$. Massive neutrinos eventually become non-relativistic. There is, however, going to be a difference later on in the temperatures of the neutrinos and the photons even in the case of neutrinos of zero rest mass. This phenomenon is explained below:

Let us consider the dynamics of the universe, from $T = 10^{12} K$ to $T = 10^9 K$. In this phase, we have photons, $e^{\pm}$ pairs and the neutrinos, each with a distribution function given earlier in the high temperature approximation. Therefore,

$$\rho_{matter(rel)} = \rho_{\nu_e} + \rho_{\bar{\nu}_e} + \rho_{\nu_\mu} + \rho_{\bar{\nu}_\mu} + \rho_{e^+} + \rho_{e^-} + \rho_\gamma.$$

To know the g-factor, we have,

$$g = 1(\nu_e)\ \ 1(\bar{\nu}_e)\ \ 1(\nu_\mu)\ \ 1(\bar{\nu}_\mu)\ \ 2(e^+)\ \ 2(e^-)\ \ \&\ \ 2(\gamma)$$

Thus, the effective 'g' $= \frac{7}{8}g_f + g_b = 9$, and hence

$$\rho = \frac{9}{2}aT^4. \tag{74}$$

So, the temperature – time relationship will get altered from (52) to

$$T = \left(\frac{c^2}{48\pi aG}\right)^{1/4} t^{-1/2}. \tag{75}$$

$$i.e., \quad T_{10} = 1.04 \times t_s^{-1/2}. \tag{76}$$

Until now the temperature has not come down to the rest temperature of the electron, $T_e \simeq 6 \times 10^9 K$. So, the question arises, what happens between $10^{10} K$ and $10^9 K$?

Earlier we had $e^+ + e^- \rightleftharpoons 2\gamma$ but now only annihilations take place $e^+ + e^- \rightarrow 2\gamma$. So the net effect is that the energies residing in $e^{\pm}$ are given to the photons but not to the neutrinos as they have already decoupled. Thus the photon temperature shoots up above the neutrino temperature. One particular reaction may be possible : $e^+ + e^- \rightarrow \nu + \bar{\nu}$, but its probability is very small. At $10^{10} K$ we had a situation when $T_\gamma = T_\nu \propto \frac{1}{S}$, but as more energy is pumped into the photons we expect $T_\gamma > T_\nu$. How do we estimate the effect quantitatively?

We have seen previously that $\sigma = S^3(p+\rho)/T$ is conserved. So, if we can calculate σ for $10^{10} K$ and $10^9 K$ then we can get an idea by what fraction the ratio T_γ/T_ν has risen above unity. In the initial relativistic phase,

$$\sigma_i = \frac{4S_i^3}{3T_i}(\rho_{\bar{e}} + \rho_e + \rho_\gamma)$$

$$= \frac{11}{3}\frac{S^3}{T_i}aT_i^4 = \frac{11}{3}(T_iS_i)^3.$$

When $e^{\pm}$ are annihilated and only photons are left, we have,

$$\sigma_f = \frac{4}{3}a(ST_\gamma)^3_f$$

Now, σ being a conserved quantity.

$$\sigma_i = \sigma_f.$$

Again, $T_\nu = B/S$ (B = a constant)

$$\sigma_i = \frac{11}{3}aB^3(\frac{T_i}{T_\nu})^3 = \frac{11}{3}aB^3 \quad \text{as} \quad T_i = T_\nu,$$

$$\text{and,} \quad \sigma_f = \frac{4}{3}aB^3(\frac{T_\gamma}{T_\nu})^3 = \sigma_i = \frac{11}{3}aB^3.$$

$$\implies (\frac{T_\gamma}{T_\nu})^3 = (11/4).$$

Thus we have,

$$\frac{T_\gamma}{T_\nu} = 1.4. \tag{77}$$

This ratio will remain unchanged all the way to the present epoch. Hence if the present photon temperature (of CMBR) is $\sim 2.7K$, the corresponding neutrino temperature would be $\sim 2K$.

Next we consider the baryons. Although dynamically they do not contribute to the expansion of the universe, yet their numbers matter in deciding the nuclear composition of the universe.

3.4. NEUTRON TO PROTON RATIO

Neutron and proton have rest mass temperatures that are pretty high so they are both non-relativistic for $T < 10^{13}K$. However, their number ratio depends on the difference $T_n - T_p$ as a fraction of T.

Thus we get,

$$N_p = \frac{2}{\hbar^3}\left(\frac{m_p KT}{2\pi}\right)^{3/2} \exp\left(-\frac{T_p}{T}\right),$$

$$N_n = \frac{2}{\hbar^3}\left(\frac{m_n KT}{2\pi}\right)^{3/2} \exp\left(-\frac{T_n}{T}\right),$$

$$\text{i.e.,} \quad \frac{N_n}{N_p} \cong \exp\left(\frac{T_p - T_n}{T}\right) = \exp\left(-\frac{1.5}{T_{10}}\right). \tag{78}$$

The ratio therefore changes with temperature in the following way :

T	N_N/N_p
$T_{13} \leq 1$	1
$T_{11} = 1$	5/6
$T_{10} = 3$	3/5

The neutron to proton number ratio critically influences the subsequent nucleosynthesis of hydrogen and helium.

For thermodynamic equilibrium to be maintained amongst these nuclei reactions that convert neutrons to protons and vice-versa have to be rapid enough compared to the rate at which the universe expands. Typically such reactions are

$$n \to p + e^- + \bar{\nu},$$

$$\text{or,} \quad n + \nu \to p + e^-, \text{etc.}$$

So long as neutrinos are present, these reactions can happen but when neutrinos decouple then we cannot use the above formula for N_n/N_p. Notice, however, that here we are considering interactions of neutrinos with baryons and not so much with leptons as earlier. Let us denote the $n \leftrightarrow p$ reaction rate as η which we want to compare with Hubble's constant. The cross-section comes out to be,

$$\Sigma_{n \leftrightarrow p} \propto T.$$

The Hubble constant changes as per (72). The effective decoupling temperature T_* at which the reaction rate is just about equal to H is $< 10^{10} K$. If the universe was expanding faster, T would be higher and the ratio at decoupling would be higher.

Once the thermodynamic equilibrium ceases to be maintained, the ratio is not given by the previous formula, but by detailed consideration of specific reactions involving the neucleons, including the rate at which a free neutron decays.

If X_n denotes the fraction of neutrons,

$$X_n = \frac{N_n}{N_n + N_p}. \tag{79}$$

Our purpose is to obtain a differential equation for X_n. If $\lambda(n \leftrightarrow p)$ denotes the rate at which neutrons are converted to protons, then X_n satisfies the equation,

$$\frac{dX_n}{dt} = (1 - X_n)\lambda(p \to n) - X_n\lambda(n \to p). \tag{80}$$

(Remember that $1 - X_n$ denotes the proton fraction)

As the universe expands and cools down to lower temperatures the pairs dissappear, but it is still possible for the neutron to decay via the reaction,

$$n \to p + e^- + \bar{\nu}_e.$$

As the temperature goes lower the neutrons and proton do not remain free but combine to form deuterium atoms which can capture neutrons and protons to form higher nuclei.

So, ultimately it becomes a many-body problem which we consider next.

3.5. THE PRIMORDIAL NUCLEOSYNTHESIS

A typical nucleus Q is described by two quantities: A = atomic mass and Z = atomic number; and is written as

$$Q_Z^A$$

This nucleus has Z protons land A-Z neutrons. If m_Q is the mass of the nucleus, it's binding energy is given by

$$B_Q = [Zm_p + (A - Z)m_n - m_Q]c^2. \tag{81}$$

We use the approximation $m_p \approx m_n = m$, and write

$$X_p = \frac{N_n}{N_N}, X_n = \frac{N_n}{N_N}, X_Q = A\frac{N_Q}{N_N}, \tag{82}$$

where N_N=number density of all nucleons of which N_p is in the form of free protons, N_n as free neutrons and N_Q as bound nuclei Q. The X's are called mass fractions of their respective species.

As we are now concerned with relative number densities, we can no longer ignore the chemical potentials. So,

$$N_Q = g_Q\left(\frac{m_Q KT}{2\pi\hbar^2}\right)^{3/2} \exp\left(\frac{\mu_Q - m_Q c^2}{KT}\right), \text{ etc.} \tag{83}$$

We know that the chemical potential satistfy the relation

$$\mu_Q = (A - Z)\mu_n + Zm_p. \tag{84}$$

Now, using (82) for n, p and Q and (80), (83) to eliminate the values μ_Q, μ_n, μ_p we get,

$$X_Q = \frac{1}{2}g_Q A^{5/2} X_p^Z X_N^{A-Z} \xi^{(A-1)} \exp(\frac{B_Q}{KT}), \tag{85}$$

$$\text{where,} \quad \xi = \frac{1}{2} N_N \left(\frac{mKT}{2\pi\hbar^2}\right)^{-3/2}. \tag{86}$$

T must drop to a low enough value to make $\exp(B/KT)$ large enough to compensate for the smallnes of $\xi^{(A-1)}$. This occurs for nucleus Q when T has dropped down to

$$T_Q \sim \frac{B_Q}{k(A-1)|ln\xi|}. \tag{87}$$

We apply the above formula to He^4, its binding energy being 4.3×10^{-5} $ergs$ $= 28.29$ Mev, to find that $T_Q \approx 3 \times 10^9 K$. At this low temperature the number densities of participating nucleons is so low, however, that the probability of four body collisions leading to the formation of helium is very small. So, we try using two body collisions to describe the buildup of heavier nuclei, and He^4 is formed as a result of the chain reactions :

$$p + n \leftrightarrow d + \gamma,$$
$$d + d \leftrightarrow He^3 + n \leftrightarrow H^3 + p,$$
$$H^3 + d \rightarrow He^4 + n, \text{etc}...$$

Although at this temperature nucleosynthesis does proceed rapidly enough, it cannot go beyond He^4 since, there are no stable nuclei with $A = 5$ or, 8.

The primordial process therefore cannot give us heavier nuclei. So, the observed abundances of the heavier nuclei are due to the evolution of stars, where further nucleosynthesis can occur beginning with the reaction

$$3He^4 \quad \rightarrow \quad C^{12*} \quad \rightarrow \quad C^{12}.$$

Although it is a three – body reaction its rarity is compensated for by its being a resonant reaction. This resonant reaction was theoretically predicted by Hoyle in the mid-1950s.

(i) *Abundances of light nuclei :* Returning to the primordial scenario, the bulk of nucleosynthesis is over at $\sim 8 \times 10^8 K$; and at this temperature all the neutrons have been gobbled up by helium nuclei. Denoting the mass fraction of the primordial helium by Y_P, we get $Y_P = 2X_n$. To this must be added the helium generated in stars, say Y_S before we can compare with the presently observed mass fraction of cosmic helium. We can write,

$$Y_{obs} = Y_P + Y_S. \tag{88}$$

Observations put an upper limit on Y_P in the range $0.23 - 0.24$. The theoritical value should depend on the total number of nucleons in the universe. We define a parameter η related to the nucleon density :

$$\eta = \left(\frac{\rho_N}{2.7 \times 10^{-26}\text{gm.cm}^{-3}}\right)\left(\frac{3}{T}\right)^3. \tag{89}$$

Then, it can be shown that

$$\rho = \eta T_9^3 \quad , \quad T_9 < 3. \tag{90}$$

In Fig.6 is a plot of Y for different values of η for different cosmological models. The figure also gives abundances of the other light nuclei like deuterium, He^3, lithium etc. which are created in very small quantities in the primordial process.

The deuterium that was originally created is depleted and so the present abundance is a lower limit to the primordial value, which, in turn puts an upper limit on the baryon number density. It is observed that X_d now is $\sim 10^{-5}$. If the baryon number density is too high, then, as seen from Fig.6 almost no deuterium is produced. Thus we have a limit on the baryonic density parameter Ω_B. It can be shown that for $h_0 = 1, \Omega_B \leq 0.12$ that is, the baryonic matter density is 12% of the closure density.

(ii) *Limits on neutrino species* The helium abundances of 0.24 was based upon 2 neutrino types (ν_μ, ν_e). But if we have a larger group of symmetries leading to 3 neutrino types $(\nu_e, \nu_\mu, \nu_\tau)$ then because of the increase of the coefficient g in the time – temperature relationship all the above calculations will change. Thus,

$$u = (g/2)aT^4 \tag{91}$$

and so, if g increases, u increases and the universal expansion rate goes up.

To see how the number of neutrinos affect the mass fractions, consider the ratio (77) at decoupling temperature.

$$x = \frac{N_n}{N_p} = \exp(-\frac{1.5}{T_{*10}}). \tag{78}$$

If we alter x we will alter the value of Y . Now since the expansion rate H goes as $g^{1/2}$, the decoupling temperature goes as

$$T_* \propto g^{1/4}. \tag{92}$$

If we increase g, x increases, so we will get more helium; for, $Y = 2N_n/(N_n + N_p)$.

It can be easily shown that a small increase of δg in g leads to

$$\delta Y = -\frac{x \ln x}{(1 + x^2)} \frac{\delta g}{g}. \tag{93}$$

Doing the calculation, $\delta Y \cong 0.02$ (for each degree of neutrino) So, 2% more helium should be expected from the universe if we increase the number of neutrino types by 1. The limits set by observations on Y_P seem to rule out more than 3 species. It is interesting to note that the accelerator experiments also suggest that there are only three neutrino flavours.

3.6. MASSIVE NEUTRINOS

It was pointed out in 1972 by Cowsik and McClelland, that if we consider neutrinos to have even a very small mass ($\sim$ a few eV), when they decouple, they will slow down and they will be massive and come to rest and will contribute to the matter density at the present epoch. How much will they contribute? The answer can be expressed in the following form :

Let us write ρ_ν = density of neutrinos at present, and define Ω_ν as ρ_ν/ρ_c. Using the high temperature approximation fixes the number density of neutrinos at decoupling. This is scaled down as S^{-3} by the expansion, so that now

$$\Omega_\nu = \frac{m_\nu}{150}\left(\frac{T_0}{3}\right)^3 h_0^{-2} , \tag{94}$$

where m_ν = mass of neutrino in eV and T_0 = present temperature of the CMBR.

Further, since there are antineutrinos as well with a similar distribution and also there may be three neutrino species, we have to multiply the above estimate of Ω_ν by 6. If $m_\nu = 25\ eV$, then we are 'closing the universe' with neutrinos alone. In that case the actual density will be higher than the luminious density, thereby pointing to a substantial contribution of 'dark matter'.

Relic neutrinos tell us two important facts :

1. Depending on the number of their species, they will alter the level of helium abundance.
2. If they have mass, then the presence of dark matter can be explained.

3.7. THE COSMIC MICROWAVE BACKGROUND RADIATION

The process of nucleosynthesis took place when the temperature was around $10^9 K$. The universe then cooled as it expanded with the radiation temperature dropping as S^{-1}. The presence of free subatomic particles and nuclei did not have much effect on the dynamics of the universe but, the electrons frequently acted as scattering centres for photons thereby keeping them thermalized and the universe was optically thick.

As the universe cooled further the electron – proton electrical attraction began to assert itself and neutral atoms formed. To find out the number densities of free electrons (N_e), protons $(N_p = N_e)$ and H atoms (N_H) at a given temperature we take the help of Saha's ionization equation,

$$\frac{N_E^2}{N_H} = \left(\frac{m_e KT}{2\pi\hbar^2}\right)^{3/2} \exp(-B/KT) \tag{95}$$

where, m_e= electron mass ; B= Binding energy of hydrogen nuclei $(= 13.59eV)$. Let, $x = \frac{N_e}{N_B}$ (N_B = total baryonic density). Then because $N_H = N_B - N_e$, we have from (94)

$$\frac{x^2}{1-x} = \frac{1}{N_B}\left(\frac{m_e KT}{2\pi\hbar^2}\right)^{3/2} \exp(-B/KT). \tag{96}$$

We can solve for x as a function of T. The results show that x drops sharply from 1 to ~ 0 around the temperature $10^3 K$. For example, if we consider $\Omega_0 h_0^2 = 0.1$, then $x = 0.003$ at temperature $T = 3000K$. The consequence of this lowering of temperature will be that the electrons will be bound and will not be available for scattering the photons. The universe will then become transparent. The photon background will be decoupled from matter and cooled with a Planckian temperature $T \propto S^{-1}$. The cosmic microwave background has a planckian spectrum with the temperature $\sim 2.7K$. If this is the relic of the hot early epochs then the above 'recombination epoch' turns out to have a redshift $\sim 10^3$.

We know the universe changed over from being radiation dominated to matter – dominated around the same epoch. This instance of both these phenomena occuring at around the same time appears a coincidence that cannot be explained in a natural way.

Another puzzling result is the observed ratio of photons to baryons

$$\frac{N_\gamma}{N_B} = 4.57 \times (\Omega_0 h_0^2)^{-1} (T_0/3)^2. \tag{97}$$

This ratio has been conserved since the time the universe became essentially transparent. Why this ratio has this value and not any other is still a mystery. Why are there so many photons for every baryon in the universe? The clue to this issue may lie in even earlier epochs, (i.e., prior to the nucleosynthesis epoch) which we will consider next.

4. The very early Universe

The history of the universe based on the current ideas is diagrammatically represented in Fig.6. To study the origin of the baryons and to get insight into the ratio (97) we have to resort to ideas in particle physics and the analysis of different interactions : (i) Q.E.D. (ii) Weak interactions and (iii) Strong interactions at very high energies.

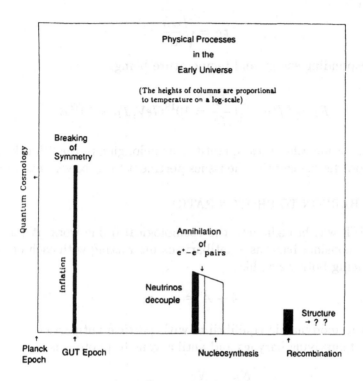

Figure 6. The time evolution of the standard hot big bang model. The time axis is on a logarithmic scale. The crucial epochs are the Planck epoch, the GUTs epoch, the neutrino decoupling epoch, the $e^{\pm}$ annihilation epoch, the nucleosynthesis epoch, the recombination epoch and the epoch when discrete structures begin to appear. This last stage is still poorly understood

In 1968 the electromagnetic and weak interactions were unified through the symmetry group $SU(2)$ and we got the electro – weak interaction. It was found that the energy at which this unification takes place is around 100 GeV, which has been tested through man – made accelarators, by the detection of massive bosons $W^{\pm}$ and Z. Extrapolating theoretically it has been predicted that, if we increase our energy to $\sim 10^{15}$ GeV, then all the 3 basic interactions may be unified. This theory, often called the 'Grand Unified Theory' is not yet known but is expected to be based on the gauge group symmetries, the simplest one being given by the group $SU(5)$.

The temperature corresponding to the GUT era is $\sim 10^{27} - 10^{26} K$. So, from the above diagram, we can say that nothing of notable importance happened between $10^{26} K$ and $10^{16} K$. Another energy range which is important is that in the quantum gravity epoch. Then we can construct a time scale

$$t_P = \sqrt{\frac{G\hbar}{c^5}}. \tag{98}$$

The corresponding energy and temperature being,

$$E_P \sim \hbar/t_P = \sqrt{\frac{c^5\hbar}{G}} = 10^{19} GeV, T_P \sim 10^{32} K. \tag{99}$$

The subscript identifies these quantities as belonging to the 'Planck epoch'. We will now discuss some of the issues pertinent to these very early epochs.

4.1. THE BARYON TO PHOTON RATIO

Before GUT was brought into the cosmological frame work, it was found that, if we consider baryons – antibaryons interacting with each other, the reaction being both ways, like,

$$A + \bar{A} \rightleftharpoons \gamma + \gamma,$$

then, in thermodynamic equilibrium with particle antiparticle symmetry, the ratio of surviving baryons and antibaryons to photons is as low as

$$\frac{N_B}{N_\gamma} = \frac{N_{\bar{B}}}{N_\gamma} = 10^{-18}. \tag{100}$$

Now, as seen from (97), the observed ratio is : $10^{-10} - 10^{-8}$ and no antibaryons are to be found when we observe galaxies.

To get rid of these difficulties, GUT was brought in. For example, the group $SU(5)$ allows us to describe any particular particle in terms of quarks and leptons, with a large number of bosons (generally called the X - bosons). Thus there could have been situations when baryons lost their identities and become leptons and pions. This allows for baryon decay and creation, occuring at the GUTs epoch: *i.e.*, the baryon number is not conserved. Further, somewhere along the long journey of our universe from big – bang to the present epoch we have to introduce particle – antiparticle assymmetry, which is better known as CP violation.

If the rates are suitably adjusted, then we can break the thermal equilibrium and produce more baryons and assume that after this the universe has expanded very fast without giving opportunity to destroy these extra baryons. Some contrived scenarios are able to produce N_B/N_γ in the narrower range of $10^{-4} - 10^{-12}$.

However, there are still some problems with this standard big bang (SBB) model which we now highlight.

4.2. SOME PROBLEMS OF SBB

(a) *The flatness problem :* First discussed by Dicke and Peebles and high-lighted by Guth, this problem is illustrated in Fig.7. There we see a number of curves all describing Friedman models with $k = 0, \pm 1$. Which is the correct one?

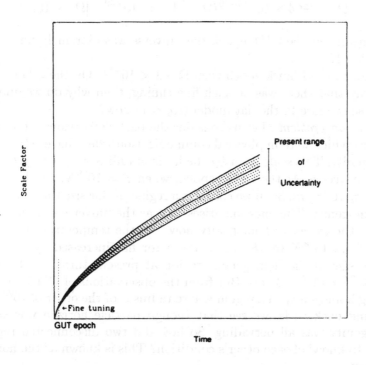

Figure 7. The flatness problem is highlighted above. The curves passing through the shaded region diverge at the present epoch but were strongly bunched around the $k = 0$ curve in the GUT epoch. Why did this fine tuning around the flat model occur?

The present observations allow for the Ω_0 parameter in the range 0.01 to 10, say. The curves lying in this region (shaded in Fig.8) include the unique actual model. How was the model described? If we are to go by the arguments of the SBB the outcome may have been decided in the early Planck epoch, or the GUT epoch.

Suppose at the early epoch, $t \ll t_0$, the value of the density parameter was somehow fixed as $\Omega(t)$. How is it related to the present value Ω_0? Taking stock of the Friedman equations at t and t_0 we get

$$(\Omega_0 - 1) = (\Omega - 1)\dot{S}^2/S_0{}^2. \tag{101}$$

Putting in numbers one can show that

$$(\Omega - 1) \simeq 4 \times 10^{-15} T_{\text{MeV}}^{-2} (\Omega_0 - 1). \qquad (102)$$

$$T \sim 10^{15} GeV \;\; = \;\; 10^{18} MeV$$

so that,

$$\Omega - 1 \cong 4 \times 10^{-15-36} (\Omega_0 - 1) \;\; < \;\; 10^{-49} \quad [\Omega_0 \sim 10].$$

This means, at the GUT epoch the universe was extremely fine tuned near $\Omega = 1$.

If we go to the Planck epoch then $\Omega - 1 < 10^{-57}$. On the other hand, if we say that there was no such fine tuning, then why do we find the universe so close to the flat model $(\Omega_0 = 1)$ now?

(b) *The horizon problem* : Let us consider the particle horizons, at small t. Regions which were in physical communication would have established homogenity. This scale is set by the horizon radius $\approx ct$, where $t =$ age of the universe. At the GUTs epoch, when $T = 10^{28} K$, $t = 10^{-37}$ sec then $r \simeq 10^{-27} cm$. So, if we consider a region of this size then there will be homogenity. The question arises that as the universe expands what will be the extent of homogenity now? As the temperature has come down from $10^{28} K$ to $3K$, the scale factor has increased by 3×10^{27}. So the size of the homogenous region at present turns out to be $\sim$ $3 \times 10^{-27} \times 10^{27} = 3$ cms. But from the observations of CMBR we are finding homogenity in a region whose radius is of the order of $10^{28} cms$. Working backwards, we see that though particle horizon was small, homogenity was all pervading. So how did two disconnected regions 'come to know' of each other's condition? This is known as the horizon problem.

(c) *The monopole problem* : This problem arose from a property of group theory. When a large local group such as $SU(5)$, (under the breakdown of the symmetry) splits into smaller groups, including the $U(1)$ group, *e.g.*,

$$
\begin{aligned}
SU(3) &\rightarrow \text{strong interaction} \\
SU(2)_L &\rightarrow \text{weak interaction} \\
U(1) &\rightarrow \text{electromagnetic interaction}
\end{aligned}
$$

$$SU(5) = SU(3) \times SU(2)_L \times U(1)$$

then some solutions are inevitably generated that will be like the 'magnetic monopole solution'. Dirac had studied the modification of

Maxwell's equations for monopole charges and derived quantization conditions on the monopole charge. If it is formed at the GUT epoch then one would expect at least one monopole of mass $\mathcal{M}$ in a volume $\frac{4\pi}{3}r_H{}^3$ at the GUTs epoch, r_H being the horizon radius. As the universe expands, what would be the density of monopole matter now? At the GUTs epoch it was

$$\rho_{\mathcal{M}} = \frac{3\mathcal{M}}{4\pi r_H{}^3} \sim 1.5 \times 10^{65} \text{gm.cm}^3.$$

This is scaled down to

$$(\rho_{\mathcal{M}})_0 = 5 \times 10^{-18} \text{g.cm}^{-3}. \tag{103}$$

which though small, is much greater than ρ_c(closure density) $= 2 \times 10^{-29}$g.cm^{-3}. The monopoles are indestructible and can easily destroy the magnetic field in the inter – galactic region (10^{-6}Gauss). They are clearly absent, contrary to the above prediction.

(d) *The entropy problem :* This is again related to the photon to baryon ratio. The entropy density s in the early universe is given by

$$s = \frac{2\pi^2}{45}T^3 g(T). \tag{104}$$

Also, during expansion $S^3 s = $ constant $= \mathcal{F}$. Thus for the present epoch,

$$\mathcal{F}_0 = S_0{}^3 s_0 \approx 10^{87} \gg 1. \tag{105}$$

Why should such a large number be present at the early epoch, when photons and other particles were on equal footing?

(e) *The domain wall problem :* There are certain particles, which play mediating role in the symmetry breaking process of the GUT – type interaction; they are known as Higgs bosons (ϕ). When the symmetry breakdown occurs there can be two values of $\phi \longrightarrow \phi_1$ and ϕ_2, say, and the very nature of phase transitions is such that we have continuous regions of $\phi = \phi_1$ and $\phi = \phi_2$ with the boundary wall as a discontinuity. This is the domain wall and if it intersects some part of our observing universe we will see some large scale astronomical effect, which is not observed. In other words, there is no observational evidence for any topological discontinuity of space.

In 1981, Guth proposed a modification of the standard big bang scenario that claimed to cure it of these defects. We will consider this interesting idea next.

4.3. THE INFLATIONARY UNIVERSE

The idea of inflation depends on phase transition in the very early universe and its dynamical impact on the spacetime geometry. We will illustrate it with a simple example:

When we describe a gauge theory, at any particular level we need some scalar particles 'ϕ' (Higgs particles) whose action functional may be given by ;

$$Action = S_{\text{Higgs}} = \int_v [\tfrac{1}{2}\phi_i\phi^i - V(\phi)]d^4x \quad \text{where,} \quad \phi_i = \frac{\partial\phi}{\partial x^i}. \tag{106}$$

Suppose V(ϕ) has a minimum at $\phi = \phi_0 \neq 0$.

In realistic gauge theories, the scalar field will not be a single entity. One normally works with a set of Higg's scalar fields ϕ^A, where $A = 1, 2, ..., N$, N being the number of generators of the gauge group. Thus, if τ_A are the generating matrices,

$$\phi = \phi^A \tau_A$$

and,

$$V = -\frac{1}{2}\mu^2 \, Tr\phi^2 + \frac{1}{4}a(Tr\phi^2)^2 + \frac{1}{2}bTr\phi^4 + \frac{1}{3}Tr\phi^3. \tag{107}$$

For example, when $SU(5) \longrightarrow SU(3) \otimes SU(2)_L \otimes U(1)$, then

$$\langle\phi\rangle = \Phi\text{diag}(1,1,1,-3/2,-3/2), \quad \Phi = 4 \text{ dimensional scalar.} \tag{108}$$

If we had $SU(5) \rightarrow SU(4) \otimes U(1)$, then

$$\langle\phi\rangle = \sigma\text{diag}(1,1,1,1,-4). \tag{109}$$

Note that $Tr\phi$ in each case $= 0$.

In the realistic case, quantum fluctuations will affect the potential $V(\phi)$, thereby affecting the spacetime geometry. So, cosmologists are interested in the effective potential which is averaged over the fluctuations. We may write it as

$$V_{\text{eff}}(\phi) = \alpha\phi^2 - \beta\phi^4 + \gamma\phi^4 \ln(\phi^2/\sigma^2). \tag{110}$$

where α, β, γ are the constants.

In the very early phase of the universe, we have to deal with a very high temperature. If we include theramal fluctuations it leads to additional temperature dependant terms in (109) $e.g.$,

$$V_{\text{thermal}}(\phi) = \frac{18T^4}{\pi^2} \int_0^\infty dx \; x^2 \ln\left[1 - \exp\left(-\left(x^2 + a\frac{\phi^2}{T^2}\right)^{1/2}\right)\right]. \tag{111}$$

The potential $V(\phi) = V_{\text{eff}}(\phi) + V_{\text{thermal}}(\phi)$ is shown in Fig.8.

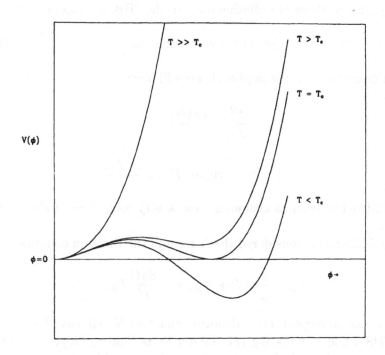

T >> T_e

T > T_e

T = T_e

T < T_e

V(φ)

φ=0

φ→

Figure 8. The potential energy of the ϕ field has a local minimum at $\phi = 0$. This is also a global minimum for $T > T_c$ while for $T < T_c$ a new set of minima appears at energies lower than that at $\phi = 0$.

For $T = T_c$ the value $V(\phi) = 0$ is attained at two positions, at $\phi = 0$ and at $\phi = \phi_0$. The $\phi = 0$ is the classical vacuum and is the state of lowest energy for $T > T_c$. Normally in the case of the classical theory $V(\phi) = 0$ gives the minimum energy whereas, here the $V_{\min} = V_0 < 0$ for $T < T_c$. Below T_c the lowest energy is at ϕ_0 and not at $\phi = 0$. So there is a possibility of transition of the system : if the Higgs boson system is cooling in the universe, the lower energy state and in the process it will dump the energy in the surroundings. This is quite analogous to the process of supercooling of steam, where going below the temperature of $100°C$ does not convert steam into water but after further lowering of temperature the steam transforms into droplets of water and releases heat. If the system is supercooled it may still reamin at higher energy level and being unstable, suddenly change its phase and dump the energy.

Consider the Friedmann equations (with $c = 1$):

$$\frac{\dot{S}^2}{S^2} + \frac{k}{S^2} = \frac{8\pi G}{3}[\rho(\phi) + \rho_{\text{other}}].$$

(112)

Here ρ_{other} is the classical radiation term of the SBB. It drops as $1/S^4$. Let

$$\rho(\phi = 0) = \epsilon_0 = \text{constant}. \tag{113}$$

So, the dominating term is $\rho(\phi)$ and, we will have

$$\frac{\dot{S}^2}{S^2} \sim \frac{8\pi G \epsilon_0}{3}$$

$$\Rightarrow S \propto e^{H_0 t} \quad \text{where} \quad H_0^2 = \frac{8\pi G \epsilon_0}{3}. \tag{114}$$

This solution has been in cosmology for a very long time, under various contexts.

In 1917, de-Sitter considered the Λ term in the Einstein equations, $i.e.$,

$$R_{ik} - \frac{1}{2} g_{ik} R + \Lambda g_{ik} = -\frac{8\pi G}{c^4} T_{ik}. \tag{115}$$

where Λ = cosmological term, denotes some sort of repulsive force.

In 1948 while formulating the Steady State Theory Hoyle introduced certain term on the right hand side of (115) instead of the Λ term to arrive at the de-Sitter model.

The Λ term was also anticipated by W. H. McCrea in 1950 from processes in the vacuum, although particle theorists were not prepared for it! The difference now is in the order of magnitude, the present Λ is 10^{108} times greater than the previous ones thought out by cosmologists!

Thus as T drops below T_c, for a while the universe is in the $\phi = 0$ state which now has the status of a false vacuum. While in this state the universe will temporarily expand exponentially (thus the word 'inflation', $i.e.$, something faster than 'expansion'). The inflation is over and the universe reverts to SBB after the phase transition is completed.

Due to this inflation a bubble is formed at $\phi = \phi_0$ and in this region phase transition goes on to a lower state while outside $\phi = 0$. So, a bubble was obtained by inflating a small region, and it may not occur simultaneously everywhere. All the bubbles thus formed are expected to collide and coalasce after which we will get a universe which will expand as per the Friedmann prescription.

It is worth pointing out that in 1966, while considering the concept of baryon creation in the C-field cosmology, Hoyle and Narlikar had arrived at the notion of 'Friedmann Bubbles' in the ambient de-Sitter (steady state) universe in much the same way as in the present inflationary scenario.

We now consider some details of Guth's model.

(a) *The entropy problem* : The inflation can account for the large entropy. Suppose the expansion by inflation occurs over a time τ. This leads to an increase of S by $Z = \exp H_0\tau$. To make it as high as $S^3 s = 10^{87}$, we need $Z^3 = 10^{87}$, *i.e.*, $Z = 10^{29}$. This implies $H_0\tau = 29 \ln 10 \cong 67$. Whatever H_0 we may have, after 67 Hubble epochs S^3 will be very high and the energy dumping process will provide the extra entropy.

(b) *The flatness problem* : In the Friedmann model k/S^2 term ($k = \pm 1$) could have been important. However, with the sudden inflation the scale factor S has increased by $\sim 10^{29}$ and the value of k/S^2 has been reduced by 10^{58}. So, even if we started from a large curvature term there will be no fine tuning necessary to arrive at the 'nearly flat' universe.

(c) *The horizon problem* : Due to inflation the small size particle horizon is increased by a factor of 10^{29}, which solves the problem.

So, we need sufficient time to inflate but we also need the bubbles to coalasce. In the Guth model there were problems on the second count. So, a newer version was proposed.

4.4. THE NEW INFLATIONARY MODEL

In Guth's scenario the bubbles tend to increase around according to the Friedmann expansion rate ($t^{1/2}$) whereas the outside will expand as $e^{H_0 t}$. The problem therefore was that the bubble centres are moving away and they don't coalasce. We need the rate of bubble formation to be large compared to that of the expansion of the universe, but, it was found that the rate was not so fast. To ensure the desired effect, it needed again a fine tuning of parameters which we want to avoid.

So a new idea came from Linde and from Albrecht and Steinherdt, to look at a different potential, given by Coleman and Weinberg :

$$
\begin{aligned}
V(\phi, T) \;=\;& \tfrac{25}{16}\alpha^2\left[\phi^4 \ln \tfrac{\phi^2}{\sigma^2} + \tfrac{1}{2}(\sigma^4 - \phi^4)\right] \\
+\;& \tfrac{18}{\pi^2}T^4 \int_0^\infty x^2 \ln\left(1 - \exp\left[-(x^2 + \tfrac{5}{12}\phi^2 g^2/T^2)^{1/2}\right]\right) dx.
\end{aligned}
$$
(116)

At $T = 0$, $V(\phi, 0)$ has a maximum at $\sigma = 1.2 \times 10^{15}\,\text{GeV}$, and,

$$
\begin{aligned}
\alpha^2 \;=\;& \text{strong coupling constant} \\
=\;& g^2/4 = \tfrac{1}{45} \text{for } SU(5).
\end{aligned}
$$
(117)

and we get, (see Fig.9),

$$
V(0) = \frac{25}{32}\alpha^2\sigma^4 > V(\sigma) = 0.
$$
(118)

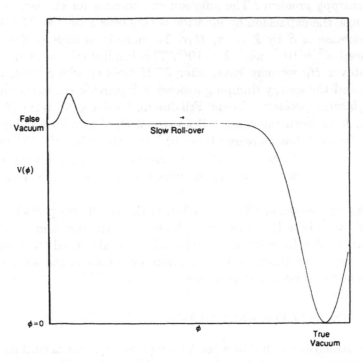

Figure 9. The potential function for the so called new inflationary model. It has a false vacuum at $\phi = 0$, followed by a high temperature local peak near $\phi > 0, 1$ followed by a slowly sloping plateau which later has a sharp drop to the true vacuum state

The dynamics follows the action principle and the equation looks like

$$\Box \phi = -\frac{\partial V}{\partial \phi}. \tag{119}$$

In the Robertson-Walker model

$$\ddot{\phi} + 3\frac{\dot{S}}{S}\dot{\phi} = -\frac{\partial V}{\partial \phi}. \tag{120}$$

The finite temperature correction implies a barrier of height $\propto T^4$ at $\phi = 0$ and with a curvature, $(5/4)g^2T^2$.

What kind of universal expansion will it produce?

Initially, at high temperature, it will have a ϕ value ≈ 0; and it will tunnel through the barrier as the universe cools.

Therefore,

(i) the field is at $\phi = 0$ for $T >> T_c$.

(ii) as $T \to T_c$, ϕ tunnels through the barrier to ϕ_i

(iii) Afterwards ($T \leq T_c$) ϕ rolls down from ϕ_i to σ, first slowly down the plateau and then rapidly and while falling it executes some oscillations around $\phi = \sigma$,

(iv) ϕ settles down at $\phi = \sigma$, after a series of damped oscillations .

At the early stage, when the energy was at higher state, the de Sitter expansion was going on.

$$\frac{\dot{S}^2}{S^2} + \frac{k}{S^2} = \frac{8\pi G}{3}(\rho(\phi) + \rho_m) \quad \text{where} \quad \rho(\phi) >> \rho_m. \tag{121}$$

This de Sitter expansion can be called inflation, while the released energy and the entropy are dumped into radiation through the damped oscillations thus solving the entropy problem. People have done calculations numerically, since no analytic method was possible. The results are

$$\phi_i \simeq 0$$
Roll over time$t \geq 190 H_0^{-1} \quad \rightarrow \quad$ duration of de Sitter phase.
$$Z \simeq \exp(190) = 10^{50} \quad \rightarrow \quad \text{inflation in size.}$$
$$\tau_{osc} = 4.8 \times 10^{-4} H_0^{-1}$$

The small coefficient indicates the rapid behaviour around σ.

The original size of the horizon $= 10^{-26}$cm becomes inflated at the time of GUT epoch to 10^{24}cm. Then, due to Friedmann expansion, the increase in size will be to $10^{24} \times 10^{27}$cm $= 10^{51}$cm $>> 10^{28}$cm. So, we have got a homogenity on a much larger scale that we observe. The monopole density has also been reduced by a factor of Z^3, *i.e.*, 10^{-150}.

The problem with this new inflationary model is that the fine tuning of ϕ_i/σ is needed. So, we need $\phi_i/\sigma < 10^{-5}$ and Higgs boson mass $m \leq 10^{-5}\sigma$. If $m \geq 10^9$GeV then inflation won't work. One positive contribution this model has made is the idea of fluctuations in the ϕ field which may lead to pregalactic inhomogeneities.

Growth of fluctuations: Consider the spectrum of fluctuations :

$$\delta\phi = \int \delta\phi(k) e^{ikx} \frac{d^3\bar{k}}{(2\pi)^3}. \tag{122}$$

This could have arisen before the Planck epoch, for example. We are building up complex fluctuations in terms of differing scales (k). Our interest is the nature of growth of (k). Work in this field has been done by S. Hawking and others, who obtain:

$$\delta\phi(k) = \left[\frac{H_0^2}{16\pi^3} \left(1 + \frac{k^2}{H_0^2} e^{-2H_0 t} \right) \right]^{1/2}. \tag{123}$$

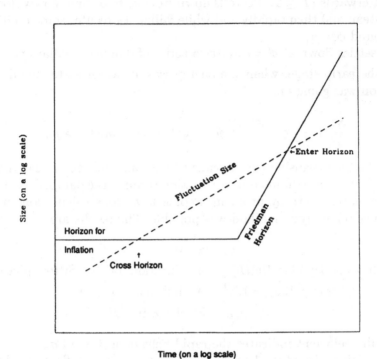

Figure 10. The fluctuation size is shown in relation to the 'horizon'. First the fluctuation size grows and 'crosses' the horizon (which is constant in size) during inflation. Subsequently the universe switches over to the Friedman state when the horizon overtakes the fluctuation size. This is when the fluctuation 'enters' the horizon.

Fig.10 illustrates what happens to these fluctuations in relation to the actual horizon.

In metric term k corresponds to the wavelength $2\pi S(t)/k \equiv \lambda$. λ goes out of the horizon and then comes back in as the universe changes over from the de Sitter to the Friedmann model. Let t_1 = time at which $\lambda H_0 = 1$. We then find that at t_1, $\delta\phi(k)$ = constant (not dependant on k). Therefore, whatever fluctuations we start with when λ leaves the horizon it is causally disconnected (t_1) and when it reenters (t_2) they will come into the Friedmann horizon with the same value.

Thus, after t_2, $\delta\phi$ is again almost independent of k, and one can relate $\delta\phi$ to the density contrast

$$\frac{\delta\rho}{\rho}\Big|_{t=t_2} = \sqrt{\frac{4\gamma}{3\pi^3}} \ln\left(\frac{H_0}{k}\right)^{3/2} \tag{124}$$

where,

$$V_{\text{eff}}(\phi) = V_{\text{eff}}(0) - \frac{1}{2}\gamma\phi^4, \quad \text{at} T = 0. \tag{125}$$

This work was done by Guth and Pi and leads to the important conclusion that density fluctuations are scale independent.

From an analysis of galaxy correlation functions Zeldovich and Harrison in the 1970s had independently suggested that there should be a scale invariant spectrum of matter fluctuations in the universe.

There, is however, a problem with the above calculation. As the de Sitter model has only an event horizon and the Friedmann model has only a particle horizon, so the concept of 'causal' connection is quite vague in the above arguement. Further the actual $\delta\rho/\rho$ turns out to be ~ 50 in this calculation while the observed value $< 10^{-4}$ (from limits on the fluctuations of CMBR).

Thus the saga of inflation continues with further inputs from particle physics. One such idea is of chaotic inflation in which the universe begins to inflate at the Planck epoch. Consider a field ϕ at $t_P \simeq \sqrt{\frac{G\hbar}{c^5}}$ and then find $\Delta\phi$ from quantum fluctuations. It is found to behave in a chaotic manner, since, quantum domain does not allow us to fix our initial condition precisely.

Finally, the Λ-term of the inflationary stage is given by

$$\Lambda = (10^{15}\text{GeV})^4 \text{Mp}^{-2}, \tag{126}$$

while its present observational value is $\leq (10^{-12}\text{GeV})^4\text{Mp}^{-2}$. This means when the transition took place the Λ term dropped by a huge factor of $\sim 10^{108}$. This is another fine tuning factor !!

In short,

"Inflation has not lived up to it's original promise. "

It may not be true but it is well contrived.

-GIORDANO BRUNO

It isn't that they can't see the solution. It is that they can't see the problem.

-GILBERT KEITH CHESTERTON

Science is built up with facts, as a house is with stones. But a collection of facts is no more a science than a heap of stones is a house.

-JULES HENRI POINCARÉ

We used to think that if we knew one, we knew two, because one and one are two. We are finding that we must learn a great deal more about 'and'.

-ARTHUR STANLEY EDDINGTON

8. THE COSMOLOGICAL CONSTANT: A TUTORIAL

PATRICK DASGUPTA
Physics Department
Delhi University
Delhi, India

A pedagogical treatment to the effect of cosmological constant in the big-bang model is presented. It is argued that quantum fluctuations of the vacuum contributes to the cosmological constant and, essentially, leads to the cosmological constant problem. The equation of state corresponding to the cosmological constant is derived using the conservation of energy-momentum tensor in the Friedman models. The epoch after which the cosmological constant starts dominating over the non-relativistic matter is calculated. The evolution of the expansion factor as a function of cosmic time is discussed for the flat model case when Λ is positive. The ensuing age of the universe since the birth of high redshift QSOs is compared with the ages of the globular clusters. Collapse of a spherical dust ball and its virialization is considered. The flatness problem in the presence of a non-zero cosmological constant is discussed.

1. Introduction

In 1917, Einstein introduced the cosmological constant Λ in the equations of motion for the geometry of the space-time in order to obtain a static solution, assuming that the universe we live in is static. But in 1920s, it was clear from the works of Slipher and Hubble that the universe is expanding, so that much of the original motivation for adding the cosmological constant term to the Einstein equation is now no longer there. Interestingly enough, subsequent developments in quantum field theory and observational cosmology have given rise to arguments that make the wishing away of the cosmological constant difficult (See Weinberg (1989) for a detailed analysis of these points). In these notes, we provide a pedagogical description of the role played by the cosmological constant in an expanding, homogeneous and isotropic universe. Since this is really a **tutorial**, I have also sowed a handful of problems at several places along with the corresponding solutions (Readers interested in the details of Relativistic Cosmological models, in general, are referred to J.V.Narlikar's article in this volume).

Einstein's theory of gravitation that reduces to the Newtonian gravity in the static and weak field limit is embodied in the following equation,

$$R^\mu_{\ \nu} - \frac{1}{2}g^\mu_{\ \nu}R = -\frac{8\pi G}{c^4}T^\mu_{\ \nu}, \tag{1a}$$

where $T_{\mu\nu}$ is the energy-momentum tensor corresponding to the matter fields that act as the source of the space-time curvature. For instance, in the Friedman-Robertson-Walker (FRW) models one usually takes the energy-momentum tensor corresponding to a perfect fluid consisting of a mixture of radiation and matter in thermal equilibrium.

Following Einstein (1917), one may add the cosmological constant term $\Lambda g^\mu_{\ \nu}$ to the left-hand side of the eq (1a),

$$R^\mu_{\ \nu} - \frac{1}{2}g^\mu_{\ \nu}R + \Lambda g^\mu_{\ \nu} = -\frac{8\pi G}{c^4}T^\mu_{\ \nu}. \tag{1b}$$

It is clear from eq (1b) that Λ has the dimensions of $(length)^{-2}$, and that if the energy and momentum associated with matter are conserved then Λ necessarily has to be a constant. The last part follows from the fact that the covariant derivatives of Einstein tensor, $G_{\mu\nu}$ ($= R_{\mu\nu} - \frac{1}{2}g_{\mu\nu}R$), as well as the energy-momentum tensor, $T_{\mu\nu}$, vanish so that having a covariant differentiation on both sides of eq (1b) yields,

$$(\Lambda g^\mu_{\ \nu})_{;\mu} = \Lambda_{,\mu}g^\mu_{\ \nu} = \Lambda_{,\nu} = 0, \tag{1c}$$

implying thereby that the cosmological constant is truly a constant. Of course, one way to make Λ depend on space-time coordinates is to give up the conservation of energy and momentum corresponding to the matter fields (note that since $G^\mu_{\ \nu;\mu}=0$ is a mathematical identity we can only tamper with the energy-momentum tensor so that $T^\mu_{\ \nu;\mu} \propto \Lambda_{,\nu}$).

The other important thing to note is that we can always bring the cosmological constant term (in eq (1b)) to the right-hand side so that,

$$R^\mu_{\ \nu} - \frac{1}{2}g^\mu_{\ \nu}R = -\frac{8\pi G}{c^4}(T^\mu_{\ \nu} + \lambda^\mu_{\ \nu}), \tag{2a}$$

where,

$$\lambda_{\mu\nu} = \frac{\Lambda c^4}{8\pi G}g_{\mu\nu}, \tag{2b}$$

and thereby interpret the theory of gravitation *with* the cosmological constant as a theory *without* the cosmological constant but having an omnipresent additional gravitational source characterised by the energy-momentum tensor $\lambda_{\mu\nu}$ given by eq (2b).

2. Vacuum and the cosmological constant

Now, let us make a small digression into quantum field theory (QFT). In QFT, the vacuum is defined to be the ground state of the energy operator. From Lorentz invariance it follows that the mean energy-momentum tensor of the vacuum is given by (Weinberg(1989)),

$$(T_{\mu\nu})_{\text{vac}} \equiv \langle T_{\mu\nu} \rangle = \langle \epsilon \rangle g_{\mu\nu}. \qquad (3a)$$

where $\langle A \rangle$ corresponds to the expectation value in the vacuum state of the operator A, ϵ is the energy density operator and $g_{\mu\nu}$ is the metric tensor.

In general, $\langle \epsilon \rangle$ is not zero but is equal to the summation of zero-point energies of all the normal modes of the fields involved (which, in non-supersymmetric theories, blows up to infinity but is generally made finite by introducing an upper momentum cutoff). This can be understood in a heuristic manner by the following argument that makes use of Heisenberg's uncertainty principle.

The zero-point energy of a quantum field essentially can be thought of arising because of **virtual** particles produced in the vacuum spontaneously. Since, conservation of energy is a fundamental principle, creation of such particles can take place only within the limits imposed by the energy-time uncertainty relation. This immediately tells us that the virtual quanta necessarily have to be short-lived. For instance, let us consider a virtual particle that lives for a time interval $\sim \tau$. Then clearly, according to the uncertainty principle, its energy $E_\tau \gtrsim \hbar/\tau$. Such particles can move only upto a distance $\sim c\tau$ while they live, so that one can think of a cell of volume $\sim (c\tau)^3$ around each of them. Then, the energy density associated with such quanta is $\sim \hbar c/(c\tau)^4$. The smallest length scale below which the notion of space-time continuum may very well break down is characterized by the Planck length $l_{\text{P}} \equiv \sqrt{G\hbar/c^3} = 1.6 \times 10^{-33}$ cm. Taking $c\tau = l_{\text{P}}$ we find that the energy density corresponding to the virtual particles have to be larger than,

$$\frac{\hbar c}{l_{\text{P}}^4} = 4.8 \times 10^{114} \ erg \ cm^{-3}. \qquad (3b)$$

The above argument suggests that the value of $\langle \epsilon \rangle$ be at least of the order given by eq (3b). Thus, the **vacuum** has a non-zero and very large value (infinite, if Planck length cut-off is not imposed, i.e., $\tau = 0$) of energy density associated with itself. This makes the vacuum energy-momentum tensor non-trivial which, as we will see below, adds to the celebrated **Cosmological constant problem** (see section 4).

According to eqs (3a) and (3b), the energy-momentum tensor corresponding to the vacuum cannot be set to zero, and strictly speaking $(T_{\mu\nu})_{\text{vac}}$ ought to be included in eq (2a) as a source for gravitation so that the Einstein equation takes the following form,

$$R^{\mu}_{\nu} - \frac{1}{2}g^{\mu}_{\nu}R = -\frac{8\pi G}{c^4}(T^{\mu}_{\nu} + (\lambda^{\mu}_{\nu})_{\text{eff}}), \qquad (4a)$$

where,

$$(\lambda_{\mu\nu})_{\text{eff}} = \frac{c^4}{8\pi G}\left(\Lambda + \frac{8\pi G}{c^4}\langle\epsilon\rangle\right)g_{\mu\nu}, \qquad (4b)$$

is the combined energy-momentum tensor of the cosmological constant and the vacuum.

It is evident from eq(4b) that the vacuum energy density acts like a cosmological constant so that the effective cosmological constant is simply,

$$\Lambda_{\text{eff}} = \Lambda + \frac{8\pi G}{c^4}\langle\epsilon\rangle. \qquad (5a)$$

Intuitively, eqs (4a) and (4b) imply that as far as (non-quantum) cosmology is concerned it sees only the Λ_{eff} and not the individual terms that appear in the right-hand side of eq (5a). In other words, using cosmological observations one may only constrain Λ_{eff} and not Λ or $\langle\epsilon\rangle$.

Since, $g^{\mu}_{\nu} = \delta^{\mu}_{\nu}$, it follows from eqs (4b) and (5a) that,

$$(\lambda^0_0)_{\text{eff}} = (\lambda^1_1)_{\text{eff}} = (\lambda^2_2)_{\text{eff}} = (\lambda^3_3)_{eff} = \frac{c^4}{8\pi G}\Lambda_{\text{eff}}, \qquad (5b)$$

all the other components being zero.

We will come back to this interplay of vacuum energy density and the bare cosmological constant in section 4 when we discuss the cosmological constant problem. But before that we need to describe FRW models in somewhat more detail.

3. Energy-momentum tensors in FRW models

The FRW models begin with the basic premise that the universe at large scales is homogeneous and isotropic, which in the framework of general relativity implies that the geometry of the space-time is described by the Robertson-Walker line-element,

$$ds^2 = c^2dt^2 - S^2(t)\left[\frac{dr^2}{1 - kr^2} + r^2(d\theta^2 + \sin^2\theta\, d\phi^2)\right], \qquad (6a)$$

where $S(t)$ is the expansion scale factor at the cosmic epoch t. The epoch $t = 0$ corresponds to the big-bang singularity when the universe is thought to have been originated.

Reading off the metric from the line-element given in eq (6a), one obtains (e.g. see Narlikar (1983)),

$$R^0{}_0 = \frac{3}{c^2} \frac{\ddot{S}}{S}, \tag{6b}$$

$$R^1{}_1 = R^2{}_2 = R^3{}_3 = \frac{1}{c^2}\left(\frac{\ddot{S}}{S} + 2\frac{\dot{S}^2 + kc^2}{S^2}\right), \tag{6c}$$

while all the other components of the Ricci tensor vanish. The scalar curvature then is,

$$R = \frac{6}{c^2}\left(\frac{\ddot{S}}{S} + \frac{\dot{S}^2 + kc^2}{S^2}\right) \tag{6d}$$

Problem 1 : *Using eqs (6b) to (6d) in the Einstein equation given by eq (4a) argue that the energy-momentum tensor that gives rise to the Robertson-Walker line-element satisfies the following conditions,*

$$T^1{}_1 = T^2{}_2 = T^3{}_3, \tag{7a}$$

$$T^\mu{}_\nu = 0, \qquad for \ \ \mu \neq \nu. \tag{7b}$$

Solution : *Let us define the following tensor,*

$$\tilde{G}^\mu{}_\nu = R^\mu{}_\nu - \frac{1}{2}g^\mu{}_\nu R + \Lambda_{\text{eff}} g^\mu{}_\nu. \tag{8a}$$

Using eqs (6b)-(6d) and the fact that $g^\mu{}_\nu = \delta^\mu{}_\nu$, it is obvious that,

$$\tilde{G}^1{}_1 = \tilde{G}^2{}_2 = \tilde{G}^3{}_3, \tag{8b}$$

$$\tilde{G}^\mu{}_\nu = 0, \qquad for \ \ \mu \neq \nu. \tag{8c}$$

Now, the Einstein equation (eq (1b)) can be rewritten using eq (8a) as,

$$\tilde{G}^\mu{}_\nu = -\frac{8\pi G}{c^4}T^\mu{}_\nu. \tag{8d}$$

The conditions given by eqs (7a) and (7b) follow from eqs (8b)-(8d), and basically reflect the symmetries of the Robertson-Walker line element.

For a perfect fluid, the energy-momentum tensor is given by,

$$T^{\mu\nu} = (p + \epsilon)u^\mu u^\nu - pg^{\mu\nu}, \tag{9a}$$

where p, ϵ and u^{μ} are the pressure, energy density and 4-velocity of the fluid, respectively. Making use of eqs $(7a)$ and $(7b)$ in eq $(9a)$, it is easy to show that (see Problem 2),

$$T^1_1 = T^2_2 = T^3_3 = -p, \tag{9b}$$

$$T^0_0 = \epsilon. \tag{9c}$$

Problem 2 : *Prove eqs (9b) and (9c).*
Solution : *From eq (9a), we have,*

$$T^{\mu}_{\nu} = (p + \epsilon)u^{\mu}u_{\nu} - p\delta^{\mu}_{\nu}, \tag{10a}$$

Eq (7b) along with the above equation for T^0_i leads to,

$$(p + \epsilon)u^0 u_i = 0, \tag{10b}$$

implying that,
$$u^i = 0. \tag{10c}$$

As $u^{\mu}u_{\nu} = 1$, it also follows from eq (10c) that,

$$u^0 = 1. \tag{10d}$$

Physical implication of eqs (10c) and (10d) is that the coordinates r, θ and ϕ represent the co-moving coordinates, (i.e., in this coordinate system a fluid element does not have any streaming motion) and the cosmic time t is also the proper time for the fluid element.

Eqs (10c) and (10d) when used in eq (10a) leads us to the result given by eqs (9b) and (9c).

With the non-zero components of the energy-momentum tensor given by eqs $(9b)$ and $(9c)$, and the Ricci tensor given by eqs $(6b)$ and $(6c)$, the Einstein equation (eq $(8d)$) can be written as,

$$\frac{\dot{S}^2 + kc^2}{S^2} = \frac{8\pi G}{3c^2}\epsilon + \frac{1}{3}\Lambda_{\text{eff}}c^2, \tag{11a}$$

$$2\frac{\ddot{S}}{S} + \frac{\dot{S}^2 + kc^2}{S^2} = -\frac{8\pi G}{c^2}p + \Lambda_{\text{eff}}c^2. \tag{11b}$$

It is interesting to note from eqs $(11a)$ and $(11b)$ that $\frac{\Lambda_{\text{eff}}c^4}{8\pi G}$ and $-\frac{\Lambda_{\text{eff}}c^4}{8\pi G}$ can be looked upon as the energy density, ϵ_{Λ}, and the pressure, p_{Λ}, respectively, corresponding to the effective cosmological constant. In other words, the equation of state for the cosmological constant is given by (also, see Problem 3),

$$p_{\Lambda} = -\epsilon_{\Lambda}. \tag{12}$$

Problem 3 : *In the standard Friedman models, where the cosmological constant is set to zero, the evolution of the scale factor is determined by the following equations (see eqs (11a) and (11b)),*

$$\frac{\dot{S}^2 + kc^2}{S^2} = \frac{8\pi G}{3c^2}\epsilon, \qquad (13a)$$

$$2\frac{\ddot{S}}{S} + \frac{\dot{S}^2 + kc^2}{S^2} = -\frac{8\pi G}{c^2}p, \qquad (13b)$$

where ϵ and p are the energy density and the pressure, respectively, of the matter that drives the expansion.

Show that if the equation of state is given by,

$$p = -\epsilon, \qquad (13c)$$

the energy density, ϵ, remains a constant as the universe expands.

Solution : *Eqs (13a) and (13b) can be written as,*

$$\epsilon S^3 = \frac{3c^2}{8\pi G}S(\dot{S}^2 + kc^2), \qquad (14a)$$

$$2S\ddot{S} = -\frac{8\pi G}{c^2}(p + \frac{\epsilon}{3})S^2. \qquad (14b)$$

Differentiating eq (14a) with respect to the scale factor gives us,

$$\begin{aligned}\frac{d}{dS}(\epsilon S^3) &= \frac{3c^2}{8\pi G}\left[(\dot{S}^2 + kc^2) + \frac{S}{\dot{S}}\frac{d}{dt}(\dot{S}^2 + kc^2)\right] \\ &= \epsilon S^2 + \frac{3c^2}{8\pi G}2S\ddot{S}\end{aligned} \qquad (14c)$$

Using eq (14b) in eq (14c), we obtain,

$$\frac{d}{dS}(\epsilon S^3) + 3pS^2 = 0. \qquad (15a)$$

Thus, if $p = -\epsilon$, eq (15a) implies,

$$\frac{d\epsilon}{dS} = 0. \qquad (15b)$$

It is also easy to see from eq (15a) that if the energy density remains a constant as the universe expands, the equation of state necessarily has to be that given by eq (13c).

Therefore, since the energy density associated with the effective cosmological constant is proportional to the latter and thereby is a constant, it is not surprising that the pressure corresponding to the cosmological constant *is same as the corresponding energy density albeit with an opposite sign (eq (12)). With eq (12) as the equation of state for the cosmological constant, eqs (11a) and (11b) imply that eqs (13a) and (13b) are valid even in the presence of a non-zero effective cosmological constant provided ϵ and p include the contributions from the cosmological constant. Thus, eqs (14b) and (15a) are also valid when Λ_{eff} is not zero.*

We may note that eq (15a) is a general result which is very often handy in determining the rate at which the energy density changes as the universe expands. For example, using the equation of state for radiation,

$$p = \frac{\epsilon}{3}, \tag{16a}$$

one obtains from eq (15a),

$$\epsilon_r(S) \propto S^{-4}. \tag{16b}$$

Similarly, for dust ($p = 0$), eq (15a) immediately yields,

$$\epsilon_m(S) \propto S^{-3}. \tag{16c}$$

Now, for non-relativistic matter, the pressure is $\sim \rho v^2 \ll \rho c^2 = \epsilon_m$, ρ being the mass density. Hence, 'dust' approximation is a good approximation for a collection of non-relativistic objects, and one may use eq (16c) to describe the fall of their energy density as the universe expands.

We will now make use of eqs (16b) and (16c) in the following section where we discuss the hot big-bang model.

4. Hot big-bang model when $\Lambda \neq 0$

The hot big-bang model assumes that the universe in the past was hotter as well as denser, and is described in terms of FRW models. Now, if one assumes that the universe is a mixture of radiation and non-relativistic matter, the evolution of the scale-factor represented by eqs (11a) and (11b) can be expressed as,

$$\frac{\dot{S}^2 + kc^2}{S^2} = \frac{8\pi G}{3}(\rho_r + \rho_m + \rho_\Lambda), \tag{17a}$$

$$2\frac{\ddot{S}}{S} + \frac{\dot{S}^2 + kc^2}{S^2} = -\frac{8\pi G}{c^2}(p_r + p_m + p_\Lambda), \tag{17b}$$

where ρ_r, ρ_m and $\rho_\Lambda = \frac{\Lambda_{\text{eff}}c^2}{8\pi G}$ are the mass-densities associated with the radiation, non-relativistic matter and the effective cosmological constant, respectively. We can use eqs (16b) and (16c) in eqs (17a) and (17b) to obtain,

$$\frac{\dot{S}^2 + kc^2}{S^2} = \frac{8\pi G}{3}\left[(\rho_m)_0\left(\frac{S_0}{S}\right)^3 + (\rho_r)_0\left(\frac{S_0}{S}\right)^4 \right] + \frac{1}{3}\Lambda c^2, \qquad (17c)$$

$$2\frac{\ddot{S}}{S} + \frac{\dot{S}^2 + kc^2}{S^2} = -\frac{8\pi G}{3}(\rho_r)_0\left(\frac{S_0}{S}\right)^4 + \Lambda c^2, \qquad (17d)$$

where $(\rho_m)_0$ and $(\rho_r)_0$ are the mass densities of matter and radiation at the present epoch, respectively, and $S_0 \equiv S(t_0)$, t_0 being the present epoch. In arriving at eq (17d), we have also used eq (16a) for radiation, and the approximation that pressure is negligible for non-relativistic matter.

Note that for notational ease we have removed the subscript 'eff' from the cosmological constant, in eqs (17c) and (17d). **From now on we will refer to the effective cosmological constant simply as the cosmological constant and denote it by Λ.**

Let us assume that during the very early epochs, the energy densities of radiation and matter were very large compared to that of the cosmological constant. Then, it is clear from eq (17c) that immediately after the big-bang when the scale-factor is very small the evolution of the scale-factor $S(t)$ is governed largely by the radiation energy density. Subsequently, as the universe expands the energy density of the radiation falls faster than that of the non-relativistic matter, and a time comes ($t \gg t_{eq}$) when the latter starts dominating over the radiation. But as the time progresses, even the energy density of the matter falls below that of the cosmological constant (because, the energy density associated with the cosmological constant remains always a constant). Therefore, it is likely that the far-future evolution of $S(t)$ is solely governed by the cosmological constant, if it is non-zero. In what follows, we will quantify the above scenario.

First, let us define the following kinematical quantities associated with the expansion of the universe :

$$H(t) \equiv \frac{\dot{S}}{S}, \qquad (18a)$$

$$q(t)H^2(t) \equiv -\frac{\ddot{S}}{S}. \qquad (18b)$$

Essentially, $H(t)$ and $q(t)$ represent the expansion and deceleration rates, respectively. At the present epoch, $H(t_0) \equiv H_0$ and $q(t_0) \equiv q_0$ are simply the Hubble constant and the deceleration parameter, respectively. A given set of values of H_0, q_0 and Λ completely determine the space-time geometry of the universe for all times $\gg t_{eq}$. Hence, determination of H_0, q_0 and Λ from observations is a very important aspect of cosmology.

Using the above definitions (eqs (18a) and (18b)) for H and q in eqs (17a) and (17b), we get,

$$H^2 + \frac{kc^2}{S^2} = \frac{8\pi G}{3}\rho, \tag{19a}$$

$$H^2(1 - 2q) + \frac{kc^2}{S^2} = -\frac{8\pi G}{c^2}p, \tag{19b}$$

where $\rho \equiv \rho_r + \rho_m + \rho_\Lambda$ and $p \equiv p_r + p_\Lambda$ are the total mass density and the total pressure, respectively.

From eq (19a) it is clear that if at **any** instant t the total mass density satisfies,

$$\rho(t) = \rho_c(t) \equiv \frac{3H^2(t)}{8\pi G}, \tag{20a}$$

then, automatically, k is forced to be zero and thereby, eq (20a) holds good for **every** epoch. The mass density given by eq (20a) is therefore very special and is called the critical density, ρ_c. Again, it is obvious from eqs (19a) and (20a) that if ρ is less than ρ_c then $k = -1$ while if ρ is greater than ρ_c then $k = +1$. It is convenient to express the total mass density in terms of a density parameter Ω and the critical density ρ_c,

$$\rho(t) \equiv \rho_c(t)\Omega(t). \tag{20b}$$

It is quite transparent from the definition of the total mass density $\rho(t)$ that,

$$\Omega(t) = \Omega_r(t) + \Omega_m(t) + \Omega_\Lambda(t), \tag{20c}$$

with $\Omega_i \equiv \rho_i/\rho_c$, with i=r,m,$\Lambda$,...... .

Using eqs (20b) and (20c) in the first of the Einstein equations (eq (19a)), we obtain,

$$\frac{kc^2}{S^2} = H^2(\Omega_m + \Omega_r + \Omega_\Lambda - 1). \tag{21a}$$

For the present epoch eq (21a) gives us,

$$\frac{kc^2}{S_0^2} = H_0^2((\Omega_m)_0 + (\Omega_r)_0 + (\Omega_\Lambda)_0 - 1). \tag{21b}$$

Problem 4 : *Show that the deceleration parameter at any time is given by,*

$$q(t) = 0.5(\Omega_m(t) + 2\Omega_r(t) - 2\Omega_\Lambda(t)). \tag{21c}$$

Solution : *Using in eq (19b) the fact that $p_r = \epsilon_r/3$ and $p_\Lambda = -\Lambda c^4/8\pi G$, we obtain,*

$$\frac{kc^2}{S^2} = H^2(2q - 1 - \Omega_r + 3\Omega_\Lambda). \tag{21d}$$

By making use of eq (21a) in the above equation, one can easily arrive at eq (21c).

Using eq (20a) in eq (17c), we get,

$$\left(\frac{\dot{S}}{S}\right)^2 = H_0^2\left[(\Omega_m)_0\left(\frac{S_0}{S}\right)^3 + (\Omega_r)_0\left(\frac{S_0}{S}\right)^4 + (\Omega_\Lambda)_0\right] - \frac{kc^2}{S^2}, \tag{22a}$$

so that,

$$\dot{S} = \pm H_0 S_0[S_{\text{eff}}] \tag{22b}$$

where,

$$S_{\text{eff}} = \left[(\Omega_m)_0(S_0/S) + (\Omega_r)_0(S_0/S)^2 + +(\Omega_\Lambda)_0(S/S_0)^2 - kc^2/(S_0 H_0)^2\right]^{\frac{1}{2}}.$$

Assuming that till the present epoch the universe has been expanding, we need to retain only the positive root of the R.H.S. of eq (22b) so that,

$$dt = \frac{1}{H_0 S_0}\frac{dS}{S_{\text{eff}}}. \tag{22c}$$

If t_1 and t_2 correspond to the epochs when the expansion factor is S_1 and S_2, respectively, the time elapsed between these two epochs then is obtained by integrating cq (22c),

$$t_2 - t_1 = \frac{1}{H_0 S_0}\int_{S_1}^{S_2}\frac{dS}{S_{\text{eff}}} \tag{22d}$$

The expression given in eq (22d) comes very handy when we wish to compare the age of some galactic source (say, globular clusters) with the time elapsed since the light rays left a distant object (say, a QSO) to reach us. We will see more of this in the later part of this section.

Let us now make contact with observations to get a feel for the numbers associated with various cosmological quantities. In particular, at the present epoch the critical density defined in eq (20a) is simply,

$$(\rho_c)_0 = 1.9 \times 10^{-29}h^2 \; gm \; cm^{-3}, \tag{23a}$$

so that the total density using eq (20b) is,

$$(\rho)_0 = 1.9 \times 10^{-29}(\Omega)_0 h^2 \; gm \; cm^{-3}, \tag{23b}$$

where the h appearing in eqs (23a) and (23b) is related to the Hubble constant H_0 in the following manner,

$$H_0 = 100 \ h \ km \ s^{-1} \ Mpc^{-1}, \tag{23c}$$

with h lying between 0.5 and 1 because of observational uncertainties.

As for the matter density now, we may write it in terms of the matter density parameter at the present epoch, $(\Omega_m)_0$, and the critical density given by eq (23a),

$$(\rho_m)_0 = 1.9 \times 10^{-29} (\Omega_m)_0 h^2 \ gm \ cm^{-3}, \tag{24a}$$

From the dynamics of galaxies in clusters, observations suggest that $(\Omega_m)_0$ lies in the range 0.1 - 0.2 (Knapp and Kormendy (1987)).

Now, concerning the radiation energy density, COBE results imply a temperature of $T_0 = 2.735 \ \pm \ 0.06°$K for the relic cosmic microwave background radiation (CMBR), suggesting a mass density of,

$$(\rho_r)_0 \simeq 5 \times 10^{-34} \ gm \ cm^{-3}, \tag{24b}$$

for the radiation, so that $(\Omega_r)_0$ is $\sim 2.6 \times 10^{-5} \ h^{-2}$.

Problem 5 : *Show that the redshift, $z_{\rm eq}$, at which the energy densities of radiation and matter become comparable is given by,*

$$1 + z_{\rm eq} \simeq 3.8 \times 10^4 \ (\Omega_m)_0 \ h^2. \tag{25a}$$

Solution : *Now, $\rho_r(S) \simeq \rho_m(S)$ by virtue of eqs (16b) and (16c) implies,*

$$(\rho_r)_0 \frac{S_0}{S_{\rm eq}} \simeq (\rho_m)_0. \tag{25b}$$

Since, $1 + z = \frac{S_0}{S}$, eq (25b) leads to,

$$1 + z_{\rm eq} = \frac{(\rho_m)_0}{(\rho_r)_0}. \tag{25c}$$

Making use of the values (see eqs (24a) and (24b)) for the mass densities in eq (25c), one easily obtains the result given by eq (25a).

Eq (25a) tells us that for redshifts $\ll z_{\rm eq}$, (*i.e.*, epochs later than $t_{\rm eq}$), radiation does not play a very crucial role in the evolution of the large-scale geometry of the universe. While $t \ll t_{\rm eq}$ corresponds to the time when radiation is the dominant component, and is usually referred to as the **radiation dominated era**. We can similarly determine the epoch, t_Λ, at which the cosmological constant term is comparable to the matter term in the right-hand side of eq (17c) (we assume that Λ is positive; motivation for this choice will be clear from the discussion following eq (27)). At this epoch,

$$\frac{\Lambda c^2}{3} \simeq \frac{8\pi G}{3}\rho_m(S_\Lambda), \tag{26a}$$

so that, making use of eq (16c) for $\rho_m(S)$, we have,

$$(\rho_m)_0\left(\frac{S_0}{S_\Lambda}\right)^3 = \frac{\Lambda c^2}{8\pi G}. \tag{26b}$$

Identifying the right-hand side of eq (26b) as the mass-density, ρ_Λ, associated with the cosmological constant, we can write this equation as,

$$1 + z_\Lambda = \left(\frac{\rho_\Lambda}{(\rho_m)_0}\right)^{\frac{1}{3}}. \tag{26c}$$

Making use of the definitions of the density parameters and eq (24a), we can re-write eq (26c) as,

$$1 + z_\Lambda = 2.08\left(\frac{(\Omega_\Lambda)_0}{0.9}\right)^{\frac{1}{3}}\left(\frac{(\Omega_m)_0}{0.1}\right)^{-\frac{1}{3}}. \tag{27}$$

Hence, for $t \gg t_\Lambda$, cosmological constant takes over and becomes a dominating factor in determining the evolution of the expansion factor. Now, the question is : What is the value of Λ ?

Lahav et al (1991) have recently attempted to constrain the $((\Omega_m)_0, (\Omega_\Lambda)_0)$ parameter space, using basically the big bang origin of the universe and the age constraint. According to the results of Sandage and Cacciari (1990) and few others, the ages of some of the globular clusters are in the range $\sim$ 14 - 19 Gyr. There has also been an indication that the Hubble constant is likely to be large, $\approx 75\ km\ s^{-1}\ Mpc^{-1}$ (Jacoby, Ciardullo and Ford (1990); Fukugita and Hogan (1990)), in which case the age of the universe turns out to be embarrassingly small, $\sim$ 9 Gyr, unless the cosmological constant is positive and sufficiently large. The age constraint more or less rules out a negative cosmological constant. However, Λ cannot be so large as to prohibit the growth of density perturbations through gravitational instabilities that is believed to give rise to galaxies, stars and eventually us! Such an 'anthropic' consideration leads to an upper bound for Λ so that $(\Omega_\Lambda)_0$ is less than $\sim$ 400 $(\Omega_m)_0$ (Weinberg (1987,1989)).

Now, even if we assume that the cosmological constant has the maximum possible value allowed by the 'anthropic' upper bound, we find that the energy density associated with Λ is given by,

$$\begin{aligned} \epsilon_\Lambda &= \rho_\Lambda c^2 \simeq 400\ (\Omega_m)_0(\rho_c)_0 c^2 \\ &= 6.84 \times 10^{-6}\ (\Omega_m)_0 h^2\ erg\ cm^{-3} \end{aligned} \tag{28a}$$

But as discussed in section 2, the effective cosmological constant, Λ, essentially is a sum of the bare cosmological constant and a term proportional to the vacuum energy density (see eq (5a)). However, according to eq (3b), the vacuum energy density with a Planck scale cut-off is $\sim 10^{114}$ erg/cub.cm, which is very large. So, in order to have a value as small as $\sim 10^{-6}$ erg/cub.cm for the energy density corresponding to the effective cosmological constant, the energy density associated with the bare cosmological constant has to cancel ϵ_{vac} with sufficient precision. That is,

$$1 + \frac{\epsilon_{bare}}{\epsilon_{vac}} \simeq 10^{-120} \quad ! \tag{28b}$$

This problem of fine tuning is often referred to as the **cosmological constant problem**. We will not describe the various mechanisms proposed by many to solve this problem but instead will refer to the excellent review article by Weinberg (1989) and the references therein.

The most common value of $(\Omega_\Lambda)_0$ (between 0.8 and 0.9) in the literature usually originates because of two reasons: (1) Inflationary scenario which requires $\Omega_0=1$, and (2) dynamics of galaxies in clusters which require $(\Omega_m)_0$ to lie in the range 0.1 - 0.2. People also use the number counts of galaxies along with the ages of the globular clusters among other constraints to obtain best fit value for the cosmological constant (Fukugita *et al* (1990);Turner (1991)). Now, $(\Omega_\Lambda)_0$ falling in the range 0.8 - 0.9 implies that for redshifts $\lesssim 1$ (see eq (27)), the cosmological constant starts playing an important role as far as the large-scale geometry of the universe is concerned.

Let us now come to the evolution of the expansion factor for epochs $\gg t_{eq}$, when the effect of radiation can be neglected. For simplicity we will concentrate on the flat FRW model. Under such conditions, eq (22d) reduces to,

$$t - t_1 \simeq \frac{1}{H_0 S_0} \int_{S_1}^{S} \frac{dS}{\sqrt{(\Omega_m)_0(S_0/S) + (\Omega_\Lambda)_0(S/S_0)^2}}, \tag{29a}$$

where we assume that S_1 corresponds to the epoch $t_1 \gg t_{eq}$. The integration in the R.H.S. of eq (29a) is quite straightforward and we obtain,

$$t - t_1 = \frac{2}{3H_0} \frac{1}{\sqrt{(\Omega_\Lambda)_0}} \left[\sinh^{-1}\left(\sqrt{\frac{(\Omega_\Lambda)_0 S^3}{(\Omega_m)_0 S_0^3}}\right) - \sinh^{-1}\left(\sqrt{\frac{(\Omega_\Lambda)_0 S_1^3}{(\Omega_m)_0 S_0^3}}\right) \right]. \tag{29b}$$

Now, for $t_1 \ll t_\Lambda$, we have,

$$\rho_\Lambda \ll \rho_m(t_1) = (\rho_m)_0(S_0/S_1)^3, \tag{29c}$$

so that by dividing on both sides of eq $(29c)$ by $(\rho_c)_0$, we obtain,

$$(\Omega_\Lambda)_0 \ll (\Omega_m)_0 (S_0/S_1)^3. \qquad (30a)$$

Eq $(30a)$ in eq $(29b)$ implies that,

$$t - t_1 \approx \frac{2}{3H_0} \frac{1}{\sqrt{(\Omega_\Lambda)_0}} \sinh^{-1}\left(\sqrt{\frac{(\Omega_\Lambda)_0 S^3}{(\Omega_m)_0 S_0^3}}\right). \qquad (30b)$$

Thus, for epochs much later than the radiation dominated era, we have from eq $(30b)$,

$$S(t) \simeq S_0 \left(\frac{(\Omega_m)_0}{(\Omega_\Lambda)_0}\right)^{\frac{1}{3}} \sinh^{\frac{2}{3}}\left[\frac{3}{2} H_0 \sqrt{(\Omega_\Lambda)_0}(t - t_1)\right]. \qquad (30c)$$

For epochs,

$$t \gg t_1 + \frac{2}{3H_0 \sqrt{(\Omega_\Lambda)_0}},$$

eq $(30c)$ reduces to,

$$S(t) \simeq S_0 \left(\frac{(\Omega_m)_0}{4(\Omega_\Lambda)_0}\right)^{\frac{1}{3}} \exp[H_0 \sqrt{(\Omega_\Lambda)_0}(t - t_1)]. \qquad (30d)$$

Hence, at late times the geometry of the universe resembles that of the De Sitter space-time, $i.e.$, the expansion factor grows exponentially with time.

Problem 6 : *Show that when in eq (30c), $\Lambda \longrightarrow 0$, $S(t) \propto (t - t_1)^{\frac{2}{3}}$, as is expected in the standard flat FRW model during the matter dominated era.*

Solution : *As Λ becomes vanishingly small, $(\Omega_\Lambda)_0$ also tends to zero, so that the argument of sine-hyperbolic function in eq (30c) takes a small value. Now, for small arguments x,*

$$\sinh(x) \simeq x. \qquad (31a)$$

Using the above approximation in eq (30c), we obtain,

$$S(t) \simeq S_0 \, (\Omega_m)_0^{\frac{1}{3}} \left[\frac{3H_0}{2}(t - t_1)\right]^{\frac{2}{3}}. \qquad (31b)$$

Since, we are working in the framework of flat model, $\Omega_m = 1$ for zero cosmological constant, so that eq (31b) gives us the well known result corresponding to the matter dominated era.

We can make use of the result given by eq (29b) to obtain the age of an object formed at a redshift $z \ll z_{eq}$. Using the redshift-expansion factor relation $1 + z = S_0/S$ in eq (29b), we get,

$$t_0 - t(z) = \frac{2}{3H_0} \frac{1}{\sqrt{(\Omega_\Lambda)_0}} \left[\sinh^{-1}\left(\sqrt{\frac{(\Omega_\Lambda)_0}{(\Omega_m)_0}}\right) - \sinh^{-1}\left(\sqrt{\frac{(\Omega_\Lambda)_0}{(\Omega_m)_0(1+z)^3}}\right) \right].$$

(32a)

Setting $(\Omega_\Lambda)_0 = 0.9$ and $(\Omega_m)_0 = 0.1$, we obtain,

$$t_0 - t(z) = 1.28 \times 10^{10}\ h^{-1}\ \left[1 - 0.55 \sinh^{-1}(3(1+z)^{-\frac{3}{2}})\right]\ yrs. \quad (32b)$$

Taking the redshift to be $z=5$ (corresponding to a very distant QSO), the time elapsed since then is given by,

$$t_0 - t(z = 5) = 1.14 \times 10^{10}\ h^{-1}\ yrs, \quad (32c)$$

so that for $h=0.75$ (corresponding to $H_0=75$ km/sec/Mpc) the time elapsed turns out to be about 15 billion years, which is not in conflict with the constraint posed by ages of the globular clusters.

Now, we turn to the problem of a dust-ball undergoing spherical infall in an expanding universe.

5. Virial radius of a spherically collapsing dust-ball

Let us consider a spherical region S_R characterized by $r \leq R$, in an expanding FRW model, r being the radial coordinate in the comoving coordinate system. As the universe expands, only the physical or the proper radius of this region increases as $\sim RS(t)$, the coordinate radius remains a constant. We choose to work in the **post** radiation dominated phase during which the dominant role is played only by the non-relativistic matter and the cosmological constant. Now, neglecting the radiation density in the right hand side of eq (17c), and multiplying the same equation on both sides by r^2, we obtain,

$$\frac{1}{2}\left[\frac{d}{dt}(rS)\right]^2 - \frac{GM(r)}{rS} - \frac{1}{6}\Lambda c^2(rS)^2 = -\frac{1}{2}kc^2r^2, \quad (33a)$$

where,

$$M(r) \equiv \frac{4\pi}{3}(rS)^3 \rho_m \quad (33b)$$

is the mass enclosed in the sphere of radius r. Note that $M(r)$ is a constant in time because of $\rho_m \propto S^{-3}$. Since, the right hand side of eq (33a) is a constant for a given sphere, this equation can be thought to be representing the conservation of energy per unit mass for a spherical mass shell of radius r. The term,

$$V_\Lambda(r) = -\frac{1}{6}\Lambda c^2 (rS)^2, \tag{34a}$$

represents the potential due to the cosmological constant, while the quantity,

$$V_G(r) = -\frac{GM(r)}{rS}, \tag{34b}$$

is the usual Newtonian potential due to a spherically symmetric distribution of matter having a mass $M(r)$.

Problem 7 : *Determine the force experienced by a test particle of mass m_0 due to the potential V_Λ.*

Solution : *The potential energy of the test particle at a distance rS is given by $m_0 V_\Lambda(r)$. The force is obtained simply by taking the derivative of the potential energy with respect to rS and then putting a negative sign in front. The result, then, turns out to be,*

$$F_\Lambda = \frac{1}{3}\Lambda c^2 (rS). \tag{35}$$

As expected, for a positive value for the cosmological constant, eq (35) implies a repulsive force and vice versa.

Now, the potential energies for the region S_R is given by,

$$K_i(S) = \int_0^{SR} V_i(r)\rho_m 4\pi (rS)^2 d(rS), \tag{36a}$$

for $i=\Lambda$ and G. It is easy to work out the integrals for constant matter density so that,

$$K_G(S) = -\frac{3}{5}\frac{G(M(R))^2}{SR}, \tag{36b}$$

and,

$$K_\Lambda(S) = -\frac{1}{10}\Lambda c^2 M(R)S^2 R^2. \tag{36c}$$

From eqs (36b) and (36c) it is clear that as the physical size of S_R expands K_G increases while K_Λ decreases (provided $\Lambda > 0$), implying that the Newtonian gravitation tries to decelerate the expansion whereas the presence of a positive cosmological constant contributes to its acceleration.

Suppose, due to statistical fluctuations the centre of S_R develops an excess matter density because of which the expanding region attains a maximum physical size, D_{max}, and then starts collapsing. This will happen if the excess density is high enough to stop the cosmological expansion of the region S_R at some 'turn around' epoch t_{ta}. Then, the maximum physical radius as a function of the 'turn around' epoch t_{ta} is given by,

$$D_{\max} = RS(t_{ta}). \tag{37a}$$

As the region S_R starts collapsing, it is likely to get virialized (may be due to violent relaxation or some other mechanism) and attain a dynamical equilibrium characterized by its final physical size D and its dispersion speed σ. In the absence of a cosmological constant it is a well known result that,

$$D = 0.5 D_{\max}. \tag{37b}$$

Let us see how the above result gets modified when $\Lambda \neq 0$ (Lahav et al (1991)).

The basic idea involved is that during the epoch t_{ta}, the expansion of the region S_R gets halted so that its total energy E at that moment is purely in the form of potential energy,

$$\begin{aligned} E &= K_G(S_{ta}) + K_\Lambda(S_{ta}), \\ &= -\frac{3}{5}\frac{G(M(R))^2}{D_{\max}} - \frac{1}{10}\Lambda c^2 M(R) D_{\max}^2 \end{aligned} \tag{38a}$$

where we have made use of the relation between $S(t_{ta})$ and $D_{\max}$ (eq (37a)).

Now, as the region collapses and gets virialized, its energy is going to remain a constant (unless the dissipative forces are large) so that,

$$E = \frac{1}{2}M(R)\sigma^2 - \frac{3}{5}\frac{G(M(R))^2}{D} - \frac{1}{10}\Lambda c^2 M(R) D^2, \tag{38b}$$

assuming that upon virialization the dispersion speed and the characterstic size of the region S_R are σ and D, respectively, so that the average kinetic energy is $\frac{1}{2}M(R)\sigma^2$.

According to the virial theorem, if the potential energy K is $\propto D^{-\alpha}$ then upon virialization,

$$\langle T \rangle = -\frac{\alpha}{2}\langle K \rangle, \tag{39a}$$

where T is the total kinetic energy of the system. Using the result of eq (39a) and the fact that $K_G \propto D^{-1}$ and $K_\Lambda \propto D^2$, we obtain,

$$\frac{1}{2}M(R)\sigma^2 = \frac{3}{10}\frac{G(M(R))^2}{D} - \frac{1}{10}\Lambda c^2 M(R) D^2. \tag{39b}$$

We can eliminate the variables E and σ by making use of eqs (38a), (38b) and (39b), and obtain the following equation for D in terms of $D_{\max}$,

$$2\Lambda c^2 D^3 - D\left(\frac{6GM(R)}{D_{\max}} + \Lambda c^2 D_{\max}^2\right) + 3GM(R) = 0. \tag{40a}$$

Denoting the matter density during the 'turn around' epoch by ρ_{ta}, we have,

$$M(R) = \frac{4\pi}{3} D_{max}^3 \rho_{ta}. \tag{40b}$$

The relative strength of the cosmological constant and the matter at the epoch t_{ta} is characterised by the ratio of the respective energy densities,

$$\mu = \frac{\Lambda c^2}{8\pi G \rho_{ta}}. \tag{40c}$$

Using eqs (40b) and (40c) in eq (40a), we get,

$$4\mu \left(\frac{D}{D_{max}} \right)^3 - 2(1+\mu)\left(\frac{D}{D_{max}} \right) + 1 = 0. \tag{41}$$

Problem 8 : *Show that,*

$$
\begin{aligned}
\mu &= \frac{(\Omega_\Lambda)_0}{(\Omega_m)_0}(1 + z_{ta})^{-3}, \\
&= 9 \times 10^{-3} \left(\frac{(\Omega_\Lambda)_0}{0.9} \right) \left(\frac{(\Omega_m)_0}{0.1} \right)^{-1} \left(\frac{1+z_{ta}}{10} \right)^{-3}
\end{aligned}
\tag{42a}
$$

where z_{ta} is the redshift at which the region S_R started collapsing.

Solution : *Since ρ_{ta} corresponds to the density of non-relativistic matter at the epoch t_{ta}, we have,*

$$
\begin{aligned}
\rho_{ta} &= (\rho_m)_0 \left(\frac{S_0}{S_{ta}} \right)^3, \\
&= (\Omega_m)_0 (\rho_c)_0 (1 + z_{ta})^3.
\end{aligned}
\tag{42b}
$$

Using eq (42b) in eq (40c), it is easy to obtain the result given in eq (42a).

From eq (42a) it is evident that the value of μ is very sensitive to the redshift at which the 'turn around' occured. For example, if we choose z_{ta} to be ~ 4, then $\mu \sim 0.07$. But as long as z_{ta} is larger than unity, μ is less than 1. For μ less than 0.5, there are solutions to eq (41) corresponding to turning around of S_R. The minimum value of D/D_{max} is 0.366 when μ is 0.5. An approximate solution to eq (41) is given by,

$$D \simeq D_{max}\left(\frac{1-\mu}{2-\mu} \right). \tag{43}$$

As expected, eq (43) agrees with eq (37b) in the limit Λ goes to zero. A positive value for the cosmological constant implies a smaller virial radius, essentially because $\Lambda > 0$ corresponds to a repulsive force (see Problem 7) so that only when the size is smaller can the attractive gravitational force dominate over that of the former, to keep the system bound.

6. The Flatness problem

We had remarked earlier that if the total density that contributes to the curvature of the space-time geometry is exactly equal to the critical density then the geometry corresponds to the Robertson-Walker line-element of eq (6a) with $k = 0$ (Flat FRW model). It is by **no** means clear from observations that $(\rho)_0 = (\rho_c)_0$. It is therefore interesting to ask if at the present epoch the total density differs from the critical density by a given amount, what is the difference at very early epochs. Since,

$$\rho(t) - \rho_c(t) = \rho_c(t)(\Omega(t) - 1), \tag{44a}$$

a good way of dealing with this question is to obtain a relation between $\Omega(t) - 1$ and $\Omega_0 - 1$. Basically, the quantity $\Omega(t) - 1$ is an indicator of the departure from the **flat model** at the epoch t.

We begin by making use of eq (20b) in eq (19a) and re-writing the latter as,

$$H^2 + \frac{kc^2}{S^2} = H^2\Omega(t), \tag{44b}$$

which leads to,

$$kc^2 = S^2 H^2(\Omega(t) - 1). \tag{45a}$$

As the left-hand side of the above equation is independent of the epoch, by equating the right hand side of eq (45a) to that corresponding to the present epoch we get,

$$\Omega(t) - 1 = \left(\frac{S_0}{S}\right)^2 \left(\frac{H_0}{H(t)}\right)^2 (\Omega_0 - 1). \tag{45b}$$

Since we are interested in very early epochs when radiation is the dominating component, it is useful to express the radiation density in terms of the corresponding temperature by making use of the temperature-scale factor relation,

$$T \propto \frac{1}{S}. \tag{46a}$$

Using eqs (16b) and (46a), we get,

$$\rho_r = (\rho_r)_0 \left(\frac{T}{T_0}\right)^4, \tag{46b}$$

where T_0 is the observed CMBR temperature (see the discussion preceding eq (24b)). Similarly, using eq (16c) and (46a) the matter density at any epoch can be written as,

$$\rho_m = (\rho_m)_0 \left(\frac{T}{T_0}\right)^3. \tag{46c}$$

Now, there is a very interesting relation between the radiation density, temperature, matter density at the present epoch and the redshift at which the radiation density and the matter density are equal. The relation is as follows (see Problem 9),

$$\rho_r = \frac{(\rho_m)_0}{1 + z_{eq}}\left(\frac{T}{T_0}\right)^4. \tag{47a}$$

Problem 9 : *Prove the result given in eq (47a).*

Solution : *At t_{eq}, we have from eq (25c),*

$$(\rho_r)_0 = \frac{(\rho_m)_0}{1 + z_{eq}}, \tag{47b}$$

which along with eq (46b) leads to eq (47a).
From eq (47b) it is easy to see that,

$$(\Omega_r)_0 = \frac{(\Omega_m)_0}{1 + z_{eq}}. \tag{47c}$$

Making use of eqs (46c) and (47a) in eq (19a), we find that,

$$H^2 + \frac{kc^2}{S^2} = \frac{8\pi G}{3}\left[(\rho_m)_0\left(\frac{T}{T_0}\right)^3\left(1 + \frac{1}{1 + z_{eq}}\left(\frac{T}{T_0}\right)\right) + \rho_\Lambda\right]. \tag{48a}$$

Using the definition of the critical density (eq (20a)) for the present epoch, we can express eq (48a) in the following way,

$$H^2 = H_0^2\left[(\Omega_m)_0\left(\frac{T}{T_0}\right)^3\left(1 + \frac{1}{1 + z_{eq}}\left(\frac{T}{T_0}\right)\right) + (\Omega_\Lambda)_0\right] - \frac{kc^2}{S_0^2}\left(\frac{T}{T_0}\right)^2. \tag{48b}$$

Making use of eqs (21b) and (47c) in eq (48b), we obtain,

$$\begin{aligned} H^2 = {}& H_0^2\left(\frac{T}{T_0}\right)^2\left[(\Omega_m)_0\left\{\frac{T}{T_0} + \frac{1}{1 + z_{eq}}\left(\frac{T}{T_0}\right)^2 - \frac{1}{1 + z_{eq}} - 1\right\}\right. \\ & \left. - (\Omega_\Lambda)_0\left\{1 - \left(\frac{T}{T_0}\right)^{-2}\right\} + 1\right]. \end{aligned} \tag{49a}$$

Hence, making use of eqs (46*a*) and (49a) in eq (45*b*), we get,

$$\Omega(t) - 1 = (\Omega_0 - 1)/\left[(\Omega_m)_0\left\{\frac{T}{T_0} + \frac{1}{1+z_{eq}}\left(\frac{T}{T_0}\right)^2 - \frac{1}{1+z_{eq}} - 1\right\}\right.$$
$$\left. - (\Omega_\Lambda)_0\left\{1 - \left(\frac{T}{T_0}\right)^{-2}\right\} + 1\right]. \quad (49b)$$

Suppose, we wish to estimate the departure from **flatness** during the epoch when strong, weak and electromagnetic forces were comparable as predicted by the Grand Unified theories (GUTs). Now, most GUTs predict that around the energy scale $\approx 10^{15}$ Gev, the running coupling constants corresponding to electro-weak force and strong force meet. Thus, when the universe was so hot that the temperature was $\sim 10^{28}$ degree-Kelvin, these gauge forces had equal strength.

Then, with the temperature $T_0 \sim 2.7$ degree-Kelvin corresponding to the present epoch, we have,

$$\frac{T_{GUTs}}{T_0} \simeq 3.7 \times 10^{27}, \quad (50a)$$

so that,

$$(\Omega(t) - 1)_{GUTs} \simeq (\Omega_0 - 1)\left[(\Omega_m)_0\frac{1}{1+z_{eq}}\left(\frac{T_{GUTs}}{T_0}\right)^2 - (\Omega_\Lambda)_0 + 1\right]^{-1}. \quad (50b)$$

Making use of the result of Problem 5 (eq (25*a*)) in eq (50*b*), we obtain,

$$(\Omega(t) - 1)_{GUTs} \simeq (\Omega_0 - 1)\left[3.6 \times 10^{50}h^{-2} - (\Omega_\Lambda)_0 + 1\right]^{-1}. \quad (50c)$$

Note that eq (50*c*) is independent of $(\Omega_m)_0$. Since we do not expect $(\Omega_\Lambda)_0$ to be larger than unity, eq (50*c*) implies that,

$$(\Omega(t) - 1)_{GUTs} \simeq 2.8 \times 10^{-51} h^2 (\Omega_0 - 1). \quad (51)$$

This means that to produce the universe observed today, the density parameter $\Omega(t)$ ought to have been close to unity within 51 decimal places at the GUT epoch! This problem of fine tuning constitutes the celebrated **flatness problem** of the hot big-bang model. (One of the major successes of Inflationary Universe scenario (Guth (1981)) was to solve this problem in a natural way).

However, if due to some peculiar reason, $(\Omega_\Lambda)_0 \approx 10^{50}$, (*i.e.*, exceeding the 'anthropic' bound!) then, it is evident from eq (50*c*) that the problem of fine tuning the density parameter at the GUTs epoch does not arise. This will require,

$$\epsilon_\Lambda \approx 1.7 \times 10^{42} erg\ cm^{-3}, \quad (52)$$

which is still much less compared to the vacuum energy density (see eq $(3b)$). Therefore, the problem of fine tuning the value of the bare cosmological constant to cancel the one arising from the vacuum effects will still remain.

7. Conclusion

Einstein had introduced a positive cosmological constant in order to have a repulsive force counteracting the attractive force due to gravitation, so that the general theory of relativity (GTR) admits a solution representing a static universe. The observed redshifts of extragalactic sources, on the other hand, indicate that the universe is expanding, overruling the idea of a universe that is static. However, the fact that a cosmological constant term can be added to the equations of GTR making the latter mathematically richer, is a great virtue in itself.

Richness of the structure apart, we saw in sections 2 and 4 that the very vacuum corresponding to the quantum fields leads to a large cosmological constant-like quantity that needs to be cancelled by a bare cosmological constant with an opposite sign, in a manner so that the effective Λ is small. The big-bang scenario along with the age constraint arising from the observations of globular clusters indicate that Λ is positive, while 'anthropic' considerations impose an upper bound on its value. A positive cosmological constant implies (i) a De Sitter like expansion at late phases for an expanding, homogeneous and isotropic universe, and (ii) smaller virial radius for collapsing matter (section 5). The flatness problem remains unless the cosmological constant is far larger than the 'anthropic' upper bound (section 6).

The most challenging problem that Λ poses is that: Why is the ratio of the bare cosmological constant and the one emerging because of the vacuum, close to unity within 1 part in 10^{120}? The answer may very well be linked with the quantum theory of gravity if at all there is one.

Acknowledgements

I thank Prof. J.V.Narlikar for clarifying certain conceptual issues during the IUCAA graduate school, when the prelimnary work for these notes had begun. It also gives me a great pleasure to thank Dr. B.R.Iyer for his incessant encouragement to complete the notes. Finally, I thank C.S.I.R., New Delhi, for supporting this research work.

References

1. Einstein, A., 1917, Sitzungsber, *Preuss. Akad. Wiss. Phys.- Math. K1.* 142
2. Fukugita, M. and Hogan, C., 1990, *Nature*, **347**, 120

3. Fukugita, M., Takahara, F., Yamashita, K. and Yoshi, Y., 1990, *Astrophys. J.*, **361**, L1
4. Guth, A. H., 1981, *Phys. Rev. D*, **23**, 347
5. Jacoby, G. H., Ciardullo, R. and Ford, H. C., 1990, *Astrophys. J.*, **356**, 332
6. Knapp, G. R. and Kormendy, 1987, Eds., *Dark Matter in the Universe*, I.A.U. Symposium No. 117 (Reidel, Dordrecht)
7. Lahav, O., Lilje, P. B., Primack, J. R. and Rees, M. J., 1991, *Mon. not. R. astr. Soc.*, **251**, 128
8. Narlikar, J. V., 1983, *Introduction to Cosmology*, (Jones and Bartlett Publishers Inc., Boston)
9. Narlikar, J. V., *Relativistic Cosmology*, in this volume
10. Sandage, A. R. and Cacciari, C., 1990, *Astrophys. J.*, **350**, 645
11. Turner, M. S., 1991, *Proceedings of the IUPAP conference on Primordial Nucleosynthesis and the Early evolution of the Universe*, Ed. K. Sato (Kluwer, Dordrecht)
12. Weinberg, S., 1987, *Phys. Rev. Lett.*, **59**, 2607
13. Weinberg, S., 1989, *Rev. Mod. Phys.*, **61**, 1

INDEX

Nothing puzzles me more than time and space; and yet nothing troubles me less, as I never think about them.

–CHARLES LAMB

If it works it's out of date.

–STAFFORD BEER

If a professor thinks what matters most
Is to have gained an academic post
Where he can earn a livelihood, and then
Neglect research, let controversy rest,
He's but a petty tradesman at the best,
Selling retail the work of other men.

–KALIDASA

Fundamental Theories of Physics

Series Editor: Alwyn van der Merwe, *University of Denver, USA*

1. M. Sachs: *General Relativity and Matter.* A Spinor Field Theory from Fermis to Light-Years. With a Foreword by C. Kilmister. 1982   ISBN 90-277-1381-2
2. G.H. Duffey: *A Development of Quantum Mechanics.* Based on Symmetry Considerations. 1985   ISBN 90-277-1587-4
3. S. Diner, D. Fargue, G. Lochak and F. Selleri (eds.): *The Wave-Particle Dualism.* A Tribute to Louis de Broglie on his 90th Birthday. 1984   ISBN 90-277-1664-1
4. E. Prugovečki: *Stochastic Quantum Mechanics and Quantum Spacetime.* A Consistent Unification of Relativity and Quantum Theory based on Stochastic Spaces. 1984; 2nd printing 1986   ISBN 90-277-1617-X
5. D. Hestenes and G. Sobczyk: *Clifford Algebra to Geometric Calculus.* A Unified Language for Mathematics and Physics. 1984
ISBN 90-277-1673-0; Pb (1987) 90-277-2561-6
6. P. Exner: *Open Quantum Systems and Feynman Integrals.* 1985   ISBN 90-277-1678-1
7. L. Mayants: *The Enigma of Probability and Physics.* 1984   ISBN 90-277-1674-9
8. E. Tocaci: *Relativistic Mechanics, Time and Inertia.* Translated from Romanian. Edited and with a Foreword by C.W. Kilmister. 1985   ISBN 90-277-1769-9
9. B. Bertotti, F. de Felice and A. Pascolini (eds.): *General Relativity and Gravitation.* Proceedings of the 10th International Conference (Padova, Italy, 1983). 1984
ISBN 90-277-1819-9
10. G. Tarozzi and A. van der Merwe (eds.): *Open Questions in Quantum Physics.* 1985
ISBN 90-277-1853-9
11. J.V. Narlikar and T. Padmanabhan: *Gravity, Gauge Theories and Quantum Cosmology.* 1986   ISBN 90-277-1948-9
12. G.S. Asanov: *Finsler Geometry, Relativity and Gauge Theories.* 1985
ISBN 90-277-1960-8
13. K. Namsrai: *Nonlocal Quantum Field Theory and Stochastic Quantum Mechanics.* 1986   ISBN 90-277-2001-0
14. C. Ray Smith and W.T. Grandy, Jr. (eds.): *Maximum-Entropy and Bayesian Methods in Inverse Problems.* Proceedings of the 1st and 2nd International Workshop (Laramie, Wyoming, USA). 1985   ISBN 90-277-2074-6
15. D. Hestenes: *New Foundations for Classical Mechanics.* 1986
ISBN 90-277-2090-8; Pb (1987) 90-277-2526-8
16. S.J. Prokhovnik: *Light in Einstein's Universe.* The Role of Energy in Cosmology and Relativity. 1985   ISBN 90-277-2093-2
17. Y.S. Kim and M.E. Noz: *Theory and Applications of the Poincaré Group.* 1986
ISBN 90-277-2141-6
18. M. Sachs: *Quantum Mechanics from General Relativity.* An Approximation for a Theory of Inertia. 1986   ISBN 90-277-2247-1
19. W.T. Grandy, Jr.: *Foundations of Statistical Mechanics.*
Vol. I: *Equilibrium Theory.* 1987   ISBN 90-277-2489-X
20. H.-H von Borzeszkowski and H.-J. Treder: *The Meaning of Quantum Gravity.* 1988
ISBN 90-277-2518-7
21. C. Ray Smith and G.J. Erickson (eds.): *Maximum-Entropy and Bayesian Spectral Analysis and Estimation Problems.* Proceedings of the 3rd International Workshop (Laramie, Wyoming, USA, 1983). 1987   ISBN 90-277-2579-9

Fundamental Theories of Physics

Fundamental Theories of Physics

43. W.T. Grandy, Jr. and L.H. Schick (eds.): *Maximum-Entropy and Bayesian Methods.* Proceedings of the 10th International Workshop (Laramie, Wyoming, USA, 1990). 1991
ISBN 0-7923-1140-X
44. P.Pták and S. Pulmannová: *Orthomodular Structures as Quantum Logics.* Intrinsic Properties, State Space and Probabilistic Topics. 1991
ISBN 0-7923-1207-4
45. D. Hestenes and A. Weingartshofer (eds.): *The Electron.* New Theory and Experiment. 1991
ISBN 0-7923-1356-9
46. P.P.J.M. Schram: *Kinetic Theory of Gases and Plasmas.* 1991
ISBN 0-7923-1392-5
47. A. Micali, R. Boudet and J. Helmstetter (eds.): *Clifford Algebras and their Applications in Mathematical Physics.* 1992
ISBN 0-7923-1623-1
48. E. Prugovečki: *Quantum Geometry.* A Framework for Quantum General Relativity. 1992
ISBN 0-7923-1640-1
49. M.H. Mac Gregor: *The Enigmatic Electron.* 1992
ISBN 0-7923-1982-6
50. C.R. Smith, G.J. Erickson and P.O. Neudorfer (eds.): *Maximum Entropy and Bayesian Methods.* Proceedings of the 11th International Workshop (Seattle, 1991). 1993
ISBN 0-7923-2031-X
51. D.J. Hoekzema: *The Quantum Labyrinth.* 1993
ISBN 0-7923-2066-2
52. Z. Oziewicz, B. Jancewicz and A. Borowiec (eds.): *Spinors, Twistors, Clifford Algebras and Quantum Deformations.* Proceedings of the Second Max Born Symposium (Wrocław, Poland, 1992). 1993
ISBN 0-7923-2251-7
53. A. Mohammad-Djafari and G. Demoment (eds.): *Maximum Entropy and Bayesian Methods.* Proceedings of the 12th International Workshop (Paris, France, 1992). 1993
ISBN 0-7923-2280-0
54. M. Riesz: *Clifford Numbers and Spinors* with Riesz' Private Lectures to E. Folke Bolinder and a Historical Review by Pertti Lounesto. E.F. Bolinder and P. Lounesto (eds.). 1993
ISBN 0-7923-2299-1
55. F. Brackx, R. Delanghe and H. Serras (eds.): *Clifford Algebras and their Applications in Mathematical Physics.* Proceedings of the Third Conference (Deinze, 1993) 1993
ISBN 0-7923-2347-5
56. J.R. Fanchi: *Parametrized Relativistic Quantum Theory.* 1993
ISBN 0-7923-2376-9
57. A. Peres: *Quantum Theory: Concepts and Methods.* 1993
ISBN 0-7923-2549-4
58. P.L. Antonelli, R.S. Ingarden and M. Matsumoto: *The Theory of Sprays and Finsler Spaces with Applications in Physics and Biology.* 1993
ISBN 0-7923-2577-X
59. R. Miron and M. Anastasiei: *The Geometry of Lagrange Spaces: Theory and Applications.* 1994
ISBN 0-7923-2591-5
60. G. Adomian: *Solving Frontier Problems of Physics: The Decomposition Method.* 1994
ISBN 0-7923-2644-X
61 B.S. Kerner and V.V. Osipov: *Autosolitons.* A New Approach to Problems of Self-Organization and Turbulence. 1994
ISBN 0-7923-2816-7
62. G.R. Heidbreder (ed.): *Maximum Entropy and Bayesian Methods.* Proceedings of the 13th International Workshop (Santa Barbara, USA, 1993) 1996
ISBN 0-7923-2851-5
63. J. Peřina, Z. Hradil and B. Jurčo: *Quantum Optics and Fundamentals of Physics.* 1994
ISBN 0-7923-3000-5
64. M. Evans and J.-P. Vigier: *The Enigmatic Photon.* Volume 1: The Field $B^{(3)}$. 1994
ISBN 0-7923-3049-8
65. C.K. Raju: *Time: Towards a Constistent Theory.* 1994
ISBN 0-7923-3103-6
66. A.K.T. Assis: *Weber's Electrodynamics.* 1994
ISBN 0-7923-3137-0

Fundamental Theories of Physics

KLUWER ACADEMIC PUBLISHERS – DORDRECHT / BOSTON / LONDON